YEAR
BOOK
1991

Daily Mail

YEAR

BOOK

1991

EDITED BY
Michael and Caroline Fluskey

CHAPMANS
1990

Chapmans Publishers Ltd

141-143 Drury Lane,

London WC2B 5TB

First published by Chapmans for Associated Newspapers plc 1990

(c) Associated Newspapers plc 1990

ISBN 1 85592 701 2

Typeset by Serif Publishing Services

Printed in England by Clays Ltd, St Ives plc

Please address all enquiries and comments about this publication to:

The Editor
Daily Mail Year Book
Chapmans Publishers Ltd
141-143 Drury Lane
London WC2B 5TB

CONTENTS

CONTENTS

CONTENTS

CALENDAR AND ALMANAC

1991

JANUARY						
S	.	6	13	20	27	.
M	.	7	14	21	28	.
T	1	8	15	22	29	.
W	2	9	16	23	30	.
T	3	10	17	24	31	.
F	4	11	18	25	.	.
S	5	12	19	26	.	.

FEBRUARY						
S	.	3	10	17	24	.
M	.	4	11	18	25	.
T	.	5	12	19	26	.
W	.	6	13	20	27	.
T	.	7	14	21	28	.
F	1	8	15	22	.	.
S	2	9	16	23	.	.

MARCH						
S	.	3	10	17	24	31
M	.	4	11	18	25	.
T	.	5	12	19	26	.
W	.	6	13	20	27	.
T	.	7	14	21	28	.
F	1	8	15	22	29	.
S	2	9	16	23	30	.

APRIL						
S	.	7	14	21	28	.
M	1	8	15	22	29	.
T	2	9	16	23	30	.
W	3	10	17	24	.	.
T	4	11	18	25	.	.
F	5	12	19	26	.	.
S	6	13	20	27	.	.

MAY						
S	.	5	12	19	26	.
M	.	6	13	20	27	.
T	.	7	14	21	28	.
W	1	8	15	22	29	.
T	2	9	16	23	30	.
F	3	10	17	24	31	.
S	4	11	18	25	.	.

JUNE						
S	.	2	9	16	23	30
M	.	3	10	17	24	.
T	.	4	11	18	25	.
W	.	5	12	19	26	.
T	.	6	13	20	27	.
F	.	7	14	21	28	.
S	1	8	15	22	29	.

JULY						
S	.	7	14	21	28	.
M	1	8	15	22	29	.
T	2	9	16	23	30	.
W	3	10	17	24	31	.
T	4	11	18	25	.	.
F	5	12	19	26	.	.
S	6	13	20	27	.	.

AUGUST						
S	.	4	11	18	25	.
M	.	5	12	19	26	.
T	.	6	13	20	27	.
W	.	7	14	21	28	.
T	1	8	15	22	29	.
F	2	9	16	23	30	.
S	3	10	17	24	31	.

SEPTEMBER						
S	1	8	15	22	29	.
M	2	9	16	23	30	.
T	3	10	17	24	.	.
W	4	11	18	25	.	.
T	5	12	19	26	.	.
F	6	13	20	27	.	.
S	7	14	21	28	.	.

OCTOBER						
S	.	6	13	20	27	.
M	.	7	14	21	28	.
T	1	8	15	22	29	.
W	2	9	16	23	30	.
T	3	10	17	24	31	.
F	4	11	18	25	.	.
S	5	12	19	26	.	.

NOVEMBER						
S	.	3	10	17	24	.
M	.	4	11	18	25	.
T	.	5	12	19	26	.
W	.	6	13	20	27	.
T	.	7	14	21	28	.
F	1	8	15	22	29	.
S	2	9	16	23	30	.

DECEMBER						
S	1	8	15	22	29	.
M	2	9	16	23	30	.
T	3	10	17	24	31	.
W	4	11	18	25	.	.
T	5	12	19	26	.	.
F	6	13	20	27	.	.
S	7	14	21	28	.	.

1990

```
JANUARY              FEBRUARY             MARCH                APRIL
S  .  7 14 21 28  .  S  .  4 11 18 25  .  S  .  4 11 18 25  .  S  1  8 15 22 29  .
M  1  8 15 22 29  .  M  .  5 12 19 26  .  M  .  5 12 19 26  .  M  2  9 16 23 30  .
T  2  9 16 23 30  .  T  .  6 13 20 27  .  T  .  6 13 20 27  .  T  3 10 17 24  .  .
W  3 10 17 24 31  .  W  .  7 14 21 28  .  W  .  7 14 21 28  .  W  4 11 18 25  .  .
T  4 11 18 25  .  .  T  1  8 15 22  .  .  T  1  8 15 22 29  .  T  5 12 19 26  .  .
F  5 12 19 26  .  .  F  2  9 16 23  .  .  F  2  9 16 23 30  .  F  6 13 20 27  .  .
S  6 13 20 27  .  .  S  3 10 17 24  .  .  S  3 10 17 24 31  .  S  7 14 21 28  .  .

MAY                  JUNE                 JULY                 AUGUST
S  .  6 13 20 27  .  S  .  3 10 17 24  .  S  1  8 15 22 29  .  S  .  5 12 19 26  .
M  .  7 14 21 28  .  M  .  4 11 18 25  .  M  2  9 16 23 30  .  M  .  6 13 20 27  .
T  1  8 15 22 29  .  T  .  5 12 19 26  .  T  3 10 17 24 31  .  T  .  7 14 21 28  .
W  2  9 16 23 30  .  W  .  6 13 20 27  .  W  4 11 18 25  .  .  W  1  8 15 22 29  .
T  3 10 17 24 31  .  T  .  7 14 21 28  .  T  5 12 19 26  .  .  T  2  9 16 23 30  .
F  4 11 18 25  .  .  F  1  8 15 22 29  .  F  6 13 20 27  .  .  F  3 10 17 24 31  .
S  5 12 19 26  .  .  S  2  9 16 23 30  .  S  7 14 21 28  .  .  S  4 11 18 25  .  .

SEPTEMBER            OCTOBER              NOVEMBER             DECEMBER
S  .  2  9 16 23 30  S  .  7 14 21 28  .  S  .  4 11 18 25  .  S  .  2  9 16 23 30
M  .  3 10 17 24  .  M  1  8 15 22 29  .  M  .  5 12 19 26  .  M  .  3 10 17 24 31
T  .  4 11 18 25  .  T  2  9 16 23 30  .  T  .  6 13 20 27  .  T  .  4 11 18 25  .
W  .  5 12 19 26  .  W  3 10 17 24 31  .  W  .  7 14 21 28  .  W  .  5 12 19 26  .
T  .  6 13 20 27  .  T  4 11 18 25  .  .  T  1  8 15 22 29  .  T  .  6 13 20 27  .
F  .  7 14 21 28  .  F  5 12 19 26  .  .  F  2  9 16 23 30  .  F  .  7 14 21 28  .
S  1  8 15 22 29  .  S  6 13 20 27  .  .  S  3 10 17 24  .  .  S  1  8 15 22 29  .
```

1992

```
JANUARY              FEBRUARY             MARCH                APRIL
S  .  5 12 19 26  .  S  .  2  9 16 23  .  S  1  8 15 22 29  .  S  .  5 12 19 26  .
M  .  6 13 20 27  .  M  .  3 10 17 24  .  M  2  9 16 23 30  .  M  .  6 13 20 27  .
T  .  7 14 21 28  .  T  .  4 11 18 25  .  T  3 10 17 24 31  .  T  .  7 14 21 28  .
W  1  8 15 22 29  .  W  .  5 12 19 26  .  W  4 11 18 25  .  .  W  1  8 15 22 29  .
T  2  9 16 23 30  .  T  .  6 13 20 27  .  T  5 12 19 26  .  .  T  2  9 16 23 30  .
F  3 10 17 24 31  .  F  .  7 14 21 28  .  F  6 13 20 27  .  .  F  3 10 17 24  .  .
S  4 11 18 25  .  .  S  1  8 15 22 29  .  S  7 14 21 28  .  .  S  4 11 18 25  .  .

MAY                  JUNE                 JULY                 AUGUST
S  .  3 10 17 24 31  S  .  7 14 21 28  .  S  .  5 12 19 26  .  S  .  2  9 16 23 30
M  .  4 11 18 25  .  M  1  8 15 22 29  .  M  .  6 13 20 27  .  M  .  3 10 17 24 31
T  .  5 12 19 26  .  T  2  9 16 23 30  .  T  .  7 14 21 28  .  T  .  4 11 18 25  .
W  .  6 13 20 27  .  W  3 10 17 24  .  .  W  1  8 15 22 29  .  W  .  5 12 19 26  .
T  .  7 14 21 28  .  T  4 11 18 25  .  .  T  2  9 16 23 30  .  T  .  6 13 20 27  .
F  1  8 15 22 29  .  F  5 12 19 26  .  .  F  3 10 17 24 31  .  F  .  7 14 21 28  .
S  2  9 16 23 30  .  S  6 13 20 27  .  .  S  4 11 18 25  .  .  S  1  8 15 22 29  .

SEPTEMBER            OCTOBER              NOVEMBER             DECEMBER
S  .  6 13 20 27  .  S  .  4 11 18 25  .  S  1  8 15 22 29  .  S  .  5 12 21 28  .
M  .  7 14 21 28  .  M  .  5 12 19 26  .  M  2  9 16 23 30  .  M  .  6 13 22 29  .
T  1  8 15 22 29  .  T  .  6 13 20 27  .  T  3 10 17 24  .  .  T  .  7 14 23 30  .
W  2  9 16 23 30  .  W  .  7 14 21 28  .  W  4 11 18 25  .  .  W  1  8 15 24 31  .
T  3 10 17 24  .  .  T  1  8 15 22 29  .  T  5 12 19 26  .  .  T  2  9 16 25  .  .
F  4 11 18 25  .  .  F  2  9 16 23 30  .  F  6 13 20 27  .  .  F  3 10 17 26  .  .
S  5 12 19 26  .  .  S  3 10 17 24 31  .  S  7 14 21 28  .  .  S  4 11 18 27  .  .
```

ANNIVERSARIES, PUBLIC AND BANK HOLIDAYS, 1991

Bank and Public Holidays

England, Wales, and Northern Ireland

New Year	January 1
St. Patrick (N. Ireland only)	March 17
Good Friday	March 29
Easter Monday	April 1
May Day	May 6
Spring	May 27
Orangeman's Day - Battle of the Boyne (N. Ireland only)	July 12
Summer	August 26
Christmas	December 25 & 26

Scotland

New Year	January 1 and 2
Good Friday	March 29
Spring	March 21
May Day	May 27
Summer	August 5
Christmas	December 25 & 26

Other Days and Anniversaries

Australia Day	January 26
Accession of Queen Elizabeth (1952)	February 6
Prince Andrew's Birthday (1960)	February 19
Ash Wednesday	February 13
Commonwealth Day	March 11
Prince Edward's Birthday (1964)	March 10
Easter Day	March 31
The Queen's Birthday (1926)	April 21
Ascension Day	May 9
Whit Sunday (Pentecost)	May 19
Duke of Edinburgh's Birthday (1921)	June 10
The Queen's Official Birthday	June 8
Trinity Sunday	May 26
Princess of Wales's Birthday (1961)	July 1
Canada Day	July 1
Independence Day (U.S.A.)	July 4
The Queen Mother's Birthday (1900)	August 4
The Princess Royal's Birthday (1950)	August 15
Islamic New Year (1412)	July 13
Jewish New Year (5752)	September 9
Remembrance Sunday	November 10
Prince of Wales's Birthday (1948)	November 14
First Sunday in Advent	December 1

Quarter Days (English)

Lady Day	March 25
Midsummer	June 24
Michaelmas	September 29
Christmas	December 25

Quarter Days (Scottish)

Candlemas	February 2
Whitsunday	May 15
Lammas	August 1
Martinmas	November 11

Law Sittings

Hilary	Jan. 11- April 11
Easter	April 24- May 25
Trinity	June 5- July 31
Michaelmas	Oct. 1-Dec. 21

Golden Number	XVI
Solar Cycle	12
Epact	14
Roman Indiction	14
Dominical Letter	F
Julian Period	6704

JULIAN PERIOD

A period of 7980 (dating from 4713 b.c.) Julian years, the result of multiplying the number of years in the Metonic Cycle, the Solar Cycle and the cycle of the Roman Indiction (19x28x15).

GOLDEN NUMBER

This is a number indicating the position of a year in the Metonic Cycle. The Athenian astronomer Meton discovered that after a period of nineteen years the phases of the Moon recur on almost the same days. To calculate the Golden Number, add 1 to the year, divide by 19, and the remainder is the Golden Number. If there is no remainder the Golden Number is 19. In old calendars the number was printed in gold, hence the name Golden Number. Nowadays it is used only for calculating the date of moveable feasts in the church calendar.

DOMINICAL LETTER

The seven letters A to G denote the Sundays of the year. If the first day of the year is a Sunday, the Dominical Letter is A, if the second day, B and so on. Leap year has two Dominical Letters; the first showing the first Sunday in January, but from March 1 the preceding letter is used.

SOLAR CYCLE

The number of the cycle gives the position of the year in a period of twenty-eight years. The days of the week recur on the same dates in the month in the corresponding year of the Solar Cycle of twenty-eight years.

EPACT

The age of the moon at the beginning of the year, used formerly to determine Easter.

ROMAN INDICTION

The position of the year in a cycle of fifteen years, dating from a.d. 312.

COMMONWEALTH DAY

COMMONWEALTH DAY was formerly called Empire Day and celebrated on May 24, Queen Victoria's birthday. Between 1966 and 1976 it was observed on the same day as the Queens official birthday, usually the second Saturday in June. In 1977 it was decided that in future Commonwealth Day would be celebrated on the second Monday in March.

ECLIPSES 1991

1. An annular eclipse of the Sun on January 15-16 is visible as a partial eclipse from the south eastern part of the Indian Ocean, the Southern Ocean, Oceania, Australasia, the western part of Antarctica and the Pacific Ocean. The eclipse begins on January 15 at 20h 51m and ends on January 16 at 02h 55m. The annular phase begins on January 15 at 22h 00m just off the west coast of Australia, crosses the extreme south western part of Australia, Tasmania, the central part of New Zealand and ends on January 16 at 01h 46m in the South Pacific Ocean. The maximum duration of the annular phase is 7m 55s.

2. A total eclipse of the Sun on July 11. The path of totality begins in the Northern Pacific Ocean, passes along the western coast of Central America, crosses the centre of Columbia and ends in the centre of Brazil. The partial phase is visible from the Pacific Ocean, the southern half of North America, Central America, the Caribbean, South America except the extreme south, and the Atlantic Ocean. The eclipse begins at 16h 29m and ends at 21h 43m, the total phase begins at 17h 23m and ends at 20h 49m. The maximum duration of totality is 6m 54s.

3. A partial eclipse of the Moon on December 21 is visible from Iceland, Greenland, Arctic regions, north west of South America, Central America, North America, the Pacific Ocean except the extreme eastern part, Australasia except the extreme west, Asia except the south western part of the extreme north of Scandinavia. The eclipse begins at 10h 01m and ends at 11h 05m. The time of maximum eclipse is 10h 33m when 0.09 of the Moon's diameter is obscured.

THE UNION FLAG

THE flag is flown on the anniversaries of the following days on Government and public buildings (from 8 a.m. to sunset):

February 6 (1952). Her Majesty's Accession.
February 19 (1960). Birthday of Prince Andrew.
March 1 St. David's Day (see note (a)).
March 10 (1964). Birthday of the Prince Edward.
April 21 (1926). Birthday of Her Majesty the Queen.
April 23 St. George's Day (see note (b)).
June 2 (1953). Coronation Day.
June 10 (1921). Birthday of the Duke of Edinburgh.
July 1 (1961). Birthday of the Princess of Wales.
August 4 (1900). Birthday of Her Majesty Queen Elizabeth the Queen Mother.
August 15 (1950). Birthday of the Princess Royal.
August 21 (1930). Birthday of the Princess Margaret.
November 14 (1948). Birthday of the Prince of Wales.
November 20 (1947). Her Majesty's Wedding Day.
November 30 St. Andrew's Day (see note (c)).

Also on the occasion of Commonwealth Day (March 12, 1990), the Queen's official birthday (June 9, 1990), Remembrance Sunday (November 11, 1990) and the opening and closing of Parliament whether actually performed by Her Majesty or not. Some public buildings traditionally fly the flag every day.

The flag should be flown at half-mast at the following times:
  (i) From the announcement of the death up to the funeral of the Sovereign, except on Proclamation Day, when it is hoisted right up from 11 a.m. to sunset.
  (ii) The funerals of members of the Royal Family, subject to special commands from Her Majesty in each case.
  (iii) The funerals of Foreign Rulers, subject to special commands from Her Majesty in each case.
  (iv) The funerals of Prime Ministers and ex-Prime Ministers of Great Britain.
  (v) Other occasions by special command of Her Majesty.

Notes
  (a) Flags should be flown on this day in Wales only.
  (b) Flags should be flown on this day in England only.
  (c) Flags should be flown on this day in Scotland only.

Where a building has two or more flagstaffs the appropriate national flag may be flown in addition to the Union Flag but not in a superior position.

BRITISH SUMMER TIME 1991

Summer Time in Great Britain and Northern Ireland in 1991, one hour in advance of GMT, will be kept from 01.00 Sunday, March 31 to 01.00 Sunday, October 27.

At the time of going to press there was much uncertainty as to what system of British Summer Time would be used in 1991. The Home office were undertaking surveys into the following possibilities:

1. Having the clocks one hour ahead of GMT throughout the year.
2. Having the clocks one hour of GMT in the winter months and two hours ahead of GMT in the summer months.

The dates for BST given above are those calculated on the present system.

SEASONS 1991

Vernal Equinox : Spring begins March 21, 03h 02m
Summer Solstice : Summer begins June 21, 21h 19m
Autumnal Equinox: Autumn begins Sept. 23, 12h 48m.
Winter Solstice : Winter begins Dec. 22, 08h 54m
The longest day is June 21.
The shortest day is December 21.

LEAP YEAR

A year actually consists of 365.2422 days, the time occupied by the Earth in revolving round the Sun. Because of this, every fourth year has an extra day in it, which is placed in February. When this occurs the year is called a leap year. This correction, however, is a little too much, so that every 100th year is not a leap year, but only those of which the first two figures of which are divisible by 4. Otherwise, every year, the last two figures of which are divisible by 4, is a leap year.

TIDAL CONSTANTS AROUND THE COAST

The following average time differences when applied to the time of high water at London Bridge will give the approximate time of high water at the designated location. All times are G.M.T.

		h	m
Aberdeen	Sub	0	21
Aberystwyth	Sub	6	09
Ayr	Sub	1	53
Belfast	Sub	2	45
Berwick-upon-Tweed	Add	0	56
Blackpool (St. Anne's)	Sub	2	49
Bournemouth *	Sub	5	03
Bridlington	Add	3	01
Brighton	Sub	2	50
Bude Haven	Add	3	59
Cromer	Add	5	16
Dartmouth	Add	4	37
Dornoch (Portmahomack)	Sub	2	06
(Meikle Ferry)	Sub	1	41
Douglas (I.O.M.)	Sub	2	43
Dover	Sub	2	52
Eastbourne	Sub	2	50
Fishguard	Add	5	46
Gairloch	Add	5	16
Gorleston (Great Yarmouth)	Sub	5	00
Holyhead	Sub	3	27
Ilfracombe	Add	4	22
Llandudno	Sub	3	09
Lowestoft	Sub	4	25
Lyme Regis	Add	4	55
Margate	Sub	1	52
Morcambe	Sub	2	32
Newlyn	Add	3	08
Newquay	Add	3	34
North Shields	Add	1	49
Oban	Add	4	17
Plymouth	Add	4	05
Porthcawl	Add	4	39
Portland	Add	5	10
Portsmouth	Sub	2	23
Pwllheli	Sub	5	46
Rhyl	Sub	2	59
Scarborough	Add	2	31
Scrabster	Sub	5	23
Skegness	Add	4	32
Southend	Sub	1	22
Stonehaven	Sub	0	11
Tenby	Add	4	27
Thurso (see Scrabster)			
Torquay	Add	4	40
Ventnor	Sub	2	50
Weston-super-Mare	Add	5	07
Whitby	Add	2	20
Wick	Sub	2	28

* 1st High Water at Springs

Certain calendar and astronomical information contained on this and the following almanac pages is reproduced, with permission, from data supplied by the Science and Engineering Research Council.

Tidal predictions for London Bridge have been computed by the Institute of Oceanographic Sciences: copyright reserved.

JANUARY

**DERIVES ITS NAME FROM JANUS
A ROMAN GOD   31 DAYS**

CAPRICORN

HIGH TIDE (London Bridge)* G.M.T.

Morn.	Ht.	Aft.	Ht.		DATE	
h m	m	h m	m			
01 41	6.8	14 04	7.1	Tue.	1	Bank Holiday, U.K
02 29	6.9	14 54	7.3	Wed.	2	Bank Holiday, Scotland
03 15	7.1	15 42	7.5	Thur.	3	Alaska became 49th State of American Union, 1959
04 00	7.2	16 28	7.5	Fri.	4	Louis Braille b. 1809
04 44	7.2	17 13	7.3	Sat.	5	Edward the Confessor d. 1066
05 26	7.0	17 58	7.0	**Sun.**	**6**	**Epiphany**
06 10	6.7	18 43	6.6	Mon.	7	Catherine of Aragon, first wife of Henry VIII, d. 1536
06 55	6.4	19 33	6.2	Tue.	8	Food rationing began in Britain in World War 2, 1940
07 48	6.1	20 29	6.0	Wed.	9	Anthony Eden resigned as Prime Minister, 1957
08 54	5.8	21 34	5.9	Thur.	10	Penny Post introduced, 1840
10 10	5.8	22 48	5.9	Fri.	11	Sir Isaac Newton elected a fellow of Royal Society, 1672
11 27	5.9	23 51	6.1	Sat.	12	Edmund Burke b. 1729
** **	***	12 22	6.1	**Sun.**	**13**	**First Sunday after Epiphany**
00 39	6.2	13 07	6.3	Mon.	14	Charles Lutwidge Dodgson (Lewis Carroll) d. 1898
01 20	6.5	13 45	6.5	Tue.	15	Elizabeth I crowned, 1559
01 57	6.7	14 22	6.7	Wed.	16	Prohibition came into effect in America, 1920
02 33	6.8	14 58	6.9	Thur.	17	David Lloyd George b. 1863
03 08	7.0	14 34	7.0	Fri.	18	Hugh Gaitskell d. 1963
03 42	7.0	16 09	7.0	Sat.	19	Paul Cezanne b. 1839
04 14	7.0	16 42	6.9	**Sun.**	**20**	**Second Sunday after Epiphany**
04 45	6.8	17 18	6.7	Mon.	21	British Airways Concorde made first commercial flight, 1976
05 18	6.7	17 54	6.5	Tue.	22	Queen Victoria d. 1901
05 54	6.5	18 38	6.2	Wed.	23	First national water strike began, 1983
06 39	6.3	19 33	6.0	Thur.	24	Frederick the Great b. 1712
07 45	6.1	20 50	5.9	Fri.	25	**Conversion of St. Paul**
09 14	6.0	22 13	6.0	Sat.	26	Australia Day
10 41	6.1	23 30	6.3	**Sun.**	**27**	**Septuagesima Sunday**
** **	***	12 01	6.4	Mon.	28	Henry VIII, d. 1547
00 36	6.5	13 04	6.8	Tue.	29	Victoria Cross instituted, 1856
01 31	6.8	13 58	7.1	Wed.	30	Adolph Hitler became Chancellor of Germany, 1933
02 19	7.0	14 46	7.3	Thur.	31	Queen Beatrix of the Netherlands, b. 1938

SUNRISE AND SUNSET (Times in G.M.T. except between 01.00 on March 31 and 01.00 on October 27 when times are in B.S.T.   1 hour in advance of G.M.T.) Sundays 1991.

London	Rise	Set	Belfast	Rise	Set	Birmingham	Rise	Set	MOON'S PHASES (G.M.T.)	
	h m	h m		h m	h m		h m	h m		
Jan. 6	08 05	16 08		08 45	16 14		08 17	16 09	Last Quarter	
Jan. 13	08 02	16 17		08 40	16 25		08 13	16 19	Jan.7	18.35
Jan. 20	07 55	16 28		08 32	16 38		08 06	16 31	New Moon	
Jan. 27	07 47	16 40		08 22	16 51		07 57	16 43	Jan.15	23.50
									First Quarter	
Cardiff	Rise	Set	**Glasgow**	Rise	Set	**Manchester**	Rise	Set	Jan.23	14.21
	h m	h m		h m	h m		h m	h m	Full Moon	
Jan. 6	08 18	16 20		08 46	16 00		08 24	16 06	Jan.30	06.10
Jan. 13	08 14	16 29		08 40	16 11		08 19	16 16		
Jan. 20	08 08	16 41		08 32	16 24		08 12	16 28	* See Tidal	
Jan. 27	07 59	16 53		08 21	16 39		08 03	16 41	constants on page 9	

FEBRUARY

WAS NAMED FROM A GOD, FEBRUUS
28 DAYS

AQUARIUS

HIGH TIDE (London Bridge)* G.M.T.

Morn.		Ht.	Aft.		Ht.	DATE			
h	m	m	h	m	m				
03	03	7.2	15	29	7.5	Fri.	1	First employment exchanges opened, 1910	
03	42	7.3	16	10	7.5	Sat.	2	**Purification. Candlemas (Scottish Quarter Day)**	
04	21	7.3	16	49	7.3	**Sun.**	**3**	**Fourth Sunday after Epiphany**	
04	59	7.1	17	26	7.0	Mon.	4	Edward Heath resigned as leader of the Conservative Party, 1975	
05	36	6.9	18	04	6.6	Tue.	5	Prince of Wales declared Prince Regent, 1811	
06	14	6.5	18	43	6.3	Wed.	6	Accession of Queen Elizabeth II, 1952	
07	02	6.1	19	33	6.0	Thur.	7	Sir Thomas More b. 1478	
08	02	5.8	20	33	5.6	Fri.	8	Jules Verne b. 1828	
09	14	5.5	21	42	5.5	Sat.	9	Edward Carson b. 1854	
10	48	5.5	23	11	5.6	**Sun.**	**10**	**Quinquagesima Sunday**	
**	**	***	12	00	5.8	Mon.	11	John Buchan, Lord Tweedsmuir, d. 1940	
00	12	6.0	12	46	6.1	Tue.	12	**Shrove Tuesday**	
00	57	6.3	13	24	6.5	Wed.	13	**Ash Wednesday**	
01	35	6.6	14	01	6.8	Thur.	14	St. Valentine's Day	
02	12	6.9	14	36	7.0	Fri.	15	Decimalisation of British currency, 1971	
02	46	7.1	15	11	7.2	Sat.	16	Nylon patented, 1937	
03	19	7.2	15	45	7.3	**Sun.**	**17**	**Quadragesima Sunday. First Sunday in Lent**	
03	52	7.2	16	19	7.2	Mon.	18	The Pilgrim's Progress published, 1678	
04	23	7.1	16	52	6.9	Tue.	19	Prince Andrew b. 1960	
04	57	6.9	17	29	6.6	Wed.	20	Edward VI crowned, 1547	
05	33	6.7	18	10	6.3	Thur.	21	Edwina, Countess Mountbatten of Burma, d. 1962	
06	19	6.4	19	01	6.0	Fri.	22	The Duchess of Kent b. 1933	
07	27	6.0	20	19	5.8	Sat.	23	Samuel Pepys b. 1633	
08	58	5.9	21	48	5.9	**Sun.**	**24**	**Second Sunday in Lent**	
10	31	6.1	23	13	6.2	Mon.	25	Pope Pius V excommunicated Queen Elizabeth, 1570	
11	53	6.5	**	**	***	Tue.	26	Victor Hugo b. 1802	
00	22	6.6	12	55	6.9	Wed.	27	The burning of the Reichstag, 1933	
01	17	6.9	13	45	7.2	Thur.	28	Relief of Ladysmith, 1900	

SUNRISE AND SUNSET (Times in G.M.T. except between 01.00 on March 31 and 01.00 on October 27 when times are in B.S.T. 1 hour in advance of G.M.T.) Sundays 1991.

London

	Rise	Set
	h m	h m
Feb. 3	07 37	16 53
Feb. 10	07 25	17 06
Feb. 17	07 12	17 18
Feb. 24	06 58	17 31

Cardiff

	Rise	Set
	h m	h m
Feb. 3	07 49	17 05
Feb. 10	07 37	17 18
Feb. 17	07 24	17 31
Feb. 24	07 10	17 43

Belfast

	Rise	Set
	h m	h m
Feb. 3	08 10	17 05
Feb. 10	07 57	17 20
Feb. 17	07 42	17 34
Feb. 24	07 26	17 49

Glasgow

	Rise	Set
	h m	h m
Feb. 3	08 09	16 54
Feb. 10	07 54	17 09
Feb. 17	07 39	17 24
Feb. 24	07 22	17 40

Birmingham

	Rise	Set
	h m	h m
Feb. 3	07 47	16 56
Feb. 10	07 34	17 10
Feb. 17	07 21	17 23
Feb. 24	07 06	17 36

Manchester

	Rise	Set
	h m	h m
Feb. 3	07 52	16 55
Feb. 10	07 39	17 08
Feb. 17	07 25	17 22
Feb. 24	07 09	17 36

MOON'S PHASES (G.M.T.)

Last Quarter	
Feb.6	13.52
New Moon	
Feb.14	17.32
First Quarter	
Feb.21	22.58
Full Moon	
Feb.28	18.25

* See Tidal Constants on page 9

MARCH

NAMED FROM MARS, THE GOD OF WAR
31 DAYS

PISCES

HIGH TIDE (London Bridge)* G.M.T.

Morn.		Ht.	Aft.		Ht.			
h	m	m	h	m	m	DATE		
02	04	7.1	14	30	7.4	Fri.	1	St. David's Day (Wales)
02	43	7.3	15	10	7.5	Sat.	2	Battle of the Bismark Sea began, 1943
03	21	7.3	15	46	7.4	Sun.	3	Third Sunday in Lent
03	56	7.3	16	20	7.2	Mon.	4	Royal National Lifeboat Institution founded, 1824
04	30	7.1	16	51	6.9	Tue.	5	Joseph Stalin d. 1953
05	02	6.9	17	23	6.7	Wed.	6	Elizabeth Barrett Browning b. 1806
05	39	6.6	17	58	6.4	Thur.	7	Alexander Graham Bell patented the first telephone, 1876
06	22	6.2	18	41	6.1	Fri.	8	Accession of Queen Anne, 1702
07	17	5.8	19	35	5.7	Sat.	9	Yuri Gagarin, first astronaut, b. 1934
08	27	5.4	20	46	5.4	Sun.	10	Fourth Sunday in Lent. Prince Edward's dirthday
09	55	5.3	22	14	5.4	Mon.	11	Commonwealth Day
11	22	5.6	23	37	5.7	Tue.	12	United States Post Office established, 1789
**	**	***	12	14	6.0	Wed.	13	Sir Hugh Walpole b. 1884
00	25	6.2	12	53	6.5	Thur.	14	First television transmission in Scotland, 1952
01	06	6.6	13	31	6.7	Fri.	15	Clothes rationing ended, 1949
01	42	6.9	14	06	7.1	Sat.	16	The new London Bridge opened, 1973
02	18	7.2	14	43	7.3	Sun.	17	Fifth Sunday in Lent. St. Patrick's Day (Ireland)
02	51	7.3	15	18	7.4	Mon.	18	Torrey Canyon aground at Lands End, 1967
03	25	7.4	15	53	7.3	Tue.	19	Sydney Harbour Bridge opened, 1932
04	00	7.3	16	30	7.0	Wed.	20	Sir Isaac Newton d. 1727
04	40	7.1	17	08	6.6	Thur.	21	The London Planetarium opened, 1950
05	23	6.7	17	51	6.3	Fri.	22	National Gallery founded, 1888
06	17	6.3	18	48	5.9	Sat.	23	World Meteorological Organisation founded, 1950
07	27	6.0	20	05	5.8	Sun.	24	Sixth Sunday in Lent. Palm Sunday
08	51	6.0	21	28	5.9	Mon.	25	Annunciation. Lady Day
10	20	6.2	22	54	6.2	Tue.	26	David Lloyd George d. 1945
11	37	6.7	**	**	***	Wed.	27	Wilhelm Konrad Rontgen b. 1845
00	03	6.6	12	38	7.1	Thur.	28	Maundy Thursday
00	57	7.0	13	27	7.3	Fri.	29	Good Friday
01	41	7.1	14	08	7.4	Sat.	30	Vincent Van Gogh b. 1853. Passover
02	20	7.2	14	44	7.3	Sun.	31	Easter Day

SUNRISE AND SUNSET (Times in G.M.T. except between 01.00 on March 31 and 01.00 on October 27 when times are in B.S.T. 1 hour in advance of G.M.T.) Sundays 1991.

London	Rise	Set	Belfast	Rise	Set	Birmingham	Rise	Set
	h m	h m		h m	h m		h m	h m
Mar. 3	06 43	17 44		07 10	18 03		06 51	17 49
Mar. 10	06 27	17 56		06 52	18 17		06 35	18 02
Mar. 17	06 12	18 08		06 35	18 30		06 18	18 14
Mar. 24	05 56	18 20		06 17	18 44		06 02	18 27
Cardiff	Rise	Set	**Glasgow**	Rise	Set	**Manchester**	Rise	Set
	h m	h m		h m	h m		h m	h m
Mar. 3	06 55	17 56		07 05	17 54		06 54	17 50
Mar. 10	06 40	18 08		06 47	18 09		06 37	18 03
Mar. 17	06 24	18 20		06 29	18 24		06 20	18 16
Mar. 24	06 08	18 32		06 10	18 38		06 03	18 29

MOON'S PHASES (G.M.T.)

Last Quarter
Mar.8 10.32
New Moon
Mar.16 08.10
First Quarter
Mar.23 06.03
Full Moon
Mar.30 07.17

* See Tidal Constants on page 9

APRIL

SECOND MONTH OF ROMAN YEAR (APRILIS)
30 DAYS

ARIES

HIGH TIDE (London Bridge)* G.M.T.

Morn.		Ht.	Aft.		Ht.	DATE		
h	m	m	h	m	m			
02	56	7.2	15	18	7.2	Mon.	1	Easter Monday
03	29	7.2	15	49	7.1	Tue.	2	Hans Christian Andersen b. 1805
04	00	7.0	16	17	6.9	Wed.	3	Richard D'Oyly Carte d. 1901
04	33	6.8	16	47	6.7	Thur.	4	Martin Luther King assassinated 1968
05	09	6.6	17	19	6.5	Fri.	5	Richard Crossman d. 1974
05	50	6.3	17	58	6.2	Sat.	6	Phineas Taylor Barnum d 1891
06	39	5.9	18	46	5.8	**Sun.**	**7**	**First Sunday after Easter. Low Sunday**
07	41	5.6	19	48	5.5	Mon.	8	Entente Cordiale established between Britain and France, 1904
09	01	5.4	21	17	5.4	Tue.	9	Isambard Kingdom Brunel b. 1806
10	23	5.6	22	41	5.6	Wed.	10	Evelyn Waugh, writer, d. 1966
11	26	6.0	23	40	6.0	Thur.	11	Napoleon abdicated, 1814
**	**	***	12	14	6.4	Fri.	12	The Tatler first published, 1709
00	27	6.5	12	56	6.8	Sat.	13	Samuel Beckett b.1906
01	07	6.8	13	35	7.1	**Sun.**	**14**	**Second Sunday after Easter**
01	45	7.1	14	13	7.2	Mon.	15	Malta awarded the George Cross by King George VI, 1942
02	23	7.3	14	51	7.3	Tue.	16	The Battle of Culloden, 1746
03	03	7.5	15	29	7.3	Wed.	17	Premium Bonds introduced, 1956
03	45	7.4	16	12	7.0	Thur.	18	San Francisco devastated by earthquake, 1906
04	30	7.2	16	57	6.7	Fri.	19	Primrose Day. Charles Darwin d. 1882
05	22	6.9	17	46	6.3	Sat.	20	Adolph Hitler b. 1889
06	21	6.5	18	45	6.1	**Sun.**	**21**	**Third Sunday after Easter. Birthday of Queen Elizabeth II**
07	27	6.3	19	52	6.0	Mon.	22	Sir Yehudi Menuhin b. 1916
08	40	6.2	21	07	6.0	Tue.	23	**St George's Day (England)**
09	59	6.4	22	27	6.2	Wed.	24	Marriage of Princess Alexandra and Hon. Angus Ogilvy, 1963
11	13	6.7	23	37	6.6	Thur.	25	**St. Mark.** Anzac Day
**	**	***	12	12	7.0	Fri.	26	Daniel Defoe d. 1731
00	32	6.9	13	02	7.1	Sat.	27	London Zoological Gardens opened, 1828
01	17	7.0	13	42	7.1	**Sun.**	**28**	**Fourth Sunday after Easter**
01	57	7.0	14	19	7.1	Mon.	29	British Aerospace Corporation established, 1977
02	32	7.0	14	50	7.0	Tue.	30	First performance of My Fair Lady at Drury Lane, 1958

SUNRISE AND SUNSET (Times in G.M.T. except between 01.00 on March 31 and 01.00 on October 27 when times are in B.S.T. 1 hour in advance of G.M.T.) Sundays 1991.

London	Rise	Set	Belfast	Rise	Set	Birmingham	Rise	Set
	h m	h m		h m	h m		h m	h m
Apr. 7	06 24	19 43		06 42	20 11		06 29	19 52
Apr. 14	06 08	19 55		06 25	20 24		06 13	20 03
Apr. 21	05 54	20 06		06 09	20 37		05 58	20 16
Apr. 28	05 43	20 15		05 53	20 51		05 43	20 28

Cardiff	Rise	Set	Glasgow	Rise	Set	Manchester	Rise	Set
	h m	h m		h m	h m		h m	h m
Apr. 7	06 36	19 55		06 34	20 06		06 29	19 54
Apr. 14	06 21	20 07		06 16	20 20		06 13	20 07
Apr. 21	06 06	20 19		05 58	20 35		05 57	20 20
Apr. 28	05 52	20 30		05 42	20 49		05 42	20 33

MOON'S PHASES (G.M.T.)

Last Quarter	
Apr.7	06.45
New Moon	
Apr.14	19.38
First Quarter	
Apr.21	12.39
Full Moon	
Apr.28	20.58

* See Tidal Constants on page 9

MAY

**NAMED FROM MAIA, MOTHER OF MERCURY
31 DAYS**

TAURUS

HIGH TIDE (London Bridge)* G.M.T.

Morn.	Ht.	Aft.	Ht.			
h m	m	h m	m	DATE		
03 04	6.9	15 19	6.9	Wed.	1	**St. Philip and St. James**
03 36	6.8	15 46	6.8	Thur.	2	Catherine, the Great Empress of Russia, b. 1729
04 10	6.7	16 17	6.7	Fri.	3	Margaret Thatcher became first woman Prime Minister, 1979
04 47	6.5	16 51	6.5	Sat.	4	The Daily Mail first published, 1896
05 27	6.3	17 29	6.3	**Sun.**	**5**	**Fifth Sunday after Easter. Rogation Sunday**
06 11	6.1	18 12	6.0	Mon.	6	May Day
07 03	5.9	19 03	5.8	Tue.	7	Lusitania torpedoed by German submarine, 1915
08 06	5.7	20 12	5.6	Wed.	8	Harry S. Truman, American President, b. 1884
09 21	5.7	21 36	5.7	Thur.	9	**Ascension Day - Holy Thursday**
10 30	6.0	22 45	6.0	Fri.	10	House of Commons badly damaged by incendiary bombs, 1941
11 27	6.4	23 42	6.3	Sat.	11	The musical Cats first produced, London, 1981
** **	***	12 18	6.7	**Sun.**	**12**	**Sunday after Ascension**
00 31	6.7	13 04	6.9	Mon.	13	(Frank James) Gary Cooper, actor, d. 1961
01 16	6.9	13 47	7.0	Tue.	14	Kennedy memorial at Runnymede inaugurated, 1965
02 10	7.2	14 30	7.1	Wed.	15	Herbert Wilcox, film director, d. 1977
02 46	7.3	15 14	7.1	Thur.	16	Wheel clamps first used by Metropolitan Police, 1983
03 55	7.4	16 00	7.0	Fri.	17	Guildford Cathedral consecrated, 1961
04 27	7.3	16 49	6.9	Sat.	18	Napoleon proclaimed Emperor of France, 1804
05 20	7.1	17 42	6.6	**Sun.**	**19**	**Whit Sunday. Pentecost.**
06 17	6.9	18 35	6.4	Mon.	20	Christopher Columbus d. 1506
07 16	6.6	19 33	6.3	Tue.	21	Linbergh's solo trans-Atlantic flight, 1927
08 18	6.5	20 37	6.2	Wed.	22	Airplane patented, 1906
09 28	6.4	21 52	6.2	Thur.	23	Avonmouth Bridge opened, 1974
10 40	6.5	23 04	6.4	Fri.	24	Amy Johnson landed in Australia after flying from London, 1920
11 42	6.7	** **	***	Sat.	25	Coventry Cathedral consecrated, 1962
00 03	6.6	12 32	6.8	**Sun.**	**26**	**Trinity Sunday**
00 52	6.6	13 16	6.8	Mon.	27	John Calvin d. 1564
01 33	6.7	13 52	6.8	Tue.	28	Mermaid Theatre, London opened, 1959
02 11	6.7	14 25	6.8	Wed.	29	Oak-apple Day - restoration of Charles II, 1660
02 46	6.7	14 56	6.7	Thur.	30	**Corpus Christi**
03 19	6.7	15 27	6.7	Fri.	31	Battle of Jutland

SUNRISE AND SUNSET (Times in G.M.T. except between 01.00 on March 31
and 01.00 on October 27 when times are in B.S.T.   1 hour in advance
of G.M.T.)   Sundays 1991.

London			**Belfast**			**Birmingham**			**MOON'S**	
	Rise	Set		Rise	Set		Rise	Set	**PHASES**	
	h m	h m		h m	h m		h m	h m	**(G.M.T.)**	
May 5	05 26	20 30		05 38	21 04		05 30	20 40	Last Quarter	
May 12	05 14	20 41		05 24	21 17		05 17	20 51	May.7	00.46
May 19	05 04	20 51		05 12	21 29		05 06	21 02	New Moon	
May 26	04 55	20 51		05 02	21 40		04 57	21 12	May.14	04.36
									First Quarter	
Cardiff			**Glasgow**			**Manchester**			May.20	19.46
	Rise	Set		Rise	Set		Rise	Set	Full Moon	
	h m	h m		h m	h m		h m	h m	May.28	11.37
May 5	05 38	20 42		05 26	21 03		05 28	20 45		
May 12	05 27	20 53		05 12	21 16		05 15	20 57		
May 19	05 16	21 03		04 59	21 19		05 03	21 09	* See Tidal	
May 26	05 08	21 13		04 48	21 41		04 54	21 19	Constants on page 9	

JUNE

LATIN: JUNIUS WAS NAMED FROM JUNO
3O DAYS

GEMINI

HIGH TIDE (London Bridge)* G.M.T.

Morn. h m	Ht. m	Aft. h m	Ht. m	DATE	
03 55	6.7	15 59	6.6	Sat. 1	Marilyn Monroe (Norma Jean Mortenson), actress, b. 1926
04 31	6.6	16 34	6.5	**Sun. 2**	**First Sunday after Trinity. Coronation Day.**
05 09	6.5	17 11	6.4	Mon. 3	Marriage of Duke of Windsor and Mrs. Wallis Warfield, 1937
05 49	6.4	17 49	6.3	Tue. 4	Tonga became independent, 1970
06 32	6.2	18 32	6.1	Wed. 5	Robert Kennedy shot (he died 25 hours later), 1968
07 21	6.0	19 23	5.9	Thur. 6	Princess Margaret married Anthony Armstrong Jones, 1960
08 23	5.9	20 33	5.8	Fri. 7	George Bryan 'Beau' Brummel, dandy, b. 1778
09 35	6.0	21 50	6.0	Sat. 8	The Queen's Official Birthday
10 42	6.2	22 58	6.2	**Sun. 9**	**Second Sunday after Trinity (Third after Pentecost)**
11 43	6.5	23 58	6.5	Mon. 10	Birthday of Prince Philip, Duke of Edinburgh
** **	***	12 38	6.7	Tue. 11	**St. Barnabas**
00 53	6.7	13 28	6.8	Wed. 12	Anthony Eden, first Earl of Avon, statesman, b. 1897
01 47	7.0	14 16	6.9	Thur. 13	Ludgwig II, King of Bavaria, drowned himself, 1886
02 39	7.2	15 04	7.0	Fri. 14	Henley Regatta held for the first time, 1839
03 29	7.4	15 52	7.1	Sat. 15	King John sealed the Magna Carta at Runnymede, 1215
04 20	7.5	16 40	7.1	**Sun. 16**	**Third Sunday after Trinity (Fourth after Pentecost)**
05 11	7.4	17 27	7.0	Mon. 17	The Opera House burnt down, 1789
06 01	7.1	18 15	6.8	Tue. 18	Battle of Waterloo, 1815
06 52	6.8	19 06	6.6	Wed. 19	Charlie Drake b. 1925
07 47	6.5	20 02	6.4	Thur. 20	Queen Victoria ascended the throne, 1837
08 47	6.3	21 08	6.2	Fri. 21	Longest Day
09 56	6.2	22 23	6.1	Sat. 22	Coronation of George V, 1911
11 05	6.3	23 32	6.2	**Sun. 23**	**Fourth Sunday after Trinity. (English Quarter Day)**
** **	***	12 03	6.3	Mon. 24	The training of nurses began at St. Thomas's Hospital, 1860
00 28	6.3	12 49	6.4	Tue. 25	Battle of Little Big Horn, 1876
01 13	6.4	13 30	6.5	Wed. 26	The Automobile Association was founded, 1905
01 54	6.5	14 05	6.6	Thur. 27	Bonnie Prince Charlie escaped to Skye disguised as a maid, 1746
02 30	6.6	14 39	6.7	Fri. 28	Treaty of Versailles signed, 1919
03 05	6.7	15 12	6.7	Sat. 29	**St. Peter**
03 41	6.7	15 48	6.7	**Sun. 30**	**Fifth Sunday after Trinity. (Sixth after Pentecost)**

SUNRISE AND SUNSET (Times in G.M.T. except between 01.00 on March 31
and 01.00 on October 27 when times are in B.S.T. 1 hour in advance
of G.M.T.) Sundays 1991.

London	Rise h m	Set h m	Belfast	Rise h m	Set h m	Birmingham	Rise h m	Set h m	MOON'S PHASES (G.M.T.)	
June 2	04 49	21 09		04 54	21 49		04 50	21 21	Last Quarter	
June 9	04 45	21 15		04 49	21 57		04 46	21 28	June 5.	15.30
June 16	04 43	21 20		04 47	22 02		04 44	21 32	New Moon	
June 23	04 44	21 22		04 47	22 04		04 44	21 34	June.12	12.06
June 30	04 47	21 21		04 51	22 03		04 48	21 34	First Quarter	
									June.19	04.19
Cardiff	Rise h m	Set h m	**Glasgow**	Rise h m	Set h m	**Manchester**	Rise h m	Set h m	Full Moon	
June 2	05 01	21 21		04 39	21 51		04 46	21 28	June 27	02.58
June 9	04 57	21 28		04 34	21 59		04 41	21 35		
June 16	04 55	21 32		04 31	22 05		04 39	21 40		
June 23	04 56	21 34		04 31	22 07		04 40	21 42	* See Tidal	
June 30	04 59	21 34		04 35	22 06		04 43	21 41	Constants on page 9	

JULY

**NAMED FOR JULIUS CAESAR BY
MARK ANTONY   31 DAYS**

CANCER

HIGH TIDE (London Bridge)* G.M.T.

Morn. h	m	Ht. m	Aft. h	m	Ht. m	DATE		
04	16	6.7	16	21	6.7	Mon.	1	Canada Day. The Princess of Wales b. 1961
04	51	6.7	16	54	6.6	Tue.	2	Ernest Hemingway d. 1961
05	26	6.6	17	27	6.5	Wed.	3	Israeli commando raid on Entebbe Airport, 1976
06	03	6.4	18	03	6.4	Thur.	4	American Independence Day
06	43	6.2	18	45	6.2	Fri.	5	Cecil Rhodes, statesman, b.1893
07	35	6.0	19	42	6.0	Sat.	6	Louis Armstrong d. 1971
08	46	5.9	21	01	6.0	**Sun.**	**7**	**Sixth Sunday after Trinity (Seventh after Pentecost)**
10	00	6.0	22	21	6.1	Mon.	8	Count Zeppelin, inventor, b. 1838
11	12	6.2	23	34	6.4	Tue.	9	Wimbledon Lawn Tennis Championships inaugurated, 1877
**	**	***	12	17	6.5	Wed.	10	Telstar, communications satellite launched, 1962
00	42	6.6	13	14	6.6	Thur.	11	Battle of Oudenarde, 1708
01	40	6.9	14	06	6.8	Fri.	12	Orangeman's Day - Battle of the Boyne
02	32	7.2	14	54	7.0	Sat.	13	First cat show held, 1871
03	21	7.4	15	39	7.2	**Sun.**	**14**	**Seventh Sunday after Trinity (Eighth after Pentecost)**
04	07	7.5	16	24	7.3	Mon.	15	**St. Swithin's Day**
04	54	7.4	17	06	7.2	Tue.	16	Muslim era began, 622
05	37	7.2	17	49	7.0	Wed.	17	The Royal family adopted the name of Windsor, 1917
06	21	6.8	18	34	6.7	Thur.	18	Dr. W.G. Grace, cricketer, b. 1848
07	07	6.5	19	23	6.4	Fri.	19	Henry VIII's flagship, the Mary Rose, sank, 1545
08	01	6.2	20	22	6.1	Sat.	20	G. M. Trevelyan d. 1962
09	01	6.0	21	34	5.9	**Sun.**	**21**	**Eighth Sunday after Trinity (Ninth after Pentecost)**
10	14	5.8	22	59	5.8	Mon.	22	**St. Mary Magdalen**
11	30	5.9	**	**	***	Tue.	23	The Battle of Shrewsbury, 1403
00	05	6.0	12	25	6.1	Wed.	24	International Finance Corporation established, 1956
00	55	6.2	13	09	6.3	Thur.	25	**St. James**
01	35	6.4	13	47	6.5	Fri.	26	Prince Charles created Prince of Wales, 1958
02	12	6.6	14	22	6.7	Sat.	27	Revolution broke out in Paris, 1830
02	46	6.8	14	56	6.9	**Sun.**	**28**	**Ninth Sunday after Trinity (Tenth after Pentecost)**
03	21	6.9	15	29	6.9	Mon.	29	Marriage of the Prince of Wales and Lady Diana Spencer, 1981
03	55	6.9	16	02	6.9	Tue.	30	Emily Bronte born, 1818
04	27	6.9	16	31	6.8	Wed.	31	Franz Liszt, composer, d. 1886

SUNRISE AND SUNSET (Times in G.M.T. except between 01.00 on March 31 and 01.00 on October 27 when times are in B.S.T. 1 hour in advance of G.M.T.) Sundays 1991.

London

	Rise h m	Set h m
July 7	04 52	21 19
July 14	04 59	21 13
July 21	05 08	21 05
July 28	05 18	20 56

Cardiff

	Rise h m	Set h m
July 7	05 04	21 31
July 14	05 11	21 25
July 21	05 20	21 18
July 28	05 30	21 08

Belfast

	Rise h m	Set h m
July 7	04 57	21 59
July 14	05 05	21 53
July 21	05 15	21 44
July 28	05 27	21 33

Glasgow

	Rise h m	Set h m
July 7	04 41	22 02
July 14	04 50	21 54
July 21	05 01	21 45
July 28	05 13	21 33

Birmingham

	Rise h m	Set h m
July 7	04 53	21 31
July 14	05 01	21 25
July 21	05 01	21 17
July 28	05 20	21 07

Manchester

	Rise h m	Set h m
July 7	04 49	21 38
July 14	04 57	21 32
July 21	05 06	21 23
July 28	05 17	21 13

**MOON'S
PHASES
(G.M.T.)**

Last Quarter	
Jul.5	02.50
New Moon	
Jul.11	19.06
First Quarter	
Jul.18	15.11
Full Moon	
Jul.26	18.24

* See Tidal
Constants on page 9

LEO

AUGUST

IN HONOUR OF AUGUSTUS CAESAR
31 DAYS

HIGH TIDE (London Bridge)* G.M.T.

Morn.		Ht.	Aft.		Ht.	DATE	
h	m	m	h	m	m		
04	59	6.7	17	02	6.7	Thur. 1	Slavery abolished in British Empire, 1834
05	33	6.5	17	34	6.6	Fri. 2	Enrico Caruso d. 1921
06	11	6.3	18	15	6.4	Sat. 3	Henry Hudson discovered Hudson Bay, 1610
06	57	6.0	19	07	6.1	**Sun. 4**	**Tenth Sunday after Trinity (Eleventh after Pentecost).**
							Birthday of Queen Elizabeth the Queen Mother
08	02	5.8	20	27	5.9	Mon. 5	Scottish Bank Holiday
09	27	5.8	21	57	6.0	Tue. 6	**Transfiguration**
10	48	6.1	23	23	6.3	Wed. 7	Dornford Yates b. 1885
**	**	***	12	03	6.4	Thur. 8	Richard Nixon announced resignation as US President ., 1974
00	35	6.7	13	03	6.7	Fri. 9	The Arts Council of Great Britain incorporated, 1946
01	31	7.1	13	54	7.0	Sat. 10	The Battle of Otterburn, 1388
02	20	7.3	14	39	7.2	**Sun. 11**	**Eleventh Sunday after Trinity (Twelfth after Pentecost)**
03	05	7.5	15	21	7.4	Mon. 12	The Glorious Twelfth, Grouse Shooting begins
03	48	7.5	16	02	7.4	Tue. 13	The Battle of Blenheim, 1704
04	28	7.4	16	41	7.3	Wed. 14	John Galsworthy, writer, b. 1867
05	08	7.1	17	19	7.0	Thur. 15	The Princess Royal b. 1950
05	46	6.7	17	58	6.7	Fri. 16	The Peterloo Massacre, 1819
06	25	6.4	18	42	6.3	Sat. 17	First balloon crossing of Atlantic in Double Eagle II, 1978
07	10	6.1	19	40	6.0	**Sun. 18**	**Twelfth Sunday after Trinity (Thirteenth after Pentecost)**
08	08	5.8	20	49	5.7	Mon. 19	Sir Henry Wood d. 1944
09	17	5.6	22	21	5.6	Tue. 20	William Booth, founder of the Salvation Army, d. 1912
10	51	5.6	23	42	5.9	Wed. 21	Princess Margaret b. 1930
**	**	***	12	00	5.9	Thur. 22	Claude Achille Debussy b. 1862
00	32	6.2	12	45	6.3	Fri. 23	Treat of Prague, 1866
01	12	6.5	13	23	6.6	Sat. 24	**St. Bartholomew**
01	47	6.7	13	57	6.8	**Sun. 25**	**Thirteenth Sunday after Trinity (Fourteenth after Pentecost)**
02	20	6.9	14	30	7.0	Mon. 26	August Bank Holiday
02	53	7.0	15	03	7.1	Tue. 27	Admiral of the Fleet Earl Mountbatten assassinated, 1979
03	27	7.1	15	34	7.1	Wed. 28	Prince William of Gloucester killed in air crash, 1972
03	59	7.1	16	04	7.1	Thur. 29	The Ashes instituted, 1882
04	31	6.9	16	37	6.9	Fri. 30	First night-time launch of U.S. space shuttle, 1983
05	05	6.6	17	13	6.7	Sat. 31	Queen Wilhelmina of the Netherlands b. 1880

SUNRISE AND SUNSET (Times in G.M.T. except between 01.00 on March 31 and 01.00 on October 29 when times are in B.S.T. 1 hour in advance of G.M.T.) Sundays 1991.

London	Rise	Set	Belfast	Rise	Set	Birmingham	Rise	Set
	h m	h m		h m	h m		h m	h m
Aug. 4	05 28	20 45		05 39	21 20		05 31	20 55
Aug. 11	05 39	20 32		05 51	21 05		05 42	20 42
Aug. 18	05 50	20 18		06 04	20 50		05 54	20 28
Aug. 25	06 01	20 04		06 17	20 34		06 06	20 12

Cardiff	Rise	Set	Glasgow	Rise	Set	Manchester	Rise	Set
	h m	h m		h m	h m		h m	h m
Aug. 4	05 40	20 57		05 26	21 19		05 29	21 01
Aug. 11	05 51	20 44		05 39	21 04		05 40	20 47
Aug. 18	06 02	20 30		05 53	20 48		05 53	20 32
Aug. 25	06 13	20 16		06 07	20 30		06 05	20 16

MOON'S PHASES (G.M.T.)

Last Quarter	Aug.3	11.25
New Moon	Aug.10	02.28
First Quarter	Aug.17	05.01
Full Moon	Aug.25	09.07

* See Tidal Constants on page 9

SEPTEMBER

MEANT THE SEVENTH MONTH FROM MARCH
30 DAYS

VIRGO

HIGH TIDE (London Bridge)* G.M.T.

Morn.		Ht.	Aft.		Ht.			
h	m	m	h	m	m	**DATE**		
05	43	6.3	17	54	6.4	**Sun.**	**1**	**Fourteenth Sunday after Trinity (Fifteenth after Pentecost)**
06	29	6.0	18	52	6.1	Mon.	2	Great Fire of London began in Pudding Lane, 1666
07	34	5.7	20	15	5.9	Tue.	3	Start of World War II
09	04	5.7	21	48	6.0	Wed.	4	Forth Road Bridge opened, 1964
10	31	6.0	23	15	6.4	Thur.	5	Treaty of Portsmouth signed, 1905
11	49	6.5	**	**	***	Fri.	6	Pilgrim Fathers sailed to New England, 1620
00	22	6.9	12	48	6.9	Sat.	7	Elizabeth I b. 1533
01	17	7.3	13	37	7.2	**Sun.**	**8**	**Fifteenth Sunday after Trinity (Sixteenth after Pentecost)**
02	04	7.4	14	19	7.3	Mon.	9	Jewish New Year (5752)
02	46	7.5	14	58	7.4	Tue.	10	The Battle of Lake Erie, 1813
03	25	7.4	15	36	7.4	Wed.	11	Halley's Comet first observed at Heidelberg in 1909
04	02	7.2	16	13	7.3	Thur.	12	Queen Mother appointed Lord Warden of the Cinque Ports, 1978
04	35	7.0	16	48	7.0	Fri.	13	Chiang Kai Shek elected President of Chinese Republic, 1943
05	08	6.7	17	25	6.7	Sat.	14	Her Serene Highness Princess Grace of Monaco d. 1982
05	43	6.4	18	07	6.3	**Sun.**	**15**	**Sixteenth Sunday after Trinity (Seventeenth after Pentecost)**
06	24	6.0	19	00	5.9	Mon.	16	Two-tier postal system came into operation, 1968
07	17	5.7	20	08	5.5	Tue.	17	Arnhem Day
08	27	5.4	21	34	5.5	Wed.	18	Day of Atonement (Yom Kippur)
09	59	5.4	23	05	5.7	Thur.	19	The Battle of Poitiers, 1356
11	22	5.8	23	58	6.1	Fri.	20	QE2 launched from Clydebank, 1967
**	**	***	12	12	6.2	Sat.	21	**St. Matthew**
00	39	6.5	12	50	6.6	**Sun.**	**22**	**Seventeenth Sunday after Trinity (Eighteenth after Pentecost)**
01	16	6.7	13	26	6.9	Mon.	23	Tabernacles (Succoth)
01	49	7.0	13	59	7.1	Tue.	24	Horace Walpole b. 1717
02	23	7.1	14	32	7.2	Wed.	25	Relief of Lucknow, 1857
02	57	7.2	15	05	7.3	Thur.	26	New Zealand declared a Dominion in 1907
03	31	7.2	15	39	7.3	Fri.	27	Opening of Stockton-Darlington railway, 1825
04	06	7.0	16	17	7.1	Sat.	28	Harpo Marx d. 1965
04	42	6.7	16	59	6.8	**Sun.**	**29**	**Eighteenth Sunday after Trinity (Nineteenth after Pentecost)**
05	25	6.3	17	49	6.4	Mon.	30	Radio One and Radio Two began, 1967

SUNRISE AND SUNSET (Times in G.M.T. except between 01.00 on March 31 and 01.00 on October 27 when times are in B.S.T. 1 hour in advance of G.M.T.) Sundays 1991.

London	Rise	Set	**Belfast**	Rise	Set	**Birmingham**	Rise	Set	**MOON'S PHASES (G.M.T.)**	
	h m	h m		h m	h m		h m	h m		
Sept. 1	06 12	19 48		06 30	20 17		06 17	19 57	Last Quarter	
Sept. 8	06 23	19 33		06 42	19 59		06 29	19 40	Sept.1	18.16
Sept. 15	06 35	19 17		06 55	19 42		06 41	19 24	New Moon	
Sept. 22	06 46	19 00		07 08	19 24		06 52	19 07	Sept.8	11.01
Sept. 29	06 57	18 44		07 21	19 06		07 04	18 51	First Quarter	
									Sept.15	22.01
Cardiff	Rise	Set	**Glasgow**	Rise	Set	**Manchester**	Rise	Set	Full Moon	
	h m	h m		h m	h m		h m	h m	Sept.23	11.08
Sept. 1	06 24	20 00		06 20	20 13		06 17	20 00		
Sept. 8	06 36	19 45		06 34	19 54		06 29	19 43		
Sept. 15	06 47	19 29		06 47	19 36		06 41	19 26		
Sept. 22	06 58	19 13		07 01	19 18		06 54	19 09	* See Tidal	
Sept. 29	07 09	18 56		07 15	18 59		07 06	18 52	Constants on page 9	

OCTOBER

WAS THE ROMANS' EIGHTH MONTH
31 DAYS

LIBRA

HIGH TIDE (London Bridge)* G.M.T.

Morn.	Ht.	Aft.	Ht.	DATE	
h m	m	h m	m		
06 15	5.9	18 52	6.1	Tue. 1	Helmut Kohl became Chancellor of W. Germany, 1982
07 24	5.7	20 12	5.9	Wed. 2	The first Rugby Football match played at Twickenham in 1909
08 49	5.8	21 38	6.2	Thur. 3	St. Francis of Assisi d. 1226
10 14	6.1	22 59	6.6	Fri. 4	The Boys' Brigade founded at Glasgow, 1882
11 29	6.6	** **	***	Sat. 5	Philip III, King of France d. 1285
00 05	7.0	12 27	7.0	**Sun. 6**	**Nineteenth Sunday after Trinity (Twentieth after Pentecost)**
00 57	7.3	13 14	7.2	Mon. 7	Battle of Lepanto, 1571
01 42	7.4	13 57	7.3	Tue. 8	Polish Parliament voted to dissolve all trade unions, 1982
02 23	7.3	14 36	7.3	Wed. 9	Che Guevara d. 1967
02 58	7.3	15 11	7.3	Thur. 10	General Election, 1974
03 32	7.1	15 46	7.2	Fri. 11	The Great Chicago Fire ended, 1871
04 03	6.9	16 20	6.9	Sat. 12	Nurse Edith Cavell executed, 1915
04 34	6.6	16 57	6.6	**Sun. 13**	**Twentieth Sunday after Trinity (Twenty-first after Pentecost)**
05 06	6.4	17 37	6.3	Mon. 14	50 pence coins issued for the first time, 1969
05 43	6.1	18 25	5.9	Tue. 15	Sir Winston Churchill awarded Nobel Prize for Literature, 1953
06 31	5.8	19 27	5.6	Wed. 16	Food and Agriculture Organisation established, 1945
07 37	5.5	20 43	5.6	Thur. 17	Charles II sold Dunkirk to French, (Treaty of Dunkirk)
09 03	5.4	22 03	5.6	Fri. 18	**St. Luke**
10 24	5.6	23 09	6.0	Sat. 19	Auguste Lumiere, pioneer in photography, b. 1862
11 25	6.0	23 57	6.4	**Sun. 20**	**Twenty-first Sunday after Trinity**
** **	***	12 10	6.4	Mon. 21	Battle of Trafalgar and death of Nelson, 1805
00 38	6.7	12 49	6.8	Tue. 22	Sarah Bernhardt b. 1845
01 16	6.9	13 26	7.0	Wed. 23	Battle of Edgehill, 1642
01 52	7.1	14 04	7.2	Thur. 24	United Nations Day
02 29	7.2	14 42	7.4	Fri. 25	**St. Crispin's Day.** Battle of Agincourt, 1415
03 07	7.2	15 21	7.4	Sat. 26	William Hogarth d. 1764
03 46	7.1	16 06	7.3	**Sun. 27**	**Twenty-second Sunday after Trinity (Ninth before Christmas)**
04 30	6.8	16 54	7.0	Mon. 28	**St. Simon and St. Jude**
05 18	6.4	17 50	6.6	Tue. 29	Sir Walter Raleigh executed, 1618
06 12	6.1	18 53	6.3	Wed. 30	Fire at the Tower of London, 1841
07 17	5.9	20 04	6.2	Thur. 31	Hallowe'en

SUNRISE AND SUNSET (Times in G.M.T. except between 01.00 on March 31 and 01.00 on October 27 when times are in B.S.T. 1 hour in advance of G.M.T.) Sundays 1991.

London	Rise	Set	**Belfast**	Rise	Set	**Birmingham**	Rise	Set	**MOON'S PHASES (G.M.T.)**	
	h m	h m		h m	h m		h m	h m		
Oct. 6	07 09	18 28		07 34	18 49		07 16	18 34	Last Quarter	
Oct. 13	07 20	18 13		07 48	18 32		07 28	18 18	Oct.1	00.30
Oct. 20	07 32	17 58		08 01	18 15		07 41	18 03	New Moon	
Oct. 27	06 44	16 44		07 15	16 59		06 53	16 48	Oct.7	21.39
									First Quarter	
Cardiff	Rise	Set	**Glasgow**	Rise	Set	**Manchester**	Rise	Set	Oct.15	17.33
	h m	h m		h m	h m		h m	h m	Full Moon	
Oct. 6	07 21	18 41		07 29	18 41		07 19	18 35	Oct.23	11.08
Oct. 13	07 32	18 25		07 43	18 23		07 31	18 19	Last Quarter	
Oct. 20	07 44	18 10		07 57	18 06		07 44	18 03	Oct.30	07.10
Oct. 27	06 57	16 56		07 12	16 49		06 58	16 48	* See Tidal Constants on page 9	

1

NOVEMBER

**NINTH MONTH OF THE EARLY ROMANS
30 DAYS**

SCORPIO

HIGH TIDE (London Bridge)* G.M.T.

Morn.	Ht.	Aft.	Ht.	DATE		
h m	m	h m	m			
08 30	6.0	21 19	6.3	Fri.	1	**All Saints Day**
09 49	6.2	22 35	6.6	Sat.	2	Marie Antoinette, Queen of France, b. 1755
11 02	6.6	23 40	7.0	Sun.	3	**Twenty-third Sunday after Trinity (Eighth before Christmas)**
** **	***	12 03	6.9	Mon.	4	Gen. Dwight D. Eisenhower elected President of the U.S.A., 1952
00 34	7.1	12 52	7.1	Tue.	5	Guy Fawkes Day (1605)
01 20	7.2	13 35	7.1	Wed.	6	Alfred Sax, inventor of the Saxophone, b. 1814
01 59	7.1	14 13	7.1	Thur.	7	Marie Curie b. 1867
02 34	7.0	14 50	7.1	Fri.	8	John Milton, poet, d. 1674
03 05	7.0	15 24	7.0	Sat.	9	Neville Chamberlain, d. 1940
03 36	6.8	15 59	6.9	Sun.	10	**Twenty-fourth Sunday after Trinity. Remembrance Sunday (Seventh Sunday before Christmas) (Scottish Quarter Day)**
04 06	6.6	16 35	6.6	Mon.	11	Armistice Day (1918)
04 40	6.4	17 15	6.4	Tue.	12	Statute of Earl Attlee unveiled in House of Commons, 1979
05 16	6.2	17 58	6.1	Wed.	13	Robert Louis Stevenson b. 1850
05 58	6.0	18 49	5.9	Thur.	14	The Prince of Wales b. 1948
06 49	5.7	19 49	5.7	Fri.	15	The Treaty of London, 1831
07 55	5.5	21 00	5.6	Sat.	16	Boston Tea Party, 1773
09 15	5.6	22 06	5.9	Sun.	17	**Twenty-fifth Sunday after Trinity (Sixth before Christmas)**
10 24	5.9	23 05	6.2	Mon.	18	Marcel Proust d. 1922
11 20	6.2	23 56	6.5	Tue.	19	Charles I b. 1600
** **	***	12 10	6.6	Wed.	20	Wedding Anniversary of The Queen and Duke of Edinburgh, 1947
00 42	6.8	12 55	6.9	Thur.	21	Construction began on Forth Road Bridge, 1958
01 26	7.0	13 40	7.1	Fri.	22	Charles de Gaulle b. 1890
02 08	7.1	14 25	7.3	Sat.	23	Crippin executed at Pentonville, 1910
02 51	7.1	15 11	7.4	Sun.	24	**Sunday Next before Advent (Fifth Sunday before Christmas)**
03 36	7.1	16 00	7.4	Mon.	25	First performance of The Mousetrap, 1952
04 23	7.0	16 52	7.2	Tue.	26	William Cowper b. 1731
05 12	6.8	17 46	7.0	Wed.	27	Eugene O'Neill d. 1953
06 04	6.5	18 43	6.7	Thur.	28	Royal Society founded, 1600
07 02	6.4	19 45	6.5	Fri.	29	Thanksgiving Day, U.S.A.
08 05	6.3	20 51	6.4	Sat.	30	**St. Andrew's Day (Scotland)**

SUNRISE AND SUNSET (Times in G.M.T. except between 01.00 on March 31 and 01.00 on October 27 when times are in B.S.T. 1 hour in advance of G.M.T.) Sundays 1991.

London	Rise	Set	Belfast	Rise	Set	Birmingham	Rise	Set
	h m	h m		h m	h m		h m	h m
Nov. 3	06 57	16 31		07 29	16 45		07 06	16 35
Nov. 10	07 09	16 19		07 43	16 31		07 19	16 23
Nov. 17	07 21	16 09		07 57	16 20		07 32	16 12
Nov. 24	07 33	16 01		08 10	16 10		07 44	16 04

Cardiff	Rise	Set	Glasgow	Rise	Set	Manchester	Rise	Set
	h m	h m		h m	h m		h m	h m
Nov. 3	07 09	16 43		07 27	16 34		07 11	16 34
Nov. 10	07 21	16 32		07 42	16 20		07 24	16 21
Nov. 17	07 33	16 22		07 56	16 07		07 37	16 10
Nov. 24	07 45	16 14		08 10	15 57		07 50	16 01

MOON'S PHASES (G.M.T.)

New Moon	
Nov.6	11.11
First Quarter	
Nov.14	14.02
Full Moon	
Nov.21	22.56
Last Quarter	
Nov.28 15.21	

* See Tidal Constants on page 9

SAGITTARIUS

DECEMBER

TENTH MONTH OF THE EARLY ROMANS
31 DAYS

HIGH TIDE (London Bridge)* G.M.T.

Morn.		Ht.	Aft.		Ht.	DATE			
h	m	m	h	m	m				
09	15	6.3	22	03	6.5	Sun.	1	**First Sunday in Advent**	
10	28	6.4	23	11	6.7	Mon.	2	Battle of Austerlitz, 1805	
11	34	6.6	**	**	***	Tue.	3	Robert Louis Stevenson d. 1894	
00	08	6.8	12	29	6.7	Wed.	4	Royal Courts of Justice London opened by Queen Victoria, 1882	
00	56	6.8	13	16	6.8	Thur.	5	Prohibition laws in U.S.A. repealed in 1933	
01	37	6.8	13	55	6.8	Fri.	6	Columbus discovered Haiti in 1492	
02	13	6.8	14	33	6.9	Sat.	7	Japanese attack on Pearl Harbour, 1941	
02	46	6.8	15	08	6.9	Sun.	8	**Second Sunday in Advent**	
03	17	6.8	15	45	6.8	Mon.	9	Dame Edith Sitwell d. 1964	
03	49	6.7	16	20	6.7	Tue.	10	Royal Academy of Arts founded, 1768	
04	23	6.6	16	57	6.6	Wed.	11	King Edward VIII abdicated, 1936	
04	58	6.4	17	34	6.4	Thur.	12	Douglas Fairbanks, Sr., actor, d. 1939	
05	34	6.3	18	15	6.2	Fri.	13	The Battle of the River Plate, 1939	
06	14	6.1	19	00	6.0	Sat.	14	Captain Roald Amundsen reached the South Pole, 1911	
07	00	5.9	19	55	5.8	Sun.	15	**Third Sunday in Advent**	
08	01	5.7	21	04	5.8	Mon.	16	Boston Tea Party, 1773	
09	19	5.8	22	13	6.0	Tue.	17	New Royal Mint at Llantrisant opened, 1968	
10	30	6.0	23	15	6.3	Wed.	18	Abolition of Slavery in the United States, 1865	
11	33	6.4	**	**	***	Thur.	19	Sir Stanley Unwin, publisher, b. 1884	
00	12	6.6	12	32	6.7	Fri.	20	Peter the Great reformed the Russian Calendar, 1699	
01	06	6.8	13	26	7.0	Sat.	21	**St. Thomas**	
01	54	7.0	14	16	7.3	Sun.	22	**Fourth Sunday in Advent**	
02	42	7.1	15	05	7.5	Mon.	23	Sir Richard Arkwright b. 1732	
03	28	7.2	15	55	7.6	Tue.	24	**Christmas Eve**	
04	14	7.2	16	44	7.5	Wed.	25	**Christmas Day**	
05	01	7.1	17	33	7.3	Thur.	26	**St. Stephan. Boxing Day**	
05	49	6.9	18	24	6.9	Fri.	27	**St. John the Evangelist**	
06	36	6.7	19	17	6.6	Sat.	28	**Holy Innocents**	
07	31	6.5	20	15	6.4	Sun.	29	**First Sunday after Christmas**	
08	34	6.3	21	21	6.3	Mon.	30	Rudyard Kipling b. 1865	
09	48	6.1	22	33	6.2	Tue.	31	**New Year's Eve**	

SUNRISE AND SUNSET (Times in G.M.T. except between 01.00 on March 31 and 01.00 on October 27 when times are in B.S.T. 1 hour in advance of G.M.T.) Sundays 1991.

London

	Rise	Set
	h m	h m
Dec. 1	07 43	15 56
Dec. 8	07 52	15 52
Dec. 15	07 59	15 52
Dec. 22	08 04	15 54
Dec. 29	08 06	15 59

Cardiff

	Rise	Set
	h m	h m
Dec. 1	07 55	16 08
Dec. 8	08 05	16 04
Dec. 15	08 12	16 04
Dec. 22	08 16	16 06
Dec. 29	08 19	16 12

Belfast

	Rise	Set
	h m	h m
Dec. 1	08 22	16 03
Dec. 8	08 32	15 59
Dec. 15	08 39	15 58
Dec. 22	08 44	16 00
Dec. 29	08 46	16 05

Glasgow

	Rise	Set
	h m	h m
Dec. 1	08 22	15 49
Dec. 8	08 33	15 44
Dec. 15	08 41	15 43
Dec. 22	08 46	15 46
Dec. 29	08 48	15 50

Birmingham

	Rise	Set
	h m	h m
Dec. 1	07 55	15 58
Dec. 8	08 04	15 54
Dec. 15	08 11	15 53
Dec. 22	08 16	15 55
Dec. 29	08 18	16 00

Manchester

	Rise	Set
	h m	h m
Dec. 1	08 01	15 54
Dec. 8	08 11	15 50
Dec. 15	08 18	15 49
Dec. 22	08 23	15 51
Dec. 29	08 25	15 57

MOON'S PHASES (G.M.T.)

New Moon
Dec.6   03.56
First Quarter
Dec.14   09.32
Full Moon
Dec.21   10.23
Last Quarter
Dec.28   01.55

* See Tidal Constants on page 9

THE ROYAL FAMILY

THE HOUSE OF WINDSOR

Her Majesty Queen Elizabeth II

Princess Elizabeth Alexandra Mary, elder daughter of his late Majesty King George VI and of H.M. Queen Elizabeth The Queen Mother, born April 21, 1926. Married, November 20, 1947, H.R.H. the Duke of Edinburgh. Ascended the Throne, February 6, 1952. Crowned in Westminster Abbey, June 2, 1953.

H.R.H. The Prince Philip, Duke of Edinburgh

Prince Philip, only son of their late Royal Highnesses Prince and Princess Andrew of Greece, born June 10, 1921. Naturalized a British subject and adopted surname of Mountbatten 1947. Created Baron Greenwich, Earl of Merioneth, and Duke of Edinburgh in November, 1947. Granted style and titular dignity of a Prince of the United Kingdom 1957.

H.R.H. The Prince of Wales

Prince Charles Philip Arthur George, eldest son of H.M. The Queen and H.R.H. The Duke of Edinburgh, born November 14, 1948. Married, July 29, 1981, Lady Diana Frances Spencer, daughter of the 8th Earl Spencer, born July 1, 1961. Two sons:

H.R.H. Prince William Arthur Philip Louis (Prince William of Wales), born June 21, 1982.

H.R.H. Prince Henry Charles Albert David (Prince Henry of Wales), born September 15, 1984.

H.R.H. The Princess Royal

Princess Anne Elizabeth Alice Louise, only daughter of H.M. The Queen and H.R.H. The Duke of Edinburgh, born August 15, 1950. Married, November 14, 1973, Capt. Mark Phillips, The Queen's Dragoon Guards, son of Mr. and the late Mrs. Peter Phillips, born September 22, 1948. Two children:

Peter Mark Andrew Phillips, born November 15, 1977.

Zara Anne Elizabeth Phillips, born May 15, 1981.

H.R.H. The Duke of York

Prince Andrew Albert Christian Edward, second son of H.M. The Queen and H.R.H. The Duke of Edinburgh, born February 19, 1960. Married, July 23, 1986, Miss Sarah Margaret Ferguson, daughter of Major Ronald Ferguson and Mrs. Hector Barrantes, born October 15, 1959. Two daughters:

H.R.H. Princess Beatrice of York, born August 18, 1988.

H.R.H. Princess Eugenie Victoria Helena of York, born March 23, 1990

H.R.H. The Prince Edward Antony Richard Louis

Youngest son of H.M. The Queen and H.R.H. The Duke of Edinburgh, born March 10, 1964.

November 6, 1935, H.R.H. the Prince Henry, Duke of Gloucester, third son of his late Majesty King George V, and who died June 10, 1974. Two sons:

H.R.H. Prince William Henry Andrew Frederick, born December 18, 1941: died August 28, 1972.

H.R.H. the 2nd Duke of Gloucester (Prince Richard Alexander Walter George) born August 26, 1944. Married, July 8, 1972, Miss Brigitte Eva Van Deurs, daughter of Asger Preben Wissing Henriksen and Vivian Van Deurs, whose surname she assumed, born June 20, 1946. Three children: Alexander Patrick Gregers Richard (Earl of Ulster), born October 24, 1974; Lady Davina Elizabeth Alice Benedikte Windsor, born November 19, 1977; Lady Rose Victoria Brigitte Louise Windsor, born March 1, 1980.

H.M. Queen Elizabeth
The Queen Mother

Lady Elizabeth Angela Marguerite Bowes-Lyon, daughter of the 14th Earl of Strathmore and Kinghorne, born August 4, 1900. Married, April 26, 1923, H.R.H. the Duke of York, who ascended the Throne as King George VI on December 11, 1936. Crowned in Westminster Abbey, May 12, 1937.

H.R.H. The Princess Margaret,
Countess of Snowdon

Princess Margaret Rose, younger daughter of his late Majesty King George VI and of H.M. Queen Elizabeth The Queen Mother, born August 21, 1930. Married, May 6, 1960, Antony Charles Robert Armstrong-Jones, born March 7, 1930, created 1st Earl of Snowdon, October, 1961 (marriage dissolved, 1978). Two children:

David Albert Charles (Viscount Linley), born November 3, 1961.

Lady Sarah Frances Elizabeth Armstrong-Jones, born May 1, 1964.

H.R.H. Princess Alice,
Duchess of Gloucester

Lady Alice Christabel Montagu-Douglas-Scott, daughter of the 7th Duke of Buccleuch and Queensberry, born December 25, 1901. Married,

H.R.H. The Duke of Kent

Prince Edward George Nicholas Paul Patrick, 2nd Duke of Kent, elder son of their late Royal Highnesses the Duke and Duchess of Kent, born October 9, 1935. Married, June 8, 1961, Miss Katharine Lucy Mary Worsley, born February 22, 1933, daughter of the late Sir William Worsley, 4th Bt. Three children:

George Philip Nicholas (Earl of St. Andrews), born June 26, 1962. Married January 9, 1988, Miss Sylvana Tomaselli, born May 28, 1957, daughter of Max Tomaselli. One son:

Edward Edmund Maximilian George, Lord Downpatrick, born December 2, 1988.

Lady Helen Marina Lucy Windsor, born April 28, 1964.

Lord Nicholas Charles Edward Jonathan Windsor, born July 25, 1970. H.R.H. Princess Alexandra Helen Elizabeth Olga Christabel, daughter of their late Royal Highnesses the Duke and Duchess of Kent, born December 25, 1936. Married, April 24, 1963, Hon. Sir Angus James Bruce Ogilvy, K.C.V.O., son of the 12th Earl of Airlie, born September 14, 1928. Two children: James Robert Bruce Ogilvy, born February 29, 1964. Married, July 30, 1988, Miss Julia Caroline Rawlinson, born October 28, 1964, daughter of Charles Frederick Melville Rawlinson; Marina Victoria Alexandra Ogilvy, born July 31, 1966. Married February 2, 1990, Paul J. Mowatt.

H.R.H. Prince Michael George Charles Franklin, younger son of their late Royal Highnesses the Duke and Duchess of Kent, born July 4, 1942. Married, June 30, 1978, Baroness Marie-Christine Agnes Hedwig Ida, daughter of Baron Gunther Hubertus von Reibnitz, and formerly wife of Thomas Troubridge, born January 15, 1945. Two children: Lord Frederick Michael George David Louis Windsor, born April 6, 1979; Lady Gabriella Marina Alexandra Ophelia Windsor, born April 23, 1981.

Illustrations of coats of arms are reproduced by permission of Burke's Peerage Limited

2 THE ROYAL FAMILY

The Royal Year

by Hugo Vickers

The highlight of 1990 was the ninetieth birthday of Queen Elizabeth The Queen Mother. Though other members of the Royal Family have reached this age in the past, it is the first time that a Queen Consort has done so. Queen Elizabeth has been the most active Queen Dowager, the first to travel on official tours abroad for the Queen, the first to ascend in a Comet, and to serve as a Counsellor of State. In her ninetieth year, her energy was undimmed, and she continued to take an active part in royal life. She visited West Berlin to present the shamrock to the Irish Guards on St. Patrick's Day, and in June she gamely walked down the hill in the annual Garter procession.

The birthday was celebrated in a number of ways. The Queen Mother did not want a special service in St. Paul's Cathedral, but there was a luncheon at Guildhall given by the Lord Mayor of London, to which she was accompanied by Princess Margaret. The following night there was an extravaganza on Horse Guards Parade in which took part representatives of regiments, charities and other organizations associated with the Queen Mother. Some 4,500 people marched past, including Jerry Hall and Susan Hampshire representing the National Trust, many nurses, members of the George Cross Association, and finally the Chelsea Pensioners (none of whom had achieved the Queen Mother's age). Two days later Her Majesty visited the Black Watch in Northern Ireland. She was also present at a gala performance at the London Palladium, called "The Queen Mother's 90th Birthday Tribute". Sir John Gielgud, Dame Peggy Ashcroft, Dame Kiri Te Kanawa, Placido Domingo and others took part. The Queen, Prince Philip and Princess Margaret joined the Queen Mother in the Royal Box. In Guildhall, Windsor, a special exhibition covered the Queen Mother's life. This was opened by the Queen on 3 August.

Perhaps as exciting as any of this for the Queen Mother was her winning of the Grand Military Gold Cup at Sandown with her horse *The Argonaut*.

In July 1989 the President of the Arab Emirates paid a State Visit to the Queen in London. Shortly afterwards Queen Beatrix of the Netherlands paid a three day official visit to London to mark the end of the celebrations of William and Mary's Tercentenary. The Queen appointed Queen Beatrix a Lady of the Garter, and in June she came to Windsor to be installed (along with the first ever Lady Companion, Lavinia, Duchess of Norfolk, the Duke of Wellington, and Field Marshal Lord Bramall).

In September the Queen paid a visit to Singapore, before attending the Commonwealth Conference in Malaysia. Christmas was again spent at Sandringham. A few days earlier the Queen had the name of President Ceausescu removed from the role of the Knights Grand Cross of the Order of the Bath. The President, who had received the honour on his 1976 State Visit, was executed in Romania, following a revolution.

The Queen and Prince Philip made an extensive tour of the Antipodes in February. In Waitingi, the Queen was briefly in some danger as a Maori protester threw what turned out to be a black tee-shirt into the Queen's car.

In April the Queen greeted Ramaswami Venkataraman, the 79 year old President of India on a State Visit to Britain. Due to a false alarm, a bomb scare, the traditional carriage drive from Victoria to Buckingham Palace was cancelled, and the President arrived by car. At the end of May the Queen visited Eton College in connexion with their 550th Anniversary (the 500th having occurred in the thick of war). The Duke and Duchess of Gloucester were there throughout the day. The Queen Mother arrived by barge for the fireworks and the Provost, Lord Charteris of Amisfield, a former Private Secretary to the Queen, was heard to greet her with the endearing phrase: "Come on. Shall we stagger up here together?" The very next day the Queen Mother left for a private visit to Brittany.

As Captain General of the Royal Marines, Prince Philip read the lesson at a memorial service for the eleven musicians of the Royal Marines School of Music, killed in an I.R.A. bomb attack at their barracks at Deal.

In September 1989 the Prince of Wales published his book, *A Vision of Britain*, in which he analyzed the decline of post-war architecture, and presented his own concept of a more harmonious future. There was also an exhibition at the Victoria and Albert Museum. In February the Prince went to Florida and then on to Washington where he again delivered a broadside to the architects. In May he introduced a television documentary on the environment. The Princess of Wales attended a memorial service for those that died when the pleasure cruiser, The Marchioness, sank in the Thames. Prince Harry joined his brother at Wetherby School. In November the Waleses visited Indonesia and then Hong Kong, a trip originally threatened by the political scene in China. (Their proposed visit to China did not take place). The Prince opened a new £200 million convention and exhibition centre. In March the Waleses made a visit to West Africa, paying the first royal visit to Nigeria since its independence nearly thirty years ago. Then they went to Hungary, where the Prince of Wales welcomed the country back into western civilization. In a speech with political implications, he spoke of the Soviet Union's "horrendous totalitarianism".

In June Prince Charles was badly injured in a polo match, breaking his arm at Cirencester. Normally special photographs are released on royal birthdays. This year, on the Princess of Wales's 29th birthday, it was the Prince himself who was released - from hospital. The Waleses attended the wedding of the Princess's brother, Viscount Althorp to model Victoria Lockwood in September 1989.

At the end of August 1989, it was announced that the Princess Royal and Captain Mark Phillips were to separate officially. The Palace announcement confirmed that this was "on terms agreed between them", adding: "There are no plans for divorce proceedings". Princess Anne was attending a meeting of the Olympic Committee in Puerto Rico at the time. The plan was that Captain Phillips should continue to live on the Gatcombe estate in order to run the farm, and the annual horse show. If precedent is followed divorce will eventually be granted due to the separation, thus alleviating the need to discuss it further.

Besides maintaining her traditionally heavy round of engagements, Princess Anne paid the first official visit of a member of the Royal Family to Russia (Prince Philip, Prince Edward and Princess Anne herself had been there for other reasons before). The Princess went in connection with the Save the Children Fund, and had a fifteen minute meeting with President Gorbachev. The highlight of her visit was an address she gave to students of Moscow University, which earned her a standing ovation.

Following a tour of Canada in July 1989, the Duke and Duchess of York were in Venice in August in connexion with the work of the Venice in Peril Fund.

On 23 March the Duchess of York gave birth to a second baby daughter, christened Eugenie Victoria Helena. The child's official style is Her Royal Highness Princess Eugenie of York, and she is sixth in line to the Throne. Not long after the birth, the Duchess took both her daughters on a holiday in Balmoral. During the course of the year the Duchess remained concerned for the health of her stepfather, erstwhile polo player, Hector Barrantes.

Prince Edward's time was spent mostly working for the Really Useful theatre Company. This took him to the United States in the summer of 1989 for the New York opening of *Aspects of Love*. Prince Edward undertook various engagements for the Duke of Edinburgh's Award Scheme. In October 1989 he was present at the memorial service for Lord Olivier in Westminster Abbey. In the new year he attended the opening of the Commonwealth Games in Auckland, New Zealand. In July 1990 Prince Edward paid a visit to Canada to open the West Canada Summer Games.

Princess Alice, Duchess of Gloucester, a year younger than the Queen Mother, carried out various engagements including attending the ceremony of the Order of the Bath at Westminster Abbey. The Princess was appointed the first ever Dame Grand Cross in 1975. The Queen was present this time as Sovereign, and the Prince of Wales as Grand Master. All wore scarlet robes of the Order.

The young Duchess of Gloucester went to Denmark for the fiftieth birthday of Queen Margrethe. There was a glittering of royalty, including King Olav of Norway, who not long afterwards suffered a serious stroke.

In November 1989 the Duke of Kent was present at a ceremony at Neuve Chapelle to mark the 75th anniversary of that grim battle. In the summer the Duke and Duchess visited Houston, Texas for their International Festival.

Prince Michael of Kent was on a speeding offence, an unfortunate thing at the best of times but worse for him as he is President of the R.A.C.

Princess Alexandra had a particularly difficult year. In the latter months of 1989 her daughter Marina announced that she was pregnant by her boyfriend, Mr. Paul Mowatt, a photographer. The family rift between the Ogilvys and the Mowatts was extensively aired in the lesser tabloids, but finally Miss Ogilvy and Mr. Mowatt decided to marry. Princess Alexandra and Sir Angus Ogilvy attended the wedding in February, accompanied by their son James, and his wife Julia. Princess Alexandra was elegant in purple velvet, sometimes deemed the colour of royal mourning. On 26 May the Mowatt baby girl was born, and, the rift somewhat healed, the Ogilvys went to the new born.

In June Princess Alexandra, Sir Angus, and the young Ogilvys were present at the memorial service for Mrs Jill Mann, wife of the former Dean of Windsor, a tribute to the help he gave them during their difficult family crisis.

Viscount Linley successfully sued *Today* newspaper for describing him as an "upper class lager lout". This was a rare appearance of a member of the Royal Family in the courtroom.

The Prince and Princess of Liechtenstein died within weeks of each other. Close friends of our Royal family, the Queen sent Prince Edward and the Princess of Wales to the funerals. The King of Greece celebrated his twenty-fifth wedding anniversary, and later his fiftieth birthday, both occasions attended by a great number of our Royal Family. It was a year when many of the Queen's cousins were in the news as communism subsided, and it appeared that possibly some of the exiled Kings might return to their countries. The Romanian Royal family were very busy undertaking relief work in Romania, though King Michael himself was not allowed to return to his country. Another active exile was Crown Prince Alexander of Yugoslavia, who, unlike some of his colleagues, studiously refused to take the title of King on the death of his father.

Interestingly the Queen Mother is not officially the oldest member of the Royal Family on the Lord Chamberlain's List. Colonel Sir Henry Abel Smith became ninety in March. For 59 years he has been married to Queen Mary's niece, the former Lady May Cambridge, daughter of the Earl of Athlone and Princess Alice, Countess of Athlone.

THE QUEEN'S HOUSEHOLD

LORD CHAMBERLAIN: The Rt. Hon. the Earl of Airlie, K.T., G.C.V.O.
LORD STEWARD: The Viscount Ridley
MASTER OF THE HORSE: The Earl of Westmorland, K.C.V.O.
TREASURER OF THE HOUSEHOLD: Tristan Garel-Jones, M.P.
COMPTROLLER OF THE HOUSEHOLD: Alastair Goodlad, M.P.
VICE-CHAMBERLAIN OF THE HOUSEHOLD: Anthony Durant, M.P.
GOLD STICK: Maj.-Gen. Lord Michael Fitzalan Howard, G.C.V.O., C.B., C.B.E., M.C.; General Sir Desmond Fitzpatrick, G.C.B., D.S.O., M.B.E., M.C.
VICE-ADMIRAL OF THE UNITED KINGDOM: Admiral Sir Anthony Griffin, G.C.B.
REAR-ADMIRAL OF THE UNITED KINGDOM: Admiral Sir Anthony Morton, G.B.E., K.C.B.
MISTRESS OF THE ROBES: The Duchess of Grafton, G.C.V.O.
LADIES OF THE BEDCHAMBER: The Countess of Airlie, C.V.O., The Lady Farnham
WOMEN OF THE BEDCHAMBER: The Hon. Mary Morrison, D.C.V.O., The Lady Susan Hussey, D.C.V.O., Mrs. John Dugdale, D.C.V.O., The Lady Elton
PRIVATE SECRETARY: The Rt. Hon. Sir William Heseltine, G.V.C.O., K.C.B., A.C.
DEPUTY PRIVATE SECRETARY: Sir Robert Fellowes, K.C.V.O., C.B.
ASSISTANT PRIVATE SECRETARY: Sir Kenneth Scott, K.C.V.O., C.M.G.
PRESS SECRETARY: Robin Janvrin, L.V.O.
KEEPER OF THE PRIVY PURSE AND TREASURER TO THE QUEEN: Major Sir Shane Blewitt, K.C.V.O.
DEPUTY KEEPER AND ASSISTANT TREASURER TO THE QUEEN: John C. Parsons.
MASTER OF THE HOUSEHOLD: Rear-Admiral Sir Paul Greening, K.C.V.O.

DEPUTY MASTER OF THE HOUSEHOLD: Lt. Col. Blair Stewart-Wilson, C.V.O.
COMPTROLLER, LORD CHAMBERLAIN'S OFFICE: Lt. Col. George West, C.V.O.
ASSISTANT COMPTROLLER, LORD CHAMBERLAIN'S OFFICE: Lt. Col. Malcolm Ross, O.B.E.
LORDS-IN-WAITING: Lt.-Col. The Rt. Hon. Lord Charteris of Amisfield, G.C.B., G.C.V.O., O.B.E., Q.S.O. (Permanent), The Lord Somerleyton, The Viscount Boyne, The Viscount Long, The Viscount Ullswater, The Lord Reay, The Earl of Strathmore and Kinghorne, The Baroness Blatch C.B.E. (Baroness in Waiting).
MARSHAL OF THE DIPLOMATIC CORPS: Lt.-Gen. Sir John Richards, K.C.B.
SECRETARY, CENTRAL CHANCERY OF THE ORDERS OF KNIGHTHOOD: Lt. Col. Malcolm Ross, O.B.E.
CAPTAIN, GENTLEMEN-AT-ARMS: The Rt. Hon. Lord Denham.
CAPTAIN, YEOMEN OF THE GUARD: The Viscount Davidson.
CROWN EQUERRY: Lt. Col. Seymour Gilbart-Denham

THE DUKE OF EDINBURGH'S HOUSEHOLD
PRIVATE SECRETARY AND TREASURER: Brian McGrath, C.V.O.
EQUERRY: Major Sir Guy Acland, Bt.

THE PRINCE AND PRINCESS OF WALES'S HOUSEHOLD
EQUERRY TO THE PRINCE OF WALES: Commander Alastair Watson, R.N.
EXTRA EQUERRIES TO THE PRINCE OF WALES: Sqdn. Ldr. Sir David Checketts, K.C.V.O., The Hon. Edward Adeane, C.V.O., Gerald Ward, C.B.E., General John Winter, L.V.O.
EQUERRY TO THE PRINCESS OF WALES: Lt.Cdr. Patrick Jephson, R.N.
LADY IN WAITING AND ASSISTANT PRIVATE SECRETARY TO THE PRINCESS OF WALES : Miss Anne Beckwith-Smith, L.V.O.
EXTRA LADIES IN WAITING: Mrs. George West, Viscountess Campden, Mrs. Max Pike, Miss Alexandra Loyd, The Hon. Miss Vivian Baring, Mrs. James Lonsdale.
PRIVATE SECRETARY AND TREASURER TO THE PRINCE AND PRINCESS OF WALES: Sir John Riddell, Bt.

ENGLISH KINGS BEFORE THE CONQUEST

	Accession	Died
Egbert	827	839
Ethelwulf	839	858
Ethelbald	858	860
Ethelbert	858	866
Ethelredt	866	871
Alfred the Great	871	901
Edward the Elder	901	925
Athelstan	925	940
Edmund	940	946
Edred	946	955
Edwy	955	959
Edgar	959	975
Edward the Martyr	975	978
Ethelred II	978	1016
Edmund Ironside	1016	1016
Canute the Dane	1017	1035
Harold I	1035	1040
Hardicanute	1040	1042
Edward the Confessor	1042	1066
Harold II	1066	1066

QUEEN ELIZABETH THE QUEEN MOTHER'S HOUSEHOLD
LORD CHAMBERLAIN: The Earl of Dalhousie, K.T., G.C.V.O., G.B.E., M.C.
MISTRESS OF THE ROBES: Vacant
PRIVATE SECRETARY: Lt.-Col. Sir Martin Gilliat, G.C.V.O., M.B.E.
TREASURER: Major Sir Ralph Anstruther, Bt., K.C.V.O., M.C.
COMPTROLLER: Captain Sir Alastair Aird, K.C.V.O.
PRESS SECRETARY: Major John Griffin, C.V.O.

THE ROYAL ARMS

TODAY the Royal Arms defy the rules of heraldry. Usually, when Arms are borne by a woman they are on a lozenge - a diamond shape - instead o73 of a shield. The shield is considered a masculine, war-like emblem.

But the Queen, as sovereign, is above the laws of heraldry. She has her Arms on a shield surmounted by another masculine emblem, a helmet.

The Royal Arms quarter the ancient Coats of the three parts of the United Kingdom: England, Scotland, and Ireland.

England: The first and fourth quarters both show three lions *passant guardant* (full-faced and walking) in *pale* (vertically) on a *gules* (red) background.
Scotland: The second quarter has a lion rampant within a double *tressure flory counter flory* (a border adorned with fleurs-de-lis pointing alternately in and out).

Ireland: The third quarter is a harp on an *azure* (blue) background.

And the whole Coat is encircled by the *garter* - a blue buckled riband.

The supporters are: *Dexter* (on the right), a lion rampant guardant, imperially crowned. *Sinister* (left), a unicorn *argent* (silver), *armed, crined,* and *ungeuled* (horn, hooves and mane a different colour from the rest of the beast), *gorged* (encircled round the throat) with a coronet and with a chain attached.

For use in Scotland, the Arms are different. The positions of the supporters are reversed. The unicorn is crowned and carries the banner of St. Andrew, the lion, the banner of St. George. The Scottish lion occupies the first and fourth quarters.

THE ROYAL FAMILY 2

ENGLISH RULERS

	Accession	Died
House of Normandy:		
William I	1066	1087
William II	1087	1100
Henry I	1100	1135
Stephen	1135	1154
House of Plantagenet:		
Henry II	1154	1189
Richard I	1189	1199
John	1199	1216
Henry III	1216	1272
Edward I	1272	1307
Edward II	1307	1327
Edward III	1327	1377
Richard II	1377	dep 1399
Henry IV	1399	1413
Henry V Lancaster	1413	1422
Henry VI	1422	dep 1461
Edward IV	1461	1483
Edward V York	1483	1483
Richard III	1483	1485
House of Tudor:		
Henry VII	1485	1509
Henry VIII	1509	1547
Edward VI	1547	1553
Jane	1553	1554
Mary I	1553	1558
Elizabeth	1558	1603

SCOTTISH RULERS

	Accession	Died
Malcolm III (Canmore)	1057	1093
Donald Ban	1093	-
Duncan II	1094	1094
Donald Ban	1094	1097
Edgar	1097	1107
Alexander I	1107	1124
David I	1124	1153
Malcolm IV (The Maiden)	1153	1165
William I (The Lion)	1165	1214
Alexander II	1214	1249
Alexander III	1249	1286
Margaret, Maid of Norway	1286	1290
John Baliol	1292	1296
Robert (I) Bruce	1306	1329
David II	1329	1371
Robert II (Stewart)	1371	1390
Robert III	1390	1406
James I	1406	1437
James II	1437	1460
James III	1460	1488
James IV	1488	1513
James V	1513	1542
Mary	1542	1587
James VI (ascended the Throne of England in 1603)	1567	1625

BRITISH RULERS

	Accession	Died	Age	Reigned
House of Stuart				
James I (VI of Scotland)	1603	1625	59	22
Charles I	1625	executed 1649	48	24
Commonwealth and Protectorate				
Oliver Cromwell, Lord Protector	1653-8	-	-	-
Richard Cromwell, Lord Protector	1658-9	-	-	-
House of Stuart (restored)				
Charles II	1660	1685	55	25
James II (VII of Scotland)	1685	deposed 1688	68	3
Interregnum Dec 11 1688 to Feb 13 1689				
William III and	1689	1702	5	13
Mary II	1689	1694	33	6
Anne	1702	1714	49	12
House of Hanover				
George I	1714	1727	67	13
George II	1727	1760	77	33
George III	1760	1820	81	59
George IV	1820	1830	67	10
William IV	1830	1837	71	7
Victoria	1837	1901	81	63
House of SaxeCoburg				
Edward VII	1901	1910	68	9
House of Windsor				
George V	1910	1936	70	25
Edward VIII	1936	1972	77	325 days
George VI	1936	1952	56	15
Elizabeth II	1952	-	-	-

THE ROYAL FAMILY

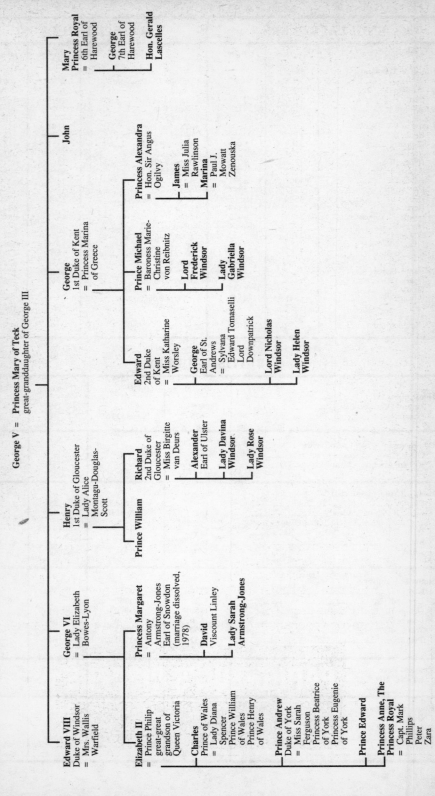

George V = **Princess Mary of Teck**
great-granddaughter of George III

Edward VIII
Duke of Windsor
= Mrs. Wallis
Warfield

George VI
= Lady Elizabeth
Bowes-Lyon

Elizabeth II
= Prince Philip
great-great
grandson of
Queen Victoria

Charles
Prince of Wales
= Lady Diana
Spencer
Prince William
of Wales
Prince Henry
of Wales

Prince Andrew
Duke of York
= Miss Sarah
Ferguson
Princess Beatrice
of York
Princess Eugenie
of York

Prince Edward

Princess Anne, The
Princess Royal
= Capt. Mark
Phillips
Peter
Zara

Princess Margaret
= Antony
Armstrong-Jones
Earl of Snowdon
(marriage dissolved,
1978)

David
Viscount Linley

Lady Sarah
Armstrong-Jones

Henry
1st Duke of Gloucester
= Lady Alice
Montagu-Douglas-
Scott

Prince William

Richard
2nd Duke of
Gloucester
= Miss Birgitte
van Deurs

Alexander
Earl of Ulster

Lady Davina
Windsor

Lady Rose
Windsor

John

George
1st Duke of Kent
= Princess Marina
of Greece

Edward
2nd Duke
of Kent
= Miss Katharine
Worsley

George
Earl of St.
Andrews
= Sylvana
Edward Tomaselli
Lord
Downpatrick

Lord Nicholas
Windsor

Lady Helen
Windsor

Prince Michael
= Baroness Marie-
Christine
von Reibnitz

Lord
Frederick
Windsor

Lady
Gabriella
Windsor

Princess Alexandra
= Hon. Sir Angus
Ogilvy

James
= Miss Julia
Rawlinson

Marina
= Paul J.
Mowatt
Zenouska

Mary
Princess Royal
= 6th Earl of
Harewood

George
7th Earl of
Harewood

Hon. Gerald
Lascelles

PARLIAMENT

THE CABINET
(As at 23rd July 1990)

Prime Minister and First Lord of the Treasury and Minister for the Civil Service (£52,627)
Rt. Hon. Margaret Thatcher, F.R.S., M.P.

Lord President of the Council and Leader of the House of Commons (£52,627)
Sir Geoffrey Howe, M.P.

Lord Chancellor (£87,250)
The Rt. Hon. Lord Mackay of Clashfern.

Secretary of State for Foreign and Commonwealth Affairs (£52,627)
Rt. Hon. Douglas Hurd, C.B.E., M.P.

Chancellor of the Exchequer (£52,627)
Rt. Hon. John Major, M.P.

Secretary of State for the Home Department (£52,627)
Rt. Hon. David Waddington, M.P.

Secretary of State for Defence (£52,627)
Rt. Hon. Tom King, M.P.

Secretary of State for Trade and Industry and President of the Board of Trade (£52,627)
Rt. Hon. Peter Lilley, M.P.

Chancellor of the Duchy of Lancaster (Chairman of the Conservative Party) (£52,627)
Rt. Hon. Kenneth Baker, M.P.

Secretary of State for Health (£52,627)
Rt. Hon. Kenneth Clarke, Q.C.,M.P.

Secretary of State for Education and Science (£52,627)
Rt. Hon. John MacGregor, O.B.E., M.P.

Secretary of State for Scotland (£52,627)
Rt. Hon. Malcolm Rifkind, Q.C., M.P.

Secretary of State for Transport (£52,627)
Rt. Hon. Cecil Parkinson, M.P.

Secretary of State for Energy (£52,627)
Rt. Hon. John Wakenham, M.P.

Lord Privy Seal and Leader of the House of Lords (£42,357)
The Rt. Hon. Lord Belstead, M.P.

Secretary of State for Social Security (£52,627)
Rt. Hon. Anthony Newton, O.B.E., M.P.

Secretary of State for the Environment (£52,627)
Rt. Hon. Christopher Patten, M.P.

Secretary of State for Northern Ireland (£52,627)
Rt. Hon. Peter Brooke, M.P.

Minister of Agriculture, Fisheries and Food (£52,627)
Rt. Hon. John Gummer, M.P.

Chief Secretary to the Treasury (£52,627)
Rt. Hon. Norman Lamont, M.P.

Secretary of State for Employment (£52,627)
Rt. Hon. Michael Howard, Q.C., M.P.

Secretary of State for Wales (£52,627)
Rt. Hon. David Hunt, M.B.E.,M.P.

LAW OFFICERS

Attorney-General (£54,827)
Rt. Hon. Sir Patrick Mayhew, Q.C., M.P.

Lord Advocate (£40,508)
The Rt. Hon. Lord Fraser of Carmyllie, Q.C.

Solicitor-General (£48,107)
The Rt. Hon. Sir Nicholas Lyell, Q.C., M.P.

Solicitor-General for Scotland (£34,956)
Alan Rodger Esq, Q.C.

MINISTERS NOT IN THE CABINET

Parliamentary Secretary to the Treasury (£37,047)
Rt. Hon. Tim Renton Esq., M.P.

Minister of State, Privy Council Office (Minister for the Arts) (£42,357)
Rt. Hon. David Mellor, M.P.

Minister for Overseas Development (£42,357)
Rt. Hon. Lynda Chalker, M.P.

Ministers of State, Foreign and Commonwealth Office (£42,357)
Rt. Hon. William Waldegrave, M.P.
Rt. Hon. Francis Maude, M.P.
Tristan Garel-Jones Esq, M.P.

Paymaster General (£42,357)
Richard Ryder Esq, O.B.E., M.P.

Financial Secretary to the Treasury (£36,367)
Rt. Hon. Francis Maude, M.P.

Ministers of State, Home Office (£42,347)
Rt. Hon. John Patten, Esq., M.P.
Rt. Hon. Angela Rumbold, C.B.E., M.P.
Rt. Hon. Earl Ferrers, D.L.

Minister of State, Ministry of Defence (Minister of State for the Armed Forces) (£42,347)
Hon. Archibald Hamilton, M.P.

Minister of State, Ministry of Defence (Minister of State for Defence Procurement) (£42,347)
Hon. Alan Clark, M.P.

Ministers of State, Department of Trade and Industry (£42,347)
Minister for Industry and Enterprise.
Hon. Douglas Hogg, Q.C. M.P.

Ministers for Trade (£42,347)
Hon. Tim Sainsbury, M.P.
Lord Hesketh

Minister of State, Department of Health (£42,347)
Mrs. Virginia Bottomley, M.P.

Minister of State, Department of Education and Science (£42,347)
Tim Eggar Esq., M.P.

Ministers of State, Scottish Office (£42,347)
Ian Lang, M.P.
Lord Sanderson of Bowden

Minister of State, Department of Transport (Minister for Public Transport) (£42,347)
Roger Freeman Esq., M.P.

Minister of State, Department of Energy (£42,347)
Lord Brabazon of Tara

Minister of State, Department of Social Security (£42,347)
Rt. Hon. Nicholas Scott, Esq., M.B.E., M.P.

Minister of State, Department of Environment (Minister for Housing and Planning) (£42,347)
Michael Spicer Esq., M.P.

Minister of State, Department of Environment (Minister for Environment and Countryside) (£42,347)
David Trippier, Esq., J.P. M.P.

Minister of State, Department of Environment (Minister for Local Government and Inner Cities) (£42,347)
Michael Portillo, Esq., M.P.

Minister of State, Northern Ireland Office (£42,347)
Rt. Hon. John Cope, M.P.

Minister of State, Ministry of Agriculture, Fisheries and Food (£42,347)
Baroness Trumpington

Minister of State, Welsh Office (£42,347)
Sir Wyn Roberts, M.P.

DEPARTMENTS OF STATE AND MINISTERS

AGRICULTURE, FISHERIES AND FOOD, MINISTRY OF -
Parliamentary Secretaries (£36,367)
Minister - **Rt. Hon. John Gummer, M.P.**
Minister of State - **Baroness Trumpington**
Parliamentary Secretaries - **David Maclean, M.P. David Curry, M.P.**

ARTS AND LIBRARIES, OFFICE OF -
Minister for the Arts - **Rt. Hon. David Mellor, M.P.**

CHANCELLOR OF THE DUCHY OF LANCASTER -
Rt. Hon. Kenneth Baker, M.P.

CIVIL SERVICE, OFFICE OF THE MINISTER FOR -
Prime Minister and Minister for the Civil Service - **Rt. Hon. Margaret Thatcher, F.R.S., M.P.**

DEFENCE -
Secretary of State - **Rt. Hon. Tom King, M.P.**
Minister of State for Defence Procurement - **Hon. Alan Clarke, M.P.**
Minister of State for the Armed Forces - **Hon. Archibald Hamilton, M.P.**

Parliamentary Under-Secretary of State for the Defence Procurment - **Kenneth Carlisle Esq, M.P.**
Parilamentary Under-Secretary of State for the Armed Forces - **Earl of Arran.**

EDUCATION AND SCIENCE -
Secretary of State - **Rt. Hon. John MacGregor, O.B.E., M.P.**
Minister of State - **Tim Eggar Esq, M.P.**
Parliamentary Under-Secretaries of State - **Alan Howarth, M.P., Michael Fallon, M.P.**

EMPLOYMENT -
Secretary of State - **Rt. Hon. Michael Howard, M.P.**
Parliamentary Under-Secretaries of State - **Robert Jackson Esq, M.P.; Eric Forth Esq, M.P.; Viscount Ullswater.**

ENERGY -
Secretary of State - **Rt. Hon. John Wakenham, M.P.**
Parliamentary Under-Secretaries of State - **Tony Baldry Esq., M.P.; Hon Colin Moynihan, M.P.**

ENVIRONMENT -
Secretary of State - **Rt. Hon. Christopher Patten, M.P.**
Ministers of State -
Minister for the Environment and Countryside - **David Trippier Esq., R.D., M.P.**
Minister for Local Government and Inner Cities - **Michael Portillo Esq., M.P.**
Minister for Housing and Planning - **Michael Spicer Esq., M.P.**
Parliamentary Under-Secretaries of State - **David Heatcote-Amory Esq., M.P.; Patrick Nicholls Esq., M.P.; Lord Strathclyde.**
Minister for Sport - **Robert Atkins Esq, M.P.**

FOREIGN AND COMMONWEALTH AFFAIRS -
Secretary of State - **Rt. Hon. Douglas Hurd, C.B.E., M.P.**
Minister for Overseas Development - **Rt. Hon. Lynda Chalker, M.P.**
Ministers of State - **Rt. Hon. William Waldegrave, M.P.; Rt. Hon Earl of Caithness; Tristan Garel-Jones Esq, M.P.**
Parliamentary Under-Secretary of State - **Hon. Mark Lennox-Boyd, M.P.**

HEALTH -
Secretary of State for Health - **Rt. Hon. Kenneth Clarke, Q.C. M.P.**
Minister of State - **Mrs. Virgina Bottomly, M.P.**
Parliamentary Under-Secretaries of State - **Stephen Dorrell Esq., M.P., Baroness Hooper.**

HOME OFFICE -
Secretary of State for the Home Department - **Rt. Hon David Waddington, Q.C., M.P.**
Ministers of State - **Rt. Hon. John Patten Esq., M.P. David Mellor; Rt. Hon. Earl Ferrers, D.L.; Mrs Angela Rumbold, C.B.E., M.P.**
Parliamentary Under-Secratary of State - **Peter Lloyd Esq., M.P.**

LAW OFFICERS' DEPARTMENT -
Attorney-General - **Rt. Hon. Sir Patrick Mayhew, Q.C. M.P.**
Solicitor-General - **Rt. Hon. Sir Nicholas Lyell, Q.C. M.P.**

LORD ADVOCATE'S DEPARTMENT -
Lord-Advocate - **Rt. Hon Lord Fraser of Carmyllie, Q.C.**
Solicitor-General for Scotland - **Alan Rodger Esq., Q.C.**

LORD CHANCELLOR -
Rt. Hon. Lord Mackay of Clashfern.

NORTHERN IRELAND OFFICE -
Secretary of State for Northern Ireland - **Rt. Hon. Peter Brooke, M.P.**
Minister of State - **Rt. Hon. John Cope, M.P.**
Parliamentary Under-Secretaries of State - **Richard Needham, M.P. Dr. Brian Mawhinney, M.P. Lord Skelmersdale.**

PAYMASTER GENERAL -
Rt. Hon. Earl of Caithness

PRIVY COUNCIL OFFICE -
Lord President of the Council and Leader of the House of Commons - **Sir Geoffrey Howe, Q.C., M.P.**
Lord Privy Seal and Leader of the House of Lords - **Rt. Hon. Lord Belstead D.L.**
Minister of State - **Rt. Hon. David Mellor, Q.C., M.P.**

SCOTTISH OFFICE -
Secretary of State for Scotland - **Rt. Hon. Malcolm Rifkind, Q.C. M.P.**
Ministers of State - **Ian Lang Esq., M.P. Lord Sanderson of Bowden.**
Parliamentary Under-Secretaries of State -
Minister for Home Affairs and the Environment - **Lord Douglas- Hamilton, M.P.**
Minister for Health - **Michael Forsyth, M.P.**

SOCIAL SECURITY -
Secretary of State for Social Security - **Rt. Hon. Anthony Newton, O.B.E., M.P,**
Minister of State for Social Security and the Disabled - **Rt. Hon. Nicholas Scott, M.B.E., M.P.**
Parliamentary Under-Secretaries of State - **Lord Henley. Mrs. Gillian Shephard, M.P.**

TRADE AND INDUSTRY -
Secretary of State for Trade and Industry and President of the Board of Trade - **Rt. Hon. Peter Lilley, M.P.**
Ministers of State -
Minister for Trade - **Hon. Tim Sainsbury, M.P.**
Minister for Industry and Enterprise - **Hon. Douglas Hogg, Q.C. M.P.**
Parliamentary Under-Secretaries of State -
Parliamentary Under-Secretary of State for Industry and Consumer Affairs -
Parliamentary Under-Secretary of State for Corporate Affairs - **John Redwood Esq., M.P.**

TRANSPORT -
Secretary of State for Transport - **Rt. Hon. Cecil Parkinson, M.P.**
Minister of State -
Minister for Public Transport - **Roger Freeman Esq., M.P.; Lord Brabazon of Tara**
Parliamentary Under-Secretaries of State -
Minister for Roads and Traffic - **Christopher Chope Esq, M.P.**
Minister for Aviation and Shipping - **Patrick McLoughlin, M.P.**

TREASURY -
Prime Minister, First Lord of the Treasury and Minister for the Civil Service - **Rt. Hon. Margaret Thatcher, F.R.S., M.P.**
Chancellor of the Exchequer - **Rt. Hon. John Major, M.P.**
Chief Secretary - **Rt. Hon. Norman Lamont, M.P.**
Paymaster General - **Richard Ryder Esq, O.B.E., M.P.**
Financial Secretary - **Hon Francis Maude, M.P.**
Economic Secretary - **John Maples, M.P.**
Parliamentary Secretary to the Treasury - **Rt. Hon. Tim Renton, M.P.**
Lord Commissioners - **David Lightbrown Esq., M.P. John M. Taylor Esq., M.P. Hon. Tom Sackville**
Assistant Whips - **Sydney Chapman Esq., M.P. Greg Knight Esq., M.P. Irvine Patnick Esq., O.B.E., M.P. Nicholas Baker Esq., M.P. Timothy Wood Esq., M.P.**

WELSH OFFICE -
Secretary of State for Wales - **Rt. Hon. David Hunt, M.B.E., M.P.**
Minister of State - **Sir Wyn Roberts Esq,. M.P.**
Parliamentary Under-Secretary of State - **Ian Grist, M.P.**

LEADER OF THE OPPOSITION -
Rt. Hon. Neil Kinnock, M.P.

Salaries shown are those in effect from January 1, 1989.

PRIME MINISTERS OF THE TWENTIETH CENTURY

REIGN OF EDWARD VII

Marquess of Salisbury (Cons)	1901-1902
Arthur J. Balfour (Cons)	1902-1905
Sir Henry Campbell-Bannerman (Lib)	1905-1901
Herbert H. Asquith (lib)	1908-1910

REIGN OF GEORGE V

Herbert H. Asquith (Lib)	1910-1915
Herbert H. Asquith (Coalition)	1915-1916
D. Lloyd George (Coalition)	1916-1922
A. Bonar Law (Cons)	1922-1923
Stanley Baldwin (Cons)	1923-1924
J. Ramsay MacDonald (Lab)	1924
Stanley Baldwin (Cons)	1924-1929
J. Ramsay MacDonald (Lab)	1929-1931
J. Ramsay MacDonald (Nat. Govt.)	1931-1935
Stanley Baldwin (Nat. Govt.)	1935-1936

REIGN OF EDWARD VIII

Stanley Baldwin (Nat. Govt.)	1936

REIGN OF GEORGE VI

Stanley Baldwin (Nat. Govt.)	1936-1937
Neville Chamberlain (Nat. Govt.)	1937-1940
Winston S. Churchill (Coalition)	1940-1945
Clement R. Atlee (Lab)	1945-1951
Winston S. Churchill (Cons)	1951-1952

REIGN OF ELIZABETH II

Sir Winston S. Churchill (Cons)	1952-1955
Sir Anthony Eden (Cons)	1955-1957
Harold Macmillan (Cons)	1957-1963
Sir Alec Douglas-Home (Cons)	1963-1964
Harold Wilson (Lab)	1964-1970
Edward Heath (Cons)	1970-1974
Harold Wilson (Lab)	1974-1976
James Callaghan (Lab)	1976-1979
Margaret Thatcher (Cons)	1979-

MEMBERS OF PARLIAMENT

(Listed alphabetically by Members' names. Numbers refer to the constituency lists on pages 39 - 48).

A

Abbott, Ms. D.J.; (Lab) Hackney North and Stoke Newington, *282*
Adams, G.; (SF) Belfast West, *41*
Adams, A.; (Lab) Paisley North, *452*
Adley, R.J.; (C) Christchurch, *141*
Aitken, J.W.P.; (C) Thanet South, *572*
Alexander, R.T.; (C) Newark, *415*
Alison, M.J.H.; (C) Selby, *504*
Allason, R.W.S.; (C) Torbay, *577*
Allen, G.W.; (Lab) Nottingham North, *441*
Alton, D.P.P.; (LD) Liverpool Mossley Hill, *377*
Amery, H.J.; (C) Brighton Pavilion, *94*
Amess, D.A.; (C) Basildon, *27*
Amos, A.T.; (C) Hexham, *313*
Anderson, D.; (Lab) Swansea East, *564*
Arbuthnot, J.N.; (C) Wanstead and Woodford, *600*
Archer, P.K.; (Lab) Warley West, *603*
Armstrong, Ms. H.J.; (Lab) Durham North West, *209*
Arnold, J.A.; (C) Gravesham, *276*
Arnold, T.R.; (C) Hazel Grove, *302*
Ashby, D.G.; (C) Leicestershire North West, *363*
Ashdown, J.J.D.; (LD) Yeovil, *648*
Ashley, J.; (Lab) Stoke-on-Trent, *545*
Ashton, J.W.; (Lab) Bassetlaw, *29*
Aspinwall, J.H.; (C) Wansdyke, *599*
Atkins, R.J.; (C) South Ribble, *527*
Atkinson, D.A.; (C) Bournemouth East, *76*

B

Baker, K.W.; (C) Mole Valley, *405*
Baker, N.B.; (C) Dorset North, *192*
Baldry, A.B.; (C) Banbury, *20*
Banks, R.G.; (C) Harrogate, *294*
Banks, T.L.; (Lab) Newham North West, *423*
Barnes, H.; (Lab) Derbyshire North East, *182*
Barnes, Mrs. R.S.; (SDP) Greenwich, *280*
Barron, K.J.; (Lab) Rother Valley, *488*
Batiste, S.L.; (C) Elmet, *229*
Battle, J.D.; (Lab) Leeds West, *359*
Beaumont-Dark, A.M.; (C) Birmingham Selly Oak, *57*
Beckett, Mrs. M.M.; (Lab) Derby South, *181*
Beggs, J.R.; (UU) Antrim East, *10*
Beith, A.J.; (LD) Berwick-upon-Tweed, *43*
Bell, S.; (Lab) Middlesbrough, *401*
Bellingham, H.C.; (C) Norfolk North West, *430*
Bendall, V.W.H.; (C) Ilford North, *330*
Benn, A.N.W.; (Lab) Chesterfield, *135*
Bennett, A.F.; (Lab) Denton and Reddish, *179*
Bennett, N.J.; (C) Pembroke, *455*
Benyon, W.R.; (C) Milton Keynes, *403*
Bermingham, G.E.; (Lab) St. Helens South, *498*
Bevan, A.D.G.; (C) Birmingham Yardley, *60*
Bidwell, S.J.; (Lab) Ealing Southall, *212*
Biffen, W.J.; (C) Shropshire North, *516*
Blackburn, J.G.; (C) Dudley West, *199*
Blair, A.C.L.; (Lab) Sedgefield, *503*
Blaker, Sir Peter; (C) Blackpool South, *65*
Blunkett, D.; (Lab) Sheffield Brightside, *507*
Boateng, P.; (Lab) Brent South, *84*
Body, Sir Richard; (C) Holland with Boston, *317*
Bonsor, Sir Nicholas; (C) Upminster, *587*
Boothroyd, Miss B.; (2ndDCWM) West Bromwich West, *616*
Boscawen, R.T.; (C) Somerton and Frome, *520*
Boswell, T.E.; (C) Daventry, *176*
Bottomley, Mrs. V.H.B.M.; (C) Surrey South West, *560*
Bottomley, P.J.; (C) Eltham, *230*
Bowden, A.; (C) Brighton Kempton, *93*
Bowden, G.F.; (C) Dulwich, *200*
Bowis, J.C.; (C) Battersea, *32*
Boyes, R.; (Lab) Houghton and Washington, *322*
Boyson, Sir Rhodes; (C) Brent North, *85*
Bradley, K.J.C.; (Lab) Manchester Withington, *394*
Braine, Sir Bernard; (C) Castle Point, *126*
Brandon-Bravo, N.M.; (C) Nottingham South, *442*
Bray, J.W.; (Lab) Motherwell South, *413*
Brazier, J.W.H.; (C) Canterbury, *117*
Bright, G.F.J.; (C) Luton South, *387*
Brooke, P.L.; (C) City of London and Westminster South, *143*

Brown, J.G.; (Lab) Dunfermline East, *205*
Brown, M.R.; (C) Brigg and Cleethorpes, *92*
Brown, N.H.; (Lab) Newcastle upon Tyne East, *419*
Brown, R.D.M.; (Lab) Edinburgh Leith, *223*
Browne, J.E.D.; (C) Winchester, *625*
Bruce, I.; (C) Dorset South, *193*
Bruce, M.G.; (LD) Gordon, *272*
Buchan, N.F.; (Lab) Paisley South, *453*
Buchanan-Smith, A.L.; (C) Kincardine and Deeside, *344*
Buck, Sir Anthony; (C) Colchester North, *149*
Buckley, G.J.; (Lab) Hemsworth, *303*
Budgen, N.W.; (C) Wolverhampton South West, *634*
Burns, S.H.M.; (C) Chelmsford, *129*
Burt, A.J.H.; (C) Bury North, *105*
Butcher, J.P.; (C) Coventry South West, *161*
Butler, C.J.; (C) Warrington South, *605*
Butterfill, J.V.; (C) Bournemouth West, *77*

C

Caborn, R.G.; (Lab) Sheffield Central, *508*
Callaghan, J.; (Lab) Heywood and Middleton, *314*
Campbell, R.; (Lab) Blyth Valley, *68*
Campbell, W.M.; (LD) Dumbarton, *247*
Campbell-Savours; D.R. (Lab), Workington, *640*
Canavan, D.A.; (Lab) Falkirk West, *240*
Carlile, A.C.; (LD) Montgomery, *409*
Carlisle, J.R.; (C) Luton North, *386*
Carlisle, K.M.; (C) Lincoln, *371*
Carr, M.; (Lab) Bootle, *74*
Carrington, M.H.M.; (C) Fulham, *251*
Cartiss, M.R.H.; (C) Great Yarmouth, *278*
Cartwright, J.C.; (SDP) Woolwich, *636*
Cash, W.N.P.; (C) Stafford, *531*
Chalker, Mrs. L.; (C) Wallasey, *593*
Channon, G.P.G.; (C) Southend West, *524*
Chapman, S.B.; (C) Chipping Barnet, *138*
Chope, C.R.; (C) Southampton Itchen, *521*
Churchill, W.S.; (C) Davyhulme, *177*
Clark, A.K.M.; (C) Plymouth Sutton, *462*
Clark, D.G.; (Lab) South Shields, *528*
Clark, M.; (C) Rochford, *482*
Clark, Sir William; (C) Croydon South, *168*
Clarke, K.H.; (C) Rushcliffe, *492*
Clarke, T.; (Lab) Monklands West, *407*
Clay, R.A.; (Lab) Sunderland North, *555*
Clelland, D.G.; (Lab) Tynebridge, *584*
Clwyd, Mrs. A.; (Lab) Cynon Valley, *172*
Cohen, H.M.; (Lab) Leyton, *370*
Coleman, D.R.; (Lab) Neath, *414*
Colvin, M.K.B.; (C) Romsey and Waterside, *484*
Conway, D.L.; (C) Shrewsbury and Atcham, *515*
Cook, F.; (Lab) Stockton North, *541*
Cook, R.F.; (Lab) Livingston, *381*
Coombs, A.M.V.; (C) Wyre Forest, *647*
Coombs, S.C.; (C) Swindon, *566*
Cope, John; (C) Northavon, *436*
Corbett, R.; (Lab) Birmingham Erdington, *51*
Corbyn, J.B.; (Lab) Islington North, *335*
Cormack, P.T.; (C) Staffordshire South, *534*
Couchman, J.R.; (C) Gillingham, *257*
Cousins, J.M.; (Lab) Newcastle upon Tyne Central, *418*
Cox, T.M.; (Lab) Tooting, *576*
Cran, J.D.; (C) Beverley, *45*
Critchley, J.M.G.; (C) Aldershot, *4*
Crowther, J.S.; (Lab) Rotherham, *487*
Cryer, G.R.; (Lab) Bradford South, *80*
Cummings, J.S.; (Lab) Easington, *213*
Cunliffe, L.F.; (Lab) Leigh, *364*
Cunningham, J.A.; (Lab) Copeland, *154*
Currie, Mrs. E.; (C) Derbyshire South, *183*
Curry, D.M.; (C) Skipton and Ripton, *517*

D

Dalyell, T; (Lab) Linlithgow, *373*
Darling, A.; (Lab) Edinburgh Central, *221*
Davies, D.J.D.; (Lab) Llanelli, *382*
Davies, J.Q.; (C) Stamford and Spalding, *537*
Davies, R.; (Lab) Caerphilly, *109*
Davis, D.M.; (C) Boothferry, *73*
Davis, T.A.G.; (Lab) Birmingham, Hodge Hill, *53*
Day, S.R.; (C) Cheadle, *128*
Dean, Sir Paul; (1stDCWM) Woodspring, *635*
Devlin, T.R.; (C) Stockton South, *542*
Dewar, D.C.; (Lab) Glasgow Garscadden, *261*
Dickens, G.K.; (C) Littleborough and Saddleworth, *374*
Dicks, T.P.; (C) Hayes and Harlington, *301*
Dixon, D.; (Lab) Jarrow, *338*

Johnson Smith, Sir Geoffrey; (C) Wealden, 610
Johnston, Sir David; (LD) Inverness, Nairn and Lochaber, 332
Jones, G.H.; (C) Cardiff North, 119
Jones, I.W.; (PC) Ynys Mon, 649
Jones, M.D.; (Lab) Clwyd South West, 146
Jones, R.B.; (C) Hertfordshire West, 311
Jones, S.B.; (Lab) Alyn and Deeside, 7
Jopling, T.M.; (C) Westmorland and Lonsdale, 620

K

Kaufman, G.B.; (Lab) Manchester Gorton, 393
Kellett-Bowman, Mrs. M.E.; (C) Lancaster, 352
Kennedy, C.P.; (LD) Ross, Cromarty and Skye, 485
Key, S.R.; (C) Salisbury, 501
Kilfedder, J.A.; (UPUP) Down North, 196
King, R.D.; (C) Birmingham Northfield, 55
King, T.J.; (C) Bridgwater, 90
Kinnock, N.G.; (Lab) Islwyn, 337
Kirkhope, T.J.R.; (C) Leeds North East, 356
Kirkwood, A.J.; (LD) Roxburgh and Berwickshire, 489
Knapman, R.; (C) Stroud, 551
Knight, Dame Jill; (C) Birmingham Edgbaston, 50
Knight, G.; (C) Derby North, 180
Knowles, M.; (C) Nottingham East, 440
Knox, D.L.; (C) Staffordshire Moorlands, 533

L

Lambie, D.; (Lab) Cunninghame South, 171
Lamond, J.A.; (Lab) Oldham Central and Royton, 446
Lamont, N.S.H.; (C) Kingston upon Thames, 345
Lang, I.B.; (C) Galloway and Upper Nithsdale, 254
Latham, M.A.; (C) Rutland and Melton, 493
Lawrence, I.J.; (C) Burton, 104
Lawson, N.; (C) Blaby, 62
Leadbitter, E.; (Lab) Hartlepool, 297
Lee, J.R.L.; (C) Pendle, 456
Leigh, E.J.E.; (C) Gainsborough and Horncastle, 253
Leighton, R.; (Lab) Newham North East, 422
Lennox-Boyd, M.A.; (C) Morecambe and Lunesdale, 411
Lester, J.T.; (C) Broxtowe, 101
Lestor, Miss J.; (Lab) Eccles, 219
Lewis, T.; (Lab) Worsley, 641
Lightbown, D.L.; (C) Staffordshire South East, 535
Lilley, P.B.; (C) St. Albans, 496
Litherland, R.K.; (Lab) Manchester Central, 392
Livingstone, K.R.; (Lab) Brent East, 84
Livsey, R.A.L.; (LD) Brecon and Radnor, 83
Lloyd, A.J.; (Lab) Stretford, 550
Lloyd, P.R.C.; (C) Fareham, 242
Lloyd, Sir Ian; (C) Havant, 300
Lofthouse, G.; (Lab) Pontefract and Castleford, 463
Lord, M.N.; (C) Suffolk Central, 552
Loyden, E.; (Lab) Liverpool Garston, 376
Luce, R.N.; (C) Shoreham, 514
Lyell, N.W.; (C) Bedfordshire Mid, 35

M

MacDonald, C.A.; (Lab) Western Isles, 618
Macfarlane, Sir D. Neil; (C) Sutton and Cheam, 562
MacGregor, J.R.R.; (C) Norfolk South, 431
MacKay, A.J.; (C) Berkshire East, 42
Maclean, D.J.; (C) Penrith and The Border, 457
Maclennan, R.A.R.; (LD) Caithness and Sutherland, 110
Madden, M.F.; (Lab) Bradford West, 81
Madel, W.D.; (C) Bedfordshire South West, 37
Maginnis, K.; (UU) Fermanagh and South Tyrone, 245
Mahon, Mrs. A; (Lab) Halifax, 285
Major, J.; (C) Huntingdon, 328
Malins, H.J.; (C) Croydon North West, 167
Mallon, S.; (SDLP) Newry and Armagh, 427
Mans, K.D.R.; (C) Wyre, 646
Maples, J.C.; (C) Lewisham West, 369
Marek, J.; (Lab) Wrexham, 644
Marland, P.; (C) Gloucestershire West, 271
Marlow, A.R.; (C) Northampton North, 434
Marshall, D.; (Lab) Glasgow Shettleston, 268
Marshall, J.; (Lab) Leicester South, 361
Marshall, J.L.; (C) Hendon South, 305
Marshall, R.M.; (C) Arundel, 14
Martin, D.; (C) Portsmouth South, 467
Martin, M.J.; (Lab) Glasgow Springburn, 269
Martlew, E.A.; (Lab) Carlisle, 122
Mates, M.J.; (C) Hampshire East, 289
Maude, F.A.A.; (C) Warwickshire North, 607
Mawhinney, Dr. B.S.; (C) Peterborough, 459

Maxton, J.A.; (Lab) Glasgow Cathcart, 259
Maxwell-Hyslop, R.J.; (C) Tiverton, 574
Mayhew, Sir Patrick; (C) Tunbridge Wells, 581
McAllion, J.; (Lab) Dundee East, 203
McAvoy, T.; (Lab) Glasgow Rutherglen, 267
McCartney, I.; (Lab) Makerfield, 390
McCrea, Rev. R.T.W.; (UDUP) Mid Ulster, 586
McCrindle, R.A.; (C) Brentwood and Ongar, 88
McFall, J.; (Lab) Dumbarton, 201
McGrady, E.K.; (SDLP) Down South, 197
McKay, A.; (Lab) Barnsley West and Penistone, 25
McKelvey, W.; (Lab) Kilmarnock and Loudoun, 343
McLoughlin, P.A.; (C) Derbyshire West, 184
McNair-Wilson, P.M.E.D.; (C) New Forest, 421
McNair-Wilson, Sir Michael; (C) Newbury, 416
McNamara, J.K.; (Lab) Hull North, 326
McWilliam, J.D.; (Lab) Blaydon, 67
Meacher, M.H.; (Lab) Oldham West, 447
Meale, J.A.; (Lab) Mansfield, 396
Mellor, D.J.; (C) Putney, 470
Meyer, Sir Anthony; (C) Clwyd North West, 145
Michael, A.E.; (Lab) Cardiff South and Penarth, 120
Michie, Mrs. J.R.; (LD) Argyll and Bute, 13
Michie, W.; (Lab) Sheffield Heeley, 510
Miller, Sir H.D.; (C) Bromsgrove, 99
Mills, I.C.; (C) Meriden, 399
Miscampbell, N.A.; (C) Blackpool North, 64
Mitchell, A.J.B.; (C) Gedling, 256
Mitchell, A.V.; (Lab) Great Grimsby, 277
Mitchell, Sir David.B.; (C) Hampshire North West, 290
Moate, R.D.; (C) Faversham, 243
Molyneaux, J.H.; (UU) Lagan Valley, 350
Monro, Sir Hector; (C) Dumfried, 202
Montgomery, Sir Fergus; (C) Altrincham and Sale, 6
Moonie, Dr.L.G.; (Lab) Kircaldy, 347
Moore, J.E.M.; (C) Croydon Central, 165
Morgan, H.R.; (Lab) Cardiff West, 121
Morley, E.; (Lab) Glanford and Scunthorpe, 258
Morris, A.; (Lab) Manchester Wythenshawe, 395
Morris, J.; (Lab) Aberavon, 1
Morris, M.W.L.; (C) Northampton South, 435
Morrison, Sir Charles.A.; (C) Devizes, 185
Morrison, P.H.; (C) Chester, 134
Moss, M.D.; (C) Cambridgeshire North East, 113
Mowlam, Miss M.; (Lab) Redcar, 474
Moynihan, C.B.; (C) Lewisham East, 368
Mudd, W.D.; (C) Falmouth and Camborne, 241
Mullin, C.J.; (Lab) Sunderland South, 556
Murphy, P.P.; (Lab) Torfaen, 578

N

Neale, G.A.; (C) Cornwall North, 156
Needham, R.F.; (C) Wiltshire North, 623
Nellist, D.J.; (Lab) Coventry South East, 160
Nelson, R.A.; (C) Chichester, 136
Neubert, M.J.; (C) Romford, 483
Newton, A.H.; (C) Braintree, 82
Nicholls, P.C.M.; (C) Teignbridge, 570
Nicholson, D.J.; (C) Taunton, 568
Nicholson, Miss E.H.; (C) Devon West and Torridge, 187
Norris, S.J.; (C) Epping Forest, 233

O

Oakes, G.J.; (Lab) Halton, 286
O'Brien, W.; (Lab) Normanton, 433
O'Neill, M.J.; (Lab) Clackmannan, 144
Onslow, C.G.D.; (C) Woking, 630
Oppenheim, P.A.C.L.; (C) Amber Valley, 8
Orme, S.; (Lab) Salford East, 500
Owen, Dr. D.A.L.; (SDP) Plymouth Devonport, 460

P

Page, R.L.; (C) Hertfordshire South West, 310
Paice, J.E.T.; (C) Cambridgeshire South East, 114
Paisley, Rev. I.R.K.; (UDUP) Antrim North, 11
Parkinson, C.E.; (C) Hertsmere, 312
Parry, R.; (Lab) Liverpool Riverside, 378
Patchett, T.; (Lab) Barnsley East, 24
Patnick, C.I.; (C) Sheffield Hallam, 509
Patten, C.F.; (C) Bath, 30
Patten, J.H.V.; (C) Oxford West and Abingdon, 451
Pattie, G.E.; (C) Chertsey and Walton, 132
Pawsey, J.F.; (C) Rugby and Kenilworth, 490
Peacock, Mrs. E.J.; (C) Batley and Spen, 31
Pendry, T.; (Lab) Stalybridge and Hyde, 536
Pike, P.L.; (Lab) Burnley, 103

Porter, D.; (C) Waveney, 609
Porter, G.B.; (C) Wirral South, 627
Portillo, M.D.X.; (C) Enfield Southgate, 232
Powell, R.; (Lab) Ogmore, 444
Powell, W.R.; (C) Corby, 155
Prescott, J.L.; (Lab) Hull East, 325
Price, Sir David; (C) Eastleigh, 216
Primarolo, Ms.D.; (Lab) Bristol South, 97

Q

Quin, Miss J.G.; (Lab) Gateshead East, 255

R

Radice, G.H.; (Lab) Durham North, 208
Raffan, K.W.; (C) Delyn, 178
Raison, T.H.F.; (C) Aylesbury, 18
Randall, S.J.; (Lab) Hull West, 327
Rathbone, J.R.; (C) Lewes, 366
Redmond, M.; (Lab) Don Valley, 191
Redwood, J.A.; (C) Wokingham, 631
Rees, M.; (Lab) Leeds South and Morley, 358
Reid, J.; (Lab) Motherwell North, 412
Renton, R.T.; (C) Mid Sussex, 561
Rhodes James, R.V.; (C) Cambridge, 112
Rhys Williams, Sir Brandon; (C) Kensington, 340
Richardson, Miss Jo; (Lab) Barking, 22
Riddick, G.E.G.; (C) Colne Valley, 151
Ridley, N.; (C) Cirencester and Tewkesbury, 142
Ridsdale, Sir Julian; (C) Harwich, 298
Rifkind, M.L.; (C) Edinburgh Pentlands, 224
Roberts, I.W.P.; (C) Conwy, 153
Robertson, G.I.M.; (Lab) Hamilton, 287
Robinson, G.; (Lab) Coventry North West, 159
Robinson, P.D.; (UDUP) Belfast, East, 38
Roe, Mrs. M.A.; (C) Broxbourne, 100
Rogers, A.R.; (Lab) Rhondda, 477
Rooker, J.W.; (Lab) Birmingham Perry Bar, 56
Ross, E.; (Lab) Dundee West, 204
Ross, W.; (UU) Londonderry East, 383
Rossi, Sir Hugh; (C) Hornsey and Wood Green, 320
Rost, P.L.; (C) Erewash, 235
Rowe, A.J.B.; (C) Mid Kent, 341
Rowlands, E.; (Lab) Merthyr Tydfil and Rhymney, 400
Ruddock, Mrs. J.M.; (Lab) Lewisham Deptford, 367
Rumbold, Mrs. A.C.R.; (C) Mitcham and Morden, 404
Ryder, R.; (C) Mid Norfolk, 428

S

Sackville, T.G.; (C) Bolton West, 72
Sainsbury, T.A.D.; (C) Hove, 323
Salmond, A.E.A.; (SNP) Banff and Buchan, 21
Sayeed, J.; (C) Bristol East, 95
Scott, N.P.; (C) Chelsea, 130
Sedgemore, B.C.J.; (Lab) Hackney South and Shoreditch, 283
Shaw, D.L.; (C) Dover, 195
Shaw, Sir John.G.D.; (C) Pudsey, 469
Shaw, Sir Michael; (C) Scarborough, 502
Sheerman, B.J.; (Lab) Huddersfield, 324
Sheldon, R.E.; (Lab) Ashton-under-Lyne, 17
Shelton, W.J.M.; (C) Streatham, 549
Shephard, Mrs. G.P.; (C) Norfolk South West, 432
Shepherd, C.R.; (C) Hereford, 307
Shepherd, R.C.S.; (C) Aldridge-Brownhills, 5
Shersby, J.M.; (C) Uxbridge, 589
Shore, P.D.; (Lab) Bethnal Green and Stepney, 44
Short, Ms.C.; (Lab) Birmingham Ladywood, 54
Sillars, J.; (SNP) Glasgow, Govan, 262
Sims, R.E.; (C) Chislehurst, 139
Skeet, Sir Trevor; (C) Bedfordshire North, 36
Skinner, D.E.; (Lab) Bolsover, 69
Smith, A.D.; (Lab) Oxford East, 450
Smith, Sir Cyril; (LD) Rochdale, 481
Smith, C.R.; (Lab) Islington South and Finsbury, 336
Smith, J.; (Lab) Monklands East, 406
Smith, J.W.P.; (Lab) Vale of Glamorgan, 590
Smith, Sir Dudley; (C) Warwick and Leamington, 606
Smith, T.J.; (C) Beaconsfield, 33
Smyth, Rev. W.M.; (UU) Belfast South, 40
Snape, P.C.; (Lab) West Bromwich East, 615
Soames, A.N.W.; (C) Crawley, 162
Soley, C.S.; (Lab) Hammersmith, 288
Spearing, N.J.; (Lab) Newham South, 424
Speed, H.K.; (C) Ashford, 16
Speller, A.; (C) Devon North, 186
Spicer, Sir James.W.; (C) Dorset West, 194

Spicer, W.M.H.; (C) Worcestershire South, 639
Squire, R.C.; (C) Hornchurch, 319
Stanbrook, I.R.; (C) Orpington, 449
Stanley, J.P.; (C) Tonbridge and Malling, 575
Steel, Sir David.; (LD) Tweeddale, Ettick & Lauderdale, 582
Steen, A.D.; (C) South Hams, 525
Steinberg, G.N.; (Lab) Durham City, 207
Stern, M.C.; (C) Bristol North West, 96
Stevens, L.D.; (C) Nuneaton, 443
Stewart, A.S.; (C) Sherwood, 512
Stewart, B.H.I.H.; (C) Hertfordshire North, 309
Stewart, J.A.; (C) Eastwood, 218
Stokes, Sir J.H.R.; (C) Halesowen and Stourbridge, 284
Stott, R; (Lab) Wigan, 622
Stradling Thomas J.; (C) Monmouth, 408
Strang, G.S.; (Lab) Edinburgh East, 222
Straw, J.W.; (Lab) Blackburn, 63
Sumberg, D.A.G.; (C) Bury South, 106
Summerson, H.H.F.; (C) Walthamstow, 597

T

Tapsell, Sir Peter; (C) Lindsey East, 372
Taylor, E.M.; (C) Southend East, 523
Taylor, I.C.; (C) Esher, 237
Taylor, J.D.; (UU) Strangford, 546
Taylor, J.M.; (C) Solihull, 519
Taylor, M.O.J.; (LD) Truro, 580
Taylor, Mrs. W.A.; (Lab) Dewsbury, 188
Tebbit, N.B.; (C) Chingford, 137
Temple-Morris; (C) Leominster, 365
Thatcher, Mrs. M.H.; (C) Finchley, 248
Thomas, D.W.; (PC) Meirionnydd Nant Conwy, 398
Thompson, D.; (C) Calder Valley, 111
Thompson, H.P.; (C) Norwich North, 437
Thompson, J.; (Lab) Wansbeck, 598
Thorne, N.G.; (C) Ilford South, 331
Thornton, G.M.; (C) Crosby, 164
Thurnham, P.G.; (C) Bolton North East, 70
Townend, J.E.; (C) Bridlington, 91
Townsend, C.D.; (C) Bexleyheath, 47
Tracey, R.P.; (C) Surbiton, 557
Tredinnick, D.A.S.; (C) Bosworth, 75
Trimble, D.; (UU) Upper Bann 588
Trippier, D.A.; (C) Rossendale and Darwen, 486
Trotter, N.G.; (C) Tynemouth, 585
Turner, D.; (Lab) Wolverhampton South East, 633
Twinn, I.D.; (C) Edmonton, 227

V

Vaughan, Sir Gerard; (C) Reading East, 472
Vaz, N.K.A.S.; (Lab) Leicester East, 360
Viggers, P.J.; (C) Gosport, 273

W

Waddington, D.C.; (C) Ribble Valley, 478
Wakeham, J.; (C) Colchester South and Maldon, 150
Waldegrave, W.A.; (C) Bristol West, 98
Walden, G.G.H.; (C) Buckingham, 102
Walker, A.C.; (UU) Belfast North, 39
Walker, H.; (CWM) Doncaster Central, 189
Walker, P.E.; (C) Worcester, 637
Walker, W.C.; (C) Tayside North, 569
Wall, C.P.; (Lab) Bradford North, 79
Wallace, J.R.; (LD) Orkney and Shetland, 448
Waller, G.P.A.; (C) Keighley, 339
Walley, Ms. J.L.; (Lab) Stoke-on-Trent North, 544
Walters, Sir Dennis; (C) Westbury, 617
Ward, J.D.; (C) Poole, 465
Wardell, G.L.; (Lab) Gower, 274
Wardle, C.F.; (C) Bexhill and Battle, 46
Wareing, R.N.; (Lab) Liverpool West Derby, 380
Warren, K.R.; (C) Hastings and Rye, 299
Watson, M; (Lab) Glasgow Central 260
Watts, J.A.; (C) Slough, 518
Weatherill, B.B.; (Speaker) Croydon North East, 166
Wells, P.B.; (C) Hertford and Stortford, 308
Welsh, A.; (SNP) Angus East, 9
Welsh, M.C.; (Lab) Doncaster North, 190
Wheeler, Sir John .D.; (C) Westminster North, 619
Whitney, R.W.; (C) Wycombe, 645
Widdecombe, Miss A.N.; (C) Maidstone, 389
Wiggin, A.W.; (C) Weston-Super-Mare, 621
Wigley, D.W.; (PC) Caernarfon, 108
Wilkinson, J.A.D.; (C) Ruislip Northwood, 491
Williams, A.J.; (Lab) Swansea West, 565
Williams, A.W.; (Lab) Carmarthen, 123

Wilshire, D.; (C) Spelthorne, 530
Wilson, B.D.H.; (Lab) Cunninghame North, 170
Winnick, D.J.; (Lab) Walsall North, 595
Winterton, Mrs. J.A.; (C) Congleton, 152
Winterton, N.R.; (C) Macclesfield, 388
Wise, Mrs. A.; (Lab) Preston, 468
Wolfson, G.M.; (C) Sevenoaks, 505
Wood, T.J.R.; (C) Stevenage, 538
Woodcock, M.; (C) Ellesmere Port and Neston, 228

Worthington, A.; (Lab) Clydebank and Milngavie, 147
Wray, J.; (Lab) Glasgow Provan, 266

Y

Yeo, T.S.K.; (C) Suffolk South, 554
Young, D.W.; (Lab) Bolton, South-East, 71
Young, Sir George; (C) Ealing Acton, 210
Younger, G.K.H.; (C) Ayr, 19

THE HOUSE OF COMMONS

STATE OF THE PARTIES IN THE HOUSE OF COMMONS AS AT 7 JUNE 1990

Conservative	372
Labour	227
Liberal Democrats	19
Ulster Unionists	9
Scottish National Party	4
Plaid Cymru	3
Social Democratic and Labour Party	3
Social Democrats	3
Ulster Democratic Unionist Party	3
Labour-Independent	1
Sinn Fein	1
Ulster Popular Unionist	1
The Speaker and 3 Deputy Speakers	4
Vacant seats	0
Total	**650**

(The total number of women MPs is 43)

Members of Parliament elected at the General Election on June 11, 1987 or at by-election since then, are shown below in Constituency order.

The political affiliations of Members are indicated as follows:

A	Alliance
C	Conservative
CD	Christian Democrat
Comm	Communist
Dem	Democrat
DUP	Democratic Unionist Party
Ex Lab Mod	Ex-Labour Moderate
G	Green Party
H	Humanist
Ind	Independent
L	Liberal
Lab	Labour
Lab Co-op	Labour Co-operative
Loony	Official Monster Raving Loony Party
ML	Moderate Labour Party
NPR	National People's Rally
OSM	Orkney & Shetlands Movements
OUP	Official Unionist Party
PC	Plaid Cymru
PRP	Protestant Reformation Party
Real U	Real Unionist Party
RF	Red Front
SDLP	Social Democratic and Labour Party
SDP	Social Democratic Party
SE	Spare the Earth
SF	Sinn Fein
SLD	Social & Liberal Democrats
SNP	Scottish National Party
WP	Workers Party
WRP	Workers Revolutionary Party

The Public Information Office, House of Commons, London SW1 (071-219 4272) answers enquiries from the general public about the work and history of the House of Commons. Enquiries regarding the House of Lords are dealt with by The Information Office, House of Lords, London SW! (071-219 3107)

PARLIAMENTARY CONSTITUENCIES

Members, in alphabetical order, appear on pages 35 - 39

	Constituency	Member	Party
1	Aberavon,	Morris, J.;	(Lab)
2	Aberdeen North,	Hughes, R.;	(Lab)
3	Aberdeen South,	Doran, F.;	(Lab)
4	Aldershot,	Critchley, J.M.G.;	(C)
5	Aldridge-Brownhills,	Shepherd, R.C.S.;	(C)
6	Altrincham and Sale,	Montgomery, Sir Fergus;	(C)
7	Alyn and Deeside,	Jones, S.B.;	(Lab)
8	Amber Valley,	Oppenheim, P.A.C.L.;	(C)
9	Angus East,	Welsh, A.;	(SNP)
10	Antrim East,	Beggs, J.R.;	(OUP)
11	Antrim North,	Paisley, Rev. I.R.K.;	(DUP)
12	Antrim South,	Forsythe, C.;	(OUP)
13	Argyll and Bute,	Michie, Mrs. J.R.;	(SLD/All)
14	Arundel,	Marshall, R.M.;	(C)
15	Ashfield,	Haynes, D.F.;	(Lab)
16	Ashford,	Speed, H.K.;	(C)
17	Ashton-under-Lyne,	Sheldon, R.E.;	(Lab)
18	Aylesbury,	Raison, T.H.F.;	(C)

	Constituency	Member	Party
20	Banbury,	Baldry, A.B.;	(C)
21	Banff and Buchan,	Salmond, A.E.A.;	(SNP)
22	Barking,	Richardson, Miss Jo;	(Lab)
23	Barnsley, Central,	Illsley, E.R.;	(Lab)
24	Barnsley East,	Patchett, T.;	(Lab)
25	Barnsley West and Penistone,	McKay, A.;	(Lab)
26	Barrow and Furness,	Franks, C.S.;	(C)
27	Basildon,	Amess, D.A.;	(C)
28	Basingstoke,	Hunter, A.R.F.;	(C)
29	Bassetlaw,	Ashton, J.W.;	(Lab)
30	Bath,	Patten, C.F.;	(C)
31	Batley and Spen,	Peacock, Mrs. E.J.;	(C)
32	Battersea,	Bowis, J.C.;	(C)
33	Beaconsfield,	Smith, T.J.;	(C)
34	Beckenham,	Goodhart, Sir Philip;	(C)
35	Bedfordshire Mid,	Lyell, N.W.;	(C)
36	Bedfordshire North,	Skeet, Sir Trevor;	(C)
37	Bedfordshire South West,	Madel, W.D.;	(C)
38	Belfast East,	Robinson, P.D.;	(UDUP)
39	Belfast North,	Walker, A.C.;	(OUP)
40	Belfast South,	Smyth, Rev. W.M.;	(OUP)
41	Belfast West,	Adams, G.;	(PSF)
42	Berkshire East,	MacKay, A.J.;	(C)
43	Berwick-upon-Tweed,	Beith, A.J.;	(SLD/All)
44	Bethnal Green and Stepney,	Shore, P.D.;	(Lab)
45	Beverley,	Cran, J.D.;	(C)
46	Bexhill and Battle,	Wardle, C.F.;	(C)
47	Bexleyheath,	Townsend, C.D.;	(C)
48	Billericay,	Gorman, Mrs. T.E.;	(C)
49	Birkenhead,	Field, F.;	(Lab)
50	Birmingham Edgbaston,	Knight, Dame Jill;	(C)
51	Birmingham Erdington,	Corbett, R.;	(Lab)
52	Birmingham Hall Green,	Hargreaves, A.R.;	(C)
53	Birmingham, Hodge Hill,	Davis, T.A.G.;	(Lab)
54	Birmingham Ladywood,	Short, Ms.C.;	(Lab)
55	Birmingham Northfield,	King, R.D.;	(C)
56	Birmingham Perry Bar,	Rooker, J.W.;	(Lab)
57	Birmingham Selly Oak,	Beaumont-Dark, A.M.;	(C)
58	Birmingham Small Heath,	Howell, D.H.;	(Lab)
59	Birmingham Sparkbrook,	Hattersley, R.S.G.;	(Lab)
60	Birmingham Yardley,	Bevan, A.D.G.;	(C)
61	Bishop Aukland,	Foster, D.;	(Lab)
62	Blaby,	Lawson, N.;	(C)
63	Blackburn,	Straw, J.W.;	(Lab)
64	Blackpool North,	Miscampbell, N.A.;	(C)
65	Blackpool South,	Blaker, Sir Peter;	(C)
66	Blaenau Gwent,	Foot, M.M.;	(Lab)
67	Blaydon,	McWilliam, J.D.;	(Lab)
68	Blyth Valley,	Campbell, R.;	(Lab)
69	Bolsover,	Skinner, D.E.;	(Lab)
70	Bolton North East,	Thurnham, P.G.;	(C)
71	Bolton, South-East,	Young, D.W.;	(Lab)
72	Bolton West,	Sackville, T.G.;	(C)
73	Boothferry,	Davis, D.M.;	(C)
74	Bootle,	Carr, M.;	(Lab)
75	Bosworth,	Tredinnick, D.A.S.;	(C)
76	Bournemouth East,	Atkinson, D.A.;	(C)
77	Bournemouth West,	Butterfill, J.V.;	(C)
78	Bow and Poplar,	Gordon, Ms.M.;	(Lab)
79	Bradford North,	Wall, C.P.;	(Lab)
80	Bradford South,	Cryer, G.R.;	(Lab)
81	Bradford West,	Madden, M.F.;	(Lab)
82	Braintree,	Newton, A.H.;	(C)
83	Brecon and Radnor,	Livsey, R.A.L.;	(SLD/All)
84	Brent East,	Livingstone, K.R.;	(Lab)
85	Brent North,	Boyson, Sir Rhodes;	(C)
86	Brent South,	Boateng, P.;	(Lab)
87	Brentford and Isleworth,	Hayhoe, Sir Barney;	(C)
88	Brentwood and Ongar,	McCrindle, R.A.;	(C)
89	Bridgend,	Griffiths, W.J.;	(Lab)
90	Bridgwater,	King, T.J.;	(C)
91	Bridlington,	Townend, J.E.;	(C)
92	Brigg and Cleethorpes,	Brown, M.R.;	(C)
93	Brighton Kempton,	Bowden, A.;	(C)

	Constituency	Member	Party
94	Brighton Pavilion,	Amery, H.J.;	(C)
95	Bristol East,	Sayeed, J.;	(C)
96	Bristol North West,	Stern, M.C.;	(C)
97	Bristol South,	Primarolo, Ms.D.;	(Lab)
98	Bristol West,	Waldegrave, W.A.;	(C)
99	Bromsgrove,	Miller, Sir H.D.;	(C)
100	Broxbourne,	Roe, Mrs. M.A.;	(C)
101	Broxtowe,	Lester, J.T.;	(C)
102	Buckingham,	Walden, G.G.H.;	(C)
103	Burnley,	Pike, P.L.;	(Lab)
104	Burton,	Lawrence, I.J.;	(C)
105	Bury North,	Burt, A.J.H.;	(C)
106	Bury South,	Sumberg, D.A.G.;	(C)
107	Bury St.Edmunds,	Griffiths, Sir Eldon	(C)
108	Caernarfon,	Wigley, D.W.;	(PC)
109	Caerphilly,	Davies, R.;	(Lab)
110	Caithness and Sutherland,	Maclennan, R.A.R.;	(Sld/All)
111	Calder Valley,	Thompson, D.;	(C)
112	Cambridge,	Rhodes James, R.V.;	(C)
113	Cambridgeshire North East,	Moss, M.D.;	(C)
114	Cambridgeshire South East,	Paice, J.E.T.;	(C)
115	Cambridgeshire South West,	Grant, Sir Anthony;	(C)
116	Cannock and Burntwood,	Howarth, J.G.D.;	(C)
117	Canterbury,	Brazier, J.W.H.;	(C)
118	Cardiff Central,	Grist, I.;	(C)
119	Cardiff North,	Jones, G.H.;	(C)
120	Cardiff South and Penarth,	Michael, A.E.;	(Lab)
121	Cardiff West,	Morgan, H.R.;	(Lab)
122	Carlisle,	Martlew, E.A.;	(Lab)
123	Carmarthen,	Williams, A.W.;	(Lab)
124	Carrick, Cumnock and Doon Valley,	Foulkes, G.;	(Lab)
125	Carshalton and Wallington,	Forman, F.N.;	(C)
126	Castle Point,	Braine, Sir Bernard;	(C)
127	Ceredigion and Pembroke North,	Howells, G.W.;	(SLD/All)
128	Cheadle,	Day, S.R.;	(C)
129	Chelmsford,	Burns, S.H.M.;	(C)
130	Chelsea,	Scott, N.P.;	(C)
131	Cheltenham,	Irving, C.G.;	(C)
132	Chertsey and Walton,	Pattie, G.E.;	(C)
133	Chesham and Amersham,	Gilmour, Sir Ian;	(C)
134	Chester,	Morrison, P.H.;	(C)
135	Chesterfield,	Benn, A.N.W.;	(Lab)
136	Chichester,	Nelson, R.A.;	(C)
137	Chingford,	Tebbit, N.B.;	(C)
138	Chipping Barnet,	Chapman, S.B.;	(C)
139	Chislehurst,	Sims, R.E.;	(C)
140	Chorley,	Dover, D.R.;	(C)
141	Christchurch,	Adley, R.J.;	(C)
142	Cirencester and Tewkesbury,	Ridey, N.;	(C)
143	City of London and Westminster South,	Brooke, P.L.;	(C)
144	Clackmannan,	O'Neill, M.J.;	(Lab)
145	Clwyd North West,	Meyer, Sir Anthony;	(C)
146	Clwyd South West,	Jones, M.D.;	(Lab)
147	Clydebank and Milngavie,	Worthington, A.;	(Lab)
148	Clydesdale,	Hood, J.;	(Lab)
149	Colchester North,	Buck, Sir Anthony;	(C)
150	Colchester South and Maldon,	Wakeham, J.;	(C)
151	Colne Valley,	Riddick, G.E.G.;	(C)
152	Congleton,	Winterton, Mrs. J.A.;	(C)
153	Conwy,	Roberts, I.W.P.;	(C)
154	Copeland,	Cunningham, J.A.;	(Lab)
155	Corby,	Powell, W.R.;	(C)
156	Cornwall North,	Neale, G.A.;	(C)
157	Cornwall South East,	Hicks, R.A.;	(C)
158	Coventry North East,	Hughes, J.;	(Lab)
159	Coventry North West,	Robinson, G.;	(Lab)
160	Coventry South East,	Nellist, D.J.;	(Lab)
161	Coventry South West,	Butcher, J.P.;	(C)
162	Crawley,	Soames, A.N.W.;	(C)
163	Crewe and Nantwich,	Dunwoody, Mrs. G.P.;	(Lab)
164	Crosby,	Thornton, G.M.;	(C)
165	Croydon Central,	Moore, J.E.M.;	(C)
166	Croydon North East,	Weatherill, B.B.;	(Speaker)
167	Croydon North West,	Malins, H.J.;	(C)

	Constituency	Member	Party
168	Croydon South,	Clark, Sir William;	(C)
169	Cumbernauld and Kilsyth,	Hogg, N.;	(Lab)
170	Cunninghame North,	Wilson, B.D.H.;	(Lab)
171	Cunninghame South,	Lambie, D.;	(Lab)
172	Cynon Valley,	Clwyd, Mrs. A.;	(Lab)
173	Dagenham,	Gould, B.C.;	(Lab)
174	Darlington,	Fallon, M.;	(C)
175	Dartford,	Dunn, R.J.;	(C)
176	Daventry,	Boswell, T.E.;	(C)
177	Davyhulme,	Churchill, W.S.;	(C)
178	Delyn,	Raffan, K.W.;	(C)
179	Denton and Reddish,	Bennett, A.F.;	(Lab)
180	Derby North,	Knight, G.;	(C)
181	Derby South,	Beckett, Mrs. M.M.;	(Lab)
182	Derbyshire North East,	Barnes, H.;	(Lab)
183	Derbyshire South,	Currie, Mrs. E.;	(C)
184	Derbyshire West,	McLoughlin, P.A.;	(C)
185	Devizes,	Morrison, C.A.;	(C)
186	Devon North,	Speller, A.;	(C)
187	Devon West and Torridge,	Nicholson, Miss E.H.;	(C)
188	Dewsbury,	Taylor, Mrs. W.A.;	(Lab)
189	Doncaster Central,	Walker, H.;	(Lab)
190	Doncaster North,	Welsh, M.C.;	(Lab)
191	Don Valley,	Redmond, M.;	(Lab)
192	Dorset North,	Baker, N.B.;	(C)
193	Dorset South,	Bruce, I.;	(C)
194	Dorset West,	Spicer, J.W.;	(C)
195	Dover,	Shaw, D.L.;	(C)
196	Down North,	Kilfedder, J.A.;	(Pop U)
197	Down South,	McGrady, E.K.;	(SDLP)
198	Dudley East,	Gilbert, J.W.;	(Lab)
199	Dudley West,	Blackburn, J.G.;	(C)
200	Dulwich,	Bowden, G.F.;	(C)
201	Dumbarton,	McFall, J.;	(Lab)
202	DumfrieS,	Monro, Sir Hector;	(C)
203	Dundee East,	McAllion, J.;	(Lab)
204	Dundee West,	Ross, E.;	(Lab)
205	Dunfermline East,	Brown, J.G.;	(Lab)
206	Dunfermline West,	Douglas, R.G.;	(Lab)
207	Durham City,	Steinberg, G.N.;	(Lab)
208	Durham North,	Radice, G.H.;	(Lab)
209	Durham North West,	Armstrong, Ms. H.J.;	(Lab)
210	Ealing Acton,	Young, Sir George;	(C)
211	Ealing North,	Greenway, H.;	(C)
212	Ealing Southall,	Bidwell, S.J.;	(Lab)
213	Easington,	Cummings, J.S.;	(Lab)
214	Eastbourne,	Gow, I.R.E.;	(C)
215	East Kilbride,	Ingram, A.P.;	(Lab)
216	Eastleigh,	Price, Sir David;	(C)
217	East Lothian,	Home Robertson, J.D.;	(Lab)
218	Eastwood,	Stewart, J.A.;	(C)
219	Eccles,	Lestor, Miss J.;	(Lab)
220	Eddisbury,	Goodlad, A.R.;	(C)
221	Edinburgh Central,	Darling, A.;	(Lab)
222	Edinburgh East,	Strang, G.S.;	(Lab)
223	Edinburgh Leith,	Brown, R.D.M.;	(Lab)
224	Edinburgh Pentlands,	Rifkind, M.L.;	(C)
225	Edinburgh South,	Griffiths, N.;	(Lab)
226	Edinburgh West,	Douglas-Hamilton, Lord James;	(C)
227	Edmonton,	Twinn, I.D.;	(C)
228	Ellesmere Port and Neston,	Woodcock, M.;	(C)
229	Elmet,	Batiste, S.L.;	(C)
230	Eltham,	Bottomley, P.J.;	(C)
231	Enfield North,	Eggar, T.J.C.;	(C)
232	Enfield Southgate,	Portillo, M.D.X.;	(C)
233	Epping Forest,	Norris, S.J.;	(Lab)
234	Epsom and Ewell,	Hamilton, A.G.;	(C)
235	Erewash,	Rost, P.L.;	(C)
236	Erith and Crayford,	Evennett, D.A.;	(C)
237	Esher,	Taylor, I.C.;	(C)
238	Exeter,	Hannam, J.G.;	(C)
239	Falkirk East,	Ewing, H.;	(Lab)
240	Falkirk West,	Canavan, D.A.;	(Lab)
241	Falmouth and Camborne,	Mudd, W.D.;	(C)

Constituency	Member	Party
242 Fareham,	Lloyd, P.R.C.;	(C)
243 Faversham,	Moate, R.D.;	(C)
244 Feltham and Heston,	Ground, R.P.;	(C)
245 Fermanagh and South Tyrone,	Maginnis, K.;	(OUP)
247 Dumbarton,	Campbell, W.M.;	(SLD/All)
248 Finchley,	Thatcher, Mrs. M.H.;	(C)
249 Folkestone and Hythe,	Howard, M.;	(C)
250 Foyle,	Hume, J.;	(SDLP)
251 Fulham,	Carrington, M.H.M.;	(C)
252 Fylde,	Jack, J.M.;	(C)
253 Gainsborough and Horncastle,	Leigh, E.J.E.;	(C)
254 Galloway and Upper Nithsdale,	Lang, I.B.;	(C)
255 Gateshead East,	Quin, Miss J.G.;	(Lab)
256 Gedling,	Mitchell, A.J.B.;	(C)
257 Gillingham,	Couchman, J.R.;	(C)
258 Glanford and Scunthorpe,	Morley, E.;	(Lab)
259 Glasgow Cathcart,	Maxton, J.A.;	(Lab)
261 Glasgow Garscadden,	Dewar, D.C.;	(Lab)
262 Glasgow, Govan,	Sillars, J.;	(SNP)
263 Glasgow Hillhead,	Galloway, G.;	(Lab)
264 Glasgow Maryhill,	Fyfe, Mrs. M.;	(Lab)
265 Glasgow Pollok,	Dunnachie, J.;	(Lab)
266 Glasgow Provan,	Wray, J.;	(Lab)
267 Glasgow Rutherglen,	McAvoy, T.;	(Lab)
268 Glasgow Shettleston,	Marshall, D.;	(Lab)
269 Glasgow Springburn,	Martin, M.J.;	(Lab)
270 Gloucester,	French, D.;	(C)
271 Gloucestershire West,	Marland, P.;	(C)
272 Gordon,	Bruce, M.G.;	(SLD/All)
273 Gosport,	Viggers, P.J.;	(C)
274 Gower,	Wardell, G.L.;	(Lab)
275 Grantham,	Hogg, D.M.;	(C)
276 Gravesham,	Arnold, J.A.;	(C)
277 Great Grimsby,	Mitchell, A.V.;	(Lab)
278 Great Yarmouth,	Cartiss, M.R.H.;	(C)
279 Greenock and Port Glasgow,	Godman, N.A.;	(Lab)
280 Greenwich,	Barnes, Mrs. R.S.;	(SDP/All)
281 Guildford,	Howell, D.A.R.;	(C)
282 Hackney North and Stoke Newington,	Abbott, Ms. D.J.;	(Lab)
283 Hackney South and Shoreditch,	Sedgemore, B.C.J.;	(Lab)
284 Halesowen and Stourbridge,	Stokes, Sir J.H.R.;	(C)
285 Halifax,	Mahon, Mrs. A;	(Lab)
286 Halton,	Oakes, G.J.;	(Lab)
287 Hamilton,	Robertson, G.I.M.;	(Lab)
288 Hammersmith,	Soley, C.S.;	(Lab)
289 Hampshire East,	Mates, M.J.;	(C)
290 Hampshire North West,	Mitchell, D.B.;	(C)
291 Hampstead and Highgate,	Finsberg, Sir Geoffrey;	(C)
292 Harborough,	Farr, Sir John;	(C)
293 Harlow,	Hayes, J.	(C)
293 Harlow,	Jayes, J.J.J.;	(C)
294 Harrogate,	Banks, R.G.;	(C)
295 Harrow East,	Dykes, H.J.M.;	(C)
296 Harrow West,	Hughes, R.G.;	(C)
297 Hartlepool,	Leadbitter, E.;	(Lab)
298 Harwich,	Ridsdale, Sir Julian;	(C)
299 Hastings and Rye,	Warren, K.R.;	(C)
300 Havant,	Lloyd, Sir Ian;	(C)
301 Hayes and Harlington,	Dicks, T.P.;	(C)
302 Hazel Grove,	Arnold, T.R.;	(C)
303 Hemsworth,	Buckley, G.J.;	(Lab)
304 Hendon North,	Gorst, J.M.;	(C)
305 Hendon South,	Marshall, J.L.;	(C)
306 Henley,	Heseltine, M.R.D.;	(C)
307 Hereford,	Shepherd, C.R.;	(C)
308 Hertford and Stortford,	Wells, P.B.;	(C)
309 Hertfordshire North,	Stewart, B.H.I.H.;	(C)
310 Hertfordshire South West,	Page, R.L.;	(C)
311 Hertfordshire West,	Jones, R.B.;	(C)
312 Hertsmere,	Parkinson, C.E.;	(C)
313 Hexham,	Amos, A.T.;	(C)
314 Heywood and Middleton,	Callaghan, J.;	(Lab)
315 High Peak,	Hawkins, C.J.;	(C)
316 Holborn and St.Pancras,	Dobson, F.G.;	(Lab)

3

Constituency	Member	Party
317 Holland with Boston,	Body, Sir Richard;	(C)
318 Honiton,	Emery, Sir Peter;	(C)
319 Hornchurch,	Squire, R.C.;	(C)
320 Hornsey and Wood Green,	Rossi, Sir Hugh;	(C)
321 Horsham,	Hordern, Sir Peter;	(C)
322 Houghton and Washington,	Boyes, R.;	(Lab)
323 Hove,	Sainsbury, T.A.D.;	(C)
324 Huddersfield,	Sheerman, B.J.;	(Lab)
325 Hull East,	Prescott, J.L.;	(Lab)
326 Hull North,	McNamara, J.K.;	(Lab)
327 Hull West,	Randall, S.J.;	(Lab)
328 Huntingdon,	Major, J.;	(C)
329 Hyndburn,	Hargreaves, J.K.;	(C)
330 Ilford North,	Bendall, V.W.H.;	(C)
331 Ilford South,	Thorne, N.G.;	(C)
332 Inverness, Nairn and Lochaber,	Johnston, Sir David;	(SLD/All)
333 Ipswich,	Irvine, M.F.;	(C)
334 Isle of Wight,	Field, B.;	(C)
335 Islington North,	Corbyn, J.B.;	(Lab)
336 Islington South and Finsbury,	Smith, C.R.;	(Lab)
337 Islwyn,	Kinnock, N.G.;	(Lab)
338 Jarrow,	Dixon, D.;	(Lab)
339 Keighley,	Waller, G.P.A.;	(C)
340 Kensington,	Fishburn, JD.;	(C)
340 Kensington,	Rhys Williams, Sir Brandon;	(C)
341 Mid Kent,	Rowe, A.J.B.;	(C)
342 Kettering,	Freeman, R.N.;	(C)
343 Kilmarnock and Loudoun,	McKelvey, W.;	(Lab)
344 Kincardine and Deeside,	Buchanan-Smith, A.L.;	(C)
345 Kingston upon Thames,	Lamont, N.S.H.;	(C)
346 Kingswood,	Hayward, R.A.;	(C)
347 Kircaldy,	Moonie, Dr.L.G.;	(Lab)
348 Knowsley North,	Howarth, G.E.;	(Lab)
349 Knowsley South,	Hughes, S.F.;	(Lab)
350 Lagan Valley,	Molyneaux, J.H.;	(OUP)
351 Lancashire West,	Hind, K.H.;	(C)
352 Lancaster,	Kellett-Bowman, Mrs. M.E.;	(C)
353 Langbaurgh,	Holt, J.R.;	(C)
354 Leeds Central,	Fatchett, D.J.;	(Lab)
355 Leeds East,	Healey, D.W.;	(Lab)
356 Leeds North East,	Kirkhope, T.J.R.;	(C)
357 Leeds North West,	Hampson, K.;	(C)
358 Leeds South and Morley,	Rees, M.;	(Lab)
359 Leeds West,	Battle, J.D.;	(Lab)
360 Leicester East,	Vaz, N.K.A.S.;	(Lab)
361 Leicester South,	Marshall, J.;	(Lab)
362 Leicester West,	Janner, G.E.;	(Lab)
363 Leicestershire North West,	Ashby, D.G.;	(C)
364 Leigh,	Cunliffe, L.F.;	(Lab)
365 Leominster,	Temple-Morris;	(C)
366 Lewes,	Rathbone, J.R.;	(C)
367 Lewisham Deptford,	Ruddock, Mrs. J.M.;	(Lab)
368 Lewisham East,	Moynihan, C.B.;	(C)
369 Lewisham West,	Maples, J.C.;	(C)
370 Leyton,	Cohen, H.M.;	(Lab)
371 Lincoln,	Carlisle, K.M.;	(C)
372 Lindsey East,	Tapsell, Sir Peter;	(C)
373 Linlithgow,	Dalyell, T;	(Lab)
374 Littleborough and Saddleworth,	Dickens, G.K.;	(C)
375 Liverpool Broad Green,	Fields, T.;	(Lab)
376 Liverpool Garston,	Loyden, E.;	(Lab)
377 Liverpool Mossley Hill,	Alton, D.P.P.;	(SLD/All)
378 Liverpool Riverside,	Parry, R.;	(Lab)
379 Liverpool Walton,	Heffer, E.S.;	(Lab)
380 Liverpool West Derby,	Wareing, R.N.;	(Lab)
381 Livingston,	Cook, R.F.;	(Lab)
382 Llanelli,	Davies, D.J.D.;	(Lab)
383 Londonderry East,	Ross, W.;	(OUP)
384 Loughborough,	Dorrell, S.J.;	(C)
385 Ludlow,	Gill, C.J.F.;	(C)
386 Luton North,	Carlisle, J.R.;	(C)
387 Luton South,	Bright, G.F.J.;	(C)
388 Macclesfield,	Winterton, N.R.;	(C)
389 Maidstone,	Widdecombe, Miss A.N.;	(C)

	Constituency	Member	Party
390	Makerfield,	McCartney, I.;	(Lab)
391	Manchester Blackley,	Eastham, K.;	(Lab)
392	Manchester Central,	Litherland, R.K.;	(Lab)
393	Manchester Gorton,	Kaufman, G.B.;	(Lab)
394	Manchester Withington,	Bradley, K.J.C.;	(Lab)
395	Manchester Wythenshawe,	Morris, A.;	(Lab)
396	Mansfield,	Meale, J.A.;	(Lab)
397	Medway,	Fenner, Dame Peggy;	(C)
398	Meirionnydd Nant Conwy,	Thomas, D.W.;	(PC)
399	Meriden,	Mills, I.C.;	(C)
400	Merthyr Tydfil and Rhymney,	Rowlands, E.;	(Lab)
401	Middlesbrough,	Bell, S.;	(Lab)
402	Midlothian,	Eadie, A.	(Lab)
403	Milton Keynes,	Benyon, W.R.;	(C)
404	Mitcham and Morden,	Rumbold, Mrs. A.C.R.;	(C)
405	Mole Valley,	Baker, K.W.;	(C)
406	Monklands East,	Smith, J.;	(Lab)
407	Monklands West,	Clarke, T.;	(Lab)
408	Monmouth,	Stradling Thomas J.;	(C)
409	Montgomery,	Carlile, A.C.;	(L/All)
410	Moray,	Ewing, Mrs. W.M.;	(SNP)
411	Morecambe and Lunesdale,	Lennox-Boyd, M.A.;	(C)
412	Motherwell North,	Reid, J.;	(Lab)
413	Motherwell South,	Bray, J.W.;	(Lab)
414	Neath,	Coleman, D.R.;	(Lab)
415	Newark,	Alexander, R.T.;	(C)
416	Newbury,	McNair-Wilson, Sir Michael;	(C)
417	Newcastle-under-Lyme,	Golding, Mrs. N.;	(Lab)
418	Newcastle upon Tyne Central,	Cousins, J.M.;	(Lab)
419	Newcastle upon Tyne East,	Brown, N.H.;	(Lab)
420	Newcastle upon Tyne North,	Henderson, D.J.;	(Lab)
421	New Forest,	McNair-Wilson, P.M.E.D.;	(C)
422	Newham North East,	Leighton, R.;	(Lab)
423	Newham North West,	Banks, T.L.;	(Lab)
424	Newham South,	Spearing, N.J.;	(Lab)
425	Newport East,	Hughes, R.J.;	(Lab)
426	Newport West,	Flynn, P.P.;	(Lab)
427	Newry and Armagh,	Mallon, S.;	(SDLP)
428	Mid Norfolk,	Ryder, R.;	(C)
429	Norfolk North,	Howell, R.F.;	(C)
430	Norfolk North West,	Bellingham, H.C.;	(C)
431	Norfolk South,	MacGregor, J.R.R.;	(C)
432	Norfolk South West,	Shephard, Mrs. G.P.;	(C)
433	Normanton,	O'Brien, W.;	(Lab)
434	Northampton North,	Marlow, A.R.;	(C)
435	Northampton South,	Morris, M.W.L.;	(C)
436	Northavon,	Cope, John;	(C)
437	Norwich North,	Thompson, H.P.;	(C)
438	Norwich South,	Garrett, J.L.;	(Lab)
439	Norwood,	Fraser, J.D.;	(Lab)
440	Nottingham East,	Knowles, M.;	(C)
441	Nottingham North,	Allen, G.W.;	(Lab)
442	Nottingham South,	Brandon-Bravo, N.M.;	(C)
443	Nuneaton,	Stevens, L.D.;	(C)
444	Ogmore,	Powell, R.;	(Lab)
445	Old Bexley and Sidcup,	Heath, E.R.G.;	(C)
446	Oldham Central and Royton,	Lamond, J.A.;	(Lab)
447	Oldham West,	Meacher, M.H.;	(Lab)
448	Orkney and Shetland,	Wallace, J.R.;	(SLD/All)
449	Orpington,	Stanbrook, I.R.;	(C)
450	Oxford East,	Smith, A.D.;	(Lab)
451	Oxford West and Abingdon,	Patten, J.H.V.;	(C)
452	Paisley North,	Adams, A.;	(Lab)
453	Paisley South,	Buchan, N.F.;	(Lab)
454	Peckham,	Harman, Ms.H.;	(Lab)
455	Pembroke,	Bennett, N.J.;	(Con)
456	Pendle,	Lee, J.R.L.;	(C)
457	Penrith and The Border,	Maclean, D.J.;	(C)
458	Perth and Kinross,	Fairbairn, N.H.;	(C)
459	Peterborough,	Mawhinney, Dr. B.S.;	(C)
460	Plymouth Devonport,	Owen, Dr. D.A.L.;	(SDP/All)
461	Plymouth Drake,	Fookes, Miss J.E.;	(C)
462	Plymouth Sutton,	Clark, A.K.M.;	(C)
463	Pontefract and Castleford,	Lofthouse, G.;	(Lab)

	Constituency	Member	Party
464	Pontypridd,	Howells. K.S.;	(Lab)
465	Poole,	Ward, J.D.;	(C)
466	Portsmouth North,	Griffiths, P.H.S.;	(C)
467	Portsmouth South,	Martin, D.;	(C)
468	Preston,	Wise, Mrs. A.;	(Lab)
469	Pudsey,	Shaw, J.G.D.;	(C)
470	Putney,	Mellor, D.J.;	(C)
471	Ravensbourne,	Hunt, J.L.;	(C)
472	Reading East,	Vaughan, Sir Gerard;	(C)
473	Reading West,	Durant, R.A.B.;	(C)
474	Redcar,	Mowlam, Miss M.;	(Lab)
475	Reigate,	Gardiner, G.A.;	(C)
476	Renfrew West and Inverclyde,	Graham, T.;	(Lab)
477	Rhondda,	Rogers, A.R.;	(Lab)
478	Ribble Valley,	Waddington, D.C.;	(C)
479	Richmond and Barnes,	Hanley, J.J.;	(C)
480	Richmond, Yorks,	Hague, W.J.:	(C)
481	Rochdale,	Smith, Sir Cyril;	(SLD/All)
482	Rochford,	Clark, M.;	(C)
483	Romford,	Neubert, M.J.;	(C)
484	Romsey and Waterside,	Colvin, M.K.B.;	(C)
485	Ross, Cromarty and Skye,	Kennedy, C.P.;	(SLD/All)
486	Rossendale and Darwen,	Trippier, D.A.;	(C)
487	Rotherham,	Crowther, J.S.;	(Lab)
488	Rother Valley,	Barron, K.J.;	(Lab)
489	Roxburgh and Berwickshire,	Kirkwood, A.J.;	(SLD/All)
490	Rugby and Kenilworth,	Pawsey, J.F.;	(C)
491	Ruislip Northwood,	Wilkinson, J.A.D.;	(C)
492	Rushcliffe,	Clarke, K.H.;	(C)
493	Rutland and Melton,	Latham, M.A.;	(C)
494	Ryedale,	Greenway, J.R.;	(C)
495	Saffron Walden,	Haselhurst, A.G.B.;	(C)
496	St. Albans,	Lilley, P.B.;	(C)
497	St. Helens North,	Evans, J.;	(Lab)
498	St. Helens South,	Bermingham, G.E.;	(Lab)
499	St. Ives,	Harris, D.A.;	(C)
500	Salford East,	Orme, S.;	(Lab)
501	Salisbury,	Key, S.R.;	(C)
502	Scarborough,	Shaw, Sir Michael;	(C)
503	Sedgefield,	Blair, A.C.L.;	(Lab)
504	Selby,	Alison, M.J.H.;	(C)
505	Sevenoaks,	Wolfson, G.M.;	(C)
506	Sheffield Attercliffe,	Duffy, A.E.P.;	(Lab)
507	Sheffield Brightside,	Blunkett, D.;	(Lab)
508	Sheffield Central,	Caborn, R.G.;	(Lab)
509	Sheffield Hallam,	Patnick, C.I.;	(C)
510	Sheffield Heeley,	Michie, W.;	(Lab)
511	Sheffield Hillsborough,	Flannery, M.H.;	(Lab)
512	Sherwood,	Stewart, A.S.;	(C)
513	Shipley,	Fox, Sir Marcus;	(C)
514	Shoreham,	Luce, R.N.;	(C)
515	Shrewsbury and Atcham,	Conway, D.L.;	(C)
516	Shropshire North,	Biffen, W.J.;	(C)
517	Skipton and Ripton,	Curry, D.M.;	(C)
518	Slough,	Watts, J.A.;	(C)
519	Solihull,	Taylor, J.M.;	(C)
520	Somerton and Frome,	Boscawen, R.T.;	(C)
521	Southampton Itchen,	Chope, C.R.;	(C)
522	Southampton Test,	Hill, S.J.A.;	(C)
523	Southend East,	Taylor, E.M.;	(C)
524	Southend West,	Channon, G.P.G.;	(C)
525	South Hams,	Steen, A.D.;	(C)
526	Southport,	Fearn, R.C.;	(SLD/All)
527	South Ribble,	Atkins, R.J.;	(C)
528	South Shields,	Clark, D.G.;	(Lab)
529	Southwark and Bermondsey,	Hughes, S.H.W.;	(SLD/All)
530	Spelthorne,	Wilshire, D.;	(C)
531	Stafford,	Cash, W.N.P.;	(C)
532	Mid Staffordshire,	Sheal, S.;	(L)
533	Staffordshire Moorlands,	Knox, D.L.;	(C)
534	Staffordshire South,	Cormack, P.T.;	(C)
535	Staffordshire South East,	Lightbown, D.L.;	(C)
536	Stalybridge and Hyde,	Pendry, T.;	(Lab)
537	Stamford and Spalding,	Davies, J.Q.;	(C)

	Constituency	Member	Party
538	Stevenage,	Wood, T.J.R.;	(C)
539	Stirling,	Forsyth, M.B.;	(C)
540	Stockport,	Favell, A.R.;	(C)
541	Stockton North,	Cook, F.;	(Lab)
542	Stockton South,	Devlin, T.R.;	(C)
543	Stoke-on-Trent Central,	Fisher, M.;	(Lab)
544	Stoke-on-Trent North,	Walley, Ms. J.L.;	(Lab)
545	Stoke-on-Trent,	Ashley, J.;	(Lab)
546	Strangford,	Taylor, J.D.;	(OUP)
547	Stratford-on-Avon,	Howarth, A.T.;	(C)
548	Strathkelvin and Bearsden,	Galbraith, S.;	(Lab)
549	Streatham,	Shelton, W.J.M.;	(C)
550	Stretford,	Lloyd, A.J.;	(Lab)
551	Stroud,	Knapman, R.;	(C)
552	Suffolk Central,	Lord, M.N.;	(C)
553	Suffolk Coastal,	Gummer, J.S.;	(C)
554	Suffolk South,	Yeo, T.S.K.;	(C)
555	Sunderland North,	Clay, R.A.;	(Lab)
556	Sunderland South,	Mullin, C.J.;	(Lab)
557	Surbiton,	Tracey, R.P.;	(C)
558	Surrey East,	Howe, Sir Geoffrey;	(C)
559	Surrey North West,	Grylis, W.M.J.;	(C)
560	Surrey South West,	Bottomley, Mrs. V.H.B.M.;	(C)
561	Mid Sussex,	Renton, R.T.;	(C)
562	Sutton and Cheam,	Macfarlane, Sir D. Neil;	(C)
563	Sutton Coldfield,	Fowler, P.N.;	(C)
564	Swansea East,	Anderson, D.;	(Lab)
565	Swansea West,	Williams, A.J.;	(Lab)
566	Swindon,	Coombs, S.C.;	(C)
567	Tatton,	Hamilton, M.N.;	(C)
568	Taunton,	Nicholson, D.J.;	(C)
569	Tayside North,	Walker, W.C.;	(C)
570	Teignbridge,	Nicholls, P.C.M.;	(C)
571	Thanet North,	Gale, R.J.;	(C)
572	Thanet South,	Aitken, J.W.P.;	(C)
573	Thurrock,	Janman, T.S.;	(C)
574	Tiverton,	Maxwell-Hyslop, R.J.;	(C)
575	Tonbridge and Malling,	Stanley, J.P.;	(C)
576	Tooting,	Cox, T.M.;	(Lab)
577	Torbay,	Allason, R.W.S.;	(C)
578	Torfaen,	Murphy, P.P.;	(Lab)
579	Tottenham,	Grant, B.;	(Lab)
580	Truro,	Taylor, M.O.J.;	(SLD/All)
581	Tunbridge Wells,	Mayhew, Sir Patrick;	(C)
582	Tweeddale, Ettick and Lauderdale,	Steel, D.;	(SLD)
583	Twickenham,	Jessel, T.F.H.;	(C)
584	Tynebridge,	Clelland, D.G.;	(Lab)
585	Tynemouth,	Trotter, N.G.;	(C)
586	Mid Ulster,	McCrea, Rev. R.T.W.;	(DUP)
587	Upminster,	Bonsor, Sir Nicholas;	(C)
588	Upper Bann,	Trimble, D.;	(OUP)
589	Uxbridge,	Shersby, J.M.;	(C)
590	Vale of Glamorgan,	Smith, J.W.P.;	(Lab)
591	Vauxhall,	Hoey, K.;	(Lab)
592	Wakefield,	Hinchlife, D.M.;	(Lab)
593	Wallasey,	Chalker, Mrs. L.;	(C)
594	Wallsend,	Garrett, W.E.;	(Lab)
595	Walsall North,	Winnick, D.J.;	(Lab)
596	Walsall South,	George, B.T.;	(Lab)
597	Walthamstow,	Summerson, H.H.F.;	(C)
598	Wansbeck,	Thompson, J.;	(Lab)
599	Wansdyke,	Aspinwall, J.H.;	(C)
600	Wanstead and Woodford,	Arbuthnot, J.N.;	(C)
601	Wantage,	Jackson, R.V.;	(C)
602	Warley East,	Faulds, A.M.W.;	(Lab)
603	Warley West,	Archer, P.K.;	(Lab)
604	Warrington North,	Hoyle, E.D.H.;	(Lab)
605	Warrington South,	Butler, C.J.;	(C)
606	Warwick and Leamington,	Smith, Sir Dudley;	(C)
607	Warwickshire North,	Maude, F.A.A.;	(C)
608	Watford,	Garel-Jones, W.A.T.T.;	(C)
609	Waveney,	Porter, D.;	(C)
610	Wealden,	Johnson Smith, G;	(C)
611	Wellingborough,	Fry, P.D.;	(C)

Constituency	Member	Party
612 Wells,	Heathcoat-Amory, D.P.;	(C)
613 Welwyn Hatfield,	Evans, D.H.;	(C)
614 Wentworth,	Hardy, P.;	(Lab)
615 West Bromwich East,	Snape, P.C.;	(Lab)
616 West Bromwich West,	Boothroyd, Miss B.;	(Lab)
617 Westbury,	Walters, Sir Dennis;	(C)
618 Western Isles,	MacDonald, C.A.;	(Lab)
619 Westminster North,	Wheeler, J.D.;	(C)
620 Westmorland and Lonsdale,	Jopling, T.M.;	(C)
621 Weston-Super-Mare,	Wiggin, A.W.;	(C)
622 Wigan,	Stott, R;	(Lab)
623 Wiltshire North,	Needham, R.F.;	(C)
624 Wimbledon,	Goodson-Wickes, Dr.C.;	(C)
625 Winchester,	Browne, J.E.D.;	(C)
626 Windsor and Maidenhead,	Glyn, Dr. A.;	(C)
627 Wirral South,	Porter, G.B.;	(C)
628 Wirral West,	Hunt, D.J.F.;	(C)
629 Witney,	Hurd, D.R.;	(C)
630 Woking,	Onslow, C.G.D.;	(C)
631 Wokingham,	Redwood, J.A.;	(C)
632 Wolverhampton North East,	Hicks, Mrs. M.;	(C)
633 Wolverhampton South East,	Turner, D.;	(Lab)
634 Wolverhampton South West,	Budgen, N.W.;	(C)
635 Woodspring,	Dean, Sir Paul;	(C)
636 Woolwich,	Cartwright, J.C.;	(SDP/All)
637 Worcester,	Walker, P.E.;	(C)
638 Mid Worcestershire,	Forth, M.E.;	(C)
639 Worcestershire South,	Spicer, W.M.H.;	(C)
640 Workington,	Campbell-Savours; D.R.	(Lab)
641 Worsley,	Lewis, T.;	(Lab)
642 Worthing,	Higgins, T.L.;	(C)
643 The Wrekin,	Grocott, B.;	(Lab)
644 Wrexham,	Marek, J.;	(Lab)
645 Wycombe,	Whitney, R.W.;	(C)
646 Wyre,	Mans, K.D.R.;	(C)
647 Wyre Forest,	Coombs, A.M.V.;	(C)
648 Yeovil,	Ashdown, J.J.D.;	(SLD/All)
649 Ynys Mon,	Jones, I.W.;	(PC)
650 York,	Gregory, C.R.;	(C)

BY-ELECTIONS AND NEW MPS SINCE THE GENERAL ELECTION OF JUNE 1987

Vacancy	Cause	Date of By Election	New Member	Introduction
Kensington	Death of Sir B Rhys Williams (C) (18.5.88)	14.7.88	Mr. D. Fishburn (C)	19.7.88
Epping Forest	Death of Sir J. Biggs- Davison (C) (17.9.88)	15.12.88	Mr. S. Norris (C)	20.12.88
Glasgow Govan	Resignation of Rt. Hon B. Millan (L) (18.10.88)	10.11.88	Mr. J. Sillars (SNP)	14.11.88
Pontypridd	Death of Mr. B. John (L) (13.12.88)	23.2.89	Dr. K. Howells (L)	1.3.89
Richmond (Yorks)	Resignation of Rt. Hon. L. Brittan (C) (31.12.88)	23.2.89	Mr. W. Hague (C)	28.2.89
Vale of Glamorgan	Death of Sir R. Gower (C) (22.2.89)	4.5.89	Mr. J.W.P. Smith (L)	9.5.89
Glasgow Central	Death of Mr. R McTaggart (L) (23.3.89)	15.6.89	Mr. M. Watson. (L)	20.6.89
Vauxhall	Resignation of Mr. S. Holland (L) (18.5.89)	15.6.89	Ms K. Hoey (L)	27.689
Mid Staffordshire	Death of Mr. J. Heddle (C) 19.12.89	22.3.90	Mrs S Heal (L)	27.3.90
Upper Bann	Death of Mr. H. McCusker (UU) (11.2.90)	17.590	Mr. D. Trimble (UU)	22.590
Bootle	Death of Mr. A. Roberts (L) 21.3.90	24.5.90	Mr. M. Carr (L)	5.9.90

MAIN POLITICAL PARTIES

Conservative Central Office: 32 Smith Square, London SW1P 3HH. Telephone: 071-222 9000. Chairman: Rt. Hon. Kenneth, M.P. Deputy Chairman: David Trippier, M.P.

Green Party: 10 Station Parade, Balham High Road, London SW12 9AZ. Telephone: 081-673 0045. Office Manager: John Bishop. Press Officer: Rowland Morgan.

Labour Party: 150 Walworth Road, London SE17 1JT. Telephone: 071-703 0833. General Secretary: J. L. Whitty. Director of Organisation: Joyce Gould. Director of Campaigns and Communications: John Underwood. Director of Policy Development: Geoff Bish. Director of Personnel, Resources and Training: Mike Watts

Plaid Cymru (Party of Wales): 51 Cathedral Road, Cardiff CF1 9HD. Telephone: Cardiff 231944. President: Dafydd Elis Thomas, M.P. Chairman: Dafydd Huws. General Secretary: Dafydd Williams.

Scottish National Party: 6 North Charlotte Street, Edinburgh EH2 4JH. Telephone: 031-226 3661. Gordon Wilson (Due to stand down in September 1990). President: Winifred Ewing, MEP. National Secretary: John Swinney.

Liberal Democrats: 4 Cowley Street, London SW1P 3NB. Telephone: 071-222 7999. General Secretary: Graham Ellis

THE PRIVY COUNCIL

THE BRITISH Constitution has a record of gradual change from a royal to a parliamentary executive. The sovereign in carrying out the executive functions of government was accustomed to be guided by the advice of certain Privy Counsellors chosen by himself. The Privy Council still plays a very important part in the Constitution. Apart from the many functions vested in it by statute, it is the body on whose advice the Queen in Council exercises certain prerogative powers and a large number of powers vested in Her Majesty by statute. Privy Counsellors are still appointed by the sovereign, and may be removed at will, though such removals are exceedingly rare. On being nominated they take the oath of office, binding themselves among other things to keep the Queen's council secret. Membership is a coveted distinction, every Privy Counsel lor being entitled to be addressed as Right Honourable. The principal officer is the Lord President of the Council, who is always a member of the Cabinet.

Clerk of the Council: G. I. de Deney

H.R.H. The Prince Philip Duke of Edinburgh
H.R.H. The Prince of Wales

Aberdare, Lord
Ackner, Lord
Adams-Schneider, L. R.
Ademola, Sir Adetokunbo
Airlie, Earl of
Aldington, Lord
Alebua, Ezekie
Alison, Michael
Alport, Lord
Amery, Julian
Anthony, John Douglas
Archer, Peter
Armstrong, Ernest
Arnold, Sir John
Ashdown, Jeremy John Durham (Paddy)
Ashley, Jack
Avonside, Lord
Aylestone, Lord
Azikiwe, Nnamdi

Bacon, Baroness
Baker, Kenneth
Balcombe, Sir John
Barber, Lord
Barnett, Lord
Barwick, Sir Garfield
Beldam, Sir Alexander
Belstead, Lord
Benn, Anthony Wedgwood
Bennett, Sir Frederic
Bevins, John R.
Biffen, John
Bingham, Sir Thomas
Bird, Vere
Bisson, Gordon, Ellis
Blaize, Hon. Herbert
Blaker, Sir Peter
Blanch, Rt. Rev. Lord
Booth, Albert Edward
Bottomley, Lord
Boyd-Carpenter, Lord
Boyson, Sir Rhodes
Braine, Sir Bernard
Brandon of Oakbrook, Lord
Bridge of Harwich, Lord
Brightman, Lord
Brittan, Sir, Leon

Brooke, Peter
Brown, Sir Stephen
Browne, Sir Patrick
Browne-Wilkinson, Sir Nicolas
Broxbourne, Lord
Buchanan-Smith, Alick
Buckley, Sir Denys
Butler, Sir Adam
Butler-Sloss, Dame Elizabeth

Callaghan of Cardiff, Lord
Cameron of Lochbroom, Lord
Campbell of Croy, Lord
Canterbury, The Archbishop of
Caradon, Lord
Carlisle of Buclow, Lord
Carr of Hadley, Lord
Carrington, Lord
Casey, Maurice
Castle, Barbara
Cato, Robert Milton
Chalfont, Lord
Chalker, Lynda
Chan, Sir Julius
Channon, Henry Paul Guinness
Charteris of Amisfield, Lord
Chataway, Christopher
Clarke, Kenneth
Cledwyn of Penrhos, Lord
Cockfield, Lord
Cocks of Hartcliffe, Lord
Coggan, Rt. Rev. Lord
Colman, Hon. Frazer
Colnbrook, Lord
Colyton, Lord
Compton, John George Melvin
Concannon, John Dennis
Cooke, Sir Robin
Cooper, Sir Frank
Cope, John
Corfield, Sir Frederick
Cowen, Sir Zelman
Craigton, Lord
Crawford and Balcarres, Earl of
Crickhowell, Lord
Cromer, Earl of
Croom-Johnson, Sir David

Cross of Chelsea, Lord
Cumming-Bruce, Sir Roualeyn

Davies, Denzil
Davison, Sir Ronald
Deedes, Lord
De L'Isle, Viscount
Dell, Edmund
Denham, Lord
Denning, Lord
Devlin, Lord
Devonshire, Duke of
Diamond, Lord
Dillon, Sir Brian
Donaldson, Sir John
Douglas, Sir William
du Cann, Sir Edward
Duff, Sir Antony
Dunn, Sir Robin

Eccles, Viscount
Eden of Winton, Lord
Edmund-Davies, Lord
Eichelbaum, Sir Johann Thomas
Ellison, Rt. Rev. Gerald
Emslie, Lord
Ennals, Lord
Erroll of Hale, Lord
Esquivel, Hon. Manuel
Eveleigh, Sir Edward

Farquharson, Sir Donald Henry
Fernyhough, Ernest
Ferrers, Earl
Fletcher, Lord
Foot, Michael
Fowler, Norman
Fox, Sir Michael
Franks, Lord
Fraser, Carmyllie
Fraser, Malcolm
Freeman, John
Freeson, Reginald

Gairy, Eric
Gardiner, Lord
Georges, Telford
Gibbs, Sir Harry
Gibbs, Sir Humphrey
Gibson, Sir Ralph (Brian)
Gibson-Watt, Lord
Gilbert, John William
Gilmour, Sir Ian, Bt.
Glenamara, Lord
Glendevon, Lord
Glidewell, Sir Iain
Goff, Sir Robert
Gordon, John Bowie
Gorton, Sir John Grey,
Gowrie, Earl of
Gray of Contin, Lord
Griffiths, Lord
Grimond, Lord
Gummer, John Selwyn

Hailsham of St. Marylebone, Lord
Harrison, Walter
Hart, Baroness
Harvington, Lord
Hasluck, Sir Paul
Hattersley, Roy
Havers of St. Edmundsbury, Lord

Hayhoe, Barney
Healey, Denis
Heath, Edward
Herbison, Margaret
Heseltine, Michael
Heseltine, Sir William (Frederick Payne)
Higgins, Terence
Holderness, Lord
Home of the Hirsel, Lord
Hope, Lord
Houghton of Sowerby, Lord
Howard, Michael
Howe, Sir Geoffrey (Lord President of the Council)
Howell, David
Howell, Denis
Hughes, Lord
Hunt, Jonathan
Hurd, Douglas
Hutton, Sir James

Irvine, Sir Bryant Godman

Jauncey, Lord
Jay, Lord
Jellicoe, Earl
Jenkin of Roding, Lord
Jenkins of Hillhead, Lord
Jones, Aubrey
Jones, Sir Edward Warburton
Jopling, Michael
Joseph, Lord
Jugnauth, Sir Anerood

Kaufman, Gerald
Keith of Kinkel, Lord
Kelly, Sir Basil
Kenilorea, Sir Peter
Kerr, Sir John
Kerr, Sir Michael
Kilbrandon, Lord
King, Thomas
Kinnock, Neil
Kitto, Sir Frank

Lamont, Norman Stewart
Lane, Lord
Lange, David
Lansdowne, Marquess of
Latey, Sir John
Lauti, Toaripi
Lawson, Nigel
Lawton, Sir Frederick
Lee of Asheridge, Baroness
Leggatt, Sir Andrew
Leigh-Pemberton, Robert
Lever of Manchester, Lord
Listowel, Earl of
Llewelyn-Davies of Hastoe, Baroness
Lloyd, Sir Anthony
London, The Bishop of
Longford, Earl of
Louis Y, Allan
Lowry, Lord
Luce, Richard Napier
Lyell, Sir Nicholas

Mabon, Jesse Dickson
McCarthy, Sir Thaddeus
MacDermott, John
MacGregor, John
MacIntyre, Duncan

Mackay of Clashfern, Lord
MacKenzie, Gregor
Maclean, Lord
McMullin, Duncan
McTiernan, Sir Edward
Major, John
Manley, Michael Norman
Mann, Michael
Mara, Sir Kamisese
Marsh, Lord
Martonmere, Lord
Mason, Lord
Maude of Stratford-upon-Avon, Lord
May, Sir John
Mayhew, Sir Patrick
McCowan, Sir Anthony
Megarry, Sir Robert
Megaw, Sir John
Mellish, Lord
Millan, Bruce
Mitchell, Hon. James
Molson, Lord
Molyneaux, James
Moore, John Edward
Moore, Sir Philip
Morris, Alfred
Morris, Charles Richard
Morris, John
Morrison, Peter Hugh
Moyle, Roland
Muirshiel, Viscount
Muldoon, Sir Robert
Mulley, Lord Frederick William
Murray, Lord
Murray of Epping Forest, Lord
Murray, Donald Bruce
Murton of Lindisfarne, Lord
Mustill, Sir Michael

Nairne, Sir Patrick
Neill, Sir Brian
Newton, Antony
Nicholls, Sir Donald
Northumberland, Duke of
Nott, Sir John
Nourse, Sir Martin
Nugent of Guildford, Lord
Nutting, Sir Anthony, Bt.

Oakes, Gordon James
O'Brien of Lothbury, Lord
O'Connor, Sir Patrick
O'Donnell, Turlough
O'Flynn, Francis Duncan
Oliver, Sir Peter
Onslow, Cranley Gordon Douglas
Oppenheim-Barres, Sally
Orme, Stanley
Ormrod, Sir Roger
Orr, Sir Alan
Owen, David

Palliser, Sir Michael
Palmer, Geoffrey Winston Russell
Parker, Sir Roger
Parkinson, Cecil
Patten, Sir Christopher
Patten, John
Pattie, Sir Geoffrey
Pearce, Lord
Percival, Sir Ian
Perth, Earl of
Peyton of Yeovil, Lord
Pindling, Sir Lynden
Poole, Lord
Powell, Enoch
Prentice, Reginald Ernest
Price, George
Prior, Lord
Puapua, Dr. Tomasi
Purchas, Sir Francis
Pym, Lord

Raison, Timothy
Ramsden, James
Rawlinson of Ewell, Lord
Rees, Merlyn
Rees, Lord
Reigate, Lord
Renton, Lord
Renton, Ronald Timothy
Richardson of Duntisbourne, Lord
Richardson, Sir Ivor Lloyd Morgan
Richmond, Sir Clifford
Ridley, Nicholas
Rifkind, Malcolm

Rippon of Hexham, Lord
Robens of Woldingham, Lord
Robinson, Sir Kenneth
Rodgers, William
Roskill, Lord
Ross, Lord
Rowling, Sir Wallace Edward
Russell, Sir Patrick

St. Aldwyn, Earl
St. Brides, Lord
St. John of Fawsley, Lord
Salmon, Lord
Sandiford, Lloyd Erskine
Scarman, Lord
Scott, Nicholas
Seaga, Edward
Seear, Baroness
Selkirk, Earl of
Shackleton, Lord
Shawcross, Lord
Shearer, Hugh
Sheldon, Robert
Shepherd, Lord
Shore, Peter
Silkin of Dulwich, Lord
Simmonds, Hon. Dr. Kennedy
Simon of Glaisdale, Lord
Sinclair, Ian
Slade, Sir Christopher
Smith, John
Somare, Michael
Somers, Edward
Stanley, John
Staughton, Sir Christopher
Stephen Thomas Jonathan Thayer
Steel, David
Stephen, Sir Ninian
Stephenson, Sir John
Stevenson, Sir Melford
Stewart, Donald
Stewart of Fulham, Lord
Stewart, Ian
Stocker, Sir John
Stodart of Leaston, Lord
Stott, Lord
Strauss, Lord

Stuart-Smith, Sir Murray

Talboys, Brian
Taylor, Sir Peter
Tebbit, Norman
Templeman, Lord
Thatcher, Margaret, Hilda
Thomas of Gwydir, Lord
Thomson, David
Thomson of Monifieth, Lord
Thorneycroft, Lord
Thorpe, Jeremy
Tizard, Robert
Tonypandy, Viscount
Tranmire, Lord
Trefgarne, Lord
Turner, Sir Alexander

Varley, Eric

Waddington, David
Wakeham, John
Waldegrave, William
Walker, Harold
Walker, Peter
Waller, Sir George
Watkins, Sir Tasker
Watkinson, Viscount
Weatherill, Bernard
Welensky, Sir Roland
Whitelaw, Viscount
Wilberforce, Lord
Williams, Alan John
Williams, Shirley
Willis, Eustace George
Wilson of Langside, Lord
Wilson of Rievaulx, Lord
Windlesham, Lord
Wingti, Pairas
Withers, Reginald
Woodhouse, Sir Owen
Woolf, Sir Harry
Wylie, Lord

York, The Archbishop of

Young, Baroness
Young of Graffham, Lord
Younger, George

THE PARLIAMENTARY COMMISSIONER FOR ADMINISTRATION

Sir Anthony Barrowclough, Q.C.

THE PARLIAMENTARY Commissioner for Administration is empowered to investigate complaints referred to him by Members of the House of Commons from members of the public who claim to have sustained injustice in consequence of maladministration in connection with administrative actions taken by or on behalf of Government departments, or certain non-departmental public bodies (NDPB).

Almost all Government departments and most NDPBs are included, but the Police, Hospitals and personnel questions in the Armed Forces and Civil Service are among the exceptions. Actions taken by local authorities and nationalised industries are also excluded. Any member of the public may submit a complaint intended for the Commissioner to a Member of Parliament.

The complaint must be made by the person aggrieved himself, but exceptions may be allowed if the person has died or is unable to act for himself.

Unless the Commissioner decides that an exception can be made, the complaint must be made to a Member of Parliament within twelve months of the time when the person aggrieved first had notice of the matters alleged in the complaint.

The complaint must be made in writing to a Member of the House of Commons and include:

1. A statement that the person making the complaint gives his consent for the M.P. to refer it to the Parliamentary Commissioner for Administration.

2. Name and full address of complainant.

3. Identity of Government department or body against whose action the complaint is made.

4. Statement of circumstances in which complainant claims to have sustained injustice.

The Commissioner's office will answer general enquiries from the public as to whether a particular Government department or body or a particular type of action is within his scope of jurisdiction. Such enquiries should be addressed to: The Office of the Parliamentary Commisioner for Administration, Church House, Great Smith Street, London SW1P 3BW. 01-276 2130.

THE COMMISSION FOR LOCAL ADMINISTRATION: LOCAL OMBUDSMEN

There are three Local Ombudsmen in England. They are independent people who investigate complaints against local authorities (except Town or Parish Councils), police authorities, the Commission for New Towns and New Town Development Corporations (housing functions), Urban Development Corporations (town and country planning functions) and fire authorities. There are separate Local Ombudsmen for Scotland, Wales and Northern Ireland.

The Local Ombudsmen cannot question what an Authority have done just because someone does not agree with it. There must be a complaint that something went wrong and caused injustice to the person who has complained. There is no charge for the service and investigations are made in private.

Complaints can be sent direct to the Local Ombudsmen or through a Councillor. The Local Ombudsman will not consider a complaint unless the Council has had an opportunity to investigate and reply to the complaint first. A free booklet about the Local Ombudsman and how to make a complaint is available from Council offices and Citizens Advice Bureaux or from the Commission's office at 21 Queen Anne's Gate, London SW1H 9Bu. 071-222 5622.

HEALTH SERVICE COMMISSIONERS

THE THREE Health Service Commissioners (for England, for Scotland and for Wales) are appointed by the Crown in the same way as the Parliamentary Commissioner. The function of the Health Service Commissioners is to investigate complaints from members of the public that they have suffered injustice or hardship as a result of a failure in a service provided by the health authority, or a failure to provide a service which it was their duty to provide, or maladministration by one of these authorities. The authorities concerned include Regional Health Authorities, District Health Authorities, Health Boards in Scotland and Family Practitioner Committees. Complaints do not have to be routed through an MP but before the Commissioner can investigate, the complaint must have been brought to the attention of the authority concerned, and an adequate opportunity given to investigate it and reply.

Matters which are outside his jurisdiction include action taken solely in the exercise of clinical judgment and the actions of doctors, dentists, pharmacists or opticians taken in connection with the general services they provide.

The complaint must be made in writing to: The Health Service Commissioner, Church House, Great Smith Street, London SW1P 3PW. 071 276 2035; The Health Service Commissioner's Office, 2nd Floor, 11 Melville Crescent, Edinburgh EH3 7LU. 031 225 7465; The Health Service Commissioner's Office, 4th Floor, Pearl Assurance House, Greyfriars Road, Cardiff CF1 3AG. 0222 394621.

Complaints should include:
1. The complainant's full name and address;
2. The health authority concerned; and
3. A full account of the circumstances and the name and address of the place where the matters complained occurred.

THE NATIONAL DEBT

THE NATIONAL Debt consists of the financial obligations of the State. The British National Debt dates from the time of William III when in 1694 a loan of £1,000,000 was raised on Government security to pay for the wars with France. Borrowing on a large scale by the Government has usually been undertaken to finance deficits during or immediately after a war. Marlborough's campaign cost about £38,000,000 and so it went on until the Napoleonic wars, when the Debt had reached over 800,000,000. By 1900 it had been reduced to £600,000,000 but the 1914-18 War sent it up again to nearly £8,000,000,000. The Second World War increased the Debt to over £23,000,000,000. On March 31, 1990, the British National Debt stood at £192,553,000,000. This figure was about £3,365 per head of the population. Of the current Debt, £4,257,000,000 was payable in foreign currencies; the Sterling Debt of £188,296,000,000 consists of a wide variety of short-, medium-, and long-term securities, including Government Stocks, Treasury Bills, National Savings securities.

If Timmy could write a Will, he would probably leave something to us.

You see, he's an arthritis sufferer. He's one of about 15,000 children in our country today who, along with over 8 million people of all other ages, are seriously affected by the disease. And, young as he is, Timmy knows we're his only hope.

We are the Arthritis and Rheumatism Council, the only UK charity financing medical research into all aspects of arthritis. Currently, we spend over £11 million annually on our research and legacies are a major source of our income. We rely entirely on voluntary contributions, receive no State aid whatsoever and spend a mere 2½p in the £ on administration.

We've made many advances in treatment through our research, but as yet there's no cure. With your help, though, we'll find one. Please do what Timmy would do: remember us in your Will.

You'd be helping us achieve the goal of ensuring future generations of Timmy's don't have to suffer this dreadful disease. Talk to your solicitor today; or alternatively, complete and return the coupon below for our Legacy leaflet.

THE ARTHRITIS AND RHEUMATISM COUNCIL FOR RESEARCH
Working to find an earlier cure

See local telephone directory or Yellow Pages for local ARC Representative.

To: The Arthritis and Rheumatism Council for Research, 41 Eagle Street, London WC1R 4AR

I would like to remember ARC in my Will. Please send me your legacy leaflet

NAME

ADDRESS

POSTCODE   DMYB 91

Patron: HRH The Duchess of Kent   *Registered Charity No. 207711*

RELIGION

ANGLICAN TRADITION

THE CHURCH OF ENGLAND

The General Synod of the Church of England Church House, Great Smith Street, Westminster, SW1P 3NZ. 071-222 9011.

Presidents - The Archbishop of Canterbury. The Archbishop of York.
Prolocutor of the Lower House of the Convocation of Canterbury - The Archdeacon of Leicester.
Prolocutor of the Lower House of the Convocation of York - Canon P. H. Boulton.
Chairman of the House of Laity - Prof. J. D. McClean.
Vice-Chairman of the House of Laity - Mrs Jill Dann.
Secretary-General - W. D. Pattinson.
Financial Secretary - T. M. Robinson.

Assistant Secretary-General - L. G. Wadeson, O.B.E.
Standing Counsel - J. Packenham-Walsh, C.B.
Legal Adviser and Joint Registrar of the Provinces of Canterbury and York (Registrar of the General Synod) - B. J. T. Hanson.
Assistant Legal Adviser - Miss I. E. Slaughter
Joint Registrar of the Province of Canterbury - Frank Robson, 16 Beaumont Street, Oxford OX1 2LZ. 0865 241974.
Registrar of the Province of York - L.P.M. Lennox, The Registry, 1 Peckitt St, York YO1 1SG. 0904 623487.
Synodical Secretary of the Convocation of Canterbury - Canon G. Dodson, Reepham Rectory, Norwich. NR10 4LJ. 0603 870220.
Synodal Secretary of the Convocation of York - Canon D. T. I. Jenkins, Church House, West Walls, Carlisle CA3 8UF. 0228 22573.

PROVINCE OF CANTERBURY

CANTERBURY

*102nd Archbishop and Primate of All England and Metropolitan (£37,800): Most Rev. and Rt. Hon. Robert Alexander Kennedy Runcie, P.C., M.C., D.D., M.A., Lambeth Palace, London. SE1 7JU. 071-928 8282. Signature: *Robert Cantuar.*

* *It was announced on 25th July 1990 that Dr George Carey, Bishop of Bath and Wells, was to be the next Archbishop of Canterbury*

Bishops Suffragan:
Dover: Rt. Rev. Richard Henry McPhail Third, M.A., Upway, St. Martin's Hill, Canterbury, Kent. CT1 1PR. 0227 464537.
Maidstone: Rt. Rev. David James Smith, Bishop's House, Pett Lane, Charing, Ashford, Kent TN27 0DL. 023 371 2950.
Honorary Assistant Bishops: Rt. Rev. and Rt. Hon. F. D. Coggan, M.A., D.D. (The Lord Coggan); Rt. Rev. R. S. Hook, M.C., D.Litt; Rt. Rev. W.A. Franklin; Rt. Rev. Dr. D. Say, K.C.V.O.
Dean: Very Rev. J. A. Simpson, M.A., The Deanery, 11 The Precints, Canterbury. CT1 2EH. 0227 65983.

LONDON

Bishop (£30,805): Rt. Rev. and Rt. Hon. Graham Douglas Leonard, M.A., D.D., London House, 8 Barton Street, London. SW1P 3NE. 071-222 8661. Signature: *Graham Londin.*

Area Bishops:
Kensington: Rt. Rev. John George Hughes, M.A., Ph.D., 19 Campden Hill Square, London. W8 7LA. 071-727 9818.
Willesden: Rt. Rev. Thomas Frederick Butler, M.Sc., Ph.D., 173 Willesden Lane, London. NW6 7YN. 081-451 0189.
Edmonton: Rt. Rev. Brian John Masters, M.A., 1 Regents Park Terrace, London. NW1 7EE. 071-267 4455.
Stepney: Rt. Rev. James Lawton Thompson, M.A., F.C.A., 63 Coborn Rd., London E3 2DB. 081-981 8015.
Fulham: Rt. Rev. Charles John Klyberg, A.R.I.C.S., 4 Cambridge Place, London W8 5PB.
Assistant Bishops: Rt. rev. Maurice Wood; Rt. Rev. M. E. Marshall, M.A..
Dean of St. Paul's: Very Rev. (Thomas) Eric Evans, M.A., 9 Amen Court, London. EC4M 7BU. 071-236 2827.
Dean of Westminster: Very Rev. Michael Clement Otway Mayne, M.A., The Deanery, Westminster, London. SW1. 071-222 2953.

WINCHESTER

Bishop (£22,585): Rt. Rev. Colin Clement Walter James, M.A., Wolvesey, Winchester. SO23 9ND. 0962 54050. Signature: *Colin Winton.*
Bishops Suffragan:
Basingstoke: Rt. Rev. Michael Richard John Manktelow, M.A., 1 The Close, Winchester. SO23 9LS. 0962 69374.
Southampton: Rt. Rev. John Freeman Perry, 'Ham House', The Crescent, Romsey, Hants. SO51 7NG. 0794 516005.
Honorary Assistant Bishops: Rt. Rev. H. B. Dehqani-Tafti, D.D.; Rt. Rev. L.L. Rees.
Dean: Very Rev. Trevor Beeson, M.A., The Deanery, Winchester. SO23 9LS. 0962 53738.

BATH AND WELLS

Bishop (£20,350): Rt. Rev. George Leonard Carey, The Palace, Wells, Somerset. BA5 2PD. 0749 72341. Signature: *George Bath et Wells.*
Bishop Suffragan:
Taunton: Rt. Rev. Nigel Simeon McCulloch, M.A., Sherford Farm House, Sherford, Taunton, Somerset. TA1 3RF. 0823 288759.

Honorary Assistant Bishop: Rt. Rev. J. S. Waller, M.A.
Dean: The Dean's Lodging, 25 The Liberty, Wells, Somerset. BA5 2SZ. 0749 72192.

BIRMINGHAM

Bishop (£20,350): Rt. Rev. Mark Santer, M.A., Bishop's Croft, Harborne, Birmingham. B17 0BG. 021-427 1163. Signature: *Mark Birmingham.*
Assiatant Bishop: The Rt. Rev. M.D. Whinney, c/o The o73 Diocesan Office, 175 Harborne Park Road, Harborne B17 OBH.
Provost: Very Rev. Peter Austin Berry, M.A., B.Th., 10 Carisbrooke Road, Edgbaston, Birmingham B17 8NW. Cathedral Office, Colmore Row, Birmingham. B3 2QB. 021-236 6323.

BRISTOL

Bishop (£20,350): Rt. Rev. Barry Rogerson, B.A., Bishop's House, Clifton Hill, Bristol. BS8 1BW. 0272 730222. Signature: *Barry Bristol.*
Bishop Suffragan:
Malmesbury: Rt. Rev. Peter James Firth, M.A., 7 Ivywell Road, Bristol BS9 1NX. 0272 685931.
Dean: Very Rev. (Arthur) Wesley Carr, M.A., Ph.D., The Deanery, 20 Charlotte Street, Bristol. BS1 5PZ. 0272 22443.

CHELMSFORD

Bishop (£20,350): Rt. Rev. John Waine, B.A., Bishops court, Main Road, Margaretting, Ingatestone, Essex CM4 0HD. 0277 352001.Signature: *John Chelmsford.*

Not every Bishop takes the full stipend to which he is entitled

4

Bishops Suffragan:
    Colchester: Rt. Rev. Michael Edwin, Vickers, M.A., 1 Fitzwalter Rd., Lexden, Colchester, Essex CO3 3SS. 0206 576648
    Barking: Rt. Rev. James William Roxburgh, M.A.(Retires Autumn 1990). Barking Lodge, 28A Connaught Avenue, Loughton, Essex. IG10 4DS. 081-508 6680.

Bradwell: Rt. Rev. Charles Derek Bond, A.K.C., 21 Elmhurst Ave., Benfleet, Essex SS7 5RY. 0268 755175.

Provost: Very Rev. John Henry Moses, Ph.D., The Provost's House, 3 Harlings Grove, Waterloo Lane, Chelmsford, Essex. CM1 1YQ. 0245 354318.

CHICHESTER

Bishop (£20,350): Rt. Rev. Eric Waldram Kemp, M.A., D.D., Beacon House, Berwick, Polegate, East Sussex BN26 6ST. 0243 782161. Signature: *Eric Cicestr.*
Bishops Suffragan:
    Lewes: Rt. Rev. Peter John Ball, C.G.A., M.A., Litlington Rectory, Polegate, East Sussex. BN26 5RB. 0323 870387.
    Horsham: Rt. Rev. Ivor Colin Docker, M.A., Bishop's Lodge, Worth, Crawley, West Sussex. RH10 4RT. 0293 883051.
Honorary Assistant Bishops: Rt. Rev. W. W. Hunt, M.A.; Rt. Rev. M. Green, M.C., M.A.; Rt. Rev. S. W. Phipps,M.C.,M.A.; Rt. Rev. E.G. Knapp-Fisher; Rt. Rev. M.H. St. J. Maddocks.
Dean: Very Rev. John David Treadgold, The Deanery, Chichester, West Sussex. PO19 1PX. 0243 783286 (Home), 787337 (Office).

COVENTRY

Bishop (£20,350): Rt. Rev. Simon Barrington-Ward, M.A., Bishop's House, 23 Davenport Road, Coventry. CV5 6PW. 0203 72244. Signature: *Simon Coventry.*
Bishop Suffragan:
    Warwick: Rt. Rev. Keith Appleby Arnold, M.A.(Retires October 1990. Bishop-elect: Ven. G.C. Handford., Warwick House, 139 Kenilworth Road, Coventry, CV4 7AF. 0203 416200. o73
Honorary Assistant Bishops: Rt. Rev. V. S. Nicholls; Rt. Rev. J. C. S. Daly.
Provost: Very Rev. John Fitzmaurice Petty, M.A., Provost's Lodge, 10A Priory Row, Coventry. CV1 5ES. 0203 27597.

DERBY

Bishop (£20,350): Rt. Rev. Peter Spencer Dawes, B.A., The Bishop's House, 6 King Street, Duffield, Derby. DE6 4EY. 0332 46744. Signature: *Peter Derby.*
Bishop Suffragan:
    Repton: Rt. Rev. Francis Henry Arthur Richmond, M.A., B.Th., B.Litt., Repton House, Lea, Matlock, Derbyshire. DE4 5JP. 062 984 644.
Honorary Assistant Bishop: Rt. Rev. K. J. F. Skelton, C.B.E., M.A.
Provost: Very Rev. Benjamin Hugh Lewers, M.A., The Provost's House, 9 Highfield Road, Derby. DE3 1GX. 0332 42971 (Home), 41201 (Office).

ELY

Bishop (£20,350): Rt. rev. S.W. Sykes, M.A., The Bishop's House, Ely, Cambs. CB7 4DW. 0353 662749.
Bishop Suffragan:
    Huntingdon: Rt. Rev. William Gordon Roe, M.A., D.Phil., 14 Lynn Road, Ely, Cambs. CB6 1DA. 0353 662137.
Dean: Very Rev. William James Patterson, M.A., Whitgift House, The College, Ely, Cambs. CB7 4DP. 0353 662432.

DIOCESE IN EUROPE

Bishop (£20,350): Rt. Rev. John Richard Satterthwaite, B.A., 5A Gregory Place, London. W8 4NG. 081-937 2796. Signature: *John Gibraltar.*
Bishop Suffragan: Rt. Rev. Edward Holland, 11 Lanark Road, London W9 1DD. 081-937 2796.
Auxiliary Bishops: Rt. Rev. E. M. H. Capper, O.B.E., L.Th.; Rt. Rev. D. de Pina Cabral; Rt. Rev. A.W.M. Weekes

EXETER

Bishop (£20,350): Rt. Rev. Geoffrey Hewlett Thompson, M.A., The Palace, Exeter. EX1 1HY. 0392 72362. Signature: *Hewlett Exon.*
Bishops Suffragan:
    Crediton: Rt. Rev. Peter Everard Coleman, LL.B., 10 The Close, Exeter. EX1 1EZ. 0392 73509.
    Plymouth: Rt. Rev. Richard Stephen Hawkins, M.A., B.Phil., 15 Stoneleigh Close, Pitt Hill Rd., Highweek, Newton Abbot, Devon TQ12 1PX. 0626 63860.
Assistant Bishops: Rt. Rev. R. C. O. Goodchild; Rt. Rev. P. J. Pasterfield; Rt. Rev. Richard Fox Cartwright
Dean: Very Rev. Richard Montague Stephens Eyre, M.A., The Deanery, Exeter. EX1 1HT. 0392 52891.

GLOUCESTER

Bishop (£20,350): Rt. Rev. John Yates, M.A., Bishops court, Pitt Street, Gloucester. GL1 2BQ. 0452 24598. Signature: *John Gloucestr.*
Bishop Suffragan:
    Tewkesbury: Rt. Rev. Geoffrey David Jeremy Walsh, M.A., Green Acre, 166 Hempstead Lane, Gloucester GL2 6LG. Gloucester 21824.
Dean: Very Rev. Kenneth Neal Jennings, M.A., The Deanery, Gloucester. GL1 2BP. Gloucester 24167.

GUILDFORD

Bishop (£20,350): Rt. Rev. Michael Edgar Adie, M.A., Willow Grange, Woking Road, Guildford, Surrey. GU4 7QS. Guildford 573922. Signature: *Michael Guildford.*
Bishop Suffragan:
    Dorking: Rt. Rev. David Peter Wilcox, 13 Pilgrims Way, Guildford, Surrey GU4 8AD. Guildford 570829.
Honorary Assistant Bishop: Rt. Rev. Kenneth D. Evans, M.A.
Dean: Very Rev. Alexander Gillan Wedderspoon, The Deanery, 1 Cathedral Close, Guildford. GU2 5TL. Guildford 60328.

HEREFORD

Bishop (£20,350): See Vacant. Bishop-elect: Ven. J.K. Oliver, Bishop's House, The Palace, Hereford, HR4 9BN. Hereford 271355. Signature: *John Hereford.*
Bishop Suffragan:
    Ludlow: Rt. Rev. Ian MacDonald Griggs, M.A., Bishop's House, Halford, Craven Arms, Shropshire SY8 9BT. 058 82 3571.
Dean: Very Rev. Peter Haynes, M.A., The Deanery, The Cloisters, Hereford. HR1 2NG. 0432 272525.

LEICESTER

Bishop (£20,350): Rt. Rev. Cecil Richard Rutt, C.B.E., M.A. Bishop's Lodge. 10 Springfield Road, Leicester LE2 3BD. Signature: *Richard Leicester.*
Assistant Bishop: Rt. Rev. G.W.E.C. Ashby, B.D., Ph.D., Bisopsmead, 554 Bradgate Road, Newton Linford, Leicester LE6 0HB. 0530 242955.
Honorary Assistant Bishop: Rt. Rev. J.E.L. Mort, C.B.E., M.A.
Provost: Very Rev. Alan Christopher Warren, M.A., Provost's House, 1 St. Martin's East, Leicester. LE1 5FX. 0533 25294/5.

LICHFIELD

Bishop (£20,350): Rt. Rev. Keith Norman Sutton, M.A., Bishop's House, 22 The Close, Lichfield. WS13 7LG. 0543 262251. Signature: *Keith Lichfield.*
Bishops Suffragan:
    Shrewsbury: Rt. Rev. John Dudley Davies, M.A., Athlone House, 68 London Road, Shrewsbury, Shropshire. SY2 6PG. 0743 235867.
    Stafford: Rt. Rev. Michael Charles Scott-Joynt, M.A., Ash Garth, Broughton Crescent, Barlaston, Stoke on Trent, Staffs. ST12 9DD. 078 139 3308.
    Wolverhampton: Rt. Rev. Christopher John Mayfield, M.A., 61 Richmond Road, Merridale, Wolverhamp ton. WV3 9JH. 0902 23008.
Dean: Very Rev. John Harley Lang, M.A., B.D., L.R.A.M., The Deanery, Lichfield, Staffs. WS13 7LD. 0543 262044.

LINCOLN
Bishop (£20,350): Rt. Rev. Robert Maynard Hardy, M.A., Bishop's House, Eastgate, Lincoln. LN2 1QQ. 0522 534701. Signature: *Robert Lincoln.*
Bishops Suffragan:
  Grimsby: Rt. Rev. David Tustin, M.A., 43 Abbey Park Road, Grimsby, South Humberside. DN32 0HS. 0472 358223.
  Grantham: Rt. Rev. William Ind, B.A., Fairacre, 243 Barrowby High Road, Grantham, Lincs. NG31 8NP. 0476 64722.
Honorary Assistant Bishops: Rt. Rev. G. F. Colin, M.A.; Rt. Rev. H.R. Darby.
Dean: Very Rev. Brandon Donald Jackson, The Deanery, Lincoln. LN2 1PX. 0522 23608.

NORWICH
Bishop (£20,350): Rt. Rev. Peter John Nott, M.A., Bishop's House, Norwich. NR3 1SB. 0603 629001. Signature: *Peter Norvic.*
Bishops Suffragan:
  Lynn: Rt. Rev. David Edward Bentley, B.A., The Old Vicarage, Castle Acre, King's Lynn, Norfolk, PE32 2AA. 07605 553.
  Thetford: Rt. Rev. Timothy Dudley-Smith, M.A., Rectory Meadow, Bramerton, Norwich. NR14 7DW. 05088 251.
Dean: Very Rev. John Paul Burbridge, M.A., The Deanery, Norwich. NR1 4EG. 0603 760140 (Home), 620715 (Office).

OXFORD
Bishop (£20,350): Rt. Rev. Richard Douglas Harris, M.A., Diocesan Church House, North Hinksey, Oxford OX2 0NB. 0865 244566. Signature: *Richard Oxon.*
Bishops Suffragan:
  Reading: Rt. Rev. John Frank Bone, Greenbanks, Old Bath Road, Sonning-on-Thames, Reading. RG4 0SY. (0734) 692187.
  Dorchester: R. Rev. Anthony John Russell, B.A., D.Phil., Holmby House, Sibford Ferris, nr. Banbury, Oxon OX15 5RG. 0865 244566.
  Buckingham: Rt. Rev. Simon Hedley Burrows, M.A., Sheridan, Grimms Hill, Great Missenden, Bucks. HP16 9BD. (02406) 2173.
Honorary Assistant Bishops: Rt. Rev. Albert Kenneth Cragg, D.Phil.; Rt. Rev. Eric Wild; Rt. Rev. Leonard Ashton.
Dean of Christ Church: Very Rev. Eric William Heaton, M.A., The Deanery, Christ Church, Oxford. OX1 1DP. (0865) 247122.
Dean of Windsor: Rt. Rev. Patrick Reynolds Mitchell, The Deanery, Windsor Castle, Berks. SL4 1NJ. (0753) 865561.

PETERBOROUGH
Bishop (£20,350): Rt. Rev. William John Westwood, M.A., The Palace, Peterborough. PE1 1YA. 0733 62492. Signature: *William Petriburg.*
Bishop Suffragan: Rt. Rev. Paul Everarad Barber, 4 The Avenue, Dallington, Northampton NN5 7AN. 0604 759423.
Dean: Very Rev. Randolph George Wise, V.R.D., M.A., The Deanery, Peterborough. PE1 1NS. 0733 62780.

PORTSMOUTH
Bishop (£20,350): Rt. Rev. Timothy John Bavin, Bishopswood, Fareham, Hants. PO14 1NT. 0329 280247. Signature: *Timothy Portsmouth.*
Honorary Assistant Bishops: Rt. Rev. Ernest Edwin Curtis, C.B.E., B.Sc.; Rt. Rev. W. W. Hunt, M.A.
Provost: Very Rev. David Staffurth Stancliffe, M.A., Provost's House, Pembroke Road, Old Portsmouth, Hants. PO1 2NS. 0705 824400 (Home); 823300 (Office).

ROCHESTER
Bishop (£20,350): Rt. Rev. Anthony Michael Arnold Turnbull, M.A., Bishopscourt, Rochester. ME1 1TS. 0634 42721. Signature: *Michael Roffen.*
Bishop Suffragan:
  Tonbridge: Rt. Rev. David Henry Bartleet, M.A., Bishop's Lodge, 48 St. Botolph's Road, Sevenoaks, Kent. TN13 3AG. 0736 456070.

Assistant Bishops: Rt. Rev. J. W. H. Flagg.
Dean: Very Rev. Edward Frank Shotter, The Deanery, King's Orchard, Rochester, Kent. ME1 1TG. 0634 44023.

ST. ALBANS
Bishop (£20,350): Vacant.
Bishops Suffragan:
  Hertford: Rt. Rev. Kenneth Harold Pillar, M.A., Hertford House, Abbey Mill Lane, St. Albans, Herts. AL3 4HE. St. 0727 66420.
  Bedford: Rt. Rev. David John Farmbrough, M.A., 168 Kimbolton Road, Bedford, MK41 8DN. 0234 57551.
Dean: Very Rev. Peter Clement Moore, M.A., D. Phil., The Deanery, Sumpter Yard, St. Albans, AL1 1BY. 0727 52120.

ST. EDMUNDSBURY AND IPSWICH
Bishop (£20,350): Rt. Rev. John Dennis, M.A., Bishop's House, 4 Park Road, Ipswich. IP1 3ST. 0473 52829. Signature: *John St. Edm. and Ipswich.*
Bishop Suffragan:
  Dunwich: Rt. Rev. Eric Nash Devenport, B.A., The Old Vicarage, Church Rd., Stowupland, Stowmarket, Suffolk IP14 4BQ. 0449 678234
Provost: Very Rev. Raymond Furnell, The Provost's House, Bury St. Edmunds, Suffolk. IP33 1RS. 0284 4852.

SALISBURY
Bishop (£20,350): Rt. Rev. John Austin Baker, M.A., B.Litt., South Canonry, 71 The Close, Salisbury. SP1 2ER. 0722 334031. Signature: *John Sarum.*
Area Bishops:
  Ramsbury: Rt. Rev. Peter St George Vaughan, Bishop's House, High Street, Urchfont, Devizes, Wilts SN10 4QH. 038084 373.
  Sherborne: Rt. Rev. John Dudley Galtrey Kirkham, M.A., Little Bailie, Sturminster Marshall, Wimborne, Dorset. BH21 4AD. 025885 7659.
Dean: Very Rev. and Hon. Hugh Dickinson, The Deanery, 7 The Close, Salisbury, SP1 2EF. 0722 22457.

SOUTHWARK
Bishop (£20,350): Rt. Rev. Ronald Oliver Bowlby, M.A., Bishop's House, 38 Tooting Bec Gardens, London. SW16 1QZ. 081-769 3256. Signature: *Ronald Southwark.*
Bishops Suffragan:
  Kingston: Rt. Rev. Peter Stephen Maurice Selby, M.A., B.D., Ph.D., Kingston Episcopal Area Office, Whiteland College, West Hill, London SW15 3SN. 01 780 2308.
  Woolwich: Rt. Rev. Albert Peter Hall, M.A., 8B Hilly Fields Crescent, Brockley, London SE4 1QA. 081-469 0013.
  Croydon: Rt. Rev. Wilfred Denniston Wood, J.P., 53 Stanhope Road, Croydon, Surrey CR0 5NS. 081-681 5496/7.
Honorary Assistant Bishops: Rt. Rev. E. M. H. Capper, O.B.E.; Rt. Rev. A. R. McD. Gordon; Rt. Rev. J. Hughes C.B.E. M.A.; Rt. Rev. H.W. Montefiore, M.A.; Rt. Rev. J. Neale; Rt. Rev. S. Phipps.
Provost: Very Rev. David Lawrence Edwards, M.A., Provost's Lodging, 51 Bankside, London. SE1 9JE. 071-407 3708/9.

TRURO
Bishop (£20,350): The Rt. Rev. M.T. Ball, C.G.A., M.A., Lis Escop, Truro, Cornwall. TR3 6QQ. (0872) 862657. Signature: *Truron.*
Bishop Suffragan:
  St. Germans: Rt. Rev. John Richard Allen Llewellin, M.A.. 32 Falmouth Road, Truro, Cornwall. TR1 2HX. (0872) 73190.
Dean: Very Rev. David John Shearlock, B.A., The Deanery, Lemon Street, Truro, Cornwall. TR1 2PE. (0872)72661.

WORCESTER
Bishop (£20,350): Rt. Rev. Philip Harold Ernest Goodrich, M.A., Bishop's House, Hartlebury Castle, Kidderminster, Worcs. DY11 7XX. (0299) 250214. Signature: *Philip Worcester.*

Bishop Suffragan:
  Dudley: Rt. Rev. Anthony Charles Dumper, M.A., Bishop's House, 366 Halesowen Road, Cradley Heath, Warley, West Midlands. 021-550 3407.
Honorary Assistant Bishops: Rt. Rev. David Howard Nicholas Allenby, M.A.; Rt. Rev. Kenneth Woollcombe.
Dean: Very Rev. R. M. C. Jeffery, B.D., The Deanery, 10 College Green, Worcester. WR1 2LH. (0905) 23501.

PROVINCE OF YORK

YORK
95th Archbishop and Primate of England (£33,080): Most Rev. and Rt. Hon. John Stapylton Habgood, M.A., Ph.D., D.D., Bishopthorpe Palace, Bishopthorpe, York. YO2 1QE. (0904) 707021/2. Signature: *John Ebor.*
Bishops Suffragan:
  Selby: Rt. Rev. Clifford Conder Barker, T.D., M.A., Dip.Th. Greenriggs, 8 Bankside Close, Upper Poppleton, York. YO2 6LH. (0904) 795342.
  Whitby: Rt. Rev. Gordon Bates, 60 West Green, Stokesley, Middlesbrough, Cleveland. TS9 5BD. (0642) 710390.
  Hull: Rt. Rev. Donald George Snelgrove, T.D., M.A., o73 Hullen House, Woodfield Lane, Hessle. HU13 0ES. (0482) 649019.
Assistant Bishops: Rt. Rev. George Eyles Irwin Cockin, B.A.; Rt. Rev. Richard Knyvet Wimbush, M.A.; Rt. Rev. Richard James Wood; Rt. Rev. Ronald Graham.
Dean: Very Rev. John Eliot Southgate, B.A., The Deanery, York. YO1 2JD. (0904) 623608.
Registrar: Lionel Lennox, The Registry, 1 Peckitt Street, York. YO1 1SG. (0904) 623487.

DURHAM
Bishop (£27,150): Rt. Rev. David Edward Jenkins, M.A., D.D., Auckland Castle, Bishop Auckland, Co. Durham. DL14 7NR. (0388) 602576. Signature: *David Dunelm.*
Bishop Suffragan:
  Jarrow: Vacant. Bishop-elect: Canon Alan Smithson, Melkridge House, Gilesgate, Durham. DH1 1JB. 091-384 3797.
Dean: Very Rev. John Robert Arnold. The Deanery, Durham. DH1 3EQ. 091-384 7500.

BLACKBURN
Bishop (£20,350): Rt. Rev. Alan David Chesters, B.A., M.A., Bishop's House, Ribchester Road, Blackburn, Lancs. BB1 9EF. (0254) 48234. Signature: *Alan Blackburn.*
Bishops Suffragan:
  Lancaster: Tt. Rev. Jack Nicholls, A.K.C.. Wheatfield, 7 Dallas Road, Lancaster LA1 1TN. (0524) 32897
  Burnley: Rt. Rev. Ronald James Milner, Palace House, 458 Padiham Road, Burnley, Lancs BB12 6TD. (0282) 23564.
Provost: Very Rev. Lawrence Jackson, A.K.C., Provost's House, Preston New Road, Blackburn. BB2 (0254) 52502.

BRADFORD
Bishop (£20,350): Rt. Rev. Robert Kerr Williamson, Bishopscroft, Ashwell Road, Bradford. BD9 4AU. (0274) 545414. Signature: *Robert Bradford.*
Assistant Bishop: Rt. Rev. David Richard John Evans, 30 Grosvenor Road, Shipley, West Yorks BD18 4RN. 0274 582033.
Provost: Provost's House, Cathedral Close, Bradford. BD1 4EG. (0274) 732023.

CARLISLE
Bishop (£20,350): Rt. Rev. Ian Harland, Rose Castle, Dalston, Carlisle. CA5 7BZ. (06996) 274. Signature: *Ian Carliol.*
Bishop Suffragan:
  Penrith: Rt. Rev. George Lanyon Hacker, M.A., Great Salkeld Rectory, Penrith, Cumbria. CA11 9NA. (076 883) 273.
Dean: Very Rev. Henry Edward Champneys Stapleton.

CHESTER
Bishop (£20,350): Rt. Rev. Michael Alfred Baughen, B.D., Bishop's House, Chester. CH1 2JD. (0244) 350864. Signature: *Michael Cestr.*

Bishops Suffragan:
  Birkenhead: Rt. Rev. Ronald Brown, B.A., Dip.Th., Trafford House, Victoria Crescent, Queen's Park, Chester. CH4 7AX. o73 (0244) 675895.
  Stockport: Rt. Rev. Frank Pilkington Sargeant, B.A., 32 Park Gates Drive, Cheadle Hulme, Cheshire SK8 7DF. 061-486 9715.
Dean: Very Rev. Stephen Stewart Smalley, M.A., B.D., Ph.D., The Deanery, 7 Abbey Street, Chester. CH1 2JF. (0244) 25920.

LIVERPOOL
Bishop (£20,350): Rt. Rev. David Stuart Sheppard, M.A., Bishop's Lodge, Woolton Park, Liverpool. L25 6DT. 051-708 9480. Signature: *David Liverpool.*
Bishop Suffragan:
  Warrington: Rt. Rev. Michael Henshall, B.A., Dip.Th., Martinsfield, Elm Avenue, Great Crosby, Liverpool. L23 2SX. 051-708 9480.
Honorary Assistant Bishop: Rt. Rev. William Scott Baker, M.A.
Dean: Very Rev. Rhys Derrick Chamberlain Walters, B.Sc., The Cathedral, Liverpool. L1 7AZ. 051-709 6271.

MANCHESTER
Bishop (£20,350): Rt. Rev. Stanley Eric Francis Booth-Clibborn, M.A., Bishopscourt, Bury New Road, Manchester. M7 0LE. 061-792 2096. Signature: *Stanley Manchester.*
Bishops Suffragan:
  Hulme: Rt. Rev. Colin John Fraser Scott, M.A., 1 Raynham Avenue, Didsbury, Manchester M20 0BW. 061-445 5922.
  Middleton: Rt. Rev. Donald Alexander Tytler, M.A., The Hollies, Manchester Road, Rochdale. OL11 3QY. (0706) 358550.
  Bolton: Rt. Rev. David George Galliford, M.A., 4 Sandfield Drive, Lostock, Bolton BL6 4DY. (0204) 43400.
Honorary Assistant Bishops: Rt. Rev. K. V. Ramsey, M.A., B.D.; Rt. Rev. E. R. Wickham, B.D.
Dean: Very Rev. Robert Murray Waddington, M.A., The Deanery, 44 Shrewsbury Road, Prestwich, Manchester M25 8GQ. 061-773 2959.

NEWCASTLE
Bishop (£20,350): Rt. Rev. Andrew Alexander Kenny Graham, M.A., The Bishop's House, 29 Moor Road South, Gosforth, Newcastle upon Tyne. NE3 1PA. 091-285 2220. Signature: *A. Newcastle.*
Assistant Bishop: Rt. Rev. K. E. Gill, The Bishop's House, 29 Moor Road South, Gosforth, Newcastle upon Tyne. NE3 1PA. 091-285 2220.
Provost: Very Rev. Christopher Garnett Howsin Spafford, M.A., Cathedral Vicarage, 23 Montagu Avenue, Gosforth, Newcastle upon Tyne. NE3 4HY. 091-285 3472.

RIPON
Bishop (£20,350): Rt. Rev. David Nigel de Lorentz Young, M.A., Bishop Mount, Ripon, North Yorks. HG4 5DP. (0765) 2045. Signature: *David Ripon.*
Bishop Suffragan:
  Knaresborough: Rt. Rev. Malcolm James Menin, M.A.,16 Shaftesbury Ave., Roundhay, Leeds LS8 1DT. (0532) 664800.
Honorary Assistant Bishops: Rt. Rev. John W.A. Howe, D.D.; Rt. Rev. Ralph Emmerson, A.K.C., B.D.
Dean: Very Rev. Christopher Russell Campling, M.A., The Minster House, Ripon. HG4 1PE. (0765) 3615.

SHEFFIELD
Bishop (£20,350): Rt. Rev. David Ramsay Lunn, M.A., Bishopscroft, Snaithing Lane, Sheffield. S10 3LG. (0742) 302170. Signature: *David Sheffield.*
Bishop Suffragan:
  Doncaster: Rt. Rev. William Michael Dermot Persson, M.A., Bishop's Lodge, Hooton Roberts, Rotherham, South Yorks. S65 4PF. (0709) 853370.
Honorary Assistant Bishop: Rt. Rev. K. J. F. Skelton, C.B.E., M.A.
Provost: Very Rev. John Warren Gladwin, Provost's Lodge, 22 Hallam Gate Road, Sheffield. S10 5BS. (0742) 662373.

SODOR AND MAN

Bishop (£20,350): Rt. Rev. Noel Debroy Jones, C.B., The Bishop's House, Quarterbridge Road, Douglas, Isle of Man. 0624 22108.

SOUTHWELL

Bishop (£20,350): Rt. Rev. Patrick Burnet Harris, M.A, Sherwood House, High Oakham Road, Mansfield, Notts. NG18 5AJ. (0636) 812112. Signature: *Patrick Southwell*
Bishop Suffragan:
Sherwood: Rt. Rev. Alan Wyndham Morgan, Durham House, Westgate, Southwell, Notts. NG25 0JL.
Provost: Very Rev. John Murray Irvine, M.A., The Residence, Vicars' Court, Southwell, Notts. NG25 0HP. (0636) 812593.

WAKEFIELD

Bishop (£20,350): Rt. Rev. David Michael Hope, D.Phil., Bishop's Lodge, Woodthorpe Lane, Wakefield, West Yorks. WF2 6JJ. (0924) 255349. Signature: *David Wakefield.*
Bishop Suffragan:
Pontefract: Rt. Rev. Thomas Richard Hare, M.A., Highfield, 306 Barnsley Road, Sandal, Wakefield. WF2 6AX. (0924) 256935.
Provost: Very Rev. John Edward Allen, M.A., 3 Cathedral Close, Margaret Street, Wakefield. WF1 2DQ. (0924)372402. 7Å3 è

THE CHURCH IN WALES

MONMOUTH

Bishop: Rt. Rev. Royston Clifford Wright, Bishopstow, Newport, Gwent. Signature: *Clifford Monmouth.*
Dean: Very Rev. Frank Graham Jenkins, M.A., The Deanery, Stow Hill, Newport, Gwent. 0633 63338.

BANGOR

Bishop: Rt. Rev. John Cledan Mears, M.A., Ty'r Esgob, Bangor, Gwynedd. Signature: *Cledan Bangor.*
Dean: Very Rev. T.E.P. Edwards, B.A., The Deanery, Bangor, Gwynedd, 0248 370693

LLANDAFF

Bishop: Rt. Rev. Roy Thomas Davies, B.A., B.Litt., Llys Esgob, The Cathedral Green, Llandaff, Cardiff. Signature: *Roy Llandav.*
Dean: Very Rev. Alun Radcliffe Davies, M.A., The Deanery, Llandaff, Cardiff. 0222 561545.

ST. ASAPH

Bishop: Rt. Rev. Alwyn Rice Jones, M.A., Esgobty, St. Asaph, Clwyd. Signature: *Alwyn St. Asaph.*
Dean: Very Rev. Charles Raymond Renowden, M.A., The Deanery, St. Asaph, Clwyd. 0745 583597.

ST. DAVIDS

Bishop and Archbishop of Wales: Most Rev. Dr. George Noakes, B.A., Llys Esgob, Abergwili, Carmarthen. Signature: *George St. Davids.*
Assistant Bishop: Rt. Rev. John Ivor Rees, B.A., Llys Dewi, 45 Clover Park, Uzmaston Road, Haverfordwest, Dyfed SA61 1UE. 0437 67750
Dean: Very Rev. Bertie Lewis, M.A., The Deanery, St. Davids, Dyfed. 0437 720202.

SWANSEA AND BRECON

Bishop: Rt. Rev. Dewi Morris Bridges, M.A., Ely Tower, Brecon, Powys. 0874 2008. Signature: *Dewi Swansea and Brecon*
Dean: Very Rev. D. Huw Jones, M.A., Blackstone, 25 Pendre, Brecon. 0874 4876.

CHURCH OF IRELAND

ARMAGH

Archbishop and Primate of All Ireland: Most Rev. Robert Henry Alexander Eames, Ph.D., LL.D., The See House, Cathedral Close, Armagh. BT61 7EE. Armagh 522851.

DUBLIN AND GLENDALOUGH

Archbishop: Most Rev. Donald Arthur Richard Caird, H.DipEd., D.D., The See House, 17 Temple Road, Milltown, Dublin 6. Dublin 977849.

MEATH AND KILDARE

Bishop: Most Rev. Walton Newcombe Francis Empey, B.A.,B.D., Ivy House, Leixlip, Co. Kildare. Dublin 244650.

CONNOR

Bishop: Rt. Rev. Samuel Greenfield Poyntz, B.D., Ph.D., Bishop's House, 22 Deramore Park, Belfast. BT9 5JU. Belfast 668442.

CASHEL AND OSSORY

Bishop: Rt. Rev. Noel Vincent Willoughby, M.A., The Palace, Kilkenny, Ireland. Kilkenny 21560. o73

DOWN AND DROMORE

Bishop: Rt. Rev. Gordon McMullan, A.C.I.S., B.Sc. (Econ.), Dip. Rel. Stud. (Cantab)., Ph.D., Th.D., The See House, 32 Knockdene Park, South Belfast. BT5 7AB. Belfast 471973.

DERRY AND RAPHOE

Bishop: Rt. Rev. James Mehaffey, B.D., Ph.D., The See House, Culmore Road, Londonderry. BT48 8JF. Londonderry 351206.

KILMORE

Bishop: Rt. Rev. William Gilbert Wilson, M.A., B.D., Ph.D., The See House, Cavan. Cavan 31336.

LIMERICK AND KILLALOE

Bishop: The Rt. Rev. Edward Flewett Darling, M.A., Bishop's House, North Circular Road, Limerick, Limerick 51532.

TUAM

Bishop: Rt. Rev. John Robert Winder Neill, M.A., The Bishop's House, Knockglass, Crossmolina, Co. Mayo. Ballina 31317.

CLOGHER

Bishop: Rt. Rev. Brian Desmond Anthony Hannon, M.A., The See House, Fivemiletown, Co. Tyrone, BT75 OQP. Five-mile-town 21265.

CORK, CLOYNE AND ROSS

Bishop: Rt. Rev. Robert Alexander Warke, B.D., The Palace, Bishop Street, Cork. Cork 271214.

THE EPISCOPAL CHURCH IN SCOTLAND

ABERDEEN AND ORKNEY

Bishop (£12.780): Rt. Rev. Frederick Charles Darwent, Bishop's House, 430 King Street, Aberdeen, 0224-572169.

ARGYLL AND THE ISLES

Bishop (£12,780): Most Rev. George Kennedy Buchanan Henderson, M.B.E., B.A., Benvoulin, 7 Achnelea, Onich, by Fort William, PH33 6SA. 08553 240.

BRECHIN
Bishop (£12,780): Rt. Rev. Robert Taylor Halliday, M.A., B.D..

EDINBURGH
Bishop (£12,780): Rt. Rev. Richard Frederick Holloway, B.D., Kingsburgh Road, Edinburgh EH12.

GLASGOW AND GALLOWAY
Bishop (£12,780): Rt. Rev. Derek Alec Rawcliffe, O.B.E., B.A., 14 Clevedon Crescent, Glasgow. G12 0PB. 041-339 0554.

MORAY, ROSS AND CAITHNESS O73
Bishop (£12,780): Rt. Rev. George Minshull Sessford, M.A., Bishop's House, 96 Fairfield Road, Inverness. Inverness 31059.

ST. ANDREWS, DUNKELD AND DUNBLANE
Bishop (£12,780): Rt. Rev. Michael Geoffrey Hare Duke, Bishop's House, Fairmount Road, Perth. Perth 21580.
Registrar of the Episcopal Synod: I. R. Guild, C.B.E., W.S., 16 Charlotte Square, Edinburgh. EH2 4YS.

ORTHODOX CHURCHES

Armenian Church. *The Rt. Rev. Bishop Yeghishe Gizirian,* Church of St. Sarkis, Iverna Gardens, London. W8 6TP. 071-937 0152. Hon President: G.S.Kurkjian O.B.E. President: J.B.N. Kurkjian. Church of St. Peter, Cranley Gardens, London. S.W.7. 071-373 3565. Chairman of the Church: Garo Krikorian

Greek Orthodox *Archdiocese of Thyateira and Great Britain. His Eminence Archbishop Gregorios, Archbishop of Thyateira and Great Britain,* Thyateira House, 5 Craven Hill, London. W2 3EN. 071-723 4787.

Russian Orthodox Church in Exile. *His Grace Bishop Mark,* 14 Saint Dunstan's Road, Baron's Court, London W6 (081-748 4232. Missions Administrator Archimandrite Alexis, St. Edward Brotherhood, Brook wood, Woking, Surrey GU24 0BL. Brookwood (04867) 87763.

Russian Orthodox Church. *His Grace Metropolitan Anthony of Sourozh,* Cathedral of the Dormition and All Saints, 67 Ennismore Gardens, London. SW7 1NH. 071- 584 0096.

ROMAN CATHOLIC HIERARCHY

ENGLAND AND WALES

WESTMINSTER
Archbishop: His Eminence Cardinal George Basil Hume, Archbishop's House, London. SW1P 1QJ. 071-834 4717.
Area Bishops: Rt. Rev. Victor Guazzelli; Rt. Rev. Gerald Mahon, M.H.M.; Rt. Rev. Philip Harvey; Rt. Rev. James O'Brien; Rt. Rev. John Crowley.

BIRMINGHAM
Archbishop: Most Rev. Maurice Couve de Murville, 57 Mearse Lane, Barnt Green, Birmingham. B45 8HJ. 021-445 1467.
Auxiliaries: Rt. Rev. Philip Pargeter.

CARDIFF
Archbishop: Most Rev. John Aloysius Ward, O.F.M.Cap., Archbishop's House, 41-43 Cathedral Road, Cardiff CF1 9HD, (0222) 20411.

LIVERPOOL
Archbishop: Most Rev. Derek Worlock, Archbishop's House, 87 Green Lane, Mossley Hill, Liverpool. L18 2EP. 051-722 2379.
Auxiliaries: Rt. Rev. Kevin O'Connor; Rt. Rev. John Rawsthorne, Rt. Rev. Vincent Malone.

SOUTHWARK
Archbishop: Most Rev. Michael George Bowen, Archbishop's House, St. George's Road, Southwark, London. SE1 6HX. 071-928 2495.
Auxiliaries: Rt. Rev. Charles Henderson; Rt. Rev. John Jukes, O.F.M. Conv.; Rt. Rev. Howard George Tripp.

ARUNDEL AND BRIGHTON
Bishop: Rt. Rev. Cormac Murphy-O'Connor, St. Joseph's Hall, Greyfriars Lane, Storrington, Pulborough, West Sussex. RH20 4HE. (090 66) 2172.

BRENTWOOD
Bishop: Rt. Rev. Thomas McMahon, Bishop's House, Stock, Ingatestone, Essex. CM4 9BU. (0277) 840268.

CLIFTON
Bishop: Rt. Rev. Mervyn Alexander, St. Ambrose, North Road, Leigh Woods, Bristol. BS8 3PW. (0272) 733072.

EAST ANGLIA
Bishop: Rt. Rev. Alan Charles Clark, The White House, 21 Upgate, Poringland, Norwich. NR14 7SH. (050 86) 2202.

HALLAM
Bishop: Rt. Rev. Gerald Moverley, Quarters, Carsick Hill Way, Sheffield. S10 3LT. (0742) 301596.

HEXHAM AND NEWCASTLE
Bishop: Rt. Rev. Hugh Lindsay, Bishop's House, East Denton Hall, 800 West Road, Newcastle upon Tyne. NE5 2BJ. (091) 742007.
Auxiliary: Rt. Rev. Owen Francis Swindlehurst.

LANCASTER
Bishop: Rt. Rev. John Brewer, Bishop's House, Cannon Hill, Lancaster. LA1 5NG. (0525) 32231.

LEEDS
Bishop: Rt. Rev. David Konstant, Bishop's House, 13 North Grange Road, Headingly, Leeds LS6 2BR (0532 304533).

MENEVIA
Bishop: Rt. Rev. Daniel Mullins, Maes-Gwyn, 63 Margam Road, Port Talbot, West Glamorgan, SA13 2HR. (0639) 883323.

MIDDLESBROUGH
Bishop: Rt. Rev. Augustine Harris, Bishop's House, 16 Cambridge Road, Middlesbrough, Cleveland. TS5 5NN. (0642) 818253.
Auxiliary: Rt. Rev. Thomas Kevin O'Brien.

NORTHAMPTON
Bishop: Rt. Rev. Patrick Leo McCartie, Bishop's House, Marriott Street, Northamton. NN2 6AW. (0604) 715635.

NOTTINGHAM
Bishop: Rt. Rev. James McGuinness, Bishop's House, 27 Cavendish Road East, The Park, Nottingham. NG7 1BB. (0602) 474786.

PLYMOUTH
Bishop: Rt. Rev. Hugh Christopher Budd, Vescourt, Hartley Road, Plymouth. PL3 5LR. (0752) 772950.

PORTSMOUTH
Bishop: Rt. Rev. Crispian Hollis, Bishop's House, Edinburgh Road, Portsmouth, Hants. PO1 3HG. (0705) 820894.

SALFORD
Bishop: Rt. Rev. Patrick Altham Kelly, Wardley Hall, Worsley, Manchester. M28 5ND. 061-794 2825.

SHREWSBURY
Bishop: Rt. Rev. Joseph Gray, Bishop's House, Eleanor Road, Birkenhead, Merseyside. L43 7QW. 051-653 3600.

WREXHAM
Bishop: Rt. Rev. James Hannigan, Bishop's House, Sontley Road, Wrexham, Clwyd LL13 7EW. (0978) 262726.

BISHOPRIC OF THE FORCES
Bishop: Rt. Rev. Francis Joseph Walmsley, C.B.E., 26 The Crescent, Farnborough, Hampshire. GU14 7AS. (0252) 543649.

UKRAINIAN EXARCHATE
Bishop: Rt. Rev. Michel Hrynchyshyn, 22 Binney Street, London. W1Y 1YN. 071-629 1073.

SCOTLAND

ST. ANDREWS AND EDINBURGH
Archbishop: Most Rev. Keith Michael Patrick O'Brien, St. Bennet's, 42 Greenhill Gardens, Edinburgh. EH10 4BJ. 031-447 3337.
Auxiliary: Rt. Rev. James Monaghan.

GLASGOW
Archbishop: Most Rev. Thomas Winning, Archbishop's House, 40 Newlands Road, Glasgow. G43 2JD. 041-332 1680.
Auxiliaries: Rt. Rev. Charles Renfrew.

ABERDEEN
Bishop: Rt. Rev. Mario Joseph Conti, Bishop's House, 156 King's Gate, Aberdeen. AB2 6BR. Aberdeen 39154.

ARGYLL AND THE ISLES
Bishop: Rt. Rev. Colin MacPherson, Bishop's House, Esplanade, Oban, Argyll. Oban 62010.

DUNKELD
Bishop: Rt. Rev. Vincent Logan, Bishop's House, 29 o73 Roseangle, Dundee. DD1 4LX. Dundee 24327.

GALLOWAY
Bishop: Rt. Rev. Maurice Taylor, Candida Casa, 8 Corse hill Road, Ayr. KA7 2ST. Ayr 266750.

MOTHERWELL
Bishop: Rt. Rev. Joseph Devine, Bishop's House, 17 Viewpark Road, Motherwell. ML1 3ER. Motherwell 63715.

PAISLEY
Bishop: Rt. Rev John Aloysius Mone, Bishop's House, Porterfield Road, Kilmacolm, Renfrewshire, Kilmacolm 2494.

NORTHERN IRELAND

One Roman Catholic Hierarchy exists covering the whole of Ireland. Some of the dioceses shown partly extend into the Republic of Ireland.

ARMAGH
Archbishop: His Eminence Cardinal Tom As O Fiaich, Ara Coeli, Armagh. BT61 7QY. Armagh (0861) 522045.

CLOGHER
Bishop: Most Rev. Joseph Duffy, Bishop's House, Monaghan, Monaghan (047) 81019.

DERRY
Bishop: Most Rev. Edward Daly, Bishop's House, St. Eugene's, Derry. BT48 9AP. Derry (0504) 262302.
Auxiliary: Most Rev. Francis Lagan.

DOWN AND CONNOR
Bishop: Most Rev. Cahal B. Daly, Lisbreen, Somerton Road, Belfast. BT15 4DJ. Belfast (0232) 776185.
Auxiliaries: Auxiliary: Most Rev. Patrick Walsh; Most Rev. Anthony Farquhar.

DROMORE
Bishop: Most Rev. Francis Gerard Brooks, Bishop's House, Newry, Co. Down. BT35 6PN. Newry (0693) 2444.

REPUBLIC OF IRELAND

DUBLIN
Archbishop: Most Rev. Desmond Connell, Primate of Ireland, Archbishop's House, Dublin, 9. Dublin (01) 373732.
Auxiliaries: Most Rev. James Kavanagh; Most Rev. Dermot O'Mahony; Most Rev. Donal Murray; Most Rev. Desmond Williams.

CASHEL
Archbishop: Most Rev. Dermot Clifford, Archbishop's House, Thurles, Co. Tipperary. Thurles (0504) 21512.

TUAM
Archbishop: Most Rev. Joseph Cassidy, St. Jarlath's, o73 Tuam, Ireland. Tuam (093) 24166.

ACHONRY
Bishop: Most Rev. Thomas Flynn, St. Nathy's, Ballaghaderreen, Co. Roscommon, Ireland. Ballaghaderreen (0907) 60021.

ARDAGH
Bishop: Most Rev. Colm O'Reilly, Bishop's House, St. Michael's, Longford, Ireland. Longford (043) 46432.

CLONFERT
Bishop: Most Rev. John Kirby, St. Brendan's, Coorheen, Loughrea, Co. Galway. 091-41560.

CLOYNE
Bishop: Most Rev. John Magee, Bishop's House, Cobh, Co. Cork. Cork (021) 811430.

CORK
Bishop: Most Rev. Michael Murphy, Diocesan Office, Bishop's House, Redemption Road, Cork. Cork (021) 501717/501282.
Auxiliary: Most Rev. John Buckley.

ELPHIN
Bishop: Most Rev. Dominic Conway, St. Mary's, Sligo. Sligo (071) 2670.

FERNS
Bishop: Most Rev. Brendan Comiskey, Bishop's House, Wexford, Ireland. Wexford (053) 22657.

GALWAY
Bishop: Most Rev. Eamon Casey, Mount St. Mary's, Galway. Office: Galway (091) 63566 and 62255.

KERRY
Bishop: Most Rev. Diarmuid O Suilleabhain, Bishop's House, Killarney, Co. Kerry. Killarney (064) 31168.

4

KILDARE
Bishop: Most Rev. Laurence Ryan, Bishop's House, Carlow. Carlow (0503) 31102.

KILLALA
Bishop: Most Rev. Thomas Finnegan, St. Muredach's, Ballina, Co. Mayo. Ballina (096) 21518.

KILLALOE
Bishop: Most Rev. Michael Harty, Westbourne, Ennis, Co. Clare. Ennis (065) 21638.

KILMORE
Bishop: Most Rev. Francis McKiernan, Bishop's House, Cullies, Cavan, Ireland. Cavan (049) 31496.

LIMERICK
Bishop: Most Rev. Jeremiah Newman, Kilmoyle, North Circular Road, Limerick. Limerick (061) 45856 (office), 51433 (residence).

MEATH
Bishop: Most Rev. John McCormack, Bishop's House, Mullingar, Co. Westmeath. Mullingar (044) 48841. Co-adjutor: Most Rev. Michael Smith

OSSORY
Bishop: Most Rev. Laurence Forristal, Sion House, Kilkenny. Kilkenny (056) 21060.

RAPHOE
Bishop: Most Rev. Seamus Hegarty, Ard Adhamhnain, Letterkenny, Co. Donegal. Letterkenny (074) 21208.

WATERFORD
Bishop: Most Rev. Michael Russell, Bishop's House, John's Hill, Waterford. Waterford (051) 74463.

IRISH EPISCOPAL CONFERENCE

Executive Secretary: Rev. Gerard Clifford.
Executive Office: 'Iona', 65 Newry Road, Dundalk, Co. Louth. Dindalk (042) 38087.

PRESBYTERIAN CHURCHES

THE CHURCH OF SCOTLAND

Moderator of General Assembly: The Right Rev. Robert Davidson, D.D. (Appointed each year.)
Principal Clerk: The Rev. James L. Weatherhead, M.A., LL.B., 121 George Street, Edinburgh. EH2 4YN. (031-225 5722).
Depute Clerk: The Rev. A. Gordon McGillivray, M.A., B.D., S.T.M.
Procurator: George Penrose, Q.C.

EDINBURGH HIGH KIRK, St. Giles *Minister:* The Very Rev. G. I. Macmillan, M.A., B.D.

GLASGOW CATHEDRAL *Minister:* The Rev. W. J. Morris, B.D., Ph.D., LL.D.

LONDON, ST. COLUMBA *Minister:* The Rev. John McIndoe, M.A., B.D., S.T.M..

LONDON CROWN COURT *Minister:* The Rev. Dr. Kenneth G Hughes, T.D.,M.A.,B.D.

Lord High Commissioner to the General Assembly of the Church of Scotland: The Rt. Hon. Lord Ross, F.R.S.E., LL.D., D. Univ.

OTHER PRESBYTERIAN CHURCHES

Presbyterian Church in Ireland, Church House, Belfast (Belfast 322284) Moderator: Rt. Rev. Dr. R.F.G. Holmes.

Presbyterian Church of Wales (Calvinistic Methodist Church of Wales):
General Assembly:
Moderator: (1988-89) Mr. R.M. Edwards, LL.B., Llwyn, Queen's Park, Croesoswallt, Salop SY11 2JD
Secretary: 1983-1990; Rev. D. H. Owen, B.Sc., B.D., 53 Richmond Road, Cardiff. CF2 3UP.
The Association: North Wales, 1988-89:
Moderator: Mr. R. Aled Roberts, Afallon, Y Felinheli, Gwynedd, LL55 1LR. South Wales, 1988-89:
Moderator: Dr. B.F. Roberts, Hengwrt, Llanbadarn Road, Aberystwyth, Dyfed SY23 1HB The East (English), 1987-88:
Moderator: Rev. J.E. Wynne Davies, B.A., B.D., Garth Owen, Iorwerth Avenue, Aberystwyth, Dyfed SY23 1EW.

Free Church of Scotland, The Mound, Edinburgh. EH1 2LS. (031-226 5286/7) *Clerk of Assembly:* Rev. Prof. C. Graham, M.A., B.D.

United Free Church of Scotland, 11 Newton Place, Glasgow G3 7PR. (041-332 3435) *Moderator:* Rev. Graeme B. Bruce, LTh.

THE METHODIST CHURCH

Methodist Conference, 1 Central Buildings, Westminster, London, SW1H 9NH. (071-222 8010) *President:* Rev. Dr. Donald English. *Secretary:* The Rev. Brian Beck.

Methodist Church in Ireland *Secretary:* Rev. Edmund T.I. Mawhinney, 3 Upper Malone Road, Belfast. BT9 5TD. (Belfast 668458).

Independent Methodist Churches, Resource Centre, Fleet Street, Lamberhead Green, Wigan WN5 8EZ.
General Secretary: Rev. John M. Day, Old Police House, Croxton, Stafford. ST21 6PE.
President: Mr. R.A. Jackson, 625G Ripponden Road, Oldham OL1 4JU

Wesleyan Reform Union, 123 Queen Street, Sheffield. S1 2DU. 721938) President: Rev. M. Nicholls, J.P.
General Secretary and Connexional Editor: Rev. D. A. Morris, Th.B.

INDEPENDENT CHURCHES

Congregational Federation, The Congregational Centre, 4 Castle Gate, Nottingham. NG1 7AS. (0602 413801.)
President: Rev. Dr. Janet Wootton, 19a Compton Terrace, Islington, London N1 2UN
Secretary: Pastor Graham M. Adams, 8 St. Mary's Close, Southam, Leamington Spa, Warks CV33 0EW.

Congregational Union of Scotland, Church House, P.O. Box 189, Glasgow G1 2BQ (041-332 7667)
President: Rev. Thomas Stout.
General Secretary: Rev. Robert Waters, M.A.

Baptist Union of Great Britain, Baptist House, P.O. Box 44, 129 Broadway, Didcot, Oxon OX11 8RT (0235 512077)
President: Rev. Dr. D.J. Tidball, B.A., B.D. until April 1991
Secretary: The Rev. Bernard Green, M.A., B.D. until April 1991

Baptist World Alliance *President,* 1990/94 Rev. Dr. K. Wimpelmann, 6733 Curran Street, McLean, Virginia 22101, U.S.A.

The Salvation Army, 101 Queen Victoria Street, London
EC4P 4EP. (071- 236 5222)
General: Eva Burrows.
Chief of the Staff: Commissioner Ron A. Cox.
British Commissioner: Commissioner Harry Read.
Scotland: Houldsworth Street, Glasgow G3 8DU. (041- 221 3378).
Territorial Commander: Colonel Dinsdale Pender.

United Reformed Church in the United Kingdom, 86
Tavistock Place, London. WC1H 9RT. (071-837 7661.)
Moderator: Rt. Rev. Graham Cook.
General Secretary: The Rev. Bernard G. Thorogood, M.A.

OTHER CHURCHES AND ORGANISATIONS

Brotherhood and Sisterhood Movement (Inc.), Spencer
Yard, Spencer Street, Leamington Spa, CV31 3NE.
(Leamington Spa 422496) *National President:* Mr. John
H. Taylor. *National Secretary:* John Clark.

Christian Science, 108 Palace Gardens Terrace, London.
W8 4RT. (071-221 5650) *District Manager, Committees
on Publication:* Graham Phaup.

Church of Jesus Christ of Latter-day Saints (Mormons),
751 Warwick Road, Solihull, West Midlands, B91 3DQ
(021-711 2244) *Director of Public Communications:* Bryan
J. Grant.

Free Church Federal Council, 27 Tavistock Square, London.
WC1H 9HH. (071-387 8413 Fax: 071-383 0150))
Moderator: Rev Prof. J. Tudno Williams, M.A., Ph.D.,
from 1991/1992 Moderator will be Rev. Dr. William R.
Davies, M.A., B.D. *General Secretary:* Rev. David Staple,
M.A., B.D.

Friends of the Western Buddhist Order, London Buddhist
Centre, 51 Roman Road, London E2 0HU. (081-981 1225)

Jehovah's Witnesses, Watch Tower House, The Ridgeway,
London. NW7 1RN. (081-906 2211) *Presiding Minister,
Great Britain:* W. Gooch.

Moravian Church House, 5 Muswell Hill, London. N10
3TJ. (081-883 3409) *Chairman of the Provincial Board:*
Rev. F. Linyard, B.A.,B.D.

New Church (Swedenborgian), 20 Bloomsbury Way,
London. WC1A 2TH. (071-229 9340) *General Conference
Secretary:* G. S. Kuphal, B.A., 20 Red Barn Road,
Brightlingsea, Colchester, Essex. CO7 0SH. (Brightlingsea
2932.)

Religious Society of Friends (Quakers), Friends House,
173-177 Euston Road, London. NW1 2BJ. (071-387 3601)
Recording Clerk: Donald H. D. Southall.

Reorganised Church of Jesus Christ of Latter Day Saints,
Region Office: 769 Yardley Wood Road, Billesley,
Birmingham. B13 0PT. (021- 444 5243). *British Isles
Region President:* Barrie Fox, 144 Sutton Road, Kirkby-
in-Ashfield, Notts N17 8HY. (0623 553150). *Central
District President:* Roy D. A. Oakman, 144 Lavender Hill,
Enfield, Middx. EN2 8RP (081-366 1446). *North West
District President:* Roy Bancroft, 30 Scott Road, Denton,
Manchester, M34 1FT (061-336 2094). *South West District
President:* Richard C. James, 108 Coalbrook Road,
Gravesend, Swansea SA4 2GS (0792 898591).

Seventh-day Adventist Church, British Headquarters,
Stanborough Park, Watford, Herts. (0923 672251)
President: M. L. Anthony, Secretary: D. W. McFarlane.
Treasurer: B. J. Powell.

Spiritualists' National Union, Redwoods, Stansted Hall,
Essex. CM24 8UD. (Bishop's Stortford 816363) *President:*
G. M. Higginson, 218 Lightwood Road, Longton, Stoke-
on-Trent. (Stoke-on-Trent 312306.) *General Secretary:*
C.S. Coulston, Redwoods, Stansted Hall, Stansted, Essex
CM24 8UD

Unitarian and Free Christian Churches, 1-6 Essex Hall,
Essex Street, London. WC2R 3HY. (071-240 2384) *General
Secretary:* Dr. Roy W. Smith.

THE JEWISH COMMUNITY

Board of Deputies of British Jews
President: Dr. Lionel Kopelowitz, J.P..
Secretary General: Hayim Pinner, O.B.E..
Office: Woburn House, Tavistock Square, London. WC1H
0BZ. (071-387 3952). Telex 262666 BOD G

Office of the Chief Rabbi
Chief Rabbi: Very Rev. Rabbi Lord Jakobovits of Regents
Park.
Secretary: Jennifer Wagner.
Office: Adler House, Tavistock Square, London. WC1H 0EP.
(071-387 1066.)

The Beth Din
Registrar: Rabbi B. Berkovits. o73
Office: Adler House, Tavistock Square, London. WC1 0EP.
(071-387 5772.)

Spanish and Portuguese Jews' Congregation, London
(established 1675). Rabbis: Rabbi Dr. Abraham Levy:
Dayan Pinhas Toledano.
Office: 2 Ashworth Road, London. W.9. (071-286 4189.)

Central Enquiry Desk (071-387 4044) A telephone
information service on any aspect of Jewish communal or
religious life.

The Jewish population of Great Britain is estimated at 330,000.

In its religious aspect, the major part of the community, which
is orthodox, is under the jurisdiction of the Chief Rabbi of the
United Hebrew Congregations of the British Commonwealth
of Nations. His authority is also recognised by provincial
congregations. The chief religious organisation is the United
Synagogue, founded in 1870, which includes the majority of
important synagogues in the metropolis.

In London the main synagogue groups have head offices at
the following addresses:

United Synagogue: Woburn House, Tavistock Square, London
WC1H 0EP. (071-387 4300)

Spanish and Portuguese Synagogue: 2 Ashworth Road, W.9.
(071-289 2573.)

Union of Orthodox Hebrew Congregations: 40 Queen
Elizabeth Walk, N.16. (081-802 6226.)

Reform Synagogues: Manor House Centre for Judaism, 80
East End Road, London, N3 2SY. (081-349 9307.)

Liberal and Progressive Synagogues: 109 Whitfield Street,
W.1. (071- 580 1663.)

The representative organisation of the community is the
Board of Deputies of British Jews, founded in 1760. Its
members, 480 in number, are elected by synagogues and by
various secular organisations.

Religious matters in dispute are referred to the Beth Din,
Court of the Chief Rabbi. The Court consists of the Chief
Rabbi and five Assessors (Dayanim). The decisions are based
on Jewish religious law and English courts have recognised it
in purely religious matters.

ARCHBISHOPS OF CANTERBURY SINCE A.D. 1114

1114 Ralph d'Escures	1349 Simon Islip	1583 John Whitgift	1828 William Howley
1123 William de Corbeil	1366 Simon Langham	1604 Richard Bancroft	1848 John Bird Sumner
1139 Theobald	1368 William Whittlesey	1611 George Abbot	1862 Charles Thomas
1162 Thomas Becket	1375 Simon Sudbury	1633 William Laud	Longley
1174 Richard (of Dover)	1381 William Courtney	1645-1660 Vacant	1868 Archibald Campbell
1185 Baldwin	1396 Thomas Arundel	1660 William Juxon	Tait
1193 Hubert Walter o73	1398 Roger Walden	1663 Gilbert Sheldon	1883 Edward White Benson
1207 Stephen Langton	1399 Thomas Arundel	1678 William Sancroft	1896 Frederick Temple
1229 Richard le Grant (of	(restored)	1691 John Tillotson	1903 Randall Thomas
Wetharshed)	1414 Henry Chichele	1695 Thomas Tenison	Davidson
1234 Edmund Rich	1443 John Stafford	1716 William Wake	1928 Cosmo Gordon Lang
1245 Boniface of Savoy	1452 John Kemp	1737 John Potter	1942 William Temple
1273 Robert Kilwardby	1454 Thomas Bourchier	1747 Thomas Herring	1945 Geoffrey Francis
1279 John Pecham	1486 John Morton	1757 Matthew Hutton	Fisher
(Peckham)	1501 Henry Dean	1758 Thomas Secker	1961 Arthur Michael
1294 Robert Winchelsey	1503 William Warham	1768 Hon. Frederick	Ramsey
1313 Walter Reynolds	1533 Thomas Cranmer	Cornwallis	1974 Frederick Donald
1328 Simon Mepcham	1556 Reginald Pole	1783 John Moore	Coggan
1333 John Stratford	1559 Matthew Parker	1805 Charles Manners	1980 Robert Alexander
1349 Thomas Bradwardine	1576 Edmund Grindal	Sutton	Kennedy Runcie

COUNCIL OF CHURCHES FOR BRITAIN AND IRELAND

The Council of Churches for Britain and Ireland (formerly known as the British Council of Churches), inaugurated in 1990, is the official instrument of Anglican, Roman Catholic, Orthodox, Presbyterian, Black-led and Free Churches in Britain and Ireland for furthering the growth of the churches in unity and common witness and for facilitating common action by the churches and cooperation in the study of social and religious issues.

The Assembly meets every two years under the leadership of six Presidents, representing the church traditions in Britain and Ireland, to coordinate the work of Churches Together in England, ACTS (Action of Churches Together in Scotland), CYTUN (Churches Together in Wales) and Irish ecumenical bodies.

A Church Representatives Meeting, two or three times a year, composed of senior representatives appointed by member churches and associations of churches, will assist the churches to develop their commitment to closer cooperation and united effort.

The General Secretary is the Revd. John Reardon, Inter-Church House, 35-41 Lower Marsh, London SE1 7RL. 071-620 4444.

EDUCATION

UNIVERSITY OF OXFORD

Full Terms, 1991:
13 Jan.-9 Mar.; 21 Apr.-15 June;13 Oct.-7 Dec.
Number of students in residence: Undergraduates 1O,755; postgraduates 3,773 (Michaelmas 1989).

UNIVERSITY OFFICERS
(Year of appointment shown in brackets)
Chancellor: The Rt. Hon. The Lord Jenkins of Hillhead, D.C.L., Balliol (1987).
High Steward: The Rt. Hon. Lord Goff of Chieveley, D.C.L., F.B.A., Lincol & New (1990).
Vice-Chancellor: Sir Richard Southwood, M.A.,D.Sc.,F.R.S., Merton (1989).
Registrar: A.J. Dorey, M.A., D.Phil., Linacre (1979)

COLLEGES AND HALLS
(Date of foundation shown in brackets)
Colleges
** **All Souls (1438)** *Warden:* Sir Patrick Neill, Q.C., B.C.L., M.A., Hon. D.C.L.
Balliol (1263) *Master:* B.S. Blumberg, M.A., D.Phil.
Brasenose (15O9) *Principal:* The Rt. Hon. Lord Windlesham, P.C., C.V.O., M.A.
Christ Church (1546) *Dean:* Very Rev. E.W. Heaton, M.A.
Corpus Christi (1517) *President:* Sir. Keith Thomas, M.A., F.B.A.
Exeter (1314) *Rector:* Sir Richard Norman, K.B.E., M.A., D.Phil., D.Sc., F.R.S., F.R.Sc.
Green (1979) *Warden:* Sir Crispin Ticke;;, G.C.M.G., K.C.V.O., M.A.
Hertford (1282 originally, present college 1874) *Principal:* E.C. Zeeman, M.A., Ph.D., F.R.S
Jesus (1571) *Principal:* P.M. North, C.B.E.,M.A., D.C.L.
Keble (1868) *Warden:* G.B. Richardson, C.B.E., M.A., Hon. D.C.L.
Lady Margaret Hall (1878) *Principal:* D.M. Stewart, M.A.
Linacre (1962) *Principal:* Sir Bryan Cartledge, K.C.M.G., M.A.
Lincoln (1427) *Rector:* Sir Maurice Shock, M.A.
Magdalen (1458) *President:* A.D. Smith, C.B.E., M.A.
Merton (1264) *Warden:* J.M. Roberts, M.A., D.Phil.
New College (1379) *Warden Harvey McGregor, Q.C., D.C.L.*
Nuffield (1937) *Warden Sir David Cox, M.A., F.R.S.*
Oriel (1326) *Provost:* E.W. Nicholson, D.D., F.B.A., M.Sc.
Pembroke (1624) *Master:* Sir Roger Bannister, C.B.E., M.Sc., D.M., F.R.C.P.
Rowley House (1990) *President:* G.P. Thomas, M.A.
The Queen's (1340) *Provost:* J. Moffatt, M.A., D.Phil.
St. Anne's (1952) (founded 1879 as Society of Oxford Home-students) *Principal:* Dr. Claire Palley, M.A.
St. Antony's (1948) *Warden Sir Ralf Dahrendorf, M.A., F.B.A.*
St. Catherine's (1963) *Master:* E.B. Smith, M.A., D.Sc.
St. Cross (1965) *Master:* R.C. Repp, M.A., D.Phil.
St. Edmund Hall (1270) *Principal:* J.C.B. Gosling, B.Phil., M.A.
* **St. Hilda's** (1893) *Principal:* Miss E.M. Llewellyn-Smith, C.B., M.A. (Women only)
St. Hugh's (1886) *Principal:* Miss M.R. Trickett, M.A.
St. John's (1555) *President:* W. Hayes, M.A., D.Phil.
St. Peter's (1929) *Master:* G.E. Aylmer, M.A., D.Phil, F.B.A.
* **Somerville** (1879) *Principal:* Miss C.E. Pestell, C.M.G., M.A. (Women only)
Trinity (1554) *President:* Sir John Burgh, K.C.M.G., C.B., M.A.
University (1249) *Master:* W.J. Albery, M.A., D.Phil., F.R.S.
Wadham (1612) *Warden:* Sir Claus Moser, K.C.B., C.B.E., M.A., F.B.A.
Wolfson (1965) *President:* Sir Raymond Hoffenberg, K.B.E., M.A., F.R.C.P.

Worcester (1714) *Provost:* The Right Hon. The Lord Briggs, M.A., F.B.A.

Permanent Private Halls
Campion Hall (1896) *Master:* Rev. J.A. Munitiz, M.A.
Greyfriars (191O) *Warden Rev. T.M. Mann, M.A.*
Mansfield College (1886) *Principal:* D.J. Trevelyan, C.B., M.A., F.R.S.A.
Regent's Park College (1927) *Principal:* Rev. P.S. Fiddes, M.A., DPhil.
St. Benet's Hall (1897) *Master:* Rev. P.F. Cowper, O.S.B., M.A., M.Sc.
Manchester (1889) *Principal:* Rev. R. Waller, M.A.
Ripon College, Cuddesdon (1975) *Principal:* Rev. Canon J.H. Garton, M.A.
St. Stephen's House (1876) *Principal:* Rev. E.R. Barnes, M.A.
Wycliffe Hall (1877) *Principal:* Rev. R.T. France, M.A.
Blackfriars (1921) *Regent of Studies:* Rev. B.E.A. Davies, M.A.
Templeton (1984) *President:* U. Kitzinger, C.B.E., M.A., M.Litt.

*All colleges except those marked * admit both men and women.*
 # For graduates only.
*** For Fellows only.*

UNIVERSITY OF CAMBRIDGE

Full Terms, 1990/91:
9 Oct.-7 Dec. 1990; 15 Jan.-15 Mar; 23 Apr.-14 Jun. 1991.
Number of students: 1O,243 undergraduates; 2,975 full-time postgraduate students (December 1989).

UNIVERSITY OFFICERS
(Year of election shown in brackets)
Chancellor: H.R.H. The Prince Philip, Duke of Edinburgh, K.G., K.T., P.C., O.M., G.B.E., Hon.LL.D., Trinity (1977)
High Steward: The Lord Devlin, P.C., M.A., Hon.LL.D., Christ's (1966). *Vice-Chancellor:* Professor D.G.T. Williams, President of Wolfson (1989). *Regis trary:* S.G. Fleet, M.A., Ph.D., Downing (1983).
Secretary-General: J.R.G. Wright, M.A., St. Catharine's (1987).
Public inquiries: G.B. Skelsey, M.A., The Old Schools, Cambridge CB2 1TN, (Assistant to the Vice-Chancellor) (1977).

COLLEGES
(Date of foundation shown in brackets)
Men and Women:
Christ's (15O5) *Master:* Professor Sir Hans Kornberg, Sc.D., F.R.S.
Churchill (196O) *Master:* Professor A.N. Broers, Ph.D., F.R.S., F.Eng. (1990)
Clare (1326) *Master:* Professor R.C.O. Matthews, M.A., F.B.A.
Corpus Christi (1352) *Master:* M.W. McCrum, M.A.
Downing (18OO) *Master:* P. Mathias, C.B.E., M.A., F.B.A.
Emmanuel (1584) *Master:* Professor C.P. Wroth, Ph.D., D.Sc., F.Eng. (1990)
Fitzwilliam (1869) *Master:* (Vacant)
Girton (1869) *Mistress:* Lady Warnock, D.B.E., M.A.
Gonville and Caius (1348) *Master:* Professor P. Gray, Sc.D, F.R.S.
Homerton (1895) (for B.Ed.students only) *Principal:* A.G. Bamford, M.A.
Hughes Hall (1885) *President:* T.D. Hawkins, M.A.
Jesus (1496) *Master:* Professor A.C. Renfrew, Sc.D., F.B.A.
King's (1441) *Provost:* Professor P.P.G. Bateson, Sc.D., F.R.S.

5

Magdalene (1542) Master D. Calcutt, Q.C., M.A.

Pembroke (1347) *Master:* Professor Lord Adrian, M.D., F.R.S.

Peterhouse (1284) *Master:* Professor H. Chadwick, D.D., F.B.A.

Queens' (1448) (Re-founded 1465) *President:* Rev. J.C. Polkinghorne, Sc.D., F.R.S.

Robinson (1977) *Warden Professor Lord Lewis, Sc.D., F.R.S.*

St. Catharine's (1473) *Master:* Professor B.E. Supple, Ph.D., F.B.A.

St. John's (1511) *Master:* Professor R.A. Hinde, C.B.E., Sc.D, F.R.S.

Selwyn (1882) *Master:* Professor Sir Alan Cook, M.A., Ph.D., F.R.S.

Sidney Sussex (1596) *Master:* Professor D.H. Northcote, Sc.D., F.R.S.

Trinity (1546) *Master:* Sir Michael Atiyah, Ph.D., F.R.S. (1990)

Trinity Hall (135O) *Master:* Sir John Lyons, M.A., Ph.D., F.B.A.

Women:

Lucy Cavendish (1965) *President:* Dame Anne Warburton, D.C.V.O., C.M.G., M.A.

New Hall (1954) *President:* Dr. V.L. Pearl, Ph.D.

Newnham (1871) *Principal:* Miss S.J. Browne, M.A., C.B.

Graduate Colleges (Men and Women):

Clare Hall (1966) *President:* Professor D.A. Low, Ph.D.

Darwin (1964) *Master:* Professor G.E.R. Lloyd, Ph.D., F.B.A.

St. Edmund's (1896) *Master:* Dr. R.M. Laws, C.B.E., Ph.D., F.R.S.

Wolfson (1965) *President:* Professor D.G.T. Williams, M.A., LL.B.

UNIVERSITY OF LONDON

Senate House, Malet Street, London WC1E 7HU.

University Terms, 1991:

7 Jan.-15 Mar.; 22 Apr.-28 Jun.; 7 Oct.-13 Dec.

Number of students: The number of internal students reading for degrees and diplomas in the session 1988-89 was 44,640 full-time; 9,881 part-time. In addition there were 25,000 registered external students.

UNIVERSITY OFFICERS

Chancellor: H.R.H. The Princess Royal, G.C.V.O., F.R.S.

Vice-Chancellor: Professor S.R. Sutherland, M.A.; L.H.D.

Chairman of Convocation: Professor C.D. Cowan, C.B.E., M.A.(Camb), Ph.D.

Chairman of Court: The Rt. Hon. Lord Goff of Chieveley, D.C.L., M.A., D.LITT., F.B.A.

Principal: P. Holwell, B.Sc.(Econ.), M.B.C.S., F.C.A.

SCHOOLS OF THE UNIVERSITY

(Date of foundation shown in brackets)

Birkbeck College (1823) *Master:* The Baroness Blackstone, B.Sc.(Soc), Ph.D.

British Postgraduate Medical Federation (1945), 33 Millman Street, London WC1N 3EJ *Director:* Professor M.J. Peckham, M.D., M.R.C.P., F.R.C.P.(G), F.R.C.R. Comprises The National Heart & Lung Institute, Hunterian Institute and Institutes of Cancer Research, Child Health, Dental Surgery, Neurology, Ophthalmology, Psychiatry.

Charing Cross and Westminster Medical School (Charing Cross 1818; Westminster 1834) *Dean:* Mr. J. Pendower, M.B., B.S., F.R.C.S.

Goldsmiths' College *Warden:* A. Rutherford, B.Litt., M.A.

Heythrop College* (1926) *Principal:* Rev. B.A. Callaghan, S.J., M.A., M.Th., M.Phil., F.R.S.M.

Imperial College of Science, Technology and Medicine (inc. St Mary's Hospital Medical School) (1907) *Rector:* Professor E.A. Ash, C.B.E., Ph.D., F.R.S.

Institute of Education, University of London (1987) *Director:* Sir Peter Newsam, D.I.P. Ed, M.A.

King's College London (King's 1829; Queen Elizabeth 1908; Chelsea 1891) *Principal:* Professor J.D.E. Beynon, M.Sc., Ph.D., F.Eng, F.I.E.E.

The London Hospital Medical College (1785) *Dean:* Professor R. Duckworth, M.D., F.R.C.S., F.D.S., F.R.C.Path.

The London School of Economics and Political Science (1895) *Director:* Professor J.M. Ashworth, Ph.D.(Leic), M.A., D.Sc.(Oxford), F.I.Biol.

London School of Hygiene and Tropical Medicine (1889) *Dean:* Prof. R.G. Feachem, PH.D.

Queen Mary College (1887) *Principal:* Professor I. Butterworth, C.B.E., Ph.D., F.R.S.

Royal Free Hospital School of Medicine (1874) *Dean:* Prof. A.J. Zuckerman, M.D., D.Sc., F.R.C.P., F.Rc.Path.

Royal Holloway and Bedford New College (Royal Holloway 1886; Bedford 1849) *Principal:* Professor N. Gowar, B.Sc., M.Phil., F.I.M.A.

Royal Postgraduate Medical School (1931) *Dean:* Professor D.N.S. Kerr, M.B., Ch.B., M.Sc., F.R.C.P.

Royal Veterinary College (1791) *Principal and Dean:* Prof. L.E. Lanyon, B.V.Sc., Ph.D., M.R.C.V.S.

St. Bartholomew's Hospital Medical College (1662) *Dean:* Prof. Lesley H. Rees, M.Sc., M.D., M.R.C.Path, F.R.C.P.

St. George's Hospital Medical School (1751) *Dean:* A.W. Asscher, B.Sc., M.D., B.S., F.R.C.P.

The School of Oriental and African Studies (1916) *Director:* Mr. M.W. McWilliam, B.Litt., M.A.

The School of Pharmacy (1842) *Dean:* Prof. A.T. Florence, D.Sc., F.R.Sc., F.R.S.E., F.R.Pharms.

United Medical and Dental Schools of Guy's and St. Thomas's Hospitals (Guy's 1724; St. Thomas's 16th century) *Principal:* Prof. I.R. Cameron, D.M. Oxf., F.R.C.S.

University College London (1826) *Provost:* Dr. D.N. Roberts, C.B.E., F.R.S., F.Eng.

Wye College (1893) *Principal:* Prof. J.H.D. Prescott, Ph.D., F.Inst Biol., F.R.Ag.S.

SENATE INSTITUTES

(Date of foundation shown in brackets)

British Institute in Paris (1927) *Director:* Professor C.L. Campos, L.sL., Ph.D.

Courtauld Institute of Art (1932) *Director:* Professor C.M. Kauffmann, M.A., Ph.D., F.M.A.

Institute of Advanced Legal Studies (1947) *Director:* Professor T.C. Daintith, M.A.

Institute of Classical Studies (1953) *Director:* Professor J.P. Barron, M.A., D.Phil., F.S.A.

Institute of Commonwealth Studies (1949) *Director:* Professor Shula E. Marks, B.A., Ph.D.

Institute of Germanic Studies (1950) Hon. *Director:* Professor M.W. Swales, M.A., Ph.D.

Institute of Historical Research (1921) *Director:* Professor P.K. O'Brian, B.Sc. Econ(London), M.A., D.Phil(Oxon).

Institute of Latin American Studies (1965) *Director:* Professor L.M. Bethell, B.A., Ph.D.

Institute of Romance Studies (1989) *Director:* Professor M.M. Bowie, M.A., D.Phil.

Institute of United States Studies (1965) *Director:* Professor P.J. Parish, B.A.

Institute of Zoology (1989) *Director:* Professor A.P.F. Flint, Ph.D., D.Sc., F.I.Biol.

School of Slavonic and East European Studies (1915) *Director:* Professor M.A. Branch, B.A., Ph.D.

Warburg Institute (1944) *Director:* Professor J.B. Trapp, M.A., F.B.A.

There are in addition five institutions having Recognised Teachers:

Jews' College *Principal:* (Appointment yet to be announced)

London Business School *Principal:* Professor G.S. Bain, D.Phil.

Royal Academy of Music *Principal:* Sir David Lumsden, Mus.B., M.A., D.Phil.

Royal College of Music *Director:* M.G. Matthews, F.R.C.M., A.R.C.O., F.R.S.A.

Trinity College of Music *Principal:* P. Jones, C.B.E., F.G.S.M., F.R.C.M., F.R.N.C.M., A.R.C.M.

* *School not in receipt of UGC grant.*

UNIVERSITY OF ABERDEEN (1495)

Regent Walk, Aberdeen AB9 1FX.

Terms, 1990-91:

Arts and Social Studies, Science, Engineering Divinity and Law students.

2 Oct.-14 Dec.; 7 Jan.-15 Mar.; 15 Apr.-21 June.

Medical students (Dates on application to University).
Number of students: (1989-90) 6,500.
Chancellor: Sir Kenneth Alexander, DLitt, B.Sc., F.R.S.E.
Principal and Vice-Chancellor: Professor George P. McNicol, Ph.D., M.D., D.Sc., F.R.S.E., F.R.C.P.E., F.R.C.P., F.R.C.Path., F.R.C.P.G., F.A.C.P. (Until 30th November 1991)
Vice-Principals: Professor Derek Ogston, M.A., M.D., Ph.D., D.Sc., D.T.M.&H., F.R.C.P., F.R.C.P.E., F.R.S.E. (1987-91); Professor W. Allan Hamilton, B.Sc., Ph.D, F.I. Biol., F.R.S.E.; Professor William Ritchie, B.Sc., Ph.D., F.R.I.C.S., F.R.S.G.S., F.R.S.E.
Secretary: Norman R.D. Begg, M.A., LL.B..

ASTON UNIVERSITY (1966)
Aston Triangle, Birmingham B4 7ET.
Terms, 1990-91:
30 Sep.-8 Dec.; 6 Jan.-16 Mar.; 14 Apr.-22 June.
Number of students: (1989-9O) 3637 full-time.
Chancellor: Sir Adrian Cadbury, M.A., Hon.D.Sc., Hon.LL.B.
Vice-Chancellor: Professor Sir Frederick Crawford, M.Sc., Ph.D., D.Eng., D.Sc., F.Eng.

UNIVERSITY OF BATH (1966)
Claverton Down, Bath BA2 7AY.
Terms, 1989-90:
1 Oct.-17 Dec.; 17 Jan.-15 Mar.; 15 Apr.-21 June.
Number of students: (1989-90) full-time/sandwich 2,621 men; 1,442 women.
Chancellor: Lord Kearton of Whitchurch, Kt., O.B.E., M.A., F.R.S.
Vice-Chancellor: J.R. Quayle, M.A., B.Sc., Ph.D., F.R.S.
Secretary and Registrar: R.M. Mawditt, O.B.E., M.Sc., F.C.C.A., F.B.I.M., F.R.S.A.

THE QUEEN'S UNIVERSITY OF BELFAST (1908)
Belfast, Northern Ireland BT7 1NN.
University *Terms, 1990-91:*
1 Oct.-14 Dec.; 7 Jan.-15 Mar.; 15 Apr.-14 June.
Number of students: (1988-89) 4,308 male; 3,375 female; part-time 1,687.
Chancellor: Sir Rowland Wright, K.B., C.B.E., B.Sc., LL.D, D.Sc., C.Chem., F.R.S.C., C.B.I.M., F.I.Chem.E.
Pro-Chancellors: Robert A. Hamilton, C.B.E., Dip.Agric., B.Sc., B.Agr., D.Sc., A.I.C.T.A., D.Sc.; John B. McGuckian, B.Sc.(Econ);
Miss Clare Macmahon, O.B.E., B.Sc., M.I.Biol.
President and Vice-Chancellor: Gordon S.G. Beveridge, B.Sc., Ph.D., A.R.C.S.T., F.Eng., F.I.Chem.E., F.R.S.E.

THE UNIVERSITY OF BIRMINGHAM (1900)
Edgbaston, Birmingham B15 2TT.
Session, 1990-91:
1 Oct.-14 Dec.; 14 Jan.-22 Mar.; 29 Apr.-5 July.
Number of students: (Dec. 1989) 10,860.
Chancellor: Sir Alex Jarratt, C.B., B.Com., Hon.LL.D., Hon.D.Sc., Hon.D.Univ.
Pro-Chancellor: Sir Julian Bullard, G.C.M.G., M.A. Oxon
Vice-Chancellor and Principal: Professor M.W. Thompson, B.Sc., D.Sc.Liv., F.Inst.P.
Registrar & Secretary: D.R. Holmes, M.A.Oxon.

UNIVERSITY OF BRADFORD
(1966)
Bradford, West Yorkshire BD7 1DP.
Terms, 1990-91:
8 Oct.-14 Dec.; 14 Jan.-22 Mar.; 22 Apr.-28 June
Number of students: (1998-90) 4,550 full-time, 578 part-time.
Chancellor: Sir John Harvey-Jones, M.B.E., Hon.D.Sc.
Vice-Chancellor and Principal: Professor David Johns, Ph.D., D.Sc., C.Eng., F.R.A.e.S., F.I.O.A., F.C.I.T.
Registrar: D.W. Granger, M.B.E., B.Sc., M.I.P.M.

UNIVERSITY OF BRISTOL (1909)
Senate House, Bristol BS8 1TH.
Session, 1990-91):
4 Oct.-14 Dec.; 11 Jan.-22 Mar.; 22 Apr.-21 June.
Number of students: full-time (1990-91) 4,366 men; 3,378 women.
Chancellor: Sir Jeremy Morse, K.C.M.G.
Vice-Chancellor: Sir John Kingman, M.A., Sc.D., D.Sc., F.R.S.
Secretary: J.H.M. Parry, M.A.
Registrar: Mrs. C.M. Cunningham, B.A.

BRUNEL UNIVERSITY (1966)
Uxbridge, Middlesex, UB8 3PH.
Terms, 1990-91:
1 Oct.-14 Dec.; 7 Jan.-27 Mar.; 22 Apr.-28 June.
Number of students: (1989-90) 2,645 undergraduates; 1,095 postgraduates; 279 research.
Chancellor: The Earl of Halsbury, F.R.S.
Vice-Chancellor and Principal: Professor M. Kogan, M.A.
Secretary General and Registrar: D. Neave, B.A., LL.M.

UNIVERSITY OF BUCKINGHAM (1983)
Hunter Street, Buckingham MK18 1EG.
Terms, 1991:
21 Jan.-22 Mar.; 8 Apr.-21 June; 15 July-13 Sept.; 30 Sept.-13 Dec.
Number of students: (1990) 763.
Chancellor: The Lord Hailsham of St. Marylebone, K.G., P.C., C.H., D.C.L., F.R.S.
Vice-Chancellor: Dr. Michael Barrett, Ph.D., F.I.Biol., F.R.S.A.
Executive Pro-Vice-Chancellor: Professor P.L. Watson, M.Sc., F.C.A.
Pro-Vice-Chancellor: Professor B.C. Collins, B.A., M.A., Ph.D.
Secretary and Registrar: Dr. M.E. Lavis, B.A., Ph.D.
Librarian: J.E. Pemberton, M.A., F.L.A., F.R.S.A.

THE CITY UNIVERSITY (1966)
Northampton Square, London EC1V 0HB.
Terms, 1990-91:
8 Oct.-14 Dec.; 14 Jan.-22 Mar.; 22 Apr.-28 June.
Number of students: (1989-90) 4,219.
Chancellor: The Lord Mayor of London.
Vice-Chancellor and Principal: Professor R.N. Franklin, M.E., M.A., D.Phil., D.Sc., C.B.I.M., C.Eng., F.I.E.E., C.Phys., F.Inst.P., F.I.M.A.
Academic Registrar: A.H. Seville, M.A., Ph.D.

THE UNIVERSITY OF DUNDEE (1967)
Dundee DD1 4HN.
Terms, 1990-91:
8 Oct.-14 Dec.; 7 Jan.-15 Mar.; 15 Apr.-21 June.
Number of students: (1989-90) 2,260 men; 1,709 women.
Chancellor: The Right Hon. The Earl of Dalhousie, K.T., G.B.E., G.C.V.O., M.C., LL.D.
Principal and Vice-Chancellor: M.J. Hamlin, B.Sc., F.Eng., F.I.C.E., F.I.W.E.M., F.R.S.E.
Rector: Paul H. Scott, C.M.G., M.A., M.Litt.
Secretary: R. Seaton, M.A., LL.B.
Librarian: J.M. Bagnall, M.A., Dip.Lib., M.I.Inf.Sc., A.I.L.

THE UNIVERSITY OF DURHAM (1832)
Old Shire Hall, Durham DH1 3HP.
Terms, 1990-91:
3 Oct.-5 Dec.; 10 Jan.-13 Mar.; 18 Apr.-19 June.
Number of students: (December 1989) 4,577 undergraduates; 754 graduates (full time).
Chancellor: Dame Margot Fonteyn de Arias, D.B.E., Litt.D., D.Mus., LL.D., D.Litt.
Vice-Chancellor and Warden: Professor E.A.V. Ebsworth, M.A., D.Sc., F.R.S.E., F.R.S.C.

Pro-Vice-Chancellor and Sub-Warden: J.P. Barber, J.P., M.A., Ph.D.
Pro-Vice-Chancellor: G.E. Rodmell, B.A., Ph.D.
Registrar and Secretary: J.C.F. Hayward, M.A., F.B.I.M.
University College Master: E.C. Salthouse, B.Sc., Ph.D., C.Eng., F.I.E.E., F.R.S.A.
Hatfield College Master: J.P. Barber, J.P., M.A., Ph.D.
Grey College Master: V.E. Watts, M.A.
Van Mildert College Principal: Judith Turner B.Sc., M.A., Ph.D.
Collingwood Master: G.H. Blake, J.P., M.A., Ph.D.
St. Chad's College Principal: D. Jasper, M.A., B.D., Ph.D.
St. John's College Principal: Rev. A. Thiselton, B.D., M.Theol., Ph.D.
College of St. Hild and St. Bede Principal: J.V. Armitage, B.Sc., Ph.D., F.I.M.A., F.R.A.S.
St. Cuthbert's Society Principal: S.G.C. Stoker, B.A., M.Ed.
St. Mary's College Principal: Joan M. Kenworthy, B.Litt., M.A.
St. Aidan's College Principal: To be appointed.
Trevelyan College Principal: Deborah Lavin, M.A.
The Graduate Society Principal: M. Richardson, B.Sc., Ph.D.
Ushaw College President: Rt. Rev. Mgr. Canon P.F.J. Walton, B.A.

UNIVERSITY OF EAST ANGLIA (1963)

Norwich NR4 7TJ.
Full Terms, 1990-91:
4 Oct.-14 Dec.; 14 Jan.-22 Mar.; 22 Apr.-28 June
Number of students: (1989-90) 5,254.
Chancellor: The Rev. Professor W.O. Chadwick, O.M., K.B.E., D.D., F.B.A.
Vice-Chancellor: Professor D.C. Burke, B.Sc., Ph.D., Hon.LL.D.
Deputy Vice-Chancellor and Pro-Vice-Chancellor: Dr. J.R. Tarrant, B.Sc., Ph.D.
Pro-Vice-Chancellors: Professor J.G. Miller, LLb., LLm., Ph.D.; Professor P.M. Stocker, M.Sc., F.I.M.A., F.B.C.S., C.Eng.
Registrar and Secretary: M.G.E. Paulson-Ellis, M.A., F.C.A.

UNIVERSITY OF EDINBURGH (1583)

Old College, South Bridge, Edinburgh EH8 9YL.
Full Terms, 1990-91:
8 Oct.-14 Dec.; 7 Jan.-15 Mar.; 16 Apr.-21 June.
Number of matriculated students: (1988-89) 12,521
Chancellor: H.R.H. The Prince Philip, Duke of Edinburgh, K.G., K.T., P.C., O.M., G.B.E.
Principal and Vice-Chancellor: Sir David Smith, M.A., D.Phil., Hon.D.Sc., F.R.S.
Rector: Muriel Gray (Until March 1991)
Secretary to the University: Dr. Martin J.B. Lowe

UNIVERSITY OF ESSEX (1964)

Wivenhoe Park, Colchester CO4 3SQ.
Terms, 1990-91:
4 Oct.-15 Dec.; 14 Jan.-23 Mar.; 22 Apr.-29 Jun..
Chancellor: Rt. Hon. Sir Patrick Nairne, G.C.B., M.C., M.A., LL.D., D.U.
Pro-Chancellors: R.D. Hart, B.Sc. Wales, C.PHYS., M.Inst.P.; Sir Andrew Stark, K.C.M.G., C.V.O., M.A. Edin., D.L.
Pro-Chancellor and Chairman of the Council: Sir Andrew Stark, K.C.M.G., C.V.O., M.A., D.L.
Vice-Chancellor: Professor Martin Harris, B.A., PhD.
Pro-Vice-Chancellors: Professor David Lockwood (Academic), B.Sc. (Econ.), Ph.D. Lond., M.A. Camb., F.B.A.; Dr. J.G. Tillett, B.Sc., Ph.D., Ph.D., D.Sc., F.R.S.C.
Treasurer: R.D. Hart, B.Sc., C.Phys., M.Inst.P.
Registrar: E. Newcomb, B.A., Dip.Ed.

UNIVERSITY OF EXETER (1955)

Northcote House, The Queen's Drive, Exeter EX4 4QJ.
Terms, 1990-91:
1 Oct.-7 Dec.; 7 Jan.-15 Mar.; 22 Apr.-28 Jun.
Number of students: (1988-89) 6,000.
Chancellor: Sir Rex Richards, D.Sc., F.R.S., F.R.Sc.

Vice-Chancellor: D. Harrison, C.B.E., M.A., Ph.D., Sc.D., F.Eng., F.R.Sc., F.I.Chem.E.
Academic Registrar and Secretary: I.H.C. Powell, M.A.

UNIVERSITY OF GLASGOW (1451)

Gilmorehill, Glasgow G12 8QQ.
Terms, 1990-91:
4 Oct.-14 Dec.; 7 Jan.-15 Mar.; 15 Apr.-21 June.
Number of students: (1989-90) 7,757 men; 6,106 women.
Chancellor: Sir Alexander Kirkland Cairncross, K.C.M.G., M.A., Ph.D., LL.D., D.Litt., D.Sc.(Econ), D.Univ., F.B.A.
Principal: Sir William Kerr Fraser, G.C.B., M.A., LLD., F.R.S.E.
Secretary: Robert Ewen O.B.E., T.D., M.A..

HERIOT-WATT UNIVERSITY (1966)

Edinburgh EH14 4AS.
Terms, 1991:
Faculties of Science, Engineering, Economic and Social Studies:
7 Jan.-15 Mar.; 15 Apr.-21 June; 7 Oct.-13 Dec.
Faculties of Art and Design and Environmental Studies:
7 Jan.-22 Mar.; 16 Apr.-28 June; 7 Oct.-20 Dec.
Faculty of Textiles:
7 Jan.-29 Mar.; 15 Apr.-28 Jun.; 1 Oct.-20 Dec.
Number of students: (1989-90) 4,898.
Chancellor: The Lord Thomson of Monifieth, K.T., P.C., F.R.S.E.
Principal and Vice-Chancellor: Professor A.G.J. MacFarlane, C.B.E., F.Eng., F.R.S.
Secretary: Mr. Peter L. Wilson, B.Sc., M.A., F.B.I.M.

THE UNIVERSITY OF HULL (1954)

Hull HU6 7RX.
Terms, 1990-91:
8 Oct.-15 Dec.; 14 Jan.-23 Mar.; 29 Apr.-6 July.
Number of students: (1989-90) 5,809
Chancellor: The Lord Wilberforce, P.C., C.M.G., O.B.E., M.A., D.C.L., LL.D.
Vice-Chancellor: Sir Professor W. Taylor, C.B.E., B.Sc.(Econ)., Ph.D., D.Sc., D.Litt., Litt.D., D.C.L., D.Univ.
Registrar & Secretary: F.T. Mattison, M.A., LL.B.

UNIVERSITY OF KEELE (1962)

Keele, Staffs ST5 5BG.
Terms, 1990-91:
11 Oct.-15 Dec.; 10 Jan.-19 Mar.; 25 Apr.-2 July
Number of students: (1989-90) 3.092
Chancellor: Sir Claus Moser, K.C.B., C.B.E., F.B.A.
Vice-Chancellor: Brian E.F. Fender, B.Sc., Ph.D.
Registrar: D. Cohen, M.A., Ph.D., C.Chem., F.R.S.C.

UNIVERSITY OF KENT AT CANTERBURY (1965)

Canterbury, Kent CT2 7NZ.
Terms, 1989-90:
4 Oct.-14 Dec.; 10 Jan.-22 Mar.; 18 Apr.-21 June.
Number of students: 3,936 undergraduates; 773 postgraduates (as at 31.12.88).
Chancellor: The Lord Grimond, P.C., D.C.L.
Pro-Chancellor: The Rt. Rev. R.D. Say, M.A., D.D., D.C.L.
Vice-Chancellor: D.J.E. Ingram, M.A., D.Phil., D.Sc., F.Inst.P.
Registrar and Finance Officer: A.D. Linfoot, M.A.

THE UNIVERSITY OF LANCASTER (1964)

University House, Lancaster LA1 4YW.
Full Terms, 1990-91:
5 Oct.-14 Dec.; 11 Jan.-22 Mar.; 19 Apr.-28 June.
Number of full-time students: (1989-90) 5,200 approx.
Chancellor: H.R.H. Princess Alexandra, the Hon. Mrs. Angus Ogilvy.
Vice-Chancellor: Professor H.J. Hanham, M.A., Ph.D.
Secretary of the University: G.M. Cockburn, M.A.
Registrar: M.D. Forster, M.A., B.Sc.(Econ.).

THE UNIVERSITY OF LEEDS (1904)

Leeds, West Yorkshire LS2 9JT.
Session, 1990-91:
3 Oct.-14 Dec.; 14 Jan.-22 Mar.; 22 Apr.-28 June.
Number of students: (October 1989) full-time 11,631.
Chancellor: H.R.H. The Duchess of Kent, G.C.V.O., LL.D.
Vice-Chancellor: Sir Edward Parkes, Sc.D., F.Eng.
Pro-Chancellor: Colonel Alan C. Roberts, M.B.E., T.D., J.P., D.L., M.Phil., Ph.D.
Pro-Vice-Chancellor: Professor Alan G. Wilson, M.A.
Treasurer: Group Captain F.W. Morgan, M.B.E., B.Sc.(Eng.), M.I.Mech.E., M.I.B.M.
Registrar: James Walsh, M.A., F.R.S.A. *Bursar:* Raymond Head, F.C.A.

THE UNIVERSITY OF LEICESTER (1957)

University Road, Leicester LE1 7RH.
*Full Terms, 1990-91:*y
2 Oct.-14 Dec.; 7 Jan.-15 Mar.; 22 Apr.-28 June.
Number of students: (December 1989) 5,671 full-time.
Chancellor: Sir George Porter, P.R.S., M.A., Ph.D., D.Sc.
Vice-Chancellor: K.J.R. Edwards, B.Sc., M.A., Ph.D.
Executive Pro-Vice Chancellor & Registrar: Professor G. Bernbaum, B.Sc.(Econ), F.R.S.A.

THE UNIVERSITY OF LIVERPOOL (1903)

P.O. Box 147, Liverpool L69 3BX.
Session, 1990-91:
8 Oct.-14 Dec.; 14 Jan.-22 Mar.; 22 Apr.-5 July.
Number of students: (December 1989) 9,659.
Chancellor: The Viscount Leverhulme, K.G., T.D., J.P., B.A., LL.D., K.St.J.
Pro-Chancellor: Bertram Lyle Rathbone, LL.D.
Vice-Chancellor: Professor Graeme John Davies, B.E., M.A., Ph.D., Sc.D., C.Eng., F.I.M., M.I.Mech.E.
President of the Council: Anthony Michael Mould, J.P.
Vice-President of the Council: Lawrence Holden, LL.B
Treasurer: William Stothart, M.A., F.C.I.S.
Deputy Treasurer: Edward John Billington, R.D. C.B.I.M.
Pro-Vice-Chancellors: John Nelson Tarn, B.Arch., Ph.D., R.I.B.A., F.R.Hist.S., F.S.A., John David Parsons, B.Sc., M.Sc.(Eng), D.Sc.(Eng), C.Eng., F.I.E.E., M.I.E.R.E.; Dorothy Sherman Severin, A.M., Ph.D.

LOUGHBOROUGH UNIVERSITY OF TECHNOLOGY (1966)

Ashby Road, Loughborough LE11 3TU.
Terms, 1990-91:
10 Oct.-7 Dec.; 7 Jan.-15 Mar.; 29 Apr.-5 July.
Number of students: (1989-90) 6,363.
Chancellor: Sir Denis Rooke, C.B.E., B.Sc.(Eng.), F.R.S., F.Eng.
Vice-Chancellor: Professor D.E.N. Davies, C.B.E., B.Sc., M.Sc., Ph.D., D.Sc., F.I.E.E., F.Eng., F.R.S.
Registrar (Academic & General): D.E. Fletcher, B.A., Ph.D.

THE UNIVERSITY OF MANCHESTER (1851)

Oxford Road, Manchester M13 9PL.
Terms, 1989-80:
2 Oct.-15 Dec.; 15 Jan.-23 Mar.; 30 Apr.-22 June.
Number of students: (1988-89) 18,412 men and women (including postgraduates and part-time students and Faculties of Technology (UMIST) and Business Administration.
Chancellor: Professor J.A.G. Griffith, LL.D., F.B.A.
Vice-Chancellor: Sir Mark Richmond, B.A., M.Sc., Ph.D., Sc.D., F.R.C.Path., F.R.S.
Registrar: K.E. Kitchen, B.A., M.A.(Econ.).
Director of Estates and Services: Robert Hargreaves, C.Eng., M.I.Mech.E., M.C.I.B.S.
Director of Finance: G.H. Roberts, B.Sc.(Econ).

THE UNIVERSITY OF MANCHESTER INSTITUTE OF SCIENCE AND TECHNOLOGY (UMIST) (1956)

P.O. Box 88, Manchester M60 1QD.
(Faculty of Technology in the University of Manchester.)
Session, 1989-90: As for the University of Manchester.
President: Sir John Mason, C.B., D.Sc., F.R.S.
Principal: Professor H.C.A. Hankins, B.Sc.(Tech.), Ph.D., C.Eng., F.I.E.E.
Secretary and Registrar: P.C.C. Stephenson, M.A.

UNIVERSITY OF NEWCASTLE UPON TYNE (1852)

6 Kensington Terrace, Newcastle upon Tyne NE1 7RU.
Terms, 1991:
14 Jan.-22 Mar.; 22 Apr.-28 June; 10 Oct.-13 Dec.
Number of students: (1989-90) 8,317.
Chancellor: Viscount Ridley, T.D.
Vice-Chancellor: Professor L.W.Martin, M.A., Ph.D.
Pro-Vice-Chancellors: Professor J.R. Ringrose, M.A., Ph.D., F.R.S.; Professor D.G. Murchison, B.Sc., Ph.D., F.G.S., Hon.F.R.M.S., F.R.S.E.
Dean of Medicine: Professor A.L. Crombie, M.B., ChB., F.R.C.S.Ed.
Registrar: D.E.T. Nicholson, M.A. School of Education (M. & W.) *Professor of Education and Head of School:* A.D. Edwards, M.A., M.Phil., Ph.D.
Director of the Centre for Curriculum Evaluation and Management: J.J.C. McCabe, B.Sc., M.Ed.

THE UNIVERSITY OF NOTTINGHAM (1948)

University Park, Nottingham NG7 2RD.
Session, 1990-91
Number of students: (1989-90) 8,000.
Chancellor: Sir Gordon Hobday, Ph.D., LL.D., F.R.S.C., H.M. Lord Lt. for Nottinghamshire
Vice-Chancellor: Mr. Colin M. Campbell LL.B
Registrar: G.E. Chandler, B.A.

THE UNIVERSITY OF READING (1926)

Whiteknights, Reading RG6 2AH.
Session, 1990-91:
7 Oct.-13 Dec.; 13 Jan.-20 Mar.; 4 May -10 July
Number of students: (November 1989) 3,780 men; 3,613 women full-time.
Chancellor: Rt. Hon. The Lord Sherfield, G.C.B., G.C.M.G., D.C.L., LL.D., D.Litt., F.I.C.E., F.R.S.
Vice-Chancellor: E.S. Page, M.A., B.Sc., Ph.D.
Registrar: T. Bottomley, B.A.

UNIVERSITY OF ST. ANDREWS (1411)

College Gate, St. Andrews, Scotland KY16 9AJ.
Terms, 1990-91:
7 Oct.-14 Dec.; 7 Jan.-15 Mar.; 8 Apr.-7 June.
Number of students: (Session 1989-90) 4,185 full-time;
Chancellor and President of the General Council: Professor Sir Kenneth James Dover, M.A., D.Litt., LL.D., F.B.A., F.R.S.E.
Principal and Vice-Chancellor: Professor Struther Arnott, B.Sc., Ph.D., F.I.Biol., F.R.S.C., F.R.S.E., F.R.S.
Secretary and Registrar: M.J.B. Lowe, B.Sc., Ph.D.
Secretary of Court and Clerk of Senate: D.P. Dorward, M.A., LL.B.

COLLEGES

United College of St. Salvator and St. Leonard *Master:* Professor J.R. MacCallum, B.Sc., Ph.D., D.Sc., C.Chem., F.R.S.C., F.R.S.E.
St. Mary's College *Principal:* Professor D.W.D. Shaw, M.A., LL.B., B.D.
St. Leonard's College *Provost:* Professor T.C. Smout, M.A., Ph.D., F.B.A., F.R.S.E.

UNIVERSITY OF SALFORD (1967)

Salford M5 4WT.
Terms, 1990-91:
2 Oct.-14 Dec.; 14 Jan.-22 Mar.; 22 Apr.-28 June.
Number of students: (1989-90) full-time undergraduates, 3,612; full-time postgraduates, 484; part-time undergraduates, 146; part-time postgraduates, 606.
Chancellor: H.R.H. The Duchess of York
Vice-Chancellor: Prof. T.M. Husband, B.Sc., M.A., Ph.D., F.I.Prod.E., F.I. Mech.E., F.Eng.
Registrar: S.R. Bosworth, O.B.E., B.A.

THE UNIVERSITY OF SHEFFIELD (1905)

Sheffield S10 2TN.
Terms, 1990-91:
1 Oct.-8 Dec.; 7 Jan.-16 Mar.; 22 Apr.-29 June.
Number of students: (1989-90) 8,513 full-time.
Chancellor: The Right Hon. The Lord Dainton of Hallam Moors, Kt., M.A., B.Sc., Ph.D., Sc.D., C.Chem., F.R.S.C., F.R.S.
Pro-Chancellors: J.E. Eardley, J.P., P.W. Lee.
Vice-Chancellor: Professor G.D. Sims, O.B.E., M.Sc., Ph.D., D.Sc., F.Eng., F.I.E.E., F.C.G.I.
Registrar and Secretary: J.S. Padley, B.Sc., Ph.D.

THE UNIVERSITY OF SOUTHAMPTON (1952)

Highfield, Southampton SO9 5NH.
Full Terms, 1990-91:
29 Sept.-9 Dec.; 8 Jan.-17 Mar.; 23 Apr.-30 June.
Number of students: (1990-91) 6,960 (including 1,092 postgraduates).
Chancellor: The Earl Jellicoe, K.B.E., P.C., D.S.O., M.C., LL.D.
Vice-Chancellor: G.R. Higginson, B.Sc., Ph.D., F.I.C.E., F.I.Mech.E.
Secretary and Registrar: D.A. Schofield, M.A.
Academic Registrar: Miss A.E. Clarke, J.P., B.A.

UNIVERSITY OF STIRLING (1967)

Stirling FK9 4LA.
Semester dates, 1990-91:
18 Sept.-21 Dec.; 12 Feb.-1 June.
Number of students: (1989-90) 2,874 undergraduates; 865 postgraduates.
Chancellor: Lord Balfour of Burleigh, CEng, F.I.E.E., F.R.S.E., D.Univ.
Principal: A.J. Forty, Ph.D., D.Sc., F.R.S.E.
Secretary: R.G. Bomont, J.P., B.Sc.(Econ.), I.P.F.A.

UNIVERSITY OF STRATHCLYDE (1964)

16 Richmond Street, Glasgow G1 1XQ.
Terms, 1990-91:
28 Sep.-21 Dec.; 7 Jan.-22 Mar.; 8 Apr.-14 June.
Number of students: (1988-89) full-time 6,320 undergraduates; 1,443 postgraduates; part-time 1,000 postgraduates.
Chancellor: The Lord Todd, O.M., M.A., D.Sc., D.Phil., LL.D., C.Chem., F.R.S.C., P.P.R.S.
Principal and Vice-Chancellor: G. Hills, Ph.D., D.Sc., Sc.D., LL.D., C.Chem., F.R.S.C., F.R.S.E.
Secretary to the University: Peter W.A. West, M.A.

UNIVERSITY OF SURREY (1966)

Guildford, Surrey GU2 5XH.
Terms, 1991-92:
14 Oct.-20 Dec.; 13 Jan.-20 Mar.; 27 Apr.-3 Jul.
8 Oct. for 1st year students.
Number of students: (1991-92) 3,270 and 1,652 postgraduate (729 full-time).
Chancellor: H.R.H. The Duke of Kent, K.G., G.C.M.G., G.C.V.O.
Vice-Chancellor: Professor A. Kelly, C.B.E., Ph.D., Sc.D., F.Inst.P., F.I.M., F.Eng., F.R.S.
Secretary: L.J. Kail, I.P.F.A.

THE UNIVERSITY OF SUSSEX (1961)

Sussex House, Falmer, Brighton, Sussex BN1 9RH.
Dates of Terms, 1989-90:
9 Oct.-15 Dec.; 8 Jan.-16 Mar.; 23 Apr.-29 June.
Number of students: (December 1988) 4,935.
Chancellor: The Earl of March and Kinrara, F.C.A., D.L.
Senior Pro-Chancellor: Lord Trafford, M.B., B.S., F.R.C.P.
Pro-Chancellor: Sir Richard Attenborough, C.B.E.
Treasurer: M.R. Toynbee, J.P.
Vice-Chancellor: Sir Leslie Fielding, K.C.M.G., M.A.
Senior Pro-Vice-Chancellor: Professor F.J. Bayley, M.Sc., Ph.D., D.Sc., F.I.Mech.E
Registrar and Secretary: G. Lockwood, B.Sc.(Econ.), D.Phil.
Finance Officer: M.A. Sims, F.C.A.
Deputy Secretary: P.A. Tear, LL.B.

* UNIVERSITY OF ULSTER (1984)

Cromore Road, Coleraine, Co. Londonderry, BT52 1SA.
(A Charter was granted for the University of Ulster, with effect from October 1, 1984.)
Terms, 1990-91:
1 Oct.-14 Dec.; 7 Jan.-22 Mar.; 15 Apr.-14 June.
Number of students: (1988-89) 12,110 full-time and part-time.
Chancellor: The Lord Grey of Naunton, G.C.M.G., G.C.V.O., O.B.E., D.Litt, LL.D., D.Sc.
Pro-Chancellors: The Hon. Sir Robert Carswell, S. O'Dwyer, O.B.E., J.P., A.C.I.S.
Vice-Chancellor: Sir Derek Birley, M.A.
Secretary: J.A. Hunter, M.A.
Librarian: B.G. Baggett, B.Sc., M.I.Inf.Sc.

UNIVERSITY OF WALES (1893)

Prifysgol Cymru
University Registry, Cathays Park, Cardiff, South Glamor Glamorgan CF1 3NS.
Chancellor: H.R.H. The Prince of Wales, K.G., K.T.
Pro-Chancellor: The Lord Cledwyn of Penrhos, P.C., C.H., LL.D.
Vice-Chancellor: Professor E. Sutherland, M.A., Ph.D.
Registrar: M.A.R. Kemp, B.Sc., Ph.D.

COLLEGES AND SCHOOLS
(Dates show Michaelmas, Lent and Easter Terms)
Aberystwyth, University College of Wales
Principal: K.O. Morgan, M.A., D.Lit., F.B.A.
2 Oct.-14 Dec. 1990, 8 Jan-22 Mar., 30 Apr.-26 June 1991
Bangor, University College of North Wales *Principal:* E. Sunderland, M.A., Ph.D
3 Oct.-14 Dec. 1990, 14 Jan.-22 Mar., 22 Apr.-21 June 1991.
Cardiff, University of Wales College of Cardiff *Principal:* Sir Aubrey Trotman Dickenson, M.A., Ph.D., D.Sc.
3 Oct.-14 Dec. 1990, 14 Jan.-22 Mar., 22 Apr.-28 June 1991.
Cardiff, University of Wales College of Medicine *Provost:* Professor Sir Herbert L. Duthie, M.D., Ch.M., F.R.C.S.
1 Oct.-14 Dec. 1990, 14 Jan.-22 Mar., 22 Apr.-28 June 1991.
Swansea, University College of Swansea *Principal:* Professor B.L. Clarkson, B.Sc., Ph.D., D.Sc., C.Eng., F.R.Ae.S.
3 Oct.-15 Dec. 1990; 3 Jan.-16 Mar.; 17 Apr.-28 Jun. 1991
Lampeter, St. David's University College *Principal:* The Lord Morris of Castle Morris, M.A., D.Phil.
5 Oct.-14 Dec., 1990; 11 Jan.-15 Mar., 12 Apr.-28 June, 1991.

UNIVERSITY OF WARWICK (1965)

Coventry CV4 7AL.
Full Terms, 1989-90:
3 Oct.-10. Dec., 9 Jan-18 Mar., 24 Apr.-1 July
Number of students: (1987-88) 6,278 including 1,021 post graduates.
Chancellor: The Rt. Hon. Lord Scarman, P.C., O.B.E., M.A.
Pro-Chancellor: Sir Arthur Vick, O.B.E., B.Sc., Ph.D.
Vice-Chancellor: C.L. Brundin, B.S., M.A., Ph.D.
Pro-Vice-Chancellors: A.G. Ford, M.A., D.Phil.; J. Gard Gardner, M.A., Ph.D., F.S.A., F.R.S.A.; T.J. Kemp, M.A., D.Phil., D.Sc.
Treasurer: P.W. Martin, M.A.
Registrar: M.L. Shattock, O.B.E., M.A.
Librarian: P.E. Tucker, M.A., B.Litt.

UNIVERSITY OF YORK (1963)

Heslington, York YO1 5DD.
Terms, 1990-91:
10 Oct.-14 Dec.; 9 Jan.-15 Mar.; 24 Apr.-28 June.
Number of students: (1989-90) 4,410
Chancellor: The Lord Swann, M.A., Ph.D.(Cantab), D.Univ.(York), F.R.S., F.R.S.E.
Pro-Chancellors: The Most Rev. and Rt. Hon. John Habgood, M.A., Ph.D.(Cantab), Hon. DD(Durham), Hon. DD(Cantab), Archbishop of York; Sir Donald Bar ron, B.Com., C.A., D.Univ.(York), C.A.; Kenneth. H.M. Dixon, B.A.(Manchester)
Vice-Chancellor: Professor Berrick Saul, B.Com., Ph.D.(Birmingham), DR honoris causa(Ediinburgh)
Registrar: D.J. Foster, B.A.(Dunelm)

ROYAL COLLEGE OF ART

Kensington Gore, London S.W.7.
(Founded in 1837 and granted university status, 1967)
Terms, 1990-91:
1 Oct.-14 Dec.; 7 Jan.-22 Mar.; 15 Apr.-5 July.
Number of students: (1989-90) 599.
Visitor: H.R.H. The Duke of Edinburgh, K.G., K.T., P.C., O.M., G.B.E.
Provost: The Right Hon. The Earl of Gowrie, PC.
Rector and Vice-Provost: Jocelyn Stevens, F.R.S.A.
Pro-Rector: Professor John Hedgecoe, Dr.R.C.A., F.S.I.A.D., F.C.S.O.
Registrar: Keith Reid.

OPEN UNIVERSITY (1969)

Walton Hall, Milton Keynes MK7 6AA.
Approximate number of students in 1990: 100,000; number of study packs sold: 70,000
Chancellor: J.S. Daniel, M.A. DesSc., Hon. D. Litt., Hon. DesSc.
Secretary: D.J. Clinch, B.A., M.B.A.

The University exists to provide educational opportunities for adults over the age of 18 who wish to study in their own homes and in their own time. There are no formal academic requirements for entry except for some postgraduate courses.

Many students join as undergraduates with the intention of gaining a B.A. degree. In the academic year February to November 1990 five first-year foundation courses are available in Arts (Humanities), Mathematics, Science, Social Sciences and Technology; there are also over 140 second, third and fourth level courses including some in Educational Studies.

Others, however join as Associate students to study a single course for its own sake, whether for personal enrichment, vocational training, profes sional updating or help with everyday practical problems. Some of these courses are available as packs of material which can be bought without the need to register as a student. Through the Open Business School a range of courses in the area of management education are also offered, including an MBA.

Courses are taught by a variety of methods, such as, correspondence texts, weekly radio and television broadcasts, audio and video cassettes, face to face tuition and attendance at residential schools.

Postgraduate degrees and diplomas are also offered, either by research or taught courses.

The broadcasts are prepared in partnership with the BBC, whose producers work with the University's academic staff.

Over 250 Study Centres throughout the United Kingdom provide television and radio facilities, and a place for students to meet specialised subject tutors as well as their own counsellors.

THE UNIVERSITY OF DUBLIN TRINITY COLLEGE (1592)

Dublin 2.
Statutory Terms, 1990-91:
10 Sept.-14 Dec.; 7 Jan.-15 Mar.; 2 Apr.-12 July.
Number of students: (1989-90) 8,614 (including higher degree and part-time).
Chancellor: F.J.C. O'Reilly, B.A., B.A.I., LL.D.(h.c.).
Pro-Chancellors: D.C. Cruise O'Brien, B.A., Ph.D., Litt.D.(h.c.), D.Litt.(h.c.); The Marchioness of Normanby, LL.D.(h.c.) R.P. Willis, M.A.; Sir Peter Froggatt, M.A., M.D., Ph.D., LL.D.(h.c.), D.Sc.(h.c.).
Provost: W.A. Watts, M.A., Sc.D.; W.J.L. Ryan, M.A., Ph.D, D.Econ.Sc.(h.c.)
Registrar: T.B.H. McMurray, M.A., Ph.D., Sc.D., C.Chem.
Deans:
Arts (Humanities): P.H. Kelly, M.A., Ph.D.
Arts (Letters): Barbara Wright, CHEV. DE L'ORDRE DU MERITE, M.A., LL.B., Ph.D.
Business Economic and Social Studies: B. Torode, B.A., Ph.D.
Engineering and Systems Sciences: S.H. Perry, B.Sc.,(Eng), M.A., Ph.D., C.Eng.
Health Sciences: I.J. Temperley, M.A., M.D..
Science: D.L. Weaire, M.A., Ph.D., C.Phys.
Graduate Studies: Helga H.W. Robinson-Hammerstein, M.A., Dr.Phil.
Overseas and Visiting students: R.F. Cox, M.A., Ph.D.

NATIONAL UNIVERSITY OF IRELAND (1908)

Ollscoil na h Eireann
49 Merrion Square, Dublin 2.
The academic year in each College (October until June) consists of three Terms.
Vice-Chancellor: Michael P. Mortell, M.Sc., Ph.D.
Registrar: John Nolan M.A., M.P.A., L.L.D.

CONSTITUENT COLLEGES
Dublin, University College *President:* Patrick Masterson, M.A., Ph.D.
Cork, University College *President:* Michael P. Mortell, M.S., Ph.D.
Galway, University College *President:* Colm O h Eocha, Ph.D., M.Sc., LL.D.

CRANFIELD INSTITUTE OF TECHNOLOGY

Cranfield, Bedford MK43 0AL. Tel: 0908 672974
The Institute was incorporated by Royal Charter in 1969. It has six faculties: Engineering; Management and Administration; Manufacturing Technology and Production Management; Science and Technology; Military Science, Technology and Management; Agricultural Engineering, Food Production and Rural Land Use.
Terms, 1990-91:
2 Oct. -15 Dec.; 13 Jan. -20 Mar.; 23 Apr. -5 July.
(Above dates may vary for particular courses)

Visitor: H.R.H. The Duke of Kent, K.G., G.C.M.G., G.C.V.O., A.D.C., F.Eng., F.R.S.
Chancellor: The Lord Kings Norton, Ph.D., D.I.C., D.Sc., F.Eng.
Pro-Chancellor: The Lord Tombs, B.Sc.(Econ.), F.Eng.
Treasurer: Mr. J.A. Rigg, C.B.E., F.C.A..
Vice-Chancellor: Professor Frank Hartley, D.Sc., C.Chem., F.R.S.C.
Pro-Vice-Chancellors: Professor R.S. Fletcher, B.Sc., Ph.D., D.I.C.; Prof. Hancock, Bsc.Tech, Ph.D.
Secretary and Registrar: J.K. Pettifer, M.A., C.Eng., F.I.E.E.
Director of Finance: D.H. Bate, F.C.A.

BOYS' SCHOOLS

The following list of public schools for boys has been compiled from the schools which are members of the Headmasters' Conference and the Governing Bodies Association.

School	Number of Pupils	Termly Fees		Head
		Boarding	Day	
GREATER LONDON				
* Alleyn's School, Dulwich, S.E.22	924	n/a	1,400	D. A. Fenner
City of London, E.C.4	848	n/a	1,360	B.G. Bass
Colfe's School, SE12 8AW	700	n/a	1,010	Dr. D. Richardson
Dulwich College, S.E.21	1,395	2,640	1,320	A.C.F. Verity
Eltham College, S.E.9	723	2,432	1,232	M. Green
Emanuel School, SW11 1HS	743	n/a	1,099	P.F. Thomson
Forest School, Nr. Snaresbrook, E17 3PY	447	1,815	1,231	J. C. Gough
Hampton School, TW12 3HD	852	n/a	1,040	G.G. Able
Harrow School, HA1 3HW	765	3,000	n/a	I.D.S. Beer
Highgate School, N.6	583	2,545	1,460	R.P. Kennedy
John Lyon School, The, HA2 OHN	508	n/a	1,020	Rev. T.J. Wright
* King Alfred School, Manor Wood NW11 7HY	489	n/a	1,349	F.P. Moran
King's College School, S.W.19	660	n/a	1,326	R. M. Reeve
* Kingston Grammar School, Surrey HT2 6PY	592	n/a	1,220	A.B. Creber
Latymer Upper School, W6 9LR	1,051	n/a	1,130	M. C Pavey
Merchant Taylors' School, HA6 2HT	705	2,350	1,500	D.J. Skipper
Mill Hill School, N.W.7	539	2,550	1,690	A. C. Graham
St. Benedict's, W.5 (R.C.)	813	n/a	1,055	Dr. A. Dachs
St. Dunstan's College, S.E.6	822	n/a	1,030	B. Dance
Trinity School, Croydon CR9 7AT	822	n/a	1,105	R.J. Wilson
St. Paul's School, S.W.13	762	1,591	1,630	Canon P. Pilkington
University College, N.W.3	518	n/a	1,425	G. D. Slaughter
Westminster, S.W.1	605	3,300	2,200	D. M. Summerscale
Whitgift School, South Croydon CR2 6YT	906	n/a	1,140	D.A. Raeburn
COUNTRY				
* Abbotsholme School, Uttoxeter ST14 5BS	261	2,484	1,656	D.J. Farrant
Abingdon School, Abingdon OX14 1DE	724	2,090	1,069	M. St.John Parker
Aldenham School, Elstree, Herts WD6 3AJ	371	2,697	2,083	M. Higginbottom
* Allhallows School, Lyme Regis DT7 3RA	294	2,588	1,360	P. Larkman
Ampleforth College (R.C.), York YO6 4ER	702	2,610	2,158	Rev. D.L. Milroy
* Ardingly College, Sussex RH17 6SQ	487	2,560	2,015	J.W. Flecker
Arnold School, Blackpool FY4 1JG	1,183	1,593	845	J.A.B. Kelsall
Ashville College, Harrogate HG2 9JR	647	1,963	1,067	M.H. Crosby
* Bancroft's School, Woodford Green IG8 ORF	723	n/a	1,170	Dr. P.C.D. Southern
Bangor Grammar Schoo, County Down BT20 5HJ	1,025	n/a	638	T.W. Patton
Barnard Castle School, Co. Durham DL12 8UN	580	1,761	1,024	F.S. McNamara
Batley Grammar School, Batley WF17 0AD	635	n/a	750	C.S. Parker
* Battle Abbey Achool, Battle, E. Sussex TN33 0AD	239	1,990	990	D.J.A. Teall
* Bedales School, Petersfield GU32 2DG	394	2,719	1,949	E.A.M. MacAlpine
Bedford Modern School, Bedford MK14 7NT	1,002	n/a	1,677	P.J. Squire
Bedford School, Bedford MK40 2TU	878	2,253	1,412	M.E. Barlen
* Belfast Royal Academy, Belfast BT14 6JL	1,575	n/a	750	W.M. Sillery
Berkhampstead Schhol, Herts HP4 2BB	483	2,138	1,339	Revd. K.H. Wilkinson
Birkenhead School, Birkenhead L43 2JA	1,010	n/a	827	S.J. Haggett
Bishop's Stortford College, Herts CM23 2QZ	367	2,420	1,880	S.G.G. Benson
Bloxham School, Oxon OX15 4PE	354	2,555	1,748	M.W. Vallance
Blundell's School, Devon EX16 14DN	477	2,800	1,700	A.J.D. Rees
Bolton School (Boys Div.), Bolton BL1 4PA	997	n/a	929	A.W. Wright
* Bootham School, York YO3 7BU	335	2,278	1,525	I.M. Small
Bradfield College, Reading RG7 6AR	534	2,750	2,062	P.B. Smith
* Bradford Grammar School, Bradford BD9 4JP	1,160	n/a	912	D.A.G. Smith
Brentwood School, Essex CM15 8AS	890	2,148	1,228	J.A.E. Evans
* Brighton College, Brighton BN2 2AL	487	2,145	1,590	J.D. Leach
Bristol Cathedral School, Bristol BS1 5TS	428	n/a	935	R.A. Collard
* Bristol Grammar School, Bristol BS8 1SR	986	n/a	896	C.E. Martin
* Bromsgrove School, Bromsgrove B61 7DU	535	2,228	1,396	T.M. Taylor
* Bryanston School, Blandford DT11 OPX	662	2,860	1,906	T.D. Wheare
Bury Grammar School, Bury BL9 OHN	750	n/a	737	K. Richards
Campbell College, Belfast BT4 2ND	417	2,052	1,062	Dr. R.J. Pollack
Canford School, Wimborne, Dorset BH21 3AD	522	2,755	1,960	M.M. Marriott
Charterhouse, Godalming GU7 2DJ	698	2,900	2,410	P.J. Attenborough
* Cheadle Hulme School, Cheadle SK8 6EF	1,079	1,970	914	D.J. Wilkinson
Cheltenham College, Cirencester GL17 1TV	547	2,720	2,040	R.M. Morgan
Chigwell School, Essex 1GF 6QF	326	2,064	1,954	A.R.M. Little
Christ College, Brecon LD3 8AG	360	1,860	1,410	S.W. Hockey
* Christ's Hospital, Horsham RH13 7LS	844	2,250	n/a	R.C. Poulton
Churcher's College, Petersfield GU31 4AS	448	2,016	1,129	G.W. Buttle
* City of London Freeman's School, Ashtead Park KT21 1ET	673	2,020	1,375	D.C. Haywood
* Clifton College, Bristol BS8 3JH	673	2,890	1,220	A.H. Mouro

School	Number of Pupils	Termly Fees		Head
		Boarding	Day	
Coleraine Academical Institution, Coleraine BT51 3LA	855	1,282	578	R.S. Forsythe
Colston's School, Bristol BS16 1BJ	319	1,840	1,145	S.B. Howarth
* Coventry School, Coventry CV1 4AU	1,925	n/a	770	R. Cooke
* Culford School, Bury St. Edmunds IP28 6TX	695	2,103	1,369	D. Robson
Dame Allan's School, Newcastle-upon-Tyne NE3 9YJ	452	n/a	843	T.A. Willcocks
Daniel Stewart's & Melville Coll., Edinburgh EH4 3EZ	781	1,782	924	P.F.J. Tobin
* Dauntsey's School, Nr. Devizes SN10 4HE	600	2,290	1,410	C.R. Evans
* Dean Close School, Cheltenham GL51 6HE	439	2,565	1,675	C.J. Bacon
* Denstone College, Uttoxeter ST14 5HN	342	2,330	1,660	R.M. Ridley
* Dollar Academy, Clackmananshire FK14 7DU	1,108	1,876	860	L. Harrison
Douai School (R.C.), Reading RG7 5Th	305	2,271	1,431	Rev. G. Scott
* Dover College, Kent CT17 9RH	290	2,550	1,685	J.K. Ind
Downside School (R.C.), Bath BA3 4RJ	465	2,402	1,537	Dom P.Webb
* Dundee High School, Dundee DD1 9BP	1,138	n/a	876	R. Nimmo
* Durham School, Durham DH1 4SZ	387	2,144	1,681	M.A. Lang
Eastbourne College, Eastbourne BN21 4JX	542	2,238	1,647	C.J. Saunders
Edinburgh Academy, The, Edinburgh EH3 5BL	579	2,315	1,205	L.E. Ellis
Elizabeth College, Guernsey	758	1,315	495	J.H.M. Doulton
Ellesmere College, Shropshire SY12 9AB	398	2,400	1,700	D.R. Du Croz
Epsom College, Surrey KT17 4JQ	665	2,560	1,790	Dr. J.B. Cook
Eton College, Windsor SL4 6DW	1,272	2,832	n/a	Dr. W.E.K. Anderson
Exeter School, Exeter EX2 4NS	682	1,668	905	G.T. Goodall
* Fettes College, Edinburgh EH4 1QX	375	2,785	1,870	M.T. Thyne
Fort Augustus Abbey School (R.C.), Inverness PH32 4DB	58	2,100	1,281	Revd. T.E. Delepine
* Framlington College, Suffolk IP13 9EY	442	2,119	1,360	J.F.X. Miller
* Frensham Heights, Farnham GU10 4EA	261	2,720	1,710	A.L. Pattinson
* Friends' School, Middleborough TS9 6BN	186	2,019	936	D. Cook
* George Heriot's School, Edinburgh EH3 9EQ	1,441	n/a	860	K.P. Pearson
* George Watson's College, Edinburgh EH10 5EG	2,130	1,782	924	F.E. Gerstenberg
* Giggleswick School, Settle BD24 0DE	290	2,470	1,650	P. Hobson
Glasgow, The High School of, Glasgow G13 1PL	955	n/a	890	R.G. easton
Glasgow Academy, Glasgow G12 8HE	830	n/a	987	C.W. Turner
Glenalmond College, Perthshire PH1 3RY	319	2,750	n/a	S.R.D. Hall
* Gordonstoun School, Moray IV30 2RF	451	2,900	1,860	M.C.S.R. Pyper
* Gresham's School, Norfolk NR25 6EA	477	2,665	1,970	H.R. Wright
Haberdashers' Aske's School, Borehamwood, Herts WD6 3AF	1,104	n/a	1,314	K. Dawson
Haileybury, Hertford SG13 7NU	655	2,833	1,870	D.J. Jewell
* Hereford Cathedral School, Hereford HR1 2NN	599	1,705	995	Dr. H.C. Tomlinson
Hulme Grammar School, Lancs OL8 4BX	867	n/a	812	G.F. Dunkin
Hurstpierpoint College, West Sussex BN6 9JS	414	2,070	1,610	S.A. Watson
* Hutcheson's Grammar School, Glasgow G41 4NW	1,623	n/a	753	D.R. Ward
Hymer's College, Hull, N. Humberside HU3 1LW	900	n/a	796	B.G. Bass
Ipswich School, Ipswich IP1 3SG	622	1,954	1,166	Dr. J.M. Blatchly
* Kelly College, Devonshire PL19 0HZ	356	2,510	1,660	C.H. Hirst
Kelvinside Academy, Glasgow G12 0SW	663	n/a	910	J.H. Duff
* Kent College, Canterbury CT2 9DT	553	2,329	1,254	R.J. Wicks
* Kimbolton School, Huntingdon PE18 0EA	701	1,995	1,119	R.V. Peel
King Edward VI School, Southampton SO9 3FP	963	n/a	995	T.R. Cookson
King Edward VII School, Lancs FY8 1DT	647	n/a	763	D. Heap
King Edward's School, Bath BA2 6HU	661	n/a	942	J.P. Wroughton
King Edward's School, Birmingham B15 2UA	766	n/a	960	M.J.W. Rogers
* King William's College, Isle of Man	381	2,210	1,555	S. A. Westley
* Kingswood School, Bath BA1 5RG	483	2,385	1,550	G.M. Best
King's College, Taunton, Somerset TA1 3DX	475	2,560	1,904	R.S. Funnell
King's School, Bruton, Somerset BA10 0ED	333	2,520	1,800	A.H. Beadles
* King's School, Cambridgeshire CB7 4DB	411	2,586	1,737	H.Ward
* King's School, Canterbury CT1 2ES	696	2,695	1,885	Canon A.C.J. Phillips
King's School, Chester CH4 7QL	578	n/a	920	A.R.D. Wickson
King's School, Macclesfield SK10 1DA	996	n/a	955	A.G. Silcock
King's School, Rochester ME1 1TD	371	2,205	1,325	Dr. I.R. Walker
King's School, The, Worcester WR1 2LH	708	1,854	1,169	Dr. J.M. Moore
* Kirkham Grammar School, Preston, Lancs PR4 2BH	511	1,360	740	M.J. Summerlee
Lancing College, Sussex BN15 0RW	556	2,640	1,836	J.S. Woodhouse
Leeds Grammar School, Leeds LS6 1AN	1,169	n/a	7966	B. W. Collins
Leighton Park School, Reading RG2 7DH	347	2,640	1,953	J.A. Chapman
Leys School, The, Cambridge CB2 2AD	386	2,633	1,955	J.C.A. Barrett
Liverpool College, Liverpool L18 8BE	664	1,755	974	R.V. Haygarth
* Llandovery College, Dyfed SA20 0EE	241	1,595	953	Dr. Claude E. Evans
* Lomond School, Dunbartonshire G84 9JX	490	2,115	928	A.D. Macdonald
* Lord Wandsworth College, Basingstoke RG25 1TB	440	2,100	1,640	G.A.G. Dodd
Loretto School, East Lothian EH21 7RE	306	2,650	1,881	Rev. N.W. Drummond

5

School	Number of Pupils	Termly Fees		Head
		Boarding	Day	
Loughborough Grammar School, Loughborough LE11 2DU	882	1,833	976	D.N. Ireland
Magdalen College School, Oxford OX4 1DZ	505	1,892	989	W.B. Cook
Malvern College, Worcs WR14 3DF	582	2,695	1,960	R. de C. Chapman
Manchester Grammar School, Manchester M13 0XT	1,449	n/a	957	J.G. Parker
Marlborough College, Wilts SN8 1PA	887	2,970	n/a	D.R. Cope
Merchant Taylors' School, Liverpool L23 0QP	801	n/a	928	S.J.R. Dawkins
Merchiston Castle School, Edinburgh EH13 0PU	369	2,560	1,650	D.M. Spawforth
* Methodist College, Belfast BT9 6BY	2,163	985	353	Dr. J. Kincade
* Millfield Senior School, Somerset BA16 0YD	1,240	2,885	1,635	C.S. Martin
Monkton Coombe School, Bath BA2 7HG	330	2,575	1,875	M.J. Cuthbertson
Monouth School, Monmouth NP5 3XP	620	1,867	1,132	R.D. Lane
* Morrison's Academy, Perthshire PH7 3AN	765	1,960	790	H.A. Ashmall
Mount St. Mary's College (R.C.), Sheffield S31 9YL	288	1,948	1,316	Rev. J.F.M. Grumitt
* Newcastle-under-Lyme School, Staffs ST5 1DB	1,387	n/a	787	D.M. Reynolds
Norwich School, Norwich NR1 4DQ	762	1,660	955	C.D. Brown
Nottingham High School, Nottingham NG7 4ED	827	n/a	965	Dr. D.T. Witcombe
* Oakham School, Rutland LE15 6DT	984	2,609	1,397	G. Smallbone
Oratory School (R.C.), The, Reading RG8 OPJ	395	2,506	1,753	M.K. Lynn
Oundle School, Peterborough PE8 4EN	727	2,900	n/a	D.B. McMurray
Pangbourne College, Reading RG8 8LA	358	2,470	1,730	A.B.E. Hudson
* Park School, The, Bournemouth BH8 9BJ	232	n/a	686	Mrs. J. Carter
Perse School, Cambridge CB2 2QF	488	1,955	1,013	Dr. G.M. Stephen
Plymouth College, Plymouth PL4 6RN	685	2,010	1,055	A.M. Joyce
Pocklington School, York YO4 2NJ	707	1,906	1,031	A.D. Pickering
* Portora Royal School, Co. Fermanagh BT74 7HA	326	1,440	769	R.L. Bennett
Portsmouth Grammar School, Portsmouth PO1 2LN	749	n/a	948	A.C.V. Evans
* Prior Park College, Bath BA2 5AH,	386	2,245	1,242	J.W.R. Golding
Queen Elizabeth Grammar School, Wakefield WF1 3QY	738	1,486	913	R.P. Mardling
Queen Elizabeth's Grammar School, Blackburn BB2 6DF	1,236	n/a	875	P.F. Johnston
Queen Elizabeth's Hospital, Bristol, BS8 1JX	475	1,580	944	Dr. R. Gliddon
* Queen's College, Taunton, Somerset TA1 4QS	437	1,995	1,360	A.P. Hodgson
Radley College, Abingdon OX14 2HR	606	2,750	n/a	D.R.W. Silk
* Ratcliffe College (R.C.), Leicester LE7 8SG	418	1,998	1,332	Rev. L.G. Hurdidge
Reed's School, Cobham, Surrey KT11 2ES	351	2,215	1,600	D.E. Prince
Reigate Grammar School, Surrey RH2 0QS	849	n/a	1,011	J.G. Hamlin
Rendcomb College, Nr. Cirencester GL7 7HA	263	2,350	n/a	J.N. Tolputt
Repton School, Derby DE6 5PA	562	2,630	1,950	G.E. Jones
Robert Gordon's College, Aberdeen AB9 1FR	1,150	1,280	580	G.A. Allan
* Rossall School, Lancs FY7 8JW	482	2,568	1,792	R. D. W. Rhodes
Royal Belfast Academical Inst., Belfast BT1 6DL	907	n/a	550	T.J. Garrett
Royal Grammar School, Guildford GU1 3BB	789	n/a	1,255	J. Daniel
Royal Grammar School, Worcester WR1 1HP	872	1,725	1,035	T.E. Savage
Rugby School, Warwickshire CV22 6QU	688	2,850	1,650	O.R.S. Bull
* Rydal School, Colwyn bay LL29 7BP	346	2,065	1,570	P.F. Watkinson
* Ryde School, Isle of Wight PO33 3BE	417	1,915	1,042	M. D. Featherstone
Sedburgh School, Cumbria LA10 5HG	490	2,540	1,780	Dr. R.G. Baxter
* Sevenoaks School, Sevenoaks TN13 1HU	911	3,102	1,965	R.P. Barker
Sherborne School, Dorset DT9 3AP	657	2,825	2,150	P.H. Lapping
Shrewsbury School, Shrewsbury SY3 7BA	674	2,700	1,905	F.E. Maidment
Sibford School, Banbury OX15 5QL	350	2,065	1,053	J. Dunston
Silcoates School, Wakefield WF2 0PD	550	2,160	1,230	J.C. Baggaley
Stamford School, Lincs PE9 2BS	571	1,760	880	G.J. Timm
Stoneyhurst College (R.C.), Blackburn BB6 9PZ	435	n/a	1,289	Dr. R.G.G. Mercer
Stowe School, Buckingham MK18 5EH	585	2,886	2,020	J.G.L. Nichols
* Strathallan School, Perth PH12 9EG	549	2,550	n/a	C.D. Pighills
St. Albans School, At. Albans AL3 4HB	670	n/a	1,145	S.C. Wilkinson
St. Anselm's College (R.C.), Birkenhead L43 1UQ	819	n/a	712	Rev. C.J. Sreenan
St. Augustine's College (R.C.), Westgate-on-Sea CT8 8NL	123	2,060	1,310	K.C. Doherty
St. Bede's College (R.C.), Manchester M16 8HX	1,031	1,554	854	J. Byrne
* St. Bees School, Cumbria CA27 ODU	360	2,370	1,655	P.A. Chamberlain
* St. Edmund's College, Ware, Herts SG11 1DS	606	2,058	1,323	D.J.J. McEwen
* St. Edmund's School, Canterbury CT2 8HU	312	2,535	1,621	J.V. Tyson
St. Edward's College (R.C.), Liverpool L12 1LF	868	n/a	763	Rev. B.D. Sassi
St. Edward's School, Oxford OX2 7NN	562	2,755	2,070	D. Christie
St. George's College (R.C.), Weybridge KT15 2QS	469	2,065	1,394	Rev. J.W. Munton
St. John's College (R.C.), Southsea PO5 3QW	882	1,500	750	Rev. Brother Cyril
St. John's School, Leatherhead KT22 8SP	480	2,194	1,584	D.E. Brown
St. Joseph's College (R.C.), Ipswich IP2 9DR	709	1,702	934	Rev. D. Hennessy
* St. Lawrence College, Ramsgate CT11 7AE	373	2,370	1,585	J.H. Binfield
* St. Mary's College (R.C.), Merseyside L23 3AB	798	n/a	915	Rev. P.E. Ryan
* St. Peter's School, York YO3 6AB	467	2,332	1,471	R.N. Pittman
* Sutton Valence School, Maidstone ME17 3HL	410	2,450	1,633	M.R. Haywood
* Taunton School, Somerset TA2 6AD	566	2,584	1,673	B.B. Sutton

School	Number of Pupils	Termly Fees		Head
		Boarding	**Day**	
* Tettenhall College, Wolverhamton WV6 8QX	458	2,042	1,258	W.J. Dale
* Thetford Grammar School, Norfolk IP24 3AF	316	n/a	939	J.R. Weeks
Trent College, Nottingham NG10 4AD	610	2,262	1,378	J.S. Lee
Truro School, Cornwall TR1 3QN	863	1,815	1,150	B.K. Hobbs
* Uplands School, Parkstone, Poole BH14 9JY	353	n/a	880	Miss C.E. Kirkpatrick
Uppingham School, Leics LE15 9QE	662	2,850	n/a	N.R. Bomford
Victoria College, St. Helier, Jersey	596	2,108	430	M.H. Devenport
Warwick School, Warwick CV34 6PP	978	2,030	1,003	P.J. Cheshire
* Wellingborough School, Northants NN8 2BX	440	2,035	1,312	G. Garrett
Wellington College, Crowthorne RG11 7PU	821	2,800	1,990	C.J. Driver
* Wellington School, Somerset TA21 8NT	794	1,730	971	J. MacG. Kendall-Carpenter
* Wells Cathedral School, Wells BA5 2ST	595	1,968	1,159	J.S. Baxter
* West Buckland School, Barnstaple EX32 0SX	556	1,906	1,089	M. Downward
William Hulme's Grammar School, Manchester M16 8PR	792	n/a	975	P.D. Briggs
Winchester College, Hampshire SO23 9NA	655	2,886	2,165	J.P. Sabben-Clare
Wolverhampton Grammar School, W. Midlands WV3 9RB	623	n/a	1,072	P.H. Hutton
* Woodbridge School, Suffolk IP12 4JH	542	2,010	1,218	Dr. D. Younger
* Woodhouse Grove School, Bradford BD10 0NR	570	1,835	1,125	D.A. Miller
* Worcester College for the Blind, Worcester WR5 2JX	110	4,353	2,539	Rev B.R. Manthop
* Worksop College, Notts S80 3AP	416	2,340	1,595	R.D.V. Knight
Worth School (R.C.), Crawley RH10 4SD	405	2,445	n/a	Rev. R.S. Ortiger
* Wrekin College, Shropshire TF1 3BG	386	2,465	1,686	J.H. Arkell
Wycliffe College, Stonehouse, Gloucs GL10 2JQ	302	2,074	1,381	A.P. Millard

* Co-educational

GOVERNING BODIES ASSOCIATION (G.B.A.)

Founded in 1941. Most independent scondary schools for boys and co-educational schools are members of the G.B.A. Current membership 285 schools in cluding six schools in Europe of a similar character.

GIRLS' SCHOOLS

The following list of schools for girls has been compiled from the schools which are members of the Association of Governing Bodies of Girls' Schools, the Schools of the Girls' Public Day School Trust, the Woodard Corporation and the Church Schools' Company Limited.

School	Number of Pupils	Termly Fees		Head
		Boarding	**Day**	
LONDON				
Channing School, N6 5HF	446	n/a	1,188	Mrs. I. R. Raphael
Francis Holland School, Clarence Gate, NW1 6XR	351	n/a	1,080	Mrs P. Parksonson
Francis Holland School, SW1W 8LF	337	n/a	1,120	Mrs. J. A. Anderson
Godolphin and Latymer, W6 0PG	698	n/a	1,191	Miss M.F. Rudland
Queen's College, W1N 2BT	408	1,675	1,165	Mrs. P. J. Fleming
St. Paul's Girls' School, W6 7BS	634	n/a	1,300	Mrs. Helen Williams
Girls' Public Day School Trust:				
Blackheath High School SE3 0TF,	538	n/a	900	Miss R.K. Musgrove
Notting Hill and Ealing High School, W13 8AX	766	n/a	900	Mrs. C. J. Fitz
Putney High School, SW15 6BH	825	n/a	900	Mrs. P. A. Penney
South Hampstead High School, NW3 5SS	668	n/a	900	Mrs. D. A. Burgess
Streatham Hill and Clapham High School, SW2 3SR	529	n/a	900	Miss G. M. Ellis
Sydenham High School, SE26 6BL	659	n/a	900	Mrs. G. Baker
Wimbledon High School SW19 4AB	714	n/a	969	Mrs. R. A. Smith
COUNTRY				
Abbey School, The, Reading, RG1 5DZ	1,081	n/a	950	Miss S. M. Hardcastle
Abbots Bromley (School of S. Mary and S. Anne), Rugeley, Staffs, WS15 3BW	276	1,810	1,140	Mrs. B. Harbron
Abbot's Hill, Hemel Hempstead HP3 8RP	146	2,220	1,300	Mrs. J. Kingsley
Alice Ottley School, Worcester WR14 3HE	677	1,890	980	Miss C. Sibbit
Ashford School, Kent, TN24 8PB	536	1,938	1,120	Mrs. A. T. D. Macaire
Badminton School, Bristol, BS9 3BA	354	2,475	1,360	C. J. T. Gould
Bedford High School, Bedford, MK40 2BS	1,047	1,534	840	Mrs. D. M. Willis
Bedgebury School, Cranbrook, Kent, TN17 2SH	394	2,328	1,380	Mrs M. E. A. Kaye
Benenden School, Cranbrook, Kent, TN17 4AA	402	2,750	n/a	Mrs. G. duCharme
Berkhamsted School for Girls, Herts, HP4 3BG	573	1,782	1,064	Miss V. E. M. Shepherd
Bolton School (Girls Div.), Bolton, BL1 4PB	1,128	n/a	878	Mrs. M. A. Spurr
Bradford Girls Grammar School, W. Yorks, BD96RB	897	n/a	816	Miss L. J. Warrington
Bruton School for Girls, Somerset, BA10 0NT	548	1,450	800	Mrs J. M. Wade
Bury Girls Grammar School, Bury BL9 0HH	1,129	n/a	737	Miss J. M. Lawley

School	Number of Pupils	Termly Fees		Head
		Boarding	Day	
Casterton School, Kirkby Lonsdale, Cumbria, LA6 2SG	388	1,767	1,067	G. Vinestock
Charters-Ancaster College, Bexhill-on-Sea, TN40 2JQ	385	1,825	900	Mrs. K. Lewis
Cheltenham Ladies' College, Cheltenham, GL50 3EP	845	2,650	1,685	Miss E. Castle
Clifton High School for Girls, Bristol, BS8 3JD	746	1,920	1,035	Mrs. J. D. Walters
Cobham Hall School, Kent, DA12 3BL	288	2,900	1,940	Mrs. R.J. McCarthy
Colston's Girls' School, Bristol, BS6 5RD	658	n/a	705	Miss A. C. Parkin
Croft House School, Blandford, DT11 0QS	194	2,090	1,452	Mrs. Susan Rawlinson
Croham Hurst School, South Croydon, CR2 7YN	580	n/a	894	Miss J. M. Shelmerdine
Dame Alice Harpur School, The, Bedford, MK42 0BX	1,042	n/a	689	Miss S. M. Morse
Dame Allan's Girls' School, Newcastle upon Tyne, NE4 3RJ	447	n/a	788	T. A. Willcocks
Derby High School for Girls, Derby DE3 7DT,	481	n/a	985	Dr. G. H. Goddard
Downe House, Newbury, Berks, RG16 9JJ	461	2,350	1,770	Miss S.R. Cameron
Durham High School, Durham, DH1 4SZ,	450	n/a	825	Miss B. E. Stephenson
Edgbaston High School for Girls Birmingham	897	n/a	966	Mrs S. J. Horsman
Edgehill College, Bideford, Devon, EX39 3LY	529	1,985	1,152	Mrs E. M. Burton
Ellerslie School, Malvern, Worcs, WR14 3HF	233	2,400	1,600	Mrs. E. Baker
Elmslie Girls School, Blackpool, FY3 9HL	365	n/a	858	Miss E. M. Smithies
Felixstowe College, Suffolk, IP11 7NQ	297	2,375	1,455	Mrs A.F.E. Woodings
Godolphin School Salisbury, Wilts, SP1 2RA	315	2,350	1,395	Mrs. H.A. Fender
Haberdashers' Aske's School, The, Elstree, WD63AF	1,096	n/a	1800	Mrs. S. Wiltshire
Haberdashers' Monmouth School, Monouth, NP53XT	635	1,757	997	Miss H. L. Gichard
Harrogate Ladies College, Harrogate, HG1 2QG,	397	2,010	1,338	Mrs. J. C. Lawrance
Headington School, Oxford, OX3 7TD	684	1,845	993	Miss E. M. Tucker
Howell's School, Denbigh, LL16 3EN,	351	2,270	1,420	Miss P. Dixon
Hulme Grammar School for Girls, Oldham, OL8 4BX	589	n/a	860	Mrs. A. Groom
Hunmanby Hall School, Filey, YO14 OJA,	199	2,170	1,170	Miss J. Rutherford
Huyton College, Liverpool, L36 5XQ	320	2,240	1,041	Miss W. E. Edwards
King's High School for Girls, Warwick, CV32 4HJ	525	n/a	804	Mrs. J. M. Anderson
Kingsley School, Leamington Spa,	498	1,770	929	Mrs. M.A. Webster
Lady Eleanor Holles School, Middlesex, TW12 3HF	803	n/a	1,045	Miss E. M. Candy
Lawnside School, Great Malvern, WR14 3AJ	114	2,340	1,450	Miss D. M. M. Stewart
Loughborough High School, Leics, LE11 2DU	524	1,390	878	Miss J. E. L. Harvatt
Malvern Girls College, Worcs, WR14 3BA	511	2,475	1,650	Dr. V. B. Payne
Manchester High School for Girls, Manchester, M14 6HS	986	n/a	876	Miss M. M. Moon
Mary Erskine School, Ravelston, Edinburgh, EH43NT	562	1,782	924	P.F.J. Tobin
Maynard School, Exeter, EX1 1SJ	529	n/a	953	Miss F. Murdin
Merchant Taylors' School for Girls, Crosby,.L23 5SP	819	n/a	928	Miss E. J. Panton
Micklefield School, Seaford, BN25 4LP	208	2,160	1,250	E. Reynolds
Mount School, The, York, YO14 0JA	300	2,278	1,525	Miss B. J. Windle
Newcastle upon Tyne Church High School, NE2 3BA	612	n/a	858	Miss P. E. Davies
Northampton High School for Girls, Northants, NN1 1UN	782	n/a	957	Miss L. A. Mayne
North London Collegiate School, Edgware, HA8 7RJ	889	n/a	1,088	Mrs. J. L. Clanchy
Northwood College, Middlesex, HA6 2YE	545	1,761	1,043	Mrs D. K. Dalton
Oakdene School, Beaconsfield, HP9 2BS	260	1,980	1,150	Miss A. M. Tippett
Ockbrook School, Nr. Derby, DE7 3RJ	362	1,389	781	Dr. M. Rennie
Park School, Glasgow, G3 6EX	368	n/a	891	Mrs. M. E. Myatt
Park School, The, Yeovil, BA20 1DH	208	1,580	730	Mrs M. J. Hannon
Penrhos College, Colwyn Bay, LL28 4DA	426	2,125	1,420	N. C. Peacock
The Perse School for Girls, Cambridge, CB2 1HF	703	n/a	928	Miss H.S. Smith
Polam Hall School, Darlington, DL1 5PA	340	1,865	965	Mrs. H. C. Hamilton
Princess Helena College, Hitchin, SG4 7RT	177	2,200	1,590	Dr. Donald Clarke
Queen Anne's School, Caversham, RG4 0DX	403	2,400	1,500	Miss A. M. Scott
Queen Ethelburga's School, Harrogate, HG3 2SG	179	2,135	1,280	Mrs. J.M. Town
Queen Margaret's School, York, YO14 6EU	357	2,250	1,425	C. S. McGarrigle
Queen Mary School, Lytham, FY8 1DS	694	n/a	634	Miss M. C. Ritchie
Queen's School, Chester, CH1 2NN	577	n/a	810	Miss D.M. Skilbeck
Queenswood School, Hatfield, AL9 6NS	388	2,500	n/a	Mrs. Audrey Butler
Redland High School, Bristol, BS6 7EF	620	n/a	851	Mrs. Carol Lear
Red Maids' School, Bristol, BS9 3AW	470	1,700	850	Miss S. Hampton
Roedean School, Brighton, BN2 5RQ	462	2,885	n/a	Mrs. A. R. Longley
Rosemead School, Littlehampton, BN17 6AL	260	2,200	1,275	Mrs J. Bevis
Royal Naval School, Haslemere, GU27 1HQ	296	2,022	1,348	Dr J. L. Clough
St. Alban's High School, Herts, AL1 3SJ	689	n/a	1,172	Miss E. M. Diggory
St. Anne's School, Windermere, LA23 1NW	404	2,253	1,476	M. P. Hawkins
St. Audries School, W. Quantoxhead Nr. Taunton, TA4 4DU	175	2,061	1,230	Mrs. A Smith
St. Catherine's School, Guildford, GU5 0DF	452	2,100	1,280	J. R. Palmer
St. Columba's School, Kilmacolm, Renfrewshire, PA13 4AU	450	n/a	759	Mr. A. H. Livingstone
St. David's School, Ashford, Middlesex TW15 3DZ	315	1,506	874	Mrs. Judith Osborne
St. Dunstan's Abbey, Plymouth, PL1 5DH	337	1,455	940	Miss H. L. Abley
St. Elphin's School, Matlock, DE4 2HA	351	2,130	1,240	A. P. C. Pollard
St. Felix School, Southwold, Suffolk, IP18 6SD	343	2,235	1,381	Miss M. A. Claydon

School	Number of Pupils	Termly Fees Boarding	Termly Fees Day	Head
St. George's School, Southwold, Suffolk, IP18 6SD	63	1,531	851	Mrs W. Martin
St. Helen's School, Northwood, Middx, HA6 3AS	919	1,925	1,077	Mrs Y. Burne
St. James's and The Abbey, West Malvern WR144DF	164	2,300	1,534	Miss Elizabeth Mullenger
St. Leonards School, St. Andrews, Fife, KY16 9QU	422	2,650	1,350	Mrs. L.E. James
St. Margaret's School for Girls, Aberdeen, AB9 1RH	418	n/a	760	Miss L Ogilvie
St. Margaret's School, Bushey, Herts, WD2 1DT	460	1,845	1,140	Mrs. S. Law
St. Margaret's School, Exeter, EX2 4PF	448	n/a	909	Mrs. J. M. Giddings
St. Mary's Hall, Brighton, BN2 5JF	404	2,083	1,379	Mrs. M. Teresa Broadbent
St. Mary's School, Calne, Wilts, SN11 0DF	429	2,420	1,509	Miss D. H. Burns
St. Mary's School, Wantage, Oxon, OX12 8BZ,	305	2,300	n/a	Mrs. P. H. Johns
St. Michael's School, Limpsfield, Oxted, RH8 0QR	158	2,240	1,300	Dr. Margaret Hustler
School of St. Clare, Penzance, TR18 4JR	244	1,635	905	I. Halford
Sherborne School for Girls, Dorset, DT9 3AP	464	2,465	1,645	Miss J. Taylor
Stamford High School, Lincs, PE9 2LJ	745	1,752	876	Miss G. K. Bland
Stonar School, Melksham, Wiltshire, SN12 8NT	461	2,120	1,170	Mrs. Susan Hopkinson
Talbot Heath School, Bournemouth, BH14 9NJ	575	1,910	1,048	Miss C.E. Austin-Smith
Tormead School, Guildford, GU1 2JD	532	n/a	1,097	Mrs. J. V. Crouch-Smith
Upper Chine School, Shanklin, I.O.W., PO37 6QU	246	1,930	1,070	S.H. Monard
Wadhurst College, Sussex, TN5 6JA	182	2,225	1,395	R.W. Purdom
Wakefield Girls' High School, Wakefield, WF1 2QS	755	n/a	882	Mrs P. A. Langham
Walthamstow Hall, Sevenoaks, TN13 3UL,	526	2,200	1,252	Mrs. Jacqueline Lang
Wentworth Milton Mount, Bournemouth, BH6 2DY	329	1,905	1,140	Miss M. Vokins
Westholme School, Blackburn, BB2 6PS	984	n/a	863	Mrs. L. Croston
Westonbirt School, Tetbury, Glocs, GL8 8QG	261	2,370	1,525	Mrs. G. Hylson-Smith
Wycombe Abbey School, High Wycombe, HP11 1PE	476	2,640	n/a	Mrs. J.M. Goodland
Church Schools' Co. Ltd.:				
Atherley School,The, Southampton, SO9 1GR	457	n/a	960	Mrs. M. Williams
Eothen School, Caterham, Surrey, CR3 6SG	334	n/a	1,063	Miss D. C. Raine
Guildford High School for Girls, Surrey, GU1 1SJ	566	n/a	1,130	Miss J. E. Dutton
Hull High School, Tranby Croft, Anlaby, HU10 7EH	413	1,438	988	Miss C. M. B. Radcliffe
Sunderland Church High School, Sunderland, SR2 8HY	402	n/a	890	Mrs. M. Thrush
Surbiton High School, Kingston upon Thames, KT1 2JT	678	n/a	1,066	Mrs. R. A. Thynne
York College for Girls, York, YO1 2HZ	310	n/a	986	Mrs. J. L. Clare
Girls' Public Day School Trust:				
Bath High School, Bath, BA1 5ES	614	n/a	974	Miss M. A. Winfield
Belvedere School, The, Liverpool, L8 3TF	568	n/a	796	Miss S. Downs
Birkenhead High School, Birkenhead, L43 1TY	932	n/a	796	Mrs. K. R. Irving
Brighton & Hove High School, Brighton, BN1 3AT	729	1,721	796	Miss R.A. Woodbridge
Bromley High School, Kent, BR1 2TW	694	n/a	900	Mrs. W.J. Hancock
Croydon High School, South Croydon, CR2 8YB	1,025	n/a	900	Mrs P.E. Davies
Ipswich High School, Suffolk, IP4 2UH	586	n/a	796	Miss P. M. Hayworth
Heathfield School, Pinner, Middx, HA5 1NB	494	n/a	966	Mrs. J. Merritt
Howell's School Llandaff, Cardiff, CF5 2YD	682	1,749	1,000	Miss J. P. Turner
Norwich High School, Norwich, NR2 2HU	812	n/a	861	Mrs. V. C. Bidwell
Nottingham High School for Girls, NG1 4JB	1,074	n/a	966	Mrs. C. Bowering
Oxford High School, Oxford, OX2 6XJ	650	n/a	796	Mrs. J. Townsend
Portsmouth High School, Hants, PO5 3EQ	652	n/a	796	Mrs. J. M. Dawtrey
Sheffield High School, S. Yorks, S10 2PE	671	n/a	908	Mrs. M. Houston
Shrewsbury High School, Shrewsbury, SY1 1TN	551	n/a	622	Miss E. M. Gill
Sutton High School, Surrey, SM1 2AX	836	n/a	963	Miss A. E. Cavendish

THE GOVERNING BODIES OF GIRLS SCHOOLS ASSOCIATION (G.B.G.S.A.)
Founded in 1942. Most independent secondary schools for girls are members of the G. B. G. S. A. Current membership is 26 schools.

Secretary: *Lt. Col. C. J. M. Hamilton, O.B.E., The Flat, The Lambdens, Beenham, Reading, Berks RG7 5JY. (0734) 302677.*

YOUTH ORGANISATIONS

AIR CADETS
A national voluntary youth organisation under the control of the Ministry of Defence. It is designed to promote air-mindedness, provide training which could be useful in both service and civil walks of life and develop the qualities of leadership and good citizenship through a spirit of adventure and sporting rivalry. 894 Air Training Corps Squadrons are now authorised to recruit girls. The current strength is 44,450 including 8,454 girl cadets. There are 188 CCF (RAF Sections) throughout the United Kingdom. Candidates for entry must be between 13 and 18. Adults wishing to become Civilian Instructors should be between 20-50 years. There are vacancies for female instructors at a number of units throughout the United Kingdom.
Enquiries to: HQ Air Cadets, R.A.F. Newton, Nottingham NG13 8HR.

ARMY CADET FORCE
The Army's voluntary youth organisation. Strength: 46,000 approximately. Boys and girls in selected units are eligible between the ages of 13 and 18. **Address:** Army Cadet Force Association, "E"Block, Duke of York Headquarters, London SW3 4RR. 071-730 9733/4. **General Secretary:** Brigadier R.B. MacGregor-Oakford, C.B.E., M.C.

5 EDUCATION

THE BOYS' BRIGADE
The first voluntary uniformed organisation for boys. Founded 1883 by Sir William A. Smith. Interdenominational. Object, The advancement of Christ's Kingdom among Boys'. Open to boys 6 to 18 years of age. Membership: British Isles 160,000, Overseas 420,000 in 60 countries in membership of the World Conference of The Boys' Brigade and Kindred Organisations. **Patron:** Her Majesty the Queen. **Brigade President:** The Viscount Thurso. **Brigade Secretary:** Sydney Jones, B.A. **Office:** 1 Kings Terrace, Galena Road, Hammersmith, London W6 0LT. 081-741 4001.

THE DUKE OF EDINBURGH'S AWARD SCHEME
The scheme is designed as a challenge to personal achievement for young people between the ages of 14 to 25 years. To gain an award, whether it is Bronze, Silver or Gold, activities must be chosen from the following sections: Service, Expeditions, Skills and Physical Recreation. The scheme encourages young people to widen their interests rather than specialise and genuine effort and perseverance are its chief objectives. In no way is the scheme competitive. The scheme operates through schools, youth centres, clubs, uniformed organisations of the voluntary youth services, police and armed services, church organisations and in industry. The Award programme has now spread to 48 countries. **Director:** Major General Michael Hobbs. Address: 5 Prince of Wales Terrace, London W8 5PG. 071-937 5205.

GIRL GUIDES
Membership: The United Kingdom (1989) 735,297. World Association (1987) 7,803,904. **President:** H.R.H. The Princess Margaret, Countess of Snowdon. **Chief Commissioner:** Mrs Jane Garside, J.P. **General Secretary:** Miss M.W. Hayter, B.A. **Commonwealth Headquarters:** 17-19 Buckingham Palace Road, London SW1W 0PT. 071-834 6242.

GIRLS' BRIGADE
Inter-denominational uniformed organisation for girls. Aim To help girls to become followers of the Lord Jesus Christ and through self-control, reverence and a sense of responsibility to find true enrichment of life'. **Patrons:** Queen Elizabeth the Queen Mother and Princess Alice, Duchess of Gloucester. **National Secretary:** Miss D. Cosser. **National Headquarters:** Girls' Brigade House, Foxhall Road, Didcot, Oxon. OX11 7BQ. 0235 510425.

THE METHODIST ASSOCIATION OF YOUTH CLUBS
MAYC includes youth clubs and fellowships and all non-uniformed work with young people in the Methodist Church. It plays a full part in the nation's youth service and is concerned with the development of the whole person. Membership: (13-25 age group) 90,000. **National Secretary:** The Rev. David Martin. **Address:** 2 Chester House, Pages Lane, London N10 1PR. 081-444 9845.

NATIONAL ASSOCIATION OF BOY'S CLUBS
Founded in 1925, the NABC has some 2,000 affiliated boy's clubs and a membership of 200,000. The Association helps boys during their adolescent years by developing their characters and skills through the club movement. It holds arts festivals, courses in drama and physical training and national football, boxing, athletics, cross country, badminton, angling, canoeing and chess competitions. Courses in club leadership are held regularly for full-time and part time leaders and helpers. Courses on all aspects of boys' club work and activities are also held for senior boys. Constituent organisations include Scottish and Northern Ireland Association of Boys' Clubs and Boys' Clubs of Wales. **National Director:** Derek Harris. **Address:** 369 Kennington Lane, London SE11 5QY. 071-793 0787.

THE NATIONAL FEDERATION OF YOUNG FARMERS' CLUBS
Motto: 'Good Farmers, Good Countrymen, Good Citizens.' Membership is open to ALL young people between the ages of 10 and 26 who are interested in rural life and the countryside. Total membership, 37,000 in 1,000 clubs in England and Wales. **President:** Sir John Cotterell, Bt. D.L. **Central Office:** Y.F.C. Centre, National Agricultural Centre, Kenilworth, Warwickshire CV8 2LG. 0203 696544

THE SCOUT ASSOCIATION
Total world membership, 16,000,000(est). Membership in the United Kingdom over 675,000. **President:** H.R.H. the Duke of Kent. **Chief Scout:** W. Garth Morrison, D.L. **Chief Executive Commissioner:** A.E.N. Black, O.B.E. **Secretary:** J.N. Stevenson, Baden Powell House, Queens's Gate, London SW75JS. 071-584 7030.

SEA CADET CORPS
The Sea Cadet Corps is a voluntary youth organisation for boys and girls between 12 and 18 years of age. Through its discipline and sea training the Corps sets out to help develop the qualities of self discipline, leadership and a sense of responsibility to the community and assist those who are considering a career in the Royal or Merchant Navies, The Royal Marines or the W.R.N.S. However, it is not a pre-service organisation and no cadet is obliged to join the armed forces. The activities available to cadets include sailing, canoeing and adventure training as well as visits to H.M. Ships and training courses in the square rigged sailing brig T.S. Royalist. The Corps is recognised by the Ministry of Defence and is controlled by the Sea Cadet Association. Present strength is about 20,000 cadets in some 400 units throughout the country. Some of the units incorporate Marine Cadet Detachments and have over 200 Girls Nautical Training Contingents. **Sea Cadet Corps Headquarters:** 202 Lambeth Road, Lambeth, London SE1 7JF. 071 928 8978.

YOUNG MEN'S CHRISTIAN ASSOCIATION
The YMCA is an interdenominational Christian organisation which welcomes into membership those of other faiths and those of none. Women are also welcome. It is a voluntary movement which seeks to meet the spiritual, educational, physical and social needs of young people in particular.

The YMCA is one of the world's biggest voluntary organisations with some 26 million members in nearly 100 countries. In England alone, the YMCA has over 250 centres and comes into contact with over one million young people a year. Its diversified programme includes the provision of accommodation, of fitness facilities, of training in youth leadership and of counselling, and of drugs education. It is one of the largest voluntary provider of places on the Youth Training Scheme and one of the largest voluntary providers of recreational facilities. Its National College trains Youth and Community workers. Its two National Outdoor Activity Centres provide an opportunity to discover the challenge of the countryside. Y Care International, the world development wing of the YMCA movements of England, Scotland, Ireland and Wales, seeks to involve young people in furthering development worldwide. **National Council:** 640 Forest Road, London E17 3DZ. 081-520 5599. **National General Secretary:** C. John Naylor.

YOUNG WOMEN'S CHRISTIAN ASSOCIATION OF GREAT BRITAIN
The YWCA is the largest international Christian women's organisation in the world, providing practical help to women and young people in need. This help takes many forms and includes Family Workshops, Women's Centres, Youth Clubs, further education training courses, and detached Youth and Community projects, Throughout its 135 year history, the YWCA has been humane, innovative and pioneering in its approach, conscious of the importance of personal fulfilment for all, regardless of race, creed, political views or nationality. In addition, the YWCA maintains some 4,300 places in its residences throughout Great Britain. These include the well-known hostels which provide single, and shared bedsitting rooms, self-contained flats and small houses providing a 'home from home' for young women with special needs. **Headquarters:** Clarendon House, 52 Cornmarket Street, Oxford OX1 3EJ. 0865 726110. **Executive Director:** Miss F. Elizabeth Sharples.

YOUTH HOSTELS ASSOCIATION
These organisations are formed with the object of helping young people on holiday. Facilities are provided which include beds and meals at very low rate. ENGLAND AND WALES: **National Office:** Trevelyan House, 8 St. Stephen's Hill, St. Albans, Herts AL1 2DY. 0727 55215. **Chief Executive:** Andrew Chinneck. SCOTLAND: **National Office:** 7 Glebe Crescent, Stirling FK8 2JA. 0786 51181. **General Secretary:** J. Martin. NORTHERN IRELAND: **Headquarters:** 56 Bradbury Place, Belfast BT7 1RU. 0232 324733. **Chairman:** R. Magowan.

SECTION 6

INDUSTRY AND COMMERCE

SCIENCE IN 1990

PROJECT JUNO

Late in 1989, the shortlist was announced for the first Briton in space. Our candidates were selected for Project Juno - an Anglo-Soviet mission scheduled for 1991. The four candidates - Tim Mace, Helen Sharman, Gordon Rooks, and Tim Smith were reduced to two - Major Tim Smith of the Army Air Corps and Miss Helen Sharman, a physicist. Both will have an intensive 18-month training program. One of the two will be selected to join Soviet cosmonauts on the flight.

STRANGE MATTER

Some interest was shown by physicists in 1989 in the existence of so-called 'strange matter'. 'Normal' matter has atoms in which the nuclei are composed of protons and neutrons. In turn, these particles are thought to be made up of more fundamental entities called 'quarks'.

According to the current theories of particle physics, quarks exist in six varieties, which are known as 'flavours': namely, up quarks, down quarks, charmed quarks, strange quarks, top quarks, and bottom quarks. In normal matter, protons and neutrons are made up of combinations of only two of these types - the up quarks and the down quarks - and a particle is made up of three of these quarks.

Some theoretical physicists have suggested that there might be another form of stable matter involving up quarks, down quarks, and strange quarks. Although stable, such 'strange matter' would only be formed under highly energetic conditions, such as would have occurred in the early lifetime of the universe shortly after the Big Bang. Although the conditions under which strange matter might be formed only existed for a very brief period after the Big Bang, some physicists believe that there might be remnants of this matter existing in the universe.

Various searches have been made for naturally existing strange matter in the last couple of years - so far without success. It has been suggested, for example, that 'strange stars' (stars composed of strange matter) might be formed in supernovae explosions. More recently, it has been suggested that it might be possible to produce drops of strange matter (called S-drops) in high-energy particle accelerators. One possible use of this is that the S-drops would be a source of energy, absorbing neutrons with release of gamma rays.

PRIME NUMBER

Late in 1989, a group of researchers at Amdahl Corporation, California, found the largest prime number so far known. Prime numbers are of interest to mathematicians; they are numbers that are larger than 1 and divisible only by 1 and themselves. So 2, 3, 5, 7, 11, 13, 17, ... are primes. Euclid, in 275 BC, proved that there is an infinite number of primes but there is no general formula for generating or predicting them.

John Brown and a team of mathematicians in California used a computer to test likely prime numbers and found the record prime. It has 65,087 digits and is not reproduced here; anyone interested in it can find its value by multiplying 2 x 2 x 2 x ... (216,193 times), then multiplying the result by 391,581, then subtracting 1.

MAD CAT DISEASE?

An unlikely contributor to the cause of science came to prominence in 1990. Step forward Miss Cordelia Gummer, aged 4, the daughter of the Minister of Agriculture, Fisheries, and Food, Mr John Gummer. On Wednesday, May 16 1990, Miss Gummer ate a beefburger in Ipswich in full iew of the World's press.

This media event was caused by public concern about a disease of cattle, bovine spongiform encephalopathy, known as BSE. This is a recently recognised condition that attacks the brains of cattle, leading to paralysis, insanity, and death. The popular name for it is mad-cow disease. Miss Gummer was trying to convince the public that beef is safe to eat.

Bovine spongiform encephalopathy is one of a class of diseases caused by slow viruses' - so-called because they have a long incubation period. At this point, the more sensitive reader might prefer to skip the next few paragraphs and continue to read about corn circles later.

The first slow virus to be recognised was identified by the American scientist David Gajdusek in 1963. He was studying the Fore people of New Guinea, who suffered from a localised neurological complaint that they called kuru. He showed that kuru was caused by the Fore's custom of eating the brains of their dead relatives. The disease was passed on by a virus present in the brain and central nervous system. Gajdusek also identified a similar disease - Creutzfeld-Jacob disease - which is a form of pre-senile dementia.

It has also been known for many years that sheep suffer from a similar condition, called scrapie. Anyone who has ever eaten a lamb chop has probably eaten scrapie-infected meat. There has, however, never been any concern about scrapie as a public-health hazard because it has always been considered to be a disease localised to sheep. The discovery of BSE in cattle caused concern because some people claimed that it had been transferred from sheep - in other words, that it could be a slightly changed form of the scrapie virus. Farmers in Britain do not (as far as is known) eat the brains of their dead relatives like the Fore people of New Guinea. They do, however, have a custom that is almost as quaint. They feed ground-up dead sheep to their cattle. This, some believe, is the source of BSE.

The concern about BSE was exacerbated by the discovery, early in 1990, that it could also be transmitted to cats, possibly as a result of eating pet food made from infected animals. To date, seven cats are known to have died from BSE-like brain conditions. The ministry acted quickly, banning the use of the brain and spinal cord of slaughtered animals in human foodstuffs (traditionally, it seems, these have been incorporated into pork pies). The main manufacturers of pet foods brought in a similar voluntary code of practice. The present government position is that there is no danger involved in eating British beef.

According to The Times, Miss Gummer ate her beef burger 'reluctantly'. It is not known whether she was concerned about slow viruses or whether she would have preferred chicken nuggets.

HUBBLE BUBBLE - TOIL AND TROUBLE

One of the major scientific setbacks of 1990 was the partial failure of the American Space Agency NASA on 24 April 1990.

Telescopes on Earth can, these days, be almost perfectly designed to give accurate images and information. The limitation on their use is not in the technology but in the fact that the light (and other radiation) that they collect has to pass thought the Earth's atmosphere. The atmosphere absorbs certain wavelengths of radiation and also distorts reception because of turbulence in the atmosphere or because of atmospheric pollution.

Astronomers describe the quality of the observing conditions as the 'seeing'. This quality is of paramount importance in the siting of telescopes, and explains why many of the world's main observatories are on mountains - Mount Hopkins, Mount Palomar, Mount Strombolo, Mount Wilson, etc. The Royal Greenwich Observatory, founded by Charles II in 1675, moved to Herstmonceux Castle in Sussex in 1954 because atmospheric pollution and extraneous sources of light limited the efficiency of observations. In 1984, the Royal Observatory's Isaac Newton Telescope was moved even further - to the Roque do los Muchachos Observatory in the Canary Islands.

A solution to this problem had been suggested as early as 1923 by the German rocket pioneer Hermann Oberth. He was the first to put forward the idea of a space telescope situated outside the Earth's atmosphere so that distortions caused by the atmosphere could be avoided. At the time the idea was impractical but in 1971 the Americans

started a feasibility study into placing a telescope in satellite orbit. The result was the Hubble project - a refracting telescope in orbit 600 kilometres above the ground with detectors for infrared and ultraviolet radiation as well as visible radiation.

The advantages of a space telescope are potentially enormous. The Hubble telescope was designed to have a resolution ten times greater than that of the best Earth-bound telescope and to be able to detect faint objects some 12 billion light years away. Objects at these distances would have been created early in the life of the universe, following the Big Bang, and would give us information about the conditions at the time. The telescope is named after the American astronomer Edwin Hubble (1889-1953), who first investigated the spectra of distant galaxies and correlated them with the age of the universe.

The telescope consists essentially of two concave mirrors. The primary mirror, with a diameter of 2.4 metres, reflects light and other radiation onto a smaller secondary mirror. From this it is focused onto various detecting instruments; signals from the detectors are relayed to the ground. The design problems in making these mirrors were immense. They had to be optically perfect and not to contract or expand with changes in temperature. In addition, they had to be lighter than mirrors on conventional Earth-based telescopes and have special coatings to reflect ultraviolet and infrared radiation as well as visible light.

Moreover, there are problems in aligning a space telescope to point at a given object. Sensitive gyroscopes detect small changes in the telescope's position and computers adjust the alignment. The orientation is kept steady to an angle of 0.007 arc seconds - equivalent to the angular distance between two sides of a human hair at a distance of one mile. To select a target star, Hubble uses the positions of reference stars, which are kept in a database of the coordinates of 15 million stars and 3 million galaxies.

Given the problems involved, it was a major technological achievement to put a working telescope into orbit. Unfortunately, it quickly became clear that there were problems with adjusting the focus of the telescope. The best result that the NASA scientists could reproduce was a resolution, in the visible region of the spectrum, that was only slightly better than that of the best Earth-based telescopes. It is thought that this was caused by a design flaw in the primary mirror.

This was an obvious problem for the NASA designers - estimates of the cost of the telescope range from $900 million to $1.5 billion to date. The telescope is still useful for its work in the ultraviolet region of the spectrum, but the expected advantages of extra resolution in the visible region have not been achieved. It is possible that NASA may retrieve the telescope in 1993 and replace one of the mirrors.

IS ANYBODY THERE?

Someone, I forget who, once described science as the study of everything that is interesting. One phenomenon that attracted considerable interest in 1990 was that of 'corn circles'. A typical corn (or crop) circle consists of a perfectly circular flattened area of corn or other crops appearing suddenly in a field. More complex patterns are also found - for example, a large circle with four symmetrical smaller circles surrounding it, or a circle with symmetrical rectangular areas on each side, or a spiral structure.

Such circles have been known to farmers for some time and a number of 'explanations' have been put forward to account for them. In the farming community it has always been thought that they were caused by small whirlwinds. An alternative theory has been that they were caused by hedgehogs running in ever decreasing (or possibly increasing) circles. So far there is no consensus in the scientific community as to why hedgehogs should behave in this way, or even why they should be hedgehogs rather than some other mammal.

There are other theories about the cause of crop circles. One is that they are caused by a fungus and are, in fact, some form of giant 'fairy ring'. Another is that they are caused by the landing of extra terrestrial spacecraft.

In July, a group of people set out to investigate this phenomenon scientifically. They kept a watch on a field in Wiltshire from Bratton Hill in a project called Operation Blackbird. On the night of Tuesday, July 24, they saw strange lights hovering over a field. The next day they were delighted to find circles in the cornfield. They were less pleased to find later, after releasing the news, that someone had played a trick on them, leaving ouija boards and wooden crosses as proof.

The joke caused a considerable amount of amusement in the press and on television, but it did harm to what was a genuine attempt to investigate a genuine phenomenon. Crop circles do exist and there must be a reason for them - it is the job of scientists to find it.

July was a bad month for people interested in extraterrestrial life. A project called SETI (Search for Extraterrestrial Life) proposed by NASA was turned down by the US Congress. The project involved using radio telescopes to monitor signals from space in the hope of finding intelligent life. The cost (6 million dollars per year) would not have been great (compare the cost of the Hubble telescope). However, the project will not go ahead, so step forward Republican Congressman Robert Machtley with the silliest quote of 1990, that 'money ought not to be spent on curiosity'.

THE QUEEN'S AWARDS 1990

Established in 1965 as The Queen's Award to Industry, the Scheme recognises outstanding achievement. Any branch of British industry, including agriculture and horticulture as well as exporters of services and merchants, is eligible and can apply for the Award. Firms which win the Award can display the appropriate emblem, on letterheads, flags, packaging and goods. The emblem is dated and the right to use it lapses after five years. In 1976, for the first time, there were two separate Awards: The Queen's Award for Export Achievement, and the Queen's Award for Technological Achievement. The Queen consented to the Awards being announced each year on her birthday, April 21. Out of 1355 applications in 1990 the following 175 firms received an Award.

FOR EXPORT ACHIEVEMENT 1990

Advisory Service Holdings Ltd. Group of Companies, London W1.

AgriSense-BCS Ltd, Pontypridd, Mid-Glamorgan.

Align-Rite Ltd., Bridgend, Mid-Glamorgan.

Apollo Fire Detectors Ltd., Havant, Hampshire.

Aquascutum Group Plc., London W1.

Armabord Ltd., Burnley, Lancashire.

Industrial Clutch Division of Automotive Products Plc., Leamington Spa, Warwickshire.

Baker & McKenzie, London WC2.

Bermans & Nathans Ltd., London NW1.

Biomet Ltd., Bridgend, Mid-Glamorgan.

The Body Shop International Plc., Littlehampton, West Sussex.

Bonas Machine Company Ltd., Gateshead, Tyne & Wear.

Border Holdings (UK) Ltd., Clun, Shropshire.

British Ceramic Service Company Ltd., Newcastle-under-Lyme, Staffordshire.

British Replin Ltd., Ayr, Ayrshire.

British Sidac Ltd., Wigton, Cumbria.

British Steel Stainless, Sheffield, South Yorkshire.

Butterley Brick Ltd., Ripley, Derbyshire.

C & S Antennas Ltd., Rochester, Kent.

C.B. Brook & Company Ltd., Bradford, West Yorkshire.

Caledonian Airmotive Ltd., Prestwick, Ayrshire.

Cambridge Research Biochemicals Ltd., Cambridge, Cambridgeshire.

Chaucer Foods Ltd., Ashford, Kent.

Chivas Brothers Ltd., Paisley, Renfrewshire.

The College of Petroleum Studies, Oxford, Oxfordshire.

Courtaulds Speciality Plastics, Derby, Derbyshire.

Crabtree of Gateshead Ltd., Gateshead, Tyne & Wear.

Crockett & Jones Ltd., Northampton, Northamptonshire.

Crosrol Ltd., Halifax, Yorkshire.

Crosslee Plc., Hipperholme, Halifax, Yorkshire.

Crystalox Ltd., Wantage, Oxfordshire.

Datapaq Ltd., Cambridge, Cambridgeshire.

Dent Instrumentation Ltd., Colne, Lancashire.

Douglas Laing & Company Ltd., Glasgow, Scotland.

Dunhill Scotch Whisky Sales Ltd., London NW1.

Dunkirk Metals Ltd., Nottingham, Nottinghamshire.

Eclipse Blinds Ltd., Glasgow Scotland.

Edgeworth Electronics Ltd., Darlington, C. Durham.

The Floor Care Division of Electrolux Ltd., Luton, Bedfordshire.

Ethicon Ltd., Edinburgh, Scotland.

Fairbank Brearley, Bingley, West Yorkshire.

Fairey Industrial Ceramics Ltd., Stone, Staffordshire.

Filtermist International Ltd., Bridgnorth, Shropshire.

Glaxo Holdings Plc., London W1.

Gloster Leisure Furniture Ltd., Bristol, Avon.

Gluck Engineering Company Ltd., London SE15.

Hazleton Laboratories Europe Ltd., Harrogate, North Yorkshire.

Hepco Slide Systems Ltd., Greenford, Middlesex.

Heraeus Noblelight Ltd., Cambridge, Cambridgeshire.

History Craft Ltd., Cirencester, Gloucestershire.

HMB Subwork Ltd., Great Yarmouth, Norfolk.

Hunt & Moscrop Ltd., Middleton, Manchester.

ICI Agrochemicals, Fernhurst, Surrey.

Imperial College of Science, Technology & Medicine, London SW7.

IOP Publishing Ltd., Bristol, Avon.

John Brown Engineering Ltd., Clydebank, Dunbartonshire.

John Guest Ltd., West Drayton, Middlesex.

Kodak Ltd., Hemel Hempstead, Hertfordshire.

Kvaerner (UK) Ltd., South Shields, Tyne & Wear.

The Hilton UK Hotels Division of Ladbroke Group Plc., Watford, Hertfordshire.

Laidlaw Drew Ltd., Livingstone, Scotland.

Land Rover Commercial Division of Rover group Ltd., Solihull, West Midlands.

The Special Products Division of Leslie Hartridge Ltd., Buckingham.

The London School of Economics and Political Science, London WC2

Lowe Refrigeration Company, Carryduff, County Down.

LWT (Holdings) Ltd., London SE1.

MF Industrial Ltd., Stretford, Greater Manchester.

The Pedigree Petfoods Division of Mars GB Ltd., Melton Mowbray, Leicestershire.

McLellan & Partners Ltd., West Byfleet, Surrey.

Metrotect Ltd., Cleckheaton, West Yorkshire.

Mordaunt-Short Ltd., Petersfield, Hampshire.

Morning Foods Ltd., Crewe, Cheshire.

MTM Plc., Yarm, Cleveland.

Murray Allan of Innerleithen Ltd., Innerleithen, Peeblesshire.

Neve Electronics International Plc., Melbourn, Hertfordshire.

Norbrook Laboratories Ltd., Newry, County Down.

Orthotec (UK) Ltd., Maltby, South Yorkshire.

Oyster Marine Ltd., Ipswich, Suffolk.

Pains-Wessex Ltd., Salisbury, Wiltshire.

Parker Bath developments Ltd., New Milton, Hampshire.

Pendle & Rivett Ltd t/a Fintex of London, London W1.

Phil Ayliff products Ltd., Nuneaton, Warwickshire.

Pobjoy Mint Ltd., Sutton, Surrey.

Portmeirion Potteries Ltd., Stoke-on-Trent, Staffordshire.

Premier Biscuits - a Division of Premier Brands Ltd., Birmingham, West Midlands.

Psion Plc., London W1.

Purolite International Ltd., Pontycrin, Mid-Glamorgan.

QDF Components Ltd., Derby, Derbyshire.

Quayle Dental Manufacturing Co. Ltd., Worthing, West Sussex.

R. Mears & Co. Ltd., London EC3.

Radiodetection Ltd., Bristol, Avon.

Randox Laboratories Ltd., Crumlin, County Antrim.

Rediffusion Simulation Ltd., Crawley, West Sussex.

Redwood International Ltd., Hemel Hempstead, Hertfordshire.

Reediehill Deer farm, Cupar, Fife.

Reynard Racing Cars Ltd., Bicester, Oxfordshire.

Reynolds & Kent Ltd., Westbury, Wiltshire.

Ronacrete Ltd., Dagenham, Essex.

The Automotive Electronics Division of Salford Electrical Instruments Ltd., Heywood, Lancashire.

Sandon Flexographic Printing Rollers Ltd., Runcorn, Cheshire.

Serif Cowells Plc., Ipswich, Suffolk.

Serono Diagnostics Ltd., Woking, Surrey.

Sharp Manufacturing Company of UK, Wrexham Clwyd.

Snell & Wilcox Ltd., Portsmouth, Hampshire.

Sony Manufacturing Company UK, Bridgend, Mid-Glamorgan.

Sperrin metal Products Ltd., Draperstown, County Londonderry.

Springpart Manufacturing Ltd., Redditch, Worcestershire.

Stirling Aquaculture, Stirling, Scotland.

Sunset + Vine Plc., London W1.

Supertrack Ltd., Banbury, Oxfordshire.

TSB Engineering, Cheltenham, Gloucestershire.

Tankard Carpets Ltd., Bradford, West Yorkshire.

Technophone Ltd., Camberley, Surrey.

Tiphook Group Plc., Bromley, Kent.

Trusthouse Forte Plc., London WC1.

Unipath Ltd., Bedford, Bedfordshire.

Vascutek Ltd., Inchinnan, Renfrewshire.

Vico Sutures Ltd., Bidford-on-Avon, Warwickshire.

Vitramon Ltd., High Wycombe, Buckinghamshire.

W. Harold John (Metals) Ltd., Crindau, Gwent.

Walker Filtration Ltd., Washington, Tyne & Wear.

Wellman Process Engineering Ltd., Smethwick, West Midlands.

White & Company (Earls Barton) Ltd., Earls Barton, Northamptonshire.

Willan-Wogen Alloys Ltd., Rotherham, South Yorkshire.

Wolfe Publishing Ltd., London WC1.

Yale Materials Handling Ltd., Wolverhampton, West Midlands.

FOR TECHNOLOGICAL ACHIEVEMENT 1990

The Paper Division of Allied Colloids Ltd., Bradford, West Yorkshire.

The Research Department of Allied Colloids Ltd., Bradford, West Yorkshire.

Clinical Reagents Division of Amersham International Plc., Little Chalfont, Buckinghamshire.

The Implant Division of Applied Materials, Horsham, West Sussex.

Applied Video Systems Ltd., t/a AVS Ltd., Chessington, Surrey.

Bonas Machine Company Ltd., Gateshead, Tyne & Wear.

Main Optical Networks Division (RT45) British Telecom, Research & Technology, Ipswich, Suffolk.

Chas. A Blatchford & Sons Ltd., Basingstoke, Hampshire.

Croda Application Chemicals Ltd., Goole, North Humberside.

Dowty Maritime Ocean Systems, Part of Dowty Maritime Ltd., Weymouth, Dorset.

Elcometer Instruments Ltd., Droylsden, Manchester.

EM Electronics, Brockenhurst, Hampshire.

Epichem Ltd., Wirral, Merseyside.

Gems of Cambridge Ltd., Cambridge, Cambridgeshire.

Glaxo Group research Ltd., Greenford, Middlesex.

Glencast Ltd., Leven, Fife.

GPT Telecommunications Systems Group (Switching Networks), Liverpool, Merseyside.

The Technical Department of Gullick Dobson Ltd., Wigan, Greater Manchester.

ICI Cellmark Diagnostics, Abingdon, Oxfordshire.

The Electrochemical Technology Business of ICI Chemicals & Polymers Ltd., Runcorn, Cheshire.

ICI Colours & Fine Chemicals, Blackley, Manchester.

ICI Retail Systems, Bracknell, Berkshire.

The product Development Division of INMOS Ltd., Almondsbury, Bristol.

J. McIntyre (Non Ferrous) Ltd., Dunkirk, Nottingham,

The Lister Institute of Preventive Medicine, Stanmore, Middlesex.

Actuation Division of Lucas Aerospace Ltd., Wolverhampton, West Midlands.

Lumonics Ltd., Rugby, Warwickshire.

Micro Focus Group Plc., Newbury, Berkshire.

Mineral Industries Computing Ltd., London W1.

NEI International Combustion Ltd, Derby, Derbyshire.

The NERC ICP_MS Facility, Egham, Surrey.

Oxford University Computing Laboratory, Oxford, Oxfordshire.

Pearpoint Ltd., Bordon, Hampshire.

Perkins Engines Group, Peterborough, Cambridgeshire.

Philips Components Ltd., Washington, Tyne & Wear.

Pilkington PE Ltd., St. Asaph, Clwd.

Renishaw Metrology Ltd., Wooton-under-Edge, Gloucestershire.

The Design Engineering Group of Rolls-Royce Plc., London SW1.

The Propulsion Department of The Royal Aerospace Establishment, Farnborough, Hampshire.

The Electronic Materials Division of The Royal Signals and Radar Establishment, Malvern, Worcestershire.

Sericol Group Ltd., Broadstairs, Kent.

The Flight Deck Display Systems Unit of the Cheltenham Division of Smiths Industries Aerospace and Defence Systems, Cheltenham, Gloucestershire.

STC Submarine Systems, Greenwich London SE10.

STC Technology Ltd., Harlow, Essex.

Steel Castings Research and Trade Association, Sheffield, South Yorkshire.

The Wolfson Research Laboratories of the Department of Clinical Medicine of the University of Birmingham, Birmingham, West Midlands.

VG Elemental Ltd., Winsford, Cheshire.

The Wellcome research Laboratories of the Wellcome Foundation Ltd., Beckenham, Kent.

Yarrow Shipbuilders Ltd., Scotstoun, Glasgow.

THE MacROBERT AWARD

THE MacRobert Award was established in 1968 by the MacRobert Trusts, who funded the award from 1969 until 1989 when, in the 21st year of the presentation of the award, The Fellowship of Engineering MacRobert Award Trust was inaugurated.

The £25,000 prize and gold medal are awarded annually to an individual or a team of up to five people who have made an outstanding innovation in the field of engineering which is, or will be, for the benefit of the community.

The 1989 MacRobert Award was presented to a team of five engineers from British Gas Plc for the development and exploitation of a system of on-line inspection of operational pipelines.

THE RANK PRIZES

The Rank Prize Funds were established in 1972 shortly before the death of Lord Rank to encourage research and provide awards to persons in the fields of Opto-Electronics and Nutrition. The first Prizes were awarded in 1976, but it was decided that they should not necessarily be on an annual basis nor be of a fixed sum.

The editors of the Daily Mail Year Book have been informed by The Rank prize Funds that whilst there are full details of the prizewinners, these will not be awarded until early 1991 and therefore cannot be included in this years edition of the Daily Mail Yearbook. It is hoped to include details of the prizes in next years edition.

BRITISH TRADE UNIONS

THE TRADES UNION CONGRESS is a permanent association of British trade unions which was founded in 1868 and which each year meets as an assembly of delegates for five days in September to discuss common problems. Almost all major unions in Britain are affiliates to the T.U.C. The executive body of Congress, elected each year, is a General Council which meets at least once a month.

The principal officer is the General Secretary, who is elected by Congress, but is not subject to annual re-election. Unions are represented at the annual Congress by one delegate for every 5,000 members, or fraction thereof. The General Council present a detailed report of their year's work to Congress, which is discussed in conjunction with motions submitted by unions.

All unions with more than 100,000 members are automatically represented on the General Council. The larger unions are entitled to more than one representative up to a maximum of six members for a union with more than 1.5 million members.

Smaller unions ballot among themselves at Congress for the 8 seats reserved for unions with less than 100,000 members. Unions with more than 100,000 women members must include at one woman in among the General Council representatives and further seats are reserved for smaller unions..

The General Council elect from their own membership nine standing committees, which usually meet at least once a month. These are the Finance and General Purposes Committee, International Committee, Economic Committee, Education and Training Committee, Trade Union Education Committee, Social Insurance and Industrial Welfare Committee, Employment Policy and Organisation Committee, Equal Rights Committee and the Committee for European Strategy. There are, in addition, a number of advisory committees and industry committees which consist of members of the General Council and representatives of the appropriate unions.

The General Council appoints representatives to a number of national joint advisory committees with employers and Government as well as making direct representations to Government on issues of importance to the trade union movement.

In international matters the T.U.C. is affiliated to the International Confederation of Free Trade Unions and the European Trade Union Confederation. The T.U.C. participates in the work of the Trade Union Advisory Committee to the Organisation of Economic Co-operation and Development and the Commonwealth Trade Union Council. A further task given to the T.U.C. by affiliated unions is that of adjudicating in disputes between unions.

The T.U.C. is not affiliated to any political party and has no political funds, but many of the unions are affiliated to the Labour Party.

The General Secretary is Norman Willis. Office address: Congress House, Great Russell Street, London WC1B 3LS. 01-636 4030.

The following trade unions in Great Britain are affiliated to the T.U.C. Names and addresses of Secretaries are shown, and figures in brackets indicate membership:

Amalgamated Association of Beamers, Twisters and Drawers (Hand and Machine (470)), A. H. Edmondson, 27 Every Street, Nelson, Lancs BB9 7NE. 0282 64181

Amalgamated Engineering Union (793,610), G.H. Laird, 110 Peckham Road, London SE15 5EL. 01-703 4321, Telex: 265871, Fax: 071-701 7826.

Amalgamated Society of Textile Workers and Kindred Trades (2,512), A. Hitchmough, Foxlowe, Market Place, Leek, Staffs ST13 6AD. 0538 382068

Associated Society of Locomotive Engineers and Firemen (19,065), Derek Fullick, 9 Arkwright Road, Hampstead, London NW3 6AB. 071-431 0275

Association of Cinematograph, Television and Allied Technicians (29,301), A.Sapper, 111 Wardour St, London W1V 4AY. 071-437 8506, Fax: 01-437 8268.

Association of First Division Civil Servants (9,353), E. Symons, 2 Caxton Street, London SW1H 0QH. 071-222 6242, Fax: 071-222 5926

Association of University Teachers (32,581), Ms D. Warwick, United House, 1 Pembridge Road, London W11 3HJ. 071-221 4370, Fax: 071-727 6547

Bakers, Food and Allied Workers' Union (34,032), J.R. Marino, Stanborough House, Gt. North Road, Stanborough, Welwyn Garden City, Herts AL8 7TA. 07072 60150

Banking, Insurance and Finance Union, The (168,408), L. A. Mills, Sheffield House, 17 Hillside, Wimbledon, London SW19 4NL. 081-946 9151, Fax: 081-879 3728

British Actors' Equity Association (40,388), P. Plouviez, 8 Harley Street, London W1N 2AB. 071-637 9311

British Air Line Pilots' Association, The (4,340), M. Young, 81 New Road, Harlington, Hayes, Middx UB3 5BG. 081-759 9331, Fax: 081-564 7957.

British Association of Colliery Management, The (9,684), A. Wilson, BACM House, 317 Nottingham Road, Old Basford, Nottingham NG7 7DP. 0602 785819

Broadcasting and Entertainment Trades Alliance (29,169), D. A. Hearn, 181-185 Wardour Street, London W1V 3AA. 071-439 7585.

Card Setting Machine Tenters' Society (92), G. Priestley, 36 Greenton Avenue, Scholes, Cleckheaton, West Yorks BD19 6DT. 0274 670022

Ceramic and Allied Trades Union, The (31,308), A. W. Clowes, Hillcrest House, Garth Street, Hanley, Stoke-on-Trent ST1 2AB. 0782 272755

Civil and Public Services Association, The (143,062), J.N. Ellis, 160 Falcon Road, London SW11 2JN. 01-924 2727

Communication Managers' Association (19,103), Terry Deegan, Hughes House, Ruscombe Road, Twyford, Reading RG10 9JD. 0734 342300, Fax: 0734 342087.

Confederation of Health Service Employees (218,321), H.U. MacKenzie, Glen House, High Street, Banstead, Surrey SM7 2LH. 0737 353322, Telex: 944245.

Educational Institute of Scotland, The (44,451), J. Martin, 46 Moray Place, Edinburgh EH3 6BH. 031-225 6244

Engineers' and Managers' Association (40,649), J. Lyons, Station House, Fox Lane North, Chertsey, Surrey KT16 9HW. 0932 564131, Fax: 0932 567707.

Film Artists' Association (2,094), M. Reynel, 61 Marloes Road, London W8 6LF. 071-937 4567

Fire Brigades' Union, The (45,683), K. Cameron, Bradley House, 68 Coombe Road, Kingston-on-Thames KT2 7AE. 081-541 1765, Fax: 081-546 5187.

Furniture, Timber and Allied Trades Union (46,096), C. A. Christopher, Fairfields, Roe Green, Kingsbury, London NW9 0PT. 081-204 0273

General Union of Associations of Loom Overlookers, The (1,101), E. Macro, (President), Overlookers Institute, Jude Street, Nelson, Lancs BB9 7NP. 0282 64066

General, Municipal, Boilermakers and Allied Trades Union (Merged with APEX on March 1st, 1989 to form GMB) (864,021), J. Edmonds, Thorne House, Ruxley Ridge, Claygate, Esher, Surrey KT10 0TL. 0372 62081, Telex: 27428, Fax: 0372 67164.

Health Visitors' Association (16,091), Ms Catherine Burns, 50 Southwark Street, London SE1 1UN. 071 378 7255

Hospital Consultants and Specialists Association, The (2,362), S.J. Charkham, The Old Court House, London Road, Ascot, Berkshire SL5 7EN. 0990 25052

Inland Revenue Staff Federation (53,523), C. Brooke, Douglas Houghton House, 231 Vauxhall Bridge Road, London SW1V 1EH. 071-834 8254, Fax: 071-630 6258

Institution of Professionals, Managers and Specialists (90,341), Bill Brett, 75-79 York Road, London SE1 7AQ. 071-928 5996

Iron and Steel Trades Confederation, The (66,000), R. L. Evans, Swinton House, 324 Gray's Inn Road, London WC1X 8DD. 071-837 6691, Fax: 071-278 8378

Manufacturing Science Finance (653,000), Ken Gill, 79 Camden Road, London NW1 9ES. 071-267 4422, Telex: 25226

Military and Orchestral Musical Instrument Makers' Trade Society (35), F. McKenzie, 2 Whitehouse Avenue, Borehamwood, Hertfordshire WD6 1HD.

Musicians' Union (39,598), J. Morton, 60-62 Clapham Road, London SW9 0JJ. 071-582 5566, Telex: 8814691.

National and Local Government Officers' Association (754,701), J. Daly, 1 Mabledon Place, London WC1H 9AJ. 071-388 2366.

National Association of Co-operative Officials (4,474), L. W. Ewing, Coronation House, Arndale Centre, Manchester M4 2HW. 061-834 6029.

National Association of Colliery Overmen, Deputies and Shotfirers (8,835), P. McNestry, Simpson House, 48 Nether Hall Road, Doncaster, South Yorkshire DN1 2PZ. 0302 368015, Fax: 0302 341945.

National Association of Licensed House Managers (11,851), J. Madden, 9 Coombe Lane, Raynes Park, London SW20 8NE. 081-947 3080.

National Association of Probation Officers (6,447), B. Beaumont, 3-4 Chivalry Road, London SW11 1HT. 071-223 4887.

National Association of Schoolmasters and Union of Women Teachers (117,610), F. Smithies, 22 Upper Brook Street, London W1Y 1PD. 071-629 3916/7, Fax: 01-409 1193.

National Association of Teachers in Further and Higher Education (81,752), Geoff Woolf, 27 Britannia Street, London WC1X 9JP. 071-837 3636

National Communications Union (154,410), Tony Young, Greystoke House, 150 Brunswick Road, London W5 1AW. 081-998 2981, Telex: 916257, Fax: 081-991 1410.

National Graphical Association (1982) (125,016), A. D. Dubbins, Graphic House, 63-67 Bromham Road, Bedford MK40 2AG. 0234 51521, Fax: 0234 270580.

National League of the Blind and Disabled, The (2,784), M. A. Barrett, 2 Tenterden Road, London N17 8BE. 081-808 6030

National Union of Civil and Public Servants (118,394), L. Christie, 124-130 Southwark Street, London SE1 0TU. 071-928 9671, Fax: 071-928 0751

National Union of Domestic Appliances and General Operatives, The (3,100), Tony McCarthy, Imperial Buildings, Corporation Street, Rotherham S60 1PB. 0709 382820

National Union of Footwear, Leather and Allied Trades (33,097), G. Browett, The Grange, Earls Barton, Northampton NN6 0JH. 0604 810326, Fax: 0604 812496

National Union of Hosiery and Knitwear Workers, The (43,526), Mrs Helen McGrath, 55 New Walk, Leicester LE1 7EB. 0533 556703, Fax: 0533 544406.

National Union of Insurance Workers (17,517), Ken Perry, 27 Old Gloucester Street, London WC1N 3AF. 071-405 1083.

National Union of Journalists (32,206), H. Conroy, Acorn House, 314- 320 Gray's Inn Road, London WC1X 8DP. 071-278 7916, Telex: 892384.

6

National Union of Lock and Metal Workers (5,294), M. Bradley, Bellamy House, Wilkes Street, Willenhall, West Midlands WV13 2BS. 0902 366651/2

National Union of Marine, Aviation and Shipping Transport Officers, The, (19,345), John Newman, Oceanair House, 750-760 High Road, Leytonstone, London E11 3BB. 081-989 6667, Telex: 892648 NUMAST G, Telegrams: UNIDECKENG LONDON E11, Fax: 081-530 1105.

National Union of Mineworkers (77,316), P. E. Heathfield, Holly Street, Sheffield S1 2EX. 0742 700388, Fax: 0742 766400.

National Union of Public Employees (635,070), R.K. Bickerstaffe, Civic House, 20 Grand Depot Road, London SE6 6SF. 081-854 2244, Fax: 081-316 7770.

National Union of Railwaymen (110,256), J. Knapp, Unity House, Euston Road, London NW1 2BL. 071-387 4771.

National Union of Scalemakers (882), A. F. Smith, 1st Floor, Queensway House, 57 Livery Street, Birmingham B3 1HA. 021-236 8998.

National Union of Seamen (21,575), S. McCluskie, Maritime House, Old Town, Clapham, London SW4 0JP. 071-622 5581, Telex: 8814611.

National Union of Tailors and Garment Workers (75,908), A. R. Smith, 16 Charles Square, London N1 6HP. 071-251 9406, Fax: 071-608 0666.

National Union of Teachers (171,990), Doug McAvoy, Hamilton House, Mabledon Place, London WC1H 9BD. 071-388 6191, Fax: 071-387 8458.

Northern Carpet Trades' Union (862), K. Edmondson, 22 Clare Road, Halifax HX1 2HX. 0422 360492

Power Loom Carpet Weavers' and Textile Workers' Union, The (3,200), Ron White, Callows Lane, Kidderminster DY10 2JG. 0562 823192

Prison Officers' Association (23,699), D. Evans, Cronin House, 245 Church Street, Edmonton, London N9 9HW. 081-803 0255, Fax: 081-803 1761.

Rossendale Union of Boot, Shoe and Slipper Operatives, The (2,591), M. Murray, 7 Tenterfield Street, Waterfoot, Rossendale, Lancs. BB4 7BA. 0706 215657

Scottish Prison Officers' Association (3,589), William Goodall, 21 Calder Road, Saughton, Edinburgh EH1 3PF. 031-443 8105, Fax: 031-444 0657.

Scottish Union of Power Loom Overlookers (65), J. Reilly, 3 Napier Terrace, Dundee, Tayside. 0382 612196

Sheffield Wool Shear Workers' Union (17), R. Cutler, 50 Bankfield Road, Malin Bridge, Sheffield S6 4RD.

Society of Graphical and Allied Trades '82 (183,213), B. Dean, Sogat House, 274-288 London Road, Hadleigh, Benfleet, Essex SS7 2DE. 0702 554111, Fax: 0702 559737.

Society of Shuttlemakers (31), L. Illingworth, 211 Burnley Road, Colne, Lancashire BB8 8JD.

Society of Telecom Executives (29,040), S. Petch, 1 Park Road, Teddington, Middlesex TW11 0AR, 081-943 5181, Telex: 0927162, Fax: 081-943 2532.

Transport and General Workers' Union (1,312,853), R. Todd, Transport House, Smith square, Westminster, London SW1P 3JB. 071-828 7788, Telex: 919009, Fax: 071-630 5861.

Transport Salaried Staffs' Association (37,340), Richard Rosser, Walkden House, 10 Melton Street, London NW1 2EJ. 071-387 2101

Union of Communication Workers, The, (197,616), A. D. Tuffin, UCW House, Crescent Lane, London SW4 9RN. 071-622 9977, Telex: 913585, Fax: 071-720 6853.

Union of Construction, Allied Trades and Technicians (250,042), A. Williams, UCATT House, 177 Abbeville Road, Clapham, London SW4 9RL. 071-622 2442, Fax: 071-720 4087.

Union of Shop, Distributive and Allied Workers (396,724), D.G. Davies, Oakley, 188 Wilmslow Road, Fallowfield, Manchester M14 6LJ. 061-224 2804.

United Road Transport Union (20,681), F. Griffin, 76 High Lane, Chorlton-cum-Hardy, Manchester M21 1FD. 061-881 6245.

Wire Workers' Union (5,139). A. M. Ardron, Prospect House, Alma Street, Sheffield S3 8SA. 0742 21674.

Writers' Guild of Great Britain, The (1,678), W. J. Jeffrey, 430 Edgware Road, London W2 1EH. 071-723 8074.

Yorkshire Association of Power Loom Overlookers (537), A. D. Barrow, 20 Hallfield Road, Bradford BD1 3RQ. 0274 727966

SCOTTISH TRADES UNION CONGRESS

The STUC was founded in 1897 and since that date it has been the one Trade Union centre for Scotland. In 1990 there were 57 Unions representing 854,940 members, and 48 Trades Councils affiliated to the Congress. The majority of unions are British based and affiliate on their Scottish membership. The STUC is governed by a general Council of 35 members, based on 7 industrial sections and is elected at a five-day Annual Congress in April.

The STUC is part of the traditions and distinctive character of Scottish life. The Congress speaks on behalf of all Scottish workers on social, economic and cultural matters and plays a considerable in bringing together Scottish opinion on major issues of the day.

General Secretary: Campbell Christie, 16 Woodlands Terrace, Glasgow G3 6DF. 041-332 4946. Chairperson: J.C. Lewis.

LEGAL TENDER

Legal tender is an exact method of payment which a creditor cannot refuse in payment of a debt. Coins issued by the Royal Mint are legal tender throughout the U.K. but only up to the following amounts: £10 in 20p or 50p pieces; £5 in 5p or 10p pieces; £5 in bronze coins. All Bank of England notes are legal tender up to any amount in England and wales only. £1 coins up to any amount are the only legal tender in Scotland and N. Ireland.

PASSPORTS

THESE are obtainable from the Passport Office, Clive House, 70-78 Petty France, London SW1H 9HD; or 5th Floor, India Buildings, Water St., Liverpool L2 0QZ; or 3 Northgate, 96 Milton Street, Cowcaddens, Glasgow G4 0BT; or Olympia House, Upper Dock Street, Newport, Gwent NP9 1XA; Aragon Court, Northminster Road, Peterborough PE1 1QG; or Hampton House, 47-53 High Street, Belfast BT1 2QS.

Applications must be countersigned by a Member of Parliament, Justice of the Peace, Minister of Religion, a professionally qualified person (e.g. doctor, engineer, lawyer, teacher), bank officer, established civil servant, police officer or a person of similar standing who has known the applicant personally for at least two years and who is either a British citizen, British overseas citizen, a British subject or a citizen of a Commonwealth country. A relative should not countersign.

The fee is £15 (£22.50 if particulars of spouse included), and the application must be accompanied by a birth certificate (or other documents establishing national status) and duplicate photographs.

A new passport granted to a person over 16 will normally be valid for ten years and will not be renewable. A passport granted to a child under 16 will normally be valid for an initial period of five years after which period it will be extendable for a further five years with no extra charge.

On May 1, 1973, a new type of passport first became available. Intended to meet the needs of businessmen and other frequent travellers who fill standard passports well before the ten-year validity has expired, it contains 94 pages, is valid for ten years and costs £30 (£45 if one's spouse is included).

Simplified British Visitor's Passports, valid for 12 months but not renewable, can be obtained from main Post Offices by British citizens, British dependent territories citizens or British overseas citizens.

In Northern Ireland, British Visitor's Passports are obtainable from Passport Office, Hampton House, 47-53 High Street, Belfast BT1 2QS. They are valid only for short visits to countries with which Her Majesty's Government has reached agreement for their acceptance.

Applications must be made in person. Duplicate photographs and a fee of £7.50 (£11.25 if particulars of spouse included) are required. Applicants will also be required to produce a document of identity such as their National Health Service medical card or birth certificate.

HOUSING IN THE UK

	Permanent dwellings completed	
	1988	*1989*
England and Wales:		
Houses and flats	196,044	177,384
Local authorities & Gov. Depts	16,410	13,866
Private owners	169,621	153,369
Housing authorities*	9,796	10,149
Scotland:		
Houses and flats	17,444	19,130
Local housing authorities	2,418	2,127
Private owners	13,344	15,830
Other authorities*	1,277	1,173
Northern Ireland:		
Houses and flats	10,209	10,233
Local housing authorities	1,712	1,708
Private owners	7,511	7,911
Other authorities*	986	614

* Dwellings built by certain housing associations

PRODUCTION OF MOTOR VEHICLES

Passenger cars (including taxis)	Home Market	Export	Total
1984	716,693	192,213	908,906
1985	840,302	207,671	1,047,973
1986	831,406	187,556	1,018,962
1987	946,486	226,197	1,142,683
1988	1,012,965	213,870	1,226,835
1989	1,018,353	280,729	1,299,082

Commercial road vehicles

1984	175,017	49,808	224,825
1985	200,217	65,756	265,973
1986	178,909	49,776	228,685
1987	185,992	60,736	246,728
1988	233,581	84,432	318,013
1989	231,089	95,492	326,581

REGISTERED UNEMPLOYED, 1989-1990 *(THOUSANDS)*

	Great Britain Total	Rate	North'n Ireland Total	Rate
July 1989	1,663.6	6.0	107.7	15.4
August 1989	1,634.0	5.9	107.0	15.3
September 1989	1,596.7	5.7	106.1	15.2
October 1989	1,533.9	5.5	101.8	14.6
November 1989	1,513.1	5.4	99.2	14.2
December 1989	1,539.8	5.5	99.0	14.2
January 1990	1,586.6	5.7	100.4	14.4
February 1990	1,576.7	5.7	98.9	14.2
March 1990	1,549.9	5.6	97.5	14.0
April 1990	1,528.6	5.5	97.6	14.0
May 1990	1,482.4	5.3	96.0	13.8
June 1990	1,460.5	5.3	95.0	13.6

Broad base unemployment rates are calculated by expressing the number of unemployed as a percentage of the estimated total workforce (the sum of the unemployed claimants, employees in employment, self-employed, HM Forces and participants in work-related government training programmes) at mid-1990.

BUILDING SOCIETIES

Building societies are mutual institutions, the main function of which is to attract savings from members of the public and to make long term loans to individuals wishing to buy their own homes.

At the end of 1989 there were around 126 building societies in existence in the United Kingdom. July 1989 saw the first ever conversion of a building society to a public limited company, when Abbey National shares were floated on the Stock Exchange.

In the housing and savings markets, societies have been extremely successful, and by the end of 1989 accounted for half of short-term savings and almost 60% of residential mortgage debt outstanding. These figures do not include Abbey National, which was no longer a building society at the end of 1989.

The last few years have seen major changes to building societies and the markets in which they operate; in particular the mortgage and savings markets have become much more competitive with many new institutions trying to attract customers. Building societies have reacted to this change, most notably by introducing new services themselves.

The Building Societies Act 1986
The Building Societies act passed by Parliament in 1986 came into effect at the beginning of 1987. The Act has since been significantly amended and as a result of both the original legislation and the amendments, building societies are now able to offer a wide range of services. These include financial services such as money transmission, credit cards and insurance broking and underwriting, and a range of housing and land services including housebuilding, estate agency and surveys and valuations. From 1988 societies have also been able to operate in other countries of the EEC. The Act made provision for building societies to convert from mutual to company status, but the only society so far to have taken this route is Abbey National.

Market Developments
Building societies have taken full advantage of the new rules. A number of societies have introduced interest bearing chequing accounts offering full current account services. The number of cash dispensers has been expanded significantly and societies now offer their investors over 2,500 machines in comparison with just over 100 seven years ago. Some societies have concentrated on the housing side becoming important housebuilders and making a significant contribution to alleviating the problems of inner city decay. A number of societies have moved into estate agency and by the end of 1989 probably controlled over 2,500 estate agency outlets. Building societies have also increased their involvement in the insurance markets, and most now sell a range of products far beyond their traditional life, house and contents policies. Some societies own broking subsidiaries and one owns an insurance company.

Some societies have also established 'offshore' subsidiaries enabling them to pay interest gross on investments, although new legislation will allow this facility 'onshore' in the future.

Conversion from Mutual to Company Status
One of the most controversial aspects of the 1986 Act as it was going through Parliament concerned the provision for building societies to convert from mutual to company status with the agreement of their members. This new power has been put into practice. In March 1989, the Abbey National Building Society announced that it intended to put to its members proposals to enable it to convert into a company quoted on the stock exchange. The necessary ballot of both borrowing and investing members was held in April 1989 and around 90% of those voting voted in favour of the conversion. As a result from 12 July, Abbey National was no longer a building society; rather, although the word does not appear in its title, it is now regulated as a bank, and counts as such in the various statistics on financial and monetary conditions prepared by the Bank of England.

There has been a particularly lengthy debate within the industry over the conversion issue. Some building societies have suggested that mutual status is beneficial because it enables them to act in the interests of their investors and borrowers without the need to answer to an outside class of shareholders. In contrast, other societies have emphasised the access to capital which the stock exchange quotation gives them and the relative freedom to offer services outside the confines of the building society legislation. It is possible that other societies will choose to convert in the future, but nevertheless large numbers will probably prefer to retain their current status.

Mergers
Far more common than conversion to company status are mergers between building societies. The number of building societies has decreased in recent years as mergers have taken place to form larger societies. There were four mergers in 1989 and four in the six months of 1990. Another subject of discussion within the industry, mergers commonly occur either between small-to-medium sized societies operating in similar localities or between small societies and large nationally-operating societies. In either event a 'bonus' is frequently paid to investors and a fixed term mortgage concession granted to borrowers, although this need not be the case.

The Future
However they are internally organised, those institutions which are now known as building societies face an exciting and successful future. Following the stock market crash of October 1987, building society saving accounts have significantly increased in popularity as many investors became increasingly concerned at the volatility of share prices. 1988 was thus a boom year for both savings and for mortgage lending. 1989 saw a downturn in the property market and the rise of interest rates to very high levels. Building society net receipts for 1989 did not therefore reach the peak they had achieved in 1988, but whatever the state of the market societies' strengths have enabled them to adapt and compete successfully.

Given their strengths in their traditional markets, building societies have found a high demand for the new products which they have recently introduced. One of the most pleasing aspects of this has been the changes which have been induced in the behaviour of other financial institutions. All of the major banks, for example, now offer interest bearing current accounts and are increasingly extending their opening hours to those considered normal by building societies. The coming year will prove an exciting time for societies as composite rate tax is abolished enabling societies to pay interest gross to non-taxpayers, and as the new TESSAs (tax exempt special savings accounts) for individuals are introduced. As a result of new legislation, increased competition and building societies's responses to the changes, an increased choice for the consumer and a better service for the customer new exists and will continue to grow.

The Housing Market
After the boom year of 1988 mortgage rates continued to rise sharply (between spring 1988 and December 1989 mortgage rates increased from 9.7% to 14.5% to leave real post-tax mortgage rates standing at record levels) and house price inflation wavered in the first half of 1989. After rising again in the third quarter, by the end of the year house prices were falling in most parts of the country although the average house price for the year was higher than in 1988.

The early part of 1990, with a further rise in interest rates saw a continuing fall in house prices in some parts of the country, notably the South East. Nevertheless, by the middle of 1990 there were indications that first-time buyers were re-entering the property market although an increase in house prices is not anticipated by analysts until interest rates reach a lower level.

VALUE ADDED TAX

SUBJECT to certain exceptions, Value Added Tax is payable by every person supplying goods or services on the value which is added to them during his particular stage of their production or distribution. The tax is added to the price of goods or services on the occasion of every transaction to which they are subjected until they reach the final consumer. A person supplying goods or services thus pays VAT on the goods which he purchases in the course of his business and charges tax to the person to whom he supplies the goods or services. At three-monthly or possibly monthly intervals he is required to account to the Customs and Excise for a sum equal to the tax which he has charged to his customers (his output tax) less, with certain exceptions, e.g. cars, business entertainment, the tax which he has paid on purchases for his business (his input tax).

A supplier whose taxable turnover in any period of 12 months does not exceed £25,400 is not liable to be registered and so does not have to account for VAT and cannot recover any tax.

Certain goods and services are exempt from VAT. These include insurance, financial services, education, most medical services and burial services. A supplier of exempted goods or services is not liable for VAT on their sale, but he may not be able to recoup from the Customs and Excise any tax which he has paid in the process of providing those goods or services. A person who provides only exempted goods or services cannot be registered. Other items, such as food (with some exceptions), books, newspapers and fuel and power supplies are zero-rated, i.e. the tax rate is nil. There is therefore no VAT to be accounted for on zero-rated supplies but the VAT paid on purchases (input tax) can be deducted in the normal way. VAT is charged on the tax-exclusive value of standard-rated supplies and is normally based on the price of the goods or services.

Civic Penalties
An independent Committee under Lord Keith of Kinkel reviewed the enforcement powers of the revenue departments in 1980-81. The majority of their recommendations about VAT were implemented by the Finance Act 1985. These included a balanced package of measures to decriminalise offences: a civil penalty for late registration; automatic penalties for late payment and penalties for negligence in the completion of VAT returns. The Taxpayer is protected by the right of Tribunal and by the concept that the penalties will not apply if he has reasonable excuse' for his conduct.

From October 1, 1986 three important changes were made to the VAT system:

1. Failure to make a return or pay the tax due is no longer liable to criminal prosecution; but
2. A default surcharge was introduced for persistently making late VAT returns or payments; and
3. A repayment supplement is paid by Customs and Excise where an acceptable claim for repayment of VAT is not paid within a reasonable period.

Default Surcharge
The default charge was introduced because many traders do not send in their returns or pay VAT on time, which at that time meant that about 1,200 million VAT was outstanding at any time. A default occurs if a VAT return and all the VAT due for the period it covers are not received in the VAT Central Unit by the due date shown on the return. This is usually a month after the end of the period covered by the return.

If a trader defaults twice in any 12 month period he will be sent a Surcharge Liability Notice. This warns that any further default in the following 12 months will incur a default surcharge on any VAT involved. Once a Notice has been issued it remains in force until the trader has not been in default for 12 months. Whilst the Notice is in force the trader will have to pay a surcharge each time he defaults.

For the first default after a Surcharge Liability Notice has been issued the surcharge will be 5 per cent of the VAT owed. As long as the Notice is in force the surcharge will increase by 5 per cent for each default to a maximum of 30 per cent of the VAT owed. If a surcharge has been imposed a trader can ask the local VAT office to reconsider the matter if it can be shown that the VAT return and tax were despatched in time to arrive by the due date, or if there is a reasonable excuse for the default. If the trader is not satisfied with the result he can appeal to an independent VAT tribunal.

Repayment Supplement
If a trader's input tax exceeds the output tax in the period covered by a return and the VAT Central Unit does not pay the amount due within a reasonable period, normally 30 days from the day the return is received, then they will be liable to pay the trader a supplement of 5 per cent of the payment due or 30, whichever is the greater. To qualify for the supplement the return must be received by the VAT Central Unit within one month of the due date shown on the form and all returns and payments must have been made for earlier periods.

Other important changes introduced in late 1989 will penalise inaccurate returns. They will involve an interest charge at commercial rates for underdeclared and overclaimed VAT; and a penalty of 30 per cent of the tax owed if VAT is substantially underdeclared or overclaimed.

Further information on all aspects of VAT can be obtained from local VAT offices.

NATIONAL SAVINGS

National Savings Capital Bonds (series B) provide capital growth at a rate guaranteed for five years. They are sold in multiples of £100, with a maximum aggregated holding of £100,000 for Series B and all future series (excluding Series A). Interest is earned without deduction of tax at source and capitalised each year. The rate of interest increases each year and with Series B Capital Bonds it is equivalent to 13 per cent per annum compound if the Bond is held for the full five years. But the rate will be lower if a Bond is cashed in early (three months' notice is required) and no interest will be repaid if it cashed in during the first year. Interest must be declared on income tax returns. Application forms available at Post Offices.

A National Savings Certificate of the 35th Issue costs £25 and each unit will have a value of £39.36 at the end of five years, equal to compound interest of 9.5 per cent per annum. Maximum holding 40 units (£1,000), with special facilities for additional holdings up to £10,000 for investors re-investing proceeds of their existing matured certificates. No Income Tax or Capital Gains Tax payable. These certificates are available from post offices and most banks.

Certificates kept for more than five years will continue to earn tax-free interest at the General Extension Rate for each additional three months they are held. This rate may be varied from time to time.

Index-linked Certificates of the 5th Index-linked Issue. The certificates are available from post offices and may be bought in units of £25, up to a maximum of £5,000. There is also a special facility for investors to re-invest up to a further £10,000 from earlier matured certificates. In addition to inflation-proofing in accordance with changes in the Retail Prices Index, this Issue will give a return of 4.5 per cent if the certificates are held for a full five years.

The return on these certificates is paid from the date of purchase for each full year they are held. For the first complete year the return is the Retail Price Index (RPI) only; 0.5 per cent plus RPI for the second; 1.0 per cent plus RPI for the third; 2.0 per cent plus RPI for the fourth and 4.5 per cent plus RPI at the fifth anniversary. Both the inflation-proofing and the Extra Interest are earned monthly from the date of purchase. At the annual anniversary of purchase everything earned in the previous year is added to the capital. Thus, in the following year, both the inflation-proofing and Extra Interest are earned on the new amount of capital. Repayments are free of all UK Income Tax and Capital Gains Tax. They are also free of Income Tax in the Channel Islands and the Isle of Man.

National Savings Bank Ordinary Account accepts deposits of any sum from £5 up to a limit of £10,000. The minimum deposit to open an Ordinary account is £5.

Money can readily be withdrawn if required. Interest is guaranteed for a calendar year, at two levels; the higher rate is paid on accounts which maintain a specified balance throughout the year. The first £70 of annual interest is free from Income Tax. Total interest must be declared in income tax returns.

National Savings Bank Investment Account. There is a £25,000 limit to the amount which may be held in an Investment account which pays variable interest (12.75 per cent from 3 April 1990 until further notice). Minimum deposit is £5, one month's notice required for withdrawals. Interest taxable, but not deducted at source.

National Savings Income Bonds, introduced in August 1982, are sold in multiples of £1,000 with a minimum holding of £2,000 and a maximum of £25,000 and provide a regular monthly income. Interest is taxable, but is paid in full without deduction at source. The cash value of the investment remains the same. The interest from 4 May 1990 was 13.5 per cent per annum but this will vary from time to time to keep it competitive. Application forms obtainable at post offices.

Premium Bonds are in units of £1 each, but the minimum purchase is £100. Other purchases must be in multiples of £10, and an individual 16 years of age or over may buy up to £10,000 worth. They may also be bought for children under 16 by a parent, grandparent or legal guardian, in amounts from £10 up to the same maximum holding. Instead of earning interest as do other forms of National Savings, the Bonds offer, after a qualifying period, a chance of winning a wide range of tax-free prizes in prize draws. The bonds may be bought at Savings Bank post offices and most banks.

National Savings Deposit Bonds were withdrawn from sale in November 1988. All Deposit Bonds purchased on or before that date may continue to be held until the tenth anniversary of purchase. They will continue to earn interest until then.

Yearly Plan is a scheme for regular savers offering guaranteed and tax-free returns. Applicants agree to make 12 monthly payments leading to the issue of a Yearly Plan Certificate, which can be held for at least four years. Payments must be made on the same date every month by standing order from a bank or other acceptable account. Only one payment may be made in any one month and must be in multiples of £5. Minimum monthly contribution is £20, maximum £200. Certificates earn interest compounded annually. Maximum interest is earned if the Certificate is held for the full four years. Application forms are available at post offices.

National Savings Gift Tokens were withdrawn from sale on 30 June 1989.

National Savings Stock Register. A wide range of Government Stock (Gilts) can be bought and sold through the National Savings Stock register. Commission rates are modest for most purchases - £1 for the first £250 and 50p for every additional £125 (or part). Interest (dividends) is paid without deduction of tax at source. Up to £10,000 may be invested in any particular Gilt on any one day and there is no limit to the total amount which may be held. Application forms at most post offices.

BRITISH AIRWAYS

	1990
Turnover (million)	4,838
Group profit before taxation	345
Retained profit	182
Scheduled Traffic and Operations	
Passengers carried (thousands)	25,238
Revenue passenger kms (million)	61,915
Available seat kms (million)	86,601
Cargo tonne km (million)	2,400
Average number of employees	50,320

Aircraft Fleet at 31 March 1990

Concorde	7
Boeing 747-100	16
Boeing 747-200	23
Boeing 747-400	8
Lockheed TriStar 1/50	9
Lockheed TriStar 200	8
McDonnell Douglas DC10-30	8
Boeing 767-300	4
Boeing 757-200	36
Airbus A320	8
Boeing 737-200	43
Boeing 737-300,400,500	4
BAC 1-11-500	34
BAe ATP	8
HS 748	8
Total	**224**

BRITISH RAILWAYS BOARD

Operating Results:

Rail Business	1988-9	1989-90

Passengers: before Government Grant

	1988-9	1989-90
Intercity	57.4	46.4
Network SouthEast	(137.7)	(138.1)
Provincial	(465.5)	(509.4)
Government grant	606.5	586.8
Freight	69.4	59.4
Parcels	(12.4)	(15.9)
Total Railways	110.5	29.2
Other Rail Business	(7.2)	(28.6)
Total Operating Surplus (Loss)	**107.00**	**(26.4)**
Group Operating Surplus (Loss)	**304.30**	**269.8**
Number of Employees		
Railways Total	128,476	129.696
Group Total	135,243	134,361

GOVERNMENT REVENUE   FROM BUDGET STATEMENT, MARCH 1990

The Finances of the Public Sector	(£ billion) 1989-90		(£ billion) 1990-91
	Budget Forecast	**Latest Estimate**	**Budget Forecast**
RECEIPTS			
Inland Revenue:			
Income tax	46.9	48.7	55.0
Corporation tax	22.4	21.4	20.7
Petroleum revenue tax	1.4	1.1	1.1
Capital gains tax	2.1	1.9	2.1
Inheritance tax	1.1	1.2	1.2
Stamp duties	2.4	2.1	1.9
Total Inland Revenue	**76.3**	**76.4**	**81.9**
Customs and Excise:			
Value added tax	30.0	29.7	32.1
Petrol, derv duties etc.	8.8	8.8	9.7
Tobacco duties	5.1	5.0	5.4
Alcohol duties	4.7	4.6	4.9
Betting and gaming duties	1.0	1.0	1.0
Car tax	1.4	1.5	1.5
Customs duties	1.8	1.8	1.9
Agricultural levies	0.1	0.1	0.1
Total Customs and Excise	**52.9**	**52.4**	**56.7**
Vehicle excise duties	2.9	2.9	3.0
Oil royalties	0.6	0.6	0.7
Local authority rates	19.7	20.1	12.2
Other taxes and royalties	3.7	4.4	4.4
Total taxes and royalties	**156.1**	**156.8**	**159.0**
National insurance and other contributions	34.3	33.1	35.9
Community charge	0.8	0.8	11.2
Interest and dividends	7.0	7.2	6.4
Gross trading surpluses and rent	3.3	3.0	3.0
Other receipts	4.8	2.5	3.1
General government receipts	**206.4**	**203.4**	**218.6**

GOVERNMENT EXPENDITURE   FROM BUDGET STATEMENT, MARCH 1990

The Finances of the Public Sector	(£ billion) 1989-90		(£ billion) 1990-91
	Budget Forecast	Latest Estimate	Budget Forecast
Central Government's own expenditure of which:	125.8	127.0	137.8
Social security	47.5	47.0	52.0
Health	19.8	20.0	22.1
Defence	20.1	20.6	21.2
Scotland	4.0	4.0	4.4
Wales	1.9	1.9	2.1
Northern Ireland	5.2	5.5	5.7
Central government support for local authorities	n.a.	38.0	41.8
Financing requirements of public corporations	0.8	1.6	1.4
Privatisation proceeds	-5.0	-4.2	-5.0
Reserve	n.a.	-	3.0
New planning total	**n.a.**	**162.3**	**179.0**
Local authority self financed expenditure	n.a.	13.9	13.3
Central government debt interest	17.0	17.7	17.0
Accounting adjustments	n.a.	3.9	3.4
General government expenditure	**194.3**	**197.7**	**212.7**
Recipts, expenditure and debt repayment			
General government recipts	206.4	203.4	218.6
General government expenditure	**194.3**	**197.7**	**212.7**
General government debt repayment	12.1	5.7	5.9
Public corporations market and overseas debt repayment	1.7	1.4	1.0
Public sector debt repayment	13.8	7.1	6.9

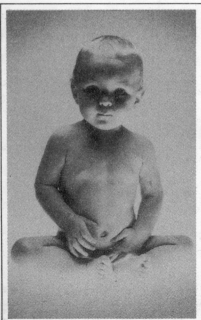

SECTION 7

PEOPLE

THE SUPREME COURT OF JUDICATURE
The Lord High Chancellor: Rt. Hon. Lord James Mackay, P.C., F.R.S.E., Q.C.,

LORDS OF APPEAL IN ORDINARY:
Rt. Hon. Lord Keith of Kinkel
Rt. Hon. Lord Bridge of Harwich
Rt. Hon. Lord Brandon of Oakbrook, M.C.
Rt. Hon. Lord Templeman, M.B.E.
Rt. Hon. Lord Griffiths, M.C.

Rt. Hon. Lord Ackner
Rt. Hon. Lord Aylmerton
Rt. Hon. Lord Chievely
Rt. Hon. Lord Jauncey of Tullichettle
Rt. Hon. Lord Lowry

ENGLAND AND WALES
COURT OF APPEAL:
The Lord High Chancellor (Rt. Hon. Lord James Mackay, P.C., F.R.S.E., Q.C.)
The Lord Chief Justice of England (Rt. Hon. Lord Lane, A.F.C.)
The Master of the Rolls (Rt. Hon. Sir John Francis Donaldson)
The President of the Family Division (Rt. Hon. Sir Stephen Brown)
The Vice-Chancellor (Rt. Hon. Sir Nicolas Christopher Henry Browne-Wilkinson)
Rt. Hon. Sir Tasker Watkins, V.C.
Rt. Hon. Sir Patrick McCarthy O'Connor
Rt. Hon. Sir Michael John Fox
Rt. Hon. Sir Michael Robert Emanuel Kerr
Rt. Hon. Sir John Douglas May
Rt. Hon. Sir Christopher John Slade
Rt. Hon. Sir Francis Brooks Purchas
Rt. Hon. Sir George Brian Hugh Dillon
Rt. Hon. Sir Roger Jocelyn Parker
Rt. Hon. Sir David Powell Croom Johnson, D.S.C., V.R.D.
Rt. Hon. Sir Anthony John Leslie Lloyd
Rt. Hon. Sir Brian Thomas Neill
Rt. Hon. Sir Michael John Mustill
Rt. Hon. Sir Martin Charles Nourse
Rt. Hon. Sir Iain Derek Laing Glidewell
Rt. Hon. Sir Alfred John Balcombe
Rt. Hon. Sir Ralph Brian Gibson

Rt. Hon. Sir John Dexter Stocker, M.C., T.D.
Rt. Hon. Sir Harry Kenneth Woolf
Rt. Hon. Sir Donald James Nicholls
Rt. Hon. Sir Thomas Henry Bingham
Rt. Hon. Sir Thomas Patrick Russell
Rt. Hon. Dame Anne Elizabeth Oldfield Butler-Sloss, D.B.E.
Rt. Hon. Sir Peter Murray Taylor
Rt. Hon. Sir Murray Stuart-Smith
Rt. Hon. Sir Christopher Stephen Thomas Jonathan Thayer Staughton
Rt. Hon. Sir Michael Mann
Rt. Hon. Sir Donald Henry Farquharson

CHANCERY DIVISION JUDGES:
Hon. Sir John Evelyn Vinelott
Hon. Sir Douglas William Falconer, M.B.E.
Hon. Sir Jean-Pierre Frank Eugene Warner
Hon. Sir Peter Leslie Gibson
Hon. Sir David Herbert Mervyn Davies, M.C., T.D.
Hon. Sir Jeremiah LeRoy Harman
Hon. Sir Richard Rashleigh Folliott Scott
Hon. Sir Leonard Hubert Hoffmann
Hon. Sir John Leonard Knox
Hon. Sir Peter Julian Millett
Hon. Sir R.A. Morritt
Hon. Sir William Aldous

QUEEN'S BENCH DIVISION JUDGES:
Hon. Sir William Lloyd Mars-Jones, M.B.E.
Hon. Sir Leslie Kenneth Edward Boreham
Hon. Sir Alfred William Michael Davies
Hon. Sir Kenneth George Illtyd Jones
Hon. Sir Haydn Tudor Evans
Hon. Sir Kenneth Graham Jupp, M.C.
Hon. Sir Walter Derek Thornley Hodgson
Rt. Hon. Sir Ronald Gough Waterhouse
Hon. Sir Frederick Maurice Drake, D.F.C.
Hon. Sir Barry Cross Sheen
Hon. Sir David Bruce McNeill
Hon. Sir Christopher James Saunders French
Hon. Sir Peter Edlin Webster
Hon. Sir Anthony James Denys McCowan
Hon. Sir Iain Charles Robert McCullough
Hon. Sir Hamilton John Leonard
Hon. Sir Alexander Roy Asplan Beldam
Hon. Sir David Cozens-Hardy Hirst
Hon. Sir John Stewart Hobhouse
Hon. Sir Andrew Peter Leggatt
Hon. Sir Michael Patrick Nolan
Hon. Sir Oliver Bury Popplewell
Hon. Sir William Alan Macpherson, T.D.
Hon. Sir Philip Howard Otton
Hon. Sir Paul Joseph Morrow Kennedy
Hon. Sir Michael Hutchison
Hon. Sir Simon Denis Brown
Hon. Sir Mark Oliver Saville
Hon. Sir Johan Van Zyl Steyn
Hon. Sir Christopher Dudley Roger Rose
Hon. Sir Richard Howard Tucker
Hon. Sir Robert Alexander Gatehouse
Hon. Sir P.N. Garland
Hon. Sir John Ormond Roch
Hon. Sir Michael John Turner
Hon. Sir Harry Henry Ognall
Hon. Sir John Downes Alliott
Hon. Sir Anthony Howell Meurig Evans
Hon. Sir Konrad Hermann Theodor Schiemann
Hon. Sir John Arthur Dalziel Owen
Hon. Sir Denis Robert Morris Henry
Hon. Sir Francis Humphrey Potts
Hon. Sir Richard George Rougier
Hon. Sir Ian Alexander Kennedy
Hon. Sir Nicholas Addison Phillips
Hon. Sir R. Ernest Auld
Hon. Sir Malcolm Thomas Pill
Hon. Sir Stuart Neil McKinnon
Hon. Sir Mark Howard Potter
Hon. Sir Henry Brooke
Hon. Sir Igor Judge
Hon. Sir Edwin Frank Jowitt
Hon. Sir Michael Morland
Hon. Sir George Mark Waller

FAMILY DIVISION JUDGES:
Hon. Sir Alfred Kenneth Hollings, M.C.
Hon. Sir John Kember Wood, M.C.
Hon. Sir Thomas Michael Eastham
Hon. Dame Margaret Myfanwy Wood Booth, D.B.E.
Hon. Sir Anthony Leslie Julian Lincoln
Hon. Sir Anthony Bruce Ewbank
Hon. Sir John Douglas Waite
Hon. Sir Anthony Barnard Hollis
Hon. Sir Swinton Barclay Thomas
Hon. Sir Matthew Alexander Thorpe
Hon. Sir Edward Stephen Cazalet
Hon. Sir Alan Hylton Ward
Hon. Sir Thomas Scott Gillespie
Hon. Sir Robert Lionel Johnson
Hon. Sir Douglas Dunlop Brown
Hon. Sir Donald Keith Rattee

NORTHERN IRELAND
Lord Chief Justice of Northern Ireland: Rt. Hon. Sir Brian Hutton

Rt. Hon. Lord Justice Sir John William Basil Kelly

Rt. Hon. Lord Justice Turlough O'Donnell

Rt. Hon. Lord Justice Sir John Clarke MacDermott

Hon. Mr. Justice Sir Donald Bruce Murray

Hon. Mr. Justice Sir John Patrick Basil Higgins

Hon. Mr. Justice Sir Robert Douglas Carswell

Hon. Mr. Justice Sir James Michael Anthony Nicholson

Hon. Mr. Justice Sir William Pascal McCollum

Hon. Mr. Justice Sir William Anthony Campbell

SCOTLAND
Lord Justice General and Lord President of the Court of Session: Rt. Hon. The Lord Emslie, M.B.E.

COURT OF SESSION
INNER HOUSE:

First Division
Rt. Hon. The Lord Emslie (Lord President)
Hon. Lord Cowie
Hon. Lord Brand
Hon. Lord Allanbridge

Second Division
Rt. Hon. Lord Ross (Lord Justice Clerk)
Hon. Lord Dunpark, T.D.
Rt. Hon. Lord Wylie
Rt. Hon. Lord Murray

OUTER HOUSE:

Hon. Lord Mayfield
Hon. Lord Davidson (Chairman, Scottish Law Commission)
Rt. Hon. Lord McCluskey
Hon. Lord Morison
Hon. Lord Sutherland

Hon. Lord Weir
Hon. Lord Clyde
Hon. Lord Cullen
Hon. Lord Prosser
Hon. Lord Kirkwood
Hon. Lord Coulsfield

Hon. Lord Milligan
Hon. Lord Dervaird
Rt. Hon. Lord Martin of Shuna
Hon. Lord Capolan
Rt. Hon. Lord Cameron of Lochbroom

LORD ADVOCATE'S DEPARTMENT:
Lord Advocate: Rt. Hon. Lord Fraser of Carmyllie, Q.C., M.P.   **Solicitor-General:** Alan F. Roger, Q.C.

CIRCUIT JUDGES

MIDLAND AND OXFORD CIRCUIT

W. A. L. Allardice, D.L.
F. A. Allen
M. J. Astill
B. J. Appleby, Q.C.
I. J. Black, Q.C.
J. F. Blythe, T.D.
F. Leo Clark, Q.C.
P. N. R. Clark
R. R. B. Cole
J. M. Coulson
P. F. Crane
Curtis Crawford, Q.C.
A. C. H. de Piro, Q.C.
T. M. Dillon, Q.C.
J. F. Evans, Q.C.

B. A. Farrer, Q.C.
J. E. Fletcher
H. G. A. Gosling
M. K. Harrison-Hall
T. R. Heald
J. R. Hopkin
R. H. Hutchinson
J. E. M. Irvine
R.P.V. Jenkins
J. Geoffrey Jones
T. O. Kellock, Q.C.
John Lee
M. H. Mander
Keith Matthewman, Q.C.
R. G. May

P. M. Medd, O.B.E., Q.C.
K. Wilson Mellor, Q.C.
Nathaniel Micklem
A. J. H. Morrison
M. D. Mott
A. J. D. Nicholl
P. C. Northcote
C. J. Pitchers
F. Malcolm Potter
D. E. Roberts
J.A.O. Shand
J. R. S. Smyth
P. J. Stretton
C. S. Stuart-White
Clive Tayler, Q.C.

Kenneth Taylor
R. J. Toyn
M. B. Ward
R. L. Ward, Q.C.
G. G. A. Whitehead, D.F.C.
D. J. R. Wilcox
D. H. Wild
Harold Wilson
John Wilson
Brian Woods
G. H. Wootton
C. G. Young

NORTH EASTERN CIRCUIT

G. F. Atkinson
Geoffrey Baker, Q.C.
P.M. Baker, Q.C.
J. M. A. Barker
G. N. Barr Young
H. G. Bennett, Q.C.
D.R. Bentley, Q.C.
D.M.A. Bryant
Bryan Bush
M. C. Carr
D.J. Charlesworth
Myrella Cohen, Q.C.

G. J. K. Coles, Q.C.
J. A. Cotton
J. Crabtree
M.T. Cracknell
W. H. R. Crawford
P.J. Fox, Q.C.
A. N. Fricker, Q.C.
M.S. Garner
H. G. Hall
W. Hannah
G. F. R. Harkins
J. A. Henham

Donald Herrod, Q.C.
Harold Hewitt
R. Hunt
V. R. Hurwitz
A. E. Hutchinson, Q.C.
J. R. Johnson
G. M. Lightfoot
A. C. MacDonald
Miss M. B. M. MacMurray, Q.C.
A. L. Myerson, Q.C.
D. A. Orde

Helen E. Paling
R. A. Percy
James Pickles
D. M. Savill, Q.C.
Alan Simpson
L. B. Stephen
Jim Stephenson
R. A. R. Stroyan, Q.C.
R. C. Taylor
G. M. Vos
Michael Walker
P. H. C. Walker

NORTHERN CIRCUIT

H. H. Andrew, Q.C.
J. R. Arthur, D.F.C.
A. W. Bell
M. S. Blackburn
A. S. Booth, Q.C.
R. Brown
I. B. Campbell
F.B. Carter, Q.C.
D. Clark
P. C. Clegg
G. P. Crowe, Q.C.
J. M. Davies, Q.C.
Miss A. E. Downey
B. R. Duckworth
S.B. Duncan

Miss A. M. Ebsworth
A. A. Edmondson
D. Marshall Evans, Q.C.
S. J. D. Fawcus
D. M. Forster
D. G. F. Franks
J. Hall
R. G. Hamilton
J. A. Hammond
R. J. Hardy
T.D.T. Hodson
Mary Holt
G. W. Humphries
A. C. Jolly
Henry Kershaw

H. L. Lachs
C. N. Lees
J. M. Lever, Q.C.
Reginald Lockett
J. H. Lord
C.J. Mahon
I. H. Morris Jones, Q.C.
F. J. Nance
G. K. Naylor
M. O'Donoghue
F. D. Paterson
R. E. I. Pickering
D. A. Pirie
A. M. Prestt, Q.C.
(Recorder of Manchester)

A.J. Proctor
M. A. G. Sachs
N. W. M. Sellers, V.R.D.
H. S. Singer
J. A. Stannard
Miss A. H. Steel
I. R. Taylor, Q.C.
E. S. Temple, M.B.E., Q.C.
(Recorder of Liverpool)
J. P. Townend
I. S. Webster
W. R. Wickham

SOUTH EASTERN CIRCUIT

M. F. Addison
F. J. Aglionby
A. K. Allen, O.B.E.
M. J. Anwyl-Davies, Q.C.
J. A. Baker
M.J.D. Baker
J.B. Baker, Q.C.
Paul Baker, Q.C.
A. F. Balston
R. M. N. Band, M.C., Q.C.
C. J. A. Barnett, Q.C.
R. A. Barr
G. A. Bathurst-Norman
P. T. S. Batterbury, T.D.
N. E. Beddard
F. E. Beezley
G. J. Binns
Michael Birks
J. C. C. Blofeld, Q.C.
John Bolland
P.C. Bowsher, Q.C.
P. N. Brandt
L. J. Bromley, Q.C.
Andrew E. Brooks
G. N. Butler, Q.C.
Neil Butter, Q.C.
H. J. Byrt, Q.C.
C. V. Callman
B. E. Capstick, Q.C.
A. W. Clark
D. J. Clarkson, Q.C.
Patricia G. Coles, Q.C.
C. C. Colston, Q.C.
C. D. Compston
M. J. Cook
R. K. Cooke, O.B.E.
G. H. Coombe
M. R. Coombe
Margaret D. Cosgrave
P. H. Counsell
A. Edward Cox
P. V. Crocker
D. L. Croft, Q.C.
I. T. R. Davidson, Q.C.
I. H. Davies
L. John Davies, Q.C.
W. L. Monro Davies, Q.C.

N. Denison, Q.C.
K. M. Devlin
G. L. S. Dobry, C.B.E., Q.C.
C. Marais Edwards
Quentin T. Edwards, Q.C.
J. K. Q. Evans
F. P. L. Evans
P. R. Faulks, M.C.
A. L. Figgis
J. J. Finney
G. C. F. Forrester
J.J. Fordham
G.C.F. Forrester
J. R. B. Fox-Andrews, Q.C.
Alan Garfitt
Leonard Gerber
S. A. Goldstein
P. W. Goldstone
M. B. Goodman
J. H. Gower, Q.C.
M. Graham, Q.C.
P. B. Greenwood
D. J. Griffiths
G.D. Grigson
R. B. Groves, T.D.
N.T. Hague, Q.C.
Miss J. Graham Hall
P. J. Halnan
John Hamilton
R. E. Hammerton
J. P. Harris, D.S.C., Q.C.
T. F. Hatton
C. L. Hawser, Q.C.
J. D. W. Hayman
A. H. Head
M. R. Hickman
J. C. Hicks, Q.C.
A. N. Hitching
Derek Holden
A. C. W. Hordern, Q.C.
Sir David Hughes-Morgan, Bt., C.B., C.B.E.
J. Hunter
M. J. Hyam
C. P. James
William Kee
M. D. Kennedy, Q.C.
A. M. Kenny
J. F. Kingham
C.F. Kolbert

L. G. Krikler
L. H. C. Lait
G.F.B. Laughland, Q.C.
R. Laurie
T. Lawrence
Christopher Lea, M.C.
E.A.G. Lewis, Q.C.
A. C. L. Lewisohn
Alan Lipfriend
D. T. Lloyd
G. D. Lovegrove, Q.C.
D. B. D. Lowe
R. H. Lownie
Noreen Lowry
R. J. Lowry, Q.C.
R. D. Lymbery, Q.C.
K. A. Machin, Q.C.
J. L. E. MacManus, T.D., Q.C.
M. J. P. Macnair
J. R. Main, Q.C.
O.S. Martin, Q.C.
K.M. McHale
I.G. McLean
M.B. McMullan
N.A. Medawar, Q.C.
D.J. Mellor
J. H. E. Mendl
A. L. Mildon, Q.C.
D. Q. Miller
Sir James Miskin, Q.C.
(Recorder of London)
E. F. Monier-Williams
D. Morton-Jack
J. I. Murchie
J. H. R. Newey, Q.C.
C. W. F. Newman, Q.C.
Mrs. H. F. Norrie
Suzanne F. Norwood
C. R. Oddie
A. Owen
D. A. Paiba
R. H. S. Palmer
M. C. Parker, Q.C.
Valerie A. Pearlman
F. H. L. Petre
A. J. Phelan
T. H. Pigot, Q.C.
(Common Serjeant in the City of London)
D. C. Pitman

P.B. Pollack
H. C. Pownall, Q.C.
B. H. Pryor, Q.C.
J. E. Pullinger
J. W. Rant, Q.C.
E. V. Paynter Reece
G. K. Rice
K.A. Richardson. Q.C.
D. A. H. Rodwell, Q.C.
G. H. Rooke, T.D., Q.C.
P. C. R. Rowntree
K. W. Rubin
T. R. G. Ryland
R. B. Sanders
J. H. A. Scarlett
J. D. Sheerin
G. J. Shindler, Q.C.
D. R. A. Sich
Mota Singh, Q.C.
John K. E. Slack, T.D.
P. M. J. Slot
F. B. Smedley, Q.C.
R. J. Southan
R. O. C. Stable, Q.C.
Eric Stockdale
C. J. Sumner
John B. Taylor, M.B.E., T.D.
D. A. Thomas, M.B.E.
A. H. Tibber
A. M. Troup
Stephen Tumim
J. T. Turner
C.J.M. Tyrer
J. E. van der Werff
L.J. Verney
A.D.R. Vick, Q.C.
Richard Vick
B. J. Wakley, M.B.E.
A. F. Waley, V.R.D., Q.C.
R. Walker
John R. Warde
D. B. Watling, Q.C.
V. B. Watts
Sir D. S. West-Russell
F. J. White
J. E. Williams
S. M. Willis
G. N. Worthington
E. G. Wrintmore

WALES AND CHESTER CIRCUIT

T. R. Crowther, Q.C.
G. H. M. Daniel
R. D. G. David, Q.C., D.L.
Lord Elystan-Morgan

T. Michael Evans, Q.C.
W. N. Francis
Michael Gibbon, Q.C.
D. Morgan Hughes
G. J. Jones
G. E. Kilfoil
T. E. I. Lewis-Bowen

D. Glyn Morgan
T.H. Moseley, Q.C.
D. A. Phillips
D. W. Powell
E. J. Prosser, Q.C.
H. W. J. ap. Robert
H. E. P. Roberts, Q.C.

J. C. Rutter
S. M. Stephens, Q.C.
David Barry Williams, T.D., Q.C.
Hugh Williams, Q.C.
R. G. Woolley

WESTERN CIRCUIT

S.T. Bates
G. B. Best
C. L. Boothman
J. W. Bracewell
M. J. L. Brodrick
R.D.H. Bursell, Q.C.
J.D. Clarke

Hazel R. Counsell
J. Anthony Cox
J.W. Da Cunha
Mark Dyer
Peter Fallon, Q.C.
P. D. Fanner
B.J.F. Galpin
I. Starforth Hill, Q.C.
G. B. Hutton

J. H. Inskip, Q.C.
A. C. Lauriston, Q.C.
Sir Ian Lewis
David McCarraher, V.R.D
H. E. L. McCreery, Q.C.
Sheila M. D. McKinney
I.S. McKintosh
J. G. McNaught
E. G. Neville

J.N.P. Rudd
David Smith, Q.C.
K. C. L. Smithies
H. J. Martin Tucker, Q.C.
D. M. Webster
J. R. Whitley
K. M. Willcock, Q.C.
J. H. Wroath

EMPLOYMENT APPEAL TRIBUNAL

4 St. James's Square, London SW1Y 4JU (01-210 3841)

Judges:
The Hon. Mr. Justice Wood M.C. (President)
The Hon. Mr. Justice French
The Hon. Mr. Justice Scott
The Hon. Mr. Justice Hutchison
The Hon. Mr. Justice Garland
The Hon. Lord Mayfield, M.C. (Scotland)

Members:
Miss J. Graham Baird
T. S. Batho

J. S. Bell
A. F. Blacklaws, O.B.E.
A. C. Blyghton
Mrs. M. L. Boyle
G. R. Carter
Miss J. W. Collerson
Ms S. Corby
L. D. Cowan
J. Daly
J. H. Galbraith, C. B.
Mr. C. Gallagher
Mr. K. Graham
Dr. D. Grieves

Miss C. Holroyd
J. D. Houston
T. H. Jenkins, C.B.E.
D. A. C. Lambert
John Langan
R. Lewis
B. McAteer, B.E.M.
Mr. W. Morris
Mrs. G. D. Mortimer
G. A. Peers, D.F.C.
R. H. Phipps
J. A. Powell
J. C. Ramsay

A. J. Ramsden
A. D. Scott
J. A. Scouller
William Sirs
S. M. Springer, M.B.E.
Mrs. M. E. Sunderland
Mrs P. Turner
Miss A. P. Vale
Ms D. Warwick
E. A. Webb, O.B.E.
G. H. Wright, M.B.E.
K. M. Young, C.B.E.

THE NEW YEAR HONOURS 1990

compiled by Philip Hancock.

Baroness *(Life Peers)*

Park, Miss Daphne Margaret Sybil Desiree; lately Principal Somerville College Oxford

Barons *(Life Peers)*

Fieldhouse, Sir John David Elliott; former Chief, Defence Staff
Tombs, Sir Francis Leonard; Chairman, Turner and Newall and Rolls Royce; Chairman, Acost.

Privy Counsellors

Lyell, Sir Nicholas Walter Q.C., Solicitor General; M.P. (C) for Mid Bedfordshire
Patten, John Haggitt Charles, Minister of State, Home Office; M.P. (C) for Oxford West and Abingdon
Waldegrave, William Arthur; Minister of State, Foreign and Commonwealth Office; M.P. (C) for Bristol West

G.B.E. *(Knight Grand Cross of the Order of the British Empire)*

Vincent, General Sir Richard; Colonel Commandant, Royal Regiment of Artillery; Honorary Colonel 100 (Yeomanry) Field Regiment; Royal Artillery (Volunteers)
Watkins, Sir Tasker; Deputy Chief Justice

Companion of Honour

Lange, David Russell, M.P.; Attorney-General and Minister of State; lately Prime Minister of New Zealand

K.C.B. *(Knight Commander of the Bath)*

Anson, John; Second Permanent Secretary, H.M. Treasury
Boulton, Clifford John; Clerk of the House, House of Commons
Coward, Vice Admiral, John Francis
Guthrie, Lieutenant General, Charles Ronald Llewelyn, Colonel Commandant, Intelligence Corps.
Hibbert, Jack, Director, Central Statistical Office
Johnson, Lieutenant General, Garry Dene, Colonel 10th Princess Mary's Own Gurkha Rifles
Kemball, Air Marshal, Richard John.
Stear, Air Marshal, Michael James Douglas.

K.C.M.G. *(Knight Commander of St. Michael and St. George)*

Jenkins, Michael Romilly Heald; H.M. Ambassador, The Hague
McColl, Colin Hugh Verel; Foreign and Commonwealth Office.

Munro, Alan Gordon; H.M. Ambassador, Riyadh.
Robson, John Adam, H.M. Ambassador, Oslo.

K.C.V.O. *(Knight Commander of the Royal Victorian Order)*

Baring, Sir John Francis Harcourt.
Macrae, Colonel Robert Andrew Scarth.
Pinker, George Douglas.
Scott, Kenneth Bertram Adam.

D.B.E. *(Dame Commander of the Order of the British Empire)*

Smith, Miss Maggie (Mrs Cross); Actress
Szaszy, Mrs Miraka Petricevich; for services to the community, New Zealand.
Waterhouse, Mrs Rachel Elizabeth; for services to consumer affairs.

K.B.E. *(Knight Commander of the Order of the British Empire)*

Cleminson, Sir James Arnold Stacey; Chairman, British Overseas Trade Board.
Delamere, Monita Eru; for services to the Maori people, New Zealand.
Gina, Lloyd Maepeza; for public service in the Solomon Islands.
Steel, David Martin Scott, M.P. (SLD), Tweeddale, Etterick and Lauderdale; for political and public service.
Swan, John William David; for public service in Bermuda.

Knights Bachelor

Alleyne, Dr. George Allanmore Ogarren; for services to medicine in Barbados
Angus, Michael Richardson; Chairman, Unilever.
Ash, Professor Eric Albert; Rector, Imperial College of Science, Technology and Medicine, University of London.
Beresford, Alexander Paul; for political and public service.
Berriman, David; Chairman North East Thames Regional Health Authority.
Brett, Charles Edward Bainbridge; for public service in Northern Ireland.
Burke, Thomas Kerry, M.P.; Speaker of the House of Representatives in New Zealand.
Chilwell, (Mr. Justice), Muir Fitzherbert; Judge of the High Court, New Zealand.
Chinn, Trevor Edwin; Vice Chairman, Wishing Well Appeal, Great Ormond Street Hospital for Sick Children.
Cons, Mr. Justice Derek; Vice President of the Court of Appeal, Hong Kong.
De-Ville, Harold Godfrey Oscar; Chairman, Meyer International.
Easton, Robert William Simpson; Chairman and Managing Director, Yarrow Shipbuilders.
Elwood, Brian George Conway; for services to local government, New Zealand.
Fairclough, John Whitaker; chief scientific advisor, Cabinet Office.
Fareed, Dr. Djamil Sheik; for services to medicine, Mauritius.
Glyn, Alan, M.P. (C) for Windsor and Maidenhead; for political service.
Graham, James Thompson; for services to the dairy industry, New Zealand.
Hardie, Douglas Fleming; deputy chairman, Scottish Development Agency.
Harrison, Donald Frederick Norris; Professor of Laryngology and Otology, University of London.

Holt, Professor James Clarke; lately Master of Fitzwilliam College and Professor of Cambridge, lately Vice President, the British Academy.

Hornby, Derek Peter, Chairman, Rank Xerox (UK); for services to export.

Irving, Charles Graham, M.P. (C) for Cheltenham; for political service.

Jones, Charles Pearce; Chairman, Yorkshire Water; Chairman Water Authorities Association.

Lampl, Frank William; Chairman, Bovis Construction.

McDowell, Eric Wallace; Chairman, Industrial Development Board for Northern Ireland.

Morton, William David; for political and public service.

Naipaul, Vidiadhar (Vidia) Surajprasad; Author.

New, Major general Lawrence Anthony Wallis; Lieutenant Governor, Isle of Man.

Prout, Christopher James, Q.C., M.E.P. (C) for Shropshire and Stafford; for political service.

Quinton, John Grand; Chairman, Barclays Bank PLC.

Rickett, Raymond Mildmay Wilson; director, Middlesex Polytechnic.

Smith, John Wilson; for services to sport.

Stirling, Colonel David Archibald; for services to the Military.

Swire, John Anthony; President, John Swire and Sons.

Taylor, Professor William; Vice Chancellor, University of Hull; Chairman, Council for the Accreditation of Teacher Education.

Turnbull, George Henry; Chairman and Chief Executive, Inchape.

Wheeler, John Daniel, M.P. (C) for Westminster North; for political service.

BIRTHDAY HONOURS 1990

Baronesses *(Life Peers)*

Castle, The Right Honourable Barbra (Anne); Former M.P. and M.E.P.

Dunn, The Honourable Dame Lydia (Selina); Chairman Hong Kong Trade Development Council.

Barons *(Life Peers)*

Haslam, Sir Robert; Chairman, British Coal Corporation.

Lane, Sir Peter; Chairman executive committee, National Union of Conservative and Unionist Associations.

Porter, Sir George; President of the Royal Society.

Runcie, The Most Reverend and Right Honourable, Robert Alexander Kennedy, Archbishop of Canterbury.

Privy Counsellors

Earl of Caithness, Malcolm Ian Sinclair, Paymaster General.

Clark, Sir William Gibson, M.P. (C) for Croydon South.

G.C.B. *(Knight Grand Cross of the Order of the Bath)*

Heseltine, Sir William Frederick Payne, Private Secretary to the Queen.

G.C.M.G. *(Knight Grand Cross of St. Michael & St. George)*

Somare, Thomas M.P.; for political services, Papua New Guinea.

G.C.V.O. *(Dame Grand Cross of the Royal Victoria Order)*

Hambledon, Patricia, Dowager Viscountess.

K.C.B. *(Knight Commander of the Order of the Bath)*

Eaton, Vice Admiral Kenneth John.

Macdonald, Kenneth Carmichael, Second Permanent Under Secretary, Ministry of Defence.

Partridge, Michael John Anthony, Permanent Secretary, Department of Social Security.

Unwin, James Brian, Chairman, Board of H.M. Customs and Excise.

Walker, Patrick Jeremy, Ministry of Defence.

Wilson, Vice Admiral Barry Nigel.

K.C.M.G. *(Knight Commander of St. Michael & St. George)*

Barrington, Nicholas John, British High Commissioner, Islamabad.

Gillmore, David Howe, Foreign and Commonwealth Office.

Jewkes, Gordon Wesley, Director General of trade and Investment, U.S.A. and H.M. Consul General, New York.

D.C.V.O. *(Dame Commander of the Royal Victorian Order)*

Campbell-Preston, Mrs. Frances Olivia.

K.C.V.O. *(Knight Commander of the Royal Victorian Order)*

Gilmour, Colonel Allan Macdonald.

Griffin, Major Arthur John Stewart.

Innes of Edingight, Malcom Rognvold.

Knox, Colonel Bryce Muir.

D.B.E. *(Dame Commander of the Order of the British Empire)*

Abaijah, Miss Josephine; for services to the community, Papua New Guinea.

Blaize, Mrs. Venetia Ursula; for services to the community, Grenada.

Hylton-Foster, Lady Audrey Pellew, Convenor Cross Bench Peers, House of Lords.

Lloyd, Miss June Kathleen, Nuffield Professor of Child Health, Institute of Child Health, University of London.

Winstone, Mrs. Dorothy Gertrude; for services to the community, New Zealand.

K.B.E. *(Knight Commander of the Order of the British Empire)*

Bennett, Air Vice Marshal Erik Peter.

Clark, Terence Joseph, former H.M. Ambassador to Baghdad.

Mace, Lieutenant General J.A., Chief of Defence Staff, New Zealand Defence Force.

Siaguru, Anthony Michael; for services to the community, Papua New Guinea.
Stuart-Paul, Air Marshal Ronald Ian.
Weatherstone, Dennis; for services to British commercial and community interests in the U.S.A.

Knights Bachelor

Amis, Kingsley William. Author.
Arnold, Thomas Richard M.P. (C) for Hazel Grove; for political service.
Bamford, Anthony Paul, Chairman and Managing Director, J.C. Bamford Excavators.
Birkin, John Derek, Chief Executive and deputy chairman, R.T.Z. Corporation.
Burton-Bradley, Dr. Burton Gyrth; for services to medicine, Papua New Guinea.
Calderwood, Robert, Chief Executive, Strathclyde Regional Council.
Crossland, Bernard, Emeritus Professor, Queens University, Belfast.
Dellow, John Albert, Deputy Commissioner, Metropolitan Police.
Doughty, William Roland, Chairman North West Thames Regional Health Authority.
Fay, (Humphrey) Michael Gerard; for services to merchant banking & yachting, New Zealand.
Foster, Norman Robert, Principal, Foster Associates.
Grierson, Ronald Hugh, Chairman, South Bank Board.
Hadlee, Richard John; for services to cricket, New Zealand.
Heatly, Peter; for services to sports administration.
Holliday, Professor Frederick George Thomas, Vice-Chancellor and Warden, University of Durham.
Honeycombe, Robert William Kerr, Emeritus Professor of Metallurgy, University of Cambridge.
Marshall, Robert Michael M.P. (C) for Arundel; for political service.
McCrindle, Robert Arthur M.P. (C) for Brentwood & Ongar; for political service.
Miller, Donald John, Chairman, South of Scotland Electricity Board.
Mitchell, professor Edgar William John, Chairman, Science and Engineering Research Council.
Morland, Robert Kenelm; for political service.
Morrison, Howard Leslie; for services to entertainment, New Zealand.
Pattinson, William Derek, Secretary General, General Synod, Church of England.
Pearce, Daniel Norton Idris; for political and public service.
Phillips, Peter John, Chairman, AB Electronics Products Group.
Pilkington, Anthony Richard, Chairman, Pilkingtons.
Ramanee, Mookteswar Baboolall Kailash; for services to trade and industry, Mauritius.
Reid, Robert Paul (Bob), Chairman and Chief Executive, Shell (UK).
Richardson, Michael John de Rougemont, former managing director of N.M. Rothschild & Sons.
Roberts, Levan Wyn Pritchard M.P. (C) for Conway; for political service.
Savile, James Wilson Vincent, Chairman Bradmoor Hospital advisory committee and Sfoke Mandeville Hospital Spinal Injuries Centre; for charitable services.
Sheppard, Allen John George, Chairman and group chief executive, Grand Metropolitan.
Shields, Robert, Professor of Surgery and head of department of surgery, University of Liverpool.
Stones, William Frederick, Managing Director, China Light and Power Company.
Tugendhat, Christopher Samuel, Chairman, Civil Aviation Authority.
Ustinov, Peter Alexander. Actor, dramatist and film director.
Williams, Edward Dillwyn, Professor of Pathology, University of Wales College of Medicine, President, Royal College of Pathologists.
Wolfson, Brian Gordon, Chairman, Wembly, Chairman, National Training Task Force.

THE HONOURS SYSTEM

Recommendation for the names of people deserving honours can be proposed by the general public. The Cabinet Office and the Honours Section at Downing Street processes all such recommendations. Where necessary they will take outside advice to confirm the suitability and merit of the person recommended. The process of selection can be quite lengthy and even a most deserving name could take a year or more to assess.

After checking a draft list of names is submitted to the Prime Minister who can amend it as much as she deems necessary. It is then forwarded to the Palace for approval.

Once the list is finalised the people named are sent a confidential letter advising them that they are being considered for an honour. This gives the person concerned the opportunity to refuse the honour as does happen on occasion.

KNIGHTS OF THE GARTER

The Most Noble Order of the Garter (1348); K.G.; Ribbon: Garter Blue. Motto: Honi Soit Qui Mal y Pense (Evil be to him who evil thinks).

Sovereign of the Order: H.M. the Queen.

Ladies of the Garter: H.M. Queen Elizabeth the Queen Mother, H.R.H. Princess Juliana of the Netherlands, H.M. the Queen of Denmark.

Knights: H.R.H. the Duke of Edinburgh, H.R.H. the Prince of Wales, H.R.H. the Duke of Kent, H.M. the King of Norway, H.M. the King of the Belgians, H.M. the King of Sweden, H.M. the King of Spain, H.R.H. the Grand Duke of Luxembourg, Viscount De L'Isle, Lord Ashburton, Sir Cennydd Traherne, the Earl of Longford, the Earl Waldegrave, the Earl of Drogheda, the Marquess of Abergavenny, Lord Shackleton, Lord Wilson of Rievaulx, the Duke of Grafton, the Earl of Cromer, Lord Elworthy, Lord Hunt, Rt. Hon. Sir Paul Hasluck, Sir Richard Hull, Lord Lewin, the Duke of Norfolk, Lord Richardson of Duntisbourne, the Marquess of Normanby, Lord Carrington, Lord Callaghan of Cardiff, Viscount Leverhulme, Lord Hailsham of St. Marylebone.

KNIGHTS OF THE THISTLE

The Most Ancient and Most Noble Order of the Thistle (1687): K.T.; Ribbon: Green. Motto: Nemo Me Impune Lacessit (No one provokes me with impunity).

Sovereign of the Order: H.M. the Queen.

Lady of the Thistle: H.M. Queen Elizabeth the Queen Mother.

Knights: H.R.H. the Duke of Edinburgh, H.R.H. the Prince of Wales, H.M. the King of Norway, Lord Home of the Hirsel, the Earl of Wemyss and March, Lord Maclean, the Earl of Dalhousie, Lord Clydesmuir, Viscount Muirshiel, Sir Donald Cameron of Lochiel, the Earl of Selkirk, Lord McFadzean, the Duke of Buccleuch and Queensberry, Lord Cameron, the Earl of Elgin and Kincardine, Lord Thomson of Monifieth, Lord Maclehose of Beoch, the Earl of Airlie, Captain Sir Ian Tennant.

THE ORDER OF MERIT

King Edward VII instituted this order in 1902. Ribbon: Blue and Crimson. The Order of Merit (O.M.) is a special distinction for both men and women but does not confer a knighthood. It is limited to 24 members (in addition to honorary members).

Members: H.R.H. the Duke of Edinburgh, Dr. Dorothy Hodgkin, Lord Zuckerman, Lord Penney, Dame Veronica Wedgwood, Sir Isaiah Berlin, Sir George Edwards, Sir Alan Hodgkin, Sir Ronald Syme, Lord Franks, Lord Todd, Lord Olivier, Group Capt. Leonard Cheshire, Sir Michael Tippett, Sir Sidney Nolan, Rev. Prof. Owen Chadwick, Sir Andrew Huxley, Graham Greene, Air Cdre Sir Frank Whittle, Frederick Sanger, Sir Yehudi Menuhin, Professor Sir Ernest Gombrich, Dr. Max Perutz.

Honorary Member: Mother Teresa.

COMPANIONS OF HONOUR

Order of the Companions of Honour (1917): C.H.: Ribbon: Carmine with Gold Edges. The number of awards is limited to 65.

Members: Tunku Abdul Rahman Putra, Rt. Hon. (John) Douglas Anthony, Rt. Hon. Jack Ashley, Lord Aylestone, Lord Carrington, Sir Hugh Casson, Lord Cledwyn of Penrhos, Dame Ninette de Valois, Viscount Eccles, Lord Elwyn-Jones, Rt. Hon. Malcolm Fraser, Lucian Freud, Lord Gardiner, Sir John Gielgud, Lord Glenamara, Lord Goodman, Rt. Hon. Sir John Gorton, Graham Greene, Lord Hailsham of St. Marylebone, Rt. Hon. Denis Healey, Lord Houghton of Sowerby, James Larkin Jones, Viscount Muirshiel, Rt. Hon. Sir Robert Muldoon, Victor Pasmore, Prof. Max Perutz, John Piper, Sir Karl Popper, Sir Philip Powell, Sir Steven Runciman, Frederick Sanger, Arnold Smith, Rt. Hon. Michael Somare, Lord Stewart of Fulham, Rt. Hon. Brian Edward Talboys, Lord Thorneycroft, Sir Michael Tippett, Pierre Trudeau, Prof. Friedrich von Hayek, Viscount Watkinson, Viscount Whitelaw, Lord Joseph, Sydney Brenneer, Sir John Summusson, George Rylands, Sir Peter Scott, Anthony Powell.

Honorary Members: Lee Kuan Yew, Dr. Joseph Luns, Jean Monnet

THE ROYAL VICTORIAN CHAIN

This Order is awarded only on special occasions, but bestows no precedence on its members. It was founded in 1902 by King Edward VII.

Members: H.M. the Queen, H.M. Queen Elizabeth the Queen Mother, H.R.H. Princess Juliana of the Netherlands, H.M. the King of Norway, H.M. the King of Thailand, H.I.H. the Crown Prince of Ethiopia, H.M. the King of Jordan, H.M. the King of Afghanistan, H.M. the Queen of Denmark, Roland Michener, H.M. the King of Nepal, H.M. the King of Sweden, Lord Coggan, H.M. the Queen of the Netherlands, Ratu Sir George Cakobau, Lord Maclean, General Antonio Eanes, H.M. King of Spain, King Faid of Saudi Arabia.

The editors would like to thank Spink & Son Ltd for their help in the reproduction of the badges shown above.

THE NOBEL PRIZES, 1989

DR. ALFRED BERNHARD NOBEL, (1833-96) was a Swedish scientist, and the inventor of dynamite. He left a fortune of £1,750,000, and a large part of this was bequeathed to a fund to provide annual prizes to those persons who had most contributed to the benefit of mankind.

There are five prizes: for Physics, awarded by the Royal Swedish Academy of Sciences, for Chemistry, awarded by the same Academy, for Medicine and Physiology, awarded by the Royal Carolinian Medico-Surgical Institute of Stockholm, for Literature, awarded by the Royal Swedish Academy of Literature, and for Peace, awarded by the Norwegian Parliament. In 1968 an Economic Science prize in memory of Alfred Nobel was established by the Swedish Riksbank and the first award was made by the Royal Swedish Academy of Sciences in 1969.

Chemistry: Awarded to S. Altman (USA); T.R. Cech (USA)

Economic Sciences: Awarded to T. Haavelmo (Norway)

Literature: Awarded to Camilo Jose Cela (Spain)

Medicine and Physiology: Awarded to J. M. Bishop (USA); H.E. Varmus (USA)

Peace: Awarded to The 14th Dalai Lama (Tenzin Gyatso) (Tibet)

Physics: Awarded to N. F. Ramsey (USA); H.G. Dehmelt (USA); W. Paul (USA)

7

THE PEERAGE
Revised by Charles Kidd
Editor of *Debrett's Peerage amd Baronetage*

A Complete Peerage of the United Kingdom is given in the following pages. Not all Peers sit in the House of Lords. Those who do not are designated by (O) against their names. (M) signifies that the Peer is a minor (who of course, does not sit); (R) denotes a Peeress in her own right; (I) a Life Peer or Peeress; and (D) a Peer who has disclaimed his title.

The House of Lords consists of all Peers (including the Royal Peers) holding creations of England, of Great Britain, or of the United Kingdom; the Archbishops of Canterbury and York; 24 of the Bishops, according to seniority of consecration (but always including the Bishops of London, Durham, and Winchester); all Life Peers; and such eldest sons of Peers as may be summoned during the lifetime of their fathers. By the Peerage Act (1963) a Peer is able to renounce his title for his lifetime and a seat in the House of Lords was also given to all Scottish Peers and all hereditary Peeresses in their own rights. The Irish Peers who used to be represented by 28 of their number (none now remaining) still cannot sit. Peers who are minors, of unsound mind, or bankrupt, cannot take their seats.

The Royal Peers are:

Duke of York		**Duke of Kent**		**Duke of Edinburgh**	
cr.	1986	cr.	1934	cr.	1947
b.	1960	b.	1935	b.	1921
Duke of Gloucester		**Duke of Cornwall**			
cr.	1928	cr.	1337*		
b.	1944	b.	1948		

This is the date of the granting of the Charter for the Dukedom, which is not an hereditary one, and can only be held by the Heir-Apparent.

Peer's Title	Born	No. of Succn.	Family Name	Peer's Title	Born	No. of Succn.	Family Name
Aberconway, Baron	1913	3	McLaren	Balfour of Inchrye, Baron	1924	2	Balfour
Abercorn, Duke of	1934	5	Hamilton	Banbury of Southam,	1953	3	Banbury
Aberdare, Baron	1919	4	Bruce	Bancroft, Baron (L)	1922	-	Bancroft
Aberdeen & Temair, Marquess of	1920	6	Gordon	Bangor, Viscount (O)	1905	7	Ward
Abergavenny, Marquess of	1914	5	Nevill	Banks, Baron (L)	1920	-	Banks
Abinger, Baron	1914	8	Scarlett	Barber, Baron (L)	1920	-	Barber
Ackner, Baron (L)	1920	-	Ackner	Barnard, Baron	1923	11	Vane
Acton, Baron	1941	4	Lyon-Dalberg-Acton	Barnett, Baron (L)	1923	-	Barnett
Addington, Baron	1963	6	Hubbard	Basing, Baron	1939	5	Sclater-Booth
Addison, Viscount	1914	3	Addison	Bath, Marquess of	1905	6	Thynne
Adrian, Baron	1927	2	Adrian	Bath and Wells, Bishop of	1935	75	Carey
Ailesbury, Marquess of	1926	8	Brudenell-Bruce	Bathurst, Earl	1927	8	Bathurst
Ailsa, Marquess of	1925	7	Kennedy	Bauer, Baron (L)	1915	-	Bauer
Airedale, Baron	1915	4	Kitson	Bearsted, Viscount	1909	4	Samuel
Airey of Abingdon, Baroness (L)	1919	-	Airey	Beatty, Earl	1946	3	Beatty
Airlie, Earl of	1926	13	Ogilvy	Beaufort, Duke of	1928	11	Somerset
Alanbrooke, Viscount	1932	3	Brooke	Beaumont of Whitley, Baron (L)	1928	-	Beaumont
Albemarle, Earl of	1965	10	Keppel	Beaverbrook, Baron	1951	3	Aitken
Aldenham, and Hunsdon of Hunsdon, Baron	1948	6&4	Gibbs	Bedford, Duke of	1917	13	Russell
Aldington, Baron	1914	1	Low	Belhaven & Stenton, Lord	1927	13	Hamilton
Alexander of Potterhill, Baron (L)	1905	-	Alexander	Bellew, Baron (O)	1920	7	Bellew
Alexander of Tunis, Earl	1935	2	Alexander	Bellwin, Baron (L)	1923	-	Bellow
Alexander of Weedon, Baron (L)	1936		Alexander	Belmore, Earl (O)	1951	8	Lowry-Corry
Allen of Abbeydale, Baron (L)	1912	-	Allen	Beloff, Baron (L)	1913	-	Beloff
Allenby, Viscount	1931	3	Allenby	Belper, Baron	1912	4	Strutt
Allendale, Viscount	1922	3	Beaumont	Belstead, Baron	1932	2	Ganzoni
Allerton, Baron	1903	3	Jackson	Benson, Baron (L)	1909	-	Benson
Alport, Baron (L)	1912	-	Alport	Berkeley, Baroness (R)	1905	22	Foley-Berkeley
Altrincham, Baron (D)	1924	2	Grigg	Berners, Baroness (R)	1901	15	Williams
Alvingham, Baron	1926	2	Yerburgh	Bernstein, Baron (L)	1899	-	Bernstein
Amherst, Earl	1896	5	Amherst	Bessborough, Earl of	1913	10	Ponsonby
Amherst of Hackney, Baron	1940	4	Cecil	Bethell, Baron	1938	4	Bethell
Ampthill, Baron	1921	4	Russell	Bicester, Baron	1932	3	Vivian Smith
Amwell, Baron	1912	2	Montague	Biddulph, Baron	1959	5	Maitland
Anglesey, Marquess of	1922	7	Paget	Birdwood, Baron	1938	3	Birdwood
Annaly, Baron	1927	5	White	Birk, Baroness (L)	-		Birk
Annan, Baron (L)	1916	-	Annan	Birkett, Baron	1929	2	Birkett
Annandale and Hartfell, Earl of	1941	11	Johnstone of Annandale and that Ilk	Birmingham, Bishop of	1936	9	Santer
Annesley, Earl (O)	1924	10	Annesley	Blackburn, Bishop of	1937	7	Chesters
Antrim, Earl of (O)	1935	9	McDonnell	Blackstone, Baroness(L)	1942	-	Blackstone
Arbuthnott, Visc. of	1924	16	Arbuthnott	Blake, Baron (L)	1916	-	Blake
Archibald, Baron (D)	1926	2	Archibald	Blakenham, Viscount	1938	2	Hare
Ardwick, Baron (L)	1910	-	Beavan	Blanch, Baron (L)	1918	-	Blanch
Argyll, Duke of	1937	12	Campbell	Blatch, Baroness (L)	1937	-	Blatch
Armstrong of Ilminster,(L)	1927		Armstrong	Blease, Baron (L)	1914	-	Blease
Arran, Earl of	1938	9	Gore	Bledisloe, Viscount	1934	3	Bathurst
Ashbourne, Baron	1933	4	Gibson	Blyth, Baron	1931	4	Blyth
Ashbrook, Viscount (O)	1905	10	Flower	Boardman, Baron (L)	1919	-	Boardman
Ashburton, Baron	1898	6	Baring	Bolingbroke and St. John, Viscount	1927	7&8	St. John
Ashby, Baron (L)	1904	-	Ashby	Bolton, Baron	1929	7	Orde-Powlett
Ashcombe, Baron	1924	4	Cubitt	Bonham-Carter,Baron(L)	1922	-	Bonham Carter
Ashton of Hyde, Baron	1926	3	Ashton	Borthwick, Lord	1905	23	Borthwick of that Ilk
Ashtown, Baron (O)	1931	6	Trench	Borwick, Baron	1917	4	Borwick
Astor, Viscount	1951	4	Astor	Boston, Baron	1939	10	Irby
Astor of Hever, Baron	1946	3	Astor	Boston of Faversham, Baron (L)	1930	-	Boston
Atholl, Duke of	1931	10	Murray	Bottomley, Baron (L)	1907	-	Bottomley
Attlee, Earl	1927	2	Attlee	Boyd of Merton, Viscount	1939	2	Lennox-Boyd
Auckland, Baron	1926	9	Eden	Boyd-Carpenter, Baron	1908	-	Boyd Carpenter
Audley, Baron	1914	25	Souter	Boyne, Viscount	1931	10	Hamilton-Russell
Avebury, Baron	1928	4	Lubbock	Brabazon of Tara, Baron	1946	3	Moore-Brabazon
Aylesford, Earl of	1918	11	Finch-Knightley	Brabourne, Baron	1924	7	Knatchbull
Aylestone, Baron (L)	1905	-	Bowden	Bradbury, Baron	1914	2	Bradbury
Aylmer, Baron (O)	1923	13	Aylmer	Bradford, Earl of	1947	7	Bridgeman
Bacon, Baroness (L)	-	-	Bacon	Bradford, Bishop of	1932	7	Williamson
Baden-Powell, Baron	1936	3	Baden-Powell	Brain, Baron	1926	2	Brain
Bagot, Baron	1914	9	Bagot	Bramall, Baron (L)	1923	-	Bramall
Baillieu, Baron	1950	3	Baillieu	Brandon of Oakbrook, Baron (L)	1920	-	Brandon
Baldwin of Bewdley, Earl	1938	4	Baldwin	Brassey of Apethorpe, Baron	1932	3	Brassey
Balfour, Earl of	1925	4	Balfour	Braybrooke, Baron	1932	10	Neville
Balfour of Burleigh,	1927	12	Bruce	Braye, Baroness (R)	1941	8	Aubrey-Fletcher
				Breadalbane, Earl of	1919	10	Campbell

Peer's Title	Born	No. of Succn.	Family Name	Peer's Title	Born	No. of Succn.	Family Name
Brentford, Viscount	1933	4	Joynson-Hicks	Carnarvon, Earl of	1924	7	Herbert
Bridge of Harwich, Baron (L)	1917	-	Bridge	Carnegy of Lour, Baroness (L)	1925	-	Carnegy of Lour
Bridgeman, Viscount	1930	3	Bridgeman	Carnock, Baron	1920	4	Nicolson of that Ilk
Bridges, Baron	1927	2	Bridges				
Bridport, Viscount	1948	4	Hood	Carr of Hadley, Baron (L)	1916	-	Carr
Briggs, Baron (L)	1921	-	Briggs	Carrick, Earl of	1931	9	Butler
Brightman, Baron (L)	1911	-	Brightman	Carrington, Baron	1919	6	Carington
Briginshaw, Baron (L)	1910	-	Briginshaw	Carter, Baron (L)	1932	-	Carter
Brimelow, Baron (L)	1915	-	Brimelow	Carver, Baron (L)	1915	-	Carver
Bristol, Marquess of	1954	7	Hervey	Castlemaine, Baron (O)	1943	8	Handcock
Bristol, Bishop of	1936	-	Rogerson	Castle Stewart, Earl(O)	1928	8	Stuart
Broadbridge, Baron	1938	3	Broadbridge	Cathcart, Earl	1919	6	Cathcart
Brocket, Baron	1952	3	Nall-Cain	Catto, Baron	1923	2	Catto
Brooke of Ystradfellte, Baroness (L)	1908	-	Brooke	Cavan, Earl of (O)	1944	13	Lambart
				Cawdor, Earl	1932	6	Campbell
Brookeborough, Viscount	1952	3	Brooke	Cawley, Baron	1913	3	Cawley
Brookes, Baron (L)	1909	-	Brookes	Cayzer, Baron (L)	1910	-	Cayzer
Brooks of Tremorfa, Baron (L)	1927	-	Brooks	Chalfont, Baron (L)	1919	-	Gwynne Jones
				Chandos, Viscount	1953	3	Lyttelton
Brougham and Vaux, Baron	1938	5	Brougham	Chapple, Baron (L)	1921	-	Chapple
				Charlemont, Viscount(O)	1934	14	Caulfeild
Broughshane, Baron	1903	2	Davison	Charteris of Amisfield, Baron (L)	1913	-	Charteris
Brownlow, Baron	1936	7	Cust				
Broxbourne, Baron (L)	1910	-	Walker-Smith	Chatfield, Baron	1917	2	Chatfield
Bruce of Donington, Baron (L)	1912	-	Bruce	Chelmer, Baron (L)	1914	-	Edwards
				Chelmsford, Bishop of	1930	7	Waine
Bruntisfield, Baron	1899	1	Warrender	Chelmsford, Viscount	1931	3	Thesiger
Buccleuch & Queensberry, Duke of	1923	9 & 11	Montagu Douglas Scott	Chesham, Baron	1941	6	Cavendish
				Chetwode, Baron	1937	2	Chetwode
				Chetwynd, Viscount (O)	1935	10	Chetwynd
Buchan, Earl of	1930	17	Erskine	Chichester, Bishop of	1915	99	Kemp
Buckinghamshire, Earl of	1944	10	Hobart-Hampden	Chichester, Earl of	1944	9	Pelham
				Chilston, Viscount	1946	4	Akers-Douglas
Buckmaster, Viscount	1921	3	Buckmaster	Chilver, Baron (L)	1926		Chilver
Bullock, Baron (L)	1914	-	Bullock	Chitnis, Baron (L)	1936	-	Chitnis
Burden, Baron	1916	2	Burden	Cholmondeley, Marquess of	1960	7	Cholmondeley
Burgh, Baron	1935	7	Leith	Chorley, Baron	1930	2	Chorley
Burnham, Baron	1920	5	Lawson	Churchill, Viscount	1934	3	Spencer
Burton, Baron	1924	3	Baillie	Churston, Baron	1910	4	Yarde-Buller
Burton of Coventry, Baroness (L)	1904	-	Burton	Citrine, Baron	1914	2	Citrine
				Clancarty, Earl of	1911	8	Le Poer Trench
Bute, Marquess of	1933	6	Crichton Stuart	Clanmorris, Baron (O)	1937	8	Bingham
Butterfield, Baron (L)	1920	-	Butterfield	Clanwilliam, Earl of	1919	7	Meade
Butterworth, Baron (L)	1918	-	Butterworth	Clarendon, Earl of	1933	7	Villiers
Buxton of Alsa, Baron(L)	1918	-	Buxton	Cledwyn of Penrhos, Baron (L)	1916	-	Hughes
Byron, Baron	1950	13	Byron	Clifford of Chudleigh, Baron	1948	14	Clifford
Caccia, Baron (L)	1905	-	Caccia	Clinton, Baron	1934	22	Fane Trefusis
Cadman, Baron	1938	3	Cadman	Clinton-Davis, Baron (L)	1928		Clinton-Davis
Cadogan, Earl	1914	7	Cadogan	Clitheroe, Baron	1929	2	Assheton
Cairns, Earl	1939	6	Cairns	Clwyd, Baron	1935	3	Roberts
Caithness, Earl of	1948	20	Sinclair	Clydesmuir, Baron	1917	2	Colville
Caldecote, Viscount	1917	2	Inskip	Cobbold, Baron	1937	2	Lytton Cobbold
Caledon, Earl of (O)	1955	7	Alexander	Cobham, Viscount	1943	11	Lyttelton
Callaghan of Cardiff, Baron (L)	1912		Callaghan	Cochrane of Cults,Baron (L)	1922	3	Cochrane
Calthorpe, Baron	1927	10	Gough-Calthorpe	Cockfield, Baron (L)	1916	-	Cockfield
				Coks of Hartcliffe, Baron (L)	1929	Cocks	
Calverley, Baron	1946	3	Muff	Coggan, Baron (L)	1909	-	Coggan
Camden, Marquess	1930	6	Pratt	Coleraine, Baron	1931	2	Law
Cameron of Lochbroom, Baron (L)	1931	-	Cameron	Coleridge, Baron	1937	5	Coleridge
Camoys, Baron	1940	7	Stonor	Colgrain, Baron	1920	3	Campbell
Campbell of Alloway, Baron (L)	1917	-	Campbell	Collison, Baron (L)	1909	-	Collison
Campbell of Croy, Baron (L)	1921	-	Campbell	Colnbrook, Baron (L)	1922		Atkins
Campbell of Eskan, Baron (L)	1912	-	Campbell	Colville of Culross, Viscount	1933	4	Colville
Camrose, Viscount	1909	2	Berry	Colwyn, Baron	1942	3	Smith
Canterbury, Archbishop of	1921	102	Runcie	Colyton, Baron	1902	1	Hopkinson
Caradon, Baron (L)	1907	-	Foot	Combermere, Viscount	1929	5	Stapleton-Cotton
Carbery, Baron (O)	1920	11	Evans-Freke	Congleton, Baron	1930	8	Parnell
Carew, Baron	1905	6	Conolly-Carew	Constantine of Stanmore,Baron (L)	1910	-	Constantine
Carlisle, Earl of	1923	12	Howard	Conyngham, Marquess	1924	7	Conyngham
Carlisle, Bishop of	1932	65	Halsey	Cork and Orrery,Earl of	1910	13	Boyle
Carlisle of Bucklow, Baron (L)	1929		Carlisle	Cornwallis, Baron	1921	3	Cornwallis
Carmichael of Kelvingrove, Baron (L)	1921	-	Carmichael	Cottenham, Earl of	1948	8	Pepys
				Cottesloe, Baron	1900	4	Fremantle
				Courtown, Earl of	1954	9	Stopford
				Coventry, Earl of	1934	11	Coventry
				Cowdray, Viscount	1910	3	Pearson
				Cowley, Earl	1934	7	Wellesley

Peer's Title	Born	No. of Succn.	Family Name
Cox, Baroness (L)	1937	-	Cox
Craigavon, Viscount	1944	3	Craig
Craigmyle, Baron	1923	3	Shaw
Craigton, Baron (L)	1904	-	Browne
Cranbrook, Earl of	1933	5	Gathorne-Hardy
Cranworth, Baron	1940	4	Gurdon
Crathorne, Baron	1939	2	Dugdale
Craven, Earl of	1961	8	Craven
Crawford and Balcarres, Earl of	1927	29& 12	Lindsay
Crawshaw, Baron	1933	4	Brooks
Crickhowell, Baron (L)	1934		Edwards
Croft, Baron	1916	2	Croft
Crofton, Baron (O)	1951	7	Crofton
Croham, Baron (L)	1917	-	Allen
Cromartie, Earl of	1948	5	Mackenzie
Cromer, Earl of	1918	3	Baring
Cromwell, Baron	1960	7	Bewicke-Copley
Crook, Baron	1926	2	Crook
Cross, Viscount	1920	3	Cross
Cudlipp, Baron (L)	1913	-	Cudlipp
Cullen of Ashbourne, Baron	1912	2	Cokayne
Cunliffe, Baron	1932	3	Cunliffe
Dacre, Baroness (R)	1929	27	Douglas-Home
Dacre of Glanton, Baron (L)	1914	-	Trevor-Roper
Dainton, Baron (L)	1914	-	Dainton
Dalhousie, Earl of	1914	16	Ramsay
Darcy de Knayth, Baroness (R)	1938	18	Ingrams
Daresbury, Baron	1928	3	Greenall
Darling, Baron	1919	2	Darling
Darnley, Earl of	1941	11	Bligh
Dartmouth, Earl of	1924	9	Legge
Darwen, Baron	1938	3	Davies
Daryngton, Baron	1908	2	Pease
Daventry, Viscount	1921	3	FitzRoy Newdegate
David, Baroness (L)	1913	-	David
Davidson, Viscount	1928	2	Davidson
Davies, Baron	1940	3	Davies
Davies of Penrhys, Baron (L)	1913	-	Davies
Dean of Beswick, Baron (L)	1922	-	Dean
Decies, Baron (O)	1915	6	de la Poer Beresford
De Clifford, Baron	1928	27	Russell
Deedes, Life Baron	1913	-	Deedes
De Freyne,	1916	-	Blackton
Delacourt-Smith of Alteryn, Baroness (L)	1927	7	French
Delamere, Baron Cholmondeley	1934	5	
De La Warr, Earl	1948	11	Sackville
Delfont, Baron (L)	1909	-	Delfont
De L'Isle, Viscount	1909	1	Sidney
De Mauley, Baron	1921	6	Ponsonby
Denbigh, and Desmond, Earl of	1943	11& 10	Feilding
Denham, Baron	1927	2	Bowyer
Denman, Baron	1916	5	Denman
Denington, Baroness (L)	1907	-	Denington
Denning, Baron (L)	1899	-	Denning
Deramore, Baron	1911	6	de Yarburgh-Bateson
De Ramsey, Baron	1910	3	Fellowes
Derby, Bishop of	1928	5	Dawes
Derby, Earl of	1918	18	Stanley
de Ros, Baron	1958	28	Maxwell
Derwent, Baron	1930	5	Vanden-Bempde-Johnstone
De Saumarez, Baron	1924	6	Saumarez
De Vesci, Viscount (O)	1955	7	Vesey
De Villiers, Baron	1911	3	de Villiers
Devlin, Baron (L)	1905	-	Devlin
Devon, Earl of	1916	17	Courtenay
Devonport, Viscount	1944	3	Kearley
Devonshire, Duke of	1920	11	Cavendish
Diamond, Baron (L)	1907	-	Diamond
Dickinson, Baron	1926	2	Dickinson
Digby, Baron	1924	12	Digby
Dilhorne, Viscount	1932	2	Manningham-Buller
Dillon, Viscount (O)	1973	22	Dillon
Donaldson of Kingsbridge, Baron (L)	1907	-	Donaldson
Donaldson of Lymington, Baron (L)	1920		Donaldson
Donegall, Marquess of	1916	7	Chichester
Doneraile, Viscount (O)	1946	10	St. Leger
Donoughmore, Earl of	1927	8	Hely-Hutchinson
Donoughue, Baron (L)	1934	-	Donoughue
Dormand of Easington, Baron (L)	1919		Dormand
Dormer, Baron	1914	16	Dormer
Dowding, Baron	1919	2	Dowding
Downe, Viscount	1935	11	Dawnay
Downshire, Marquess of	1929	8	Hill
Drogheda, Earl of	1937	12	Moore
Ducie, Earl of	1917	6	Moreton
Dudley, Earl of	1920	4	Ward
Dudley, Baroness (R)	1907	14	Hamilton
Dufferin and Clandeboye, Baron	1916	10	Blackwood
Dulverton, Baron	1915	2	Wills
Dunalley, Baron (O)	1912	6	Prittie
Dunboyne, Baron (O)	1917	28	Butler
Dundee, Earl of	1949	12	Scrymgeour
Dundonald, Earl of	1961	15	Cochrane
Dunleath, Baron	1933	4	Mulholland
Dunmore, Earl of	1913	11	Murray
Dunraven and Mount-Earl, Earl of (O)	1939	7	Wyndham-Quin
Dunrossil, Viscount	1926	2	Morrison
Dunsany, Baron (O)	1906	19	Plunkett
Durham, Bishop of	1925	92	Jenkins
Durham, Earl of (D)	1922	6	Lambton
Dynevor, Baron	1935	9	Rhys
Dysart, Countess of (R)	1914	11	Greaves
Ebbisham, Baron	1912	2	Blades
Ebury, Baron	1934	6	Grosvenor
Eccles, Viscount	1904	1	Eccles
Eden of Winton, Baron (L)	1925	-	Eden
Edmund-Davies, Baron (L)	1906	-	Edmund-Davies
Effingham, Earl of	1905	6	Howard
Eglinton and Winton, Earl of	1939	18	Montgomerie
Egmont, Earl of	1914	11	Perceval
Egremont and Leconfield, Baron	1948	2 & 7	Wyndham
Eldon, Earl of	1937	5	Scott
Elgin and Kincardine, Earl of	1924	11&15	Bruce
Elibank, Lord	1923	14	Erskine Murray
Ellenborough, Baron	1926	8	Law
Elles, Baroness (L)	1921	-	Elles
Elliot of Harwood, Baroness (L)	1903	-	Elliot
Elliot of Morpeth, Baron (L)	1920	-	Elliott
Elphinstone, Lord	1953	18	Elphinstone
Elton, Baron	1930	2	Elton
Elworthy, Baron (L)	1911	-	Elworthy
Ely, Bishop of	1919	66	Walker
Ely, Marquess of	1913	8	Tottenham
Elystan-Morgan, Baron (L)	1932	-	Morgan
Emslie, Baron (L)	1919	-	Emslie
Ennals, Baron (L)	1922	-	Ennals
Enniskillen, Earl of	1942	7	Cole
Erne, Earl of	1937	6	Crichton
Erroll, Earl of	1948	24	Hay
Erroll of Hale, Baron	1914	1	Erroll
Erskine of Rerrick, Baron	1926	2	Erskine
Esher, Viscount	1913	4	Brett
Essex, Earl of	1920	10	Capell
Evans of Claughton, Baron (L)	1928	-	Evans
Ewart-Biggs, Baroness (L)	1929	-	Ewart Biggs
Exeter, Marquess of	1935	8	Cecil
Exmouth, Viscount	1940	10	Pellew
Ezra, Baron (L)	1919	-	Ezra

7

Peer's Title	Born	No. of Succn.	Family Name	Peer's Title	Born	No. of Succn.	Family Name
Fairfax of Cameron, Lord	1956	14	Fairfax	Grantley, Baron	1923	7	Norton
Fairhaven, Baron	1936	3	Broughton	Granville, Earl	1918	5	Leveson-Gower
Faithfull, Baroness(L)	1910	-	Faithfull	Granville of Eye,			
Falkender, Baroness (L)	1932	-	Falkender	Baron(L)	1899	-	Granville
Falkland, Viscount of	1935	15	Cary	Graves, Baron (O)	1911	8	Graves
Falmouth, Viscount	1919	9	Boscawen	Gray, Lord (O)	1931	22	Campbell-Gray
Fanshawe of Richmond,	1927	-	Royle	Gray of Contin, Baron (L)	1927	-	Gray
Baron (L)				Greene of Harrow Weald,	1910	-	Greene
Faringdon, Baron	1937	3	Henderson	Baron (L)			
Farnham, Baron (O)	1931	12	Maxwell	Greenhill, Baron	1924	3	Greenhill
Fermoy, Baron (O)	1967	6	Roche	Greenhill of Harrow,	1913	-	Greenhill
Ferrers, Earl	1929	13	Shirley	Baron (L)			
Ferrier, Baron (L)	1900	-	Noel-Paton	Greenway, Baron	1941	4	Greenway
Feversham, Baron	1945	6	Duncombe	Greenwood, Viscount	1914	2	Greenwood
ffrench, Baron (O)	1956	8	ffrench	Gregson, Baron (L)	1924	-	Gregson
Fieldhouse, Baron (L)	1928	-	Fieldhouse	Grenfell, Baron	1935	3	Grenfell
Fife, Duke of	1929	3	Carnegie	Gretton, Baron (M)	1975	4	Gretton
Fisher, Baron	1921	3	Fisher	Grey, Earl	1939	6	Grey
Fisher of Rednal,	1919	-	Fisher	Grey of Codnor	1935	5	Cornwall-Legh
Baroness (L)				Grey of Naunton, Baron (L)	1910	-	Grey
Fitt, Baron (L)	1926	-	Fitt	Gridley, Baron	1906	2	Gridley
FitzWalter, Baron	1914	21	Plumptre	Griffiths, Baron (L)	1923	-	Griffiths
Fletcher, Baron (L)	1903	-	Fletcher	Grimond, Baron (L)	1913	-	Grimond
Flowers, Baron (L)	1924	-	Flowers	Grimston of Westbury,	1925	2	Grimston
Foley, Baron	1923	8	Foley	Baron			
Foot, Baron (L)	1909	-	Foot	Grimthorpe, Baron	1915	4	Beckett
Forbes, Lord	1918	22	Forbes	Guilford, Earl of	1933	9	North
Forester, Baron	1938	8	Weld-Forester				
Forres, Baron	1946	4	Williamson	Hacking, Baron	1938	3	Hacking
Forte, Baron (L)	1908	-	Forte	Haddington, Earl of	1941	13	Baillie-Hamilton
Fortescue, Earl	1922	7	Fortescue	Haden-Guest, Baron	1913	4	Haden-Guest
Forteviot, Baron	1906	3	Dewar	Haig, Earl	1918	2	Haig
Franks, Baron (L)	1905	-	Franks	Hailsham, Viscount (D)	1907	2	Hogg
Fraser of Kilmorack,	1915	-	Fraser	Hailsham of St.	1907	-	Hogg
Baron (L)				Marylebone, Baron (L)			
Freyberg, Baron	1923	2	Freyberg	Halifax, Earl of	1944	3	Wood
Furness, Viscount	1929	2	Furness	Halsbury, Earl of	1908	3	Giffard
				Hambleden, Viscount	1930	4	Smith
Gage, Viscount	1932	7	Gage	Hamilton & Brandon,	1938	15 &	Douglas-
Gainford, Baron	1921	3	Pease	Duke of		12	Hamilton
Gainsborough, Earl of	1923	5	Noel	Hamilton of Dalzell,			
Gallacher, Baron (L)	1920	-	Gallacher	Baron	1938	4	Hamilton
Galloway, Earl of	1928	13	Stewart	Hampden, Viscount	1937	6	Brand
Galpern, Baron (L)	1903	-	Galpern	Hampton, Baron	1925	6	Pakington
Galway, Viscount	1922	12	Monckton-	Hankey, Baron	1905	2	Hankey
			Arundell	Hanson, Baron (L)	1922	-	Hanson
Gardner of Parkes,	1927	-	Gardner	Hanworth, Viscount	1916	2	Pollock
Baroness (L)				Harberton, Viscount (O)	1910	10	Pomeroy
Garvagh, Baron (O)	1920	5	Canning	Harding of Petherton,	1928	2	Harding
Geddes, Baron	1937	3	Geddes	Baron			
Gerard, Baron	1918	4	Gerard	Hardinge, Viscount	1956	6	Hardinge
Gibson, Baron (L)	1916	-	Gibson	Hardinge of Penshurst,	1921	3	Hardinge
Gibson-Watt, Baron (L)	1918	-	Gibson-Watt	Baron			
Gifford, Baron	1940	6	Gifford	Hardwicke, Earl of (M)	1971	10	Yorke
Gisborough, Baron	1927	3	Chaloner	Harewood, Earl of	1923	7	Lascelles
Gladwyn, Baron	1900	1	Jebb	Harlech, Baron	1954	6	Ormsby-Gore
Glanusk, Baron	1917	4	Bailey	Harmar Nicholls, Baron (L)	1912	-	Harmar
Glasgow, Earl of	1939	10	Boyle				Nicholls
Glenamara, Baron (L)	1912	-	Short	Harmsworth, Baron	1903	2	Harmsworth
Glenarthur, Baron	1944	4	Arthur	Harrington, Earl of	1922	11	Stanhope
Glenconner, Baron	1926	3	Tennant	Harris, Baron	1920	6	Harris
Glendevon, Baron	1912	1	Hope	Harris of Greenwich,	1930	-	Harris
Glendyne, Baron	1926	3	Nivison	Baron (L)			
Glentoran, Baron	1912	2	Dixon	Harris of High Cross,	1924	-	Harris
Gloucester, Bishop of	1925	37	Yates	Baron (L)			
Goff of Chieveley,	1926	-	Goff	Harrowby, Earl of	1922	7	Ryder
Baron (L)				Hart of South Lanark,	1924	Hart	
Goodman, Baron (L)	1913	-	Goodman	Baroness (L)			
Goold, Baron (L)	1934	-	Goold	Hartwell, Baron (L)	1911	-	Berry
Gorell, Baron	1927	4	Barnes	Harvey of Prestbury,	1906	-	Harvey
Gormanston, Viscount	1939	17	Preston	Baron (L)			
Gormley, Baron (L)	1917	-	Gormley	Harvey of Tasburgh,			
Gort, Viscount (O)	1916	8	Vereker	Baron	1921	2	Harvey
Goschen, Viscount	1965	4	Goschen	Harvington, Baron (L)	1907	-	Grant Ferris
Gosford, Earl of	1942	7	Acheson	Hastings, Baron	1912	22	Astley
Gough, Viscount	1941	5	Gough	Hatch of Lusby, Baron(L)	1917	-	Hatch
Gowrie, Earl of	1939	2	Hore-Ruthven	Hatherton, Baron	1950	8	Littleton
Grade, Baron (L)	1906	-	Grade	Havers, Baron (L)	1923	-	Havers
Grafton, Duke of	1919	11	FitzRoy	Hawarden, Viscount (O)	1926	8	Maude
Graham of Edmonton,	1925	-	Graham	Hawke, Baron	1904	10	Hawke
Baron (L)				Hayter, Baron	1911	3	Chubb
Granard, Earl of	1915	9	Forbes	Hazlerigg, Baron	1910	2	Hazlerigg
Grantchester, Baron	1921	2	Suenson-Taylor	Head, Viscount	1937	2	Head

Peer's Title	Born	No. of Succn.	Family Name	Peer's Title	Born	No. of Succn.	Family Name
Headfort, Marquess of	1932	6	Taylour	Jenkins of Putney, Baron (L)	1908	-	Jenkins
Headley, Baron (O)	1902	7	Allanson-Winn	Jersey, Earl of	1910	9	Child-Villiers
Hemingford, Baron	1934	3	Herbert	Jessel, Baron	1904	2	Jessel
Hemphill, Baron	1928	5	Martyn-Hemphill	John-Mackie, Baron (L)	1909	-	Mackie
Henderson of Brompton, Baron (L)	1922	-	Henderson	Johnston of Rockport, Baron (L)	1915	-	Johnston
Henley, Baron	1953	8	Eden	Joicey, Baron	1925	4	Joicey
Henniker, Baron	1916	8	Henniker-Major	Joseph, Baron (L)	1918		Joseph
Hereford, Bishop of	1920	103	Eastaugh				
Hereford, Viscount	1932	18	Devereux	Kaberry of Adel, Baron (L)	1907	-	Kaberry
Herries of Terregles, Baroness (R)	1938	14	Cowdrey	Kadoorie, Baron (L)	1899	-	Kadoorie
Herschell, Baron	1923	3	Herschell	Kagan, Baron (L)	1915	-	Kagan
Hertford, Marquess of	1930	8	Seymour	Kearton, Baron (L)	1911	-	Kearton
Hesketh, Baron	1950	3	Fermor-Hesketh	Keith of Castleacre, Baron (L)	1916	-	Keith
Heytesbury, Baron	1931	6	Holmes a Court	Keith of Kinkel, Baron (L)	1922	-	Keith
Hill, Viscount	1931	8	Clegg-Hill	Kemsley, Viscount	1909	2	Berry
Hill Norton, Baron (L)	1915	-	Hill Norton	Kenilworth, Baron	1954	4	Siddeley
Hindlip, Baron	1912	5	Allsopp	Kennet, Baron	1923	2	Young
Hirshfield, Baron (L)	1913	-	Hirshfield	Kensington, Baron	1933	8	Edwardes
Hives, Baron	1913	2	Hives	Kenswood, Baron	1930	2	Whitfield
Holderness, Baron (L)	1920	-	Wood	Kenyon, Baron	1917	5	Tyrell-Kenyon
Hollenden, Baron	1914	3	Hope-Morley	Kershaw, Baron	1936	4	Kershaw
Holm Patrick, Baron	1928	3	Hamilton	Keyes, Baron	1919	2	Keyes
Home, Earl of (D)	1903	14	Douglas-Home	Kilbracken, Baron	1920	3	Godley
Home of the Hirsel, Baron (L)	1903	-	Douglas-Home	Killanin, Baron	1914	3	Morris
Hood, Viscount	1914	7	Hood	Killearn, Baron	1919	2	Lampson
Hooper, Baroness (L)	1939	-	Hooper	Kilmaine, Baron (O)	1948	7	Browne
Hooson, Baron (L)	1925	-	Hooson	Kilmarnock, Baron	1927	7	Boyd
Horder, Baron	1910	2	Horder	Kilmorey, Earl of (O)	1942	6	Needham
Hotham, Baron (O)	1940	8	Hotham	Kimball, Baron (L)	1928	-	Kimball
Hothfield, Baron	1904	5	Tufton	Kimberley, Earl of	1924	4	Wodehouse
Houghton of Sowerby, Baron (L)	1898	-	Houghton	Kindersley, Baron	1929	3	Kindersley
Howard de Walden, Baron	1912	9	Scott Ellis	King of Wartnaby, Baron (L)	1918	-	King
Howard of Penrith, Baron	1905	2	Howard	Kingsale, Baron (O)	1941	30	de Courcy
Howe, Earl	1951	7	Curzon	Kings Norton, Baron (L)	1902	-	Roxbee Cox
Howick of Glendale, Baron	1937	2	Baring	Kingston, Earl of (O)	1943	11	King-Tenison
Howie of Troon, Baron (L)	1924	-	Howie	Kinloss, Baroness (R)	1922	12	Freeman-Grenville
Hughes, Baron (L)	1911	-	Hughes				
Hunt, Baron (L)	1910	-	Hunt	Kinnaird, Lord	1912	13	Kinnaird
Hunt of Tanworth, Baron (L)	1919	-	Hunt	Kinnoull, Earl of	1935	15	Hay
Hunter of Newington, Baron (L)	1915	-	Hunter	Kinross, Baron	1949	5	Balfour
				Kintore, Earl of	1939	13	Baird
Huntingdon, Earl of	1901	15	Hastings	Kirkhill, Baron (L)	1930	-	Smith
Huntingfield, Baron (O)	1915	6	Vanneck	Kirkwood, Baron	1931	3	Kirkwood
Huntly, Marquess of	1944	13	Gordon	Kissin, Baron (L)	1912	-	Kissin
Hutchinson of Lullington, Baron, (L)	1915	-	Hutchinson	Kitchener of Khartoum, Earl	1919	3	Kitchener
Hylton, Baron	1932	5	Jolliffe	Knights, Baron (L)	1920		Knights
Hylton-Foster, Baroness (L)	1908	-	Hylton-Foster	Knollys, Viscount	1931	3	Knollys
				Knutsford, Viscount	1926	6	Holland-Hibbert
Iddesleigh, Earl of	1932	4	Northcote	Lambert, Viscount	1912	3	Lambert
Ilchester, Earl of	1920	9	Fox-Strangways	Lane, Baron (L)	1918	-	Lane
Iliffe, Baron	1908	2	Iliffe	Lanesborough, Earl of (O)	1918	9	Butler
Inchcape, Earl of	1917	3	Mackay	Langford, Baron (O)	1912	9	Rowley-Conwy
Inchiquin, Baron (O)	1943	18	O'Brien	Lansdowne, Marquess of	1912	8	Petty-Fitzmaurice
Inchyra, Baron	1935	2	Hoyer Millar				
Ingleby, Viscount	1926	2	Peake	Latham, Baron	1954	2	Latham
Inglewood, Baron	1951	2	Fletcher-Vane	Latymer, Baron	1926	8	Money-Coutts
Ingrow, Baron (L)	1917	-	Taylor	Lauderdale, Earl of	1911	17	Maitland
Inverforth, Baron (M)	1966	4	Weir	Lawrence, Baron	1937	5	Lawrence
Ironside, Baron	1924	2	Ironside	Layton, Baron	1947	3	Layton
Irvine of Lairg, Baron (L)	1940	-	Irvine	Leatherland, Baron (L)	1898	-	Leatherland
Iveagh, Earl of	1937	3	Guinness 126	Leathers, Viscount	1908	2	Leathers
				Leicester, Earl of	1909	6	Coke
				Leicester, Bishop of	1925	4	Rutt
Jacques, Baron (L)	1905	-	Jacques	Leigh, Baron	1935	5	Leigh
Jakobovits, Baron (L)	1921	-	Jakobovits	Leighton of Saint Mellons, Baron	1922	5	Seager
James of Rusholme, Baron (L)	1909	-	James	Leinster, Duke of	1914	8	FitzGerald
Jauncey of Tullichettle, Baron (L)	1925	-	Jauncey	Leven and Melville, Earl of	1924	14 & 13	Leslie Melville
Jay, Baron (L)	1907	-	Jay	Lever of Manchester, Baron (L)	1914	-	Lever
Jeffreys, Baron	1957	3	Jeffreys				
Jeger, Baroness (L)	1915	-	Jeger	Leverhulme, Viscount	1915	3	Lever
Jellicoe, Earl	1918	2	Jellicoe	Lewin, Baron	1920	-	Lewin
Jenkin of Roding, Baron (L)	1926		Jenkin	Lewis of Newnham, Baron (O)			
Jenkins of Hillhead, Baron (L)	1920		Jenkins		1928	-	Lewis
				Lichfield, Earl of	1939	5	Anson

Peer's Title	Born	No. of Succn.	Family Name	Peer's Title	Born	No. of Succn.	Family Name
Lifford, Viscount (O)	1949	9	Hewitt	Maclay, Baron	1942	3	Maclay
Lilford, Baron	1931	7	Powys	Maclehose of Beoch, (L)	1917	-	Maclehose
Limerick, Earl of	1930	6	Pery	Macleod of Borve, Baroness (L)	1915	-	Macleod
Lincoln, Earl of	1913	18	Fiennes-Clinton				
Lindsay, Earl of Bethune	195	16	Lindesay-	MacLeod of Fuinary, Baron (L)	1895	-	MacLeod
Lindsay of Birker, Baron	1909	2	Lindsay	McNair, Baron	1947	3	McNair
Lindsey and Abingdon, Earl of	1931	14 & 9	Bertie	Macpherson of Drumochter, Baron	1924	2	Macpherson
Linlithgow, Marquess of	1946	4	Hope	Mais, Baron (L)	1911	-	Mais
Lisburne, Earl of (O)	1918	8	Vaughan	Malmesbury, Earl of	1907	6	Harris
Lisle, Baron (O)	1903	7	Lysaght	Malvern, Viscount	1949	3	Huggins
Listowel, Earl of	1906	5	Hare	Manchester, Duke of	1938	12	Montagu
Liverpool, Bishop of	1929	6	Sheppard	Manchester, Bishop of	1924	9	Booth- Clibborn
Liverpool, Earl of	1944	5	Foljambe	Mancroft, Baron	1957	3	Mancroft
Llewelyn-Davies of Hastoe, Baroness (L)	1915	-	Llewelyn Davies	Manners, Baron	1923	5	Manners
				Mansfield and Mansfield, Earl of	1930	8	Murray
Lloyd of Hampstead, Baron (L)	1915	-	Lloyd	Manton, Baron	1924	3	Watson
				Mar, Countess of (R)	1940	31	of Mar
Lloyd of Kilgerran, Baron (L)	1907	-	Lloyd	Mar & Kellie, Earl of	1921	13 & 15	Erskine
Lloyd George of Dwyfor, Earl	1924	3	Lloyd George	Marchamley, Baron	1922	3	Whiteley
				Marchwood, Viscount	1936	3	Penny
Loch, Baron	1920	4	Loch	Margadale, Baron	1906	1	Morrison
Lockwood, Baroness (L)	1924	-	Hall	Margesson, Viscount	1922	2	Margesson
Londesborough, Baron	1959	9	Denison	Marks of Broughton, Baron	1920	2	Marks
London, Bishop of	1921	130	Leonard				
Londonderry, Marquess of	1937	9	Vane Tempest- Stewart	Marlborough, Duke of	1926	11	Spencer- Churchill
Long, Viscount	1929	4	Long	Marley, Baron	1913	2	Aman
Longford, Earl of	1905	7	Pakenham	Marsh, Baron (L)	1928	-	Marsh
Lonsdale, Earl of	1922	7	Lowther	Marshall of Goring, Baron (L)	1932	-	Marshall
Lothian, Marquess of	1922	12	Kerr				
Loudoun, Countess of (R)	1919	14	Abney Hastings	Marshall of Leeds, Baron (L)	1915	-	Marshall
Louth, Baron (O)	1929	16	Plunkett				
Lovat, Baron	1911	15	Fraser	Martonmere, Baron	1963	2	Robinson
Lovelace, Earl of	1951	5	King	Masham of Ilton, Baroness (L)	1935	-	Cunliffe-Lister
Lovell Davis, Baron (L)	1924	-	Lovell Davis				
Lowry, Baron (L)	1919	-	Lowry	Mason of Barnsley, Baron (L)	1924		Mason
Lucan, Earl of, (missing since 1974)	1934	7	Bingham				
				Massereene and Ferrard, Viscount	1914	13 & 6	Skeffington
Lucas of Chilworth, Baron	1926	2	Lucas	Massy, Baron (O)	1921	9	Massy
Lucas of Crudwell, Baroness (R)	1919	10	Palmer	Matthews, Baron (L)	1919	-	Matthews
				Maude of Stratford upon- Avon, Baron (L)	1912	-	Maude
Luke, Baron	1905	2	Lawson Johnston	May, Baron	1931	3	May
Lurgan, Baron	1911	5	Brownlow	Mayhew, Baron (L)	1915	-	Mayhew
Lyell, Baron	1939	3	Lyell	Mayo, Earl of (O)	1929	10	Bourke
Lytton, Earl of	1950	5	Lytton	Meath, Earl of	1910	14	Brabazon
Lyveden, Baron	1915	6	Vernon	Melchett, Baron	1948	4	Mond
				Mellish, Baron (L)	1913	-	Mellish
McAlpine of West Green, Baron (L)	1942	-	McAlpine	Melville, Viscount	1937	9	Dundas
				Merrivale, Baron	1917	3	Duke
MacAndrew, Baron	1945	3	MacAndrew	Mersey, Viscount	1934	4	Bigham
McCarthy, Baron (L)	1925	-	McCarthy	Merthyr, Baron (D)	1935	4	Lewis
Macaulay of Bragar, Baron (L)	19-		Macaulay	Meston, Baron	1950	3	Meston
				Methuen, Baron	1925	6	Methuen
Macclesfield, Earl of	1914	8	Parker	Mexborough, Earl of (O)	1931	8	Savile
McCluskey, Baron (L)	1929	-	McCluskey	Middleton, Baron	1921	12	Willoughby
McColl of Dulwich, Baron (L)	1933	-	McColl	Midleton, Viscount	1949	12	Brodrick
				Miles, Baron (L)	1907	-	Miles
Macdonald, Baron (O)	1947	8	Macdonald	Milford, Baron	1902	2	Philipps
Macdonald of Gwaenysgor, Baron	1915	2	Macdonald	Milford Haven, Marquess of	1961	4	Mountbatten
				Mills, Viscount	1956	3	Mills
McFadzean, Baron (L)	1903	-	McFadzean	Milne, Baron	1909	2	Milne
McFadzean of Kelvinside, Baron (L)	1915	-	McFadzean	Milner of Leeds, Baron	1923	2	Milner
				Milverton, Baron	1930	2	Richards
McFarlane of Llandaff, Baroness (L)	1926	-	McFarlane	Minto, Earl of	1928	6	Elliot- Murray- Kynynmound
McGowan, Baron	1938	3	McGowan				
McGregor of Durris, Baron (L)	1921	-	McGregor	Mishcon, Baron (L)	1915	-	Mishcon
				Molesworth, Viscount (O)	1907	11	Molesworth
McIntosh of Haringey, Baron (L)	1933	-	McIntosh	Molloy, Baron (L)	1918	-	Molloy
				Molson, Baron (L)	1903	-	Molson
Mackay of Clashfern, Baron (L)	1927	-	Mackay	Monck, Viscount	1953	7	Monck
				Monckton of Brenchley, Viscount	1915	2	Monckton
Mackenzie-Stuart, Baron (L)	1924	-	Stuart				
Mackie of Benshie, Baron (L)	1919	-	Mackie	Moncrieff, Baron	1915	5	Moncrieff
				Monk Bretton, Baron	1924	3	Dodson
Mackintosh of Halifax, Viscount	1958	3	Mackintosh	Monkswell, Baron	1947	5	Collier
				Monsell, Viscount	1905	2	Eyres Monsell

Peer's Title	Born	No. of Succn.	Family Name
Monson, Baron	1932	11	Monson
Montagu of Beaulieu, Baron	1926	3	Douglas-Scott-Montagu
Monteagle of Brandon, Baron	1926	6	Spring Rice
Montgomery of Alamein, Viscount	1928	2	Montgomery
Montrose, Duke of	1907	7	Graham
of Wolvercote, Baron (L)	1921	-	Moore
Moran, Baron	1924	2	Wilson
Moray, Earl of	1928	20	Stuart
Morley, Earl of	1923	6	Parker
Morris, Baron	1937	3	Morris
Morris of Castle Morris, Baron (L)	1930	-	Morris
Morris of Grasmere, Baron (L)	1898	-	Morris
Morris of Kenwood, Baron	1928	2	Morris
Morrison, Baron	1914	2	Morrison
Morton, Earl of	1927	21	Douglas
Morton of Shuna, Baron (L)	1930	-	Morton
Mostyn, Baron	1920	5	Lloyd Mostyn
Mottistone, Baron	1920	4	Seely
Mountbatten of Burma, Countess (R)	1924	2	Knatchbull
Mount Edgcumbe, Earl of	1939	8	Edgcumbe
Mountevans, Baron	1943	3	Evans
Mountgarret, Viscount	1936	17	Butler
Mowbray, Segrave & Stourton, Baron	1923	26, 27 & 23	Stourton
Moyne, Baron	1905	2	Guinness
Moynihan, Baron	1936	3	Moynihan
Moyola, Baron (L)	1923		Chichester-Clark
Muirshiel, Viscount	1905	1	Maclay
Baron (L)	1918	-	Mulley
Munster, Earl of	1926	7	FitzClarence
Murray of Epping Forest, Baron (L)	1922	-	Murray
Murray of Newhaven, Baron (L)	1903		Murray
Murton of Lindisfarne, Baron (L)	1914	-	Murton
Muskerry, Baron (O)	1948	9	Deane
Nairne, Baroness (R)	1912	12	Bigham
Napier & Ettrick, Baron	1930	14 & 5	Napier
Napier of Magdala, Baron	1940	6	Napier
Nathan, Baron	1922	2	Nathan
Nelson, Earl	1941	9	Nelson
Nelson of Stafford, Baron	1917	2	Nelson
Netherthorpe, Baron	1964	3	Turner
Newall, Baron	1930	2	Newall
Newborough, Baron (O)	1917	7	Wynn
Newburgh, Earl of	1942	12	Rospigliosi
Newcastle, Bishop of	1929	10	Graham
Newton, Baron	1915	4	Legh
Nicol, Baroness (L)	1923	-	Nicol
Noel Buxton, Baron	1940	3	Noel Buxton
Norbury, Earl of (O)	1939	6	Graham Toler
Norfolk, Duke of	1915	17	Fitzalan Howard
Normanby, Marquess of	1912	4	Phipps
Normanton, Earl of	1945	6	Agar
Norrie, Baron	1936	2	Norrie
Northampton, Marquess of	1946	7	Compton
Northbourne, Baron	1926	5	James
Northbrook, Baron	1915	5	Baring
Northesk, Earl of	1926	13	Carnegie
Northfield, Baron (L)	1923	-	Chapman
Northumberland, Duke of	1953	11	Percy
Norton, Baron	1915	7	Adderley
Norwich, Viscount	1929	2	Cooper
Nugent of Guildford, Baron (L)	1907	-	Nugent
Nunburnholme, Baron	1928	4	Wilson
Oaksey and Trevethin, Baron	1929	2 & 4	Lawrence
O'Brien of Lothbury, Baron (L)	1908	-	O'Brien
Ogmore, Baron	1931	2	Rees Williams
O'Hagan, Baron	1945	4	Strachey
Oliver of Aylmerton, Baron (L)	1921	-	Oliver
O'Neill, Baron	1933	4	O'Neill
O'Neill of the Maine, Baron (L)	1914	-	O'Neill
Onslow, Earl of	1938	7	Onslow
Oppenheim-Barnes, Baroness (L)	1930	-	Oppenheim-Barnes
Oram, Baron (L)	1913	-	Oram
Oranmore & Browne, Baron	1901	4	Browne
Orkney, Earl of	1919	8	Fitz-Maurice
Ormonde, Marquess of	1899	7	Butler
Orr Ewing, Baron (L)	1912		Orr Ewing
Oxford and Asquith, Earl of	1916	2	Asquith
Oxfuird, Viscount of	1934	13	Makgill
Palmer, Baron	1916	3	Palmer
Park of Monmouth, Baroness (L)	-	Park	Park
Parmoor, Baron	1929	4	Cripps
Parry, Baron (L)	1925	-	Parry
Pearce, Baron (L)	1901	-	Pearce
Peel, Earl	1947	3	Peel
Pembroke and Montgomery, Earl of	1939	17 & 14	Herbert
Pender, Baron	1933	3	Denison-Pender
Penney, Baron (L)	1909	-	Penney
Pennock, Baron (L)	1920	-	Pennock
Penrhyn, Baron	1908	6	Douglas-Pennant
Perry of Walton, Baron (L)	1921	-	Perry
Perth, Earl of	1907	17	Drummond
Peston, Baron (L)	1931	-	Peston
Petre, Baron	1942	18	Petre
Peyton of Yeovil, Baron (L)	1919	-	Peyton
Phillimore, Baron	191	4	Phillimore
Phillips, Baroness (L)	1910	-	Phillips
Piercy, Baron	1946	3	Piercy
Pike, Baroness (L)	1918	-	Pike
Pitt of Hampstead, Baron (L)	1913	-	Pitt
Platt of Writtle, Baroness (L)	1923	-	Platt
Plowden, Baron (L)	1907	-	Plowden
Plumb, Baron (L)	1925	-	Plumb
Plummer of St. Marylebone, Baron (L)	1914	-	Plummer
Plunket, Baron	1925	8	Plunket
Plymouth, Earl of	1923	3	Windsor Clive
Poltimore, Baron	1957	7	Bampfylde
Polwarth, Baron	1916	10	Hepburne-Scott
Ponsonby of Shulbrede, Baron	1930	3	Ponsonby
Poole, Baron	1911	1	Poole
Porritt, Baron (L)	1900	-	Porritt
Portal of Hungerford, Baroness (R)	1923	2	Portal
Portarlington, Earl of (O)	1938	7	Dawson-Damer
Portland, Duke of	1897	9	Cavendish-Bentinck
Portman, Viscount	1934	9	Portman
Portsmouth, Earl of	1954	10	Wallop
Powerscourt, Viscount	1935	10	Wingfield
Powis, Earl of	1925	7	Herbert
Prior, Baron (L)	1927		Prior
Pritchard, Baron (L)	1910	-	Pritchard
Prys-Davies, Baron (L)	1923	-	Davies
Pym, Baron (L)	1922	-	Pym
Queensberry, Marquess of	1929	12	Douglas
Quinton, Baron (L)	1925	-	Quinton

Peer's Title	Born	No. of Succn.	Family Name	Peer's Title	Born	No. of Succn.	Family Name
Radnor, Earl of	1927	8	Pleydell-Bouverie	Sackville, Baron	1913	6	Sackville-West
Raglan, Baron	1927	5	Somerset	Sainsbury, Baron (L)	1902	-	Sainsbury
Ranfurly, Earl of	1929	7	Knox	Sainsbury of Preston Candover, Baron (L)	1927	-	Sainsbury
Rankeillour, Baron	1935	4	Hope	St. Albans, Bishop of	1929	8	Taylor
Rathcavan, Baron	1909	2	O'Neill	St. Albans, Duke of	1939	14	Beauclerk
Rathcreedan, Baron	1905	2	Norton	St. Aldwyn, Earl	1912	2	Hicks Beach
Rathdonnell, Baron (O)	1938	5	McClintock-Bunbury	St. Davids, Viscount	1917	2	Philipps
				St. Germans, Earl of	1941	10	Eliot
Ravensdale, Baron	1923	3	Mosley	St. Helens, Baron	1945	2	Hughes-Young
Ravensworth, Baron	1924	8	Liddell	St. John of Bletso, Baron	1957	21	St. John
Rawlinson of Ewell, Baron (L)	1919	-	Rawlinson	St. John of Fawsley, Baron (L)	1929		St. John-Stevas
Rayleigh, Baron	1960	6	Strutt				
Rayne, Baron (L)	1918	-	Rayne	St. Levan, Baron	1919	4	St. Aubyn
Rayner, Baron (L)	1926	-	Rayner	St. Oswald, Baron	1919	5	Winn
Rea, Baron	1928	3	Rea	St. Vincent, Viscount	1905	7	Jervis
Reading, Marquess of	1942	4	Rufus Isaacs	Salisbury, Bishop of	1928	76	Baker
Reay, Baron	1937	14	Mackay	Salisbury, Marquess of	1916	6	Gascoyne-Cecil
Redesdale, Baron	1932	5	Mitford				
Rees, Baron (L)	1926		Rees	Salmon, Baron (L)	1903	-	Salmon
Rees-Mogg, Baron (L)	1928		Rees-Mogg	Saltoun, Lady (R)	1930	20	Fraser
Reigate, Baron (L)	1905	-	Vaughan-Morgan	Samuel, Viscount	1922	3	Samuel
				Sanderson of Ayot, Baron (D)	1931	2	Sanderson
Reilly, Baron (L)	1912	-	Reilly				
Reith, Baron (D)	1928	2	Reith	Sanderson of Bowden, Baron (L)	1933	-	Sanderson
Remnant, Baron	1930	3	Remnant				
Rendlesham, Baron (O)	1915	8	Thellusson	Sandford, Baron	1920	2	Edmondson
Rennell, Baron	1935	3	Rodd	Sandhurst, Baron	1920	5	Mansfield
Renton, Baron (L)	1908	-	Renton	Sandwich, Earl of (D)	1906	10	Montagu
Renwick, Baron	1935	2	Renwick	Sandys, Baron	1931	7	Hill
Rhodes, Baron (L)	1895	-	Rhodes	Savile, Baron	1919	3	Lumley-Savile
Richardson, Baron (L)	1910	-	Richardson	Saye and Sele, Baron	1920	21	Fiennes
Richardson of Duntisbourne, Baron (L)	1915	-	Richardson	Scanlon, Baron (L)	1913	-	Scanlon
				Scarbrough, Earl of	1932	12	Lumley
Richmond & Gordon, Duke of	1929	10 & 5	Gordon Lennox	Scarman, Baron (L)	1911	-	Scarman
				Scarsdale, Viscount	1924	3	Curzon
Ridley, Viscount	1925	4	Ridley	Schon, Baron (L)	1912	-	Schon
Ripon, Bishop of	1931	11	Young	Seafield, Earl of	1939	13	Ogilvie-Grant
Rippon of Hexham, Baron (L)	1924		Rippon	Seear, Baroness (L)	1913	-	Seear
				Seebohm, Baron (L)	1909	-	Seebohm
Ritchie of Dundee, Baron	1919	5	Ritchie	Sefton of Garston, Baron (L)	1915	-	Sefton
Riverdale, Baron	1901	2	Balfour				
Robens of Woldingham, Baron (L)	1910	-	Robens	Selborne, Earl of	1940	4	Palmer
				Selby, Viscount	1942	4	Gully
Robertson of Oakridge, Baron	1930	2	Robertson	Selkirk, Earl of	1906	10	Douglas-Hamilton
Roborough, Baron	1903	2	Lopes	Selsdon, Baron	1937	3	Mitchell-Thomson
Robson of Kiddington, Baroness (L)	1919	-	Robson				
				Sempill, Lady (R)	1920	20	Sempill
Rochdale, Viscount	1906	1	Kemp	Serota, Baroness (L)	1919	-	Serota
Rochester, Bishop of	1935	105	Turnbull	Shackleton, Baron (L)	1911	-	Shackleton
Rochester, Baron	1916	2	Lamb	Shaftesbury, Earl of	1938	10	Ashley-Cooper
Rockley, Baron	1934	3	Cecil	Shannon, Earl of	1924	9	Boyle
Roden, Earl of (O)	1909	9	Jocelyn	Sharp of Grimsdyke, Baron (L)	1916	-	Sharp
Rodney, Baron	1920	9	Rodney				
Roll of Ipsden, Baron (L)	1907	-	Roll	Sharples, Baroness (L)	1923	-	Swan
Rollo, Lord	1915	13	Rollo	Shaughnessy, Baron	1922	3	Shaughnessy
Romney, Earl of	1910	7	Marsham	Shawcross, Baron (L)	1902	-	Shawcross
Rootes, Baron	1917	2	Rootes	Sheffield, Bishop of	1930	5	Lunn
Rosebery, Earl of	1929	7	Primrose	Shepherd, Baron	1918	2	Shepherd
Roskill, Baron (L)	1911	-	Roskill	Sherfield, Baron	1904	1	Makins
Ross of Newport, Baron (L)	1926		Ross	Shrewsbury, Earl of	1952	22	Chetwynd-Talbot
Rosse, Earl of (O)	1936	7	Parsons				
Rosslyn, Earl of	1958	7	St. Clair-Erskine	Shuttleworth, Baron	1948	5	Kay-Shuttleworth
Rossmore, Baron	1931	7	Westenra				
Rothermere, Viscount	1925	3	Harmsworth	Sidmouth, Viscount	1914	7	Addington
Rotherwick, Baron	1912	2	Cayzer	Sieff of Brimpton, Baron (L)	1913	-	Sieff
Rothes, Earl of	1932	21	Leslie	Silkin, Baron (D)	1916	2	Silkin
Rothschild, Baron	1936	4	Rothschild	Silsoe, Baron	1930	2	Eve
Rowallan, Baron	1919	3	Corbett	Simon, Viscount	1902	2	Simon
Roxburghe, Duke of	1954	10	Innes-Ker	Simon of Glaisdale, Baron (L)	1911	-	Simon
Rugby, Baron	1951	3	Maffey	Simon of Wythenshawe, Baron	1913	2	Simon
Runciman of Doxford, Viscount	1934	3	Runciman				
Russell, Earl	1937	5	Russell	Sinclair, Baron	1914	17	St. Clair
Russell of Liverpool, Baron	1952	3	Russell	Sinclair of Cleeve, Baron	1953	3	Sinclair
Rutland, Duke of	1919	10	Manners	Sinha, Baron	1920	3	Sinha
Ryder of Eaton Hastings, Baron (L)	1916	-	Ryder	Skelmersdale, Baron	1945	7	Bootle-Wilbraham
				Sligo, Marquess of	1908	10	Browne
Ryder of Warsaw, Baroness (L)	1923	-	Ryder	Slim, Viscount	1927	2	Slim
				Smith, Baron (L)	1914	-	Smith

Peer's Title	Born	No. of Succn.	Family Name	Peer's Title	Born	No. of Succn.	Family Name
Snowdon, Earl of	1930	1	Armstrong Jones	Thomas of Swynnerton, Baron (L)	1931	-	Thomas
Somerleyton, Baron	1928	3	Crossley	Thomson of Fleet, Baron	1923	2	Thomson
Somers, Baron	1907	8	Cocks	Thomson of Monifieth, Baron (L)	1921	-	Thomson
Somerset, Duke of	1952	19	Seymour	Thorneycroft, Baron (L)	1909	-	Thorneycroft
Sondes, Earl	1940	5	Milles Lade	Thurlow, Baron	1912	8	Hovell Thurlow Cumming Bruce
Soper, Baron (L)	1903	-	Soper				
Soulbury, Viscount	1915	2	Ramsbotham				
Southampton, Baron	1928	6	FitzRoy				
Southborough, Baron	1922	4	Hopwood	Thurso, Viscount	1922	2	Sinclair
Southesk, Earl of	1893	11	Carnegie	Todd, Baron (L)	1907	-	Todd
Southwark, Bishop of	1926	7	Bowlby	Tollemache, Baron	1939	5	Tollemache
Southwell, Viscount (O)	1930	7	Southwell	Tombs, Baron (L)	1924	-	Tombs
Spencer, Earl	1924	8	Spencer	Tonypandy, Viscount	1909	1	Thomas
Spens, Baron	1942	3	Spens	Tordoff, Baron (L)	1928	-	Tordoff
Stafford, Baron	1954	15	Fitzherbert	Torphichen, Baron	1946	15	Sandilands
Stair, Earl of	1906	13	Dalrymple	Torrington, Viscount	1943	11	Byng
Stallard, Baron (L)	1921	-	Stallard	Townshend, Marquess of	1916	7	Townshend
Stamp, Baron	1935	4	Stamp	Tranmire, Baron (L)	1903	-	Turton
Stanley of Alderley, and Sheffield, Viscount (D)	1927	8	Stanley	Trefgarne, Baron	1941	2	Trefgarne
Stansgate, Baron	1925	2	Benn	Trenchard, Viscount	1951	3	Trenchard
				Trevor, Baron	1928	4	Hill-Trevor
Stedman, Baroness (L)	1916	-	Stedman	Trimlestown, Baron (O)	1899	19	Barnewall
Stevens of Ludgate, Baron (L)	1936	-	Stevens	Trumpington, Baroness (L)	1922	-	Barker
				Truro, Bishop of	1922	12	Mumford
Stockton, Earl of	1943	2	Macmillan	Tryon, Baron	1940	3	Tryon
Stodart of Leaston, Baron (L)	1916	-	Stodart	Turner of Camden, Baroness (L)	1927	-	Turner
Stoddart of Swindon, Baron (L)	1926	-	Stoddart	Tweeddale, Marquess of	1947	13	Hay
				Tweedsmuir, Baron	1911	2	Buchan
Stokes, Baron (L)	1914	-	Stokes				
Strabolgi, Baron	1914	11	Kenworthy	Ullswater, Viscount	1942	2	Lowther
Stradbroke, Earl of	1937	6	Rous	Underhill, Baron (L)	1914	-	Underhill
Strafford, Earl of	1936	8	Byng				
Strang, Baron	1922	2	Strang	Valentia, Viscount (O)	1929	15	Annesley
Strathalmond, Baron	1947	3	Fraser	Vaux of Harrowden, Baron	1915	10	Gilbey
Strathcarron, Baron	1924	2	Macpherson	Ventry, Baron (O)	1943	8	Daubeny de Moleyns
Strathclyde, Baron	1960	2	Galbraith				
Strathcona & Mount Royal Baron	1923	4	Howard	Vernon, Baron	1923	10	Venables Vernon
Stratheden & Campbell, Baron	1934	6	Campbell	Verulam, Earl of	1951	7	Grimston
Strathmore & Kinghorne, Earl of	1957	18	Bowes Lyon	Vestey, Baron	1941	3	Vestey
				Vickers, Baroness (L)	1907	-	Vickers
Strathspey, Baron	1912	5	Grant of Grant	Vinson, Baron (L)	1931	-	Vinson
Strauss, Baron (L)	1901	-	Strauss	Vivian, Baron	1906	5	Vivian
Stuart of Findhorn, Viscount	1924	2	Stuart				
				Wakehurst, Baron	1925	3	Loder
Sudeley, Baron	1939	7	Hanbury Tracy	Waldegrave, Earl	1905	12	Waldegrave
Suffield, Baron	1922	11	Harbord Hamond	Wallace of Campsie, Baron (L)	1915	-	Wallace
				Wallace of Coslany, Baron (L)	1906	-	Wallace
Suffolk & Berkshire, Earl of	1935	21&14	Howard	Walpole and Walpole of Wolterton, Baron	1938	10&8	Walpole
Sutherland, Duke of	1915	6	Egerton	Walsingham, Baron	1925	9	de Grey
Sutherland, Countess of (R)	1921	24	Sutherland	Walston, Baron (L)	1912	-	Walston
Swann, Baron (L)	1920	-	Swann	Walton of Detchant, Baron (L)	1922	-	Walton
Swansea, Baron	1925	4	Vivian				
Swaythling, Baron	1928	4	Montagu	Wardington, Baron	1924	2	Pease
Swinfen, Baron	1938	3	Eady	Warnock, Baroness (L)	1924	-	Warnock
Swinton, Earl of	1937	2	Cunliffe-Lister	Warwick, Earl of, and Brooke, Earl	1934	8	Greville
Sysonby, Baron	1945	3	Ponsonby	Waterford, Marquess of	1933	8	Beresford
Talbot de Malahide, Baron (O)	1931	10	Arundell	Waterpark, Baron (O)	1926	7	Cavendish
Tankerville, Earl of	1956	10	Bennet	Watkins, Baron (L)	1903	-	Watkins
Tanlaw, Baron (L)	1934	-	Mackay	Watkinson, Viscount	1910	1	Watkinson
Taylor of Blackburn, Baron (L)	1929	-	Taylor	Waverley, Viscount	1949	3	Anderson
				Wedderburn of Charlton, Baron (L)	1927	-	Wedderburn
Taylor of Gryfe, Baron (L)	1912	-	Taylor				
Taylor of Hadfield, Baron (L)	1905	-	Taylor	Wedgwood, Baron	1954	4	Wedgwood
				Weidenfeld, Baron (L)	1919	-	Weidenfeld
Taylor of Mansfield, Baron (L)	1895	-	Taylor	Weinstock, Baron (L)	1924	-	Weinstock
				Weir, Viscount	1933	3	Weir
Tedder, Baron	1926	2	Tedder	Wellington, Duke of	1915	8	Wellesley
Temple of Stowe, Earl	1924	8	Temple Gore-Langton	Wells Pestell, Baron (L)	1910	-	Wells-Pestell
Templeman, Baron (L)	1920	-	Templeman	Wemyss and March, Earl of	1912	12&8	Charteris
Tenby, Viscount	1927	3	Lloyd George				
Tennyson, Baron	1919	4	Tennyson	Westbury, Baron	1922	5	Bethell
Terrington, Baron	1915	4	Woodhouse	Westmeath, Earl of (O)	1928	13	Nugent
Teviot, Baron	1934	2	Kerr	Westminster, Duke of	1951	6	Grosvenor
Teynham, Baron	1928	20	Roper-Curzon	Westmorland, Earl of	1924	15	Fane
Thomas of Gwydir, (L)	1920	-	Thomas	Westwood, Baron	1907	2	Westwood

Peer's Title	Born	No. of Succn.	Family Name	Peer's Title	Born	No. of Succn.	Family Name
Whaddon, Baron (L)	1927	-	Page	Winstanley, Baron (L)	1918	-	Winstanley
Wharncliffe, Earl of	1953	5	Montagu Stuart Wortley	Winterbottom, Baron (L)	1913	-	Winterbottom
				Winterton, Earl of (O)	1915	7	Turnour
White, Baroness (L)	1909	-	White	Wise, Baron	1923	2	Wise
Whitelaw, Viscount	1918	1	Whitelaw	Wolfson, Baron (L)	1927	-	Wolfson
Wigoder, Baron (L)	1921	-	Wigoder	Wolverton, Baron	1938	7	Glyn
Wigram, Baron	1915	2	Wigram	Woolton, Earl of	1958	3	Marquis
Wilberforce, Baron (L)	1907	-	Wilberforce	Wraxall, Baron	1928	2	Gibbs
Williams of Elvel, Baron (L)	1933	-	Williams	Wrenbury, Baron	1927	3	Buckley
				Wrottesley, Baron	1968	6	Wrottesley
Willis, Baron (L)	1918	-	Willis	Wyatt of Weeford, Baron (L)	1918	-	Wyatt
Willoughby de Broke, Baron	1938	21	Verney	Wyfold, Baron	1915	3	Hermon-Hodge
Willoughby de Eresby, Baroness (R)	1934	27	Heathcote Drummond- Willoughby	Wynford, Baron	1917	8	Best
				Yarborough, Earl of	1920	7	Pelham
Wilson, Baron	1915	2	Wilson	York, Archbishop of	1927	95	Habgood
Wilson of Langside, Baron (L)	1916	-	Wilson	Young, Baroness (L)	1926	-	Young
				Young of Dartington, Baron (L)	1915	-	Young
Wilson of Rievaulx, Baron (L)	1916	-	Wilson	Young of Graffham, Baron (L)	1932	-	Young
Wilton, Earl of	1921	7	Egerton	Younger of Leckie, Viscount	1906	3	Younger
Wimborne, Viscount	1939	3	Guest				
Winchester, Bishop of	1926	95	James				
Winchester, Marquess of	1941	18	Paulet	Zetland, Marquess of	1937	4	Dundas
Winchilsea and Nottingham, Earl of	1936	16&11	Finch Hatton	Zouche, Baron	1943	18	Frankland
				Zuckerman, Baron (L)	1904	-	Zuckerman
Windlesham, Baron	1932	3	Hennessy				

THE ASTRONOMER ROYAL

Professor Graham Smith, F.R.S.

THE title of Astronomer Royal was formerly given to the Director of the Royal Greenwich Observatory, but in 1971 it was decided that the two titles should be separated. John Flamsteed was the first Astronomer Royal and held the position from 1675 to 1719. Sir Richard Woolley was the last holder of both titles, 1956-71. Sir Martin Ryle was Astronomer Royal, 1972-82.

In 1982 the title was conferred, by the Queen's prerogative, on Francis Graham Smith, Professor of Radio Astronomy at Manchester University.

LORD WARDEN OF THE CINQUE PORTS

H.M. Queen Elizabeth the Queen Mother

THE Lord Wardenship of the Cinque Ports is one of the oldest offices connected with the defence of the realm and dates back to before the Norman Conquest. The ports were originally five in number: Hastings, Romney, Hythe, Dover and Sandwich. Rye and Winchelsea were added later. Until the end of the fifteenth century the Cinque Ports were required to supply the Crown with ships and men for the defence of the South coast.

H.M. Queen Elizabeth the Queen Mother succeeded the late Sir Robert Menzies as Lord Warden in 1978 and was installed in 1979.

THE MASTER OF THE QUEEN'S MUSIC

Malcolm Williamson, C.B.E.

The Master of the King's or Queen's Music is attached to the Royal Household and in former times was responsible for the sovereign's band. Nowadays it is an honorary rather than an executive position.

Malcolm Williamson succeeded the late Sir Arthur Bliss as Master of the Queen's Music in 1975.

PRESIDENTS OF THE ROYAL ACADEMY OF ARTS SINCE 1768

1768	Sir Joshua Reynolds
1792	Benjamin West
1805	James Wyatt
1806	Benjamin West
1820	Sir Thomas Lawrence
1830	Sir Martin Shee
1850	Sir Charles Eastlake
1866	Sir Francis Grant
1878	Lord Leighton
1896	Sir John Millais
1896	Sir Edward Poynter
1919	Sir Aston Webb
1924	Sir Francis Dicksee
1928	Sir William Llewellyn
1938	Sir Edwin Lutyens
1944	Sir Alfred Munnings
1949	Sir Gerald Kelly
1954	Sir Albert Richardson
1956	Sir Charles Wheeler
1966	SirThomas Monnington
1976	Sir Hugh Casson
1984	Roger de Grey

THE POET LAUREATE

Ted Hughes, O.B.E.

THE Poet Laureate is attached to the court and it is customary for him to write verse in celebration of great occasions. The office developed from earlier times when minstrels and poets formed part of the retinue of the king. It was not until 1670 that the title was officially conferred by letters patent on John Dryden.

1670	John Dryden	1843	William Wordsworth
1688	Thomas Shadwell		
1692	Nahum Tate	1850	Lord Tennyson
1715	Nicholas Rowe	1890	Alfred Austin
1718	Rev. Laurence Eusden	1913	Robert Bridges
		1930	John Masefield
1730	Colley Cibber	1967	Cecil Day Lewis
1757	William Whitehead	1972	Sir John Betjeman
1790	Henry James Pye	1984	Edward (Ted) Hughes
1813	Robert Southey		

ROYAL ACADEMY OF ARTS *Burlington House, Piccadilly, London, W1V 0DS.*
President of the Royal Academy 1984 Roger de Grey

ACADEMICIANS
(with date of election)

Adams (Prof.), Norman (1972).
* Agar, Elieen (1988).
* Bawden, Edward, C.B.E. (1956).
Blackadder, Miss Elizabeth, O.B.E. (1976).
Blake, Peter, C.B.E. (1981).
Blamey, Norman (1975).
Blow, Miss Sandra (1978).
Bowey, Miss Olwyn (1975).
Bowyer, William (1981).
Bratby, John R. (1971).
Brown, Ralph (1972).
Buhler, Robert (1956).
Butler, James (1972).
* Cadbury-Brown (Prof.), H.T., O.B.E. (1975)
Camp, Jeffery B., (1984).
* Casson, Sir Hugh, C.H., K.C.V.O. (1970).
Clarke, Geoffrey (1976).
Clatworthy, Robert (1973).
Coker, Peter (1972).
* Collins, Cecil (1988).
Cooke, Miss Jean (1972).

Cuming, Frederick (1974).
Dannatt (Prof.), Trevor (1983).
de Grey, Roger (1969).
Dickson, Miss Jennifer (1976).
Dowson, Sir Philip, C.B.E. (1985).
* Dring, William (1955).
Dunstan, Bernard (1968).
* Eurich, Richard, O.B.E. (1953).
Eyton, Anthony (1986)
Fraser, Donald Hamilton (1985).
Frink, Dame Elisabeth, D.B.E. (1977).
Gore, Frederick (1972).
Green, Anthony (1977).
* Greenham, Peter G., C.B.E. (1960).
Harpley, Sydney (1981).
Hayes, Colin (1970).
* Hepple, Norman (1961).
Hogarth, Paul (1984).
Jones, Allen (1986)
Kenny, Michael (1986)
King, Prof. Philip C.B.E. (1988)
Kneale (Prof.), Bryan (1974).
* Lessore, Helen, O.B.E. (1986).
Levene, Ben (1986)
McFall, David (1963).

* Machin, Arnold, O.B.E. (1956).
Manasseh, Leonard, O.B.E. (1980).
Martin, Sir Leslie (1985).
* Medley, Robert, C.B.E. (1985).
* Moynihan, Rodrigo, C.B.E. (1954).
* Pasmore, Victor, C.H., C.B.E. (1983).
Paolozzi (Prof.), Eduardo, C.B.E. (1979).
Philipson, Sir Robin (1981).
Powell, Sir Philip, C.H., O.B.E. (1978).
Roberts-Jones, Ivor, C.B.E. (1974).
Rogers, Richard (1984).
Rosoman, Leonard, O.B.E. (1969).
* Rothenstein, Michael (1983).
* Sanders, Christopher (1961).
Scott, William, C.B.E. (1984).
* Soukop, Willi (1969).
* Spear, Ruskin, C.B.E. (1954).
Stephenson, Ian (1986).
Swanwick, Miss Betty (1979).
Tindle, David (1979).
Ward, John, C.B.E. (1965).
* Weight (Prof.), Carel, C.B.E. (1965).
Williams, Kyffin, O.B.E. (1974).

ASSOCIATES

Ackroyd, Norman (1988).
Aitchison, Craigie
Ayres, Miss Gillian, O.B.E.
Bellany, John
Christopher, Miss Ann
Crosby, Theo
Flanagan, Barry
Foster, Norman

Gowing, Prof. Sir Lawrence, C.B.E.
Hockney, David
Howard, Ken
Hoyland, John
Huxley, Prof. Paul
Kitaj, R. B.
Koralek, Paul
Lawson, Miss Sonia
McComb, Leonard
Nolan, Sir Sidney (O.M., C.B.E.)

Partridge, John, C.B.E.
Phillips, Tom
Sandle, Prof. Michael
Stirling, James
Sutton, Philip
Symons, Patrick
Tilson, Joe
Whishaw, Anthony
Wragg, John

* **Senior Academician.** **Secretary:** Piers Rodgers.

ROYAL SCOTTISH ACADEMY *The Mound, Edinburgh, EH2 2EL.*
President of the Royal Scottish Academy Sir Anthony Wheeler, O.B.E.

ACADEMICIANS
(with date of election)
* Armour, Mrs. Mary (1958)
Baille, W.J.L. (1979)
Blackadder, Miss Elizabeth, O.B.E. (1972)
Bushe, Frederick (1986)
Butler, Vincent (1977)
Cameron, Gordon S. (1971)
Campbell, Alexander (1981)
Collins, Peter (1974)
Crosbie, William (1974)
Cumming, James (1970)
Donaldson, Dr. David A. (1962)
Evans, David (1989)

* Fleming, Ian (1956)
Fraser, Alex (1989)
Glover, John Hardie, O.B.E. (1981)
* Gordon, Esm (1967)
Harvey, Jake (1989)
* Johnston, Ninian (1966)
* Kininmouth, Sir William (1956)
Knox, John (1979)
Littlejohn, William (1973)
* Lorimer, Hew, O.B.E. (1957)
McClure, David (1971)
Malcolm, Miss Ellen (1976)
Michie, David (1972)
Morris, James (1989)
Morrocco, Alberto (1963)

* Patrick J. McIntosh (1957)
Peploe, Denis (1966)
Philipson, Sir Robin (1962)
Reeves, Philip (1976)
* Reiach, Alan, O.B.E. (1986)
Richards, John, C.B.E. (1989)
Robertson, James D (1989)
Robertwson, R. Ross (1977)
Scott, Bill (1984)
Smith, Ian McKenzie Snowden, Michael (1985)
Steedman, Robert R. (1979)
Walker, Miss Frances (1983)
Wheeler, H. Anthony, O.B.E. (1975)
* Whitson, Peter (1977)

* **Honourary Retired Academician**

ASSOCIATES

Arnott, Ian
Balmer, Barbara
Boys, John
Brown, Neil Dallas
Brotherston, William
Buchan, Dennis
Busby, John
Cairns, Joyce
Campbell, A. Buchanan
Clifford, John G.
Cocker, Douglas

Crowe, Victoria
Dean, Fiona
Donald, George
Fairgreive, James
Gasson, Barry,
Haig, The Earl
Howard, Ian
Johnstone, John
Law, Graham Couper
Low, Bet
McIntosh, Iain R.

Maclean, William
McMillan, Professor Andrew
MacPherson, George
Main, Kirkland
Merrylees, Andrew
Metzstein, Isi
Mooney, John
Morrison, Dr. James
Onwin, Glen
Pelly, Frances
Pottinger, Frank

Rae, Barbara
Renton, Stuart, M.B.E.
Richards, John, C.B.E.
Ross, Alastair
Shanks, Duncan F.
Smart, Alastair
Squire, Geoffrey
Stenhouse, Andrew
Stiven, Fred
Watson, Arthur
Wedgewood, Roland

Non-resident Associates: Leon Morrocco, Charles Pulsford, Peter Womersley
Secretary: Robert R. Steedman **Treasurer:** W.J.L. Baillie **Administrative Secretary:** William T. Meikle

BIOGRAPHIES IN BRIEF

ABBADO, Claudio, former principal conductor and present musical director of London Symphony Orchestra; b. 26 June, 1933. Educated in Milan and Vienna. Musical director La Scala, Milan 1968-86, and principal conductor, Vienna Philharmonic Orchestra since 1986.

ACKNER OF SUTTON, Baron (Life Peer) (Desmond James Conrad Ackner), P.C., a Lord of Appeal in Ordinary since 1986; b. 18 Sept., 1920. Called to Bar, 1945. Q.C., 1961. Recorder of Swindon, 1962-71; a Judge of the Queen's Bench Division, 1971-80. Chairman of the Law Advisory Committee, British Council since 1980.

ACLAND, Sir Antony Arthur, G.C.M.G., K.C.V.O., British Ambassador to USA 1986; Permanent Under-Secretary of State, Foreign and Commonwealth Office, and Head of H.M. Diplomatic Service 1982 to 1986; b. 12 March, 1930. Joined Diplomatic Service, 1953 and served in Dubai, Kuwait and Geneva; Ambassador to Luxembourg, 1975-77 and to Spain, 1977-79; Deputy Under-Secretary of State, Foreign and Commonwealth Office, 1980-82.

ADIE, Rt. Rev. Michael Edgar, Bishop of Guildford since 1983; b. 22 Nov., 1929. Vicar of St. Mark, Sheffield, 1960-69; Rector of Louth, 1969-76; Vicar of Morton with Hacconby, 1976-83 and Archdeacon of Lincoln, 1977-83.

ADRIAN, 2nd Baron (Richard Hume Adrian), M.D., F.R.S., Master of Pembroke College, Cambridge, since 1981; b. 16 Oct., 1927. Reader in experimental biophysics, Cambridge University, 1968-78; Fellow of Churchill College, 1961-81; Professor of Cell Physiology since 1978. Vice-Chancellor of Cambridge University 1985 - October 1987.

AGA KHAN (IV), H.H. Prince Karim, Imam of Ismaili Muslims; son of the late Aly Khan and grandson of Aga Khan (III); b. 1936; m. Sarah Crichton-Stuart, 1969; two s; one d.

AIRLIE, 13th Earl of (David George Coke Patrick Ogilvy), K.T., P.C., G.C.V.O., Lord Chamberlain of H.M. Household since 1984; b. 17 May, 1926. Ensign, Queen's Body Guard for Scotland, Royal Company of Archers, since 1985. Chairman, Schroders plc, 1977-84. Governor, Nuffield Nursing Homes Trust since 1985.

ALEXANDER, Sir Kenneth, F.R.S.E., Principal and Vice-Chancellor of Stirling University 1981-86; b. 14 March, 1922. Professor of Economics, Strathclyde University, 1963-80. Dean of Scottish Business School, 1973-75. Chairman, Highlands and Islands Development Board, 1976-80. Trustee, National Museums of Scotland since 1985.

ALEXANDER, Rt. Rev. Mervyn Alban Newman, Bishop of Clifton (R.C.) since 1974 (Auxiliary Bishop, 1972-74); b. 29 June, 1925. R.C. Chaplain, Bristol University, 1953-67; Parish Priest, Weston-super-Mare, 1967-72.

ALISON, Rt. Hon. Michael James Hugh, P.C., M.P. (C), Second Church Estates Commissioner representing Church Commissioners; b. 27 June, 1926. Parl. Private Secretary to Prime Minister 1983-87; Parliamentary Under-Secretary of State, Department of Health and Social Security, 1970-74; Minister of State, Northern Ireland Office, 1979-81 and at Dept. of Employment, 1981-83.

ALLANBRIDGE, Hon. Lord (William Ian Stewart), a Senator of College of Justice in Scotland since 1977; b. 8 Nov., 1925. Called to Bar, 1951. Q.C. (Scot.), 1965. Solicitor-General for Scotland, 1972-74.

ALLDAY, Coningsby, C.B.E., Chairman and Chief Executive of British Nuclear Fuels 1983-86 (managing director, 1971-83); b. 21 Nov., 1920. A chemical engineer, was with I.C.I., 1939-59 and with U.K.A.E.A., 1959-71.

AMIS, Sir Kingsley, C.B.E., author; b. 16 April, 1922. Lecturer in English, University College of Swansea, 1949-61.

Fellow of Peterhouse, Cambridge, 1961-63. First novel Lucky Jim published, 1954 and filmed, 1957. 1986 Booker Prize winner with The Old Devils.

ANCRAM, Earl of (Michael Andrew Foster Jude Kerr), Parliamentary Under-Secretary of State, Scottish Office, 1983-87; b. 7 July, 1945, e.s. of Marquess of Lothian. Advocate, Scottish Bar, 1970.

ANDERSON, (William) Eric (Kinloch), Headmaster of Eton College since 1980; b. 27 May, 1936. Was on staff of Fettes College and Gordonstoun before becoming headmaster of Abingdon, 1970-75 and of Shrewsbury, 1975-80.

ANNIGONI, Pietro, Italian painter; b. 7 June, 1910. Is best known in this country for his portraits, notably those of H.M. the Queen and of Prince Philip; has exhibited at the Royal Academy.

ANOUILH, Jean, French dramatist; b. 23 June, 1910. Many of his plays have been translated for the English stage with great success; won Grand Prix du Cinema Francais for his film Monsieur Vincent.

ARMSTRONG, Rt. Hon. Ernest, First Deputy Chairman of Ways and Means, House of Commons, and an Assistant Deputy Speaker since 1981; b. 12 Jan., 1915. An Opposition Whip, 1970-73; Parl. Under-Sec. of State, Dept. of Education and Science, 1974-75 and Dept. of Environment, 1975-79.

ARMSTRONG, Baron (Life Peer) Robert Temple, G.C.B., C.V.O., Secretary of the Cabinet 1979-87 and Permanent Secretary, Management and Personnel Office, and Head of Home Civil Service 1983-1988; b. 30 March, 1927. Joined Treasury, 1950; Principal Private Secretary to Prime Minister, 1970-75; Permanent Under-Sec. of State, Home Office, 1977-79.

ARNOLD, Rt. Hon. Sir John Lewis, a Judge of the Family Division since 1972 and President of the Division since 1979; b. 6 May, 1915. Called to Bar, 1937. Q.C., 1958. A Judge of the Employment Appeal Tribunal, 1977-79.

ARNOLD, Malcolm, C.B.E., F.R.C.M., composer; b. 21 Oct., 1921. Was principal trumpet with London Philharmonic Orchestra, 1941-44, 1945-48. Awarded Oscar for music for film Bridge on the River Kwai in 1957.

ASH, Eric Albert, C.B.E., Ph.D., F.R.S., Rector of Imperial College of Science and Technology since 1985; b. 31 Jan., 1928. An engineer with Standard Telecommunication Laboratories, 1955-63; Professor of Electronic and Electrical Engineering, University College London, 1967-85. Secretary of the Royal Institution since 1984.

ASHCROFT, Dame Peggy (Edith Margaret Emily), D.B.E., actress; b. 22 Dec., 1907. First appeared with Birmingham Rep., 1926; is best known for her work in Shakespeare and the classics; has acted many times at the Old Vic, the National Theatre and the Stratford Memorial Theatre. A director of Royal Shakespeare Co. since 1968. Awarded Oscar for her part in A Passage to India, 1985.

ASHDOWN, Jeremy John Durham (Paddy), M.P. (L), leader of S.L.D. Party since 1988; b. 27 Feb., 1941. Commando Special Boat Division, Captain R.M., First Sec. U.K. Mission United Nations Geneva 19771-76.

ASHMORE, Vice-Admiral Sir Peter William Beckwith, K.C.B., K.C.V.O., D.S.C., Master of the Queen's Household, 1973-86; b. 4 Feb., 1921, b. of Admiral of the Fleet Sir Edward Ashmore. Equerry to King George VI and Extra Equerry to the Queen since 1952. Chief of Allied Staff in NATO Naval H.Q., Southern Europe, 1970-72.

ASHWORTH, John Michael, D.Sc., Vice-Chancellor of Salford University since 1981; b. 27 Nov., 1938. Lecturer in biochemistry, 1963-71 and Reader, 1971-73, Leicester University; Professor of Biology, Essex University, 1974-79; Under-Sec., Cabinet Office, 1979-81; Chief Scientist, Central Policy Review Staff, 1976-81. Chairman of the National Computing Centre since 1983.

ATTENBOROUGH, Sir David, C.B.E., F.R.S., broadcaster; b. 8 May, 1926, b. of Sir Richard Attenborough. Joined BBC, 1952; has undertaken several zoological expeditions which have been filmed and presented on TV; Controller, BBC-2 1965-68. Director, BBC TV Programmes, 1969-72. First book, Zoo Quest to Guiana, published 1956. Won Fellowship Award of British Academy of Film and Television Arts, 1980. Trustee of British Museum since 1980, and of World Wildlife Fund International since 1979.

ATTENBOROUGH, Sir Richard, C.B.E., producer and actor; b. 29 Aug., 1923, b. of David Attenborough; m. 1945, Sheila Sim. First appearance, Intimate Theatre, Palmer's Green, 1941. Formed Beaver Films with Bryan Forbes; also formed Allied Film Makers. Pro-Chancellor of Sussex University. Chairman of R.A.D.A. and Dep. Chairman, Channel Four Television, since 1980. Chairman, British Film Institute, since 1982. Awarded Oscar, 1983, for production of Gandhi. Chairman, Goldcrest Films and Television, since 1985.

AYCKBOURN, Alan, playwright. Associate Director of the National Theatre since 1986; b. 12 April, 1939. Worked in repertory as stage manager and actor; was BBC radio drama producer, Leeds, 1964-70 and is now director of productions, Theatre-in-the-Round, Scarborough. Has written many successful plays which have been produced first in Scarborough before presentation in London. Won drama awards for Absurd Person Singular, The Norman Conquests and Just Between Ourselves.

BAGNALL, General Sir Nigel (Thomas), G.C.B., C.V.O., M.C., Chief of the General Staff since 1985; b. 10 Feb., 1927. Commissioned, Green Howards, 1946 and served in Palestine, Malaya and Borneo; C.-in-C., B.A.O.R., and Commander Northern Army Group, 1983-1985. Hon. Fellow, Balliol College Oxford since 1986.

BAKER, Dame Janet Abbott, D.B.E., singer; b. 21 Aug., 1933. Won Daily Mail Kathleen Ferrier Award, 1956 and Queen's Prize, Royal College of Music, 1959. President, Royal Scottish Academy of Music and Drama, since 1983. Hon. Fellow, Downing College Cambridge since 1985.

BAKER, Rt. Rev. John Austin, Bishop of Salisbury since 1982; b. 11 January, 1928. Chaplain and Lecturer in Divinity, Corpus Christi College, Oxford, 1959-73; Lecturer in Theology, Brasenose and Lincoln Colleges, Oxford, 1959-73; Canon of Westminster, 1973-82 and Sub-Dean, 1978-82; Rector of St. Margaret's, Westminster, and Speaker's Chaplain, 1978-82.

BAKER, Rt. Hon. Kenneth Wilfred, M.P. (C), Chancellor of the Duchy of Lancaster (Chairman of the Conservative Party), Secretary of State for Education and Science, 1986-89; b. 3 Nov., 1934. P.P.S. to Leader of Opposition, 1974-75; Minister of State, Dept. of Industry, 1981-83 and Dept. of Trade and Industry, 1983-84; Minister of State, Dept. of Environment (Minister for Local Govt.), 1984-86.

BALCOMBE, Rt. Hon. Lord Justice (Rt. Hon. Sir (Alfred) John Balcombe) Lord Justice of Appeal since 1985; b. 29 Sept., 1925. Called to Bar, 1950. Q.C., 1969. Judge of the High Court of Justice, Family Division 1977-85. Member of General Council of the Bar, 1967-71. Judge of Employment Appeal Tribunal since 1983.

BANDA, Dr. Hastings, President of Malawi since 1966; Prime Minister, 1963-66; b. 1905. Practised medicine in England, 1939-53; Minister of Natural Resources and Local Govt., Nyasaland, 1961-63.

BANNISTER, Sir Roger, C.B.E., D.M. (Oxon), F.R.C.P. Master of Pembroke College, Oxford, since 1985; consultant physician, Nat. Hosp. for Nervous Diseases and St. Mary's Hosp.; b. 23 March, 1929. Educated at St. Mary's Hosp. Medical School and Exeter College, Oxford. An Olympic athlete, he set new world record for mile, 1954; chairman, Sports Council, 1971-74; president, International Council for Sport and Physical Recreation, 1976-83.

BARENBOIM, Daniel, pianist and conductor; b. 15 Nov., 1942 in Buenos Aires; m. Jacqueline du Pre 1967, d.1987.

Educated in Rome. Debut as pianist with Israel Philharmonic Orch., 1953 and with Berlin Philharmonic, 1963. Musical director, Orchestre de Paris, since 1975.

BARKWORTH, Peter Wynn, actor; b. 14 Jan., 1929. Trained at R.A.D.A. and was with Folkestone and Sheffield Rep. Cos., 1948-51; appearances on West End stage include Crown Matrimonial ; received two awards for o73 performance in TV play Professional Foul.

BARRETT, (Arthur) Michael, Ph.D., Vice-Chancellor of University of Buckingham since 1985; b. 1 April, 1932. Was with I.C.I. Ltd., 1961-70. Professor of Pharmacology, Leeds University, 1970-84. General Secretary, International Union for Pharmacology since 1981.

BARROWCLOUGH, Sir Anthony Richard, Q.C., Parliamentary Commissioner for Administration and Health Service Commissioner for England, Wales and Scotland since 1985; b. 24 June, 1924. Called to Bar, 1949. Q.C., 1974. Recorder of the Crown Court, 1972-84. Member, Council on Tribunals (Member, Scottish Committee), since 1985.

BASNETT, Baron (Life Peer) (David Basnett) General Secretary of General, Municipal, Boilermakers and Allied Trades Union, 1973-85; b. 9 Feb., 1924. A trade union official since 1948 and a member of T.U.C. General Council since 1966 (chairman, 1977-78). Member of National Economic Development Council 1973-86.

BATTEN, Sir John Charles, K.C.V.O. Physician to the Queen since 1974 and Head of H.M. Medical Household since 1982; Physician, Brompton Hosp., since 1959; b. 11 March, 1924. M.D., 1951. F.R.C.P., 1964. Physician, St. George's Hosp., 1958-79. Physician to H.M. Household, 1970-74.

BAUDOUIN I, King of the Belgians; b. 7 Sept., 1930. Succeeded to throne, 17 July, 1951; m. 1960 Dona Fabiola de Mora y Aragon. His brother is Prince Albert, b. 6 June, 1934, who married Donna Paola Ruffo di Calabria, 1959; his sister is Princess Josephine Charlotte, who m. Prince (now Grand Duke) Jean of Luxembourg, 1953.

BAUGHEN, Rt. Rev. Michael Alfred, Bishop of Chester since 1982; b. 7 June, 1930. Was with Martins Bank before ordination in 1956; Rector of Holy Trinity, Rusholme, Manchester, 1964-70; Vicar of All Souls, Langham Place, London, 1970-75 and Rector, 1975-82. Consultant editor, Hymns for Today's Church.

BAVIN, Rt. Rev. Timothy John, Bishop of Portsmouth since 1984; b. 17 Sept., 1935. Curate of Uckfield, Sussex, 1969-71; Vicar of Good Shepherd, Brighton, 1971-73; Dean and Rector, Cathedral of St. Mary the Virgin, Johannesburg, 1973-74; Bishop of Johannesburg, 1974-84.

BAWDEN, Edward, C.B.E., R.A., painter and designer; b. 1903. Official War Artist, 1940-45; was a tutor, School of Graphic Design, Royal College of Art.

BEATRIX, Queen of the Netherlands since 1980; b. 31 Jan., 1938; m. 10 Mar., 1966, Herr Claus von Amsberg (now Prince Claus of the Netherlands); three s : Prince Willem Alexander (now the Prince of Orange) b. 1967; Prince Johan Friso b. 1968; Prince Constantijn Christof b. 1969.

BEATTIE, Sir David Stuart, G.C.M.G., G.C.V.O., Q.S.O., Governor-General of New Zealand, 1980-85; b. 29 Feb., 1924 in Australia. A barrister and solicitor, he was president of Auckland Dist. Law o73 Society, 1964. Q.C., 1965. A Judge of New Zealand Supreme Court, 1969-80.

BECKETT, Sir Terence Norman, K.B.E., Director General of Confederation of British Industry 1980-86; b. 13 Dec., 1923. Educated at L.S.E. Joined Ford Motor Co., 1950 and was managing director and chief executive, 1974-80 and chairman, 1976-80. Member of National Economic Development Council since 1980. Chairman of Governing Body, London Business School, 1979-86.

BEER, Ian David Stafford, M.A., J.P., Headmaster of Harrow School since 1981; b. 28 April, 1931. Was a housemaster at Marlborough and Headmaster of Ellesmere College, 1961-69 and of Lancing College, 1969-81. Chairman, Headmasters' Conference, 1980.

BEITH, Alan James, M.P. (L), Liberal Chief Whip, 1976-85; b. 20 April, 1943. Was a lecturer in politics at University of Newcastle upon Tyne; is also a Methodist local preacher. Member of General Advisory Council of BBC since 1974.

BELDAM, Hon. Mr. Justice (Hon. Sir Alexander Roy Asplan Beldam), a Judge of the Queen's Bench Division since 1981; b. 29 March, 1925. Called to Bar, 1950. Q.C., 1969. A Recorder of the Crown Court, 1972-81. Judge of Employment Appeal Tribunal since 1984. Chairman of the Law Commission since 1985.

BELSTEAD, 2nd Baron (John Julian Ganzoni), P.C., Lord Privy Seal and Leader of the House of Lords 1988. b. 30 Sept., 1932. Parl. Under-Sec. of State, Dept. of Education and Science, 1970-73; at Northern Ireland Office, 1973-74 and Home Office, 1979-82; Minister of State, Foreign and Commonwealth Office, 1982-83. Minister of State, Min. of Agriculture, Fisheries and Food, 1983-87; Minister of State, Dept of the Environment 1987-1988.

BENN, Rt. Hon. Anthony Neil Wedgwood, M.P. (Lab); b. 3 April, 1925. Member, Nat. Exec. Com. of Labour Party, 1959-60, and since 1962. M.P. (Lab), Bristol, South-East, 1950-60, and 1963-83; for Chesterfield since 1984. Disclaimed peerage (2nd Viscount Stansgate), 1963; Postmaster-General, 1964-66; Minister of Technology, 1966-70; and of Power, 1969-70. Secretary of State for Industry, 1974-75 and for Energy, 1975-79.

BICKERSTETH, Rt. Rev. John Monier, Bishop of Bath and Wells 1975-87; Clerk of the Closet to the Queen since 1979; b. 6 Sept., 1921. Served in Army, 1941-46 and was ordained, 1951; Vicar of St. Stephen's, Chatham, 1962-70; Bishop Suffragan of Warrington, 1970-75.

BIDE, Sir Austin (Ernest), Chairman of British Leyland since 1982 and of Glaxo Holdings since 1973; b. 11 Sept., 1915. Was in Government Chemist's Dept. and joined Glaxo, 1940, as research chemist. Dep. Chairman of British Leyland, 1980-82.

BIFFEN, Rt. Hon. (William) John, M.P. (C), Lord Privy Seal 1983-87 and Leader of House of Commons 1982-87; b. 3 Nov., 1930. Formerly with Tube Investments Ltd. and Economist Intelligence Unit. Chief Secretary, Treasury, 1979-81; Secretary of State for Trade, 1981-82. Lord President of the Council, 1982-83.

BINGHAM, Rt.Hon. Lord Justice (Rt. Hon. Sir Thomas Henry Bingham), a Lord Justice of Appeal since 1986; a Judge of the Queen's Bench Division 1980-87; b. 13 Oct., 1933. Called to Bar, 1959. Q.C., 1972. A Recorder of the Crown Court, 1975-80. Chairman, Council of Legal Education since 1982.

BISHOP, Richard Evelyn Donohue, C.B.E., F.R.S., Vice-Chancellor & Principal of Brunel University since 1981; b. 1 Jan., 1925. Educated at University College, London and Stanford University, California. Professor of Mechanical Engineering, London University, 1957-81.

BLACKSTONE, Baroness (Life Peer), Master Birkbeck College since 1987, Chairman General Advisory Council B.B.C. since 1987; b. 27 Sept., 1942. Advisor Central Policy Review Staff Cabinet Office 1975-78.

BLAKE, Baron (Life Peer) (Robert Norman William Blake), Provost of The Queen's College, Oxford, since 1968; b. 23 Dec., 1916. Student and Tutor in Politics, Christ Church, 1947-68. Editor, Dictionary of National Biography, since 1980. Chairman of Royal Commission on Historical Manuscripts.

BLANCH, Baron (Life Peer) (Rt. Rev. Stuart Yarworth Blanch), P.C., Archbishop of York, 1975-83; b. 1918. In R.A.F., 1940-46. Ordained, 1949; Canon of Rochester and Warden of Rochester Theological College, 1960-66; Bishop of Liverpool, 1966-75.

BOKSENBERG, Prof. Alexander, Ph.D., F.R.S., Director of Royal Greenwich Observatory since 1981; b. 18 March, 1936. Reader in Physics, 1975-78 and Prof. of Physics, Dept. of Physics and Astronomy, 1978-81, University College London; Visiting Professor since 1981.

BOLT, Robert Oxton, C.B.E., dramatist; b. 15 Aug., 1924. Was formerly a teacher of English; first London production, Flowering Cherry, 1958; won British Film Academy Award for screenplay of Lawrence of Arabia, and Oscars for Dr. Zhivago and A Man for All Seasons.

BONDI, Prof. Sir Hermann, K.C.B., F.R.S., Master of Churchill College, Cambridge, since 1983; Professor of Mathematics, King's College, London, since 1954; b. in Vienna 1 Nov., 1919. Lecturer in mathematics, Cambridge University, 1948-54; Director-General, European Space Research Org., 1967-71; Chief Scientist, Dept. of Energy, 1977-80. Chairman, Natural Environment Research Council, 198-84.

BONINGTON, Christian John Storey, C.B.E., mountaineer; b. 6 Aug., 1934. Was in Army, 1955-61. Leader of Annapurna South Face expedition, 1970 and of British Everest expeditions, 1972 and 1975. With Norwegian expedition reached summit of Everest, 1985.

BOOTH, Hon. Mrs. Justice (Hon. Dame Margaret Myfanwy Wood Booth), D.B.E., a Judge of the Family Division since 1979; b. 1933. Called to Bar, 1956. Q.C., 1976. Chairman of Family Law Bar Association, 197678.

BOOTH-CLIBBORN, Rt. Rev. Stanley Eric Francis, Bishop of Manchester since 1979; b. 20 Oct., 1924. Leader, Lincoln City Centre team ministry, 1967-70; Vicar, University Church of St. Mary the Great, Cambridge, 1970-79.

BOREHAM, Hon. Mr. Justice (Hon. Sir Leslie Kenneth Edward Boreham), a Judge of the Queen's Bench Division since 1972; b. 1918. Called to Bar, 1947. Q.C., 1965. Recorder of Margate, 1968-71.

BORRIE, Sir Gordon Johnson, Director-General of Fair Trading since 1976; b. 13 March, 1931. Called to Bar, 1952. QC 1986. Professor of English Law and Director of Institute of Judicial Administration, Birmingham University, 1969-76. Member of Parole Board, 1971-74. Member of Consumer Protection Advisory Committee, 1973-76.

BOSCAWEN, Hon. Robert Thomas, M.C., M.P. (C), Comptroller of H.M. Household 1987-89; b. 17 March, 1923, s. of 8th Viscount Falmouth. Vice-Chamberlain of H.M. Household 1983-86. Was vice-chairman of Conservative Parliamentary Health and Social Security Committee. An Assistant Govt. Whip, 1979-81. A Lord Commissioner of the Treasury, 1981-83.

BOTHA, Pieter Willem, President of South Africa 1984-89; b. 12 Jan., 1916. Minister of Defence, 1966-80; Prime Minister and Minister of National Intelligence Service, 1978-84.

BOTHA, Roelof Frederik (Pik), Minister of Foreign Affairs, South Africa, since 1977, also Minister of Information; b. 27 April, 1932. Formerly in South African diplomatic service and was delegate to United Nations; South African Ambassador to U.S.A., 1975-77. M.P. (National Party) for Wonderboom, 1970-74 and for Westdene since 1977.

BOTTOMLEY, Peter James, M.P. (C), formerly Parl. Under-Sec of State, Northern Ireland Office. Parl. Under-Sec. of State, Dept. of Transport, 1986-89; b. 30 July, 1944. Was in industrial relations. M.P. (C) for Woolwich West, 1975-83 and for Eltham since 1983. Parl. Under-Sec. of State, Dept. of Employment, 1984-86. His wife, Mrs. Virginia Bottomley, is M.P. (C) for Surrey, South-West and a Parliamentary Under-Secretary of State for the Environment.

BOWEN, Most Rev. Michael George, Archbishop and Metropolitan of Southwark (R.C.) since 1977; b. 23 April, 1930. Ordained, 1958; teacher of theology, Beda College, Rome, 1963-66; Bishop of Arundel and Brighton, 1971-77.

BOWLBY, Rt. Rev. Ronald Oliver, Bishop of Southwark since 1980; b. 16 Aug., 1926. Vicar of St. Aidan, Billingham, 1956-66 and of Croydon, 1966-72. Bishop of Newcastle, 1973-80.

BOWNESS, Sir Alan, C.B.E., Director of the Henry Moore Foundation 1988 ; b. 11 Jan., 1928. Director of Tate Gallery 1980-1988; Joined Courtauld Institute of Art, 1957 and was dep. director, 1978-79; Prof. of History of Art, London University, 1978-79.

BOYSON, Rt. Hon. Sir Rhodes, P.C., Ph.D., M.P. (C), Minister of State, Dept. of Environment (Minister for Planning and Regional Affairs), 1986-87; b. 11 May, 1925. Educated at L.S.E. and Universities of Manchester and Cambridge; Headmaster of Robert Montefiore Secondary School, Stepney, 1961-66 and of Highbury Grove School, 1967-74. Parl. Under-Sec. of State, Dept. of Education and Science, 1979-83. Minister of State, Dept. of Health and Social Security (Minister for Social Security), 1983-84. Minister of State, Northern Ireland Office, 1984-86.

BRABAZON OF TARA, 3rd Baron (Ivon Anthony Moore-Brabazon), Parl. Under-Sec, Foreign and Commonwealth Office since 1989. Parl. UnderSec. for Aviation and Shipping from 1988-89; Parl. Under-Sec. of State, Dept. of Transport 1986-88; b. 20 Dec., 1946.

BRAGG, Melvyn, writer; b. 6 Oct., 1939. Joined BBC as radio and TV producer, 1961; presenter of Read All About It, 1976-77; presenter of ITV's The South Bank Show since 1978. First book for Want of a Nail published, 1965; also wrote screenplays for Isadora and Jesus Christ Superstar.

BRAMALL, Baron (Life Peer) (Field Marshal Sir Edwin) G.C.B., O.B.E., M.C., J.P., H.M. Lord-Lieutenant of Greater London since 1986. Chief of Defence Staff, 1982-85; b. 18 Dec., 1923. Cmdr., British Forces, Hong Kong, 1973-76; C.-in-C., U.K. Land Forces, 1976 78; Vice-Chief of Defence Staff, 1978-79. Colonel Commandant, 3rd Battalion Royal Green Jackets, 1973-84. Chief of General Staff, 1979-82.

BRAND, Hon. Lord (David William Robert Brand), a Senator of the College of Justice in Scotland since 1972; b. 21 Oct., 1923. Admitted to Faculty of Advocates, 1948. Q.C. (Scot.), 1959. Solicitor-General for Scotland, 1970-72.

BRANDON OF OAKBROOK, Baron (Life Peer) (Henry Vivian Brandon), M.C., P.C., a Lord of Appeal in Ordinary since 1981; b. 3 June, 1920. Called to Bar, 1946. Q.C., 1961. A Judge of the Probate, Divorce and Admiralty Division, 1966-71 and of the Family Division and Admiralty Court, 1971-78; a Lord Justice of Appeal, 1978-81.

BRANSON, Richard, Founder & Chairman Virgin Group; b. 18 July 1950. Founder student magazine 1968-69, Set up student advisory Centre (HELP) 1970; founder of Virgin mail order and shop; Virgin Airlines 1984; set record for fastest boat crossing in 1986.

BREWSTER, Kingman, Master of University College, Oxford from 1986-89; b. 17 June, 1919. Educated at Yale and Harvard Universities; Professor of Law, Harvard, 1953-60; Provost of Yale, 1961-63 and President 1963-77. American Ambassador to Britain, 1977-81.

BRIDGE OF HARWICH, Baron (Life Peer) (Nigel Cyprian Bridge), P.C., a Lord of Appeal in Ordinary since 1980; b. 26 Feb., 1917. Called to Bar, 1947. Junior Counsel to Treasury (Common Law), 1964-68; a Judge of Queen's Bench Division, 1968-75; a Lord Justice of Appeal, 1975-80. Chairman of Security Commission, 1982-85.

BRIGGS, Baron (Life Peer) (Asa Briggs), Provost of Worcester College, Oxford, since 1976; b. 7 May 1921. Professor of Modern History, Leeds University, 1955-61; Vice-Chancellor of Sussex University, 1967-76 and Professor

of History, 1961-76. Is a trustee of Glyndebourne Arts Trust; President of Social History Society. Chancellor of Open University 1978-88.

BRIGHTMAN, Baron (Life Peer) (John Anson Brightman), P.C., a Lord of Appeal in Ordinary 1982-86; b. 20 June, 1911. Called to Bar, 1932. Q.C., 1961. A Judge of the Chancery Division, 1970-79; a Lord Justice of Appeal, 1979-82.

BRIGSTOCKE, Mrs. Heather Renwick, High Mistress of St. Paul's Girls' School since 1974; b. 2 Sept., 1929. Was classics mistress at Francis Holland School, 1951-53 and Headmistress, 1965-74.

BRISTOW, Hon. Mr. Justice (Hon. Sir Peter Henry Rowley Bristow), a Judge of the Queen's Bench Division 1970-85; b. 1 June, 1913. Called to Bar, 1936. Q.C., 1964. Judge of the Courts of Appeal, Guernsey and of Jersey, 1965-70. A Judge of Commercial Court and Employment Appeal Tribunal, 1976-78. Presiding Judge, Western Circuit, 1979-82.

BRITTAN, Rt. Hon. Sir Leon, Q.C., b. 25 Sept., 1939. President of Cambridge Union, 1960. Called to Bar, 1962. Q.C., 1978. Minister of State, Home Office, 1979-81; Chief Secretary, Treasury, 1981-83. Home Secretary 1983-85. Secretary of State for Trade and Industry 1985-86.

BROOK, Peter Stephen Paul, C.B.E., theatrical producer; Co-Director, Royal Shakespeare Theatre; b. 21 March, 1925; m. 1951, Natasha Parry, Director of Productions, Royal Opera House, Covent Garden, 1947-50.

BROOKE, Hon. Peter Leonard, P.C., M.P. (C), Secretary of State for Northern Ireland; Chairman of the Conservative Party from 1988-89. Paymaster General from 1987-89; b. 3 March, 1934, s. of Minister of State, Treasury, 1985-87; late Baron Brooke of Cumnor. President of Oxford Union, 1957. An Assistant Government Whip, 1979-81; a Lord Commissioner of the Treasury, 1981-83. Joint Parl. Under-Sec. of State. Dept. of Education and Science, 1983-85.

BROOKS, Most Rev. Francis Gerard, Bishop of Dromore (R.C.) since 1976; b. 1924. Was formerly president of St. Colman's College, Newry.

BROWN, Hon. Mr. Justice Kilner (Hon. Sir Ralph Kilner Brown), O.B.E., Judge of the Queen's Bench Division, 1970-85; b. 28 Aug., 1909. Called to Bar, 1934. Q.C., 1958. Judge of Central Criminal Court, 1965-67; Recorder of Liverpool, 1967-69. A Judge of Employment Appeal Tribunal 1976-84.

BROWN, Hon. Mr. Justice (Hon. Sir Simon Denis Brown), a Judge of the Queen's Bench Division since 1984; b. 9 April, 1937. Called to Bar, 1961. First Junior Treasury Counsel, Common Law, 1979-84; a Recorder of the Crown Court, 1979-84.

BROWN, Rt. Hon. Lord Justice Stephen (Rt. Hon. Sir Stephen Brown), a Lord Justice of Appeal since 1983; b. 3 Oct., 1924. Called to Bar, 1949. Q.C., 1966. A Recorder of the Crown Court, 1972-75; a Judge of the Family Division, 1975-77 and of the Queen's Bench Division, 197783.

BROWNE, Sheila Jeanne, C.B., Principal of Newnham College, Cambridge, since 1983; b. 25 Dec., 1924. Educated at Lady Margaret Hall, Oxford. Was a university lecturer in French; H.M. Inspector of Schools, 196170; Senior Chief Inspector (Deputy Senior Chief Inspector, 1972-74), Dept. of Education and Science, 1974-83.

BROWNE-WILKINSON, Rt. Hon. Lord Justice (Rt. Hon. Sir Nicolas Christopher Henry Browne-Wilkinson), Vice-Chancellor of the Supreme Court since 1985 and a Lord Justice of Appeal 1983-85; b. 30 March, 1930. Called to Bar, 1953. Q.C., 1972. Junior Counsel, Dept. of Trade and Industry, 1966-72. A Judge of Jersey and Guernsey Courts of Appeal, 1976-77; a Judge of the Chancery Division, 1977-83. President of Employment Appeal Tribunal, 1981-83.

BUCHANAN-SMITH, Rt. Hon. Alick Laidlaw, M.P. (C), Minister of State, Dept. of Energy, 1983-87; b. 8 April, 1932, s. of late Baron Balerno. Parl. Under-Sec. of State. Scottish Office, 1970-74. Minister of State, Min. of Agriculture, Fisheries and Food, 1979-83.

BULLARD, Sir Julian, G.C.M.G., British Ambassador to Fed. Rep. of Germany since 1984; b. 8 March, 1928. Fellow of All Souls, 1950-57. Joined Diplomatic Service, 1953 and served in Moscow, Dubai and Bonn; Deputy to Permanent Under-Sec. of State, Foreign and Commonwealth Office, 1982-84.

BURGEN, Sir Arnold Stanley Vincent, F.R.S., Former Master of Darwin College, Cambridge; b. 20 March, 1922. Asst. Lecturer in Pharmacology, Middlesex Hosp. Medical School, 1948-49; Professor of Physiology, McGill University, Montreal, 1949-62; Shield Professor of Pharmacology, Cambridge University, 1962-71. Director of National Institute for Medical Research, 1971-82.

BURNETT, Sir John Harrison, D.Phil., F.R.S.E., Principal and Vice-Chancellor, Edinburgh University, 1979-87; b. 21 Jan., 1922. Professor of Botany, St. Andrews University, 1955-60; at King's College, Durham University, 1961-63 and at Newcastle University, 1963-68; Regius Professor of Botany, Glasgow, 1968-70; Professor of Rural Economy, Oxford, 1970-79.

BURNS, Sir Terence, Chief Economic Adviser to Treasury and Head of Government Economic Service since 1980; b. 13 March, 1944. Educated at Manchester University. Senior Lecturer in Economics, London Business School, 1974-79 and Prof. of Economics, 1979; Director, LBS Centre for Economic Forecasting, 1976-79.

BUSH, Hon. Mr. Justice (Hon. Sir Brian Drex Bush), a Judge of the Family Division since 1976; b. 5 Sept., 1925. Called to Bar, 1947. A Circuit Judge, 1969-76; member of Parole Board, 1971-74. Presiding Judge, Midland and Oxford Circuit, 1982-85.

BUSH, George Herbert Walker, President of the U.S.A. since 1989; Vice-President of U.S.A. 1981-89; b. 12 June, 1924. Elected to House of Representatives for Texas, 1966, gave up his seat in 1970. U.S. Permanent Representative at United Nations, 1971-73; chairman of Republican Party National Committee, 1973-74; director of Central Intelligence Agency, 1976-77.

BUTCHER, John Patrick, M.P. (C), Former Parl. Under-Sec. of Education and Science; b. 1946. Parl. Under-Sec. of State, Dept. of Industry, 1982-83 and Dept. of Trade and Industry 1983-1988; Former member of Birmingham City Council; entered Parliament, 1979.

BUTLER, Rt. Hon. Adam Courtauld, M.P. (C), Former Minister of State, Min. of Defence 1984 and at Northern Ireland Office, 1981-84; b. 11 Oct., 1931, s. of late Baron Butler of Saffron Walden. Was with Courtaulds Ltd., 1955-73. P.P.S. to Leader of Opposition, 1975-79. Minister of State, Dept. of Industry, 1979-81.

BUTLER, Sir Michael Dacres, G.C.M.G., U.K. Permanent Representative to European Communities, 1979-85; b. 27 Feb., 1927. Joined H.M. Foreign Service, 1950 and served in Baghdad, Paris, Geneva and Washington. Asst. Under-Sec., Foreign and Commonwealth Office, in charge of European Community Affairs, 1974-76; Director, Hambros Ltd since 1986.

BUTLER-SLOSS, Hon. Mrs. Justice (Hon. Dame (Ann) Elizabeth (Oldfield) Butler-Sloss), D.B.E., a Judge of the Family Division since 1979; b. 10 Aug., 1933, sister of Rt. Hon. Sir Michael Havers. Called to Bar, 1955. A Registrar of the Family Division, 1970-79.

BUTTERFIELD, Baron (Life Peer), Prof. (William John Hughes), O.B.E., Master of Downing College, Cambridge, 1978-87; Regius Professor of Physics since 1976; b. 28 March, 1920. Member of M.R.C. scientific staff, 1946-58; Prof. of Experimental Medicine, Guy's Hosp., 1958-63 and

Prof. of Medicine, Guy's Hosp. Medical School, 1963-71; ViceChancellor, Nottingham University, 1971-75; Chairman, Medicines Commission, 1976-81.

CAITHNESS, 20th Earl of (Malcolm Ian Sinclair), Paymaster General since 1989; Minister for Environment, Countryside and Water from 1988; b. 3 Nov., 1948. A Lord in Waiting 1984-85; Minister of State, Home Office 1986-88. Is a chartered surveyor.

CALLAGHAN, Baron (Life Peer) (Leonard James Callaghan) K.G., P.C.; b. 27 March, 1912. Parl. and Fin. Sec., Admiralty, 1950 51; Chancellor of the Exchequer, 1964-67; Home Secretary, 1967-70; Secretary of State for Foreign and Commonwealth Affairs, 1974-76; Prime Minister and First Lord of the Treasury, 1976-79; Leader of the Opposition, 197980. Knight of the Garter, 1987.

CALLIL, Carmen Therese, Chairman Virago Press since 1972 (Managing Director 1972-82); Managing Director Chatto and Whindus, The Hogarth Press since 1983; b. 15 July 1938. Founder Virago Press 1972; Member of Board of Channel 4 from 1985.

CAMERON, Hon. Lord (John Cameron), K.T., D.S.C., Senator of College of Justice in Scotland and Lord of Session since 1955; b. 1900. K.C. (Scot.), 1936; Dean of Faculty of Advocates, 1948-55.

CAMERON OF LOCHBROOM, Baron (Life Peer) (Kenneth John Cameron), P.C., Lord Advocate from 1984; b.11 June, 1931, s. of Lord Cameron. Admitted to Faculty of Advocates, 1958. Q.C. (Scot.), 1972. Chairman, Industrial Tribunals in Scotland, 1966-81; Advocate Depute, 1981-84.

CANTLEY, Hon. Mr.Justice (Hon. Sir Joseph Donaldson Cantley), O.B.E., Judge of the Queen's Bench Division 1965-85; b. 8 Aug., 1910. Called to Bar, 1933. Q.C., 1954. Judge of Salford Hundred Court of Record, 1960-65.

CARL XVI GUSTAF, King of Sweden since 1973; b.30 April, 1946, son of Prince Gustaf Adolf (d.1947) and grandson of late King Gustaf VI Adolf; m. 1976, Silvia Sommerlath; 3 children: Crown Princess Victoria; Prince Carl Philip; Princess Madeleine.

CARMICHAEL, Ian, actor; b.18 June, 1920. Trained at R.A.D.A. First appearance at People's Palace, 1939. Entered films, 1947. Appeared on TV in The World of Wooster and Lord Peter Wimsey.

CARPENTER, Very Rev. Edward Frederick, Dean of Westminster, 1974-85; b.27 Nov., 1910. Rector of Great Stanmore, 1945-51. Canon of Westminster, 1951-74 and Treasurer, 1959-74; Archdeacon of Westminster, 1963-74.

CARRINGTON, 6th Baron (Peter Alexander Rupert Caringtion), K.G., P.C., C.H., G.C.M.G., M.C., Chairman of Christies; ; b.6 June, 1919. Secretary-General of N.A.T.O. 1984-1988; High Commissioner for U.K. in Australia, 1956-59; First Lord of the Admiralty, 1959-63; Minister without Portfolio and Leader of House of Lords, 1963-64; Secretary of State for Defence, 1970-74. Leader of Opposition, House of Lords, 1964-70 and 1974-79; Secretary of State for Foreign and Commonwealth Affairs, 1979-82. Chairman of General Electric Co., 1983-84.

CARSBERG, Prof. Bryan Victor, Director-General of Telecommunications since 1984; b.3 Jan., 1939. Chartered accountant, 1960. Lecturer in Accounting, L.S.E., 1964-68; Professor of Accounting, Manchester University, 1969-81; Professor of Accounting, L.S.E., since 1981.

CARSWELL, Hon. Mr.Justice (Hon. Robert Douglas Carswell), a Judge of High Court of Justice, N. Ireland, since 1984; b.28 June, 1934. Called to N.I.Bar, 1957 and to English Bar, 1972. Q.C. (N.I.), 1971. Senior Crown Counsel in N.I., 1979-84.

CARTIER-BRESSON, Henri, b. 22 Oct., 1908. Photographer.

CARTLEDGE, Sir Bryan, K.C.M.G., British Ambassador to U.S.S.R. since 1985; b. 10 June, 1931. Entered Diplomatic Service, 1960 and served in Stockholm, Moscow and Tehran. Ambassador to Hungary, 1980-83; Assistant Under-Sec. of State, Foreign and Commonwealth Office, 1983-84; Dep. Sec. of Cabinet, 1984-85.

CASSON, Sir Hugh (Maxwell), C.H., K.C.V.O., P.R.A., architect; President of Royal Academy, 1976-84; b. 23 May, 1910. Director of Architecture, Festival of Britain, 1948-51; Professor of Environmental Design, Royal College of Art, 1953-75. Provost of Royal College of Art since 1980. Albert Medal, Royal Society of Arts, 1984.

CASTLE, Rt. Hon. Barbara, Member of European Parliament (Lab) since 1979; b. 6 Oct., 1910. M.P. (Lab) for Blackburn, 1945-50 and 1955-79; for Blackburn, East, 1950-55; Minister of Transport, 1965-68; First Secretary of State and Secretary of State for Employment, 1968-70; Secretary of State for Social Services, 1974-76.

CATHERWOOD, Sir (Henry) Frederick (Ross), Member of European Parliament (C) since 1979; b.30 Jan., 1925. A chartered accountant. Chief Executive, Richard Costain Ltd., 1955-60; Managing director, British Aluminium Co. Ltd., 1962-64. Chief Industrial Adviser, Dept. of Economic Affairs, 1964-66; Director-General, N.E.D.C., 1966-71. Chairman, British Overseas Trade Board, 1975-79.

CAULFIELD, Hon. Mr.Justice (Hon. Sir Bernard Caulfield), Judge of the Queen's Bench Division since 1968; b.24 April, 1914. Solicitor, 1940. Called to Bar, 1947. Q.C., 1961. Recorder of Coventry, 1963-68.

CHADWICK, Rev. (William) Owen, O.M., K.B.E., Master of Selwyn College, Cambridge, 1956-83 and Regius Professor of Modern History, 1968-83; b.20 May, 1916. Was a chaplain at Wellington College; Dixie Professor of Ecclesiastical History, Cambridge, 1958-68. Chairman, Archbishops' Commission on Church and State, 1966-70. President of British Academy, 1981-85. Fellow of Selwyn College since 1983. Chancellor of East Anglia University since 1985.

CHALKER, Rt. Hon. Mrs. Lynda, M.P. (C), Minister for Overseas Development since 1989; Minister of State, Foreign and Commonwealth Office, 1986-89; b.29 April, 1942. A statistician, was with Unilever, 1963-69. Parl. Under-Sec. of State, Dept. of Health and Social Security, 197982. Parl. Under-Sec. of State, 1982-83. Minister of State, Dept. of Transport, 1983-86.

CHANNON, Rt. Hon. (Henry) Paul (Guinness), M.P. (C), Secretary of State for Transport 1987-89. B. 9 Oct. 1935. Secretary of State for Trade and Industry, 1986-87; Minister of State, Northern Ireland Office, 1972; Minister for Housing and Construction, 1972-74; Minister of State, Civil Service Dept., 1979-81 and Dept. of Education and Science (Minister for the Arts), 1981-83. Minister of State, Dept. of Trade and Industry, 1983-86.

CHAPPLE, Baron (Life Peer) (Frank Joseph Chapple), General Secretary of Electrical, Electronic, Telecommunication and Plumbing Union, 1966-84; b. 1921. Member of Royal Commission on Environmental Pollution, 1973-77 and of Energy Commission, 1977-79; member of N.E.D.C., 1979-83 and of National Nuclear Corp. since 1980.

CHESHIRE, Group Captain (Geoffrey) Leonard, V.C., O.M., D.S.O., D.F.C.; b. 7 Sept., 1917; m. 1959, Susan Ryder (now Baroness Ryder of Warsaw). Was in R.A.F., 1939-45. Founder of the Cheshire Foundation Homes for the Sick.

CHRISTOPHERSON, Sir Derman Guy, O.B.E., F.R.S., Master of Magdalene College, Cambridge, 1979-85; b.6 Sept., 1915. Professor of Mechanical Engineering, Leeds University, 1949-55; Professor of Applied Science, Imperial College of Science and Technology, 1955-60. Vice-Chancellor and Warden of Durham University, 1960-78. Chairman, Royal Fine Art Commission, 1980-85.

CLARK, Rt. Rev. Alan Charles, Bishop of East Anglia (R.C.), since 1976; b.9 Aug., 1919. Parish priest, St. Mary's,

Blackheath, 1965-69; Auxiliary Bishop of Northampton, 1969-76.

CLARK, Hon. Alan Kenneth McKenzie, M.P. (C), Minister of State, Ministry of Defence since 1989; Minister of State, Dept. of Trade and Industry (Minister for Trade), 1986-89; b.13 April, 1928, s. of late Baron Clark. Called to Bar, 1955. Parl. Under-Sec. of State, Dept. of Employment, 1983-86.

CLARKE, Rt. Hon. Kenneth Harry, Q.C., M.P. (C), Secretary of State for Health; b. 2 July, 1940. Paymaster General, 1985-87; President of Cambridge Union, 1963. Called to Bar, 1963. A Lord Commissioner of the Treasury, 1974. Parl. Sec., Dept. of Transport, 1979-82. Minister of State, Dept. of Health and Social Security (Minister for Health), 1982-85. Chancellor of Duchy of Lancaster 1987-89.

CLEDWYN OF PENRHOS, Baron (Life Peer) (Cledwyn Hughes), P.C., C.H., Leader of Opposition, House of Lords, since 1982; b.14 Sept., 1916. Admitted a solicitor, 1940. M.P. (Lab) for Anglesey, 1951-79; Secretary of State for Wales, 1966-68; Minister of Agriculture, Fisheries and Food, 1968-70. Pro-Chancellor, University of Wales, since 1985.

COCKFIELD, Baron (Life Peer) (Francis Arthur Cockfield), P.C., formerly Vice-President, Commission of European Community; b.28 Sept., 1916. Called to Bar, 1942. Director of Statistics and Intelligence to Board of Inland Revenue, 1945-52. Chairman, Boots Pure Drug Co., 1961-67. Adviser on taxation policy to Chancellor of Exchequer, 1970-73; Chairman of Price Commission, 1973-77. Minister of State, Treasury, 1979-82; Secretary of State for Trade, 1982-83; Chancellor of Duchy of Lancaster, 1983-84.

COCKS, Baron (Life Peer) (Michael Francis Lovell), P.C.; b.19 Aug., 1929. Was a lecturer at Bristol Polytechnic. A Lord Commissioner of the Treasury, 1975-76; Parliamentary Secretary to the Treasury and Chief Whip, 1976-79. Chief Opposition Whip, 1979-85.

COGGAN, Baron (Life Peer) (Rt. Rev. Frederick Donald Coggan), P.C., Archbishop of Canterbury, 1974-80; b.9 Oct., 1909. Principal, London College of Divinity, 1944-56. Bishop of Bradford, 1956-61. Archbishop of York, 1961-74.

COLE, Sir (Alexander) Colin, K.C.V.O., Garter King of Arms since 1978; b.16 May, 1922. Called to Bar, 1949. Member of Court of Common Council of City of London since 1964; Registrar and Librarian, College of Arms, 1967-74; Windsor Herald of Arms, 1966-78.

COMYN, Hon. Mr. Justice (Hon. Sir James Comyn), a Judge of the Family Division, 1978-79 and of the Queen's Bench Division 1979-85; b.8 March, 1921. Called to Bar, 1942 and to Irish Bar, 1947. Q.C., 1961. Recorder of Andover, 1964-71; a Recorder of the Crown Court, 1972-77.

CONNERY, Sean, actor; b.25 Aug., 1930. First film, No Road Back, 1956.

CONRAN, Sir Terence, formerly Chairman and Chief Executive Storehouse PLC, Chairman Haibitat Group 1971, Conran Design 1971, b. 4 Oct., 1931. Designer and businessman with worldwide interests.

CONTI, Rt. Rev. Mario Joseph, Bishop of Aberdeen (R.C.) since 1977; b.20 March, 1934. Parish priest, St.Joachim's, Wick and St.Anne's, Thurso, 1962-77.

COOK, Prof. Sir Alan Hugh, F.R.S., Master of Selwyn College, Cambridge, since 1983; Jackson Professor of Natural Philosophy, Cambridge, since 1972; b.2 Dec., 1922. Was with Admiralty Signal Establishment; at Nat. Physical Laboratory, 1966-69; Professor of Geophysics, Edinburgh, 1969-72.

COOKE, (Alfred) Alistair, journalist and broadcaster; b.20 Nov., 1908, in England; is now a naturalised U.S. citizen. Commentator on American affairs for BBC. Chief correspondent in U.S. of The Guardian, 1948-72. Wrote and

7

7 PEOPLE

narrated TV series on U.S.A.; Benjamin Franklin Medal, 1973; Hon. K.B.E., 1973.

COOKE, Arthur Hafford, M.B.E., D.Phil., Warden of New College, Oxford, 1976-85; b. 13 Dec., 1912. Admiralty radar research, 1940-45. Fellow of New College, Oxford, 1946-76 and was university lecturer in physics, 1944-71; reader in physics, 1971-76.

COOPER, Kenneth Reginald, Chief Executive of British Library since 1984; b.28 June, 1931. Joined Min. of Labour, 1954.Chief Executive, Employment Services Agency, 1971-75 and of Training Services Agency, 1975-79; Director-General, Nat.Federation of Building Trades Employers, 1979-84.

COPE, John Ambrose, P.C., M.P. (C), Minister of State, Northern Ireland Office since 1989; Minister of State at the Department of Employment 1987-89; b. 13 May 1937. Treasurer of H.M. Household and Deputy Chief Whip 1983-85. In Conservative Research Dept., 1965-67; published, with Bernard Weatherill, Acorns to Oaks (Policy for Small Business), 1967. An Assistant Government Whip,1979-81; a Lord Commissioner of the Treasury, 1981-83.

CORNWELL, David John Moore (John le Carre), author; b.19 Oct., 1931. Was a schoolmaster and later was in H.M. Foreign Service, 1960-64. First book published, 1961; The Spy Who Came in from the Cold and The Looking Glass War were filmed and TV serials were made from Tinker, Tailor, Soldier, Spy and Smiley's People.

COTTON, William Frederick (Bill), O.B.E., Managing Director B.B.C. Television 1984-88, b. 23. April 1928. Chairman B.B.C. Enterprises 1982-86 and 1987-88 and various B.B.C. appointments.

COTTRELL, Sir Alan, F.R.S., Master of Jesus College, Cambridge, 1974-86; b.17 July, 1919. Professor of Physical Metallurgy, Birmingham University, 1949-55; Professor of Metallurgy, Cambridge University, 1958-65; part-time member of U.K.A.E.A., 1962-65 and since 1983. Dep. Chief Scientific Adviser (Studies), Min. of Defence, 1965-67 and Chief Adviser, 1967. Chief Scientific Adviser to H.M. Government, 1971-74. Member of Security Commission since 1981.

COUVE DE MURVILLE, Most Rev. Maurice Noel Leon, Archbishop of Birmingham (R.C.) since 1982; b.27 June, 1929.Was Catholic chaplain, Sussex University, 1961-77 and Cambridge University, 1977-82.

COWEN, Rt. Hon. Sir Zelman, G.C.M.G., G.C.V.O., Q.C., Provost of Oriel College, Oxford, since 1982; b.7 Oct., 1919.Called to Bar, 1947.Q.C., 1972.Prof. of Public Law and Dean of Faculty of Law, Melbourne University, 1951-66; Vice-Chancellor and Professor, University of New England, New South Wales, 1967-70; Vice-Chancellor, Queensland University, 1970-77. Governor-General of Australia, 1977-82.Chairman of Press Council since 1983.

COWIE, Hon. Lord (William Lorn Kerr Cowie), a Senator of College of Justice in Scotland since 1977; b.1 June, 1926.Member of Faculty of Advocates, 1952. Q.C. (Scot.), 1967.

COX, Baroness (Life Peer) (Caroline Anne Cox), a Baroness in Waiting, 1985; b.6 July, 1937. State Registered Nurse, 1958; M.Sc.in Economics, 1969. Was lecturer then head of Dept. of Sociology, Polytechnic of North London, 1969-77; director, Nursing Education Research Unit, Chelsea College, since 1977.

CRADOCK, Sir Percy, G.C.M.G., special adviser on foreign affairs to the Prime Minister since 1984; b. 26 Oct., 1923. British Ambassador to German Democratic Republic, 1976-78 and to China, 1978-83. Leader of U.K. delegation to Comprehensive Test Ban Discussions, Geneva, 1977-78.

CRAIG, Air Chief Marshal Sir David (Brownrigg), G.C.B., O.B.E., Chief of the Defence Staff; since 1988; Chief of the Air Staff 1985-88; b.17 Sept., 1929. Commissioned in R.A.F., 1951; A.O.C. No.I Group, Strike Command, 1978-80; Vice-Chief of Air Staff, 1980-82; A.O.C.-in-C., Strike Command

and C.-in-C., U.K. Air Forces, 1982-85.

CRAWFORD, Frederick William, D.Sc., Vice-Chancellor of University of Aston in Birmingham since 1980; b.28 July, 1931. Educated at Universities of London and Liverpool. Joined N.C.B. Mining Research, 1956; lecturer in electrical engineering, Birmingham, 1958-59; Stanford University, California, 1959-81, as lecturer and subsequently Chairman of Institute for Plasma Research.

CROOM-JOHNSON, Rt. Hon. Lord Justice (Rt. Hon. Sir David Powell Croom- Johnson), D.S.C., a Lord Justice of Appeal since 1984; b. 28 Nov., 1914. Called to Bar, 1938. Q.C., 1958. Recorder of Winchester, 1962-71; a Judge of the Queen's Bench Division, 1971-84. Chairman of Tribunal of Inquiry into the Crown Agents, 1978.

CROSS, Rt. Rev. (David) Stewart, was Bishop of Blackburn from 1982-88; b. 4 April, 1928. Ordained, 1955. Curate of St.Ambrose, Chorlton-onMedlock, and Assistant Chaplain, Manchester University, 1963-67; BBC producer in religious broadcasting, 1968-76; Bishop Suffragan of Doncaster, 1976-82.

CROWTHER-HUNT, Baron (Life Peer) (Norman Crowther Crowther-Hunt), Former Rector of Exeter College, Oxford, from 1982; b.13 March, 1920. Fellow and lecturer in politics, Exeter College, 1952-82. Minister of State, Dept. of Education and Science, 1974-76. Member of Fulton Committee on Civil Service, 1966-68.

CUMMING-BRUCE, Rt. Hon. Lord Justice (Rt. Hon. Sir (James) Roualeyn Hovell-Thurlow Cumming-Bruce), a Lord Justice of Appeal, 1977-85; b.9 March, 1912. Called to Bar, 1937. Recorder of Doncaster, 1957-58; of York, 1958-61; a Judge of the Family (formerly Probate, Divorce and Admiralty) Division, 1964-77; a Judge of Restrictive Practices Court, 1968-77.

CURRIE, Edwina, M.P. (C), Former Parliamentary Under-Secretary of Health, b. 13 Oct., 1946. Member of B.B.C. General Advisor Committee 1985-86; Political and Social work in Birmingham; Under-Secretary of State Department of Health and Social Security 1986-88.

DACRE OF GLANTON, Baron (Life Peer) (Hugh Redwald Trevor-Roper), Was Master of Peterhouse College, Cambridge from 1980; b.15 Jan., 1914. Student of Christ Church, Oxford, 1946-57; Regius Professor of Modern History, Oxford, 1957-80.

DAHL, Roald, b. 13 Sept., 1916. Prolific writer of stories for children and gorwn-ups, also television plays.

DAINTON, Baron (Life Peer) (Frederick Dainton), F.R.S., Chairman of British Library Board 1978-85; b. 11 Nov., 1914. Professor of Physical Chemistry, Leeds University, 1950-65; Vice-Chancellor, Nottingham University, 1965-70; Dr. Lee's Professor of Chemistry, Oxford University, 1970-73. Chairman of University Grants Committee, 1973-78.Davy Medal, Royal Society, 1969. Chancellor of Sheffield University since 1978.

DALHOUSIE, 16th Earl of (Simon Ramsay), K.T., G.C.V.O., G.B.E., M.C., Formerly Lord Chamberlain to the Queen Mother; b.17 Oct., 1914. M.P. (C) for County of Angus, 1945-50. Governor-General of the Federation of Rhodesia and Nyasaland, 1957-63. Chancellor of Dundee University since 1977.

DALY, Most. Rev. Cahal Brendan, Bishop of Down and Connor (R.C.) since 1982; b.1917.Lecturer, 1946-62 and Reader, 1962-67, in Scholastic Philosophy, Queen's University, Belfast. Bishop of Ardagh and Clonmacnois, 1967-82.

DANIEL, Sir Goronwy Hopkin, K.C.V.O., C.B., Former Chairman of Welsh Fourth TV Channel Authority since 1981; H.M. Lieutenant for Dyfed since 1978; b. 21 March, 1914. Permanent Under-Sec.of State, Welsh Office, 1964-69.Principal, Aberystwyth University College, 1969-79; Vice-Chancellor, University of Wales, 1977-79. Dep. chairman, Prince of Wales Committee, since 1980.

DARWENT, Rt. Rev. Frederick Charles, Bishop of Aberdeen and Orkney since 1978; b.20 April, 1927.Worked in bank before ordination in 1964. Rector of Strichen, 1965-71 and of Fraserburgh, 1971-78; Dean of Aberdeen and Orkney, 1973-78.

DAVIDSON, Hon. Lord (Charles Kemp Davidson), a Senator of College of Justice in Scotland since 1983; b. 13 April, 1929: Admitted to Faculty of Advocates, 1956. Q.C. (Scot.), 1969. Dean of Faculty of Advocates, 1979-83. Procurator to General Assembly of Church of Scotland, 1972-83.

DAVIES, Hon. Mr. Justice Mervyn (Hon. Sir (David Herbert) Mervyn Davies), M.C., a Judge of the Chancery Division since 1982; b.17 Jan., 1918. Admitted a solicitor, 1939. Called to Bar, 1947. Q.C., 1967. A Circuit Judge, 1978-82.

DAVIES, Hon. Mr. Justice Michael (Hon. Sir (Alfred William) Michael Davies), a Judge of the Queen's Bench Division since 1973; b.29 July, 1921. Called to Bar, 1948. Q.C., 1964. Recorder of Grantham, 1963-65 and of Derby, 1965-71.

DAVIES, Sir Peter Maxwell, C.B.E., Composer, b. 8 Sep. 1934.

DAVIS, Sir Colin (Rex), C.B.E., Musicial Director, Royal Opera House, Covent Garden, 1971-86; b.25 Sept., 1927. Assistant Conductor, BBC Scottish Orchestra, 1957-59; Principal Conductor, Sadler's Wells, 1960-65, and Musical Director, 1961-65; Chief Conductor, BBC Symphony Orchestra, 1967-71. Principal Guest Conductor of Boston Symphony and London Symphony Orchestras. Chief Conductor, Bavarian Radio Symphony Orchestra.

DAVIS, Stanley Clinton, Member, Commission of the European Communities since 1985; b.6 Dec., 1928. Admitted a solicitor, 1953. M.P. (Lab) for Hackney Central, 1970-83; Parl.Under-Sec.of State, Dept.of Trade, 1974-79.

DAY, Sir Derek, K.C.M.G., Former British High Commissioner in Canada; b. 29 Nov., 1927. High Commissioner in Cyprus, 1972-75; Ambassador to Ethiopia, 1975-78; Dep. Under-Sec. of State, Foreign and Commonwealth Office, 1980-84 and Chief Clerk, 1982-84.

DAY, Sir (Judson) Graham, Chairman of The Rover Group, since 1986; Chairman and Chief Executive, British Shipbuilders, since 1983; b.3 May, 1933. Educated in Canada and practised law in Nova Scotia, 1956-64. With Canadian Pacific, 1964-71 and Cammell Laird, Birkenhead, 1971-75; dep. chairman, organising committee for British Shipbuilders, 1975-76. Professor of Business Studies and Director, Canadian Marine Transportation Centre, Dalhousie University, 1977-81.

DAY, Sir Robin, journalist and television commentator; b. 24 Oct., 1923. President of Oxford Union, 1950. Called to Bar, 1952. Newscaster and parliamentary correspondent, Independent TV news, 1955-59; joined BBC, 1959 and was introducer of Panorama, 1967-72. Presenter, World at One, BBC Radio, and of Question Timeon TV. Won Richard Dimbleby Award, 1974.

DEAN, Sir Paul, M.P. (C), Second Deputy Chairman of Ways and Means, House of Commons and an Assistant Deputy Speaker, since 1982; b.14 Sept., 1924. With Conservative Research Dept., 1957-64; Parl. UnderSec. of State, Dept.of Health and Social Security, 1970-74.

DEARING, Sir Ronald Ernest, C.B., Chairman of Post Office Corporation 1981-87; b.27 July, 1930. Educated at Hull University and London Business School; joined civil service, 1946; Deputy Secretary, Dept.of Industry, 1976-80.

DEARNLEY, Christopher Hugh, Organist of St.Paul's Cathedral since 1968; b.11 Feb., 1930. Organist and Master of the Choristers, Salisbury Cathedral, 1957-67.

de GREY, Roger, P.R.A., President of Royal Academy since 1984; b.18 April, 1918. Senior Tutor, later Reader, in Painting, Royal College of Art, 1953-73; Principal, City and Guilds of London Art School since 1973. R.A., 1969.

DELFONT, Baron (Life Peer) (Bernard Delfont), executive chairman First Leisure Corp. (formerly Trusthouse Forte Leisure), since 1986 (chairman & chief executive 1980-86); b.5 Sept., 1909. Began in theatrical management, 1941; converted London Hippodrome into Talk of the Town restaurant, 1958. Is president of Entertainment Artistes' Benevolent Fund.

DELL, Rt. Hon Edmund, Chairman, Channel Four TV Co., since 1980; b.15 Aug., 1921. M.P. (Lab) for Birkenhead, 1964-79; Paymaster General, 1974-76; Secretary of State for Trade, 1976-78. Was with I.C.I., 1949-63; Chairman of Guinness Peat Group, 1979-82.

DEL MAR, Norman Rene, C.B.E., conductor; b.31 July, 1919. Educated at Royal College of Music and is now Conductor and Professor of Conducting. Conductor, BBC Scottish Orchestra, 1960-65 and Academy of the BBC, 1974-77.

DENHAM, 2nd Baron (Bertram Stanley Mitford Bowyer), P.C., Captain, Gentlemen at Arms and Chief Whip, House of Lords, since 1979; b.3 Oct., 1927. Opposition Chief Whip, House of Lords, 1978-79.

DENISON, (John) Michael (Terence Wellesley), C.B.E., actor; b.1 Nov., 1915; m.1939 Dulcie Gray. First appeared, Westminster Theatre, 1938. Appears on stage, screen and TV. Was a member of Arts Council Drama Panel.

DENNING, Baron (Life Peer) (Alfred Thompson Denning), P.C., Master of the Rolls, 1962-82; b. 23 Jan., 1899. Called to the Bar, 1923; K.C., 1938. A Lord Justice of Appeal, 1948-57. A Lord of Appeal in Ordinary, 1957-62.

DENT, John, C.B.E., Chairman of Civil Aviation Authority 1982-86; b.5 Oct., 1923. Chief engineer, Armstrong Whitworth Armaments Division, 1961-63; director and chief engineer. Hawker Siddeley Dynamics, 1963-67; director, Dunlop Engineering Group, 1968-76; managing director, Dunlop Ltd., 1978-82.

DE VALOIS, Dame Ninette, C.H., D.B.E., founder of The Royal Ballet and director, 1931-63; b.6 June, 1898. A prima ballerina at Covent Garden in 1919 and 1928. A member of Diaghilev Ballet, 1923-26. A leading British choreographer.

DEVINE, Rt. Rev.Joseph, Bishop of Motherwell (R.C.) since 1983; b.7 Aug., 1937.Lecturer in philosophy, St.Peter's College, Dumbarton, 1967-74; Chaplain, Glasgow University, 1974-77; Auxiliary Bishop to Archbishop of Glasgow, 1977-83.

DEVLIN, Baron (Life Peer) (Patrick Arthur Devlin), P.C., High Steward of Cambridge University since 1966; b.25 Nov., 1905.Called to Bar, 1929. K.C., 1945.Judge of the Queen's Bench Division, 1948-60; President of Restrictive Practices Court, 1956-60. Lord Justice of Appeal, 1960-61; a Lord of Appeal in Ordinary, 1961-64. Chairman of Press Council, 1964-69.

DEVONSHIRE, 11th Duke of (Andrew Robert Buxton Cavendish), P.C., M.C., Chancellor of Manchester University 1965-86; b.2 Jan., 1920. Parl. Under-Sec.of State, Commonwealth Relations, 1960-62; Minister of State for Commonwealth Relations and for Colonial Affairs, 1962-64.

DILLON, Rt. Hon. Lord Justice (Rt. Hon. Sir (George) Brian (Hugh) Dillon), a Lord Justice of Appeal since 1982; b.2 Oct., 1925. Called to Bar, 1948.Q.C., 1965. A Judge of the Chancery Division, 1979-82.

DIMBLEBY, David, broadcaster and newspaper proprietor; b.28 Oct., 1938, s. of late Richard Dimbleby. Joined BBC as news reporter in 1960 and was commentator on Current Events; presenter of 24 Hours, 1969-72; subsequently presenter of Panorama and Nationwide. Is also managing director of Dimbleby newspaper group.

DONALDSON, Baron (Life Peer) (John Francis), P.C., Master of the Rolls since 1982; b.6 Oct., 1920. Called to Bar, 1946. Q.C., 1961. A Judge of the Queen's Bench Division, 1966-79. President, National Industrial Relations Court, 1971-74. A Lord Justice of Appeal, 1979-82.

DORMAND, Baron (Life Peer) (John Donkin Dormand), chairman of Parliamentary Labour Party 1981-85; b.27 Aug., 1919. Was a teacher and education officer before entering Parliament in 1970; a Lord Commissioner of the Treasury, 1974-79.

DOWELL, Anthony James, C.B.E., senior principal, Royal Ballet, Covent Garden, since 1967; director of Royal Ballet from Sept., 1986; b.16 Feb., 1943. Trained at Royal Ballet School and joined Opera Ballet, 1960; has since toured with ballet co. to Russia, Japan and U.S.A.

DRABBLE, Margaret, C.B.E., author; b.5 June, 1939. Editor of Oxford Companion to English Literature since 1979. First book, A Summer Birdcage, published, 1963.

DRAKE, Hon. Mr. Justice (Hon. Sir (Frederick) Maurice Drake), D.F.C., a Judge of the Queen's Bench Division since 1978; b.15 Feb., 1923. Called to Bar, 1950, Q.C., 1968. A Recorder of the Crown Court, 1972 78.

du CANN, Rt. Hon. Sir Edward, K.B.E., M.P. (C) for Taunton 1987, chairman of Lonrho Ltd. since 1984; b.28 May, 1924. Founder, Unicorn Group of Unit Trusts, 1957. Economic Sec. to Treasury, 1962-63; Minister of State, Board of Trade, 1963-64; Chairman of Public Accounts Committee, 1974-79 and of Conservative 1922 Committee, 1972-84.

DUNLOP, Frank, C.B.E., Director of Edinburgh International Festival since 1984; b.15 Feb., 1927. Founder and director of Young Vic, 1969-83; associate director, National Theatre, 1967-71; has directed plays in London and New York and for Belgian National Theatre.

DUNN, Robert John, M.P. (C), Formerly Parl. Under-Sec. of State, Dept. of Education and Science, from 1983; b.1946. Was with J. Sainsbury Ltd., 1973-79. Member of Southwark Borough Council, 1974-78.

DUNPARK, Hon. Lord (Alastair McPherson Johnston), a Senator of College of Justice in Scotland since 1971; b.15 Dec., 1915. Member of Faculty of Advocates, 1946. Q.C. (Scot.), 1958. Sheriff of Dumfries and Galloway, 1966-68.

DUNROSSIL, 2nd Viscount (John William Morrison), C.M.G., Governor of Bermuda since 1983; b.22 May, 1926. Joined Commonwealth Relations Office, 1951; Counsellor, Brussels, 1975-78; High Commissioner in Fiji, 1978-82 and in Barbados, 1982-83.

DURANT, Robert Anthony Bevis (Tony), M.P. (C), Lord Commisioner and Assistant Govt. Whip 1984-87; b.9 Jan., 1928. With Conservative Party Org., 1952-67; entered Parliament 1974.

DURRELL, Gerald Malcolm, O.B.E., Zoologist and writer, b. 7 Jan., 1925. Collector of animals and nature conservationist.

EAMES, Rt. Rev. Robert Henry Alexander, Bishop of Derry and Raphoe, 1975-80; b.27 April, 1937. Research scholar and tutor, Faculty of Law, Queen's University of Belfast, 1960-63; Rector of St. Dorothea's, Belfast, 1966-74 and of St.Mark's, Dundela, 1974-75.

EASTAUGH, Rt. Rev.John Richard Gordon, formerly Bishop of Hereford; b.11 March, 1920.Vicar of Heston, 1963-67; Vicar of St.Peter, Eaton Square, 1967-73; Archdeacon of Middlesex, 1966-73.

EASTHAM, Hon. Mr. Justice (Hon. Sir (Thomas) Michael Eastham), a Judge of the Family Division since 1978; b.26 June, 1920. Called to Bar, 1947. Q.C., 1964. Recorder of Deal, 1968-71 and of Cambridge, 1971; a Recorder of the Crown Court, 1972-78.

EDWARDES, Sir Michael Owen, formerly chairman of Dunlop; b.11 Oct., 1930 in South Africa. Joined Chloride Group, 1951 and was chairman, 1974-77; non-executive chairman since 1982. Chairman and chief executive, BL Ltd. (British Leyland), 1977-82; chairman of Mercury Communications, 1982-83 and of ICL, 1984. Chief executive, Chloride Group plc since 1985.

EDWARDS, Baron (Life Peer) (Roger) Nicholas Edwards), P.C., Secretary of State for Wales 1979-87; b.25 Feb., 1934. Entered Parliament, 1970 and was Conservative spokesman on Welsh affairs, 1975-79.

EDWARDS, Prof. Sir Samuel Frederick, F.R.S., John Humphrey Plummer Professor of Physics, Cambridge University, 1972-84 and Cavendish Professor of Physics since 1984; Member of Defence Scientific Advisory Council since 1973; b.1 Feb., 1928. Professor of Theoretical Physics, Manchester University, 1963-72. Chairman, Science Research Council, 1973-77.

ELLIOTT, Charles Kennedy, Physician to the Queen since 1980; b. 1919. M.B., B.Ch., Trinity College, Dublin, 1942. Was in general practice, Wisbech, 1949-69; homoeopathic practitioner, London, 1973-80; clinical assistant, Royal London Homoeopathic Hosp., 1973-81; Sub Dean, Faculty of Homoeopathy, 1976-79.

ELLIS, Roger Wykeham, C.B.E., Master of Marlborough College, 1972-86; b.3 Oct., 1929. Assistant master, Harrow School, 1952-67; Headmaster of Rossall School, 1967-72. Chairman, Headmasters' Conference, 1983.

ELTON, 2nd Baron (Rodney Elton), b.2 March, 1930. Was a farmer, also schoolmaster and lecturer. Parl. Under-Sec. of State at Northern Ireland Office, 1979-81; at Dept. of Health and Social Security, 198182 and at Home Office, 1982-84; Minister of State, Home Office, 198485. Minister of State, Dept. of Environment, 1985-86.

EMSLIE, Baron (Life Peer) (George Carlyle Emslie), P.C., M.B.E., Lord Justice General of Scotland and Lord President of the Court of Session; b.6 Dec., 1919. Q.C. (Scot.), 1957. Sheriff of Perth and Angus, 1963-66; Dean of Faculty of Advocates, 1965-70. A Senator of the College of Justice in Scotland, 1970-72.

EURICH, Richard Ernst, O.B.E., R.A., painter; b. 14 Mar., 1903. Studied at Slade School. Official War Artist, 1941-45.

EVANS, Hon. Mr. Justice (Hon. Sir Anthony Howell Meurig Evans), a Judge of the Queen's Bench Division since 1984; b.11 June, 1934. Called to Bar, 1958.Q.C., 1971. A Recorder of the Crown Court, 197284.

EVANS, (Arthur) Mostyn, General Secretary of Transport and General Workers' Union, 1978-85; b. 13 July, 1925. National organiser, T.G.W.U., 1973-78. Member of T.U.C. General Council since 1977.

EVANS. Sir Geraint Llewellyn, C.B.E., opera singer and formerly principal baritone, Royal Opera House, Covent Garden; b.16 Feb., 1922. Educated at Guildhall School of Music and sang at Covent Garden; also at La Scala, Milan, Metropolitan Opera, New York, and other major opera houses. Is a director of Harlech Television Ltd.

EVANS, Sir Richard (Mark), K.C.M.G., British Ambassador to China since 1984; b.15 April, 1928. Joined Foreign Service, 1952 and served in Peking, Berne, Stockholm and Paris; Dep. Under-Sec.of State, Foreign Office, 1982-84.

EVELEIGH, Rt. Hon. Lord Justice (Rt. Hon. Sir Edward Walter Eveleigh), a Lord Justice of Appeal, 1977-84; b. 8 Oct., 1917. Called to Bar, 1945.Q.C., 1961. Recorder of Burton-on-Trent, 1961-64 and of Gloucester, 1964-68. A Judge of the Queen's Bench Division, 1968-77. Member of Royal Commission on Criminal Procedure, 1978-80.

EWBANK, Hon. Mr. Justice (Hon. Sir Anthony Bruce Ewbank), a Judge of the Family Division since 1980; b. 30 July, 1925. Called to Bar, 1954. Q.C., 1972. A Recorder of the Crown Court, 1975-80.

FALCONER, Hon. Mr. Justice (Hon. Sir Douglas William Falconer), M.B.E., a Judge of the Chancery Division since 1981; b. 20 Sept., 1914. Called to Bar, 1950. Q.C., 1967. Member of Standing Advisory Committees on Patents and on Trade Marks, 1975-79.

FARQUHARSON, Hon. Mr. Justice (Hon. Sir Donald Henry Farquharson), a Judge of the Queen's Bench Division since 1981; b. 1928. Called to Bar, 1952. Q.C., 1972. A Recorder of the Crown Court, 1972-81. Presiding Judge, South Eastern Circuit, since 1985.

FENNER, Mrs. Peggy, M.P. (C), b. 12 Nov., 1922. Member of Sevenoaks Urban District Council, 1957-71. M.P. for Rochester and Chatham, 1970-74 and 1979-83; for Medway since 1983. Parl. Sec., Min. of Agriculture, Fisheries and Food, 1972-74 and 1981-86.

FIELDHOUSE, Sir John (David Elliott), G.C.B., G.B.E., Admiral of the Fleet, Chief of Defence Staff 1985; b. 12 Feb., 1928; Entered Submarine Service, 1948; Flag Officer, Submarines, 1976-78; Controller of the Navy, 1979-81; C.-in-C. Fleet, 1981-82; Chief of Naval Staff and First Sea Lord, 1982-85.

FINNISTON, Sir (Harold) Montague, Ph.D., F.R.S., F.R.S.E., Chancellor of Stirling University from 1978; b. 15 Aug., 1912. Educated at Royal College of Science and Technology, Glasgow. Chief Metallurgist, U.K.A.E.A., Harwell, 1948-58; Technical director, C.A. Parsons and Co. Ltd., 1959-67; Dep. chairman, British Steel Corp., 1967-73 and chairman, 1973-76.

FISHER, Hon. Sir Henry Arthur Pears, President of Wolfson College, Oxford, 1975-85; b. 20 Jan., 1918, s. of late Most Rev. Lord Fisher of Lambeth. Called to Bar, 1947. Q.C., 1960. Recorder of Canterbury, 1962-68; a Judge of the Queen's Bench Division, 1968-70. Director of J. Henry Schroder Wagg & Co., 1970-75.

FISTOULARI, Anatole, orchestral conductor; b. Kiev, U.S.S.R., 20 Aug., 1907; now British citizen. Conducted first concert at age of seven. Founder and principal conductor of London International Orchestra and guest conductor of London Philharmonic Orchestra.

FITZGERALD, Garret, former Prime Minister (Taoiseach) of Ireland, 1981-82 and 1983-86; b. 9 Feb., 1926. A barrister, was a lecturer in political economy at University College, Dublin, Leader of Fine Gael party since 1977; Minister for Foreign Affairs, 1973-77.

FLOWERS, Baron (Life Peer) (Brian Hilton Flowers), F.R.S., Vice-Chancellor of London University since 1985; b. 13 Sept., 1924. Professor of Physics, Manchester University, 1961-72; Chairman of Science Research Council, 1967-73 and of Royal Commission on Environmental Pollution, 1973-76. Member of U.K. Atomic Energy Authority, 1971-81 and of Energy Commission, 1977-79; Rector of Imperial College of Science and Technology, 1973-85.

FOLEY, Rt. Rev. Brian Charles, Bishop of Lancaster (R.C.), 1962-85; b. 25 May, 1910. Formerly Canon of Brentwood Diocese.

FONTEYN, Dame Margot (Margot Fonteyn de Arias), D.B.E., prima ballerina; b. 18 May, 1919; m. 1955, Roberto E. Arias. Educated in China and U.S., she joined Sadler's Wells Ballet in 1934. President, Royal Academy of Dancing, since 1954. Benjamin Franklin Medal, 1974. Chancellor of Durham University since 1982.

FOOT, Rt. Hon. Michael, M.P. (Lab), Leader of the Opposition, 1980-83; b. 23 July, 1913, s. of late Rt. Hon. Isaac Foot. President of Oxford Union, 1933. Editor of Tribune, 1948-52 and 1955-60; Managing director, 1945-74; political columnist on Daily Herald, 1944-64. Secretary of State for Employment, 1974-76; Lord President of the Council and Leader of House of Commons, 1976-79. Deputy Leader of Labour Party, 1976-80 and Leader, 1980-83.

FORBES, Bryan, film producer; b. 22 July, 1926; m. 1958, Nanette Newman. Acted on stage and in films, 1948-60; with Richard Attenborough formed Beaver Films 1959 and has written, produced and directed many films. Managing director, ABPC Studios, 1969-71 and of EMI-MGM, Elstree Studios, 1970-71. Also runs a bookshop in Surrey.

FORMAN, Sir Denis, O.B.E., Chairman of Granada Television 1974-87; b. 13 Oct., 1917. Chief production officer, Central Office of Information Films, 1947; Director, British Film Institute, 1948-55. A director of Granada Group since 1964; is also a director of Royal Opera House, Covent Garden.

FOWLER, Rt. Hon. Sir (Peter) Norman, P.C., M.P. (C), Secretary of State for Employment 1988-90; b. 2 Feb., 1938. Secretary of State for Social Services 1981-87. On staff of The Times, 1961-70. Member of Parl. Select Committee on Race Relations and Immigration, 1970-74. Secretary of State for Transport, 1981 (Minister of Transport, 1979-81).

FOX, Rt. Hon. Lord Justice (Rt. Hon. Sir Michael John Fox), a Lord Justice of Appeal since 1981; b. 8 Oct., 1921. Called to Bar, 1949. Q.C., 1968. A Judge of Chancery Division, 1975-81.

FOYLE, Christina Agnes Lilian (Mrs. Ronald Batty), bookseller; b. 30 Jan., 1911. Managing director of W. & G. Foyle Ltd. Started Foyle's literary luncheons in 1930.

FRASER, Lady Antonia, writer; b. 27 Aug., 1932, d. of Earl of Longford; m. Harold Pinter, 1980. First book published King Arthur and the Knights of the Round Table, 1954; awarded James Tait Black Memorial Prize for Mary Queen of Scots, 1969. Also appears on TV and radio.

FRASER OF TULLYBELTON, Baron (Life Peer) (Walter Ian Reid Fraser), P.C., a Lord of Appeal in Ordinary, 1975-85; b. 3 Feb., 1911. Q.C. (Scot), 1953. Dean of Faculty of Advocates, 1959-64; a Senator of College of Justice in Scotland, 1964-74.

FRASER, Peter Lovat, Q.C., Solicitor-General for Scotland since 1982; b. 29 May, 1945. Called to Scottish Bar, 1969. Was a university lecturer on constitutional law. Entered Parliament, 1979. Was M.P. (C) for Angus East.

FRENCH, Hon. Mr. Justice (Hon. Sir Christopher James Saunders French), a Judge of the Family Division, 1979-82 and of the Queen's Bench Division since 1982; b. 14 Oct., 1925. Called to Bar, 1950. Q.C., 1966. A Recorder of the Crown Court, 1972-79. Presiding Judge, South Eastern Circuit, since 1982.

FRETWELL, Sir John Emsley, K.C.M.G., British Ambassador to France 1982-87; b. 15 June, 1930. Joined Diplomatic Service, 1953 and served in Hong Kong, Peking, Moscow and Warsaw; Minister, British Embassy, Washington, 1980-82.

FRY, Christopher, playwright; b. 18 Dec., 1907. Formerly a schoolmaster. Was a director of Tunbridge Wells and Oxford Rep. Theatres before success as playwright. Awarded Queen's Gold Medal for Poetry, 1962.

GALWAY, James, O.B.E., flute player; b. 8 Dec., 1939 in Northern Ireland. Trained at Royal College of Music and Guildhall School of Music; principal flute, Royal Philharmonic Orchestra, 1967-69 and principal solo flute, Berlin Philharmonic Orchestra, 1969-75.

GAREL-JONES, (William Armand Thomas) Tristan, M.P. (C), Minister of State, Foreign Office, 1990- ; Treasurer of Her Majesty's Household; Comptroller to H.M. Household until 1989; b. 28 Feb., 1941. Was principal of language school in Madrid, 1960-70, and subsequently merchant banker. Assistant to Chairman of Conservative Party, 1978-79. A Lord Commissioner of the Treasury 1983-88.

GELDOF, Bob, Hon. K.B.E., songwriter and initiator and organiser of Band-Aid, Life-Aid and Sport-Aid, b. 5 Oct., 1954. Group singer and joint founder of The Boomtown Rats, rock band. Freeman Borough of Swale 1985, Hon M.A. Kent 1985.

GIBBS, Rt. Rev. John, Bishop of Coventry, 1976-85; b. 15 March, 1917. Was in Congregational ministry before ordination in Church of England; Principal of Keswick Hall College of Education, Norwich, 1964-73; Bishop Suffragan of Bradwell, 1973-76.

GIBBS, Field Marshal Sir Roland Christopher, G.C.B., C.B.E., D.S.O., M.C., Constable of H.M. Tower of London since 1985; b. 22 June, 1921. Commissioned in 60th Rifles, 1940. C.-in-C., U.K. Land Forces, 197476; Chief of General Staff, 1976-79. Chairman, National Rifle Association since 1984.

GIBSON, Baron (Life Peer) (Richard Patrick Tallentyre Gibson), Chairman of National Trust 1977-85; b. 5 Feb., 1916. Chairman of S. Pearson and Son Ltd., 1978-83 and of The Financial Times, 1975-77. Chairman of Arts Council of Great Britain, 1972-77.

GIBSON, Sir Alexander Drummond, C.B.E., F.R.S.E., Conductor and Musical Director, Scottish National Orchestra, 1959-84; b. 11 Feb., 1926. Musical director, Sadler's Wells Opera. 1957-59; Artistic director, Scottish Opera Co., 1962-85 and Director of Music since 1985; Principal guest conductor, Houston Symphony Orchestra, 1981-83. Sibelius Medal, 1978.

GIBSON, Hon. Mr. Justice Peter (Hon. Sir Peter Leslie Gibson), a Judge of the Chancery Division since 1981; b. 10 June, 1934. Called to Bar, 1960. Junior Counsel to Inland Revenue (Chancery), 1970-72 and to Treasury (Chancery), 1972-81. Judge of Employment Appeal Tribunal since 1984.

GIBSON, Rt. Hon. Lord Justice Ralph (Rt. Hon. Sir Ralph Brian Gibson), a Judge of the Queen's Bench Division since 1977; Chairman of the Law Commission, 1981-85; b. 17 Oct., 1922. Called to Bar, 1948. Q.C., 1968. A Recorder of the Crown Court, 1972-77.

GIELGUD, Sir (Arthur) John, C.H., actor; b. 14 April, 1904. A son of Kate Terry Lewis, he is a member of the famous Terry family. First stage appearance 1921, with the Old Vic. Particularly associated with the works of Shakespeare. Has appeared in films and on television. President of R.A.D.A. since 1977.

GILMOUR, Rt. Hon. Sir Ian Hedworth John Little, Bt., M.P. (C); b. 8 July, 1926. Called to Bar, 1952. Editor of The Spectator, 1954-59. Minister of State for Defence Procurement, 1971-72 and for Defence, 1972-74; Secretary of State for Defence, 1974; Lord Privy Seal, 1979-81.

GLENARTHUR, 4th Baron (Simon Mark Arthur), Minister of State, Scottish Office, 1986-87; b. 7 Oct., 1944. Was in Army, 1963-75. British Airways helicopters captain, 1976-82. A Lord in Waiting, 1982-83. Parl. Under-Sec. of State, Dept. of Health and Social Security, 1983-85 and at Home Office, 1985. Minister of State, Foreign and Commonwealth Office since 1987.

GLIDEWELL, Rt. Hon. Lord Justice (Rt. Hon. Sir Iain Derek Laing Glidewell), a Lord Justice of Appeal since 1985; b. 8 June, 1924. Called to Bar, 1949. Q.C., 1969. A Recorder of the Crown Court, 1976-80; Judge of Appeal, Isle of Man, 1979-80. a Judge of the Queen's Bench Division, 1980-85.

GOFF, Chieveley, Baron (Life Peer) (Robert Lionel Archibald Goff), P.C., a Lord of Appeal in Ordinary, since 1986; b. 12 Nov., 1926. Called to Bar, 1951. Q.C., 1967. Fellow and Tutor, Lincoln College, Oxford, 1951-55. A Judge of the Queen's Bench Division, 1975-82.

GOODISON, Alan Clowes, C.M.G., C.V.O., former British Ambassador to Ireland; b. 20 Nov., 1926. Joined Foreign Office, 1949 and was head of South European Dept., 1973-76; Minister, Rome, 1976-80; Assistant Under-Sec. of State, Foreign and Commonwealth Office, 1981-83.

GOODLAD, Alastair Robertson, M.P. (C), Parl. Under-Sec. of State, Dept. of Energy, 1984-87; b. 4 July, 1943. Member, Select Committee on Agriculture, 1979-81; an Assistant Government Whip, 1981-82; a Lord Commissioner of the Treasury, 1982-84.

GOODMAN, Baron (Life Peer) (Arnold Abraham Goodman), C.H., Master of University College, Oxford, 1976-86; b. 21 Aug., 1913. A solicitor, was also a member of Industrial Reorganisation Corporation. Chairman of Arts Council of Great Britain, 1965-72. Chairman, Newspaper Publishers' Association, 1970-75; of National Building Agency, 1973-78 and of Housing Corporation, 1973-77. Is a director of English National Opera.

GOODRICH, Rt. Rev. Philip Harold Ernest, Bishop of Worcester since 1982; b. 2 Nov., 1929. Rector of South Ormsby group of parishes, 1961-68; Vicar of Bromley, 1968-73; Bishop Suffragan of Tonbridge, 1973-82.

GORBACHEV, Mikhail, President of the Soviet Union; b. 2 March, 1931 in Stavropol. Studied law at Moscow University; has also a degree in agriculture. First Secretary of Communist Party in Stavropol, 1970. Central Committee Secretary for Agriculture, 1978-85; member of Politburo since 1980.

GORDON, Rt.Rev. Archibald Ronald McDonald, Chief of Staff to Archbishop of Canterbury since 1984 and Bishop to the Forces since 1985; b. 19 March, 1927. Vicar of St. Peter, Birmingham, 1959-67; Residentiary Canon, Birmingham Cathedral, 1967-71; Vicar of University Church of St. Mary the Virgin, Oxford, 1971-75; Bishop of Portsmouth, 1975 84.

GOULDING, Hon. Mr. Justice (Hon. Sir (Ernest) Irvine Goulding), a Judge of the Chancery Division 1971-87; b. 1 May, 1910. Called to Bar, 1936. Q.C., 1961.

GOWRIE, 2nd Earl of (Alexander Patrick Greysteil Hore-Ruthven), P.C., Chairman of Sotheby's 1988; b. 26 Nov., 1939. Chancellor of Duchy of Lancaster and Minister for the Arts 1984-85; Was a lecturer in English and American literature. A Lord in Waiting, 1972-74; Minister of State, Dept. of Employment, 1979-81 and at Northern Ireland Office, 1981-83; Minister of State, Privy Council Office, and Minister for the Arts, 1983-84.

GRAFTON, Duchess of (Ann Fortune FitzRoy), G.C.V.O., Mistress of the Robes to the Queen since 1967; m. 1946. Earl of Euston (now 11th Duke of Grafton). Lady of the Bedchamber to the Queen, 1953 66.

GRAHAM, Rt. Rev. Andrew Alexander Kenny, Bishop of Newcastle since 1981; b. 7 Aug., 1929. Chaplain and lecturer in theology, Worcester College, Oxford, 1958-70; Warden of Lincoln Theological College, 1970-77; Bishop Suffragan of Bedford, 1977-81. Chairman of Advisory Council for Church's Ministry since 1984.

GRAHAM, Sir John Alexander Noble, Bt., K.C.M.G., U.K. Permanent Representative to N.A.T.O. in Brussels since 1982; b. 15 July, 1926. Private Sec. to Foreign and Commonwealth Secretary, 1969-72; Ambassador to Iraq, 1974-77 and to Iran, 1979-80; Dep. Under-Sec. of State, Foreign and Commonwealth Office, 1980-82.

GRAHAM, (John) Alistair, Director of the Industrial Society, since 1986; General Secretary, Civil and Public Services Association, 198286; b. 6 Aug., 1942. Was a clerical officer in hospital service; Assistant Secretary, C.P.S.A., 1966-75 and Dep. General Secretary, 1976 82. Member of T.U.C. General Council, 1982-84.

GRANDY, Formerly Marshal of the R.A.F. Sir John, G.C.V.O., G.C.B., K.B.E., D.S.O., Constable and Governor of Windsor Castle since 1978; b. 8 Feb., 1913. C-in-C., Bomber Command, 1963-65; C-in-C., Far East Command, 1965-67; Chief of the Air Staff, 1967-71. Governor of Gibraltar, 1973-78.

GRAY, Dulcie (Dulcie Winifred Catherine Denison), C.B.E., actress and writer; b. 20 Nov., 1920; m. Michael Denison. First appeared in repertory, Aberdeen, 1939.

GRAY, His Eminence Cardinal Gordon, Archbishop of St. Andrews and Edinburgh (R.C.), 1951-85; b. 10 Aug., 1910. Rector of Blairs College, Aberdeen, 1947-51.

GRAY, Rt. Rev. Joseph, Bishop of Shrewsbury (R.C.) since 1980; b. 20 Oct., 1919. Vicar-General, Birmingham, 1960-69; parish priest, St. Michael's, Birmingham, 1955-69; Auxiliary Bishop of Liverpool, 1969-80.

GRAY OF CONTIN, Baron (Life Peer) (James Hector Northey Gray), P.C., b. 28 June, 1927. M.P. (C) for Ross and Cromarty, 1970-83. A Lord Commissioner of the Treasury, 1973-74; Minister of State, Dept. of Energy, 1979 83. Minister of State, Scottish Office, 1983-86.

GREEN, Rev. Vivian Hubert Howard, D.D., Rector of Lincoln College, Oxford, 1983-87; b. 18 Nov., 1915. Ordained, 1940 and was chaplain, Exeter School, 1940-42; chaplain and asst. master. Sherborne School, 1942-51; Fellow and Tutor in History, Lincoln College, Oxford, since 1951.

GREENE, Graham, C.H., author; b. 2 Oct., 1904. Formerly a journalist on staff of The Times, 1926 30, and Literary Ed., The Spectator, 1940-41. Won Hawthornden Prize in 1940 with his novel The Power and the Glory, awarded Jerusalem Prize, 1981. Companion of Literature, 1984.

GREET, Rev. Dr. Kenneth Gerald, Secretary of Methodist Conference, 1971-84 and President, 1980-81; b. 17 Nov., 1918. Minister, Tonypandy Central Hall, 1947-54; Secretary, Dept. of Christian Citizenship of Methodist Church, 1954-71; member of British Council of Churches since 1955 and chairman of executive committee, 1977-81. Moderator, Free Church Federal Council, 1982-83.

GRIEVE, Hon. Lord (William Robertson Grieve), a Senator of College of Justice in Scotland since 1972; b. 21 Oct., 1917. Admitted to Faculty of Advocates, 1947. Q.C. (Scot.), 1957. Procurator of Church of Scotland, 1969-72.

GRIFFITHS, Baron (Life Peer) (William Hugh Griffiths), M.C., P.C., a Lord of Appeal in Ordinary since 1985; b. 26 Sept., 1923. Called to Bar, 1949. Q.C., 1964. Recorder of Margate, 1962-64 and of Cambridge, 1964-70; a Judge of the Queen's Bench Division, 1971-80; a Lord Justice of Appeal, 1980-85. Chairman of Security Commission since 1985.

GROVES, Sir Charles Barnard, C.B.E., conductor; b. 10 March, 1915. Trained at Royal College of Music. Conductor, Bournemouth Symphony Orchestra, 1954-61; musical director, Welsh National Opera Co., 1961-63; musical director and resident conductor, Royal Liverpool Philharmonic Orch., 1963-77; associate conductor, Royal Philharmonic Orch., since 1967; musical director, English National Opera, 1978-79.

GUINNESS, Sir Alec, C.B.E., actor; b. 2 April, 1914. Began career as advertisement copy writer. First professional appearance, 1933. Has played several seasons with the Old Vic. Awarded Oscar for performance in film, Bridge on the River Kwai, 1957 and special lifetime achievement Oscar, 1980.

GUMMER, Rt. Hon. John Selwyn, M.P. (C), Minister of Agriculture, Fisheries and Food; b. 26 Nov., 1939; Joint Minister of State, Min. of Agriculture, Fisheries and Food, 1985-88; chairman of Conservative Party 1983-85; President, Cambridge Union, 1962. A Lord Commissioner of the Treasury, 1981-83; Minister of State, Dept. of Employment, 1983 84. Paymaster General, 1984-85.

HABGOOD, Most Rev. and Rt. Hon. John Stapylton, Archbishop of York since 1983; b. 23 June, 1927. Demonstrator in pharmacology, Cambridge, 1950 53. Rector of St. John's Church, Jedburgh, 1962-67; Principal of Queen's College, Birmingham, 1967-73; Bishop of Durham, 1973-83.

HAGGART, Most Rev. Alastair Iain Macdonald, Former Bishop of Edinburgh; Primus of Episcopal Church in Scotland since 1977; b. 10 Oct., 1915. Provost, St. Paul's Cathedral, Dundee, 1959 71; Principal, Edinburgh Episcopal Theological College, 1971 75.

HAILSHAM OF ST. MARYLEBONE, Baron (Life Peer) (Quintin McGarel Hogg), K.G., P.C., C.H., Lord High Chancellor of Great Britain, 1970-74 and 1979-87; b. 9 Oct., 1907. Called to Bar, 1932. Q.C., 1953. First Lord of Admiralty,

1956-57; Lord President of the Council, 1957-59 and 1960-64; Leader of House of Lords, 1960-63; Minister for Science, 1959-64; Sec. of State for Education and Science, 1964. Disclaimed peerage (2nd Viscount Hailsham) 1963 and was returned as M.P. (C) for St. Marylebone. Awarded life peerage, 1970. Chancellor of University of Buckingham since 1983.

HAITINK, Bernard, Artistic Director and Permanent Conductor, Concertgebouw Orchestra, Amsterdam, since 1964; musical director, Glyndebourne Festival Opera, since 1978; b. 4 March, 1929 in Amsterdam. Started career as violinist; later became second conductor with Radio Union at Hilversum; artistic director, London Philharmonic Orch., 1967-79. Musical Director, Royal Opera House, Covent Garden, from 1986. Hon. K.B.E., 1977.

HALL, Sir Peter Reginald Frederick, C.B.E., Director, National Theatre, since 1973; Artistic Director, Glyndebourne Festival, since 1984; b. 22 Nov., 1930. Director, formerly managing-director, of Royal Shakespeare Co. at Stratford-on-Avon and Aldwych Theatre, 1960-73. Associate Professor of Drama, Warwick University, since 1966.

HAMILTON, Hon. Archibald Gavin, M.P. (C), Minister of State for the Armed Forces; b. 30 Dec., 1941, Parl. Under-Sec. of State for Defence Procurement, Ministry of Defence, 1986-1988; yr.s. of Baron Hamilton of Dalzell. Member of Kensington and Chelsea Borough Council, 1968-71. An Assistant Government Whip, 1982-84. A Lord Commissioner of the Treasury, 1984-86. Parliamentary Private Secretary to the Prime Minister since 1987.

HAMMOND, Dame Joan Hood, D.B.E., C.M.G., Australian operatic and concert singer; b. 24 May, 1912. A former golf champion. Studied violin and singing in Sydney, Australia, and made her debut there in 1929. Operatic debut, Vienna, 1939.

HAMMOND INNES, Ralph, C.B.E., author; b. 15 July, 1913. On staff of Financial News, 1934-40. Many of his books have been translated into other languages; The White South, Campbell's Kingdom and Atlantic Fury were Book Society Choices.

HANNAY, Sir David Hugh Alexander, K.C.M.G., U.K., Permanent Representative to European Communities since 1985; b. 28 Sept., 1935. Joined Foreign Office, 1959 and served in Tehran, Kabul and Brussels; Assistant Under-Sec. of State, Foreign and Commonwealth Office, 1979-84; Minister, Washington, 1984-85.

HARE DUKE, Rt. Rev. Michael Geoffrey, Bishop of St. Andrews, Dunkeld and Dunblane since 1969; b. 28 Nov., 1925. Vicar of St. Mark's, Bury, 1956 62 and of St. Paul's, Daybrook, 1964-69.

HARMAN, Hon. Mr. Justice (Hon. Sir Jeremiah LeRoy Harman), a Judge of the Chancery Division since 1982; b. 13 April, 1930. Called to Bar, 1954. Called to Hong Kong Bar, 1978 and to Singapore Bar, 1980. Q.C., 1968.

HARPER, Heather (Mary), C.B.E., soprano; b. 8 May, 1930. Has sung principal roles at Glyndebourne, Covent Garden, Sadler's Wells and at each season of Sir Henry Wood Promenade Concerts since 1957.

HARRIS, Rt. Rev. Augustine, Bishop of Middlesbrough (R.C.) since 1978; b. 27 Oct., 1917. Was formerly a prison chaplain; Auxiliary Bishop of Liverpool, 1965-78.

HARRISON, David, Sc.D., Vice-Chancellor of Exeter University since 1984; b. 3 May, 1930. Lecturer in chemical engineering, Cambridge University, 1961-79; Fellow of Selwyn College, Cambridge, since 1957. Chairman, Board of Trustees, Homerton College, Cambridge, since 1979. Vice-Chancellor of Keele University, 1979-84.

HARTWELL, Baron (Life Peer) (William Michael Berry), M.B.E., formerly Chairman and Editor-in-Chief of The Daily Telegraph and Sunday Telegraph; b. 18 May, 1911, 2nd s. of 1st Viscount Camrose. Chairman, Amalgamated Press Ltd., 1954-59.

7

HARVEY-JONES, Sir John, M.B.E., formerly Chairman of Imperial Chemical Industries; b. 16 April, 1924. Served in Royal Navy, 1937-56. Joined I.C.I., 1956 and was chairman of Petrochemicals Division, 1970-73. Chancellor of Bradford University since 1985.

HASLAM, Sir Robert, chairman of British Coal, since 1986; b. 4 Feb., 1923. Joined I.C.I. as mining engineer, 1947 and was chairman of Fibres Division, 1971; chairman of I.C.I. Americas Inc., 1978-81 and dep. chairman of I.C.I. Ltd., 1980-83. Chairman of British Steel Corp., 1983-86 and of Tate and Lyle, 1983-86.

HATTERSLEY, Rt. Hon. Roy Sydney George, M.P. (Lab.), Deputy Leader of Labour Party since 1983; b. 28 Dec., 1932. Member of Sheffield City Council, 1957-65. Minister of Defence for Administration, 1969-70; Minister of State, Foreign and Commonwealth Office, 1974-76; Secretary of State for Prices and Consumer Protection, 1976-79. Visiting Fellow, Inst. of Politics, Harvard University, 1971-72. Also columnist, The Guardian and The Listener.

HAVERS, Baron (Life Peer) (Robert) Michael (Oldfield Havers), P.C., Q.C., Attorney-General 1979-87; b. 10 March, 1923. Called to Bar, 1948. Q.C., 1964. Solicitor-General, 1972-74.

HAWKE, Robert James Lee, Prime Minister of Australia since 1983; b. 9 Dec., 1929. Educated at Universities of Western Australia and Oxford. President Australian Council of Trade Unions, 1970-80. Entered Parliament as M.P. (Lab) for Wills, Melbourne, 1980; Leader of Australian Labour Party since 1983.

HAYES, John Trevor, Ph.D., Director of Nat. Portrait Gallery since 1974; b. 21 Jan., 1929. Assistant Keeper, London Museum, 1954-70 and Director, 1970-74. Visiting Prof. in History of Art, Yale University, 1969.

HAYHOE, Rt. Hon. Sir Bernard John (Barney), M.P. (C), b. 8 Aug., 1925. Was in Inspectorate of Armaments, 1954-63; Conservative Research Dept., 1965-70. Parl. Under-Sec. of State, Min. of Defence, 1979-81. Minister of State, Treasury, 1981-85. Minister of State, Dept. of Health and Social Security (Minister for Health), 1985-86.

HEALEY, Rt. Hon. Denis Winston, C.H., M.B.E., M.P. (Lab.); b. 30 Aug., 1917. Secretary, International Dept., Labour Party, 1945-52; Councillor, Institute of Strategic Studies, 1958-61. Secretary of State for Defence, 1964-70; Chancellor of the Exchequer, 1974-79. Deputy Leader of Labour Party, 1980-83.

HEATH, Rt. Hon. Edward Richard George, M.B.E., M.P. (C); b. 9 July, 1916. Parliamentary Secretary to the Treasury and Government Chief Whip, 1955-59; Minister of Labour, 1959-60; Lord Privy Seal, 1960-63; Secretary of State for Industry, Trade and Regional Development and President of Board of Trade, 1963-64; Prime Minister and First Lord of the Treasury, 1970 74; Leader of the Opposition, 1965-70 and 1974-75.

HEATON, Very Rev. Eric William, Dean of Christ Church, Oxford, since 1979; b. 15 Oct., 1920. Tutor in theology, Official Fellow and Chaplain, St. John's College, Oxford, 1960-74; Dean of Durham, 1974-79.

HEBDITCH, Maxwell Graham, Director of Museum of London since 1977 (Deputy Director 1974-77); b. 22 Aug., 1937. Curator in Agricultural and Social History, Bristol City Museum, 1965-71; Director of Guildhall Museum, London, 1971-74.

HEDLEY, Ronald Henderson, D.Sc., Ph.D., Director of British Museum (Natural History), since 1976 (Deputy Director, 1971-76); b. 2 Nov., 1928. Joined British Museum (Natural History), 1955 and was Dep. Keeper of Zoology, 1964-71.

HEILBRON, Hon. Mrs. Justice (Hon. Dame Rose Heilbron), D.B.E., a Judge of the Family Division since 1974; b. 19 Aug., 1914. Called to Bar, 1939. Q.C., 1949.

Recorder of Burnley, 1956-71; a Recorder of the Crown Court, 1972-74. Treasurer of Gray's Inn since 1985.

HELE, James Warwick, High Master of St. Paul's School, 1973-86; b. 24 July, 1926. Was on staff of Rugby School as assistant master and housemaster, 1955-73. Chairman of Headmasters' Conference, 1982. o73

HESELTINE, Rt. Hon. Michael Ray Dibdin, M.P. (C), 21 March, 1933. Entered Parliament, 1966. Parl. Under-Sec. of State, Dept. of the Environment, 1970-72; Minister for Aerospace and Shipping, 1972-74. Secretary of State for the Environment, 1979-83. Secretary of State for Defence, 1983-86.

HESELTINE, R. Hon. Sir William, K.C.B., G.C.V.O., K.C.V.O., Private Secretary to the Queen (Assistant Private Secretary, 1972-77); b. 17 July, 1930 in West Australia. Private Sec. to Prime Minister of Australia, 1955-59; Assistant Federal Director of Australian Liberal Party, 1962-64; Press Secretary to the Queen, 1968-72.

HETHERINGTON, Sir Thomas Chalmers (Tony), K.C.B., C.B.E., Q.C., Director of Public Prosecutions since 1977; b. 18 Sept., 1926. Called to Bar, 1952. Legal Secretary in Law Officers' Dept., 1966-75; Deputy Treasury Solicitor, 1975-77.

HEWISH, Prof. Antony, F.R.S., Professor of Radio Astronomy, Cambridge University, since 1971; b. 11 May, 1924. Lecturer in Physics, Cambridge University, 1962-69 and Reader in Radio Astronomy, 1969-71. Fellow of Churchill College since 1962. Shared with Sir Martin Ryle Nobel Prize for Physics, 1974.

HEYERDAHL, Thor, author and anthropologist; b. 6 Oct., 1914. Organised and led Kon-Tiki Expedition, 1947, also Norwegian Archaeological Expedition to Easter Island and East Pacific, 1955-56. Made crossing from Morocco to West Indies in papyrus boat Ra II, 1970.

HIGGINS, Hon. Mr. Justice (Hon. John Patrick Basil Higgins), a Judge of High Court of Justice, N. Ireland, since 1984; b. 14 June, 1927. Called to N.I. Bar, 1948. Q.C (N.I.), 1967. A County Court Judge, N.I., 1971-84 and Recorder of Belfast, 1982-84.

HILDER, Rowland, painter and illustrator; b. U.S.A., 28 June, 1905, of British parents. Ed. in United States and at Goldsmiths' College School of Art, London. President of Royal Institute of Painters in Water Colours, 1964-74.

HILLARY, Sir Edmund, K.B.E., New Zealand High Commissioner to India since 1984; author and mountaineer; b. 20 July, 1919. Was a member of British Expedition to Mount Everest led by Col. John Hunt (now Lord Hunt) and with Sherpa Tensing reached the summit, May, 1953; Leader of New Zealand Trans-Antarctic Expedition, 1955-58.

HILLER, Dame Wendy, D.B.E., actress; b. 15 Aug., 1912. Began stage career with Manchester Rep. Theatre. Appeared in plays and films in this country and United States. Won Academy Award for performance in Separate Tables.

HILLERY, Dr. Patrick John, President of Ireland since 1976; b. 2 May, 1923. Qualified in medicine before entering the Dail in 1951; Minister for Labour, 1966-69; Minister for Foreign Affairs, 1969-73. Vice-President of Commission of the European Communities, with responsibility for Social Affairs, 1973-76.

HILLS, Sir Graham John, D.Sc., F.R.S.E., Principal and Vice-Chancellor of Strathclyde University since 1980; b. 9 April, 1926. Lecturer in physical chemistry, Imperial College, 1949-62; Professor of Physical Chemistry, Southampton University, 1962-80.

HINSLEY, Prof. Sir Harry, O.B.E., Formerly, Master of St. John's College, Cambridge, (President, 1975-79); Vice-Chancellor of Cambridge University, 1981-83; b. 26 Nov., 1918. Was successively lecturer in history, Cambridge University and Reader in History of International Relations; Professor of History of International Relations, 1969-83.

HIRSCH, Sir Peter (Bernhard), F.R.S., Wolfson Professor of Metallurgy, Oxford University, since 1966; b. 16 Jan., 1925. Reader in physics, Cambridge University, 1964-66; member of U.K. Atomic Energy Authority since 1982 and chairman, 1982-84. Royal Medal of Royal Society, 1977.

HIRST, Hon. Mr. Justice (Hon. Sir David Cozens-Hardy Hirst), a Judge of the Queen's Bench Division since 1982; b. 31 July, 1925. Called to Bar, 1951. Q.C., 1965. Member of Lord Chancellor's Law Reform Committee, 1966-80. Chairman of the Bar, 1978-79.

HODGKIN, Sir Alan Lloyd, O.M., K.B.E., F.R.S., Master of Trinity College, Cambridge, 1978-84; John Humphrey Plummer Professor of Biophysics, Cambridge University, 1970-81; b. 5 Feb., 1914. Foulerton Research Professor, Royal Society, 1952-69. Royal Medal of Royal Society, 1958. Joint winner of Nobel Prize for ·Medicine, 1963. Chancellor of Leicester University, 1971-85. President of Royal Society, 1970-75.

HODGKIN, Prof. Dorothy Crowfoot, O.M., F.R.S., Wolfson Research Professor, Royal Society, 1960-77; Fellow of Wolfson College, Oxford, 1977-82; b. 1910; m. Thomas Hodgkin (d. 1982). Nobel Prize for Chemistry, 1964; appointed member of Order of Merit, 1965, the second woman to receive this honour. Copley Medal of Royal Society, 1976. Chancellor of Bristol University since 1970. President of British Assoc. for Advancement of Science, 1977-78.

HODGSON, Hon. Mr. Justice (Hon. Sir (Walter) Derek (Thornley) Hodgson), a Judge of the Queen's Bench Division since 1977; b. 24 May, 1917. Called to Bar, 1946. Q.C., 1961. Judge of the Salford Hundred Court of Record, 1965-71; a Law Commissioner, 1971-77 and a Recorder of the Crown Court, 1972-77.

HOFFENBERG, Sir Raymond, K.B.E., President of Wolfson College, Oxford, since 1985; b. 6 March, 1923 in South Africa. Lecturer in Medicine, University of Cape Town and physician, Groote Schuur Hosp., 1955-67. Emigrated to U.K., 1968. Professor of Medicine, Birmingham University, since 1972; President, Royal College of Physicians, since 1983.

HOFFMANN, Hon. Mr. Justice (Hon. Sir Leonard Hubert Hoffmann), a Judge of the Chancery Division since 1985; b. 8 May, 1934. Advocate of Supreme Court of South Africa, 1958-60. Called to Bar, 1964. Q.C., 1977. A Judge of Courts of Appeal of Jersey and Guernsey, 1980-85.

HOLLIDAY, Prof. Frederick George Thomas, C.B.E., F.R.S.E., Vice-Chancellor of Durham University since 1980; b. 22 Sept., 1935. Professor of Biology, Stirling University, 1967-75; Professor of Zoology, Aberdeen University, 1975-79. A trustee of National Heritage Memorial Fund since 1980.

HOLLINGS, Hon. Mr. Justice (Hon. Sir (Alfred) Kenneth Hollings), M.C., a Judge of the Family (formerly Probate, Divorce and Admiralty) Division since 1971; b. 12 June, 1918. Called to Bar, 1947. Q.C., 1966. Recorder of Bolton, 1968; County Court Judge, 1968-71.

HOLLIS, Hon. Mr Justice (Hon. Sir Anthony Barnard Hollis), a Judge of the Family Division since 1982; b. 11 May, 1927. Called to Bar, 1951. Q.C., 1969. Chairman of Family Law Bar Association, 1974-76. A Recorder of the Crown Court, 1976-82.

HOME OF THE HIRSEL, Baron (Life Peer) (Alexander Frederick DouglasHome), K.T., P.C., b. 2 July, 1903. M.P. (U), South Lanark, 1931-45; M.P. (C), Lanark, 1950-51. Secretary of State, Commonwealth Relations, 1955-60; Lord President of the Council and Leader of House of Lords, 1957-60; Secretary of State for Foreign Affairs, 1960-63; Prime Minister and First Lord of the Treasury, 1963-64; Leader of the Opposition, 1964-65; Secretary of State for Foreign and Commonwealth Affairs, 1970-74. Disclaimed peerage (14th Earl of Home) 1963 and was returned as M.P. (C) for Kinross and West Perthshire. Awarded a life peerage, 1974. Chancellor of Heriot-Watt University, 1966-77.

HOPE, Bob (Leslie Townes Hope), actor; b. London, England,

29 May, 1903. His family emigrated to United States in 1907. First important stage part, 1932. Entered radio, 1935, and films in 1938. Hon. C.B.E., 1976.

HOPKINS, Anthony, actor; b. 31 Dec., 1937. Trained at R.A.D.A. and Cardiff College of Drama; first London appearance, 1964; with National Theatre, 1966-73.

HOPKINS, Antony, C.B.E., conductor and composer; b. 21 March, 1921. Studied at Royal College of Music and won Gold Medal, 1942. Formerly Professor of Music at City University. Has composed music for stage and cinema.

HORDERN, Sir Michael (Murray), C.B.E., actor; b. 3 Oct., 1911. Was with Educational Supply Association before stage career. First professional appearance, People's Palace, 1937; has played at Stratford and with the Old Vic; also appears on TV and radio.

HORLOCK, John Harold, F.R.S., Ph.D., Vice-Chancellor of Open University since 1981; b. 19 April, 1928. Professor of Mechanical Engineering, Liverpool University, 1958-66; Professor of Engineering, Cambridge University, 1967-74; Vice-Chancellor of Salford University, 1974-80 and Professor of Engineering, 1976-80.

HOROWITZ, Vladimir, Russian pianist; b. Kiev, 1 Oct., 1904. European debut, 1925; New York, 1928. Now lives in America. Gold Medal of Royal Philharmonic Society, 1972.

HOWARD, Prof. Michael Eliot, C.B.E., M.C., Regius Professor of Modern History, Oxford University, since 1980; b. 29 Nov., 1922. Professor of War Studies, King's College, London, 1963-68; Chichele Professor of History of War, Oxford University, 1977-80; Fellow of All Souls, 1968-80; Fellow of Oriel College since 1980.

HOWE, Rt. Hon. Sir (Richard Edward) Geoffrey, Q.C., M.P. (C), Lord President of the Council and Leader of the House of Commons; Secretary of State for Foreign and Commonwealth Affairs 1983-89; b. 20 Dec., 1926. Called to Bar, 1952. Q.C., 1965. M.P. (C) for Bebington, 1964-66; for Reigate, 1970-74 and for Surrey, East, since 1974. SolicitorGeneral, 1970-72; Minister for Trade and Consumer Affairs, 1972-74. Chancellor of the Exchequer, 1979-83.

HOYLE, Prof. Sir Fred, F.R.S., Hon. Research Professor, Manchester University, since 1972; b. 24 June, 1915. Plumian Professor of Astronomy and Experimental Philosophy, Cambridge University, 1958-72. Professor of Astronomy, Royal Institution of Great Britain, 1969-72; Visiting Associate in Physics, California Institute of Technology. Royal Medal of Royal Society, 1974.

HUGHES, Ted (Edward James), O.B.E., Poet Laureate since 1984; b. 17 Aug., 1930. Has won a number of awards for his poetry including Hawthornden Prize for Lupercal, 1961. Awarded Queen's Gold Medal for Poetry, 1974.

HUME, His Eminence Cardinal (George) Basil, Archbishop of Westminster (R.C.) since 1976; b. 2 March, 1923. Educated at Ampleforth and was on staff teaching modern languages, 1955-63; Abbot of Ampleforth, 196376.

HUNT, David James Fletcher, M.B.E., M.P. (C), Parl. Under-Sec. of State, Dept. of Energy, 1984-87; b. 21 May, 1942. Admitted a solicitor, 1968. Chairman of Young Conservatives, 1972-73. A Lord Commissioner of the Treasury, 1983 84. Treasurer of H.M. Household, Deputy Chief Whip since 1987.

HUNT, General Sir Peter Mervyn, G.C.B., D.S.O., O.B.E., Constable of H.M. Tower of London, 1980-85; b. 11 March, 1916. Commissioned, Queen's Own Cameron Highlanders, 1936; Cmdr., Far East Land Forces, 1968-70; Cmdr., Northern Army Group and C.-in-C., B.A.O.R., 1970-73; Chief of General Staff, 1973-76.

HUNTER, Hon. Lord (John Oswald Mair Hunter), a Senator of College of Justice in Scotland since 1961; b. 21 Feb. 1913. Called to Bar, 1937. Q.C. (Scot.), 1951. Admitted to Faculty of Advocates, 1937. Chairman of Scottish Law Commission, 1971-81.

HURD, Rt. Hon. Douglas Richard, C.B.E., M.P. (C), Secretary of State for Foreign and Commonwealth Affairs; b. 8 March, 1930, e.s. of late Baron Hurd. President of Cambridge Union, 1952. Was in Diplomatic Service, 1952-66; political secretary to Prime Minister, 1970-74. Minister of State, Foreign and Commonwealth Office, 1979-83; Minister of State, Home Office, 1983-84. Secretary of State for Northern Ireland, 1984-85. Is also a writer of thrillers.

HUSSEIN IBN TALAL, King of Jordan; b. 1935; m. 1st 1955, Princess Dina, d. of Prince Abd-el-Hamid Aoun of Saudi Arabia; 1 d.; m. 2nd 1961, Antoinette Gardiner (H.R.H. Princess Muna al Hussein); 2 s., twin d.; m. 3rd 1972, Alia Toukan (Queen Alia, died 1977); 1 s., 1 d., m. 4th 1978, Elizabeth Halaby (Queen Noor); 2 s., 2 d.

HUTCHINSON, Patricia Margaret, C.M.G., C.B.E., Consul-General, Barcelona, since 1983; b. 18 June, 1926. Joined Diplomatic Service, 1948 and served in Bucharest, Berne, Washington and Lima; Consul-General, Geneva, 1975-80; British Ambassador to Uruguay, 1980-83.

HUTCHISON, Hon. Mr. Justice (Hon. Sir Michael Hutchison), a Judge of the Queen's Bench Division since 1983; b. 13 Oct., 1933. Called to Bar, 1958. Q.C., 1976. A Recorder of the Crown Court, 1975-83; a Judge of Employment Appeal Tribunal since 1984.

HUTTON, Hon. Mr. Justice (Hon. James Brian Edward Hutton), a Judge of High Court of Justice, N. Ireland, since 1979; b. 29 June, 1931. Called to N.I. Bar, 1954. Q.C. (N.I.), 1970. Called to English Bar, 1972. Senior Crown Counsel in N. Ireland, 1973 79.

HUXLEY, Sir Andrew Fielding, O.M., F.R.S., President of Royal Society, 1980-85; Master of Trinity College, Cambridge, since 1984; b. 22 Nov., 1917. Assistant Director of Research, Dept. of Physiology, Cambridge University, 1951-59; Fullerian Professor of Physiology and Comparative Anatomy, Royal Institution, 1967-73; Royal Society Research Professor, Dept. of Physiology, University College London, 1969-83 (Jodrell Professor, 1960-69). Nobel Prize for Medicine and Physiology, 1963. Copley Medal, Royal Society, 1973.

INGRAM, David John Edward, D.Phil., Vice-Chancellor of University of Kent at Canterbury since 1980; b. 6 April, 1927. Reader in electronics, Southampton University, 1957-59; Professor of Physics, Keele University, 1959-73; Principal of Chelsea College, London University, 1973-80.

ISAACS, Jeremy Israel, Chairman Board of Directors of Royal Opera House, Covent Garden, 1987; b. 28 Sept., 1932. Chief Executive, Channel Four TV Co., 1981-1987 Joined Granada TV as producer, 1958; Controller of Features, Thames Television, 1968-74 and Director of Programmes, 1974-78. .

JACKSON, Glenda, C.B.E., actress; b. 9 May, 1936. Trained at R.A.D.A. and made first stage appearance, 1957. Won awards for film performances in Sunday, Bloody Sunday, Women in Love and A Touch of Class.

JACOBI, Derek George, C.B.E., actor; b. 22 Oct., 1938. Was with Birmingham Rep., 1960-63 and National Theatre, 1963-71; artistic associate, Old Vic. Co. (formerly Prospect Theatre Co.) 1976-81. Won TV award for performance in I, Claudius.

JAKOBOVITS, Baron (Life Peer), Very Rev. Rabbi Immanuel, Chief Rabbi of the United Hebrew Congregations of the British Commonwealth since 1967; b. 1921 in East Prussia. Came to London, 1936; Chief Rabbi of Ireland, 1949-58; Rabbi of Fifth Avenue Synagogue, New York, 1958-67.

JAMES, Rt. Rev. Colin Clement Walter, Bishop of Winchester since 1985; b. 20 Sept., 1926. BBC Religious Broadcasting Dept., 1959-67; Vicar of St. Peter with St. Swithin, Bournemouth, 1967-73; Bishop Suffragan of Basingstoke, 1973-77; Bishop of Wakefield, 1977-85. Chairman, BBC and IBA Central Religious Advisory Committee, 1979-84.

JARRATT, Sir Alexander Anthony, C.B., Chairman, Reed

International, 1974-85; a dep. chairman of Midland Bank since 1980; b. 19 Jan., 1924. In civil service, 1949-70 and was Secretary to Nat. Board for Prices and Incomes, 1965-68 and Dep. Under-Sec. of State, Dept. of Employment, 1968 70. Chancellor of Birmingham University since 1983.

JAUNCEY, Hon. Lord (Charles Eliot Jauncey), a Senator of College of Justice in Scotland since 1979; b. 8 May, 1925. Q.C. (Scot.), 1963. Sheriff Principal of Fife and Kinross, 1971-74; Judge of Courts of Appeal of Jersey and Guernsey, 1972-79.

JEFFERSON, Sir George, C.B.E., Chairman of British Telecommunications from 1981; b. 26 March, 1921. Joined Guided Weapons Division of English Electric Co., 1952 and became chief research engineer. Chairman and managing director, British Aircraft Corp., 1968-77; a director of British Aerospace, 1977-80.

JENKIN, Baron (Life Peer) (Charles) Patrick (Fleeming Jenkin), P.C., Secretary of State for the Environment 1983-85; b. 7 Sept., 1926. Called to Bar, 1952. Was with Distillers Co, 1957-70. Financial Sec., 1970-72 and Chief Sec., 1972-74 to Treasury; Minister for Energy, 1974. Secretary of State for Social Services, 1979-81; Secretary of State for Industry, 1981-83.

JENKINS, (David) Clive, General Secretary of Assoc. of Scientific, Technical and Managerial Staffs since 1970; b. 2 May, 1926. Started work in metallurgical test house, 1940 and became branch sec. of Assoc. of Scientific Workers, 1946. Member of Gen. Council of T.U.C. since 1974 and of British Overseas Trade Board since 1980; member of Bullock Committee on Industrial Democracy, 1975-77 and of Wilson Committee to Review Functioning of Financial Institutions, 1977-80.

JENKINS, Rt. Rev. David Edward, Bishop of Durham since 1984; b. 26 Jan., 1925. Fellow, chaplain and praelector in theology, Queen's College, Oxford, 1954-69; director, humanum studies, World Council of Churches, Geneva, 1969-73. Canon Theologian, Leicester, 1966-82; Professor of Theology, Leeds University, 1979-84; director, William Temple Foundation, Manchester, 1973-78.

JENKINS, Baron (Life Peer) (Roy Harris Jenkins), M.P. (SDP), P.C., founder member of Social Democratic Party, 1981; b. 11 Nov., 1920. M.P. (Lab) for Central Southwark, 1948-50 and for Birmingham, Stechford, 1950-76; M.P. (SDP) for Glasgow, Hillhead, 1982-87. Minister of Aviation, 1964-65; Home Secretary, 1965-67 and 1974-76; Chancellor of the Exchequer, 1967-70. Dep. Leader of Labour Party, 1970-72. President of European Commission, 1977-81.

JOHN PAUL II, His Holiness Pope (Karol Wojtyla), elected Pope, 16 Oct., 1978, the first non-Italian Pope for over 450 years; b. 18 May, 1920 in Wadowice, Poland. Ordained 1946; was professor of moral theology at Lublin and Cracow Universities; Auxiliary Bishop of Cracow, 1958-64 and Archbishop, 1964-78. Created Cardinal, 1967.

JOHNSTON, Thomas Lothian, Ph.D., F.R.S.E., Was Principal and ViceChancellor of Heriot-Watt University; b. 1 March, 1927. Educated at Edinburgh and Stockholm Universities. Lecturer in political economy, Edinburgh University, 1955-65; Professor and Head of Dept. of Economics, Heriot-Watt, 1966-76. Chairman, Manpower Services Committee for Scotland, 1977-80. Chairman of inquiry into water-workers' pay dispute, 1983.

JONES, Rt. Rev. Alwyn Rice, Bishop of St. Asaph since 1982; b. 25 March, 1934. Director of Education, diocese of Bangor, 1965-75; Vicar of Porthmadog, 1975-79; Dean of Brecon Cathedral, 1979-82.

JONES, Hon. Mr. Justice Kenneth (Hon. Sir Kenneth George Illtyd Jones), a Judge of the Queen's Bench Division since 1974; b. 26 May, 1921. Called to Bar, 1946. Q.C., 1962. Recorder of Shrewsbury, 1964-66 and of Wolverhampton, 1966-71; a Circuit Judge, 1972-73.

JOPLING, Rt. Hon. (Thomas) Michael, M.P. (C), Minister of Agriculture, Fisheries and Food 1983-87; b. 10 Dec., 1930.

A farmer, was P.P.S. to Minister of Agriculture, 1970-71; a Lord Commissioner of the Treasury, 1973-74. Parliamentary Secretary to the Treasury and Chief Whip, 1979-83.

JOSEPH, Baron (Life Peer) (Keith Sinjohn Joseph) Bt., P.C., C.H., b. 17 Jan., 1918. Called to Bar, 1946. A fellow of All Souls, 1946-60 and since 1972. Minister of Housing and Local Govt. and Minister for Welsh Affairs, 1962-64; Secretary of State for Social Services, 1970-74 and for Industry, 1979-1981. Secretary of State for Education and Science 1981-86.

JUAN CARLOS I, King of Spain since 1975; b. 5 Jan., 1938; grandson of late King Alfonso XIII; m. Princess Sofia of Greece, 1962; one s. (Prince Felipe, Prince of Asturias); two d. Nominated, 1969, by General Franco to succeed him as head of state at his death.

JULIANA, Princess, Queen of the Netherlands, 1948-80; b. 30 April, 1909; m. 7 Jan., 1937, Prince Bernhard of Lippe-Biesterfeld (now Prince of the Netherlands); four d.: Princess Beatrix, b. 31 Jan., 1938 (see Beatrix, Queen of the Netherlands); Princess Irene, b. 5 Aug., 1939 (m. Prince Carlos Hugo of Bourbon-Parma, 1964: marriage dissolved, 1981: two s., two d.); Princess Margriet, b. 19 Jan., 1943 (m. Pieter van Vollenhoven, 1967: four s.); Princess Maria Christina, b. 18 Feb., 1947 (m. Jorge Guillermo, 1975; two s. one d.).

JUPP, Hon. Mr. Justice (Hon. Sir Kenneth Graham Jupp), M.C., a Judge of the Queen's Bench Division since 1975; b. 2 June, 1917. Called to Bar, 1945. Q.C., 1966. Dep. Chairman, Cambridge and Isle of Ely Quarter Sessions, 1965-71; a Recorder of the Crown Court, 1972-75.

KAUFMAN, Rt. Hon. Gerald Bernard, M.P. (Lab); b. 21 June, 1930. Was a political journalist on Daily Mirror and New Statesman. Parl. Under-Sec. of State, Dept. of Environment, 1974-75; Minister of State, Dept. of Industry, 1975-79.

KAUNDA, (David) Kenneth, President of Zambia since 1964; formerly Prime Minister, Northern Rhodesia; b. 28 April, 1924. Minister of Local Govt. and Social Welfare, 1962-63.

KEARTON, Baron (Life Peer) (Christopher Frank Kearton), K.T., O.B.E., F.R.S., M.A., Chancellor of University of Bath since 1980; b. 17 Feb., 1911. Joined Courtaulds Ltd., 1946 and was chairman, 1964-75. Member of C.E.G.B., 1974-80 and of U.K.A.E.A., 1955-81, Chairman of Electricity Supply Research Council, 1960-77; President of RoSPA, 1973-80 and of British Association for Advancement of Science, 1978-79. Chairman of British National Oil Corp., 1976-79.

KEITH OF KINKEL, Baron (Life Peer) (Henry Shanks Keith), P.C., a Lord of Appeal in Ordinary since 1977; b. 7 Feb., 1922. Called to Bar, 1951. Q.C. (Scot.), 1962. Sheriff of Roxburgh, Berwick and Selkirk, 1970-71; a Senator of College of Justice in Scotland, 1971-77.

KELLY, Rt. Hon. Lord Justice (Rt. Hon. Sir (John William) Basil Kelly), a Lord Justice of Appeal, N. Ireland, since 1984; b. 10 May, 1920. M.P. (U) for Mid-Down, N.I. Parliament, 1964-72; Attorney-General for N.I., 1968-72; a Judge of High Court of Justice, N.I., 1973-84.

KELLY, Rt. Rev. Patrick, Bishop of Salford (R.C.) since 1984; b. 23 Nov., 1938. Curate, Lancaster Cathedral, 1964-66; lecturer in theology, 1966-79 and rector, 1979-84, St. Mary's College, Oscott.

KEMP, Rt. Rev. Eric Waldram, Bishop of Chichester since 1974; b. 27 April, 1915. Fellow, Chaplain, Tutor and Lecturer in Theology and Medieval History, Exeter College, Oxford, 1946-69; Chaplain to the Queen, 1967 69; Dean of Worcester, 1969-74.

KENDREW, Sir John Cowdery, C.B.E., Sc.D., F.R.S., President of St. John's College, Oxford, 1982-87; b. 24 March, 1917. With Min. of Aircraft Production, 1940-45; dep. chairman, M.R.C. Laboratory for Molecular Biology, Cambridge, 1946-75; director-general, European Molecular Biology Lab., 1975-82; President, International Union for Pure and Applied Biophysics, 1969-72 and of B.A.A.S., 1973 74. Nobel Prize (jointly) for Chemistry, 1962. Royal Medal of Royal Society, 1965.

KENNEDY, Edward Moore, U.S. Senator from Massachusetts since 1963; b. 22 Feb., 1932, b.. of late President John Kennedy and late Senator Robert Kennedy. Called to Massachusetts Bar, 1959. Senate majority whip, 1969-71. Candidate for Democratic Presidential nomination, 1980.

KENNEDY, Ludovic Henry Coverley, writer and television commentator; b. 3 Nov., 1919; m. 1950, Moira Shearer. Was formerly a news reader on ITV; commentator on Panorama and other current affairs programmes; introduced Did You See?

KENNEDY, Hon. Mr. Justice (Hon. Sir Paul Joseph Morrow Kennedy), a Judge of the Queen's Bench Division since 1983; b. 12 June, 1935. Called to Bar, 1960. Q.C., 1973. A Recorder of the Crown Court, 197283. Presiding Judge, North Eastern Circuit, since 1985.

KENNY, Anthony John Patrick, F.R.S.E., D.Phil., Formerly Master of Balliol College, Oxford; b. 16 March, 1931. Ordained R.C. priest, 1955 and was curate in Liverpool, 1959-63. Returned to lay state, 1963. Fellow of Balliol, 1964 78 and Senior Tutor, 1971-72 and 1976-78; University lecturer, 1965-78.

KERR, Rt. Hon. Lord Justice (Rt. Hon. Sir Michael Robert Emanuel Kerr), a Lord Justice of Appeal since 1981; b. 1 March, 1921. Called to Bar, 1948. Q.C., 1961. A Judge of the Queen's Bench Division, 1972-78. Chairman of Law Commission, 1978-81.

KINCRAIG, Hon. Lord (Robert Smith Johnston), a Senator of the College of Justice in Scotland since 1972; b. 10 Oct., 1918. Sheriff of Roxburgh, Berwick and Selkirk, 1964-70; Dean of Faculty of Advocates, 1970-72.

KING OF WARTNABY, Baron (Life Peer) (John Leonard King), Chairman of British Airways since 1981 and of Babcock International Ltd. since 1972; b. 1918. Founded Whitehouse Industries Ltd. 1945 and Ferrybridge Industries Ltd., subsequently Pollard, Ball and Roller Bearing Co. Ltd. Deputy Chairman, National Enterprise Board, 1979-81.

KING, Rt. Hon. Thomas Jeremy, M.P. (C), Secretary of State for Defence from 1989; Secretary of State for Northern Ireland, 1986-89; b. 13 June, 1933. Minister for Industrial Development, 1972-74; Minister of State for Local Govt. and Environmental Services, 1979-83; Secretary of State for Environment, Jan. June, 1983; Secretary of State for Transport, June Oct., 1983. Secretary of State for Employment, 1983-86.

KINGMAN, Sir John Frank Charles, F.R.S., Sc.D., Vice-Chancellor of Bristol University since 1985; b. 28 Aug., 1939. Professor of Mathematics, Sussex University, 1966-69; Professor of Mathematics, Oxford University, 1969-84. Chairman of Science and Engineering Research Council, 1981-85. Royal Medal of Royal Society, 1983.

KINNOCK, Rt. Hon. Neil Gordon, M.P. (Lab), Leader of Labour Party since 1983; b. 28 March, 1942. Was tutor organiser in Industrial and Trade Union Studies, W.E.A., 1966-70. Member of Nat. Exec. Committee of Labour Party since 1978.

KOHL, Helmut, Chancellor of Fed. Rep. of Germany since 1982; b. 3 April, 1930. Educated at Frankfurt and Heidelburg Universities and graduated in law. Chairman of Christian Democratic Union since 1973; Opposition leader, 1976-82.

KORNBERG, Prof. Sir Hans (Leo), F.R.S., Master of Christ's College, Cambridge, since 1982; b. 14 Jan., 1928. Educated at University of Sheffield and Yale University; Member of scientific staff, M.R.C., 1955-60; Professor of Biochemistry, Leicester University, 1960-75; Sir William Dunn Professor of Biochemistry, Cambridge, and Fellow of Christ's College since 1975.

LAIRD, Gavin Harry, General Secretary of Amalgamated Union of Engineering Workers since 1982; b. 14 March, 1933. A full-time trade union official since 1971 and a member of A.U.E.W. exec. council since 1975. Member of T.U.C. General Council, 1979-82. Member of Arts Council since 1983.

LAMONT, Rt. Hon. Norman Stewart Hughson, M.P. (C), Chief Secretary to the Treasury, since 1986; b. 8 May, 1942. President of Cambridge Union, 1964. Formerly merchant banker with N.M. Rothschild and Sons, 1968-79; Parl. Under-Sec. of State, Dept. of Energy, 1979-81. Minister of State, Dept. of Trade and Industry, 1983-85 (Dept. of Industry, 1981-83). Minister of State for Defence Procurement, 1985-86.

LANE, Baron (Life Peer) (Geoffrey Dawson Lane), P.C., A.F.C., Lord Chief Justice of England since 1980; b. 17 July, 1918. Called to Bar, 1946. Q.C., 1962. A Judge of the Queen's Bench Division, 1966-74; a Lord Justice of Appeal, 1974-79; a Lord of Appeal in Ordinary, 197980.

LANG, Ian Bruce, M.P. (C), Parl. Under-Sec. of State, Dept. of Employment, in 1986, and at the Scottish Office, Sept. 1986-87; b. 27 June, 1940. Member, Queen's Body Guard for Scotland (Royal Company of Archers), since 1974. Assistant Government Whip, 1981-83. A Lord Commissioner of the Treasury, 1983-86. Scottish Minister of State since 1987.

LANGE, David Russell, formerly Prime Minister of New Zealand; b. 4 Aug., 1942. A solicitor, has been M.P. (Lab) for Mangere, N.Z., since 1977; Leader of Opposition, 1983-84.

LASDUN, Sir Denys Louis, C.B.E., architect; b. 8 Sept., 1914. Professor of Architecture, Leeds University, 1962-63; a trustee of British Museum since 1975. Works include University of East Anglia, Royal Institute of Chartered Surveyors, Parliament Square and National Theatre. Gold Medal of R.I.B.A., 1977.

LATEY, Hon. Mr. Justice (Hon. Sir John Brinsmead Latey), M.B.E., Judge of the Family (formerly Probate, Divorce and Admiralty) Division since 1965; b. 7 March, 1914. Called to Bar, 1936. Q.C., 1957. Chairman, Lord Chancellor's Committee on Age of Majority, 1965-67.

LAWSON, Rt. Hon. Nigel, M.P. (C), former Chancellor of the Exchequer; b. 11 March, 1932. Was a financial journalist; city editor, Sunday Telegraph, 1961-63; editor, The Spectator, 1966-70. Financial Secretary, Treasury, 1979-81; Secretary of State for Energy, 1981-83.

LAWTON, Rt. Hon. Lord Justice (Rt. Hon. Sir Frederick Horace Lawton), a Lord Justice of Appeal 1972-86; b. 21 Dec., 1911. Called to Bar, 1935. Q.C., 1957. Recorder of Cambridge, 1957-61. A Judge of the Queen's Bench Division, 1961-72.

LEAHY, Sir John Henry Gladstone, K.C.M.G., British High Commissioner in Australia since 1984; b. 7 Feb., 1928. Joined Foreign Office, 1952 and was head of News Dept., 1971-73. Counsellor and Head of Chancery, Paris, 1973-75; Under-Secretary, Northern Ireland Office, 1975-76. Assistant Under-Sec. of State, 1977-79 and Deputy Under-Sec. of State, 1982-84, Foreign and Commonwealth Office; British Ambassador to South Africa, 1979-82.

LEGGATT, Hon. Mr. Justice (Hon. Sir Andrew Peter Leggatt), a Judge of the Queen's Bench Division since 1982; b. 8 Nov., 1930. Called to Bar, 1954. Q.C., 1972. Member of Top Salaries Review Body, 1979-82. A Recorder of the Crown Court, 1974-82.

LEIGH-PEMBERTON, Rt. Hon. Sir Robert (Robin), Governor of Bank of England since 1983; b. 5 Jan., 1927. Called to Bar, 1954. Member of Kent County Council, 1961-77. Lord Lieutenant of Kent since 1982. Chairman, National Westminster Bank, 1977-83.

LENNOX-BOYD, Hon. Mark Alexander, M.P. (C), Lord Commissioner of Treasury, an assistant Govt. Whip since 1984; b. 4 May, 1943, 3rd s. of 1st Viscount Boyd of Merton. Called to Bar, 1968. Entered Parliament, 1979; P.P.S. to

Secretary of State for Energy, 1981-83 and to Chancellor of Exchequer, 1983-84.

LEONARD, Rt. Rev. and Rt. Hon. Graham Douglas, Bishop of London since 1981; b. 8 May, 1921. Archdeacon of Hampstead and Rector of St. Andrew Undershaft with St. Mary Axe, City of London, 1962-64; Bishop Suffragan of Willesden, 1964-73; Bishop of Truro, 1973-81. Dean of the Chapels Royal and Prelate of Order of the British Empire since 1981. Chairman, BBC and IBA Central Religious Advisory Committee, since 1984.

LEONARD, Hon. Mr. Justice (Hon. Sir (Hamilton) John Leonard), a Judge of the Queen's Bench Division since 1981; b. 28 April, 1926. Called to Bar, 1951. Q.C., 1969. A Circuit Judge, 1978-81; Common Serjeant, City of London, 1979-81. Presiding Judge, Wales and Chester Circuit.

LEVER OF MANCHESTER, Baron (Life Peer) (Norman Harold Lever), P.C.; b. 15 Jan., 1914. Called to Bar, 1935. M.P. (Lab.) for Manchester, Exchange, 1945-50; for Manchester, Cheetham, 1950-74 and for Manchester, Central, 1974-79. Paymaster General, 1969-70; Chancellor of Duchy of Lancaster, 1974-79. Chairman of committee of inquiry into steel-workers' pay dispute, 1980.

LEVEY, Sir Michael Vincent, M.V.O., Director of the National Gallery 1973-87 (Keeper, 1968-73); b. 8 June, 1927; m. Brigid Brophy, 1954. Slade Professor of Fine Art, Cambridge, 1963-64. Awarded Hawthornden Prize, 1968, for his book Early Renaissance.

LEVI, Peter Chad Tigar, formerly Professor of Poetry, Oxford University; b. 16 May, 1931. Formerly a Jesuit priest, he resigned from priesthood, 1977. Lecturer in classics, Christ Church College, Oxford, 1979-82; Fellow of St. Catherine's College since 1977. First poems, The Gravel Ponds, published, 1960.

LIGHTHILL, Sir (Michael) James, F.R.S., Provost of University College London since 1979; b. 23 Jan., 1924. Professor of Applied Mathematics, Manchester University, 1950-59; Director of R.A.E., Farnborough, 1959-64; Royal Society Research Professor, Imperial College, 1964-69; Lucasian Professor of Mathematics, Cambridge University, 1969-79. Royal Medal of Royal Society, 1964; Gold Medal, Royal Aeronautical Soc., 1965.

LINCOLN, Hon. Mr. Justice (Hon. Sir Anthony Leslie Julian Lincoln), a Judge of the Family Division since 1979; b. 7 April, 1920. Called to Bar, 1949. Q.C., 1968. A Recorder of the Crown Court, 1974-79. Judge of Restrictive Practices Court since 1980 and President since 1982. Also a writer and has contributed articles to The Observer and Spectator.

LINDSAY, Rt. Rev. Hugh, Bishop of Hexham and Newcastle (R.C.) since 1974, formerly Auxiliary Bishop; b. 20 June, 1927. Diocesan Secretary, 1959-69.

LLOYD, Rt. Hon. Hon. Lord Justice (Rt. Hon. Sir Anthony (John Leslie) Lloyd), a Lord Justice of Appeal since 1984; b. 9 May, 1929. Called to Bar, 1955. Q.C., 1967. Attorney-General to the Prince of Wales, 1969-77; a Judge of the Queen's Bench Division, 1978-84. Member of Criminal Law Revision Committee since 1981 and of Parole Board since 1983.

LOCKWOOD, Baroness (Life Peeress) (Betty Lockwood), President, Birkbeck College, London University, since 1983; Chairman of Equal Opportunities Commission, 1975-83; b. 22 Jan., 1924. Chief Woman Officer and Asst. National Agent of Labour Party, 1967-75; Vice-Chairman, International Council of Social Democratic Women, 1969-75; editor of Labour Woman, 1967-71.

LOGAN, Rt. Rev. Vincent, Bishop of Dunkeld (R.C.) since 1981; b. 30 June, 1941. Chaplain, St. Joseph's Hospital, Rosewell, 1967-77; Parish Priest, St. Mary's, Ratho, 1977-81.

LONG, 4th Viscount (Richard Gerard Long), a Lord in Waiting since 1979; b. 30 Jan. 1929. An Opposition Whip, 1974-79.

LONGAIR, Prof. Malcolm Sim, F.R.S.E., Astronomer Royal for Scotland, Regius Prof. of Astronomy, Edinburgh University and Director of Royal Observatory, Edinburgh, since 1980; b. 18 May, 1941. University Lecturer in Physics, Cambridge, 1975-80; Official Fellow, Royal Society, 1971-80.

LONGFORD, 7th Earl of (Francis Aungier Pakenham), K.G., P.C.; b. 5 Dec., 1905. Student in Politics, Christ Church, Oxford, 1934-46 and 1952-64. Minister of Civil Aviation, 1948 51. First Lord of the Admiralty, 1951; Colonial Secretary, 1965-66; Lord Privy Seal, 1964-65 and 1966-68. Chairman of Sidgwick and Jackson, 1970-80.

LOUGHRAN, James, Principal Conductor and Musical Adviser, Halle Orchestra, 1971-83; Chief Conductor, Bamberg Symphony Orchestra, 197983; b. 30 June, 1931. Educated in Glasgow, Bonn, Amsterdam and Milan. Associate Conductor, Bournemouth Symphony Orchestra, 1964; Principal Conductor, BBC Scottish Symphony Orchestra, 1965-71.

LOVELL, Prof. Sir (Alfred Charles) Bernard, O.B.E., F.R.S., physicist and astronomer; b. 31 Aug., 1913. Prof. of Radio Astronomy, Univ. of Manchester, 1951-80; Director of Jodrell Bank Experimental Station, Cheshire, now Nuffield Radio Astronomy Laboratories, 1951-81. Reith Lecturer, 1958. Vice-President of International Astronomical Union, 1970-76. Benjamin Franklin Medal of Royal Society of Arts, 1980. Gold Medal, Royal Astronomical Society, 1981.

LOWRY, Baron (Life Peer) (Robert Lynd Erskine Lowry), P.C., Lord Chief Justice of Northern Ireland since 1971; b. 30 Jan., 1919. Called to N. Ireland Bar, 1947. Q.C. (N.I.), 1956. A Judge of High Court of Justice (N.I.), 1964-71. Chairman, N.I. Constitutional Convention, 1975.

LOWRY, Sir (John) Patrick, C.B.E., Chairman, Advisory, Conciliation and Arbitration Service 1981-87; b. 31 March, 1920. Studied at London School of Economics; was Director of Industrial Relations, British Leyland and subsequently Personnel Director, 1975-81. Member of court of inquiry into Grunwick dispute, 1977.

LUCAS OF CHILWORTH, 2nd Baron (Michael William George Lucas), Formerly Parl. Under-Sec. of State, Dept. of Trade and Industry; b. 26 April, 1926. President, League of Safe Drivers, 1976-80 and of Institute of Transport Administration, 1980-83. A Lord in Waiting, 1983-84.

LUCE, Rt. Hon. Richard Napier, M.P. (C), formerly Minister of State, Privy Council Office (Minister for the Arts), 1985 - 1990; b. 14 Oct., 1936. An Opposition Whip, 1974-75; Parl. Under-Sec. of State, Foreign and Commonwealth Office, 1979-81. Minister of State, Foreign and Commonwealth Office, 1981-82 and 1983-85.

LUMSDEN, Sir David James, Principal of Royal Academy of Music since 1982; b. 19 March, 1928. Organist and Choirmaster, St. Mary's, Nottingham, 1954-56. Fellow and organist, New College, Oxford, and lecturer in faculty of music, 1959-76; organist, Sheldonian Theatre, 1964-76. Principal, Royal Scottish Academy of Music and Drama, Glasgow, 1976-82.

LUNN, Rt. Rev. David Ramsay, Bishop of Sheffield since 1980; b. 1930. Ordained, 1956. Vicar of St. George, Cullercoats, 1970-75 and Rector, 1975-80; Rural Dean of Tynemouth, 1975-80.

LYELL, 3rd Baron (Charles Lyell), Former Parl. Under-Sec. of State, Northern Ireland Office; b. 27 March, 1939. Is a chartered accountant; a member of the Queen's Body Guard for Scotland (Royal Company of Archers). A Lord in Waiting, 1979-84.

LYELL, Sir Nicholas Walter, Q.C., M.P. (C), Solicitor General since 1987; b. Dec., 1938. Recorder 1985-87; Attorney General 1979-86; Parlimentary Under Secretary of State to D.H.S.S. 1986-87.

LYMPANY, Moura, C.B.E., concert pianist; b. 18 Aug., 1916. First public performance at Harrogate, at age of 12.

LYONS, John, Ph.D., Master of Trinity Hall, Cambridge, since 1984; b. 23 May, 1932. Lecturer in General Linguistics, Cambridge University, 1961-64; Professor of General Linguistics, Edinburgh University, 1964-76; Professor of Linguistics, 1976-84 and Pro-Vice-Chancellor, Sussex University, 1981-84.

McADOO, Most Rev. Henry Robert, Archbishop of Dublin and Primate of Ireland, 1977-85; b. 1916. Dean of Cork, 1952-62; Canon of St. Patrick's Cathedral, Dublin, 1960 62; Bishop of Ossory, Ferns and Leighlin, 1962 77.

McCARTNEY, (James) Paul, M.B.E., musician and composer; b. 18 June 1942. Founder member of The Beatles, many awards for music and films.

McCLUSKEY, Baron (Life Peer) (John Herbert McCluskey), a Senator of the College of Justice in Scotland since 1985; b. 12 June, 1929. Admitted to Faculty of Advocates, 1955. Q.C. (Scot), 1967. Sheriff Principal of Dumfries and Galloway, 1973-74; Solicitor General for Scotland, 1974-79.

McCOWAN, Hon. Mr. Justice (Hon. Sir Anthony James Denys McCowan), a Judge of the Queen's Bench Division since 1981; b. 12 Jan., 1928. Called to Bar, 1951. Q.C., 1972. A Recorder of the Crown Court, 197281. Member of Parole Board, 1982-84. Presiding Judge, South Eastern Circuit, from 1986.

McCOWEN, Alec, O.B.E., actor; b 26 May, 1925. Trained at R.A.D.A. and was in repertory theatre. 1943-50. First London appearance, Escapade at St. James's, 1952; has appeared with Royal Shakespeare Co. and National Theatre and has won awards for his acting. Solo performances of St. Mark's Gospel in 1978 and 1981.

McCRUM, Michael William, Master of Corpus Christi College, Cambridge, since 1980; b. 23 May, 1924. Tutor, Corpus Christi College, Cambridge, 1951-62; Headmaster of Tonbridge School, 1962-70 and of Eton College, 1970-80. Is a trustee of National Heritage Memorial Fund.

McCULLOUGH, Hon. Mr. Justice (Hon. Sir (Iain) Charles (Robert) McCullough), a Judge of the Queen's Bench Division since 1981; b. 31 July, 1931. Called to Bar, 1956. Q.C., 1971. A Recorder of the Crown Court, 1972-81. Member of Parole Board since 1984.

MacDERMOTT, Hon. Mr. Justice (Hon. John Clarke MacDermott), a Judge of High Court of Justice, N. Ireland, since 1973; b. 1927, s. of late Lord MacDermott, former Lord Chief Justice of N. Ireland. Called to Bar, 1949. Q.C. (N.I.), 1964.

McDONALD, Hon. Lord (Robert Howat McDonald), M.C., a Senator of College of Justice in Scotland since 1973; b. 15 May, 1916. Sheriff Principal of Ayr and Bute, 1966-71; President, Industrial Tribunals for Scotland, 1972 73. A Judge of Employment Appeal Tribunal since 1976.

MACFARLANE, Sir (David) Neil, M.P. (C), Former Parl. Under-Sec. of o73 State, Dept. of Environment (with special responsibility for sport); b. 7 May, 1936. Parl. Under-Sec. of State, Dept. of Education and Science, 1979-81.

MacGREGOR, Ian, b. 21 Sept., 1912. Educated at Glasgow University and went to U.S.A. with Min. of Supply Mission, 1940. Chairman of Amax Inc., 1966-77; partner in Lazard Freres and Co., New York, since 1978. Deputy chairman, British Leyland, 1977-80; chairman of British Steel Corp., 1980-83. Chairman of British Coal (National Coal Board) 1983-86.

MacGREGOR, Rt. Hon. John Roddick Russell, P.C., O.B.E., M.P. (C), Minister of Agriculture, Fisheries & Food 1988-89. b. 14 Feb., 1937. Chief Secretary to the Treasury, 1985-87; Head of Rt. Hon. Edward Heath's Private Office, 1965-68; a Director of Hill, Samuel and Co. Ltd., 1973-79. A Lord Commissioner of the Treasury, 1979-81; Parl. Under-Sec. of State, Dept. of Industry, 1981-83. Minister of State, Min. of Agriculture, Fisheries and Food, 1983-85 and since 1987 Cabinet Minister.

McGUINNESS, Rt. Rev. James Joseph, Bishop of Nottingham (R.C.) since 1974 (Auxiliary Bishop, 1972 74); b. 2 Oct., 1925. Curate, St. Mary's Derby, 1950-53; Parish Priest, Clifton, Nottingham, 1956-1972.

MACHIN, Arnold, O.B.E., R.A., sculptor; b. 1911. Master, Royal Academy School of Sculpture, `1958-67. Designed effigy of the Queen's head for decimal coins; also designed commemorative Silver Wedding and Silver Jubilee crowns.

McINTYRE, Very Rev. Prof. John, F.R.S.E., Professor of Divinity, Edinburgh University, since 1956; Moderator of General Assembly of Church of Scotland, 1982-83; b. 20 May, 1916. Ordained, 1941. Minister of Fenwick, Ayrshire, 1943-45. Prof. of Theology, St. Andrew's College, Sydney University, 1946-56; Dean of Order of the Thistle.

MACKAY OF CLASHFERN, Baron (Life Peer) (James Peter Hymers Mackay), P.C., Q.C., F.R.S.E., ; Lord Chancellor; b. 2 July, 1927. Admitted to Faculty of Advocates, 1955. Q.C. (Scot.), 1965. Dean of Faculty of Advocates, 1976-79. Lord Advocate, 1979-84. A Senator of the College of Justice in Scotland, 1984-85; A Lord of Appeal in Ordinary 1985-88.

MACKAY, John Jackson, Parl. Under-Sec. of State, Scottish Office, 1982-87; b. 15 Nov., 1938. Formerly a mathematics teacher. Entered Parliament, 1979.

MACKENZIE STUART, Hon. Lord (Alexander John Mackenzie Stuart), a Judge of the European Court of Justice since 1973 and President of the Court since 1984; a Senator of College of Justice in Scotland, 1972-73; b. 18 Nov., 1924. Admitted to Faculty of Advocates, 1951. Q.C. (Scot.), 1963. Sheriff-Principal of Aberdeen, Kincardine and Banff, 1971-72.

MACLEAN, Baron (Life Peer) (Charles Hector Fitzroy Maclean), Bt., K.T., P.C., G.C.V.O., K.B.E., Lord Chamberlain of H.M. Household, 1971-84; b. 5 May, 1916. Is the 27th Chief of Clan Maclean. Chief Scout of the U.K. and Overseas Branches, 1959-71; Chief Scout of the Commonwealth, 1959-75. Lord High Commissioner to General Assembly of o73 Church of Scotland, 1984 and 1985.

McLUSKEY, Very Rev. (James) Fraser, M.C., Former Minister of St. Columba's Church of Scotland, Pont Street, London; Moderator of General Assembly of Church of Scotland, 1983-84; b. 1914. Ordained, 1938. Army Chaplain, S.A.S., 1943-46 and Sub Warden Royal Army Chaplains' Training Centre, 1947-50. Minister, Broughty Ferry, East, 1950-55 and New Kilpatrick, Bearsden, 1955-60.

McNEILL, Hon. Mr. Justice (Hon. Sir David Bruce McNeill), a Judge of the Queen's Bench Division since 1979; b. 6 June, 1922. Called to Bar, 1947. Q.C., 1966. Lecturer in law, Liverpool University, 1948-58; a Recorder of the Crown Court, 1972-78. Member of Restrictive Practices Court since 1981.

McNICOL, Prof. George Paul, F.R.S.E., Principal and Vice-Chancellor of Aberdeen University since 1981; b. 24 Sept., 1929. Qualified in medicine, Glasgow University and subsequently lecturer and reader in medicine; Professor of Medicine, Leeds General Infirmary, 1971-81.

MacPHERSON, Rt. Rev. Colin, Bishop of Argyll and the Isles (R.C.) since 1968; b. 5 Aug., 1917. Parish priest, Benbecula, 1956-66, and Fort William, 1966-68.

MACPHERSON OF CLUNY, Hon. Mr. Justice (Hon. Sir William Alan Macpherson of Cluny), a Judge of the Queen's Bench Division since 1983; b. 1 April, 1926. Called to Bar, 1952. Q.C., 1971. A Recorder of the Crown Court 1972 83. Presiding Judge, Northern Circuit since 1985. Is 27th Chief of Clan Macpherson.

MADDOCKS, Rt. Rev. Morris Henry St. John, Adviser on Ministry of Health and Healing to Archbishops of Canterbury and York since 1983; Assistant Bishop in diocese of Bath and Wells since 1983; b. 28 April, 1928. Vicar of St. Martin's on the Hill, Scarborough, 1961-71; Bishop Suffragan of Selby, 1972-83.

MAJOR, Rt. Hon. John, M.P. (C), Chancellor of the Exchequer, 1990 -; Secretary of State for Foreign and Commonwealth Affairs, 1989 - 90; Chief Secretary to the Treasury from 1987-89. b. 29 March, 1943. Was in banking before entering Parliament, 1979. Member of Lambeth Borough Council, 1968-71. An Assistant Government Whip, 1983-84. A Lord Commissioner of the Treasury, 1984-86. Minister of State, Dept. of Health and Social Security (Minister for Social Security) 1986-87.

MANN, Rt. Rev. Michael Ashley, Dean of Windsor since 1976; b. 25 May, 1924. Was in Colonial Administration Service before ordination. Vicar of Christ Church, Port Harcourt, Nigeria, 1962-67; Residentiary Canon, Norwich Cathedral, 1969-74; Bishop Suffragan of Dudley, 1974-76.

MANN, Hon. Mr. Justice (Hon. Sir Michael Mann), a Judge of the Queen's Bench Division since 1982; b. 9 Dec., 1930. Called to Bar, 1953. Q.C., 1972. A Recorder of the Crown Court, 1979-82. Inspector, Vale of Belvoir Coal Inquiry, 1979-80.

MARGRETHE, Queen of Denmark since 1972; b. 16 April, 1940; m. June 10, o73 1967 Count Henri de Monpezat (now Prince Henrik of Denmark); two s.; Crown Prince Frederik, b. 1968; Prince Joachim, b. 1969.

MARKOVA, Dame Alicia (Alicia Marks), D.B.E., ballerina; b. London, 1 Dec., 1910. With Diaghilev's Russian Ballet 1925-29. Vic-Wells Ballet, 1933-35. Markova-Dolin Ballet, 1935-37. Ballet Russe, Monte Carlo, 1938-41. Co-founder and prima ballerina, Festival Ballet, 1950-51. Director, Metropolitan Opera Ballet, N.Y., 1963-69. Professor of Ballet, College-Conservatory of Music, University of Cincinnati, since 1970. Governor, Royal Ballet, since 1973. President of the London Festival Ballet, since 1986.

MARSH, Baron (Life Peer) (Richard William Marsh), P.C., Chairman of Newspaper Publishers Association since 1976; b. 14 March, 1928. M.P. (Lab.), for Greenwich, 1959-71. Minister of Power, 1966-68; Minister of Transport, 1968-69. Member of N.E.D.C. since 1971. Chairman of British Railways Board, 1971-76. Member of committee of inquiry into steelworkers' pay dispute, 1980. Chairman of TV-AM since 1983.

MARSHALL, Sir Roy, C.B.E., Vice-Chancellor of Hull University, 197985; b. 21 Oct., 1920. Called to Bar, 1947. Professor of Law, Sheffield University, 1956-69; Vice-Chancellor, University of West Indies, 1969-74; Secretary-General, Committee of Vice-Chancellors and Principals, 1974-79. Chairman, Commonwealth Education Liaison Committee, 1974-81.

MARSHALL, Sir Walter Charles, C.B.E., F.R.S., Ph.D., formerly Chairman of Central Electricity Generating Board; b. 5 March, 1932. Joined Atomic Energy Research Establishment, Harwell, 1954 and was head of Theoretical Physics Div., 1960-66, Deputy Director, 1966 68 and Director, 1968-75. Director, Research Group, U.K.A.E.A., 1969-75; Deputy Chairman, U.K.A.E.A., 1975-81 and Chairman, 1981-82. Awarded a life peerage June, 1985 and took title of Baron Marshall of Goring.

MARS-JONES, Hon. Mr. Justice (Hon. Sir William Lloyd Mars-Jones), M.B.E., a Judge of the Queen's Bench Division since 1969; b. 4 Sept., 1915. Called to Bar, 1941. Q.C., 1957. Recorder of Birkenhead, 195965; of Swansea, 1965-68; of Cardiff, 1968-69.

MARSLAND, Prof. Edward Abson, Vice-Chancellor and Principal, Birmingham University, 1981-87; b. 18 May, 1923. Qualified in dentistry, Birmingham, and was a lecturer in dental pathology; Professor of Oral Pathology, 1964-81. Director of Birmingham Dental School, 1969-74.

MASON, Baron (Life Peer) (Roy Mason), P.C.; b. 18 April, 1924. Member of Yorkshire Miners' Council, 1949-53. Minister of Power, 1968-69; President of Board of Trade, 1969-70; Secretary of State for Defence, 1974-76; Secretary of State for Northern Ireland, 1976-79.

MASSEY, Anna, actress; b. 11 Aug., 1937, d. of late Raymond Massey and of Adrianne Allen. First stage appearance, The Reluctant Debutante, 1955; entered films, 1957.

MATHER, Sir (David) Carol (Macdonell), M.C., Comptroller of H.M. Household 1983-87 (Vice-Chamberlain, 1981-83); b. 3 Jan., 1919. Commissioned in Welsh Guards, 1940; retired from Army, 1962. Was in Conservative Research Dept., 1962-70. A Lord Commissioner of the Treasury, 1979-81.

MATTHEWS, Baron (Life Peer) (Victor Collin Matthews), Deputy Chairman of Trafalgar House plc., since 1973; Chairman of Fleet Holdings 1982-85; b. 5 Dec., 1919.

MATTHEWS, Denis, C.B.E., concert pianist; b. 27 Feb., 1919. First public appearance at Queen's Hall, 1939. Professor of Music, University of Newcastle-upon-Tyne, 1971-84.

MATTHEWS, Michael Gough, Director, Royal College of Music, since 1985; b. 12 July, 1931. Trained at Royal College of Music and was Professor of Piano, 1972-75; Vice-Director, R.C.M., 1978-82. Supervisor, junior studies, Royal Scottish Academy of Music and Drama, 1964-71.

MAXWELL, Hon. Lord (Peter Maxwell), a Senator of College of Justice in Scotland since 1973; b. 21 May, 1919. Called to Scottish Bar, 1951. Q.C. (Scot.), 1961. Sheriff-Principal of Dumfries and Galloway, 1970-73. Chairman of Scottish Law Commission since 1982.

MAY, Rt. Hon. Lord Justice (Rt. Hon. Sir John Douglas May), a Lord Justice of Appeal since 1982; b. 28 June, 1923. Called to Bar, 1947. Q.C., 1965. Recorder of Maidstone, 1971. A Judge of the Queen's Bench Division, 1972-82; member of Parole Board, 1977-80 and of Employment Appeal Tribunal, 1978-82.

MAYFIELD, Hon. Lord (Ian MacDonald), M.C., a Senator of College of Justice in Scotland since 1981; b. 26 May, 1921. Called to Bar, 1952. Q.C. (Scot.), 1964. President, Industrial Tribunals for Scotland, 1973-81.

MAYHEW, Rt. Hon. Sir Patrick Barnabas Burke, Q.C., M.P. (C), Solicitor-General 1983-87; b. 11 Sept., 1929. President of Oxford Union, 1952. Called to Bar, 1955. Q.C., 1972. Parl. Under-Sec. of State, Dept. of Employment, 1979-81; Minister of State, Home Office, 1981-83. Attorney General since 1987.

MEARS, Rt. Rev. John Cledan, Bishop of Bangor since 1983; b. 8 Sept., 1922. Vicar of Cwm, 1955-58; lecturer, St. Michael's College, Llandaff and University of Wales, Cardiff, 1959-73; Vicar of St. Mark's, Gabalfa, Cardiff, 1973-82.

MEGARRY, Rt. Hon. Sir Robert Edgar, Vice-Chancellor of the Supreme Court, 1982-85; a Judge of the Chancery Division, 1967-85 and ViceChancellor, 1976-85; b. 1 June, 1910. Called to Bar, 1944. Q.C., 1956. Reader in Equity in the Inns of Court (Council of Legal Education), 1951-67; was a solicitor, 1935-41.

MELLOR, David John, M.P. (C), Minister for Arts 1990-; formerly Minister of State Department of Health; b. 12 March, 1949. Joint Minister of State, Home Office, 1986-87 Called to Bar, 1972. QC. 1987. Parl. Under-Sec. of State, Dept. of Energy, 1981-83. Parl. Under-Sec. of State, Home Office, 1983-86. Minister of State, Foreign & Commonwealth Office since 1987.

MENOTTI, Gian Carlo, composer; b. Cadegliano, Italy, 7 July, 1911. Resident in U.S.A. since 1928. His operas have twice won him a Pulitzer Prize. Teacher of composition at Curtis Institute of Music, Philadelphia, 1948-55.

MENUHIN, Sir Yehudi, O.M., K.B.E., violinist; b. New York, 22 April, 1916; took British citizenship, 1985. Studied with Enesco and Adolph Busch. Began playing at age of five. Has since played with leading orchestras all over the world. Founded Yehudi Menuhin School of Music at Stoke d'Abernon, 1963. Gold Medal of Royal Philharmonic Society, 1962. President of Royal Philharmonic Orchestra since 1982.

MERCER, Rt. Rev. Eric Arthur John, Bishop of Exeter, 1973-85; b. 6 Dec., 1917. Ordained, 1947 after service in Army. Rector, Chester St. Bridget, 1959-65; Bishop Suffragan of Birkenhead, 1965-73.

MICHELL, Keith, actor; b. 1 Dec., 1928 in Australia. Was teacher of art until first appearance on stage, Adelaide, 1947; first London appearance, 1951; has acted with Shakespeare Memorial Theatre Co.; played Henry VIII in TV series The Six Wives of Henry VIII. Director of Chichester Festival Theatre, 1974-77.

MICHELMORE, Clifford Arthur, C.B.E., television commentator and producer; b. 11 Dec., 1919; m. Jean Metcalfe. Entered TV in 1950 as a sports commentator. Introduced nightly BBC programmes Tonight and 24 Hours. Has won several TV awards.

MIDDLETON, Sir Peter, K.C.B., former Permanent Secretary, H.M. Treasury; b. 2 April, 1934. Private Sec. to Chancellor of Exchequer, 1969-72; Treasury Press Secretary, 1972-75; Under-Secretary, 1976-80 and Deputy Secretary, 1980-83.

MILES, Baron (Life Peer) (Bernard Miles), C.B.E., actor; b. 27 Sept., 1907. First stage appearance, 1930. Was in repertory for five years as designer, stage manager, and actor. Entered films, 1937. Founded Mermaid Theatre in 1950, which was later built at Puddle Dock, London, 1959.

MILLS, Sir John, C.B.E., actor and producer; b. 22 Feb., 1908; m. 1941. Mary Hayley Bell, playwright. First appearance on stage, 1929. Now acts mainly in films. Awarded Oscar for performance in Ryan's Daughter, 1971.

MILNE, Alasdair David Gordon, Director-General of the BBC 1982-87 (Deputy Director-General, 1980-82); b. 8 Oct., 1930. Joined BBC, 1954 and worked on Tonight programme; Controller, BBC Scotland, 1968-72; Director of Programmes, BBC TV, 1973-77; Managing Director, BBC Television, 1977-82.

MISKIN, His Honour Judge Sir James (Sir James William Miskin), Q.C., Recorder of London since 1975; b. 11 March, 1925. Called to Bar, 1951. Q.C., 1967. Dep. Chairman, Herts. Quarter Sessions, 1968-71; a Recorder of Crown Court, 1972-75.

MITCHELL, David Bower, M.P. (C), Former Minister of State, Dept. of Transport; b. 1928. An Opposition Whip, 1965-67; Chairman of Conservative Smaller Business Committee, 1974-79. Parl. Under-Sec. of State, Dept. of Industry, 1979-81 and at Northern Ireland Office, 1981-83. Joint Parl. Under. Sec. of State, Dept. of Transport 1983-86.

MITFORD, Jessica (Mrs. Robert Treuhaft), author; b. 11 Sept., 1917, d. of 2nd Baron Redesdale. First book Hons and Rebels published, 1960; has also written The American Way of Death and A Fine Old Conflict. Now lives in U.S.A.

MITTERAND, Francois Maurice Marie, President of France since 1981; b. 26 Oct., 1916. Deputy from Nievre, 1946-58 and 1962-81; First Secretary, Socialist Party, 1971-81. Was a candidate in French presidential elections of 1965 and 1974.

MONTEFIORE, Rt. Rev. Hugh William, Bishop of Birmingham 1978-87; b. 12 May, 1920. Fellow and Dean of Gonville and Caius College, Cambridge, 1954-63 and lecturer in New Testament, 1959-63; Vicar of Great St. Mary's, Cambridge, 1963-70; Bishop Suffragan of Kingston upon Thames, 1970-78.

MOORE, Rt. Hon. John Edward Michael, P.C., M.P. (C), Secretary of State for Social Security 1988-89; b. 26 Nov. 1937. Educated at L.S.E. Parl. Under-Sec. of State, Dept. of Energy, 1979-83; Economic Secretary, Treasury, June Oct., 1983. Financial Secretary to Treasury, 1983-86. Secretary of State for Transport 1986-87. Secretary of State for Social Services 1987-88

7

MOORE OF WOLVERCOTE, Baron (Life Peer) (Philip Moore) P.C., G.C.B., G.C.V.O., C.M.G., Private Secretary to the Queen and Keeper of H.M.'s Archives 1977-86; b.6 April, 1921. British Deputy High Commissioner, Singapore, 1963-65; Chief of Public Relations, Min. of Defence, 1955-56. Assistant Private Secretary to the Queen, 1966-72 and Deputy Private Secretary, 1972-77. Played rugby football for Oxford Univ., 1945-46 and England, 1951.

MORLEY, Robert, C.B.E., actor-dramatist; b.26 May, 1908. Studied at R.A.D.A. First appeared in Treasure Island in 1929. Entered films, 1937.

MORRISON, Hon. Peter Hugh, P.C., M.P. (C), Parliamentary Private Secretary 1990 -; former Minister of State Department of Energy and Deputy Chairman of the Conservative Party, 1986 - 90; b. 2 June, 1944, s. of 1st Baron Margadale. An Opposition Whip, 1976-79; a Lord Commissioner of the Treasury, 1979-81. Parl. Under-Sec. of State, Dept. of Employment, 1981-83. Minister of State, Dept. of Employment, 1983-85. Minister of State, Dept. of Trade and Industry, 1985-86. Minister of State, Dept of Energy since 1987.

MORTIMER, James Edward, General Secretary of Labour Party, 1982 85; b.12 Jan., 1921. Was a full-time trade union official, 1948-68. Director, London Co-operative Society, 1968-71; member, London Transport Executive, 1971-74. Chairman, Advisory, Conciliation and Arbitration Service, 1974-81.

MORTIMER, John Clifford, C.B.E., Q.C., barrister and author; b.21 April, 1923.Called to Bar, 1948. Q.C., 1966. Won the Italia Prize for his play The Dock Brief which was later filmed, and B.A.F.T.A. Writer of the Year Award, 1980. Published autobiography, Clinging to the Wreckage, 1982.

MOSER, Sir Claus, K.C.B., C.B.E., Warden of Wadham College, Oxford, since 1984; b.24 Nov., 1922 in Berlin. Educated at Frensham Heights and L.S.E. Professor of Social Statistics, L.S.E., 1961-70; director, Central Statistical Office, 1967-78; director, N.M. Rothschild and Sons since 1978; chairman of Economist Intelligence Unit, 1979-83. Chairman of board of directors, Royal Opera House.

MOVERLEY, Rt.Rev.Gerald, Bishop of Hallam (R.C.) since 1980; b.9 April, 1922. Chancellor of Leeds Diocese, 1958-68; Bishop Auxiliary of Leeds, 1968-80.

MOYNIHAN, The Hon. Colin Berkeley, M.P. (C), Energy Under Sectary 1990 -; former Parliamentary Under-Secretary Department of the Environment, Minister of Sport 1987 -90; b. 13 Sep., 1955. Oxford double blue Rowing and Boxing 1976 and 1977, outstanding athlete.

MUGABE, Robert Gabriel, Prime Minister of Zimbabwe since 1980; b.1924. Was a teacher in Northern Rhodesia and Ghana. Secretary-General of Zimbabwe African National Union and leader of Patriotic Front delegation to Lancaster House constitutional conference, 1979.

MUGGERIDGE, Malcolm, journalist; b.24 March, 1903. Formerly a university lecturer in Egypt. Has been on the staff of the Manchester Guardian, the Evening Standard, and the Daily Telegraph. Editor of Punch, 1953-57.

MULRONEY, (Martin) Brian, Prime Minister of Canada since 1984; M.P. (Progressive Conservative) for Central Nova since 1983; b.20 March, 1939. A lawyer, was president of Iron Ore Co. of Canada, 1976-83. Leader of Opposition, 1983-84.

MURDOCH, Dame (Jean) Iris (Mrs.J.O.Bayley), D.B.E., novelist; b.15 July, 1919, in Dublin. Administrative Officer, U.N.R.R.A., 1944-46; Fellow of St. Anne's College, Oxford since 1948. Her novels A Severed Head and The Italian Girl have been dramatised; The Black Prince won James Tait Black Prize, 1973 and The Sea, The Sea, won Booker Prize, 1978.

MURDOCH, (Keith) Rupert, Chairman of News International plc. (incl. the Sun and News of the World) and Times Newspapers Holdings Ltd. (The Times and the Sunday Times); b.11 March, 1931 in Australia. Is also Editor-in-Chief, New York Post and Chief Executive of News Corporation, Australia.

MURPHY-O'CONNOR, Rt. Rev.Cormac, Bishop of Arundel and Brighton (R.C.) since 1977; b.24 Aug., 1932. Secretary to Bishop of Portsmouth, 1966-70; parish priest, Parish of Immaculate Conception, Southampton, 1970-71; Rector, English College in Rome, 1971-77.

MURRAY, Hon. Mr.Justice (Hon.Donald Bruce Murray), a Judge of High Court of Justice, N. Ireland, since 1975; b.24 Jan., 1923. Called to Bar, 1945. Called to N.I.Bar, 1953 and to Inner Bar, 1964. Chairman, Gen. Council of Bar of N.I., 1972-75.

MURRAY, Rt.Hon.Lord (Rt. Hon. Ronald King Murray), a Senator of College of Justice in Scotland since 1979; b.15 June, 1922. Called to Scottish Bar, 1953. Q.C. (Scot.), 1967. M.P. (Lab.) for Edinburgh, Leith, 1970-79; Lord Advocate, 1974-79.

MURRAY OF EPPING FOREST, Baron (Life Peer) (Lionel Murray), P.C., O.B.E., General Secretary of T.U.C., 1973-84 (Asst. Gen. Sec., 1969-73); b.2 Aug., 1922. Head of Economic Dept., T.U.C., 1954-69.Member of National Economic Development Council, 1973-84 and of Committee to Review Functioning of Financial Institutions, 1977-80.

MUSTILL, Rt. Hon.Lord Justice (Rt. Hon. Sir Michael John Mustill), a Lord Justice of Appeal since 1985; b.10 May, 1931. Called to Bar, 1955. Q.C., 1968. Chairman, Civil Service Appeal Tribunal, 1971-78. A Recorder of the Crown Court, 1972-78; a Judge of the Queen's Bench Division, 1978-85.

NAIRNE, Rt. Hon. Sir Patrick, G.C.B., M.C., Former Master of St. Catherine's College, Oxford; b. 15 Aug., 1921. Entered Civil Service, 1947; Dep. Under-Sec. of State, Min. of Defence, 1970-73; Second Permanent Sec., Cabinet Office, 1973-75; Permanent Sec., Dept. of Health and Social Security, 1975-81. Chancellor of Essex University since 1983.

NEILL, Rt. Hon. Lord Justice (Rt. Hon. Sir Brian Thomas Neill), a Lord Justice of Appeal since 1984; b.2 Aug., 1923, b.. of Sir Patrick Neill. Called to Bar, 1949. Q.C., 1968. A Recorder of the Crown Court, 1972-78; a Judge of the Queen's Bench Division, 1978-84.

NEILL, Sir (Francis) Patrick, Q.C., Director of Times Newspapers Holdings 1988. Warden of All Souls College, Oxford, 1977-86; Chairman, Council for Securities Industry, since 1978; b.8 Aug., 1926; Called to Bar, 1951. Q.C., 1966., A Recorder of the Crown Court, 1975-78; a Judge of Courts of Appeal of Jersey and Guernsey since 1977. Chairman of Press Council, 1978-83.

NEUBERT, Michael Jon, M.P. (C), former Parliamentary Under-Sec. of State for defence Procurment, 1989-90; Vice Chamberlain to H.M. Household from 1988-89 b.3 Sept., 1933. Member of Bromley Borough Council, 1960-74 and was Mayor, 1972-73. P.P.S. to Secretary of State for Trade, 1982-83. A Lord Commissioner of the Treasury.

NEVILLE, Adam Matthew, M.C., D.Sc., F.R.S.E., Principal and ViceChancellor of Dundee University 1978-87; b.5 Feb., 1923. Professor of Civil Engineering, Nigerian College of Technology, 1960-62; Dean of Engineering, Calgary University, 1963-67; Professor of Civil oEngineering, Leeds University, 1968-78. Is a consultant on concrete and structural design.

NEWMAN, Sir Kenneth, Q.P.M., G.B.E., Commissioner, Metropolitan Police, 1982-87; b.1926. Served with Palestine Police, 1946-48 and Metropolitan Police, 1948-73; Chief Constable of Royal Ulster Constabulary, 1976-79; Commandant, Police Staff College, Bramshill, 1980-82.

NEWSAM, Sir Peter Anthony, Chairman of Commission for Racial Equality since 1982; b.2 Nov., 1928. Was in civil service, 1952-55 and a teacher, 1956-63; subsequently education officer in Yorkshire and Cumberland. Education Officer, Inner London Education Authority, 1977-82.

NEWTON, Antony Harold, P.C., O.B.E., M.P. (C), Secretary of State for Social Security 1989; Chancellor of The Duchy of Lancaster & Minister of Trade and Industry; b.1937. Minister of State, Dept. of Health and Social Security (Minister for Health) till 1988; An economist, was Assistant Director, Conservative Research Dept., 1970-74. An Assistant Government Whip, 1979-81 and a Lord Commissioner of the Treasury, 1981-82; Parl. Under-Sec. of State, Dept. of Health and Social Security, 1982-84. Minister for Social Security, Dept. of Health and Social Security, 1984-86.

NICHOLLS, Rt. Hon. Lord Justice (Rt. Hon. Sir Donald James Nicholls), a Judge of the Chancery Division since 1983; b.25 Jan., 1933. Called to Bar, 1958. Q.C., 1974. A Lord Justice of Appeal.

NOAKES, Most Rev. George, Archbishop of Wales since 1986 Bishop of St. Davids since 1982; b.13 Sept., 1924. Rector of Aberystwyth, 1976-79; Canon of St. Davids Cathedral, 1977-79; Archdeacon of Cardigan, 197982; Vicar of Llanychaern, 1980-82.

NOLAN, Hon. Mr. Justice (Hon. Sir Michael Patrick Nolan), a Judge of the Queen's Bench Division since 1982; b.10 Sept., 1928. Called to Northern Ireland Bar, 1974. Q.C., 1968. A Recorder of the Crown Court, 1975-82. Judge of Employment Appeal Tribunal since 1983. Presiding Judge, Western Circuit, since 1985.

NORFOLK, 17th Duke of (Miles Francis Fitzalan-Howard), K.G., C.B., C.B.E., M.C., Earl Marshal and Hereditary Marshal and Chief Butler of England, Premier Duke and Earl; b.21 July, 1915. Joined Grenadier Guards, 1937 and retired, 1967. Director, Min. of Defence, Management and Support Intelligence, 1965-66, and Service Intelligence, 1966-67.

NORTH, Peter Machin, D.C.L., Principal of Jesus College, Oxford since 1984; b.30 Aug., 1936. Tutor in Law, Keble College, Oxford, 1965-76 and a Fellow, 1965-84; member of Lord Chancellor's Committee on Legal Education, 1973-75; a Law Commissioner, 1976-84.

NORTHUMBERLAND, 10th Duke of (Hugh Algernon Percy), K.G., P.C., G.C.V.O., F.R.S., Lord Steward of H.M. Household since 1973; b.6 April, 1914. Chairman of Agricultural Research Council, 1958-68; of Medical Research Council, 1969-77. Chancellor of Newcastle University since 1964.

NOURSE, Rt. Hon. Lord Justice (Rt. Hon. Sir Martin Charles Nourse), a Lord Justice of Appeal since 1985; b.3 April, 1932. Called to Bar, 1956. Q.C., 1970. Attorney-General of Duchy of Lancaster, 1976-80; a Judge of Courts of Appeal of Jersey and Guernsey, 1977-80; a Judge of the Chancery Division, 1980-85.

NUREYEV, Rudolf, ballet dancer and choreographer; b. 1939 in E. Siberia. Joined Kirov Ballet School, and while on tour in Paris, sought political asylum, 1961; debut at Covent Garden with Dame Margot Fonteyn, 1962.

NYERERE, Julius Kambarage, President of Tanzania since 1964; of Tanganyika, 1962-64; b. 1922. Studied at Makerere and Edinburgh Universities; Prime Minister of Tanganyika, 1961-62.

O'CONNOR, Rt. Hon. Lord Justice (Rt. Hon. Sir Patrick McCarthy O'Connor), a Lord Justice of Appeal since 1980; b. 28 Dec., 1914. Called to Bar, 1940. Q.C., 1960. Recorder of King's Lynn, 1959-61 and of Southend, 1961-66; a Judge of Queen's Bench Division, 1966-80.

O'DONNELL, Rt. Hon. Lord Justice (Rt. Hon. Turlough O'Donnell), a Lord Justice of Appeal, N. Ireland, since 1979; b. 5 Aug., 1924. Called to Bar of N.Ireland, 1947; called to Inner Bar, 1964. A Judge of High Court of Justice, N. Ireland, 1971-79.

OLAV V, King of Norway, b. 2 July, 1903. Succeeded his father, Haakon VII, 21 Sept., 1957. m. 1929 Princess Martha of Sweden, b. 1901; she died, 1954; three c; Princess Ragnhild Alexandra, b. 9 June, 1930, m. 1953; Princess Astrid Ingeborg,

b. 12 Feb., 1932, m. 1961; Crown Prince Harald, b. 21 Feb., 1937, m. Sonja Haraldsen, 1968; one s; one d.

ONSLOW, Cranley Gordon Douglas, P.C., M.P. (C), chairman of Conservative 1922 Committee since 1984; b. 8 June, 1926. Was in H.M. Foreign Service, 1951-60. M.P. (C) for Woking since 1964; Minister of State, Foreign and Commonwealth Office, 1982-83.

OSBORNE, John James, dramatist and actor; b. 12 Dec., 1929. First stage appearance, Sheffield, 1948. First play produced, 1949. Awarded Oscar for screenplay, Tom Jones.

O'TOOLE, Peter, stage and film actor; b. 1932. Educated at R.A.D.A.; with Bristol Old Vic, 1955-58; first London appearance, 1956.

OTTON, Hon. Mr. Justice (Hon. Sir Philip Howard Otton), a Judge of the Queen's Bench Division since 1983; b. 28 May, 1933. Called to Bar, 1955. Q.C., 1975. A Recorder of the Crown Court, 1972-83. Presiding Judge, Midland and Oxford Circuit, from 1986.

OWEN, Rt.Hon.David Anthony Llewellyn, M.P. (SDP); b. 2 July, 1938. M.B., B. Chir., 1962. Neurological and Psychiatric Registrar, St. Thomas Hosp., 1964-66. Parl. Under-Sec. of State, Min. of Defence 1968-70; Minister of State, Dept. of Health and Social Security, 1974-76 and at Foreign and Commonwealth Office, 1976-77; Secretary of State for Foreign and Commonwealth Affairs, 1977-79. Founder member of Social Democratic Party, 1981. M.P. (Lab. 1966-81 and SDP since 1981) for Plymouth, Devonport.

PAIN, Hon. Mr. Justice (Hon. Sir Peter Richard Pain), a Judge of the Queen's Bench Division since 1975; b. 6 Sept., 1913. Called to Bar, 1936. Q.C., 1965. Chairman of Race Relations Board Conciliation Committee for Greater London since 1968. Member of Parole Board, 1978-83.

PARK, Daphne Margaret Sybil Desiree, C.M.G., O.B.E., Formerly Principal of Somerville College, Oxford; b. 1 Sept., 1921. Joined Foreign Office, 1948 and was Consul-General in Hanoi, 1969-70; at Foreign and Commonwealth Office, 1973-79.

PARK, Hon. Mr. Justice (Hon. Sir Hugh Eames Park), Judge of the Queen's Bench Division, 1973-85; of the Family Division, 1965-73; b. 24 April, 1910. Called to Bar, 1936. Q.C., 1960. Recorder of Exeter, 1960-64; of Southampton, 1964-65.

PARKER, Sir Peter, M.V.O., Chairman of Rockware Group, 1971-76 and since 1983; b. 30 Aug., 1924. Chairman of Bookers Engineering and Industrial Holdings Limited., 1966-70; of Associated British Maltsters, Ltd., 1971-73 and of Curtis Brown Ltd., 1971-76. Member of British Airways Board, 1971-81. Chairman, British Railways Board, 1976-83. Chairman, British Institute of Management, since 1984.

PARKER, Rt. Hon. Lord Justice (Rt. Hon. Sir Roger Jocelyn Parker), a Lord Justice of Appeal since 1983; b. 25 Feb., 1923. Called to Bar, 1961. Judge of Queen's Bench Division, 1977-83. Chairman of Court of Inquiry into Flixborough Explosion, 1974; conducted Windscale Nuclear Fuel Reprocessing Inquiry, 1977.

PARKES, Sir Edward Walter, Sc.D., Vice-Chancellor of Leeds University since 1983; b. 19 May, 1926. Head of Dept. of Engineering, Leicester University, 1960-65; Professor of Mechanics, Cambridge, and Professorial Fellow, Gonville and Caius Coll., 1965-74; Vice-Chancellor of City University, 1974-78.Chairman of University Grants Committee, 1978-83.

PARKINSON, Rt. Hon. Cecil Edward, M.P. (C); Secretary of State for Transport from 1989; Secretary of State for Energy since 1987-89 b. 1 Sept., 1931. Qualified as chartered accountant, 1959 and was company director, 1965-79.Minister of State, Dept. of Trade, 1979-81; Paymaster General, 1981-83 and Chancellor of Duchy of Lancaster, 198283.Chairman of Conservative Party, 1981-83; Secretary of State for Trade and Industry, 1983.

PATERSON, Very Rev. John Munn Kirk, Moderator of General Assembly of Church of Scotland, 1984-85; b. 8 Oct., 1922. Was an insurance official before ordination as Minister in Church of Scotland, 1964; Minister, St. Paul's Church, Milngavie since 1970.

PATTEN, Christopher Francis, M.P. (C), Secretary of State for the Environment from 1989; Minister of State, Foreign and Commonwealth Office and Minister for Overseas Development, 1986-89; b. 12 May, 1944. Director, Conservative Research Dept., 1974-79; P.P.S. to Chancellor of Duchy of Lancaster and Leader of House of Commons, 1979-81. Parl. Under-Sec. of State, Northern Ireland Office, 1983-85.Minister of State, Dept. of Education and Science, 1985-86.

PATTEN, John Haggitt Charles, Ph.D., M.P. (C), formerly Minister of State at the Home Office; Minister for Overseas Development until 1989; b. 17 July, 1945. Was a university lecturer. Fellow of Hertford College, Oxford, since 1972. Parl. Under-Sec. of State, Northern Ireland Office, 1981-83. Under-Sec. of State, Dept. of Health and Social Security, 1983-85. Minister of State, Home Office since 1987. Parl. Minister of State, Dept. of Environment (Minister for Housing, Urban Affairs and Construction), 1985-87.

PATTIE, Rt. Hon. Geoffrey Edwin, M.P. (C), Minister of State, Dept. of Trade and Industry, 1984-87; b. 17 Jan., 1936. Called to Bar, 1964. Member of House of Commons Public Accounts Committee, 1976-79. Parl. Under-Sec. of State, 1979-83 and Minister of State, 1983-84, Min. of Defence.

PEACOCK, Prof. Alan Turner, D.S.C., Vice-Chancellor of Buckingham University, 1983-84 (Principal of University College at Buckingham, 1980-83); b. 26 June, 1922. Professor of Economic Science, Edinburgh University, 1957-62; Professor of Economics, York University, 1962-78; Principal-designate and Professor of Economics, University College at Buckingham, 1978-80.Chief Economic Adviser, Depts.of Industry and Trade, 1973-76. Research Professor in Public Finance, Heriot-Watt University, since 1985. Chairman of committee of inquiry into BBC funding since 1985. Chairman of the Scottish Arts Council, since 1986.

PEARCE, Sir Austin William, C.B.E., Ph.D., Chairman of British Aerospace since 1980; b. 1 Sept., 1921. Joined Agwi Petroleum Corp. (later Esso Petroleum Co.), 1945; chairman of Esso Petroleum, 1972-80; member of N.R.D.C., 1973-76 and of Energy Commission, 1977-79.

PEARL, Valerie, D. Phil., President of New Hall, Cambridge, since 1981; b. 31 Dec., 1926. Educated at St. Anne's College, Oxford; research fellow and lecturer in history, Somerville College, 1965; Professor of History of London, University College London, 1976-81. Literary director, Royal Historical Society, 1975-77.

PENROSE, George William, Q.C., Procurator to General Assembly of Church of Scotland since 1984; b. 2 June, 1938. Admitted to Faculty of Advocates; is also a chartered accountant.

PEREZ DE CUELLAR, Javier, Secretary-General of United Nations since 1982; b. 1920. A Peruvian diplomat, he was Ambassador to Switzerland, 1964-66; to the U.S.S.R., 1969-71 and to Venezuela, 1978; Peru's Permanent Representative to U.N., 1971-75 and a U.N. Under-Secretary General for Special Political Affairs, 1979-81.

PHIPPS, Rt. Rev. Simon Wilton, M.C., Bishop of Lincoln 1974-87; b. 6 July, 1921. In Coldstream Guards, 1940-46.Ordained, 1950; industrial chaplain in Coventry, 1958-68; Bishop Suffragan of Horsham, 1968-74.

PINKER, George Douglas, C.V.O., Surgeon-Gynaecologist to the Queen since 1973; b. 6 Dec., 1924. Consulting gynaecological surgeon, St. Mary's and Samaritan Hospitals since 1958 and Middlesex and Soho Hospitals since 1969.

PINTER, Harold, C.B.E., actor, director and playwright; b. 10 Oct., 1930; m. Lady Antonia Fraser, 1980. His plays The Caretaker and The Birthday Party have also been filmed.Associate Director of National Theatre since 1973.

PIPER, Sir David Towry, C.B.E., Director of the Ashmolean Museum, Oxford, 1973-85; b. 21 July, 1918. Director of National Portrait Gallery, 1964-67. Slade Professor of Fine Art, Oxford, 1966-67. Director of Fitzwilliam Museum, Cambridge, 1967-73.Member of Royal Fine Art Commission since 1970 and a trustee of Leeds Castle Foundation since 1981.

PIPER, John Egerton Christmas, C.H., painter and author; b. 13 Dec., 1903. His drawings and paintings have been exhibited in London since 1925; designed windows for Coventry Cathedral and King George VI Memorial Chapel, Windsor. A Trustee of National Gallery, 1967-74 and 1975-78; member of Royal Fine Art Commission, 1959-78.

PLATT OF WRITTLE, Baroness (Life Peer) (Beryl Catherine Platt), C.B.E., Chairman of Equal Opportunities Commission since 1983; b. 18 April, 1923. Educated at Girton College, Cambridge; with Hawker Aircraft, 1943-46 and B.E.A., 1946-49. Member of Chelmsford R.D.C., 1958-74 and of Essex C.C.since 1965.

PLUMB, Baron (Life Peer) (Sir (Charles) Henry Plumb), Member of European Parliament for The Cotswolds since 1979 and leader of Democratic Group since 1982; b.27 March, 1925. President of National Farmers Union, 1970-79 and chairman of British Agricultural Council, 1975-79.

PLUMB, Sir John Harold, historian; b. 20 Aug., 1911. Tutor, Christ's College, Cambridge, 1950-59 and Vice-Master, 1964-68; Professor of Modern English History, Cambridge, 1966-74. Master of Christ's College, 1978-82. Advisory editor to American Heritage Co., and historical adviser to Penguin Books.

PONSONBY OF SHULBREDE, 3rd Baron (Thomas Arthur Ponsonby), Chief Opposition Whip, House of Lords, since 1982; b. 23 Oct., 1930. Member of Kensington and Chelsea Borough Council, 1956-65 and Alderman, 1964-74; leader of Labour Group, 1968-73.General Secretary, Fabian Society, 1964-76. Chairman, London Tourist Board, 1976-80.

POOLE HUGHES, Rt. Rev. John Richard Worthington, Bishop of Llandaff, 1976-85; b. 8 Aug., 1916. Formerly a missionary and was Home Secretary, Universities' Mission to Central Africa, 1959-62; Bishop of South-West Tanganyika, 1962-74.

POPPLEWELL, Hon. Mr. Justice (Hon. Sir Oliver Bury Popplewell), a Judge of the Queen's Bench Division since 1983; b. 15 Aug., 1927. Called to Bar, 1951. Q.C., 1969. Recorder of Burton-on-Trent, 1970-71. A Recorder of the Crown Court, 1972-83.Judge of Employment Appeal Tribunal since 1984.

PORTER, Eric (Richard), actor; b. 8 April, 1928. First appearance on London stage, 1946; with Royal Shakespeare Co., 1960-65; won an award for his performance in TV serial The Forsythe Saga.

PORTER, Sir George, F.R.S., President of Royal Society from Dec., 1985; Director of Royal Institution of Great Britain and Fullerian Professor of Chemistry since 1966 (until August 1988); b. 6 Dec., 1920. Professor of Physical Chemistry, 1955-63 and Firth Professor of Chemistry, 1963-66, Sheffield University. Joint winner of Nobel Prize for Chemistry, 1967. Davy Medal of Royal Society, 1971; Faraday Medal of Chemical Society, 1980.

PORTILLO, Michael Denzil Xavier, M.P. (C), Minister for Public Transport, b 26 May 1953. Special Advisor to the Secretary of State 1983 and to the Chancellor of the Exchequer 1983-84, Assistant Government Whip 1986-87, Parliamentary Under-Secretary of State for Health and Social Security 1987-88.

POWELL, Anthony Dymoke, C.H., C.B.E., author; b. 21 Dec., 1905; m. 1934, Lady Violet Pakenham. Published first novel, 1931. Won James Tait Black Prize for his novel At

Lady Molly's, 1957 and W. H.Smith & Son's literary award for Temporary Kings, 1974.

POWELL, Rt. Hon. (John) Enoch, M.B.E., b. 16 June, 1912. Parl. Sec., Min. of Housing, 1955-57; Financial Sec. to Treasury, 1957-58; Minister of Health, 1960-63. M.P. (C) for Wolverhampton, South-West, 195074, and Ulster Unionist for Down, South, 1974-87.

PREVIN, Andre George, composer and conductor; b.6 April, 1929 in Berlin; became American citizen, 1943. Director, Houston Symphony Orchestra, 1967-69; conductor, London Symphony Orchestra, 1968-79.Has composed music for films and won several awards. Music Director of Pittsburgh Symphony Orchestra, 1976-84; of Royal Philharmonic Orchestra since 1985 and of Los Angeles Philharmonic Orchestra from 1986.

PRIOR, Baron (Life Peer) (James Michael Leathes Prior) M.P. (C), P.C., Chairman of G.E.C. since 1984; b. 6 11 Oct., 1927. Farmer and land agent since 1951. Minister of Agriculture, Fisheries and Food, 197072; Lord President of the Council and Leader of House of Commons, 1972-74. Secretary of State for Employment, 1979-81; Secretary of State for Northern Ireland, 1981-84.

PRITCHARD, Sir John (Michael), C.B.E., Chief Conductor, BBC Symphony Orchestra since 1982; b. 5 Feb., 1921. Conductor, Glyndebourne Festivals, 1952-77; conductor and musical director, Royal Liverpool Philharmonic Orch., 1957-63; musical director, London Philharmonic Orch., 1962-66; principal conductor, Glyndebourne Opera, 1967-77; chief conductor, Cologne Opera, since 1978.

PURCHAS, Rt. Hon. Lord Justice (Rt. Hon. Sir Francis Brooks Purchas), a Lord Justice of Appeal since 1982; b. 19 June, 1919. Called to Bar, 1948. Q.C., 1965. A Recorder of the Crown Court, 1972-74. A Judge of the Family Division, 1974-82.

PYKE, Magnus, O.B.E., Ph.D., F.R.S.E., b. 29 Dec., 1908. Is an expert on nutrition and was with Min. of Food, 1941-48; Manager, Distillers' Co. Glenochil Research Station, 1955-73. Member of Council of Royal Inst. of Chemistry, 1953-55 and 1962-65; President of Inst. of Food Science and Technology of U.K., 1969-71.Secretary and Chairman of Council, British Association for Advancement of Science, 1973-77. Has published books on nutrition.

PYM, Baron (Life Peer) (Francis Leslie Pym), M.C., P.C.; b. 13 Feb., 1922. Parl. Sec. to Treasury and Chief Whip, 1970-73; Secretary of State for Northern Ireland, 1973-74; Secretary of State for Defence, 1979-81; Lord President of the Council and Leader of House of Commons, 1981-82, also Chancellor of Duchy of Lancaster and Paymaster General, 1981; Secretary of State for Foreign and Commonwealth Affairs, 198283.

QUAYLE, Sir (John) Anthony, C.B.E., actor and producer; b. 7 Sept., 1913; m. 1947, Dorothy Hyson. First appeared on stage, 1931. Director, Shakespeare Memorial Theatre, 1948-56.

QUAYLE, John Rodney, Ph.D., F.R.S., Vice-Chancellor of Bath University since 1983; b. 18 Nov., 1926. Educated at University College of North Wales and Cambridge University. Member of scientific staff, M.R.C., 1956-63; senior lecturer in biochemistry, Sheffield University, 196365; Professor of Microbiology, Sheffield, 1965-83.

QUICK, Anthony Oliver Hebert, Headmaster of Bradfield College, 197185; b. 26 May, 1924. Assistant Master at Charterhouse, 1949-61; Headmaster of Rendcomb College, 1961-71.

QUIRK, Prof. Sir (Charles) Randolph, C.B.E., Vice-Chancellor of London University, 1981-85; b. 12 July, 1920. Professor of English Language, Durham University, 1958-60 and at London University, 1960-68. Has published a number of books on language and grammar. Quain Professor of English Language and Literature, University College London, 196881.

RAE, John Malcolm, Ph.D., Director of the Laura Ashley Foundation since April 1986; b. 20 March, 1931. Assistant Master, Harrow School, 1955-66; Headmaster of Taunton School, 1966-70. Chairman of Headmasters' Conference, 1977. Headmaster of Westminster School, 1970-86.

RAINIER III, Prince of Monaco since 1949; b. 31 May, 1923; m. 19 April, 1956, Grace Kelly (Princess Grace) (d. 1982); Heir, Prince Albert, b. 14 March, 1958; two d.

RAISON, Rt. Hon. Timothy Hugh Francis, M.P. (C), b. 3 Nov., 1929. Editor of New Society, 1962-68; Parl. Under-Sec. of State, Dept. of Education and Science, 1973-74. Minister of State, Home Office, 1979-83.Minister of State, Foreign and Commonwealth Office and Minister for Overseas Development, 1983-86.

RAMPHAL, Sir Shridath Surendranath, C.M.G., Secretary-General of the Commonwealth since 1975; b. 1928. Educated at King's College, London and called to Bar, 1951. Solicitor-General, British Guiana, 1959-61; Attorney General, Guyana, 1965-73; Minister of Foreign Affairs and Justice, Guyana, 1973-75.

RATTLE, Simon, principal conductor, City of Birmingham Symphony Orchestra, since 1980; b. 1955. Won international conducting competition at age of 19; debut at Festival Hall, 1976 and at Glyndebourne, 1977; associate conductor, Royal Liverpool Philharmonic Soc., 1977-80.

RAWCLIFFE, Rt. Rev. Derek Alec, O.B.E., Bishop of Glasgow and Galloway since 1981; b. 8 July, 1921. Ordained, 1945 and was a schoolmaster in Solomon Islands. Bishop of the New Hebrides, 1975-80.

REAGAN, Ronald, President of U.S.A. 1981-89; b. 6 Feb., 1911. Was a sports announcer, 1932-37 and film and TV actor, 1937-66.Service in U.S.A.A.F., 1942-45.Governor of California, 1967-74; candidate for Republican Presidential nomination, 1976.

REDGRAVE, Vanessa, C.B.E., actress; b. 30 Jan., 1937, d. of late Sir Michael Redgrave. First appearance Frinton Summer Repertory, 1957; has acted with Royal Shakespeare Theatre Company. Awarded Oscar for performance in Julia , 1978. Was Workers' Revolutionary Party candidate in 1974 and 1979 General Elections.

REES, David Allan, D.Sc., F.R.S., Director of National Institute for Medical Research, Mill Hill, since 1982; b. 28 April, 1936. Lecturer in chemistry, Edinburgh University, 1962-70; principal scientist, Unilever Research, Colworth Lab., 1972-82.

REES, Rt. Hon. Merlyn, M.P. (Lab.); b. 18 Dec., 1920. Served in R.A.F., 1941-46; taught economics and history, 1949-60. Parl. UnderSec. of State, Min. of Defence, 1965-68 and Home Office, 1968-70; Secretary of State for Northern Ireland, 1974-76; Home Secretary, 1976-79.

REES, Baron (Life Peer) (Peter Wynford Innes Rees) P.C., Q.C., former Chief Secretary, Treasury; b. 9 Dec., 1926. Called to Bar, 1953. Q.C., 1969. Minister of State, Treasury, 1979-81 and at Dept. of Trade, 1981-83.

REES-MOGG, Baron (Life Peer) (William Rees-Mogg); b. 14 July, 1928. Educated at Balliol College and was President of Oxford Union, 1951. Joined Financial Times, 1952 and was chief leader writer, 1955-60; dep. editor, The Sunday Times, 1964-67; editor, The Times, 1967-81. Vice-chairman of BBC since 1981.

REEVE, Hon. Mr. Justice (Hon. Sir (Charles) Trevor Reeve), a Judge of the Family Division since 1973; b. 4 July, 1915. Called to Bar, 1946. Q.C., 1965. A Circuit (formerly County Court) Judge, 1968-72.

REEVES, Sir Paul Alfred, Governor-General of New Zealand since 1985; b. 6 Dec., 1932. Ordained, 1960. Was a lecturer in church history and director of Christian education in Auckland; Bishop of Waiapu, 197179. Archbishop and Primate of New Zealand, 1980-85.

7 PEOPLE

REID, Sir Robert Basil, C.B.E., former Chairman of British Railways Board 1983-90 (Chief Executive, 1980-83); b.7 Feb., 1921. Joined L.N.E.R. as traffic apprentice, 1947; general manager, Southern Region, 1974-76; executive member for marketing, B.R.B., 1977-80.

RENFREW, Prof. (Andrew) Colin, Disney Professor of Archaeology, Cambridge University, since 1981; b. 25 July, 1937. Was a lecturer and reader in pre- history and archaeology, Sheffield University, 1965-72; Professor of Archaeology, Southampton University, 1972-81; member of Historic Buildings and Monuments Commission for England.

RENTON, (Ronald) Timothy, M.P. (C), former Minister of State at The Home Office; Joint Minister of State, Foreign and Commonwealth Office, 1985-87; b. 28 May, 1932. Was P.P.S. to Rt. Hon. John Biffen and to Rt. Hon. Sir Geoffrey Howe. Parl. Under-Sec. of State, Foreign and Commonwealth Office, 1984-85. Minister of State, Home Office since 1987.

RESTIEAUX, Rt. Rev. Cyril Edward, Bishop of Plymouth (R.C.) 1955-87; b. 1910. Provost and Domestic Prelate to H.H. Pope Pius XII, 1955.

REYNOLDS, Philip Alan, Vice-Chancellor of Lancaster University, 198085; b. 15 May, 1920. Lecturer in international history, L.S.E., 194650; Professor of International Politics, University College of Wales, Aberystwyth, 1950-64; Professor of Politics, Lancaster University, 1964-80.

RICHARDS, Lt.-Gen. Sir John Charles Chisholm, K.C.B., Marshal of the Diplomatic Corps since 1982; b. 21 Feb., 1927. Joined Royal Marines, 1945 and was C.O. 42 Commando, 1970-72; Cmdr. 3rd Commando Bde., 1975-76 and Commandant General, Royal Marines, 1977-81. Chief of Staff, British Defence Staff, Washington, 1972-74.

RICHARDSON OF DUNTISBOURNE, Baron (Life Peer) (Gordon William Humphreys Richardson), K.G., P.C., M.B.E., High Steward of Westminster since 1985; b. 25 Nov., 1915. Called to Bar, 1946. Joined J. Henry Schroder Wagg, 1957 and was Chairman, 1962-72. Governor of Bank of England, 1973-83. Benjamin Franklin Medal, Royal Society of Arts, 1984.

RICHMOND, Prof. Mark Henry, Sc.D., F.R.S., Vice-Chancellor of Manchester University and Professor of Molecular Microbiology since 1981; Chairman of Committee of Vice-Chairmen & Vice-Principals since 1987.; b. 1 Feb., 1931. Reader in molecular biology, Edinburgh University, 1965-68; Prof. of Bacteriology, Bristol University, 1968-81. Member of Public Health Laboratory Service Board since 1976 and of o73 Science and Engineering Research Council since 1981.

RICKS, Prof. Christopher Bruce, Professor of English at Boston University since 1986, and Cambridge 1975-1986; b. 18 Sept., 1933. Graduated at Balliol College, Oxford; Fellow of Worcester College, Oxford, 1958-68; Professor of English, Bristol University, 1968-75.

RIDLEY, Rt. Hon. Nicholas, M.P. (C), former Secretary of State for Trade and Industry and President of the Board of Trade, 1989-90; Secretary of State for the Environment, 1986-89; b. 17 Feb., 1929, y.s. of Viscount Ridley. Is a civil engineer; Parl. Sec., Dept. of Trade and Industry, 1970-72.Minister of State, Foreign and Commonwealth Office, 1979-81; Financial Secretary, Treasury, 1981-83. Secretary of State for Transport, 1983-86.

RIFKIND, Rt. Hon. Malcolm Leslie, M.P. (C), Secretary of State for Scotland, since 1986; b. 21 June, 1946. Called to Scottish Bar, 1970. Chairman of Scottish Conservative Devolution Committee, 1976. Parl. Under-Sec. of State, Scottish Office, 1979-82 and at Foreign and Commonwealth Office, 1982-83. Minister of State, Foreign and Commonwealth Office, 1983-86.

ROBERTS, (Ieuan) Wyn (Pritchard), M.P. (C), Parl. Under-Sec.of State, Welsh Office, 1979-87; b. 10 July, 1930. Was a journalist and TV producer. P.P.S. to Secretary of State for Wales, 1970-74. Minister of State, Welsh Office since 1987.

ROBERTSON, Hon. Lord (Ian Macdonald Robertson), a Senator of College of Justice in Scotland since 1966; b. 30 Oct., 1912. Called to Scottish Bar, 1939. Q.C. (Scot.), 1954. Sheriff of Ayr and Bute, 1961-66.

RODGER, Rt. Rev. Patrick Campbell, Bishop of Oxford 1978-87; b. 28 Nov., 1920. Exec. Sec. for Faith and Order, World Council of Churches, 1961-66; Provost of St.Mary's Cathedral, Edinburgh, 1967-70.Bishop of Manchester, 1970-78.

RODGERS, Rt. Hon. William Thomas; b. 28 Oct., 1928. Gen.Sec., Fabian Society, 1953-60. Minister of State, Board of Trade, 1968-69, Treasury, 1969-70 and at Min. of Defence, 1974-76; Secretary of State for Transport, 1976-79. Founder member of Social Democratic Party, 1981. M.P. (Lab., 1962-81 and SDP, 1981-83) for Stockton.

ROGERSON, Rt. Rev. Barry, Bishop of Bristol since 1985; b. 25 July, 1936. Was with Midland Bank before ordination; lecturer, Lichfield Theological Coll., 1967-71 and vice-principal, 1971-72; Vicar, St. Thomas Wednesfield, 1975-79; Bishop Suffragan of Wolverhampton, 1979-85.

ROOKE, Sir Denis (Eric), C.B.E., F.R.S., Chairman of British Gas since 1976 (Dep. Chairman, 1972-76) President of the Fellowship of Engineering, since 1986; b. 2 April, 1924. Joined South Eastern Gas Bd., mechanical engineer, 1949. Member of British Nat. Oil Corp., 1976-82.

ROSE, Hon. Mr. Justice (Hon. Sir Christopher Dudley Roger Rose), a Judge of the Queen's Bench Division since 1985; b. 10 Feb., 1937. Called to Bar, 1960. Q.C., 1974. Recorder of the Crown Court, 1978-85.

ROSKILL, Baron (Life Peer) (Eustace Wentworth Roskill), P.C., a Lord of Appeal in Ordinary 1980-86; b. 6 Feb., 1911. Called to Bar, 1933. Q.C., 1953. A Judge of the Queen's Bench Division, 1962-71; a Lord Justice of Appeal, 1971-80.Chairman of Commission on Third London Airport, 1968-70.

ROSS, Hon. Lord (Donald MacArthur Ross), a Senator of College of Justice in Scotland since 1977; b. 29 March, 1927. Admitted to Faculty of Advocates, 1952. Q.C. (Scot.), 1964. Junior Legal Assessor to Edinburgh Burgh and Dean of Guild Courts, 1958-64; Dean of Faculty of Advocates, 1973-76. Lord Justice Clerk since 1985.

ROTHERMERE, 3rd Viscount (Vere Harold Esmond Harmsworth), Chairman of Daily Mail and General Trust plc since 1978; Chairman of Associated Newspapers plc. since 1970; launched new Daily Mail 3rd May 1971; launched the Mail on Sunday 2nd May 1982; b. 27 Aug., 1925, elder son of 2nd Viscount Rothermere, succeeded to the Viscountcy, 12 July, 1978. Educated at Eton and at Kent School, Conn., U.S.A. Trustee of Reuters and Director of Northern Star Holdings (Australia) and Power Corporation (Canada). Patron of London School of Journalism. F.R.S.A., F.B.I.M. Commander: Order of Merit (Italy); Order of Lion (Finland).

ROWSE, Alfred Leslie, historian and author; b. St. Austell, Cornwall, 4 Dec., 1903. Fellow of All Souls College, Oxford, 1925-74. First book Politics and the Younger Generation published, 1931.

RUMBOLD, Angela, M.P. (C), Minister of State, Home Office, 1990-; b.11 August 1932. Founder member of the National Association of Child in Hospital and National Chairman 1974-76.

RUNCIE, Most Rev. and Rt. Hon. Robert Alexander Kennedy, M.C., Archbishop of Canterbury since 1980; b. 2 Oct., 1921. Fellow, Dean and Asst. Tutor of Trinity Hall, Cambridge, 1956-60; Vicar of Cuddesdon and Principal of Cuddesdon College, 1960-69; Bishop of St.Albans, 1970-80.

RUSSELL, Rt. Hon. Mr. Justice (Rt. Hon. Sir (Thomas) Patrick Russell), a Judge of the Queen's Bench Division 1980-87; b. 30 July, 1926. Called to Bar, 1949. Q.C., 1971. Prosecuting Counsel to the Post Office, 1961-70; a Recorder of the Crown Court, 1972-80. Presiding Judge, Northern Circuit, since 1983. Lord Justice of Appeal since 1986.

RUTHERFORD, Andrew, Warden of Goldsmiths' College, London University, since 1984; b. 23 July, 1929. Lecturer in English, Edinburgh University, 1956-64; Second Professor of English, Aberdeen University, 1965-68, and Regius Professor of English Literature, 1968-84.

RUTT, Rt. Rev. Cecil Richard, C.B.E., Bishop of Leicester since 1979; b. 27 Aug., 1925. Served in R.N.V.R., 1943-46. Ordained, 1952. Was in Korea, 1954-74 and Bishop of Taejon, 1968-74. Bishop Suffragan of St. Germans, 1974-79.

RYDER, Richard Andrew, O.B.E., M.P. (C), Paymaster General 1990 -; Economic Secretary to the Treasury 1989-90; Former Parliamentary Secretary Department of Agriculture and Fisheries, b. 4 Feb., 1949. Political Secretary to the Leader of the Opposition 1975-79 and to the Prime Minister 1979-81, Assistant Government Chief Whip 1986-88.

SABBEN-CLARE, James Paley, Headmaster (formerly Second Master) of Winchester College since 1985; b. 9 Sept., 1941. Educated at Winchester and joined teaching staff, 1968; assistant master, Marlborough College, 1964-68.

SAINSBURY, Hon. Timothy Alan Davan, M.P. (C), Trade Minister 1990 -; Parl. Under-Sec. of State at Ministry of Foreign and Commonwealth Affairs, 1989-90; Former Parl. Under Sec. of State for Defence Procurement. Lord Commissioner to the Treasury; b. 11 June, 1932, s. of Baron Sainsbury. P.P.S. to Secretary of State for Environment, 197983.

ST.JOHN-STEVAS, Baron (Life Peer) (Norman Antony Francis St. John Stevas), M.P. (C), P.C.; b. 18 May, 1929. Called to Bar, 1952. Formerly a university lecturer and tutor; edited collected works of Walter Bagehot and was legal and ecclesiastical correspondent of The Economist. Minister of State (formerly Parl. Under-Sec.of State), Dept. of Education and Science, 1972-74; Chancellor of Duchy of Lancaster and Leader of House of Commons, 1979-81.

SAUL, Prof. Samuel Berrick, Vice-Chancellor of York University since 1979; b. 20 Oct., 1924. B.Com., 1949, Ph.D., 1953, Birmingham University. Lecturer in economic history, Liverpool University, 1951-63; Professor of Economic History, Edinburgh University, 1963-78; also Dean of Faculty of Social Sciences, 1970-75 and Vice-Principal, 1975-77.

SAUVE, Jeanne, Governor-General of Canada since 1984; b. 26 April, 1922. A journalist, she was secretary-general of Federation of Authors and Artists of Canada, 1966-72. Liberal M.P., 1972-84; Minister of Communications, 1975-79; Speaker of Canadian House of Commons, 1980-84.

SAVILLE, Hon. Mr. Justice (Hon. Sir Mark Oliver Saville), a Judge of the Queen's Bench Division since 1985; b. 20 March, 1936. Called to Bar, 1962. Q.C., 1975.

SCARMAN, Baron (Life Peer) (Leslie George Scarman), P.C., O.B.E., a Lord of Appeal in Ordinary 1977-86; b. 29 July, 1911. Called to Bar, 1936. Q.C., 1957. A Judge of the Family Division, 1961-73; a Lord Justice of Appeal, 1973-77. Chairman of the Law Commission, 1965-73. Chairman of Court of London University since 1970 and Chancellor of Warwick University since 1977.

SCHREYER, Edward Richard, Governor-General of Canada, 1979-84; b. 1935. First elected to Manitoba Legislature in 1958; he was Premier of o73 the Province, 1969-77; was federal M.P., 1965-69. Canadian High Commissioner in Australia since 1984.

SCHWARZ, Rudolf, C.B.E., orchestral conductor; b. Austria, 29 April, 1905. Principal Guest Conductor, Northern Sinfonia Orchestra, 1973-82 and of Bournemouth Symphony Orchestra, 1970-79; Chief Conductor of the BBC Symphony Orchestra, 1957-62.

SCHWARZKOPF, Elisabeth, opera and concert singer; b. 9 Dec., 1915. Has sung at Covent Garden, Vienna State Opera and La Scala, Milan, and also at Continental festivals.

SCOFIELD, (David) Paul, C.B.E., actor; Associate Director,

National Theatre, 1970-71; b. 21 Jan., 1922. Early stage career with Croydon and Birmingham Reps. and with ENSA in World War II. Appears with Royal Shakespeare and National Theatre. Awarded Oscar for film performance in A Man for all Seasons.

SCOTT, Nicholas Paul, M.B.E., M.P. (C), Minister of State Department of Social Security; b. 1933. Member of Holborn Borough Council, 1956-59 and 1962-65; Parl. Under-Sec. of State, Dept. of Employment, 1974. Parliamentary Under-Sec. of State, Northern Ireland Office, 1981-86. Minister of State for Health since 1987; Minister of State, Northern Ireland Office, 1986-8.

SCOTT, Hon. Mr. Justice (Hon. Sir Richard Rashleigh Folliott Scott), a Judge of the Chancery Division since 1983; b. 2 Oct., 1934. Called to Bar, 1959. Q.C., 1975. Attorney General of Duchy of Lancaster, 198083. Vice-Chancellor of the County Palatine of Lancaster since 1987.

SEARLE, Ronald William Fordham, artist; b. 3 March, 1920. Was P.O.W. in Siam and Malaya, 1942 45. Exhibited wartime drawings at Cambridge, 1945. Theatre artist of Punch, 1949-62.

SECOMBE, Sir Harry, C.B.E., singer and comedian; b. Swansea, 8 Sept., 1921. A popular performer on radio, TV, stage and screen. Has appeared at eight Royal Command Performances.

SEEAR, Baroness (Life Peer) (Beatrice Nancy Seear), P.C., Liberal Leader, House of Lords, since 1984; b. 7 Aug., 1913. Was a Reader in Personnel Management, London School of Economics. Chairman of Nat. Council for the Single Woman and her Dependants; member of Top Salaries Review Body.

SEROTA, Nicholas Andrew, Director of the Tate Gallery; b 27 April 1946. Director of the Whitechapel Art Gallery 1976-88, Director of the Museum of Modern Art Oxford 1973-76 and Trustee Public Art Development Council from 1983.

SESSFORD, Rt. Rev. George Minshull, Bishop of Moray, Ross and Caithness since 1970; b. 7 Nov., 1928; Priest-in-Charge, Cumbernauld New Town, 1958-66; Rector of Forres, 1966-70.

SHAW, (John) Giles (Dunkerley), M.P. (C), Minister of State, Dept. of Trade and Industry, 1986-87; b. 1931. President of Cambridge Union, o73 1954. Was Marketing Director with Rowntree Mackintosh, 1970-74. Parl. Under-Sec. of State, Northern Ireland Office, 1979-81; at Dept. of Environment, 1981-83 and Dept. of Energy, 1983-84. Minister of State, Home Office, 1984-86.

SHEEN, Hon. Mr. Justice (Hon. Sir Barry Cross Sheen), a Judge of the Queen's Bench Division since 1978; b. 31 Aug., 1918. Called to Bar, 1947. Q.C., 1966. Junior Counsel to Admiralty, 1961-66; a Recorder of the Crown Court, 1972-78.

SHELBOURNE, Sir Philip, Chairman of Britoil plc. since 1982 (British National Oil Corporation, 1980-82); b. 15 June, 1924. A barrister, was Chief Executive of Drayton Corp., 1971-72 and Chairman, 1973-74; Chairman of Samuel Montagu and Co., 1974-80.

SHELDON, Hon. Mr. Justice (Hon. Sir (John) Gervase (Kensington) Sheldon), a Judge of the Family Division since 1978; b. 4 Oct., 1913. Called to Bar, 1939. A Circuit Judge, 1968-78. Presiding Judge, Western Circuit, 1980-84.

SHELDON, Rt. Hon. Robert Edward, M.P. (Lab), chairman of Public Accounts Committee, House of Commons, since 1983; b. 13 Sept., 1923. Minister of State, Treasury, 1974-75; Financial Sec. to Treasury, 1975-79.

SHEPPARD, Rt. Rev. David Stuart, Bishop of Liverpool since 1975; b. 6 March, 1929. A former county and Test cricketer, played for England 22 times. Ordained, 1955; Warden and Chaplain of Mayflower Family Centre, Canning Town, 1957-69. Bishop Suffragan of Woolwich, 1969-75.

7 PEOPLE

SHOCK, Maurice, Vice-Chancellor of Leicester University 1977-87; Rector of Lincoln College Oxford since 1987; b. 15 April, 1926. Fellow and Praelector in Politics, University College, Oxford, 1956-77. Member of Economic and Social Research Council since 1981. Chairman, Committee of Vice-Chancellors and Principals, 1985-87.

SHORE, Rt. Hon. Peter (David), M.P. (Lab); b. 20 May, 1924. P.P.S. to Prime Minister, 1965-66. Secretary of State for Economic Affairs, 1967-69. Minister without Portfolio and Dep. Leader of House of Commons, 1969-70; Secretary of State for Trade, 1974-76 and for the Environment, 1976-79.

SHULTZ, George Pratt, U.S. Secretary of State since 1982; b. 13 Dec., 1920. Prof. of Industrial Relations, Chicago University Graduate School of Business, 1957-62 and Dean, 1962-69. Secretary of Labour, 1969-70; Director, Office of Management and Budget, 1970-72; Secretary of the Treasury, 1972-74. Chairman of President's Economic Policy Advisory Board, 1981-82.

SINDEN, Donald Alfred, C.B.E., actor; b. 9 Oct., 1923. First appearance on stage, 1941; entered films, 1952; appears with Royal Shakespeare Co. and on TV. Chairman of British Theatre Museum Assoc., 1971-77; Vice-President of London Appreciation Soc. since 1960. Member of Arts Council since 1982. Published autobiography, A Touch of the Memoirs, 1982. o73

SKELMERSDALE, 7th Baron (Roger Bootle-Wilbraham), Parl. Under-Sec. of State, Dept. of Environment, 1986-87; b. 2 April, 1945. Managing director of Broadleigh Nurseries, 1973-81. A Lord in Waiting (Government Whip) 1981-86. Under Secretary for Health since 1987.

SLACK, Rev. Dr. Kenneth, M.B.E., Minister, Kensington United Reformed Church, since 1982; b. 20 July, 1917. Ordained Presbyterian Church of England, 1941. Gen.Sec., British Council of Churches, 1955-65; Minister, St. Andrew's Church, Cheam, 1965-67. Minister of City Temple, London, 1967-75. Director, Christian Aid Division, British Council of Churches, 1975-82. Moderator of General Assembly of United Reformed Church, 1973-74 and of Free Church Federal Council, 1983-84.

SLADE, Rt. Hon. Lord Justice (Rt. Hon. Sir Christopher John Slade), a Lord Justice of Appeal since 1982; b. 2 June, 1927. Called to Bar, 1951. Q.C., 1965. Attorney-General, Duchy of Lancaster, 1972-75; a Judge of the Chancery Division, 1975-82. President of Restrictive Practices Court, 1981-82.

SLOMAN, Sir Albert Edward, C.B.E., Vice-Chancellor of Essex University 1962-87; b. 14 Feb., 1921. Reader in Spanish, Dublin University, 1947-53; Professor of Spanish, Liverpool University, 1953-62. Reith Lecturer, 1963.

SLYNN, Hon. Sir Gordon, Advocate-General, Court of Justice of European Communities, since 1981; b. 17 Feb., 1930. Called to Bar, 1956. Q.C., 1974. A Recorder of the Crown Court, 1972-76; a Judge of the Queen's Bench Division, 1976-81. President of Employment Appeal Tribunal, 1978-81.

SMITH, Cyril, M.B.E., M.P. (L), Liberal Chief Whip, 1975-76; b. 28 June, 1928. Member of Rochdale Council, 1952-75 and was Mayor, 196667. Entered Parliament, 1972.

SMITH, Prof. (Francis) Graham, F.R.S., Professor of Radio Astronomy and Director of Nuffield Radio Astronomy Laboratories, Manchester University, since 1981; b. 25 April, 1923. Telecommunications Research, 1943-46; Cavendish Laboratory, 1947-64; Professor of Radio Astronomy, Manchester University, 1964-74. Director of Royal Greenwich Observatory, 1976-81. President, Royal Astronomical Society, 1975-77. Astronomer Royal since 1982.

SOLTI, Sir Georg, K.B.E., Principal Conductor, London Philharmonic Orchestra, 1979-83; Musical Director, Chicago Symphony Orchestra, since 1970; b. 21 Oct., 1912 in Budapest; became British citizen, 1972. Musical Director, Munich State Opera, 1946-52; of Frankfurt Opera, 1952-61 and of Covent Garden Opera Co., 1961-71.

SOLZHENITSYN, Alexander Isayevitch, Russian author; b. 11 Dec., 1918. Was in Army 1941-45 and a teacher in Ryazan and Moscow. Imprisoned, 1945-53; expelled from Russia, 1974. Nobel Prize for Literature, 1970; Templeton Prize for Progress in Religion, 1983. First book, One Day in the Life of Ivan Denisovich, published, 1962.

SOPER, Baron (Life Peer) (Rev. Donald Oliver Soper), Methodist minister; b. 31 Jan., 1903. Minister, South London Mission, 1926-29; Central London Mission, 1929-36. President of the Methodist Conference, 1953; Superintendent of West London Mission, Kingsway Hall, 1936-78.

SPARK, Muriel Sarah, O.B.E., writer; b. Edinburgh. Editor, The Poetry Review, 1947-49; her novels Memento Mori and The Prime of Miss Jean Brodie have been dramatised. Awarded James Tait Black Prize for The Mandelbaum Gate, 1965.

SPENDER, Sir Stephen, C.B.E., poet and critic; b. 28 Feb., 1909. Coeditor, Encounter, 1953-67. Professor of English, University College, London, 1970-77.Queen's Gold Medal for Poetry, 1971; Companion of Literature, 1977.

SPICER, (William) Michael (Hardy), M.P. (C), Parl. Under-Sec. of State, Dept. of Transport, 1984-87; b. 22 Jan., 1943. Director, Conservative Systems Centre, 1968-70; a deputy chairman of Conservative Party since 1983. Managing director, Economic Models Ltd., 1970-80. Parliamentary Under-Secretary of State, Dept. of Energy since 1987.

STANIER, Field Marshal Sir John (Wilfred), G.C.B., M.B.E., Chief of the General Staff, 1982-85; b. 6 Oct., 1925. Commissioned in 7th Queen's Own Hussars, 1946; Vice Chief of General Staff, 1978-80; C.-in-C., U.K. Land Forces, 1981-82.

STANLEY, Rt. Hon. John Paul, M.P. (C), Minister of State, Min. of Defence, 1983-87; b. 19 Jan., 1942. P.P.S. to Leader of the Opposition, 1976-79. Minister of State for Housing and Construction, Dept. of Environment, 1979-83. Minister of State, Northern Ireland Office since 1987.

STAUGHTON, Hon. Mr. Justice (Hon. Sir Christopher (Stephen Thomas Jonathan Thayer) Staughton), a Judge of the Queen's Bench Division since 1981; b. 24 May, 1933. Called to Bar, 1957. Q.C., 1970. A Recorder of the Crown Court, 1972-81.

STAVELEY, Admiral Sir William (Doveton Minet), G.C.B., Formerly Chief of Naval Staff and First Sea Lord; b. 10 Nov., 1928. Entered Royal Navy, 1942; Chief of Staff to C.-in-C. Fleet, 1978-80; Vice-Chief of Naval Staff, 1980-82; C.-in-C. Fleet and Allied C.-in-C., Channel and Eastern Atlantic, 1982-85.

STEEL, Rt. Hon. Sir David Martin Scott, M.P. (L), formerly leader of Liberal Party; b. 31 March, 1938. Was youngest M.P. when elected for Roxburgh, Selkirk and Peebles, 1965; sponsored Private Member's Bill on abortion law reform, 1966; Liberal Chief Whip, 1970-75. Member of British Council of Churches, 1971-75. Rector of Edinburgh University, 1982-85.

STEPHEN, Rt. Hon. Sir Ninian Martin, G.C.M.G., G.C.V.O., K.B.E., Governor-General of Australia since 1982; b. 15 June, 1923. Admitted barrister and solicitor, State of Victoria, 1949; Q.C., 1966. A Judge of Supreme Court of Victoria, 1970; a Judge of High Court of Australia, 1972-82.

STEPHENSON, Rt. Hon. Lord Justice (Rt. Hon. Sir John Stephenson), a Lord Justice of Appeal, 1971-85; b. 28 March, 1910. Called to Bar, 1934. Q.C., 1960. Recorder of Winchester, 1959-62; a Judge of the Queen's Bench Division, 1962-71.

STERN, Isaac, American violinist; b. Russia, 21 July, 1920. Studied at San Francisco Conservatory. First public concert, 1934.

STEWART, (Bernard Harold) Ian (Halley), M.P. (C), Economic Secretary, Treasury, 1983-87; b. 10 Aug., 1935. A merchant banker, joined Brown Shipley and Co., 1960. Parl.Under-Sec. of State, Min. of Defence, Jan. Oct., 1983. A numismatist, has written books on coinage. Minister of State for Defence from 1987.

STEWART, Rt. Hon. Donald James, M.P. (SNP), Leader of Parliamentary Scottish National Party since 1974; b. 17 Oct., 1920. Provost of Stornoway, 1958-64 and 1968-70.

STEWART, (John) Allan, M.P. (C), b. 1 June, 1942. Was a lecturer in political economy, St. Andrews University; joined C.B.I., 1971 and was Scottish Director, 1978-79. Parl. Under-Sec. of State, Scottish Office, 1981-86.

STEYN, Hon. Mr. Justice (Hon. Sir Johan Van Zyl Steyn), a Judge of the Queen's Bench Division since 1985; b. 15 Aug., 1932 in South Africa. Was in practice at South African Bar but came to U.K. 1973. Called to Bar, Lincoln's Inn, 1973. Q.C., 1979.

STOCKER, Rt. Hon. Lord Justice (Rt. Hon. Sir John Dexter Stocker), M.C., a Judge of the Queen's Bench Division since 1973; b. 7 Oct., 1918. Called to Bar, 1948. Q.C., 1965. A Recorder of the Crown Court, 1972-73. A Lord Justice of Appeal.

STOTT, Rt. Hon. Lord (Rt. Hon. George Gordon Stott), a Senator of the College of Justice in Scotland, 1967-84; b. 22 Dec., 1909. K.C. (Scot), 1950. Sheriff of Roxburgh, Berwick and Selkirk, 1961-64; Lord Advocate, 1964-67.

STRONG, Sir Roy (Colin), formerly Director of Victoria and Albert Museum 1974-87; b. 23 Aug., 1935; m. Julia Trevelyan Oman, 1971. Director and Keeper of National Portrait Gallery, 1967-73. Has published books on Elizabethan and Jacobean portraiture. Member of Arts Council since 1983.

STUART-SMITH, Hon. Mr. Justice (Hon. Sir Murray Stuart-Smith), a Judge of the Queen's Bench Division since 1981; b. 18 Nov., 1927. Called to Bar, 1952. Q.C., 1970. A Recorder of the Crown Court, 1972-81. Presiding Judge, Western Circuit, since 1983.

SUPPLE, Prof. Barry Emanuel, Master of St. Catharine's College, Cambridge, since 1984; Professor of Economic History since 1981; b. 27 Oct., 1930. Professor of Economic and Social History, Sussex o73 University, 1962-78; Reader in Recent Social and Economic History, Oxford University, 1979-81.

SUTHERLAND, Dame Joan, D.B.E., operatic soprano singer; b. 7 Nov., 1926; m. Richard Bonynge, 1954. Debut, Sydney, Australia, 1947; joined Royal Opera House, Covent Garden, 1952.

SUTHERLAND, (Norman) Stuart, D. Phil., Principal of King's College, London since 1985; b. 26 March, 1927. Oxford University lecturer in experimental psychology, 1960-64; Professor of Experimental Psychology, Sussex University, 1965-85. Visiting Professor, Massachusetts Inst.of Technology, 1961-62 and 1964-65.

SUTTON, Rt.Rev.Keith Norman, Bishop of Lichfield since 1984; b. 23 June, 1934. Tutor and chaplain, Bishop Tucker College, Mukono, Uganda, 1968-73; Principal of Ridley Hall, Cambridge, 1973-78; Bishop Suffragan of Kingston upon Thames, 1978-84.

SWANN, Baron (Life Peer) (Michael Meredith Swann), F.R.S., F.R.S.E., Chancellor of York University 1979-90; b. 1 March, 1920. Professor of Natural History, 1952-65 and Principal and Vice-Chancellor, 196573, University of Edinburgh. Chairman of BBC, 1973-80. Provost of Oriel College, Oxford, 1980-81. Died September 1990.

SWINNERTON-DYER, Prof. Sir (Henry) Peter (Francis), Bt. F.R.S., K.B.E., Chairman of University Grants Committee since 1983; b. 2 Aug., 1927. Dean of Trinity College, Cambridge, 1963-73; Professor of Mathematics (Lecturer,

1960-71). Cambridge, University since 1971; Master of St. Catharine's College, Cambridge, 1973-83.

SWINTON, 2nd Earl of (David Yarburgh Cunliffe-Lister), b. 21 March, 1937; m. 1959, Susan Sinclair (now Baroness Masham of Ilton). Member of North Riding County Council, 1961-73 and of North Yorkshire C.C., 1973-77.Captain, Yeomen of the Guard and Dep. Chief Whip, House of Lords, 1982-86.

TAYLOR, Alan John Percivale, historian; b. 25 March, 1906. Fellow of Magdalen College, Oxford, 1938-76 and Tutor in Modern History, 1938-63. Died 1990.

TAYLOR, Rt. Rev. John Vernon, Bishop of Winchester, 1975-85; b. 11 Sept., 1914. Warden of Bishop Tucker College, Uganda, 1945-54; research worker, Int. Missionary Council, 1955-59; Africa Sec., Church Missionary Society, 1959-63 and General Sec., 1963-74.

TAYLOR, Rt. Rev. Maurice, Bishop of Galloway (R.C.) since 1981; b. 5 May, 1926. Was a lecturer in philosophy and theology. Parish priest, Our Lady of Lourdes, East Kilbride, 1974-81.

TAYLOR, Hon. Mr. Justice (Hon. Sir Peter Murray Taylor), a Judge of the Queen's Bench Division since 1980; b. 1 May, 1930. Called to Bar, 1954. Q.C., 1967. A Recorder of the Crown Court, 1972-80. Presiding Judge, North Eastern Circuit, since 1984.

TAYLOR, William, C.B.E., Ph.D., Vice-Chancellor of Hull University since 1985; b. 31 May, 1930. Educated at L.S.E. and Westminster College. Head of Education Dept., Bede College, Durham, 1961-64; Tutor and Lecturer in Education, Oxford, 1964-66; Professor of Education, Bristol University, 1966-73; Director, University of London Inst. of Education, 1973-83; Principal, University of London, 1983-85.

TEBBIT, Rt. Hon. Norman Beresford, M.P. (C), Chancellor of the Duchy of Lancaster, 1985-87; b. 29 March, 1931. After service in R.A.F., was a civil airline pilot, 1953-70; is also a journalist. Parl. Under-Sec. of State, Dept. of Trade, 1979-81; Minister of State, Dept. of Industry, 1981; Secretary of State for Employment, 1981-83. Secretary of State for Trade and Industry, 1983-85. Companion of Honour 1987.

TE KANAWA, Dame Kiri, D.B.E., opera singer; b. 6 March, 1944 in New Zealand; m. Desmond Stephen Park, 1967. Educated at St.Mary's College, Auckland, and London Opera Centre. Sings leading operatic roles at Covent Garden and in New York, Paris, Cologne and Milan.

TEMPLEMAN, Baron (Life Peer) (Sydney William Templeman), P.C., M.B.E., a Lord of Appeal in Ordinary since 1982; b. 3 March, 1920. Called to Bar, 1947. Q.C., 1964. Attorney General of Duchy of Lancaster, 1970-72. A Judge of the Chancery Division, 1972-78; a Lord Justice of Appeal, 1978-82.

TERESA, Mother (Agnes Gonxha Bojaxhiu), Roman Catholic nun; b. 27 Aug., 1910 in Yugoslavia. Joined Sisters of Loretto in Ireland, 1928 and went to India, 1929 and taught at St. Mary's High School, Calcutta. Founded Missionaries of Charity for destitute and dying, 1950. Awarded Nobel Peace Prize, 1979. Hon. O.M., 1983.

TERRY, Air Chief Marshal Sir Peter, G.C.B., A.F.C., Governor and C.-in-C.of Gibraltar since 1985; b. 18 Oct., 1926. Joined R.A.F., 1945; Vice-Chief of Air Staff, 1977-79; C.-in-C., R.A.F. Germany, 1979-81; Deputy Supreme Allied Commander, Europe, 1981-84.

THATCHER, Rt. Hon. Margaret Hilda, F.R.S., M.P. (C), Prime Minister and First Lord of the Treasury since 1979; b. 13 Oct., 1925; m. Denis Thatcher, 1951. Research chemist, 1947-51. Called to Bar, 1954. Parl. Sec., Min. of Pensions and Nat. Insurance, 1961-64. Secretary of State for Education and Science, 1970-74. Leader of the Opposition, 1975-79.

THOMAS, Dafydd Elis, M.P. (PC), President of Plaid Cymru (National Party of Wales) since 1984; b. 18 Oct., 1946. Was a university lecturer. Entered Parliament, 1974.

THOMAS, Hon. Mr. Justice (Hon. Sir Swinton Barclay Thomas), a Judge of the Family Division since 1985; b. 12 Jan., 1931. Called to Bar, 1955. Q.C., 1975. A Recorder of the Crown Court, 1975-85.

THOMPSON, Donald, M.P. (C), Former Parl. Secretary, Min. of Agriculture, Fisheries and Food; b. 13 Nov., 1931. Was formerly a member of West Riding County Council and of Calderdale District Council. An Assistant Government Whip, 1981-83. A Lord Commissioner of the Treasury, 1983-86.

THOMPSON, Rt. Rev. (Geoffrey) Hewlett, Bishop of Exeter since 1985; b. 14 Aug., 1929. Ordained, 1954. Vicar of St. Augustine's, Wisbech, 1959-66 and of St. Saviour's Folkestone, 1966-74; Bishop Suffragan of Willesden, 1974-85.

THOMPSON, Michael Warwick, D.Sc., Vice-Chancellor of East Anglia University 1980-87; Vice-Chancellor of Birmingham University since 1987; b. 1 June, 1931. Was a research scientist, A.E.R.E. Harwell, 1953-65; Professor of Experimental Physics, Sussex University, 1965-80.

THOMSON, Sir John Adam, G.C.M.G., U.K. Permanent Representative to United Nations since 1982; b. 27 April, 1927. Joined Foreign Office, 1950 and served in Damascus, Washington and Vienna; Deputy Permanent Rep. to North Atlantic Council, 1972-73; High Commissioner to India, 1977-82.

THOMSON OF MONIFIETH, Baron (Life Peer) (George Morgan Thomson), K.T., P.C., F.R.S.E., Chairman of Independent Broadcasting Authority since 1981; b. 16 Jan., 1921. M.P. (Lab.), for Dundee, East, 1952-72; Secretary of State for Commonwealth Affairs, 1967-68; Minister without Portfolio, 1968-69; Chancellor of Duchy of Lancaster, 1966-67 and 1969-70. Member, Commission of European Communities, 1973-77. First Crown Estate Commissioner, 1978-80. Chancellor of Heriot-Watt University since 1977.

THORN, John Leonard, Headmaster of Winchester College, 1968-85; b. 28 April, 1925. Assistant master, Clifton College, 1949-61; Headmaster of Repton School, 1961-68. Director of Royal Opera House, Covent Garden, 1971-76. Trustee of British Museum since 1980.

TINSLEY, Rt. Rev. Ernest John, Bishop of Bristol, 1976-85; Lecturer in Theology, Bristol University, 1976-84; b. 22 March, 1919. Lecturer in Theology, University College of Hull, 1946-61; Professor of Theology, University of Leeds, 1962 75.

TIPPETT, Sir Michael, O.M., C.H., C.B.E., composer; b. 2 Jan., 1905. Director of Music, Morley College, London, 1940-51; Artistic Director, Bath Festival, 1969-74. Cobbett Medal for Chamber Music, 1948. Gold Medal of Royal Philharmonic Society, 1976. His oratorio A Child of our Time first performed, 1944.

TODD, Baron (Life Peer) (Alexander Robertus Todd), O.M., F.R.S., President of Royal Society, 1975-80; b. 2 Oct., 1907. Prof. of Chemistry and Director of Chemical Laboratories, Manchester University, 1938-44; Professor of Organic Chemistry, Cambridge University, 194471; Master of Christ's College, Cambridge, 1963-78. Chancellor of Strathclyde University. Nobel Prize for Chemistry, 1957.

TONYPANDY, 1st Viscount (Thomas George Thomas), P.C., Speaker of House of Commons, 1976-83; Chairman of Ways and Means and Dep. Speaker, 1974-76; b. 1909. Minister of State, Commonwealth Office, 1967-68; Secretary of State for Wales, 1968-70. M. P. (Lab.) Cardiff, Central, 1945-50 and Cardiff, West, 1950-76, until elected Speaker. Awarded a viscountcy, 1983.

TREFGARNE, 2nd Baron (David Garro Trefgarne), former Minister for Trade, Trade and Industry Ministry, 1989-90; Minister of State for Defence Procurement 1988-89; b. 31 March, 1941. Has held several flying records in light aircraft. A Lord in Waiting, 1979-81; Parl. Under-Sec. of State at Dept. of Trade, 1981; at Foreign and Commonwealth Office, 1981-82 and Dept. of Health and Social Security,

198283. Parl. Under-Sec. of State, Min. of Defence, 1983-86; Minister of State, Min. of Defence, 1986-88.

TRETHOWAN, Sir (James) Ian (Raley), Chairman of Horserace Betting Levy Board since 1982; Chairman of Thames Television since 1987; b. 20 Oct., 1922. A journalist and was political commentator on The Economist and The Times ; dep. editor, Independent Television News, 1958-63. Joined BBC, 1963 and was managing director, radio, 1969-75 and managing director, television, 1976-77. Director-General of the BBC, 1977-82. An independent director of Times Newspapers Holdings since 1982.

TRILLO, Rt. Rev. Albert John, Bishop of Chelmsford, 1971-85; b. 4 July, 1915. Principal, Bishops' College, Cheshunt, 1955-63; Bishop Suffragan of Bedford, 1963-68 and of Hertford, 1968-71.

TRIPPIER, David Austin, M.P. (C), Minister for the Environment and Countryside, 1989; Parl. Under-Sec. of State, Dept. of Employment, 1986-87; b. 15 May, 1946. Member of Rochdale Council, 1969-78; P.P.S. to Minister for Health, 1982-83. Parl. Under-Sec. of State, Dept. of Trade and Industry 1983-85 and Dept. of Environment 1985-86 and since 1987.

TRUMPINGTON, Baroness (Life Peer) (Jean Alys Barker), Parl. Sec., Ministry of Agriculture, Fisheries and Food; Parl. Under-Sec. of State, Dept. of Health and Social Security, 1985-87; a Baroness in Waiting, 1983-85. Member of Cambridge City Council, 1963-73 and was Mayor, 1971-72. Chairman of Air Transport Users' Committee, 1979-80. Steward of Folkestone racecourse since 1980. Parliamentary UnderSecretary of State, Ministry of Agriculture, Fisheries and Food since 1987.

TUCKER, Hon. Mr. Justice (Hon. Sir Richard Howard Tucker), a Judge of the Queen's Bench Division since 1985; b. 9 July, 1930. Called to Bar, 1954. Q. C., 1972. A Recorder of the Crown Court, 1972-85.

TUDOR EVANS, Hon. Mr. Justice (Hon. Sir Haydn Tudor Evans), a Judge of the Family Division, 1974-78 and of Queen's Bench Division since 1978; b. 20 June, 1920. Called to Bar, 1947. Q. C., 1962. A Recorder of the Crown Court, 1972-74. A Judge of Employment Appeal Tribunal since 1982.

TUTIN, Dorothy, C.B.E., actress; b. 8 April, 1931; m. 1963, Derek Barton-Chapple (Derek Waring). Trained at Royal College of Dramatic Art. Began acting in 1950. Appears with Royal Shakespeare and National Theatre companies.

USTINOV, Sir Peter Alexander, C.B.E., actor, dramatist and film director; b. London, 16 April, 1921; m. 1972 Helene d'Allemans. He first acted in 1939. Has written a number of succesful plays in which he has appeared. Rector of Dundee University, 1968-74.

VAUGHAN, Rt. Rev. Benjamin Noel Young, Bishop of Swansea and Brecon 1976-87; b. 25 Dec., 1917. Lecturer in theology, St. David's College, Lampeter, 1952-55. Dean of Trinidad, 1955-61; Bishop Suffragan of Mandeville, 1961-67; Bishop of British Honduras, 1967-71. Dean of Bangor, 1971-76.

VINELOTT, Hon. Mr. Justice (Hon. Sir John Evelyn Vinelott), a Judge of the Chancery Division since 1978; b. 15 Oct., 1923. Called to Bar, 1953. Q. C., 1968.

WADDINGTON, Rt. Hon. David Charles, P.C., Q.C., M.P.(C), Secretary of State for the Home Department 1990- b. 2 Aug., 1929. Called to Bar, 1951. Q. C., 1971. A Recorder of the Crown Court since 1972. A Lord Commissioner of the Treasury, 1979-81; Parl. Under-Sec. of State, Dept. of Employment, 1981-83. Chief Government Whip since 1987. Minister of State, Home Office. 1983-8

WAIN, John Barrington, C.B.E., author; b. 14 March, 1925. Lecturer in English literature, University of Reading, 1947-55; Professor of Poetry, Oxford University, 1973-78. First book published, Hurry on Down, 1953; his biography of Samuel Johnson won James Tait Black Prize, 1975.

WAINE, Rt. Rev. John, Bishop of Chelmsford, formerly Bishop of Edmundsbury and Ipswich; b. 20 June, 1930. Vicar of Holy Trinity, Southport, 1964-69; Rector of Kirkby, 1969-75; Bishop Suffragan of Stafford, 1975-78.

WAITE, Hon. Mr. Justice (Hon. Sir John Douglas Waite), a Judge of the Family Division since 1982; b. 3 July, 1932. President of Cambridge Union, 1955. Called to Bar, 1956. Q. C., 1975. President, Employment Appeal Tribunal, since 1983.

WAKEHAM, Rt. Hon. John, P.C., M. P. (C), Secretary of Sate for Energy 1990-; former Lord President of the Council and Leader of the House of Commons; b. 22 June, 1932. Is a chartered accountant. Assistant Government Whip, 1979-81; a Lord Commissioner of the Treasury, 1981; Parl. Under-Sec. of State, Dept. of Industry, 1981-82; Minister of State, Treasury, 1982-83. Parliamentary Secretary to the Treasury and Chief Whip 1983-87.

WALDEGRAVE, Hon. William Arthur, M. P. (C), Minister of State Foreign & Commonwealth Affairs from 1988; b. 15 Aug., 1946, yr.s. of Earl Waldegrave. Was president of Oxford Union; a fellow of All Souls. Head of Leader of Opposition's Office, 1974-75. Parl. Under-Sec. of State, Dept. of Education and Science, 1981-83 and at Dept. of Environment, 1983-85. Minister of State, Dept. of Environment, 1986-88.

WALKER, Rt. Hon. Peter Edward, M.B.E., M.P. (C), formerly Secretary of State for Wales; b. 25 March, 1932. Nat. Chairman, Young Conservatives, 1958-60; Secretary of State for the Environment, 1970-72 and for Trade and Industry, 1972-74; Minister of Agriculture, Fisheries and Food, 1979-1983. Secretary of State for Energy 1983-87.

WALSH, Maj.-Gen. Michael John Hatley, C.B., D.S.O., Chief Scout since 1982; b. 10 June, 1927. Commissioned in K.R.R.C., 1946 and served in Malaya, Cyprus, Suez and Aden; G.O.C., 3rd Armoured Division, 1976-79; Director of Army Training, Min. of Defence, 1979-81.

WALTERS, Prof. Sir Alan Arthur, Former Economic Adviser to the Prime Minister; b. 17 June, 1926. Cassel Professor of Economics, L.S.E., 1968-76; Professor of Political Economy, Johns Hopkins University, U.S.A., since 1976.

WARBURTON, Dame Anne Marion, D.C.V.O., C.M.G., a U.K. Permanent Representative to United Nations, Geneva, 1983-85; b. 8 June, 1927. Educated in U.S.A. and Somerville College, Oxford. Joined Diplomatic Service, 1957; Counsellor, U.K. Mission to U.N. Geneva, 1970-75; Head of Guidance and Information Policy Dept., Foreign Office, 1975-76; British Ambassador to Denmark, 1976-83. President of Lucy Cavendish College, Cambridge, from 1986.

WARD, Most Rev. John Aloysius, Archbishop of Cardiff (R.C.) since 1983; b. 24 Jan., 1929. A Capuchin Franciscan friar, he was ordained in 1953. Guardian and parish priest, Peckham, 1960-66; Bishop of Menevia, 1981-83 (Bishop Coadjutor, 1980-81).

WARNER, Hon. Mr. Justice (Hon. Sir Jean-Pierre Frank Eugene Warner), a Judge of the Chancery Division since 1981; b. 24 Sept., 1924. Called to Bar, 1950. Q. C., 1972. Junior Counsel to Treasury (Chancery), 1964-72; Advocate-General, Court of Justice of European Communities, 1973-81. Judge of Restrictive Practices Court since 1982.

WARNOCK, Baroness (Life Peer) (Helen Mary Warnock), D. B. E., Mistress of Girton College, Cambridge, since 1985; b. 14 April, 1924. Tutor in philosophy, St. Hugh's College, Oxford, 1949-66 and Senior Research Fellow, 1976-84. Headmistress, Oxford High School, 1966-72. Fellow, Lady Margaret Hall, Oxford, 1972-76. Chairman, Committee of Inquiry into Human Fertilisation, 1982-84.

WATERHOUSE, Hon. Mr. Justice (Hon. Sir Ronald Gough Waterhouse), a Judge of the Family Division since 1978; b. 8 May, 1926. Called to Bar, 1952. Q. C., 1969. A Recorder of the Crown Court, 1972-77. Chairman, Local Govt. Boundary Commission for Wales, 1974-78. A Judge of

Employment Appeal Tribunal since 1980. Presiding Judge, Wales and Chester Circuit, 1980-84.

WATKINS, Rt. Hon. Lord Justice (Rt. Hon. Sir Tasker Watkins), V. C., a Lord Justice of Appeal since 1980; Senior Presiding Judge for England and Wales since 1983; b. 18 Nov., 1918. Called to Bar, 1948. Q. C., 1965. Recorder of Merthyr Tydfil. 1968-70 and of Swansea, 1970-71; a Judge of the Family Division, 1971-74 and of the Queen's Bench Division, 1974-80.

WEATHERILL, Rt. Hon. (Bruce) Bernard, M.P. (C), Speaker of the House of Commons since 1983 (Deputy Speaker, 1979-83); b. 25 Nov., 1920. Was managing director of Bernard Weatherill Ltd. (tailors). Entered Parliament, 1964; Treasurer of H.M. Household, 1973-74; Opposition Deputy Chief Whip, 1974-79.

WEBSTER, Very Rev. Alan Brunskill, Dean of St. Paul's 1978-87; b. 1918. Ordained, 1942. Warden of Lincoln Theological College, 1959-70; Dean of Norwich, 1970-78.

WEBSTER, Hon. Mr. Justice (Hon. Sir Peter Edlin Webster), a Judge of the Queen's Bench Division since 1980; b. 16 Feb., 1924. Lecturer in Law, Lincoln College, Oxford, 1950-52. Called to Bar, 1952. Q.C., 1967. A Recorder of the Crown Court, 1972-80.

WEDGWOOD, Dame (Cicely) Veronica, O.M., D.B.E., historian; b. 20 July, 1910. Her books on 17th-century history have been widely acclaimed. Won James Tait Black Prize in 1944. President of Society of Authors, 1972-77. Trustee, National Gallery, 1962-68 and 1969-76.

WEIGHT, Carel Victor Morlais, C.B.E., R.A., artist; b. 10 Sept., 1908. Professor of Painting, Royal College of Art, 1957-73, now Professor Emeritus. First exhibited at Royal Academy, 1931; first one-man show, 1934. Work purchased by galleries in London, Liverpool, Southampton and overseas.

WEINSTOCK, Baron (Life Peer) (Arnold Weinstock), Managing Director of General Electric Co. since 1963; b. 29 July, 1924. Took degree in statistics and was in Admiralty, 1944-47. Was Managing Director of Radio and Allied Holdings Ltd.; a director of Rolls-Royce (1971) Ltd., 1971-73. A trustee of British Museum since 1985.

WEST, John Clifford, C.B.E., D.Sc., Former Vice-Chancellor of Bradford University; b. 4 June, 1922. Educated at Manchester University. Professor of Electrical Engineering, Queen's University of Belfast, 1958-65; Professor of Electrical and Control Engineering, Sussex University, 1965-78. Chairman, British Philatelic Council, 1980-81.

WESTMORELAND, Earl of (David Anthony Thomas Fane), K.C.V.O., Master of the Horse since 1978; Director Sotheby Parke Benet Group, Chairman 1980-82; 31 March 1924. Lord in Waiting to the Queen 1955-78.

WESTON, Dame Margaret Kate, D.B.E., Director of Science Museum since 1973; b. 7 March, 1926. Was an engineering apprentice with General Electric Co. Joined Science Museum, 1955 and was Keeper, Dept. of Museum Services, 1967-72.

WESTWOOD, Rt. Rev. William John, Bishop of Peterborough since 1984; b. 28 Dec., 1925. Rector of Lowestoft, 1957-65; Vicar of St. Peter Mancroft, Norwich, 1965-75; Area Bishop of Edmonton, 1975-84.

WHEELER, Rt. Rev. William Gordon, Bishop of Leeds (R.C.), 1966-85; b. 5 May, 1910. Administrator of Westminster Cathedral, 1954-64; Coadjutor Bishop of Middlesbrough, 1964-66.

WHITE, Christopher John, Ph. D., Director of Ashmolean Museum, Oxford, since 1985; b. 19 Sept., 1930. Educated at Courtauld Institute of Art; on staff of British Museum, 1954-65. Director, P. and D. Colnaghi, 1965-71. Curator of Graphic Arts, National Gallery of Art, Washington, 1971-73; Director of Studies, Paul Mellon Centre for Studies in British Art, 1973-85.

WHITELAW, 1st Viscount (William Stephen Ian Whitelaw), P.C., C.H., M.C., Lord President of the Council and Leader of House of Lords 1983 to 1988; b. 28 June, 1918. M.P. (C) for Penrith and the Border, 1955-83; Chief Opposition Whip, 1964-70; Lord President of Council and Leader of House of Commons, 1970-72; Secretary of State for Northern Ireland, 1972-73 and for Employment, 1973-74; Home Secretary, 1979-83. Awarded a viscountcy, 1983.

WHITFORD, Hon. Mr. Justice (Hon. Sir John Norman Keates Whitford), Judge of the Chancery Division since 1970; b. 24 June, 1913. Called to Bar, 1935. Q. C., 1965.

WHITNEY, Raymond William, O.B.E., M.P. (C), b. 28 Nov., 1930. Was in Army, 1951-63; entered Diplomatic Service, 1964 and was head of Overseas Information Dept., 1977-78. Entered Parliament, 1978. Parl. Under-Sec. of State, Foreign and Commonwealth Office, 1983-84 and at Dept. of Health and Social Security, 1984-86.

WIGHT, James Alfred, O.B.E., veterinary surgeon; b. 3 Oct., 1916. Qualified at Glasgow Veterinary College and has been in veterinary practice in Yorkshire since 1940. As James Herriot has written a series of books on veterinary experiences which have been filmed and televised; first book *If Only They Could Talk* published, 1970.

WILKINSON, Sir Denys, F.R.S., Vice-Chancellor of Sussex University 1976-87; b. 5 Sept., 1922. Professor of Nuclear Physics, 1957-59 and Professor of Experimental Physics, 1959-76, Oxford University. Chairman, Radioactive Waste Management Advisory Committee, 1978-83. Royal Medal of Royal Society, 1980.

WILLIAMS, Sir Alwyn, F.R.S., F.R.S.E., Former Principal and ViceChancellor of Glasgow University; President of the Royal Society of Edinburgh, since 1985; b. 8 June, 1921. Lecturer in geology, Glasgow University, 1950-54; Professor of Geology, Queen's University of Belfast, 1954-74 and at Birmingham University, 1974-76.

WILLIAMS, Rt. Hon. Shirley; b. 27 July, 1930. m. Prof Richard Neustadt 20 Dec, 1987. M.P. (Lab.) for Hitchin, 1964-74 and for Hertford and Stevenage, 1974-79; M.P. (SDP) for Crosby, 1981-83. Minister of State, Dept. of Education and Science, 1967-69 and Home Office, 1969-70; Secretary of State for Prices and Consumer Protection, 1974-76; Secretary of State for Education and Science and Paymaster General, 1976-79. Founder member of Social Democratic Party.

WILLIAMSON, Air Chief Marshal Sir Keith, G.C.B., A.F.C., Chief of the Air Staff, 1982-85; b. 25 Feb., 1928. Commandant, R.A.F. Staff College, 1975-77; A.O.C.-in-C., Support Command, 1978-80 and Strike Command, 1980-82.

WILLIAMSON, Malcolm Benjamin Graham Christopher, C.B.E., composer and Master of the Queen's Music since 1975; b. 21 Nov., 1931 in Australia. Composer in Residence, Westminster Choir College, U.S.A., 1970-71. His works include operas, ballet and film scores.

WILLIAMSON, Rt. Rev. Robert Kerr, Bishop of Bradford since 1984; b. 18 Dec., 1932. Vicar of St. Paul, Hyson Green, 1966-71; of St. Ann with Emmanuel, Nottingham, 1971-76 and of St. Michael and All Angels, Bramcote, 1976-79; Archdeacon of Nottingham, 1978-84.

WILLIS, Norman David, General Secretary of T.U.C. since 1984 (Deputy Gen. Sec., 1977-84); b. 21 Jan., 1933. Joined T.G.W.U., 1949 and was Nat. Sec. for Research and Education, 1970-74. Member of Staines District Council, 1971-74.

WILSON, Alexander, Director-General of British Library Reference Division since 1980; b. 12 Feb., 1921. Director of Library and Cultural Services, Dudley and later Coventry, 1952-72; Director of Cheshire Libraries and Museums Service, 1972-79.

WILSON, Sir David Mackenzie, Director of British Museum since 1977; b. 30 Oct., 1931. Assistant Keeper, British Museum, 1954-64; Reader in Archaeology, London University, 1964-71 and Professor of Medieval Archaeology, 1971-76. Member of Ancient Monuments Board for England, 1976-84.

WILSON OF RIEVAULX, Baron (Life Peer) (James Harold Wilson), K.G., P.C., O.B.E., Prime Minister and First Lord of the Treasury, 1964-70 and 1974-76; b. 11 March, 1916. Former university lecturer in economics. M.P. (Lab) for Ormskirk, 1945-50 and for Huyton, 1950-83. Parliamentary Secretary, Ministry of Works, 1945-47; President of Board of Trade, 1947-51; Leader of the Labour Party, 1963-76. Chancellor of Bradford University, 1966-85. Leader of the Opposition, 1963-64 and 1970-74. Chairman of Committee to Review Functioning of Financial Institutions, 1976-80. Awarded a peerage July, 1983.

WINNING, Most Rev. Thomas, Archbishop of Glasgow (R.C.) since 1974. Formerly a parish priest, St. Luke, Braidhurst, Motherwell. Auxiliary Bishop of Glasgow, 1972-74.

WOOD, Hon. Mr. Justice (Hon. Sir John Kember Wood), M.C., a Judge of the Family Division since 1977; b. 8 Aug., 1922. Called to Bar, 1949. Q. C., 1969. A Recorder of the Crown Court, 1975-77.

WOOD, Rt. Rev. Maurice Arthur Ponsonby, D.S.C., Bishop of Norwich, 1971-85; b. 26 Aug., 1916. Vicar and Rural Dean of Islington, 1952-61; Principal of Oak Hill Theological College, 1961-71.

WOOLF, Rt. Hon. Lord Justice (Rt. Hon. Sir Harry Kenneth Woolf), a Judge of the Queen's Bench Division since 1979; b. 2 May, 1933. Called to Bar, 1954. A Recorder of the Crown Court, 1972-79; Treasury junior counsel (common law), 1974-79. A Lord Justice of Appeal.

WORLOCK, Most Rev. Derek John Harford, Archbishop of Liverpool (R.C.) and Metropolitan of Northern Province since 1976; b. 4 Feb., 1920. Private Sec. to Archbishop of Westminster, 1945-64; Rector, Church of SS. Mary and Michael, London, E1, 1964-65; Bishop of Portsmouth, 1965-76.

WRIGHT, Sir (John) Oliver, G.C.M.G., G.C.V.O., D.S.C., British Ambassador to U.S.A. 1982-86; b. 6 March, 1921. Ambassador to Denmark, 1966-69; Chief Clerk, H. M. Diplomatic Service, 1970-72; Dep. UnderSec. of State, Foreign and Commonwealth Office, 1972-75. Ambassador to Federal Republic of Germany, 1975-81.

WYLIE, Rt. Hon. Lord (Rt. Hon. Norman Russell Wylie), a Senator of the College of Justice in Scotland since 1974; b. 26 Oct., 1923. Advocate-Depute, 1959. Q.C. (Scot.), 1964. M.P. (C) for Edinburgh, Pentlands, 1964-74; Solicitor General for Scotland, April Oct., 1964; Lord Advocate, 1970-74.

YATES, Rt. Rev. John, Bishop of Gloucester since 1975; b. 17 April, 1925. Was in R.A.F.V.R., 1943-47. Ordained, 1951; Principal, Lichfield Theological College, 1966-72; Bishop Suffragan of Whitby, 1972-75.

YOUNG OF GRAFFHAM, Baron (Life Peer) (David Ivor Young), P.C., Secretary of State for Trade and Industry and President of the Board of Trade until 1989; b. 27 Feb. 1932. Secretary of State for Employment, 1986-87; b. of Stuart Young. Admitted a solicitor, 1956. Was chairman of Manufacturers Hanover Property Services Ltd., and president of British Org. for Rehabilitation by Training. Special adviser, Dept. of Industry, 1980-82; chairman, Manpower Services Commission, 1982-84. Secretary of State for Trade and Industry since 1987.

YOUNG, Rt. Rev. David Nigel de Lorentz, Bishop of Ripon since 1977; b. 2 Sept., 1931. Lecturer in comparative religion, Manchester University, 1967-70; Vicar of Burwell, Cambridge, 1970-75; Archdeacon of Huntingdon, 1975-77.

YOUNG, Sir George, Bt., M.P. (C), b. 16 July, 1941. Economic adviser to Post Office Corporation, 1969-74; member of G.L.C., 1970-73; Parl. Under-Sec. of State, Dept. of Health and Social Security, 1979-81. Parl. Under-Sec. of State, Dept. of Environment, 1981-86.

YOUNGER, Rt. Hon. George Kenneth Hotson, M.P. (C), Secretary of State for Defence, 1986-89; b. 22 Sept., 1931. e.s. of Viscount Younger of Leckie. Parl. Under-Sec. of State, Scottish Office, 1970-74. Secretary of State for Scotland 1979-86.

OBITUARY

October 1st 1989 - June 30th 1990

Abercorn, Dowager Duchess of, G.C.V.O. (84), Mistress of the Robes, 2/2/90

Adams, Professor Colin (61), experimental pathologist, 30/1/90

Akass, John Ewart (56), columnist and journalist, 4/6/90

Alexander, Horace Gundry (100), Indian independence, 7/10/89

Allen, Sir George 'Gubby', C.B.E. (87), cricketer, 29/11/89

Ames, Leslie, C.B.E. (84), all round cricketer, 27/2/90

Asherson, Nehemiah, F.R.C.S., F.Z.S. (91), otorhinolaryngolist, 9/11/89

Baillie, John Strachan, C.B.E. (93), former chairman of Harland & Wolff, 20/11/89

Balfour, David (86), outstanding diplomat, 18/10/89

Balfour, Lady Eve, O.B.E. (91), created concept of organic agriculture, 17/1/90

Ball, Eric (85), outstanding composer of music for brass bands, 11/10/89

Baring, Sir Charles, Second Baronet, DL (91), public service, 25/1/90

Barke, Allen (86), former Chief Executive of Ford of Britain, 29/1/90

Barker, Dennis Q.C. (63), Appellate Judge in Hon Kong, 17/11/89

Barker, Eric (78), actor and comedian, 1/6/90

Batha, Derek (60), Weight Watchers slimming clubs, 13/10/89

Bawden, Edward (86), book illustrator and war artist, 21/11/89

Beattie, Dr. John (75), distinguished social anthropologist, 25/4/90

Beauchamp, Countess (94), last of one of Worcestershire's oldest family names, 17/11/89

Beckett, Samuel (83), novelist and playwright, 22/12/89

Berkeley, Sir Lennox, C.B.E. (86), composer, 26/12/89

Bishop, Father Hugh, (82), Superior of the Community of the Resurrection, 4/10/89

Blacking, Professor John (61), Chair of Social Anthropology at Belfast University, 24/1/90

Blair-Cunynghame, Sir James, O.B.E. (76), Royal Bank of Scotland Chairman, 4/1/90

Blundy, David (44), Washington representative of The Sunday Correspondent, 18/11/89

Boomer, Aubrey (91), British member of first Ryder Cup team, 14/10/89

Booth, Lieut-Colonel Olive (98), last surviving child of General Bramwell Booth, 13/12/89

Booth, The Rev. Alan, O.B.E. (78), Director of Christian Aid, 10, 3.90

Boothby, Evelyn Basil, C.M.G. (79), diplomat, 21/2/90

Bower, Lieutenant-general Sir Roger, K.C.B., K.B.E. (86), 9/1/90

Brassey, Colonel Sir Hugh, K.C.V.O., O.B.E., M.C. (74), Lord Lieutenant of Wiltshire, 10/4/90

Braybrooke, Lord, 9th Baron, (93), appointed Masters of Magdalene College, 23/3/90

Bromley-Davenport, Sir Walter (86), 26/12/89

Bruce-Gardyne, Lord (60), former Treasury Minister, 15/4/90

Bulley, Rt. Rev. Cyril (82), sometime Bishop of Carlisle, 20/11/89

Buxton, John (76), Emeritus Fellow of New College, Oxford, 11/12/89

Caldecott, Oliver (64), publisher, 22/11/89

Campbell, Sir Ralph Abercromby (83), Chief Justice of the Bahamas, 12/10/89

Cayzer, The Hon. Anthony (69), senior member of the Cayzer shipping and airline family, 4/3/90

Ceausescu, Nicolae (71), Romanian tyrant, 25/12/89 o73

Channing-Williams, Major-general, John William, C.B., D.S.O., O.B.E. (81), 26/5/90

Chapman, Graham (48), member of Monty Python's Flying Circus, 6/10/89

Chapman, Ken (81), former president of the Rugby Football Union, 10/11/89

Charles, Canon Sebastian (57), Westminster Abbey, Parole Board and inner city, 1/11/89

Charleson, Ian (40), actor, 7/1/90

Chipperfield, James (78), head of Chipperfield Circus, 20/4/90

Cholmondeley, Dowager Marchioness of, C.B.E. (95), 26/12/89

Cholmondeley, The Marquess, G.C.V.O., M.C., D.L. (70), Lord Great Chamberlain of England, 13/3/90

Churchill, Major-General T.B.L., C.B., C.B.E., M.C. (82), 19/2/90

Clayson, Sir Eric (81), chairman Birmingham Post and Mail group, 5/10/89

Clifford, Graham Douglas, C.M.G. (76), expansion of wartime radio engineering, 9/11/89

Cooke, Canon Greville, F.R.A.M., F.S.A. (95), priest, poet and musician, 10/11/89

Coombe-Tennant, Dom Joseph, M.C. (76), soldier and Benedictine monk, 14/11/89

Coulson, Professor John Metcalfe (79), influential chemical engineer, 16/1/90

Cranstoun, Lt-Colonel Alastair 'Sandy', M.C. (79), military and diplomatic career, 28/2/90

Crisp, Professor Dennis John, C.B.E., F.R.S. (73), marine biology, 18/1/90

Dalzell, Lord Hamilton of, G.C.V.O., M.C. (78), 31/1/90

Daresbury, Lord, second Baron, third Baronet, (87), 16/2/90

Dartford, Lord Irving of (71), former Deputy Speaker of the House of Commons, 18/12/89

Davie, Sir Paul Christopher (88), Assistant Legal Advisor to the Home Office, 25/1/90

Davis, Bette (81), Hollywood film star, 9/10/89

Davis, Professor Norman, M.B.E., F.R.S. (76), professor of English at Oxford, 2/12/89

Dexter, John (64), distinguished stage director, 23/3/90

Dignam, Mark (80), actor, 5/10/89

Dodgson, Professor, John (61), outstanding scholar, 7/2/90

Doggart, James M.D., F.R.C.S (89), distinguished eye surgeon, 18/10/89

Drake, Fabia, O.B.E. (86), actress, 1/3/90

Drogheda, The Earl of, K.G., K.B.E. (79), Former Chairman of The Financial Times, 24/12/89

Dudgeon, Prof. Alastair, C.B.E., M.C. (72) advances in vaccination, 16/10/89

Earle, Air Chief Marshal Sir Alfred 'Tubby', G.B.E., C.B. (82), 27/3/90

Easthaugh, Rt. Rev. John (69), Bishop of Hereford, 16/2/90

Ekin, Major-General R.G., C.I.E. (94), 9/3/90

Elwyn-Jones, Lady (85), talent in books, stained glass and broadcasting, 29/1/90

Elwyn-Jones, Lord, P.C., C.H. (80), Nuremberg prosecutor and Lord Chancellor, 4/12/89

Emmet, Commander Heneage 'Bill' (77), career in naval Intelligence, 9/11/89 o73

Erskine, Joe (56), former British and Empire heavyweight boxing champion, 18/2/90

Ferrar, Dr. William (96), eminent mathematician, 22/1/90

Festenstein, Prof. Hilliard (59), research into immunology, 17/10/89

Freeman, Rt. Rev. Gregory (66), Abbot of Douai Abbey, Berkshire, 26/10/89

Fulham, Lord Stewart of, C.H. (83), former Labour Foreign Secretary, 10/3/90

Fussell, Dr. G.E. (100), pioneer of agricultural history, 1/1/90

Gardiner, Lord, P.C., C.H. (89), reforming Labour Lord Chancellor, 7/1/90

Garrett, Professor Denis, F.R.S. (83), Emeritus Professor of Mycology, 26/12/89

Gascoigne, Major-General Sir Julian, K.C.V.O., K.C.M.G., C.B., D.S.O. (86), 26/2/90

Gibbons, Stella (87), author of Cold Comfort Farm, 19/12/89

Gilson, Dr. John Carey, C.B.E., F.R.C.P. (77), research into asbestos poisoning, 1/12/89

Glass, Ruth (77), urban sociologist, 7/3/90

Goodman, Francis (76), society photographer, 3/10/89

Goodman, Professor Colin (62), senior scientist at STC Ltd., 5/2/90

Gordon-Finlayson, Air-Vice Marshal J.R., D.S.O., D.F.C. (75), 3/3/90

Grant, Dr. Ronald Thomson, O.B.E., F.R.S. (97), studies of wounds in wartime, 15/11/89

Granville, Sir Keith, C.B.E. (79), last Chairman of BOAC, 7/4/90

Grasmere, Lord Morris of (92), former Vice-Chancellor of Leeds University, 30/5/90

Gundry, Canon Dudley (73), churchman with skills of journalist and teacher, 24/3/90

Hall, Henry, C.B.E (91), pioneer of BBC light entertainment, 30/10/89

Hammick, Charles (62), pioneer bookseller, 1/2/90

Hargreaves, Brigadier Kenneth, C.B.E. (87), business, politics, philanthropy, 27/3/90

Harkness, Captain Kenneth, C.B.E., D.S.C. (89), distinguished naval career, 19/1/90

Harmsworth, Lord (86), publisher and painter, 2/6/90

Harrison, Sir Rex (82), actor, 2/6/90

Hastings, Lt-Colonel Robin, D.S.O. and Bar, O.B.E., M.C. (73), 28/3/90

Hatch-Barnwell, Stephen, C.B.E. (80), Indian Civil Servant, 2/11/89

Hay, Roy (79), horticultural correspondent, 23/10/89

Heddle, John (48), Conservative MP for Mid-Staffordshire, 19/12/89

Herron, Shaun (76), Irish priest, journalist and novelist, 23/10/89

Heycock, Lord Llewellyn (84), commitment to local government, 14/3/90

Hopkins, Admiral Sir Frank, K.C.B., D.S.O., D.S.C., D.L. (79), 19/4/90

Howard, William McLaren Q.C. (69), Judge Advocate of the Fleet, 9/3/90

Hutchinson, Judy (72), first woman to be made High Sheriff of Oxfordshire, 7/11/89

Hutchison, Sir Kenneth, C.B.E., F.R.S. (86), chief architect of modern gas industry, 28/11/89

Inchyra, Lord (89), diplomat, 19/10/89

Jackson, Gordon, O.B.E. (66), Scottish actor, 14/1/90

Jasper, The Very Rev. Ronald, D.D. (72), former Dean of York, 11/4/90

Jones, Dr. Sydney, C.B.E. (78), conceived idea of Advanced Passenger Train, 21/2/90 o73

Jones, Peter (60), BBC Radio senior sports commentator, 2/4/90

Kahn, Dr. Jack Harold (85), development of child psychiatry in Britain, 14/12/89

Kellett, Air Commodore Richard, C.B.E., D.F.C., A.F.C. (84), distinguished airman, 20/1/90

Kerr, Elizabeth Lamorna (85), artist, 8/3/90

Keswick, Sir William (86), prominent City of London figure, 16/2/90

Kuypers, Professor Hans, (64), distinguished neuroscientist, 3/10/89

Lane, Lieut-Colonel Michael (57), life devoted to military music, 9/11/89

Law, W. Alexander, O.B.E., F.R.C.S. (79), developed hip replacement surgery, 3/11/89

Lehmann, Rosamond, Nina, C.B.E. (89), novelist, 12/3/90

Lett, Major Gordon, D.S.O. (78), fought with Italian partisans in Second World War, 23/10/89

Lewis, Sir Ian Malcolm (64), Judge in Nigeria, 16/2/90

Livermore, Sir Harry (81), campaigning Merseyside lawyer, 4/12/89

Lock, Air Vice-Marshal Basil, C.B., C.B.E., A.F.C. (66), 20/11/89

Long, Douglas (64), top newspaper executive, 7/2/90

Loss, Joe, L.V.O., O.B.E. (80), popular bandleader, 6/6/90

Lott, Air Vice-Marshal George, C.B., C.B.E., D.S.O., D.F.C. (83), 31/12/89

Luce, Lady Margaret (81), playwright and diarist, 25/10/89

MacColl, Ewan (74), folk singer, songwriter, poet and playwright, 24/10/89

MacKenna, Sir Brian (84), Judge of the High Court, 30/10/89

Mackinnon, Norman (66), Chairman of The Drambuie Liqueur Company, 1/11/89

Maclean, Lord, Bt., K.T., G.C.V.O., K.B.E. (73), Privy Councillor, 8/2/90

MacPherson, The Rt. Rev. Colin (72), Bishop of Argyll and the Isles, 24/3/90

Marlborough, Laura Duchess of (74), society figure, 19/2/90

Marre, Sir Alan, K.C.B. (76), Ombudsman, 20/3/90

Marsham, Dr. Tom, C.B.E., F.R.S. (65), development of civil use of nuclear energy, 14/10/89

Martin, Professor Graham (69), leading radio-chemist, 22/12/89

Maskell, Eric (67), research work at Farnborough on Concorde, 31/10/89

Mather, Sir Kenneth, C.B.E., F.R.S. (78), Professor of Genetics, Birmingham University, 20/3/90

McCrindle, Alex (78), founder of Scottish Actor's Equity, 20/4/90

McCulloch, Rev. Joseph (82), radical spirit within Established Church, 4/3/90

McCusker, Harold (50), Ulster Unionist MP for Upper Bann, 12/2/90

McLachlan, Charles, C.B.E., Q.P.M. (58), HM Inspector of Constabulary for South East England, 3/4/90

McMullen, Rear-Admiral Morrice, C.B., O.B.E. (81), 18/3/90

McNeill, David Bruce (67), High Court Judge, 26/2/90

Milburn, Colin (48), Test batsman, 28/2/90

Moffat, Lord McAlpine of (82), head of the McAlpine building company, 7/1/90

Morris, Air Marshal Sir Douglas, K.C.B., C.B.E., D.S.O., D.F.C. (81), 26/3//90

Mynors, Sir Roger (86), Professor of Latin at Cambridge and Oxford, 19/10/89 o73

Newell, Kenneth Wyatt (64), Professor of Tropical Community Health at Liverpool Schoo, 13/4/90

Nicholas, Tressilian Charles, M.C., O.B.E. (010), geologist, 16/11/89

Nickerson, Sir Joseph (75), farmer and brilliant shot, 3/3/90

Norris, Vice-Admiral Sir Charles, K.B.E., C.B., D.S.O. (89), 5/1/90

Northampton, Lord Paget of, Q.C. (81), Labour politician, 2/1/90

Oulton, Lady (57), devoted life to well-being of others, 25/11/89

Parkinson, Norman, C.B.E. (76), royal portraitist, 15/2/90

Part, Sir Antony, G.C.B., M.B.E. (73), distinguished civil servant, 11/1/90

Pavitt, Laurie (75), Labour MP for Brent South, 14/12/89

Pilcher, Sir John, G.C.M.G. (77), Ambassador to Japan, 10/2/90

Pochin, Sir Edward, K.B.E. (80), International Commission on Radiological Protection, 29/1/90

Powell, Michael (84), British film maker, 19/2/90

Pritchard, Sir John, C.B.E. (68), leading British international conductor, 5/12/89

Pulvertaft, R.J.V. (93), Emeritus Professor of Clinical Pathology, London University, 30/3/90

Quayle, Sir Anthony, C.B.E. (76), actor and director, 21/10/89

Rado, Professor Richard Rado, F.R.S. (83), Emeritus Professor of Pure Mathematics, 23/12/89

Rainey, Dr. Reginald Charles, O.B.E., F.R.S. (76), study of migrant insects, 18/1/90

Ramsbotham, Rt. Rev. John Alexander (83), former Bishop of Wakefield, 16/12/89

Redmond, Liam (76), Irish actor, 22/11/89

Reindorp, The Rt. Rev. George (78), former Bishop of Guildford and Salisbury, 20/4/90

Reiss, Sir John (80), former Chairman of Associared Portland Cement Manufacturers, 13/12/89

Richmond and Gordon, The Duke of (85), active role in motor-racing, 4/11/89

Robertson, Professor John (89), Emeritus Professor of Chemistry, 3/1/90

Robins, Daniel 'Dan' Gerard (47), The Bar, anthropology and cricket, 13/10/89

Robson, Vice-Admiral Sir Geoffrey, K.B.E., C.B., D.S.O., D.S.C. (87), 25/12/89

Rothschild, Lord, G.B.E., G.M., F.R.S. (79), scientist, government adviser and MI5 agent, 20/3/90

Royle, Derek (61), actor, 23/1/90

Rutland, The Dowager Duchess of (95), public service and domestic duty, 4/12/89

Sakharov, Andrei (68), Russian dissenter, 14/12/89

Schofield, Guy (87), former editor of The Daily Mail, 14/2/90

Scott, Roger (46), BBC Radio 1 disc-jockey, 2/11/89

Scott, Sir George (86), UK's longest serving police officer, 6/11/89

Scott, William, C.B.E., R.A. (76), painter, 28/12/89

Scott-Kilvert, Ian, O.B.E. (72), Special Operations Executive, 12/10/89

Scupham, John, O.B.E. (85), helped create the Open University, 10/1/90

Semprini, Fernando Riccardo Alberto (81), pianist, 19/1/90

Sheals, Dr. John Gordon (65), pioneered research into effects of insecticides, 17/11/89 o73

Shepheard, Sir Victor, K.C.B. (96), director of naval construction, 8/12/89

Slattery, Rear-Admiral Sir Matthew, K.B.E., C.B. (88), 16/3/90

Smith, Sir Leonard, C.B.E. (82), lifelong dedicated Liberal, 13/10/89

Smith-Ryland, Sir Charles (62), Lord-Lieutenant of Warwickshire, 20/11/89

Spear, Augustus John Ruskin, C.B.E., R.A. (78), painter, 17/1/90

Stephens, Sir David, K.C.B., C.V.O. (79), Clerk of the Parliaments, 3/4/90

Stevens, Vice-Admiral Sir John, K.B.E., C.B. (89), wartime service, 10/12/89

Stirling, Duncan Alexander (90), first Chairman of National Westminster Bank, 15/4/90

Stratton, Lieutenant General Sir William, K.C.B., C.V.O., C.B.E., D.S.O (86), 25/11/89

Stuart, Peter Maxwell (67), 20th Laird of Traquir, 14/2/90

Sumner, Geoffrey, (80), actor, 2/10/89

Swaythling, Lord, 3rd Baron, O.B.E. (91), 5/1/90

Taylor, Lord William Desmond (85), archaeologist, 2/12/89

'Terry-Thomas' (Thomas Terry Hoar Stevens) (78), actor, 8/1/90

Thompson, Sir Edward (87), pioneer of nuclear power, 22/12/89

Thomson, Virgil (92), composer of operas, 2/10/89

Thorpe-Bates, Peggy (75), actress, 26/12/89

Tighe, Maj-Gen. Anthony, C.B., M.B.E. (66), distinguished service career, 28/10/89

Titterton, Sir Ernest, C.M.G. (73), helped produce Britain's atomic bombs, 8/2/90

Tollemache, Major-General Sir Humphrey, Bt, C.B., C.B.E., D.L. (92), 30/3/90

Trewin, J.C. (81), critic and author, 16/2/90

Turner, Commander Bradwell, C.V.O., D.S.O., O.B.E. (92), 21/3/90

Villiers, Vice-Admiral Michael (82), first captain of aircraft carrier Bulwark, 3/1/90

Vyner, Michael (46), artistic director of the London Sinfonietta, 20/10/89

Walker, Vice-Admiral Sir Peter, K.B.E., C.B., D.S.C., C.Eng. (78), 7/12/89

Wallace, Doreen (92), novelist, 26/10/89

Ware, Sir Henry (77), former Treasury Solicitor, 16/10/89

Waverley, Viscount, 2nd Viscount (79), 21/2/90

Wedgwood, Sir John (82), former deputy chairman of Joseph Wedgwood & Sons, 11/12/89

Wheeler, Lieutenant-Colonel Geoffrey, C.B.E., C.I.E. (92), 1/2/90

White, Air Commodore Harold, C.B.E., D.F.C., A.F.C. (66), 25/3/90

Whitehorn, Mrs Josephine (76), 'Aunty Jo' of the BBC's Children's Hour, 8/1/90

Whitlock, Lt-Cdr Peter (64), leading authority on warships in the days of sail, 25/10/89

Wilde, Cornel (74), Hollywood actor, 17/10/89

Wilkinson, Sir Martin (78), innovative chairman of the Stock Exchange, 22/1/90

Williams, The Very Rev. Harold C.N. 'Bill' (75), Provost of Coventry Cathedral, 5/4/90

Williams Keeton, George (87), development of legal education, 6/10/89

Wingfield, Lawrence, M.C., D.F.C. (91), service to aviation, 26/10/89 o73

Winterbotham, Group Captain Frederick William, C.B.E., (92), intelligence work, 28/1/90

Wynne, Greville (71), British businessman and agent of British Intelligence, 27/2/90

'Yana' (Pamela Guard) (57), stage and television star, 21/11/89

Yardley, Norman (74), test cricketer, 5/10/89

Youett, Felicity (45), interior design, sculpture and stage costume, 12/1/90

Zetland, Lord (80), revival of Redcar racecourse, 11/10/89

OTHER PEOPLE'S MONEY

This year's list of the top 100 estates (which now only includes those of over £2.6 million) is headed by the £41 million estate of Lady Teresa Agnew, followed by the £27.3m estate of the 3rd Marquess of Zetland, for many years chairman of Catterick and Redcar Racecourses. Other larger estates in the list include Lady Sarah Cohen, widow of the founder of Tesco, the Dowager Marchioness of Cholmondeley, Chatelaine of Houghton in Norfolk and the last private resident of Kensington Palace Gardens in London, and Sir George Meyrick, who had the right to stop one train each day on his Hinton Admiral estate in Hampshire.

Sir Joseph Nickerson, who founded Cherry Valley Farms, the duckling breeders, and Rothwell Plant Breeders (now owned by Shell), held the world record, which still stands, of having shot 2, 119 wild English partridge in one day with five other guns. He was a founder member of the World Wildlife Fund and a vice-president of the Royal Agricultural Society, while Sir Charles Smith-Ryland was chairman of the Council of that Society, and Sir Douglas Crossman was president of the Huntingdonshire Agricultural Society as well as being a former chairman of brewers Mann, Crossman and Paulin and later of Watney Mann. Col. Thomas Forman Hardy was a former chairman of Nottingham brewers Hardy & Hanson, and chairman of the Nottingham Evening Post for 25 years, during which time it became the first newspaper in Britain to be produced by journalists using direct input technology.

Industry is also well represented with the estates of Baron McAlpine, head of the building and construction family, Margery Hurst, founder of the Brook Street Bureau, David Roberts, chairman of the former National Provincial Bank and later of the National Westminster Bank, and Gerald Coke, former chairman of Rio Tinto Zinc and founder of the Glyndebourne Arts Trust. Simon Heller, who was a world authority on nuts, acquired a small sweet manufacturer in Rotherham, which he made famous for KP nuts, before it was acquired by United Biscuits, and another Yorkshireman Anthony Fawcett started his professional life as a joiner in his uncle's firm in Ampleforth and rose to become deputy chairman of Persimmon Homes, the well known York-based housebuilders.

Violet Abbott left probably the largest single charitable bequest of the year, being the bulk of her £3.9 million estate to the Marie Curie Memorial Foundation. Helena Levy also left 7/8ths of the residue of her £6.6 million estate to the National Trust and 1/8th to the Historic Churches Preservation Trust. Julian Layton left £125,000 to the Charity Trust bearing his name - he was a stockbroker and a o73 dedicated worker for Jewish refugees from central Europe and was instrumental in enabling thousands to escape from Nazi persecution. The Countess of Brecknock was a senior commander of the A.T.S. in the War and later became Superintendent-in-Chief of the St. John Ambulance Brigade. Lady Charlotte Bonham-Carter was a founding director of the Ballett Rambert and president of the Women's Advisory Housing Council, and Irina Moore was widow of Henry Moore the sculptor. Peter Bennett was a well known character actor and prominent in Equity, and Keith Ewart was a pioneer of television commercials, having directed over 2, 000 of them and won countless awards.

The 48 year old Conservative M.P. for Mid-Staffordshire, John Heddle, was a back bench specialist in environment, housing and local government. He was found dead in his car, and, despite leaving over £3 million gross, his net estate was a mere £12,420. Baron Inglewood was a landowner, chartered surveyor and land agent, and former Conservative M.P. for Westmoreland and Joint Parliamentary Secretary to the Ministry of Agriculture, Fisheries and Food. Aubrey Orchard-Lisle, another surveyor, was former senior partner of Healey and Baker, and a director of National Bus Properties Ltd. He was also governor of both Guy's Hospital and its medical school, and left £100,000 for research into osteoarthritis there. Charles Church founded the development company of that name, which was one of the main providers of up-market housing. He also owned five wartime Spitfires, but unfortunately died when one he was piloting crashed.

Lady Teresa Jane Agnew, of Melbury House, Dorchester Dorset, estate valued at £41,058,255 (net £40,030,307)

The Most Hon. Lawrence Aldred Mervyn Dundas, 3rd Marquess of Zetland, of Aske Hall, Richmond, North Yorkshire, estate valued at £27,336,431 (net £27,314,417)

Mr. Peter Lawrence Brake, of Rough Common Road, Canterbury, Kent, estate valued at £19,486,904 (net £19,478,690)

Lady Sarah Cohen, of Gloucester Square, London W.2, estate valued at £17,966,416 (net £17,882,476)

Lt. Col. Sir George David Eliott Tapps Gervis Meyrick, 6th Bart., M.C., of Hinton Admiral, Hants., estate valued at £13,731,817 (net £13,540,239)

Mr. James William Alston-Roberts-West, of Alscot Park, Stratford upon Avon, Warwickshire, estate valued at £12,762,577 (net £12,093,120)

The Most Hon. Sybil Rachel Cecile Betty Adele, Dowager Marchioness of Cholmondeley, C.B.E., of Houghton Hall, King's Lynn, Norfolk, estate valued at £12,451,097 (net £12,437,693)

Mr. Harold Desmond Robert Ridgeon, of Home End, Fulbourn, Cambs., estate valued at £12,240,270 (net £12,207,349)

Sir Joseph Nickerson, of Rothwell, Lincs, estate valued at £11,764,447 (net £7,479,207) o73

Mr. Richard John Stuart Hawkins, of Thinghill Court, Hereford, estate valued at £11, 151,287 (net £10,843,250)

Mr. Anthony Fawcett, of High Currah, Ampleforth, North Yorks., estate valued at £10,223,358 (net £9,976,116)

Rt. Hon. Joseph William Lionel, 17th Baron Petrie of Writtle, of Ingatestone Hall, Ingatestone, Essex, estate valued at £8,695,145 (net £8,539,604)

Mr. John Thompson Bogg, of Cave Road, Brough, North Humberside, estate valued at £8,445,318 (net £8,247,384)

Mr. Roger St. John Hart, of Hinton House, Beaconsfield, Bucks., estate valued at £8,339,578 (net £8,278,109)

Mr. Ralph Levy, of South Downs Drive, Hale, Greater Manchester, estate valued at £7,181,515 (net £7,154,399)

Mrs. Helen Katherine Greville Levy, of Cadogan Square, London S.W.1., estate valued at £6,739,074 (net £6,676,431)

Sir Douglas Peter Crossman, of Tetworth Hall, Sandy, Beds., estate valued at £6,565,302 (net £6,277,893)

Mr. Aubrey Edwin Orchard-Lisle, C.B.E., F.R.I.C.S., of Grosvenor Square, London W.1. estate valued at £6,334,391 (net £5,628,927)

Robert Edwin, Baron McAlpine of Moffat, of Benhams, Fawley Green, Bucks., estate valued at £6,326,450 (net £5,685,536)

Mr. Christopher James Sellick, of Dorneys, Eversley Cross, Hants., estate valued at £6,305,907 (net £6,301,409)

Elsa Maria Margarete Speyer, of South Parade, London W.4., estate valued at £6,270,625 (net £6,227,592)

Mrs. Phyllis Mary Currie, of Buckshorns, Great Leighs, Essex, estate valued at £6,213,363 (net £6,021,983)

Rt. Hon. Anne Lorina, Baroness Allerton, of Loddington House, Loddington, Leics., estate valued at £5,968,778 (net £5,968,201)

Mr. Frederick Horton, of Shrawley Wood House, Shrawley, Worcs., estate valued at £5,755,180 (net £5,728,141)

Mr. William James Whale, of Bushwood Lane, Lapworth, Warwickshire, estate valued at £5,732,792 (net £5,571,393)

Col. The Hon. Julian Berry, O.B.E., of Tunworth, Basingstoke, Hants., estate valued at £5,470,320 (net £4,918,776)

Mr. Thomas Schofield, of Disleys Farm, Whittle le Woods, Lancs., estate valued at £5,304,348 (net £5,281,304) o73

Sir Charles Mortimer Tollemache Smith-Ryland, K.C.V.O., of Sherbourne Park, Warwick, estate valued at £5,133,066 (net £5,091,511)

Lady Joan Terry Hanbury, of Amwellbury House, Great Amwell, Herts., estate valued at £5,082,789 (net £5,066,489)

Lady Charlotte Helen Bonham-Carter, of Wyck Place, Alton, Hants., estate valued at £5,035,570 (net £4,904,151)

Mrs. Agnes Mary Violet Graham, of Lancaster Gate, London W.1., estate valued at £5,008,843 (net £4,928,639)

Mrs. Ellen Pattinson Willson, of Westwood Park Road, Peterborough, Cambs., estate valued at £4,928,466 (net £4,883,274)

Mrs. Esme Grace Anderson, of Grosvenor Square, London W.1. estate valued at £4,908,250 (net £4,101,137)

Mr. John de Vere Hunt, of Kensington Square, London W.8., estate valued at £4,853,930 (net £4,761,305)

Mr. David Beresford Lye, of Pelham Gardens, Folkstone, Kant, estate valued at £4,777,305 (net £4,336,874)

Mr. Ronald John Hoare, C.B.E., of Boulevard d'Italie, Monaco, late of Canford Cliffs, Dorset, estate in the U.K. valued at £4,737,821 (net £4,608,335)

Mr. Walter Gerson Rothschild, of Hardwater Road, Great Doddington, Northants., estate valued at £4,722,957 (net same)

Mr. Harry Oldschool, of Broom Park, Teddington, Middlesex, estate valued at £4,614,050 (net £4,497,010)

Marjorie Minna, Countess of Brecknock, D.B.E., of Wherwell Priory, Andover, Hants., estate valued at £4,595,484 (net £4,463,771)

Mr. Simon Heller, of Cavendish Avenue, Harrogate, North Yorkshire., estate valued at £4,561,826 (net £3,838,888)

Major John Clement Godfrey Francis, R.A. retd., of Quy Hall, Stow cum Quy, Cambs., estate valued at £4,472,978 (net £4,460,212)

Mr. Cyril Montague Ernest Franklin, of West Heath Road, London N.W.£., estate valued in U.K. at £4,468,143 (net £4,343,564)

Lt. Col. Julian David Layton, O.B.E., of Lyndhurst Terrace, London N.W.3., estate valued at £4,424,158 (net £4,270,935)

Mr. Thomas Sidney Hohler, of Wolverton Park, Basingstoke, Hants., estate valued at £4,370,293 (net £4,226,642)

Mr. Harry Bardiger, of Edgeworth Crescent, London N.W.4., estate valued at £4,332,663 (net £4,243,163) o73

Mr. Nicholas John Derek de Chapeaurouge Ripley, of Hurst farm, Privett, Alton, Hants., estate valued at £4,254,617 (net £4,029,195)

Hon. Lady Aline Emily Hogg, of Sloane Square, London S.W.3., estate valued at £4,147,167 (net £4,112,621)

Mrs. Ethel Mary Cardy, of Lower Bowden, Pangbourne, Berks., estate valued at £4,103,453 (net £4,055,233)

Mrs. Elizabeth Sibylla Jones-Mortimer, of Hartsheath,

Mold, Clwyd, estate valued at £4,101,235 (net £4,049,392)

Mr. Keith Anthony Douglas Ewart, of Lancaster Avenue, London S.W.19., estate valued at £4,053,477 (net £3,599,667)

Mr. Derek Charles Howard Crouch, of Wretton Road, Stoke Ferry, Norfolk, estate valued at £4,001,692 (net £3,991,064)

Mr. Ronald Ernest Summerfield, of Bayshill Road, Cheltenham, Gloucs., estate valued at £3,967,630 (net £3,964,358)

Mr. Hedley Jack Meek, of Westfield Road, Beaconsfield, Bucks., estate valued at £3,967,168 (net £3,913,707)

Miss Violet Alice Abbott, of Sutton Road, Erdington, Birmingham, estate valued at £3,903,685 (net £3,896,806)

Mrs. Margery Hurst, O.B.E., of Long Cross, Chertsey, Surrey, estate valued at £3,826,389 (net £3,188,831)

Olive Madeleine Phillips, of Ladbroke Road, London W.11., estate valued at £3,814,000 (net £3,780,710)

Mr. Graham Henry Bartlett, of Carbone Hill, Northaw, Herts., estate valued at £3,728,763 (net £3,717,763)

Mr. John Bentley Heddle, M.P., of Lowndes Close, London S.W.1., estate valued at £3,641,523 (net £12,420)

Mr. Brian Robert Osborne Bell, of Heathgate, London N.W.11., estate valued at £3,623,568 (net £2,947,763)

Mr. David John Roberts, of Lillingstone House, Lillingstone Dayrell, Bucks., estate valued at £3,606,811 (net £3,411,796)

Mr. Pantelis Savva, of Cockfosters Road, Barnet, Herts., estate valued at £3,526,052 (net £3,069,426)

Rt. Hon. John Henrik, 3rd Baron Gretton, of Somerby House, Somerby, Leics., estate valued at £3,518,711 (net £3,462,422)

Mr. Bernard Carlyle Hackett, of Heathon, Claverley, Salop, estate valued at £3,443,485 (net £3,440,692)

Mr. Charles James Gregory Church, of Laverstock Lane, Michelldever, Hants., estate valued at £3,403,185 (net £2,298,657)

Elizabeth Florence Theodosia Royds, of manor Road, Sandbach, Cheshire, estate valued at £3,397,470 (net £3,393,511)

Mr. Geoffrey Hugh Bird, of Murray Road, London S.W.19., estate valued at £3,358,272 (net £2,745,571)

Mr. John Albert Edmonds Fryer, of Bishop's Walk, Addington, Surrey, estate valued at £3,335,372 (net £3,203,853)

Rt. Hon. Ruth Alice Hannah Mary, Countess of Halifax, of Low House, Kirby Underdale, North Humberside, estate valued at £3,310,021 (net £3,146,718)

Capt. Francis Peter Longton, M.C., retd., of Heatherwold, Burghclere, hants., estate valued at £3,300,034 (net £3,294,883)

Mr. Ronald Henry Cross, of Dulcie Road, Bournemouth, Dorset, estate valued at £3,273,187 (net £3,272,285)

Mr. Edward Douglas Good, of Church Lane, Loughton, Essex, estate valued at £3,237,583 (net £3,235,743)

Mr. Clifford James Lister, of Bawtry Road, Listerdale, South Yorks., estate valued at £3,152,767 (net £3,107,999)

Rt. Hon. William Morgan, 1st Baron Inglewood, of Hutton in the Forest, Penrith, Cumbria, estate valued at £3,118,972 (net £2,848,889)

Mrs. Edith Mildred Scrasse Glasse, of Bickington,

Barnstaple, Devon, estate valued at £3,082,224 (net £3,072,979)

Mr. Edward Augustus Whittles, of Castle Avenue, London E.4., estate valued at £3,062,072 (net £2,830,117)

Mr. Peter Egerton Bennett, of Bedford Gardens, London W.8., estate valued at £3,027,617 (net £3,012,452)

Mr. George Richard Barbour, of Bolesworth Castle, Tattenhall, Cheshire, estate valued at £2,998,336 (net £2,895,336)

Mr. Marcus William Wickham-Boynton, of Burton Agnes Hall, Burton Agnes, North Humberside, estate valued at £2,979,815 (net £2,978,240)

Col. Thomas Eben Forman Hardy, of Car Colston Hall, Bingham, Notts., estate valued at £2,935,230 (net £2,884,651)

Mr. Hyman Cen, of Portland Place, London, W.1., estate valued at £2,926,215 (net £2,663,448)

Mr. Joseph Shaw, of Gresham Gardens, London N.W.1., estate valued at £2,918,126 (net £2,917,061)

Mr. George Robert Belgium Clarke, of Melksham Court, Strinchcombe, Gloucs., estate valued at £2,888,074 (net £2,707,228)

Mrs. Irina Moore, of Perry Green, Much Hadham, Herts., estate valued at £2,879,266 (net £2,860,101)

Miss Mary Cecilia Christie-Miller, of Henleys Lane, Drayton, Abingdon, Oxon., estate valued at £2,878,541 (net £2,872,997)

Mr. Mark Hellyer, of Cherry Burton Hall, Cherry Burton, North Humberside, estate valued at £2,863,087 (net £2,852,575)

Mr. Alex William Blackwell, of Berners Street, London, W.1., Great Maplestead, Essex, and Lindford, Hants, estate valued at £2,851,977 (net £2,818,481)

Mr. Stanley Shorrock, of Higher Feniscowles Hall, Pleasington, Lancs., estate valued at £2,835,791 (net £2,526,014)

Mrs. Violet Dorothy Mills, of Ennismore Gardens, London S.W.7., estate valued at £2,834,552 (net £2,810,931)

Mr. Cecil Compton, of Ringwood Road, Parkstone, Dorset, estate valued at £2,799,311 (net £2,786,596)

Mr. James Collinson, of Scotchman Lane, Morley, West Yorks., estate valued at £2,782,080 (net £2,718,873)

Mr. Leslie Eric McLean, of Crawley Hill, Camberley, Surrey, estate valued at £2,759,879 (net £2,674,333)

Mr. Alfred Edwin Morgan, of Fairmile lane, Cobham, Surrey, estate valued at £2,739,465 (net £2,268,888)

Edith Alison Impey, of Alresford Grange, Colchester, Essex, estate valued at £2,731,397 (net £2,672,155)

Mr. Terence John Kenny, of Styvechale Avenue, Coventry, West Midlands, estate valued at £2,711,749 (net £1,284,593)

Mr. Michael Gordon Foster, M.B.E., J.P., of Leysthorpe, Oswaldkirk, North Yorks., estate valued at £2,682,960 (net £2,619,004)

Mr. John Bennett Rubens, of Park Lane, London W.1., estate valued at £2,646,798 (net £2,614,369)

Mr. Ivo Matthew Leopold Dieskau Forde, of Norther Farm, Cranleigh, Surrey, estate valued at £2,645,208 (net £2,620,730)

Mr. Gerald Edward Coke, C.B.E., of Jenkyn Place, Bentley, Hants., estate valued at £2,629,665 (net £2,575,223)

7

7 PEOPLE

Mr. Alexander Arditti, of Parkfield Road, Altrincham, Great Manchester, estate valued at £2,620,671 (net £2,575,590)

Laura, Duchess of Marlborough, of George Street, London, W.1., estate valued at £2,617,345 (net £2,585,516)

Other estates not in the above list but published this year contain several well known political figures, including two former Labour Lord Chancellors - **Lord Gardiner**, who left £39,268, and **Lord Elwyn-Jones**, who left £227,106. **Baroness Gaitskell**, widow of the former Labour Party leader, left £27,157, and **Lord Trafford**, former Minister of State for Health and M.P. for the Wrekin, and **Lady Annie Gammans**, former Conservative M.P. for Hornsey, each left over £1 million.

Viscount Runciman, who left £1.7 million, joined the board of both Imperial and British Airway in 1938 and helped forge their amalgamation into B.O.A.C., becoming in the process its Director-General. **Baroness Rendlesham**, who was a director Yves St. Laurent's first Rive Gauche boutique in this country and a former Fashion Editor of Queen, left £1.7 million, **Cecil Moores**, president and co-founder with his brother John of Littlewoods Pools, left £1.9 million, and **Sir Archibald Finlayson**, former president of the Midland Bank, left £1.2 million.

Sir Peter Scott, the artist and naturalist and founder of the Wildfowl Trust, left £593,532, **Kerrison Cooke**, former ballet master of the Festival Ballet, left £233,287, and **Dame Frances Qvist**, the internationally famous cardiologist and consulting physician to the Royal Free Hospital, left £1.6 million, with the residue left between the School of Medicine at that Hospital and the Royal College of Surgeons. Londoner **Henry Bright** left all his £1.2 million estate between four national charities and **Judith Bartram**, of Felmingham in Norfolk, left nearly all her £1.8 million estate between the church there and two others in nearby Antingham and Southrepps.

The acting profession is heavily represented with **Lord Olivier** leaving £1.3 million, **Sir Anthony Quayle** £626,664, **Cyril

Luckham £89,788, **Gordon Jackson** £742,068 and Harry Andrews £257,093. **Roger Middleton** left £59,905 and **Donald Yarranton** left 316,849. The former was actor **Maurice Colbourne**, who played Tom Howard in Howard's Way, and the latter was better known as **Howard Lang**, who played Captain Baines in another well-known nautical series The Onedin Line. **Allan McClelland**, the actor and author, left £138,020, Monty Python's **Graham Chapman**, left £393,113, and **Harry Worth** left £570,332. **Audrey Russell**, the BBC's first woman news reporter and its only accredited female war correspondent in the last war, left £427,795, and **Harry Corbett**, creator of Sooty and Sweep, left £80,918, including £2,000 to his brother Leslie 'in appreciation of his great help as Sweep's daddy'.

John Ogden, the concert pianist and composer, left £565,100, **Lady Daphne Browning** - the novelist **Daphne Du Maurier** - left £467,992, **Sir Sacheverell Sitwell**, the poet and brother of Edith and Osbert, left £161,284, and **Laurence Meynell**, the author of over 100 books ranging from thrillers to studies of cricket and cats, left £288.314. **Don Revie**, the former Leeds and England football manager, left £67,786, and **Norman Yardley**, the Yorkshire and England cricketer and later Test selector, left £203,979. Another England selector **'Gubby' Allen**, who was also president of the M.C.C., left £977,589, including a quarter o73 of the residue for various cricket charities, including the M.C.C., for encouraging youth cricket and helping old cricketers and their families in distress, the Middlesex County Cricket Club Centenary Youth trust, and the Association of Cricket Umpires.

Thomas Wright, of Wallasey, left over £2 million, while **Helen Hall**, of Rickinghall, Suffolk, **Alan Partridge**, of Drewsteignton, Devon, **Robert Adams**, of Purley, Surrey, **Henry Ellis** of Brighton, **Ronald Pearson** of Whitton, Middlesex, **Awad Sudki**, of Erdington, Birmingham, **Horace Clarke**, of Canford Cliffs, Dorset, and **Raymond Downes**, of Winchmore Hill, London, all left over £1 million. About the only thing they had in common last year was that, despite leaving an aggregate of some £12 million, each of them died without making a will.

BROADCASTING AND ENTERTAINMENT

THE BRITISH BROADCASTING CORPORATION

London Headquarters:
Broadcasting House, London W1A 1AA. 071-580 4468.

Television:
Television Centre, Wood Lane, London W12 7RJ. 081-743 8000.

Scotland:
Broadcasting House, Queen Margaret Drive, Glasgow G12 8DG. 041-330 2345.

Wales:
Broadcasting House, Llantrisant Road, Llandaff, Cardiff CF5 2YQ. 0222 573888.

Northern Ireland:
Broadcasting House, 25-27 Ormeau Avenue, Belfast BT2 8HQ. 0232 244400.

THE British Broadcasting Corporation, established as a public corporation by Royal Charter in 1927, transmits broadcasting services in sound and two of the television broadcasting services in the United Kingdom.

The BBC derives its legal powers to maintain broadcasting stations from a Licence and Agreement with the Home Secretary, who has power to control wireless transmissions under the Wireless Telegraphy Act, 1949, and earlier Acts of Parliament.

It has from the first been the settled policy of Parliament that the BBC should be free from control in the conduct of its business. The Home Secretary is answerable to Parliament on broad questions of policy. Parliament retains ultimate control but the Corporation enjoys complete independence in practice in the planning of its programmes and the matter which they contain. In its day-to-day management, the Corporation is entirely independent of the Government and Parliament.

The domestic services of the BBC are financed from (1) the revenue from the issue, by the Post Office, of broadcast receiving licences and (2), income from the sale of BBC publications including The Radio Times, and from trading activities of BBC Enterprises. The BBC's World Service is financed by an annual Grant-in-Aid from the Treasury.

For 1988-89 the deduction from licence receipts to meet the cost of collecting fees, anti-evasion measures, and dealing with complaints of electrical and other interferences, etc. was £71.3 million.

The Corporation received an income of £1,081.1 million (net) from licence receipts in 1988-89. Trading and other income (less tax) i.e. Publications, Enterprises etc. was £40.5 million and Grant-in-Aid receipts were £120.2 million.

LICENCES
Owners of receiving sets must obtain licences from the Post Office. Annual television fees are: Monochrome £24; Colour £71.00. The radio-only licence fee was abolished from February 1, 1971.

The number of current receiving licences in the United Kingdom at March 1990 was: Monochrome television 1,680,618; Colour television, 17,882,122; total 19,588,885.

RADIO
This comprises five complementary national BBC services:

Radio 1 (the pop network), Radio 2 (light music), Radio 3 (serious music and programmes reflecting the arts, including poetry and drama), Radio 4 (speech programmes, including news, drama, documentaries and features) and Radio 5 (youth, education, sport and World Service); National Regional services in Scotland, Wales and Northern Ireland and local radio.

Radio 1: Transmits every day from 5 a.m. to 2 a.m. (97-99MHz)

Radio 2: Transmits 24 hours a day. (88-90MHz)

Radio 3: Transmits every day 6.55 a.m. to 12.05 a.m. (90.2-92.4MHz) are widely available throughout United Kingdom.

Radio 4: Transmits every day 6.00 a.m. to 12.30 a.m. (92.4-94.6MHz) and 198 LW is widely available in England, and good population cover age is also provided in Scotland (92.5-95.8MHz) and Wales (94.3-104MHz), less so in Northern Ireland ((3.2-94.9MHz).

Radio 5: Transmits every day 6.00 a.m. to 12.00 a.m. (693 and 909 MW)

FM National Regional Services
Radio Scotland 92.5-99.3 MHz; Radio Ulster 93.0-95.4MHz; Radio Cymru (Welsh Language) 92.5-96.8MHz.

AM National Services
Radio Scotland 810 KHz; Radio Ulster 1341KHz; Radio Wales 882KHz.

Local Broadcasting: Thirty-eight stations will be operational: see next page. (The two that are not yet operational are Suffolk and Surrey & Berks.)

TELEVISION
The BBC started the world's first regular high-definition television service (240 and 450 lines) from Alexandra Palace, North London, on November 2nd 1936. It had been involved in experimental low-definition broadcasting (30 lines) since 1929. Apart from a war time close-down between 1939 and 1946, BBC Television has operated almost continuously since 1936.

Today, there are two nationally-networked channels, BBC-1 and BBC-2 (which started in 1964) providing colour programmes on 625 lines definition. They are broadcast from a nationwide chain of nearly 1,000 transmitting stations jointly built and operated by the BBC and the Independent Broadcasting Authority. More than 99 per cent of the population can receive their transmissions.

On average, one person in nine watches some of the 220 hours-plus of programmes, which are broadcast each week in total on BBC-1 and BBC-1, covering entertainment, news and a wide range of other interests.

In addition to networked broadcasts, programmes are also made for audiences in specific parts of Great Britain: Scotland, Wales and Northern Ireland and in England, Midlands, North East, North West, South and East, South and West.

WORLD SERVICE
The World Service broadcast over 780 hours of programmes a week in 38 languages, including English. 97 transmitters are used, 38 of them in the U.K. and 48 at relay stations overseas. In addition, through their Transcription and Topical Tapes Services, World Service supply recorded programmes in English and other languages to radio stations throughout the world. The Monitoring Service at Caversham Park, near Reading, makes available in a number of publications summaries of the output of foreign radio stations, on a subscription basis.

8

The main output services are:

World Service, which is on the air in English for 24 hours a day, directed to all parts of the world, and with additional streams of programmes specially designated for audiences in Africa, South Asia and the Caribbean at appropriate peak listening times.

African Service, which broadcasts in Swahili, Somali and Hausa.

Arabic Service, on the air for nine hours a day to the Middle East and North Africa.

Eastern Service, which broadcasts in Bengali, Burmese, Hindi, Sinhala, Nepali, Pashto, Persian, Tamil and Urdu.

Far Eastern Service, in Chinese (Cantonese and Standard Chinese), Indonesian, Japanese, Malay, Thai and Vietnamese.

Latin American Service, in Spanish and Portuguese.

German Service, directed to West and East Germany, Austria and Switzerland.

Russian Service, broadcasting 7.5 hours a day to the U.S.S.R.

Central European Service, in Polish, Hungarian, Czech, Slovak and Finnish.

South East European Service, in Bulgarian, Romanian, Serbo-Croat, Slovene, Greek and Turkish.

French and Portuguese Service, in French to Metropolitan France, Belgium, Switzerland, the Maghreb and Francophone Africa and in Portuguese to Europe and Africa.

BBC English is the largest English-teaching laboratory in the world.

BOARD OF GOVERNORS
Marmaduke Hussey (*Chairman*), Lord Barnett (*Vice Chairman*), Sir Graham Hills (*National Governor for Scotland*), John Parry (*National Governor for Wales*), Dr. James Kincade (*National Governor for Northern Ireland*), , Sir Curtis Keeble, Dr. John Roberts, Miss P.D. James, Mr. Keith Oates, Mr. Bill Jordan, Miss Jane Glover, and Mrs Shawar Sadeque.

BOARD OF MANAGEMENT
Michael Checkland (*Director-General*); John Birt (*Deputy Director-General*); John Tusa (*Managing Director, World Service*); Ron Neil (*Managing Director, Regional Broadcasting*), David Hatch (*Managing Director, Network Radio*); Paul Fox (*Managing Director, Network Television*); Roger Chase (*Director of Personnel*); Ian Phillips (*Director, Finance*); Bill Dannay (*Director of Engineering*); Howell James (*Director of Corporate Affairs*).

BBC LOCAL RADIO STATIONS

MIDLANDS REGION:
Head of Local Radio (Midlands): Owen Bentley.
Broadcasting Centre, Pebble Mill, Birmingham, B5 7SA.

CWR: Coventry Warwickshire Radio, 25 Warwick Road, Coventry CV1 2WR. 0203 525341 VHF: 94.8/103.7
DERBY: Radio Derby, 56 St. Helen's Street, Derby DE1 3HY. Derby 361111. VHF: 94.2/104.5/95.3 MHz; MF: 1116 KHz (269 m)
HEREFORD & WORCESTER: Hereford and Worcester Radio, Hylton Road, Worcester WR2 5WW. Hereford 355252; Worcester 748485. Hereford FM: 94.7 stereo; MW 819KHz/366m; Worcester FM: 104.0 stereo; MW 738KHz/406m.
LEICESTER: Radio Leicester, Epic House, Charles Street, Leicester LE1 3SH. Leicester 516688. VHF: 95.1 MHz; MF: 837 KHz (358 m)
LINCOLNSHIRE: Radio Lincolnshire, Radio Buildings, Newport, Lincoln LN1 3XY. Lincoln 511411. VHF: 94.9 MHz; MF: 1368 KHz (219 m)
NOTTINGHAM: Radio Nottingham, York House, Mansfield Road, Nottingham NG1 3JB. Nottingham 415161. VHF: 95.5/103.8 MHz; MF: 1521/1584 KHz (197/189 m)
SHROPSHIRE: Radio Shropshire, Boscobell Drive, Heath Farm, Shrewsbury, Shropshire. Shrewsbury 248484. VHF: 95.0/96.0 MHz; MF: 756/1584 KHz (397/189m)
STOKE ON TRENT: Radio Stoke on Trent, Conway House, Cheapside, Hanley, Stoke-on-Trent ST1 1JJ. Stoke-on-Trent 208080. VHF: 94 MHz; MF: 1503 KHz (200 m)
WEST MIDLANDS: Radio W.M., Pebble Mill Road, Birmingham B5 7SD. 021-414 8484. VHF: 95 MHz; MF: 1458 KHz (206 m); 828 KHz (362 m)

NORTH EAST REGION:
Head of Radio Development (North East): David Challis.
Broadcasting Centre, Woodhouse Lane, Leeds, LS2 9PX.

CLEVELAND: Radio Cleveland, P.O. Box 1548, Broadcasting House, Newport Road, Middlesbrough TS1 5DG. Middlesbrough 225211. VHF: 95.0/95.8 MHz; MF: 1548 KHz (194 m)
HUMBERSIDE: Radio Humberside, 63 Jameson Street, Hull HU1 3NU. Hull 23232. VHF: 95.9 MHz; MF: 1485 KHz (202 m)
LEEDS: Radio Leeds, Broadcasting House, Woodhouse Lane, Leeds LS2 9PN. Leeds 442131. VHF: 95.4/95.3 MHz; MF: 774 KHz (388 m)
NEWCASTLE: Radio Newcastle, Crestina House, Archbold Terrace, Newcastle upon Tyne 2 1DZ. Tyneside 2324141. VHF: 95.4/96.0/104.4 MHz; MF: 1458 KHz (206 m)

SHEFFIELD: Radio Sheffield, Ashdell Grove, 60 Westbourne Road, Sheffield S10 2QU. Sheffield 686185. VHF: 88.6/104.1 MHz; MF: 1035 KHz (290 m)
YORK: Radio York, 20 Bootham Row, York YO3 7BR. York 641351. VHF: 95.5/103.7/104.3 MHz; MF: 1260/666 KHz (238/450 m)

NORTH WEST REGION:
Head of Local Radio (North West): Donald Kerr.
New Broadcasting House, Oxford Road, Manchester, M60 1SJ.

CUMBRIA: Radio Cumbria, Hilltop Heights, London Road, Carlisle, Cumbria CA1 2NA. Carlisle 31661. VHF: 95.2/95.96.1/104.2/96.1 MHz; MF: 756 KHz (397 m). 1456 KHz (206 m); 837 KHz (358m).
LANCASHIRE: Radio Lancashire, Darwen Street, Blackburn BB2 2EA. Black burn 62411. VHF: 95.5/103.9/104.5 MHz; MF: 855/1557 KHz (351/193 m)
MANCHESTER: Radio Manchester, New Broadcasting House, Oxford Road, Manchester M60 1SJ. 061-228 3434. VHF: 95.1 MHz. MF: 1458 KHz (206 m)
MERSEYSIDE: Radio Merseyside, 55 Paradise Street, Liverpool L1 3BP. 051-708 5500. VHF: 95.8 MHz; MF: 1485 KHz (202 m)

SOUTH AND EAST REGION:
Head of Local Radio (South and East): Arnold Miller. BBC Elstree Centre, Clarendon Road, Borehamwood, Herts, WD6 1JF.

BEDFORDSHIRE: Radio Bedfordshire, P.O. Box 476, Hastings Street, Luton. Luton 45911. VHF: 95.8/103.8 MHz; MF: 630/1161 KHz.
CAMBRIDGESHIRE: Radio Cambridgeshire, Broadcasting House, 104 Hills Road, Cambridge CB2 1LD. Cambridge 315970. VHF: 95.7/96.0 MHz; MF: 1449 KHz (292/207 m); MF: 1026KHz/292m.
ESSEX: BBC Essex, 198 New London Road, Chelmsford, Essex CM2 9AB. Chelmsford 262393. VHF: 95.3/ 103.5 MHz; MF: 1530/765/729 KHz (196/392/412m).
KENT: Radio Kent, Sun Pier, Chatham, Kent ME4 4EZ. Medway 830505. VHF: 96.7/104.2 MHz; MF: 774/1035 KHz (290/388/187m).
LONDON: Greater London Radio, 35A Marylebone High Street, London W1A 4LG. 01-224 2424. VHF: 94.9 MHz; MF: 1458 KHz (206 m)
NORFOLK: Radio Norfolk, Norfolk Tower, Surrey Street, Norwich NR1 3PA. Norwich 617411. VHF: 95.1/ 104.4 MHz; MF: 855 KHz (351 m), 873 KHz (344 m)

NORTHAMPTON: Radio Northampton, P.O. Box 1107, Abington Street, Northampton NN1 2BE. Northampton 239100. VHF: 103/104.2 MHz; MF: 1107 KHz (271 m)
OXFORD: Radio Oxford, 242 Banbury Road, Summertown, Oxford OX2 7DW. Oxford 311444. VHF: 95.2 MHz; MF: 1485 KHz (202 m)
SUSSEX: Radio Sussex, Marlborough Place, Brighton, BN1 1TU. Brighton 680231. VHF: 95.3/104.0/104.5 MHz; MF: 1485/1161/1368 KHz (202/258/219 m)

SOUTH AND WEST REGION:
Head of Local Radio (South and West): Derek Woodcock. Broadcasting House, Whiteladies Road, Bristol, BS8 2LR.

BRISTOL: Radio Bristol, 3 Tyndalls Park Road, Bristol, BS8 1PP. Bristol 741111. VHF: 94.9/95.5/104.6 MHz; MF: 1548/1323 KHz (194/227 m)
CORNWALL: Radio Cornwall, Phoenix Wharf, Truro, Cornwall TR1 1UA. Truro 75421. VHF: 95.2/96.0/103.9 MHz; MF: 630/657 KHz (467/457 m); Isle of Scilly VHF: 96.0 MHz.
DEVON: Radio Devon, St. David's Hill, Exeter, Devon EX4 4DB. Exeter 215651. VHF: 96.0/94.8/95.8/103.4 MHz; MF: 855/990/1458/801 KHz (351/303/206/375 m)
GLOUCESTER: Radio Gloucestershire, London Road, Gloucester GL1 1SW. Gloucester 308585. Gloucester VHF: 104.7 MHz; Stroud & area VHF: 95.0 MHz; MF 603 KHz.
GUERNSEY: Radio Guernsey, Commerce House, Les Banques, St. Peter Port, Guernsey. Guernsey 28977. VHF: 93.2 MHz; MF: 1116 KHz (269 m)
JERSEY: Radio Jersey, Broadcasting House, Rouge Bouillon, St. Helier, Jersey. Jersey 70000. VHF: 88.8 MHz; MF: 1026 KHz (292 m)
SOLENT: Radio Solent, South Western House, Canute Road, Southampton SO9 4PJ. Southampton 631311. VHF: 96.1 MHz; MF: 999 KHz (300 m); 1359 KHz (221 m)
WILTSHIRE SOUND: Radio Wiltshire, Broadcasting House, Prospect Place; Swindon SW1 3RW. Swindon 513626. North Wiltshire VHF: 103.6 MHz; West Wiltshire VHF: 104.3 MHz; Salisbury VHF: 103.5 MHz.

INDEPENDENT BROADCASTING AUTHORITY (UNTIL 31.12.1990)

INDEPENDENT TELEVISION COMMISSION (FROM 1.1.1991)

Headquarters
70 Brompton Road, London SW3 1EY. 071-584 7011.

Senior Staff:
Lady Little, Director General (IBA)
David Glencross, Chief Executive (ITC)

Scotland:
123 Blythswood Street, Glasgow G2 4AN. 041 226 4436.
Wales and the West of England:
Elgin House, 106 St. Mary Street, Cardiff CF1 1DX. 0222 384541/2/3.
8th Floor, The Colston Centre, Colston Avenue, Bristol BS1 4UB. 0272 213672.
Northern Ireland:
Royston House, 34 Upper Queen Street, Belfast BT1 6HG. 0232 248733.
South of England and Channel Islands:
Castle Chambers, Lansdowne Hill, Southampton SO1 0EQ. 0703 331344; Lyndean House, Albion Place, Maid stone, Kent ME14 5DZ. 0622 61176; Royal London House, 153 Armada Way, Plymouth PL1 1HY. 0752 663031
North-East England, The Borders and Isle of Man:
3 Collingwood Street, Newcastle upon Tyne NE1 1JS. 091 2610148.
East of England:
24 Castle Meadow, Norwich NR1 3DH. 0603 623533.
North-West England:
Television House, Mount Street, Manchester M2 5WT. 061 834 2707.

Yorkshire:
Dudley House, Albion Street, Leeds LS2 8PN. 0532 441091.
Midlands:
Lyndon House, 62 Hagley Road, Birmingham B16 8PE. 021 454 1068.10/11 The Poultry, Nottingham NG1 2HW. 0602 585105.

UNTIL the 31 December 1990, the IBA is responsible to Parliament for Independent Television (ITV, including TV-am and Channel 4) and Independent Local radio. The IBA selects and appoints the ITV and IR programme companies; supervises the programmes provided by the con tractors - and the Channel Four Television Company - and their scheduling; controls advertising and builds, owns and operates the transmitting stations. Fifteen ITV programme companies provide programmes in the 14 Independent Television regions of the UK (two companies operate in London) and TV-am provides a national breakfast-time service.

Some 50 Independent Local Radio stations can now be heard by around 90% of the population in the UK. By the summer of 1990, 24 new radio stations should be on the air. Known as 'incrementals', because they are based in areas already covered by ILR, they will provide programming directed towards 'communities of interest' including ethnic groups, specialist music tastes and small geographic areas.

Both ITV and IR are financed mainly by the sale of advertising time and receive no part of the licence fee. In spring 1990, British Satellite Broadcasting (BSB) launched new programme services on five channels broadcast directly from satellite (DBS) into homes all over the UK. These will be funded by a combination of advertising and subscription.
During 1990, Parliament considered new legislation concerning the future structure and regulation of broadcasting, particularly commercially-funded television and radio. The Broadcasting Bill was published on 7 December 1989.

The new Independent Television Commission (ITC) and Radio Authority will succeed the IBA on 1 January 1991, and its transmission operation will be privatised. The ITC will licence and regulate all UK non-BBC TV services, including those delivered by cable and UK-linked satellite. The Radio Authority will assign frequencies, issue licences and regulate all independent radio stations.

MEMBERS OF THE INDEPENDENT BROADCASTING AUTHORITY 1990

George Russell, C.B.E. Chairman
The Rt. Hon The Lord Chalfont, O.B.E., M.C. Deputy Chairman
Professor J.F. Fulton
R.A. Grantham
Mrs P. Mathias
Lady Margaret Popplewell
P. Sheth

MEMBERS OF THE SHADOW INDEPENDENT TELEVISION COMMISSION

Professor James Ring
Professor J.F. Fulton
Lady Margaret Popplewell

TELEVISION PROGRAMME CONTRACTORS

ANGLIA TELEVISION LIMITED
Anglia House, Norwich NR1 3JG Telephone: 0603 615151 48 Leicester Square, London WC2H 7FB Telephone: 071-321 0101.
Provides programmes for the East of England during the whole week.

BORDER TELEVISION LIMITED
The Television Centre, Carlisle CA1 3NT Telephone: 0228 25101 18 Clerkenwell Close, London EC1R 0AA Telephone: 071-253 3737.
Provides programmes for the Borders during the whole week.

CENTRAL INDEPENDENT TELEVISION PLC
Central House, Broad Street, Bermingham B1 2JP
Telephone: 021-643 9898 East Midlands TV Centre,
Not tingham, NG7 2NA Telephone: 0602 863322 35-38
Portman Square, London W1A 2HZ
Telephone: 01-486 6688.
Provides programmes for the East and West Midlands during
the whole week.

CHANNEL TELEVISION
The Television Centre, St. Helier, Jersey Telephone:
0534 73999 The Television Centre, St. George's Place,
St. Peter Port, Guernsey Telephone: Guernsey 23451.
Provides programmes for the Channel Islands during the
whole week.

GRAMPIAN TELEVISION PLC
Queen's Cross, Aberdeen AB9 2XJ Telephone: 0224
646464 29 Glasshouse Street, London W1R 5RG
Telephone: 071 439 3141.
Provides programmes for North Scotland during the whole
week.

GRANADA TELEVISION LIMITED
Granada TV Centre, Manchester M60 9EA Telephone:
061-832 7211 36 Golden Square, London W1R 4AH
Telephone: 071-734 8080.
Provides programmes for North-West England during the
whole week.

HTV LIMITED
HTV Wales, The Television Centre, Culverhouse Cross,
Cardiff CF5 6XJ Telephone: 0222 590590 HTV West,
The Television Centre, Bath Road, Bristol BS4 3HG
Telephone: 0272 778366 99 Baker Street, London W1M
2AJ Telephone: 071-486 4311.
Provides programmes for Wales and West of England during
the whole week.

LONDON WEEKEND TELEVISION LIMITED
South Bank Television Centre, London SE1 9LT
Telephone: 071-620 1620 Regional Sales Office, 6th
Floor, Adamson House, Shambles Square, Manchester
M3 1RE Telephone: 061-834 6718.
Provides programmes in the London area from 5.15 p.m.
Friday till Sunday close down.

SCOTTISH TELEVISION PLC
Cowcaddens, Glasgow G2 3PR Telephone: 041-332
9999 114 St. Martins Lane, London WC2N 4AZ
Tel:071-836 1500 The Gateway, Edinburgh EH7 4AH
Telephone: 031-557 4554.
Provides programmes for Central Scotland during the whole
week.

TELEVISION SOUTH PLC
Television Centre, Southampton SO9 5HZ Telephone:
0703 34211 Television Centre, Vinters Park, Maidstone
ME14 5NZ Telephone: 0622 54945 Spencer House, 60
Buckingham Place, London SW1E 6AJ Telephone: 071-
828 9898.
Provides programmes for South and South-East England
during the whole week.

TELEVISION SOUTH WEST LIMITED
Derry's Cross, Plymouth PL1 2SP Telephone: 0752
663322 Bowater House, Knightsbride, London SW1X
7NN Telephone: 071-589 9755. Provides programmes for
South-West England during the whole week.

THAMES TELEVISION LIMITED
Thames Television House, 306 316 Euston Road,
London NW1 3BB Telephone: 071-387 9494
International House, 149 Tottenham Court Road,
London W1P 9LL Telephone: 071 387 9494 Teddington
Studios, Teddington, Middlesex TW11 9NT Telephone:
081-977 3252.
Provides programmes for London from Monday to 5.15 p.m.
Friday.

TYNE TEES TELEVISION LIMITED The Television
Centre, City Road, Newcastle upon Tyne NE1 2AL
Telephone: 0912 610181 15 Bloomsbury Square,
London WC1A 2LJ
Telephone: 071-405 5474.
Provides programmes for North-East England during the
whole week.

ULSTER TELEVISION LIMITED
Havelock House, Ormeau Road, Belfast BT7 1EB
Tel: 0232 328133 6 York Street, London W1H 1FA
Telephone: 071-486 5211.
Provides programmes for Northern Ireland during the whole
week.

YORKSHIRE TELEVISION LIMITED
The Television Centre, Leeds LS3 1JS Telephone: 0532
438283 Television House, 32 Bedford Row, London
WC1R 4HE Telephone: 071-242 1666.
Provides programmes for Yorkshire during the whole week.

BREAKFAST-TIME TELEVISION
TV-am, Breakfast Television Centre, Hawley Crescent,
London NW1 8EF Telephone: 071-267 4300.
National breakfast-time service.

CHANNEL FOUR TELEVISION COMPANY LTD
60 Charlotte Street, London W1P 2AX Telephone: 071-
631 4444
A subsidiary company of the IBA.
Provides a programme service throughout the UK (except
Wales).

INDEPENDENT TELEVISION ASSOCIATION
Knighton House, 56 Mortimer Street, London W1N
8AN Telephone: 071-636 6866.
Acts on behalf of all the Programme Companies on certain
matters of common interest.

INDEPENDENT TELEVISION NEWS LIMITED
ITN House, 48 Wells Street, London W1P 4DE
Telephone: 071-637 2424.
Provides the national and international news programmes for
all ITV areas.

SC4 THE WELSH FOURTH CHANNEL AUTHORITY

Headquarters: Clos Sophia, Caerdydd, CF1 9XY. (0222)
343412.

Chairman: John Howard Davies, C.B.E., D.L.

Members: Eleri Wynne Jones; John Parry, C.B.E.; Tom
Jones; 1 vacancy.

The Welsh Fourth Channel Authority was established under
the Broad casting Act 1980 and is answerable to Parliament
through the Home Secretary. The programme service, S4C,
started broadcasting on November 1, 1982.

The function of the Authority is to provide on S4C Welsh
language television programmes of high quality for
broadcasting during peak times through the IBA's transmitter
network on the fourth channel in Wales. The programmes are
commissioned from HTV and independent producers, about
15 hours in total. In addition, the BBC provides about 10
hours per week which is funded out of the licence fee. S4C
also reschedules most of Channel 4's programmes around the
block of Welsh programmes.

S4C is funded in the same way as Channel 4, through a levy
on the advertising revenue of the IBA companies, which is
split 20-80% between S4C and C4. Advertising on S4C is the
responsibility of HTV Wales.

The funding provisions and some regulations relating to the
management of S4C will be changed following the publication
of the new Broadcasting Act in 1990.

S4C's Chief Executive is Geraint Stanley Jones.

SATELLITE BROADCASTING

Television signals normally come from a tall transmitter tower and are picked up by an aerial made of metal rods, pointed roughly in the direction of the transmitter. The signals cannot go over the horizon, so reception distance is limited to a few tens of miles.

For many years broadcasting stations have been exchanging programmes over long distances by beaming high frequency signals into space to satellites. These work like very, very tall towers and transmit the signals back to earth over a wide area. Now the same system has been adapted for home use.

In 1987, Luxembourg, a country which has always been a pioneer in broadcasting, put up a satellite called Astra which can transmit sixteen tv channels down to earth across Europe. A dish aerial on the roof or in the garden, pointed very accurately at the satellite and without any obstruction - even leaves on a tree, is required to receive these signals. Also needed is a "receiver" which sits on top of a television set, to convert the satellite signals into a form which conventional television sets can handle.

The set-top satellite receiver also tunes between the different channels on offer. These include four programmes from the Sky service, owned by Rupert Murdoch, in addition to a Childrens' Channel and a Lifestyle programme aimed at housewives and an all-sport channel provided by W.H. Smith. There are also several foreign language channels scheduled for transmission.

The equipment needed to receive satellite signals costs several thou sand pounds to buy and needs professional installation - it is not a D.I.Y. operation. One of the Sky channels broadcasts movies and this will soon be scrambled or "encrypted" so that only viewers who pay a subscription of a few pounds a week for an extra de-scrambler box, will be able to watch. Many people hire a system, for about five pounds a week, with installation, maintenance and subscription fees included.

A British company, British Satellite Broadcasting, has a government franchise to provide a similar five channel service from a different satellite and programmes began in 1990. Because BSB uses a different satellite and different television system, even people with Astra dishes already installed need to buy and install a completely new aerial and set-top receiver if they wish to watch BSB's programmes.

Both Sky on Astra and BSB are advertising heavily to win as many viewers as possible - the battle between satellite broadcasters could be compared to the past battle between the VHS and Beta home video systems.

INDEPENDENT LOCAL RADIO STATIONS

ABERDEEN: NorthSound, 45 Kings Gate, Aberdeen AB2 6BL. 0224 632234.VHF: 96.9 MHz; MF: 1035 kHz (290 m).
AYR: West Sound, Radio House, 54 Holmston Road, Ayr KA7 3BD. 0292 283662 Ayr: VHF: 96.7 MHz; MF: 1035 kHz (290 m).Girvan: VHF: 97.5 MHz.
BELFAST: Downtown Radio, P.O. Box 96, Newtownards, Co. Down, Northern Ireland BT23 4ES. 0247 815555. VHF: 97.4 MHz; MF: 1026 kHz (293 m).
BIRMINGHAM: BRMB Radio, P.O. Box 555, Radio House, Aston Road North, Aston, Birmingham B6 4BX. 021-359 4481/9 VHF: 96.1 MHz; MF: 1152 kHz (261 m).
BORDERS: Radio Borders Ltd., Tweeside Park, Tweedbank, Melrose TD1 3RS. 0896 59444
Peebles: 103.1
Byemouth: 103.4
Selkirk: 96.8
Berwick: 97.5
BOURNEMOUTH: Two Counties Radio, 5 Southcote Road, Bournemouth BH1 3LR. 0202 294881. VHF: 97.2 MHz; MF: 828 kHz (362 m).
BRADFORD: Pennine FM, P.O. Box 235, Pennine House, Forster Square, Bradford BD1 5NP. 0274 90417.
Bradford: VHF: 97.5 MHz; MF: 1278 kHz (235 m).
Huddersfield & Halifax: VHF: 102.5 MHz; MF: 1530 kHz (196 m).

BRIGHTON: Southern Sound, Radio House, Franklin Road, Portslade BN4 2SS. 0273 422288.
Hastings: VHF: 97.5; MF: 103.5/227m;
Newhaven: VHF: 96.9 MHz;
Eastbourne: VHF: 102.4
BRISTOL: G.W.R., P.O. Box 2000, Watershed, Canons Road, Bristol BS99 7SN. 0272 279900. VHF: 96.3 MHz; MF: 1260 kHz (238 m).
BURY ST. EDMUNDS: Saxon Radio Limited in association with Radio Orwell Limited, Long Brackland, Bury St. Edmunds, Suffolk IP33 1JY. 0284 701511. VHF: 96.4 MHz; MF: 1251 kHz (240 m)
CAMBRIDGE & NEWMARKET CN.FM 103: P.O. Box 1,000, Vision Park, Chivers Way, Hinton, Camb. CB4 4WW. 0223 235255 VHF/FM: 103 MHz.
CARDIFF: Red Dragon Radio, Radio House, West Canal Wharf, Cardiff C 5JX. 0222 384041. VHF: 103.2 MHz; MF: 1359 kHz (221 m).
COVENTRY: Mercia Sound, Hertford Place, Coventry CV1 3TT. 0203 28451. VHF: 97.0 MHz; MF: 1359 kHz (220 m).
DONCASTER: Radio Hallam Ltd (Sheffield). VHF 103.4; MF 990 khz (302m)
DUMFRIES SOUTH WEST SOUND: (West Sound - Ayr address) VHF 97.2
DUNDEE/PERTH: Radio Tay, P.O. Box 123, Dundee DD1 9UF. 0382 29551.
Dundee: VHF: 95.8 MHz; MF: 1161 kHz (258 m).
Perth: VHF: 96.4 MHz; MF: 1584 kHz (189 m).
EAST KENT: Invicta Radio, 15 Station Road East, Canterbury CT1 2AB. 0227 67661.
Dover: VHF: 97.0 MHz; MF: 603 kHz (497 m).
Thanet: VHF: 95.9 MHz.
Canterbury: VHF: 102.8 MHz.
Ashford: VHF: 96.1 MHz.
EASTBOURNE/HASTINGS: Southern Sound, Radio House, P.O. Box 2000, Eastbourne BN21 4UH. 0323 43011
Eastbourne: VHF 102.4 Mhz
Hastings: VHF 97.5 Mhz
EDINBURGH: Radio Forth, Forth House, Forth Street, Edinburgh EH1 3LF. 031-556 9255. VHF: 97.3 MHz; MF: 1548 kHz (194 m).
EXETER/TORBAY: Devon Air Radio, The Studio Centre, 35/37 St. David's Hill, Exeter EX4 4DA. 0392 30703.
Exeter: VHF: 95.8 MHz; MF: 666 kHz (450 m).
Torbay: VHF: 95.1 MHz; MF: 954 kHz (314 m).
GLASGOW: Radio Clyde, Clydebank Business Park, Clydebank, Glasgow G81 2RX. 041-941 1111. VHF: 95.1 MHz; MF: 1152 kHz (261 m).
GLOUCESTER AND CHELTENHAM: Severn Sound, P.O. Box 388, Old Talbot House, 67 Southgate Street, Gloucester GL1 1TX. 0452 423791. VHF: 102.4 MHz; MF: 774 kHz (388 m).
GREAT YARMOUTH & NORWICH: Radio Broadland, St.George's Plain, Colegate, Norwich NR3 1DD. 0603 630621.VHF: 97 MHz; MF: 1152 kHz (260 m).
GUILDFORD: County Sound, The Friary, Guildford GU1 4YX. 0483 505566. VHF: 96.4 MHz; MF: 1476 kHz (203 m).
HEREFORD/WORCESTER: Radio Wyvern, 5/6 Barbourne Terrace, Worcester WR1 3JM. 0905 612212.
Hereford: VHF: 97 MHz; MF: 954 kHz (314 m).
Worcester: VHF: 102.8 MHz; MF: 1530 kHz (169 m).
HUMBERSIDE: Viking FM, Commercial Road, Hull HU1 2SG. 0482 25141.VHF: 96.9 MHz; MF: 1161 kHz (258m).
INVERNESS: Moray Firth Radio, P.O. Box 271, Inverness IV3 6SF. 0463 224433. VHF:97.4 MHz; MF:1107 kHz (271 m).
IPSWICH: Radio Orwell, Electric House, Lloyds Avenue, Ipswich IP1 3HZ. 0473 216971. VHF: 97.1 MHz; MF: 1170 kHz (257 m).
LEEDS: Radio Aire, P.O. Box 362, 51 Burley Road, Leeds LS3 1LR. 0532452299. VHF:96.9 MHz; MF:828 kHz (362 m).
LEICESTER: Leicester Sound, Granville House, Granville Road, Leicester LE1 7RW. 0533 551616. VHF: 103.2 MHz; MF: 1260 kHz (238 m).
LIVERPOOL: Radio City, P.O. Box 194, 8/10 Stanley Street, Liverpool L69 1LD. 051-227 5100. VHF: 96.7 MHz; MF: 1548 kHz (194 m).
LONDON GENERAL: Capital Radio, Euston Tower, London NW1 3DR. 071-388 1288. VHF: 95.8 MHz; MF: 1548 kHz (194.m).
LONDON NEWS: LBC, Crown House, 72 Hammersmith Road, London W1L 8YE. 071-603 2400.

8

LUTON/BEDFORD: Chiltern Radio, Chiltern Road, Dunstable, Bedfordshire LU6 1HQ. 0582 666001.
Luton: VHF: 97 MHz; MF: 828 kHz (362 m).
Bedford: VHF: 96.9 MHz; MF: 792 kHz (379 m).
MAIDSTONE/MEDWAY: Invicta Radio, 37 Earls Street, Maidstone ME14 1PS. 0622 679001. VHF: 103.1 MHz; MF: 1242 kHz (242 m).
MANCHESTER: Piccadilly Radio, 127 131 The Piazza, Piccadilly Plaza, Manchester M1 4AW. 061-236 9913. VHF: 103.0 MHz; MF: 1152 kHz (261 m).
MILTON KEYNES: Milton Keynes Broadcasting Co., Haome Farm, Old Stratford, Milton Keynes MK19 6AX 0582 666001. Expected on air Oct 1989.
NEWPORT (Gwent): Red Dragon Radio, Radio House, West Canal Wharf, Cardiff CF1 5JX. 02222 384041. VHF: 97.4 MHz; MF: 1305 kHz (230m).
NORTHAMPTON: Northants 96, 73 Abington Street, Northampton NN1 2BH. 0604 29811. VHF: 96 MHz; MF: 1557 kHz (193 m).
NOTTINGHAM: Radio Trent, 29-31 Castle Gate, Nottingham NG1 7AP. 0602 581731. VHF: 96.2 MHz; MF: 999 kHz (301 m).
Derby: VHF: 102.8 MHz; MF: 945 kHz (317 m).
OXFORD/BANBURY FOX FM: Brush House, Pony Road, Cowley OX4 2XR.
Oxford: VHF 102.6 Mhz
Banbury: VHF 97.4 Mhz
PETERBOROUGH: Hereward Radio, P.O. Box 225, 114 Bridge Street, Peterborough, Cambridgeshire PE1 1XJ. 0733 46225. VHF: 102.7 MHz; MF: 1332 kHz (225 m).
PLYMOUTH: Plymouth Sound, Earl's Acre, Alma Road, Plymouth PL3 4HX. 0752 27272, VHF: 96 MHz; MF: 1152 kHz (261 m).
Tavistock: VHF: 96 MHz.
PORTSMOUTH AND SOUTHAMPTON: Ocean Sound, Whittle Avenue, Segensworth West, Fareham, PO15 5PA.
Portsmouth: VHF: 97.5 MHz; MF 1170 MHz (257 m).
Southampton: VHF: 103.2 MHz; MF: 1557 kHz (193m).
Winchester: VHF: 96.7 MHz.
PRESTON AND BLACKPOOL: Red Rose Radio, P.O. Box 301, St. Paul's Square, Preston PR1 1YE. 0772 556301. VHF: 97.3 MHz; MF: 301 m (999 kHz).
READING: Radio 210 Thames Valley, P.O. Box 210, Reading RG3 5RZ. 0734 413131. VHF: 97.0 MHz; MF: 210 m (1431 kHz).
Basingstoke & Andover: VHF: 102.9
REIGATE AND CRAWLEY: Radio Mercury, Broadfield House, Brighton Road, Crawley RH11 9TT. 0293 519161. VHF: 102.7 MHz; MF: 1521 kHz (197m).
Horsham: VHF: 97.5 MHz.
SHEFFIELD AND ROTHERHAM: FM Hallam, P.O. Box 194, Hartshead, Sheffield S1 1GP. 0742 71188. VHF: 97.4 MHz (Sheffield). VHF: 103.4 MHz; MF 990kHz (302m) (Doncaster). VHF: 96.1 MHz (Rotherham). MF: 1548 kHz (194 m).
SOUTHEND/CHELMSFORD: Essex Radio, Radio House, Clifftown Road, Southend-on-Sea, Essex SS1 1SX. 0702 333711.
Southend: VHF: 96.3 MHz; MF: 1431 kHz (210 m).
Chelmsford: VHF: 102 MHz; MF: 1359 kHz (220 m).
STOKE-ON-TRENT: Signal Radio, Studio 257, 67 73 Stoke Road, Stoke-on-Trent, Staffordshire ST4 2SR. 0782 417111. VHF: 102 MHz; MF: 1170 kHz (257 m).
SWANSEA: Swansea Sound, Victoria Road, Gowerton, Swansea SA4 3AB. 0792 893751. VHF: 95.1 MHz; MF: 1170 kHz (257 m).
SWINDON/WEST WILTSHIRE: G.W.R., Lime Kiln Studios, High Street, Wootton Bassett, Swindon, Wiltshire SN4 7EX. Swindon 853222.
Swindon: VHF: 97.2 MHz; MF: 1161 kHz (258 m).
West Wiltshire: VHF 102 MHz; MF: 936 kHz (320 m).
TEESSIDE: T.F.M. Radio, 74 Dovecot Street, Stockton-on-Tees, Cleveland TS18 1HB. Stockton-on-Tees 615111. VHF: 96 MHz; MF: 1170 kHz (257 m).
TYNE/WEAR: Metro FM, Newcastle upon Tyne NE99 1BB. 091-488 3131.
VHF: 97.1 MHz; MF: 1152 kHz (261 m).
WOLVERHAMPTON: Beacon Radio, P.O. Box 303, 267 Tettenhall Road, Wolverhampton WV6 0DQ. 0902 757211.
Wolverhampton & Black Country: VHF: 97.2 MHz; MF: 990 kHz (303 m).
Shrewsbury & Tetford: VHF: 103.1 MHz

WREXHAM AND DEESIDE: Marcher Sound/ Sain-Y-Gororau, The Studios, Mold Road, Gwersyllt, Wrexham, Clwyd LL11 4AF. 0978 752202. VHF: 95.4 MHz; MF: 1260 kHz (238 m).
YEOVIL/TAUNTON ORCHARD FM: Haygrove House, Shoreditch, Taunton, Somerset TA3 7BT. 0823 338448. VHF 102.6

INCREMENTAL RADIO STATIONS

MANCHESTER: Sunset Radio, 23 New Mount Street, Manchester M4 4DE. 061-953 5353. VHF 102.0 Mhz
HOUNSLOW AND EALING: Sunrise Radio, Sunrise House, Crosslances Road, Hounslow, Middx. TW3 2AD. 081-574 6666. MF 1413 kHz (212m)
HARINGEY: London Greek Radio, Florentia Village, Vale Road, London N4 1TD. 081-800 8001; WNK Radio, 185b High Road, Wood Green, London N22 6BA. 081-1547.
BRADFORD: Bradford Radio City, 30 Chapel Street, Bradford BD1 5DN. 0274 735043. VHF 103.2 Mhz.
STOCKPORT: KFM Radio, First Floor, Regent House, Heaton Lane, Stock port, Cheshire SK4 1BX. 061-480 5445. VHF 104.9 Mhz.
GREATER LONDON (community of interest): Jazz FM, 26-27 Castlereagh Street, London W1H 5YR. 071-706 4100. VHF 102.2 Mhz.
THAMESMEAD: RTM (Independent Radio Thamesmead), 17-20 Tavy Bridge, London SE2 9UG. 081-311 3112. VHF 103.8 Mhz.
BRIXTON: Choice FM (South London Radio), 16-18 Trinity Gardens, Bris ton London SW9 8DP. 071-706 1619. VHF 96.9 Mhz.
BELFAST: Belfast Community Radio, Russell Court, Claremont Street, Lisburn Road, Belfast BT9 6JX. 0232 438500. VHF 96.7 Mhz.
KETTERING: KCBC Radio, P.O. Box 1530, Kettering, Northants NN16 8PU. 0536 412413. MF 1530 kHz (196m).
ISLE OF WIGHT: Isle of Wight Radio, Dodnor Park, Newport Isle of Wight PO30 5XE. 0983 822557. MF 1242 kHz (196m).
BRISTOL: FTP (For the People), 2nd Floor, 25 Portland Square, Bristol BS2 8RZ. 0272 243286. VHF 97.2 Mhz.
BIRMINGHAM: Buzz FM, The Spencers, Augusta Street, Birmingham B18 6JA. 021-236 4888. VHF 102.4 Mhz.
HEATHROW AND GATWICK AIRPORTS: Airport Information Radio, Broadfield House, Brighton Road, Crawley, West Sussex RH11 9TT. 0293 519161. MF 1584 kHz (189m).
COVENTRY: Radio Harmony, Ringway House, Hill Street, Coventry CV1 4AN. 0203 525656. VHF 102.6 Mhz.
STIRLING: CentreSound (Stirling Community Radio Association), Stirling Enterprise Park, John Player Building, Kerse Road, Stirling FK7 7RP. 0786 51188. VHF 96.7.
SUNDERLAND: Wear FM (Sunderland Community Radio Association), 53 Frederick Street, Sunderland SR1 1NF. 091-565 1566. VHF 103.4 Mhz.
TENDRING: Tendring Radio (North East Sussex Community Radio), P.O. Box 608, Clacton-on-Sea, Essex CO15 2DF. 0206 221777. MF 1557 kHz (193).
GREATER LONDON (Multi-ethnic): Spectrum Radio, Endeavour House, North Circular Road, Brent Cross, London NW2 1JT. 081-905 5000. MF 558 (538m).
EASTERHOUSE (East Glasgow): East End Radio, The Great Easterhouse Business Centre, Unit 16, Blairtummock Road, Glasgow G33 4AN. 041-774 5335.
WEST LOTHIAN (Bathgate): Radio West Lothian, 6 Mansfield Street, Bathgate, West Lothian EH48 4HU. 0506 630227. MF 1368 kHz (219m).
GREATER LONDON: Kiss Radio, 14 Blackstock Mews, 100 Blackstock Road, London N4 2DR. 071-359 2969 & 071-487 4284. VHF 100.0 Mhz.
GREATER LONDON: Melody Radio, 180 Brompton Road SW3 1HF. 071-584 1049. VHF 104.9 Mhz.

IRN INDEPENDENT RADIO NEWS

A subsidiary of LBC which acts as a news agency for all other ILR companies by providing spoken and other live material and a teleprinter service. Address as LBC in left-hand column.

ASSOCIATION OF INDEPENDENT RADIO CONTRACTORS

46 Westbourne Grove, London W2 5SH Tel: 071-727 2646.

ENTERTAINMENT AWARDS

BAFTA

The British Academy of Film and Television Awards:

The BAFTA Special Award 1990: Dame Peggy Ashcroft
Academy Fellowship: Paul Fox, C.B.E.
Michael Balcon Award: Lewis Gilbert
Desmond Davis Award: John Lloyd
The Writers Award: Andrew Davies
The Richard Dimbleby Award: Kate Adie
Best Foreign Television Programme: Hotel Terminus
Academy Award: Leslie Halliwell

FILM

Best Film: Steven Haft/Paul Junger Witt/Tony Thomas/Peter Weir; *Dead Poets' Society:*
Best Original Screenplay: Nora Ephron; *When Harry Met Sally:*
Best Adapted Screenplay: Christopher Hampton; *Dangerous Liaisons:*
Best Actress: Pauline Collins; *Shirley Valentine:*
Best Actor: Daniel Day Lewis; *My Left Foot:*
Best Supporting Actress: Michelle Pfeiffer; *Dangerous Liaisons:*
Best Supporting Actor: Ray McAnally; *My Left Foot*
Best Director: Kenneth Branagh; *Henry V*
Best Film Score: Maurice Jarre; *Dead Poets' Society*
Best Foreign Language Film: Rene Cleitman/Bertrand Tavernier; *Life And Nothing But*
Best Short Film: Peter Hewitt/David Freeman/Damian Jones; *The Candy Show*

TV PRODUCTION AND PERFORMANCE AWARDS

Best Single Drama: Geoffrey Case/Paul Kinight/Les Blair; *The Account ant*
Best Drama Series/Serial: Somin Moore/Brian Eastman/Alastair Reed; *Traffik*
Best Factual Series: Edward Mirzoeff; *Forty Minutes (Series 1)*
Best Light Entertainment Programme: Elaine Bedell/Richard Drewitt; *Clive James On The 80s*
Best Comedy Series: John Lloyd/Richard Boden/Ben Elton/Richard Curtis; *Blackadder Goes Forth*
Best News or Outside Broadcast Coverage: Steve Selman; *Tiananmen Square Massacre (BBC News)*
Best Children's Programme - Factual: Paul Appleby; *The Really Wild Show*
Best Children's Programme - Entertainment/Drama: Richard Callan/David Bell; *Maid Marion And Her Merry Men*
Best Actress: Diana Rigg; *Mother Love*
Best Actor: John Thaw; *Inspector Morse*
Best Light Entertainment Performance: Rowan Atkinson; *Blackadder Goes Forth*
Best Original T.V. Music: Christopher Gunning; *Agatha Christie's Poirot*
Huw Weldon Award: Peter Adam; *Art In The Third Reich (Omnibus)*
Flaherty Documentary Award: Kevin Sim; *Four Hours In My Lai (First Tuesday)*

CANNES FILM FESTIVAL

Major Awards of the Cannes Film Festival in May 1990.

Palme d'or (Best Film): *Wild at Heart* (USA), directed by David Lynch
Special Jury Prize: shared by *Sting of Death* (Japan), directed by Kohei Oguri and *Tilai* (Burkino Faso), directed by Idrissa Ouedraogo
Best Director: Pavel Lungin, for Taxi Blues (USSR)
Best Actor: Gerard Depardieu, for *Cyrano de Bergerac* (France), direct ed by Jean-Paul Rappeneau
Best Actress: Krystana Janda, for *Interrogation* (Poland, 1982), directed by Richard Bugajksi

IVOR NOVELLO MUSIC AWARDS

Britain's Songwriter of the Year: Mike Stock, Matt Aitkin, Pete Water man
Outstanding Contribution to British Music: David Bowie

Outstanding Service to British Music: The Kinks
Best Film Song or Theme: *Henry V - Non Nobis Domine*, written by Patrick Doyle
Best Song Musically & Lyrically: *The Living Years*, written by B.A. Robertson
Best Contemporary Song: *All Around the World*, written by Lisa Stansfield
Best Theme from a TV/Radio Production: *Ruth Rendell Mysteries*, written by Brian Bennett
Best Theme from a TV/Radio Commercial: *Abbey Endings*, written by Lionel Bart
Best Selling 'A' Side: *Too Many Broken Hearts*, written by Mike Stock, Matt Aitkin, Pete Waterman
Most Performed Work: *This Time I Know it's for Real*, written by Mike Stock, Matt Aitkin, Pete Waterman, Donna Summer
International Hit of the Year: *She Drives Me Crazy*, written by David Steele, Roland Gift
Best British Musical: *Aspects of Love*; written by Andrew Lloyd Webber, Charles Hart, Don Black
The Jimmy Kennedy Award: Mike Stock, Matt Aitkin, Pete Waterman

LAURENCE OLIVIER AWARDS
(The Society of West End Theatre)

Best Play: *Racing Demon*, David Hare
Best Comedy: *Single Spies*, Alan Bennett
Best Musical: *Return to the Forbidden Planet*, Bob Carlton
Best Actor in a New Play: Oliver Ford Davies, *Racing Demons*
Best Actress in a New Play: Fiona Shaw, Electra; *As You Like It; The Good Person of Sichuan*
Best Comedy Performance: Michael Gambon, *Man of the Moment*
Outstanding Actor Performance (Musical): Jonathan Pryce, *Miss Saigon*
Outstanding Actress Performance (Musical): Lea Salonga, *Miss Saigon*
Outstanding Performance in a Supporting Role: Michael Bryant, *Hamlet; The Voysey Inheritance; Racing Demon*
Outstanding Newcomer: Jeremy Northam, *The Voysey Inheritance*
The Most Outstanding Achievement in Opera: The Komische Opera's production of 'Orpheus and Eurydice'
The Most Outstanding Achievement in Dance: London Contemporary Dance Theatre for their production of Kim Brandstrup's 'Orfeo'
Best Director: Michael Bogdanov, Wars of the Roses
Best Designer: Bob Crowley, Ma Rainey's Black Bottom; Hedda Gabler; Ghetto; The Plantagenets
Observer Award (in memory of Kenneth Tynan): Declan Donnellan for his production of 'Fuente Ovejuna'

RADIO & TELEVISION INDUSTRIES
CLUB AWARDS 1990
BBC Television Personality of the Year: Clive James
BBC Radio Personality of the Year: Sue MacGregor
IBA Personality of the Year: Barry Humphries
BBC Television Programme of the Year: Mother Love
IBA Television Programme of the Year: The Bill
Television Comedy of the Year: A bit of a Do
Television News Presenter of the Year: Kate Adie
Best Science-based Programme of the Year: QED
Sports Presenter of the Year: Jim Rosenthal
Radio Programme of the Year: Start the Week
Best Children's Programme of the Year: Going Live

VARIETY CLUB
Show Business Personality: Lenny Henry
Best Film Actor: Sean Connery
Best Film Actress: Pauline Collins
Best Stage Actor: Jonathan Pryce
Best Stage Actress: Jane Lapotaire
BBC TV Personality: Rowan Atkinson
ITV Personality: Coronation Street
BBC Radio Personality: Simon Mayo & Sybil Ruscoe
Independent Radio Personality: Steve Jones
Recording Artiste of the Year: Lisa Stansfield
Most Promising Artiste: Michael Ball
Special Award: Sir John Gielgud

LITERARY AWARDS

THE BOOKER PRIZE

THE BOOKER PRIZE, for Fiction. It was established in 1968 and is open to authors from the British Commonwealth, Republic of Ireland, Pakistan and South Africa. A British publisher may submit up to three entries for the d15,000 Prize. Sponsored by Booker plc, an international food and agriculture business, and administered by Book Trust. The management committee appoints a panel of judges each year.

Winners

1969 **P. H. Newby** *Something to Answer For* (Faber and Faber).
1970 **Bernice Rubens** *The Elected Member* (Eyre and Methuen).
1971 **V. S. Naipaul** *In a Free State* (Deutsch).
1972 **John Berger** *G* (Weidenfeld and Nicolson).
1973 **J. G. Farrell** *The Siege of Krishnapur* (Weidenfeld and Nicolson).
1974 **Nadine Gordimer** *The Conservationist* (Cape).
1974 **Stanley Middleton** *Holiday* (Hutchinson).
1975 **Ruth Prawer Jhabvala** *Heat and Dust* (John Murray).
1976 **David Storey** *Saville* (Cape).
1977 **Paul Scott** *Staying On* (Heinemann).
1978 **Iris Murdoch** *The Sea, The Sea* (Chatto and Windus).
1979 **Penelope Fitzgerald** *Offshore* (Collins).
1980 **William Golding** *Rites of Passage* (Faber and Faber).
1981 **Salman Rushdie** *Midnight's Children* (Cape).
1982 **Thomas Keneally** *Schindler's Ark* (Hodder and Stoughton).
1983 **J. M. Coetzee** *Life and Times of Michael K* (Secker and Warburg).
1984 **Anita Brookner** *Hotel du Lac* (Jonathan Cape).
1985 **Keri Hulme** *The Bone People* (Hodder and Stoughton).
1986 **Kingsley Amis** *The Old Devils* (Hutchinson).
1987 **Penelope Lively** *Moon Tiger* (Andre Deutsch).
1988 **Peter Carey** *Oscar and Lucinda* (Faber and Faber)
1989 **Kazuo Ishiguro** *The Remains of the Day* (Faber & Faber)

WHITBREAD BOOK OF THE YEAR

WHITBREAD established their Literary Awards for the encouragement and promotion of good English literature in 1971. In 1985 the Awards were reorganised to cover five categories (novel, first novel, children's novel, biography/autobiography and poetry) with a nomination from each for selection as the Whitbread Book of the Year. Publishers may submit entries written by authors who have been resident in the United King dom or the Republic of Ireland for the preceding three years. The author of the book nominated by the judges in each category receives an award of £1.750 and the winner of the Whitbread Book of the Year, an additional £20,250. In 1990 the winners were:

Novel:	*The Chemical Wedding* by Lindsay Clarke (Jonathan Cape)
Biography and Book of the Year:	*Coleridge: early Visions* by Richard Holmes (Hodder & Stoughton)
Children's Novel:	*Why Weeps the Brogan?* by Hugh Scott (Walker Books)
First Novel:	*Gerontius* by James Hamilton Peterson (Macmillian)
Poetry:	*Shibboleth* by Michael Donaghy (Oxford University Press)

THE NCR BOOK AWARD FOR NON-FICTION

A new award with a first prize of £25,000 and three runner-up prizes of £1,500 each.

The winner was:
A Chronicle of the French revolution (Viking) by Simon Schama

Runners-up:
Pity the Nation (Deutsch) by Robert Fisk
The Godwins and the Shelleys (Faber) by William St Clair
C.S. Lewis (Collins) by A.N. Wilson

FILM CERTIFICATES

Issued by the British Board of Film Classification.

U Universal: Suitable for all

PG Parental Guidance: General viewing but some scenes may be unsuitable for young children

12 Minimum Admission Age 12: Suitable for secondary school children

15 Minimum Admission Age 15: Suitable for older teenagers

18 Minimum Admission Age 18: Suitable for adults only

R18 Adult Restricted: Screening restricted to licensed cinema clubs

TOURIST INFORMATION IN BRITAIN

British Tourist Authority: Thames Tower, Black's Road, London W6 9EL.
National Tourist Information Centre : Victoria Station Forecourt, London SW1. 081-846 9000.
Cumbria Tourist Board: Ashleigh, Holly Road, Windermere, Cumbria LA23 2AQ. 09662 4041.
East Anglia Tourist Board: Toppesfield Hall, Hadleigh, Suffolk IP7 7DN. 0473 822922.
East Midlands Tourist Board: Exchequergate, Lincoln, Lincolnshire. 0522 531521.
Heart of England Tourist Board: 2-4 Trinity Street, Worcester, Worcestershire WR1 2PW. 0905 613132.
London Tourist Board: 26 Grosvenor Gardens, London SW1W ODU. 071-730 3450.
North West Tourist Board: The Last Drop Village, Bromley Cross, Bolton, Greater Manchester BL7 9PZ. 0204 591511.
Northumbria Tourist Board: Aykley Heads, Durham DH1 5UX. 091-384 6905.
South East England Tourist Board: 1 Warwick Park, Tunbridge Wells, Kent TN2 5TA. 0892 540766.
Southern Tourist Board: 40 Chamberlayne Road, Eastleigh, Hampshire S05 5JH. 0703 620010.
Thames and Chilterns Tourist Board: The Mount House, Church Green, Witney, Oxfordshire OX8 6AZ. 0993 778800.
West Country Tourist Board: Trinity Court, 37 Southernhay East, Exeter, Devon EX1 1QS. 0392 76351.
Yorkshire and Humberside Tourist Board: 312 Tadcaster Road, York, North Yorkshire Y02 2HP. 0904 707961.

EVENTS AND EXHIBITIONS IN BRITAIN FOR 1991

JANUARY

HOME AND WORLD: JEWISH ARTISTS OF THE TWENTIETH CENTURY
Barbican Art Gallery, Barbican Centre, London EC2
January 11-6

PORTRAITS BY CHRIS GARNHAM
National Portrait Gallery, St. Martin's Place, London WC2
January 1-20

EGON SCHIELE AND HIS CONTEMPORARIES
Royal Academy of Arts, Piccadilly, London W1
January 1 -17 February

THE RAJ - INDIA AND THE BRITISH
National Portrait Gallery, St. Martin's Place, London WC2
January 1-17 March

A ROYAL MISCELLANY EXHIBITION FROM THE ROYAL LIBRARY, WINDSOR CASTLE
Queens Gallery, Buckingham Palace Road, London SW1
January 1-13

200 YEARS OF ASTRONOMY IN NORTHERN IRELAND
Armagh Observatory and other venues, Armagh, County Armagh
January 1 - April

MODEL ENGINEER AND MODELLING EXHIBITION
Alexandra Palace, Wood Green, London N22
January 1-6

HOLIDAY AND TRAVEL FAIR
National Exhibition Centre, Birmingham, West Midlands
January 3-6

MOTOR SPORTS INTERNATIONAL
National Exhibition Centre, Birmingham, West Midlands
January 3-6

LONDON INTERNATIONAL BOAT SHOW
Earls Court Exhibition Centre, Warwick Road, London SW5
January 3-13

INTERNATIONAL AMUSEMENT TRADES EXHIBITION
Olympia, Hammersmith Road, London W4
January 7-10

KNITTING AND NEEDLECRAFT EXHIBITION
Sandown Park Racecourse, High Street, Esher, Surrey
January 17-20

WEST LONDON ANTIQUES FAIR
Kensington Town Hall, Hornton Street, London W8
January 1-20

WORLD OF DRAWINGS AND WATERCOLOURS
Park Lane Hotel, Piccadilly, London W1
January 23-27

ART '91
Business Design Centre, Upper Street, Islington, London N1
January 24-27

CRUFTS DOG SHOW
National exhibition Centre, Birmingham, West Midlands
January 9-12

FOREIGN AND COLONIAL HASTINGS 66TH CHESS CONGRESS
Cinque Ports Hotel, Summerfields and Falaise Hall, Falaise Road, East Sussex
January 1-14

RUGBY UNION: WALES V ENGLAND
Cardiff Arms Park, Cardiff, South Glamorgan
January 9

FEBRUARY

CHINESE NEW YEAR CELEBRATIONS
Chinatown, Gerrard Street and Leicester Square, London W1
February 17

ROAD RACING AND SUPERBIKE SHOW
Alexandra Palace, Wood Green, London N22
February 7-10

INTERNATIONAL SILVER AND JEWELLERY FAIR AND SEMINAR
Park Lane Hotel, Piccadilly, London W1
February 8-11

ULSTER MOTOR SHOW
King's Hall, Belfast, County Antrim
February 11-16

BOAT, CARAVAN AND LEISURE SHOW
National Exhibition Centre, Birmingham, West Midlands
February 16-24

PRACTICAL WOODWORKING EXHIBITION
Wembley Exhibition Hall, Wembley, London
February 21-24

JORVIK VIKING FESTIVAL
Various venues, York, North Yorkshire
February 2-23

RUGBY UNION: SCOTLAND V WALES
Murrayfield, Edinburgh, Lothian
February 2

RUGBY UNION: ENGLAND V SCOTLAND
Rugby Union Football Ground, Twickenham, London
February 16

RUGBY UNION: WALES V IRELAND
Cardiff Arms Park, Cardiff, South Glamorgan
February 16

MARCH

DAILY MAIL IDEAL HOME EXHIBITION
Earls Court Exhibition Centre, Warwick Road, London SW5
March 15-April 7

INTERNATIONAL FESTIVAL OF SCIENCE AND TECHNOLOGY
Various venues, Edinburgh, Lothian
March 18-30

EDINBURGH INTERNATIONAL FOLK FESTIVAL
Various venues, Edinburgh, Lothian
March 22-31

HARROGATE INTERNATIONAL YOUTH MUSIC FESTIVAL
Various venues, Harrogate, North Yorkshire
March 27-April 3

WORLD CLOWN CONVENTION
Bognor Regis, West Sussex
March 12-18

HORSE RACING CHELTENHAM GOLD CUP
Cheltenham Racecourse, Prestbury, Cheltenham, Gloucestershire
March 1-14

RUGBY UNION: ENGLAND V FRANCE
Rugby Football Union Ground, Twickenham, London
March 16

RUGBY UNION: SCOTLAND V IRELAND
Murrayfield, Edinburgh, Lothian
March 16

DEVIZES TO WESTMINSTER INTERNATIONAL CANOE RACE
Starts Wharf Car Park, Wharf Street, Devizes
March 29-April 1

APRIL

BRITISH INTERNATIONAL ANTIQUES FAIR
National Exhibition centre, Birmingham, West Midlands
April 4-10

SYON PARK GARDEN SHOW
Syon Park, Isleworth, London
April 19-21

LONDON INTERNATIONAL STRING QUARTET COMPETITION
Goldsmiths' Hall, Foster Lane, London EC2
April 10-15

SHAKESPEARE THEATRE SEASON
Royal Shakespeare Theatre, Stratford-upon-Avon
April-Jan 1992

HORSE RACING GRAND NATIONAL MEETING
Aintree Racecourse, Aintree, Liverpool, Merseyside
April 4-6

LONDON WORLD CUP MARATHON
London
April 21

8

MAY

GLYNDEBOURNE FESTIVAL OPERA SEASON
Glyndebourne, near Lewes, East Sussex
May-August

PITLOCHRY FESTIVAL THEATRE SEASON
Pitlochry Festival Theatre, Pitlochry, Perthshire
May-October

MAYFEST 1991
Various venues, Festival director, 18 Albion street, Glasgow
G1 1LH
May 5-25

PERTH FESTIVAL OF THE ARTS
Various venues, Perth, Tayside
May 15-26

CATHEDRAL CLASSICS - SUMMER FESTIVAL OF MUSIC IN CATHEDRALS
Various Cathedrals in Great Britain
May 22-July 6

BATH INTERNATIONAL FESTIVAL
Various venues, Bath, Avon
May 24-June 9

GREENWICH FESTIVAL
Various venues, Greenwich, London SE10
May 31- June 16

ENGLISH RIVIERA DANCE FESTIVAL
Various venues, Torquay, Devon
May 25-June 8

CHICHESTER FESTIVAL THEATRE SEASON
Chichester, West Sussex
May-September

CHELSEA FLOWER SHOW
Royal Hospital, Chelsea, London SW3
May 21-24 (Members only on 21 and 22 May)

ROYAL ULSTER AGRICULTURAL SOCIETY 124TH ANNUAL SHOW AND INDUSTRIAL EXHIBITION
The Showgrounds, Balmoral, Belfast, County Antrim
May 21-24

MILDENHALL AIR FETE
RAF Mildenhall, Bury St. Edmunds, Suffolk
May 25-26

ROYAL BATH AND WEST SHOW
The Showground, Shepton Mallet, Somerset
May 29-June 1

HORSE RACING: 1000 GUINEAS STAKES
Newmarket Racecourse, Newmarket, Suffolk
May 2

BADMINTON HORSE TRIALS
Badminton, Avon
May 2-5

HORSE RACING: 2000 GUINEAS STAKES
Newmarket Racecourse, Newmarket, Suffolk
May 4

ROYAL WINDSOR HORSE SHOW
Home Park, Windsor, Berkshire
May 8-12

INTERNATIONAL TT MOTORCYCLE RACES
Isle of Man
May 31-June 7

JUNE

BEATING RETREAT BY THE HOUSEHOLD DIVISION
Horse Guards Parade, Whitehall, London SW1
June 4-6

TROOPING THE COLOUR THE QUEENS OFFICIAL BIRTHDAY PARADE
Horse Guard's Parade, Whitehall, London SW1
June 15

APPLEBY HORSE FAIR
Appleby, Cumbria
June 12

GROSVENOR HOUSE ANTIQUES FAIR
Grosvenor House, Park Lane, London W1
June 13-22

ALDEBURGH FESTIVAL OF MUSIC AND THE ARTS
Aldeburgh, Suffolk
June 7-23

BEVERLEY FOLK FESTIVAL
Various venues, Beverley, Humberside
June 14-16

CHARLECOTE PARK FESTIVAL
Charlecote Park, near Stratford-upon-Avon, Warwickshire
June 21-26

BOURNEMOUTH INTERNATIONAL MUSIC FESTIVAL
Various venues, Bournemouth, Dorset
June 22-July 6

SHREWSBURY INTERNATIONAL MUSIC FESTIVAL
Shrewsbury, Shropshire
June 26-July 3

STAMFORD SHAKESPEARE COMPANY '91 SEASON
Rutland Open Air Theatre, Tolethorpe Hall, Little Casterton, Stamford, Lincolnshire
June-August

BROADSTAIRS DICKENS FESTIVAL
Various venues, Broadstairs, Kent
June 15-22

ROYAL HIGHLAND SHOW
Ingliston, Newbridge, Edinburgh, Lothian
June 20-23

STELLA ARTOIS GRASS COURT TENNIS CHAMPIONSHIPS
The Queen's Club, Palliser Road, London W14
June 10-16

HORSE RACING
THE DERBY June 5
CORONATION CUP June 6
INTERNATIONAL DAY June 7
OAKS STAKES June 8
Epsom Racecourse, Epsom, Surrey

HORSE RACING ROYAL ASCOT
Ascot Racecourse, Ascot, Berkshire
June 19-22

ROYAL INTERNATIONAL HORSE SHOW
National Exhibition Centre, Birmingham, West Midlands
June 13-17

GOLF LYTHAM TROPHY
Royal Lytham and St. Anne's Golf Course, Links Gate, Lytham St. Anne's, Lancashire
June 21-22

LAWN TENNIS CHAMPIONSHIPS
All England Lawn Tennis and Croquet Club, Wimbledon, London SW19
June 24-July 7

MOTORCYCLE RACING: 125CC WORLD CHAMPIONSHIP MOTO CROSS GRAND PRIX
Killinchy, County Down
June 28-29

JULY
WARWICK ARTS FESTIVAL
Warwick, Warwickshire
July 3-14

CHELTENHAM INTERNATIONAL FESTIVAL OF MUSIC
Various venues, Cheltenham, Gloucestershire
July 6-21

CITY OF LONDON FESTIVAL
Various venues, The City, London
July 7-24

LLANGOLLEN INTERNATIONAL MUSICAL EISTEDDFOD
Eisteddfod Field, Llangollen, Clwyd
July 9-14

SOUTHERN CATHEDRALS FESTIVAL
Salisbury Cathedral, Salisbury, Wiltshire
July 11-14

HENRY WOOD PROMENADE CONCERTS 1989
Royal Albert Hall, Kensington Gore, London SW7
July 219-September 14

WELSH PROMS '91
St. David's Hall, The Hayes, Cardiff, South Glamorgan
July 20-27

ROYAL INTERNATIONAL AGRICULTURAL SHOW
National agricultural centre, Stoneleigh, Kenilworth, Warwickshire
July 1-4

CITY OF BELFAST INTERNATIONAL ROSE TRIALS
Sir Thomas and Lady Dixon Park, Upper Malone, Belfast, County Antrim
July 1-September 30

GREAT YORKSHIRE SHOW
Great Yorkshire Showground, Hookstone Oval, Wetherby Road, Harrogate, North Yorkshire
July 9-11

ROYAL TOURNAMENT
Earls Court Exhibition Centre, Warwick Road, London SW5
July 10-27

INTERNATIONAL AIR TATTOO
Royal Air Force Fairford, near Cirencester, Gloucestershire
July 20-21

ROYAL WELSH SHOW
Royal Welsh Showground, Llanelwedd, Builth Wells, Powys
July 22-25

HENLEY ROYAL REGATTA
Henley-on-Thames, Oxfordshire
July 3-7

GOODWOOD INTERNATIONAL DRESSAGE CHAMPIONSHIPS
Goodwood, Chichester, West Sussex
July 5-7

SAILING: CUTTY SARK TALL SHIPS RACE
Starts from Milford Haven, Dyfed
July 11-14

HORSE RACING: ULSTER HARP DERBY
Down Royal, Maze Racecourse, Lisburn, County Antrim
July 13

WORLD STUDENT GAMES
Various venues, Sheffield, South Yorkshire
July 14-25

GOLF OPEN CHAMPIONSHIP
Royal Birkdale Golf Club, Waterloo Road,
Southport, Merseyside
July 18-21

TENNIS: FEDERATION CUP
Nottingham University Park, Nottingham, Nottinghamshire
July 21-28

SAILING: CHAMPAGNE MUMM ADMIRAL'S CUP
The Solent, off the Isle of Wight
July 29-August 16

HORSE RACING: GOODWOOD RACES - GLORIOUS GOODWOOD
Goodwood Racecourse, Chichester, West Sussex
July 30-August 3

AUGUST
BATTLE OF FLOWERS
Jersey, Channel Islands
August 8

OUL'LAMMAS FAIR
Ballycastle, County Antrim
August 26-27

SIDMOUTH INTERNATIONAL FESTIVAL OF FOLK ARTS
Various venues, Sidmouth, Devon
August 2-9

EISTEDDFOD GENEDLAETHOL FRENHINOL CYMRU - ROYAL NATIONAL EISTEDDFOD OF WALES
Mold, Clwyd
August 3-10

ABERDEEN INTERNATIONAL YOUTH FESTIVAL
Various venues, Aberdeen, Grampian
August 7-17

EDINBURGH FESTIVAL FRINGE
Edinburgh, Lothian
August 11-31

EDINBURGH INTERNATIONAL FESTIVAL
Edinburgh, Lothian
August 11-31

PONTARDAWE INTERNATIONAL MUSIC FESTIVAL
Parc Ynsderw, Pontardawe, West Glamorgan
August 81-21

ARUNDEL FESTIVAL
Various venues, Arundel, West Sussex
August 22-September 1

EDINBURGH BOOK FESTIVAL
Charlotte Square Gardens, Edinburgh, Lothian
August 10-27

EDINBURGH MILITARY TATTOO
Edinburgh Castle, Edinburgh, Lothian
August 2-24

SUNDERLAND ILLUMINATIONS
Roker and Seaburn, Sunderland, Tyne and Wear
August 23-November 5

BLACKPOOL ILLUMINATIONS
The Promenade, Blackpool, Lancashire
August 30-October 27

SAILING COWES WEEK
Cowes, Isle of Wight
August 3-11

INTERNATIONAL POWERBOAT SHOW
Mayflower Park, Southampton, Hampshire
August 13-21

8

SEPTEMBER

SOUTHAMPTON INTERNATIONAL BOAT SHOW
Mayflower Park, Southampton, Hampshire
September 13-21

HELITECH '91
Redhill Aerodrome, Redhill, Surrey
September 24-27

SALISBURY FESTIVAL
Various venues, Salisbury, Wiltshire
September 7-21

SWANSEA MUSICAL FESTIVAL
Various venues, Swansea, West Glamorgan
September 30-October 26

JAPAN UK FESTIVAL 1991
Various venues throughout Great Britain
September-December

WORLD PLOUGHING CHAMPIONSHIPS
Limavady, County Londonderry
September 20-21

BURGHLEY HORSE TRIALS
Burghley House, Stamford, Lincolnshire
September 5-8

BRAEMAR ROYAL HIGHLAND GATHERING
Princess Royal and Duke of Fife Memorial Park, Braemar,
Grampian
September 7

GOLF: BRITISH AMATEUR CHAMPIONSHIPS
Ganton and Scarborough North Cliff Golf Clubs, Scarborough,
North Yorkshire
September 10-15

HORSE RACING: ST LEGER FESTIVAL MEETING
Doncaster Racecourse, Leger Way, Doncaster, South Yorkshire
September 11-14

OCTOBER

MOTORFAIR - THE LONDON MOTOR SHOW
Earls Court Exhibition centre, warwick road, London SW5
October 7-27

NORFOLK AND NORWICH FESTIVAL
Various venues, Norwich, Norfolk
October 10-20

CHELTENHAM FESTIVAL OF LITERATURE
Various venues, Cheltenham, Gloucestershire
October 5-20

HORSE OF THE YEAR SHOW
Wembley Arena, Wembley, London
October 7-12

NOVEMBER

LORD MAYOR'S PROCESSION AND SHOW
The City, London
November 9

AUTO TECH 1991
National Exhibition Centre, Birmingham, West Midlands
November 12-15

BELFAST FESTIVAL OF ARTS AT QUEEN'S
In and around Queen's University, Belfast, County Antrim
November 6-23

CAMBRIDGE MOZART FESTIVAL
Various venues, Cambridge, Cambridgeshire
November 10-December 5

RUGBY UNION: WORLD CUP FINAL
Rugby Union Ground, Twickenham, London
November 2

LONDON TO BRIGHTON VETERAN CAR RUN
Hyde Park, London-Brighton, East Sussex
November 3

DECEMBER

**ROYAL SMITHFIELD SHOW AND AGRICULTURAL
MACHINERY EXHIBITION**
Earls Court Exhibition Centre, Warwick Road, London SW5
December 1-5

**OLYMPIA INTERNATIONAL SHOWJUMPING
CHAMPIONSHIPS**
Olympia, Hammersmith Road, London W14
December 12-16

HOUSEHOLDERS' GUIDE

THE LEGAL ASPECT

THE FOLLOWING notes can only provide, in the space available, a bare summary of some of the main general legal principles involved in the matters dealt with. It is hoped that such outlines will be helpful and will enable anyone interested to make more detailed enquiries of a competent authority or solicitor. It is essential to obtain professional legal advice before embarking upon any action. In many cases legal advice is available as part of legal aid, as indicated below.

These legal notes are concerned with the law of England and Wales. They do not cover the law of Scotland which can differ in many respects.

HOUSING

Notice to Quit. Under the Protection from Eviction Act, 1977 and the Notice to Quit (Prescribed Information) Regulations, 1988, no notice by a landlord or tenant to quit any premises let as a dwelling is valid unless it is in writing, containing prescribed information and is given not less than 4 weeks, or more as may be necessary, before the date on which it is to take effect. Even a valid notice to quit is not effective by itself if the tenancy is a protected letting.

Legal Charges. It was formerly regarded as a custom that an incoming tenant paid the legal expenses of his landlord in preparing the agreement as well as his own. By the Costs of Leases Act 1958, this custom was abolished and now unless the parties otherwise agree in writing, there is no obligation for either party to a lease or tenancy agreement to pay any of the other party's legal costs.

Payment of Rent. With regard to the payment of rent, it is a general rule that a debtor must find his creditor and pay him. A landlord is under no obligation to collect the rent. In the case of tenancies protected by the Rent Acts rent can only become due at the beginning of the period to which it relates and if the rental period exceeds six months the rent is not payable earlier than six months before the end of such period.

Rent Books. The Landlord and Tenant Act 1985, obliges all landlords of residential premises where the rent is payable weekly to provide a rent book containing the name and address of the landlord, and certain statutory particulars. Also if the Rent Restrictions Acts apply to the tenancy, or if the tenancy is a furnished one within the limits of the Rent Acts, other statutory particulars must also be given. If the landlord is a company the tenant may require the company to furnish in writing the name and address of each of the directors and the secretary of the company, by serving a notice on the company or the company's agent. Fines are provided for breaches of this Act and the Act has no application to contracts for board and lodging provided that the value of the board to the tenant forms a substantial proportion of the whole rent payable.

Rent Restrictions. The Rent Act 1977 together with the Protection from Eviction Act 1977 consolidated and amended earlier legislation, coming into force on August 29, 1977. It is unlawful to evict any occupier of residential property except by an order of the Court, or to harass the occupier in order to try and force him to leave, and severe penalties, including imprisonment, may be inflicted upon persons who attempt to take the law into their own hands in this way.

The Rent Act 1977 protects, with exceptions, all unfurnished premises let as dwelling houses where the rateable value does not exceed 1,500 in the area covered by the Greater London Council or 750 in other parts of England and Wales.

The main cases where an order for possession can be made are (a) where suitable, alternative accommodation is available, (b) where the tenant is in arrears with his rent or in breach of an obligation of the tenancy, (c) where the tenant, his lodger or a resident is guilty of nuisance or annoyance to adjoining occupiers or of allowing the premises to be used for illegal or immoral purposes, (d) where he has sublet the whole of the premises, (e) where the landlord requires possession for a whole-time employee of his, or (f) where the landlord requires the premises for the occupation of himself or for a son or daughter of his over the age of 18 or for his father or mother or father-in-law or mother-in-law, provided that the landlord has not purchased the premises after March 23, 1965. In certain cases other dates are prescribed. In all the above cases the Court can only make an order if it considers it reasonable to do so and in the case of (f) above no order can be made if greater hardship would be caused by granting the order than by refusing it. The Court must also find it reasonable to make a possession order.

There is, however, a special provision to enable owner-occupiers of property to recover possession with reasonable certainty. A landlord who has let his own house and given written notice normally at the beginning of the letting that he may require possession under that section is entitled as of right to an order for possession on proof that the house is required for occupation by him or by a member of his family who resided with him when he last resided in the house. See Rent (Amendment) Act 1985.

Permitted Rent. The Act provides for the registration of all rents of protected tenancies with local authorities and in each area Rent Officers are appointed to whom applications may be made by either landlords or tenants to determine a fair rent. Your local authority will give you his address. After consulting with both sides the Rent Officer must then register the rent he considers to be a fair one in respect of the premises and if either the landlord or the tenant objects to his decision an appeal lies to a Rent Assessment Committee. When the fair rent has been determined in this way the registered rent will be the rent limit of the premises subject to increases increases permitted for improvements since the registration of the rent, unless and until it is altered as a result of a further application to the Rent Officer which cannot usually be made for two years.

Where the rent is not registered, the rent limit is that recoverable for the last contractual period (S.45(1) of the 1977 Act), subject to adjustments any increase in cost of services and/or furniture to be agreed with the landlord, or by the County Court (sections 46 and 47).

There is no rent limit where a protected regulated tenancy is first granted to an entirely new tenant. This excludes a person who may succeed the previous tenant as a statutory tenant.

9

Where improvements are made with the consent of the tenant the permitted rent may be increased by eight per cent or 12 per cent of the permitted rent according to the rate when they were carried out.

Protected Shorthold Tenancies. The Housing Act 1980, Section 52 introduced a new form of tenancy, granted for a period of between one and five years to a new tenant, who, before the grant, has been notified, in a form specified by Regulations, by the landlord that it is a protected shorthold tenancy. It is also necessary in London shorthold lettings for registration of a fair rent. This will enable the landlord, after a specified notice to the tenant, to recover possession easily at or after the end of the agreed term, provided there has not been a grant of a further tenancy or the tenant has not become a protected or statutory tenant under the main statute. During the term the tenant himself can terminate the letting upon giving the prescribed notice.

Repairs. Normally a landlord of an unfurnished dwelling-house is not liable for repairs unless he has undertaken to do them, but in all houses let for not more than 26 a year (40 in London) the landlord is bound by statute to keep the house fit for human habitation. If the letting was made after July 6, 1957, the respective rent limits are 52 and 80. This repairing provision does not apply where the premises are let for at least three years upon the terms that the lessee puts the premises into a condition reasonably fit for human habitation. Landlord & Tenant Act 1985.

Also in the case of many leases for less than seven years, the landlord must keep in repair the structure, exterior and service installations in the dwelling-house. Landlord & Tenant Act 1985.

But where a landlord of Rent Restricted premises is responsible for repairs and allows the premises to be in a state of disrepair and persistently fails to put matters right, the tenant can go to the local authority and make an application for a Certificate of Disrepair.

The local authority will then send representatives to inspect the house and if they consider that the house is in a state of disrepair they will issue a three-weeks' warning to the landlord. If at the end of this time he has still not carried out the repairs, the Certificate of Disrepair will be issued and the tenant will be able to make substantial reductions from the rent until the repairs are done. Enquiries should be made from the local authority as to the proper amount to be deducted from the rent and most authorities are able and willing to give advice and assistance to landlords and tenants on questions of repairs.

Premiums or 'Key Money'. All premiums on houses whose rent is controlled either by the Rent Act 1977 or by the decision of a local rent tribunal are in general illegal and may be recovered. Excessive charges for furniture or fittings are treated as premiums. Where a landlord requires an incoming tenant in the case of a tenancy protected by the Rent Acts, to pay an unreasonably high price for furniture or fails to furnish the tenant with a written inventory of the price of each piece of furniture, he commits an offence and is liable to a fine. The Court may order repayment of the premium. Furniture includes fittings and other articles (Rent Act 1977, Section 128 (1)). Local authorities have power to enter and to inspect premises where they have reasonable grounds for thinking such offences have been committed.

Furnished Lettings etc. Most of the provisions of the Rent Act did not apply to houses let at a rent which includes payments in respect of board, or attendance. But under the Rent Act 1974 (now the 1977 Act) the protection afforded to unfurnished tenancies was extended in most cases to furnished lettings.

There are other provisions in most areas throughout the country contained in the 1977 Act applicable to a tenancy of a house or part of a house, e.g. rooms, for a rent which includes payment for the use of services, such as heating, lighting, or hot water or where there is a resident landlord. Usually, provided the premises have not a net annual rateable value of more than 1,500 in London or 750 elsewhere, the tenant, landlord, or the local council may bring the terms of the tenancy before a local Rent Assessment Committee sitting as a Rent Tribunal which fixes what it considers a proper rent. The local council keeps a register in which are entered all rents fixed by the tribunal. It is illegal to demand a rent higher than the registered rent. There is nothing to prevent the landlord from giving the tenant a notice to quit. In the case of such lettings entered into before November 28, 1980, if a notice to quit is given after the letting has been referred to the tribunal, it does not take effect until six months after the tribunal's decision, unless the tribunal directs a shorter period or unless the reference is withdrawn. If not, the tribunal can extend the protection by successive extensions of six months at a time. In the case of such lettings entered into after November 27, 1980, on the making of a possession order and up to execution of the order the court can postpone possession up to three months after such an order.

Holiday accommodation is not protected and is not a type of accommodation that can be referred to a Rent Tribunal. There is also a special provision enabling an owner of furnished premises which he has let furnished to recover possession if he was previously occupying it, and has given notice at the time of the letting that he would need to occupy it again and he wants the premises for his own occupation.

Secure Tenancies. The Housing Act 1985, provides for security of tenure to tenants of local authorities and certain other public bodies and organisations. Such tenants also have certain rights to buy the freehold or a long lease of their dwelling houses. This right normally applies to a secure tenant of at least three years' standing.

Assured Tenancies. A category of 'Assured Tenancies' was created by the Housing Act 1980. This relates to a dwelling house constructed wholly or in part on or after August 8, 1980. To qualify, works involving expenditure of at least 7,000 in Greater London, or 5,000 elsewhere, must have been carried out on the building, or a proportionate amount in relation to a flat let therein. (See S.1. 1987 No.122). The interest of the landlord must belong to an 'approved body' - i.e. approved by the Secretary of State. A great number of such approvals have been made, including some to Housing Associations. The protection given to such assured tenants is in a modified form analogous to that given to business tenants under the Landlord and Tenant Act 1954. The rate limits are the same as for fully protected tenants.

Rent (Agriculture) Act 1976. This statute provides security for agricultural workers who are occupiers of protected dwelling houses under this Act. The security follows, in many respects, that provided for under the Rent Acts.

Landlord and Tenant Act 1954. Part 1 of this Act, as amended, gives security of possession to residential tenants and sub- tenants upon termination of long leases, i.e. of over 21 years. Such tenancies are normally outside the Rent Acts, but now if certain conditions laid down in the Act are fulfilled, the tenancy can be converted into a statutory tenancy on terms agreed between the landlord and tenant or, failing such agreement, on terms laid down by the Court. Even so the landlord may still apply to the Court for possession of the property after conversion on certain grounds specified in the 1954 Act. If a tenancy is not so terminated in accordance with the provisions of the Act, it will continue automatically. (See also the next paragraph.)

Part 2. Business and Professional Tenants. Where on the expiration of such a tenancy, the parties cannot agree on the granting of a new tenancy or its terms, then providing all the conditions laid down in the Act are fulfilled, the tenant may apply to the Court for a new tenancy, where either the landlord has given notice to terminate the tenancy, or the tenant has made a request for a new tenancy under the Act. The landlord can oppose such an application on specified grounds, and in certain circumstances if the landlord succeeds in his opposition the tenant can recover compensation from the landlord. The Court can also fix the terms of the new tenancy which cannot be for a period of more than 14 years and the Court also has power to order a rent renewal clause to be included in the terms.

A business tenancy cannot be converted into a protected residential tenancy merely by the tenant residing there instead of conducting a business.

Leasehold Reform Acts 1967 and 1979, as amended. These Acts enable tenants of certain leasehold houses (not flats) within a time limit to compel their landlords to allow them to purchase the freehold of their house or to grant them a further lease for 50 years. The principal conditions that have to be satisfied at the time the claim is made are:

(a) The rateable value of the house and premises must be in respect of: (i) leases granted on or before February 18, 1966, 1,500 for Greater London and 750 elsewhere, in England and Wales, or (ii) leases granted after February 18, 1966, 1,000 for Greater London and 500 elsewhere.
(b) The lease must have been for more than 21 years.
(c) The rent payable under the lease must not exceed two-thirds of the rateable value of the house.
(d) The tenant must have occupied the house as his residence under a long tenancy at a low rent for either the last three years or for three out of the last ten years.

The making of such a claim and the calculation of the purchase price to be paid to the landlord are not simple matters and if you think that you may be qualified to make such a claim and you wish to do so you would be well advised to consult a solicitor. The Landlord and Tenant Act 1987, enables the tenants of flats to acquire their landlord's interest in their flats in certain cases.

Rates (where still applicable). The General Rate Act 1967 provides that in certain cases rates may be paid by instalments instead of in lump sums. This does not apply where the rates are paid by or through the landlord. If you wish to do this you must give notice to your local authority. The Rate Rebate Regulations 1978, as amended by 1981 Regulations and local rate rebate schemes under the Local Government Act 1974, permit certain residential occupier ratepayers with very low incomes to claim a rebate on the rates due from them and if you think you may qualify for this you should consult your local authority. In certain cases a disabled person is entitled to a rate rebate in respect of accommodation related to disability under the Rating (Disabled Persons) Act 1978.

Personal Community Charge. The Personal Community Charge (Relief) (England) Regulations 1990 provides for certain limited relief in some cases of resident charge payers and also of the elderly and disabled.

Rent Rebates and Allowances. The Social Security and Housing Benefits Acts 1982 and 1983 enable a Council tenant who suffers particular hardship to apply for a rent rebate based upon earnings and income. Statutory provision is also made in certain cases for needs allowances to private tenants of unfurnished and furnished dwellings. Tenants should apply to the local housing authority for a rebate, or allowance, where applicable.

The Rent Rebate and Rent Allowances Schemes (England and Wales) Regulations 1982 have further increased the maximum rebate and maximum allowances for any week in a rebate or allowance period.

The Housing Rents and Subsidies Act 1975, and Housing Act 1985 provide for the phasing of some rent increases and also gives the Government power to limit rents in the case of both Council and private tenants. (These provisions may be affected by legislation now before Parliament).

Loans for House Purchase and Grants for Improvements. In some cases Government assistance is available to enable building societies and local authorities to advance the whole of the purchase price of a house instead of only a proportion of it. Such extra assistance is by way of loan to the purchaser and has to be repaid over a number of years as in the case of any building society mortgage. Some of the lending powers have been suspended for the time being, but if you are contemplating buying a house and you are unable to afford the difference between what the building society will lend and the purchase price, you may find it helpful to inquire from the building society or your local authority if you can qualify for assistance.

The Housing Acts permit local authorities to make substantial grants towards the cost of improvement, repair and conversion of houses. If you own an old house and you are anxious to modernise it you should consult your local authority to see if you can obtain a grant towards the cost of some or all of such improvements.

The Clean Air Act 1956 as amended by the Local Government, Planning and Land Act 1980, provides for grants towards some of the expenses of adapting fireplaces in private dwelling houses in smoke control areas. Many parts of the country have now been declared smoke control areas and if you are contemplating alterations to your grates and fireplaces it is worth while to inquire from the local authority whether the district is likely to become a smoke control area in the near future, and whether it is possible to qualify for the grant. If your district is in such an area it can be an offence if smoke is emitted from your chimneys. Modern fireplaces are essential and smokeless fuels must be used.

The Occupiers Liability Act 1957. This Act is concerned with the duties of occupiers of all premises including dwelling houses, towards persons visiting the premises regarding dangers due to the state of the premises. An occupier of premises owes the same duty of care to all his visitors, and so does a landlord towards lawful visitors of his tenant in respect of dangers arising from any breach of his obligations to maintain and repair the premises. Under the Occupiers Liability Act 1984 an occupier owes a duty of care to a non-visitor if he has reasonable grounds to believe that the latter may be in danger and that in all the circumstances it is reasonable to offer some protection, such as a warning. There is no duty to a person who accepts the risks.

Homeless Persons. Under the Housing (Homeless Persons) Act 1977, a housing authority is under a duty to provide accommodation for a person with a local connection who is not intentionally homeless.

BOUNDARY FENCES

NORMALLY the ownership of boundary fences is expressly set out in, or to be inferred from, relative deeds, conveyance or agreements. It may also be inferred from acts of ownership, e.g. where one party, or his predecessor in title, has kept the fence in good condition and repair, or in verbal admissions. In the absence of any such indications of ownership, there are legal presumptions which themselves can be rebutted by any sufficient evidence which may in the end be produced to the contrary.

In the case of wooden and similar fences, there is such a presumption that the fence belongs to the landowner on whose side the upright posts are erected. This gives him the maximum amount of land for his use. On the other hand, in the case of brick and similar walls, with protruding built in upright supporting sections, the presumption is the reverse, on the grounds that the protruding sections could not have been erected without the builder entering the neighbour's land. That would be an act of trespass which the law would presume against.

RIGHT TO LIGHT

SUBJECT to certain exceptions the owner and occupier of land has no right to enjoy natural light coming from his neighbour's land. The main exceptions include (1) where there is an express agreement, (2) where there is an implied agreement by a vendor who retains or sells land adjoining that sold and (3) by prescription. This applies to windows and openings which have enjoyed continuously for at least 20 years the benefit of light coming in from the neighbouring land. The light protected is that needed for the reasonable enjoyment of the room and not more than previously enjoyed. This is a highly complex branch of the law and in the event of any dispute or difficulty, legal advice should be sought in the light of particular facts.

TRESPASS

WITH some statutory exceptions, a person who enters upon, or interferes with, another's property including premises and land without the consent of the owner or occupier entitled to give it, is a trespasser. At common law he commits a civil wrong. This is not a crime in the absence of deliberate damage or injury. He does, however, act at his peril, and he is liable for all damage or injury caused. He must leave the property as soon as requested to do so. By Act of Parliament trespass has been made a criminal offence in specific cases. These usually refer to public property. Examples are local authority bye-laws and railway property regulations. The Government have stated their intention of introducing legislation to make trespass of private land in some cases a criminal offence.

Public footpaths running alongside the public road are usually part of the highway, and subject to the same rights and restrictions, unless there are special provisions as to its use, made under the terms of dedication or creation. Local authorities frequently have special powers to make provisions as to the user of such pathways.

Interference with property adjoining the highway can well amount to trespass.

SAFETY AND HEALTH IN THE HOME

SEVERAL Acts of Parliament dealing with these important subjects have come into force. For example it is an offence to sell oil heaters that do not comply with certain safety regulations. The Home Safety Act 1961, empowers local authorities to spend money on promoting home safety and preventing accidents in the home. The Consumer Safety Act 1978 enables the Home Secretary to make regulations for ensuring that goods sold are safe to the consumer, and prevent the risk of death or personal injury. And the Public Health Act 1961 makes it an offence for any dealer to offer for sale any verminous household article and also compels occupiers of premises to give information if requested by a Medical Officer of Health regarding any persons on the premises suffering from notifiable diseases or food poisoning.

Regulations under the Consumer Protection Act 1961 make it compulsory in law from July 1970 for the colours of wires in all three-core flexes attached to household electrical appliances offered for sale in the UK to comply with international standards.

AIR GUNS AND SHOT GUNS

THE FIREARMS ACT 1968 makes it illegal for anyone to give to any person under age of 14 an air gun or ammunition for such a gun, and it is an offence for a child under that age to accept such a gift or subject to the exceptions (a) and (b) below, to have either an air gun or ammunition for an air gun in his possession. No one under the age of 17 is now allowed to have in his possession an air gun in any public place unless it is securely fastened with a gun cover so that it cannot be fired. Exceptions to this are: (a) The use of air guns at recognised shooting clubs and shooting galleries, and (b) under the supervision of someone over the age of 21 an air gun may be used on premises provided it is not used to fire any missile beyond those premises. For example, a father may lawfully supervise his son in the use of an air gun in his own garden provided no pellets are fired at anything outside the garden at all.

No one under the age of 15 is allowed to have an assembled shot gun in his possession unless either he is under the supervision of someone over 21 or the gun is secured with a gun cover so that it cannot be fired. Punishments for offences relating to minors vary up to six months imprisonment and/or fines of 400 and by the forfeiture of the gun and ammunition.

The Act also provides very severe penalties for any person having a loaded air gun or shot gun in a public place or for having even an unloaded rifle or revolver with ammunition in a public place unless he has a lawful excuse for so doing. There is no lawful purpose for a sawn-off shotgun (R.V. Horne (1988) G.C.A. 12 339 (C.A.).

Under this Act it is an absolute offence to have possession of a firearm without holding a certificate. A firearm manufactured during this century cannot be an antique. In the case of firearms made earlier, it is a question of fact in each case whether the firearm is caught by the statute. A change of firearms, even of the same type, requires a new certificate.

Under the Firearms Act 1982, imitation firearms which are readily convertible into firearms are caught, with some savings, by the Firearms Act 1968. Ammunition not in actual use must be kept in a secure place with a view to preventing access to it by unauthorised persons, Firearms Rules. An electric stungun requires authority for possession under Firearms Act, 1968.

The Firearms Amendment Act, 1988, passed on November 15, 1988, has made further controls, inter alia, on the issue and use of firearms including shotguns, and with further powers to the police.

POLLUTION

UNDER the Control of Pollution Act 1974 the deposit on land of poisonous, noxious or polluting waste giving rise to an environmental hazard, can be an offence. There are provisions relating to polluted water and discharge of radio-active waste. Other provisions are made under the Water Act 1989.

CONTROL OF NOISE

UNDER PART III of the Control of Pollution Act 1974 the local authority and a local magistrate may take steps to control noise or vibration they consider to be a statutory nuisance on receipt of a complaint from any occupier of premises who is aggrieved by the noise; these powers now include noise made by statutory under-takers. The local authority may also set predetermined limits on noise from construction sites, on application by the contractor, and in special circumstances control noise from non-residential premises by means of a noise abatement zone.

The Secretary of State for the Environment now has the power to approve and issue codes of practice on minimisation of noise from specific sources (e.g. construction sites) under the Act. These are designed to help the local authority, magistrate or member of the public to decide whether a noisy activity is being pursued in a reasonable and considerate manner.

The Act also restricts the operation of loudspeakers in the streets for purposes of advertising.

LIMITATION OF ACTIONS

ACTIONS for damages for personal injuries from negligence, nuisance or breach of duty must generally be commenced within three years from the date when the cause of action arose, but the Court has a limited discretion to extend the time limit. The time limit for libel and slander is now 3 years. Many other actions have to be commenced within six years. See Limitations Act 1980 and the Administration of Justice Act 1985.

UNSOLICITED GOODS

IF GOODS ARE sent to your home that you have never ordered you are not obliged to acknowledge their receipt or to pay for them unless you wish to buy them. Your only obligation is to take reasonable care of them and to surrender them to the sender or his agent when he calls for them. This is subject to the Unsolicited Goods and Services Act 1971 as amended by the Unsolicited Goods and Services (Amendment) Act 1975. This provides that if unsolicited goods are sent to you and you have no reason to think that they were sent in order that you might use them for some trade or business, you may treat them as a gift and do whatever you like with them (a) after they have been in your possession for six months and during that time you have not unreasonably refused a request by the sender to be allowed to have them back, or (b) you have sent a notice to the sender (by post if you like) giving your name and address and the address from which the goods may be collected, if it is different from your address, and telling the sender that the goods were unsolicited and not wanted and during the next 30 days the goods have not been collected.

By Section 2 of the Act anyone who knows that he has sent unsolicited goods and then demands payment for them or threatens legal proceedings is guilty of an offence and is liable to a fine of up to 400. Section 4 of the Act also provides heavy fines for persons sending books, magazines, leaflets or advertising material describing human sexual techniques which they know, or ought reasonably to know, are unsolicited.

TRADE DESCRIPTIONS

UNDER THE Trade Descriptions Act 1968 it is an offence for a person in the course of his trade or business to supply without due diligence a false or misleading trade description to any goods or to supply them under such false description. Offences are also created in respect of false or misleading statements, made in the course of

business, relating to the provision and nature of services, including accommodation and facilities. The Act is enforced by the local Inspectors of Weights and Measures to whom any complaint should be made.

SALE OF GOODS

ADDED protection to shopgoers is given by the Sale of Goods Act 1979. Goods sold must correspond with their description, and this extends to goods selected by the buyer in a self-service store. Where the seller sells goods in the course of business, the goods must be of merchantable quality except as to defects known to the buyer. When the buyer makes known to the shopkeeper, expressly or by implication, the purpose for which he requires the goods, they must be reasonably fit for such purpose, except where it would be unreasonable to rely upon the seller's skill or judgement. These conditions cannot be excluded by a shopkeeper in the case of goods of a type ordinarily bought for private use and consumption and sold to an ordinary shopper. In the cases of other goods, excluding terms are unenforceable if not fair or reasonable.

Further protection to the private purchaser is given by the Unfair Contract Terms Act 1977 which prevents guarantees from restricting the consumer's right of action in relation to defective condition or negligent handling of goods purchased.

Protection analogous to that given to buyers of goods under the Sale of Goods Act has been extended to contracts for the transfer of the ownership of goods (e.g. by barter) by the Supply of Goods and Services Act 1982. This Act also gives protection in hiring contracts (apart from hire purchase agreements) and in the supply of services.

LEGAL AID

Legal Aid Schemes. There are different kinds of legal aid in England and Wales which provide for the help of a solicitor.

Full particulars about the conditions for legal aid can be obtained from the Legal Aid Head Office, Newspaper House, 8-16 Great New Street, London EC4A 3BN. It is important to appreciate that the conditions for legal aid do vary from time to time.

The amounts of disposable capital and disposable income to qualify for legal aid are under continual review. The figures given are fixed as from April 1990, but may change during the course of the year. It is usual for legal aid eligibility payments to be reviewed annually.

LEGAL ADVICE AND ASSISTANCE

which covers advice and help with any legal problem. This scheme may also provide assistance by way of representation, in most civil cases in magistrates' courts, and before the Mental Health Review Tribunals. In both cases a Green Form must be filled in through the solicitor. In the case of assistance by way of representation, the Legal Aid Office will decide whether this should be granted, on reasonable grounds. In the case of legal advice and assistance, the solicitor will decide if the applicant qualifies. To qualify, in either case, the disposable weekly income must be £135 or less and the disposable capital £935 or less. No contribution is required where the disposable income is £64 or less weekly. Between £64 and £135 weekly disposable income, the contribution varies to a maximum of £75.

In the case of Assistance by way of Representation the same income conditions apply but with savings up to £3,000.

ACCIDENT LEGAL ADVICE SERVICE

THIS free scheme, started on June 29, 1987, is designed to assist persons who have had an accident, suffered injury and/or loss and/or damage, and want to know their legal rights as to compensation. The Service provides an entirely free first interview with a solicitor. Upon the information given to him, he will advise whether a legal claim is advisable. If so, he will explain whether the applicant qualifies for legal aid; if not, he will indicate the likely cost of proceeding unaided.

The Solicitors Regional Directory shows which solicitors offer a free interview under this service. The Directory should be available at the local Citizens' Advice Bureau, local advice centres and public libraries. Alternatively, information can be obtained by letter from the Law Society, Accident Legal Advice Service, FREEPOST, London, WC2A 1BR, or by telephone, 01-242 2430.

LEGAL AID FOR CIVIL COURT PROCEEDINGS

THIS covers all the work leading up to and including the court proceedings, and representation by a solicitor and counsel where necessary. This covers most cases in the main courts and some tribunals. Application for legal is made through a solicitor. A committee of lawyers have to decide whether it is reasonable to grant the aid. To qualify, financially the disposable capital must not normally exceed £6,310, or £8,000 in personal injury claims and the disposable income £6,350 or £7,000. The applicant will not have to make a contribution from his disposable capital if it is £3,000 or less. If the disposable income is not more than £2,645, no deduction from it will be made. The maximum contribution from income is one quarter of the disposable income. The maximum contribution from capital is disposable capital over £3,000.

CRIMINAL LEGAL AID

IN the Magistrates Court, there will often be a duty solicitor available on call, to give the legal advice to a person charged with a criminal offence. In addition the Court may order legal aid in the conduct of the case. This covers the preparation of the defence and representation in Court, and on appeal, by solicitor and counsel where necessary. Application is made to the Court dealing with the case and it will grant legal aid if it considers in the interests of justice that the applicant should have legal representation and that he needs assistance to pay the costs. The Court can order that a contribution be made as a condition of legal aid where the weekly disposable income exceeds £55 and/or the disposable capital exceeds £3,000.

THE FIXED FEES INTERVIEW

IN addition to the above schemes, many solicitors will give advice, for up to half an hour, for 5 or less. Names of firms of solicitors who take part in this service are contained in the Solicitors Regional Directory. Also at Police Stations, solicitors may be paid for advice and assistance given there.

WILLS

WILLS are technical legal documents, and a solicitor should always be consulted where possible when making a will. The following is only a guide to some general matters.

Capacity. Anyone who is 18 years of age or over and who is of sound mind i.e. understands clearly what he is doing, may make a will.

Formalities. The will should be written clearly, in simple language, and without making any alterations or erasures. It should be signed at the end by the testator in the presence of two witnesses who must then also sign the will in the presence of the testator and each other. The fact that they have witnessed these signatures in each other's presence and at the testator's request and in his presence should also be recorded. None of the attesting witnesses nor their wives or husbands can receive any benefit under the will unless the will is duly executed without their attestation.

Executors. One or more persons should be appointed executors of the will and these may be relatives, friends or anyone else whom the testator wishes to administer his estate after his death. A corporate trustee may also be appointed, such as a Bank.

Revocation. Generally a will is revoked either by a subsequent will which should expressly state the testator's intention to revoke any previous will, or by being burnt, torn up, or destroyed by the testator or some other person in his presence and by his direction with the intention of revoking it. Marriage also normally revokes a will unless it was made expressly in anticipation of the marriage.

Privileged Wills. Formalities are greatly relaxed in the case of wills made by soldiers and members of the Royal Air Force on actual military service and seamen who are at sea.

By virtue of Part III of the Administration of Justice Act 1969, amending Part VIII of the Mental Health Act 1959 the Court can order a will to be made on behalf of a patient of unsound mind with testamentary capacity.

Deposit of Wills. Under the Wills (Deposit for Safe Custody) Regulations 1978 testamentary documents of living persons can be deposited for safe custody with the Principal Registry of the Family Division of the High Court.

INTESTACY

WHERE anyone dies intestate on or after March 1, 1981 leaving a husband or wife, the surviving spouse takes:

(1) The personal chattels absolutely.
(2) If there is issue, 40,000 absolutely free of death duties and costs: if there is no issue, 85,000 absolutely free of death duties and costs.
(3) If there is issue, a life interest in half the remaining estate, the rest to the issue: if there is no issue but the deceased left a parent, brother or sister, nephew or niece of the whole blood, half the remaining estate absolutely: if there is no issue and no relatives as above, all the remaining estate absolutely.

If the deceased was unmarried at the date of death or was a widow or a widower and there is no issue then the estate goes to the following persons:

(a) The deceased's natural parents in equal shares (note step-parents and in-laws are excluded).
(b) If the parents are dead then the estate goes to the following persons, if living, and in the following order:

(1) Brothers and sisters of the whole blood or their issue.
(2) Brothers and sisters of the half blood or their issue.
(3) Grandparents.
(4) Uncles and aunts of the whole blood or their issue.
(5) Uncles and aunts of the half blood or their issue.

The Family Law Reform Act 1969 provides that an illegitimate child and his parents now have the same right to share in each other's estates on an intestacy as if the child were legitimate. Where the illegitimate child dies before the intestate parent, the child's own issue can take as if the child were legitimate.

If none of the above persons is alive or none can be traced then the Estate goes to the Crown.

FAMILY PROVISION ON DEATH

UNDER the Inheritance (Provision for Family and Dependants) Act, 1975 the dependants of a deceased person are entitled to ask the Court to order reasonable provisions to be made for them out of the property of the deceased. An application under this Act must be made within six months of grant of representation but the Court now has power to extend this time limit, and such an application can now be made in the County Court, provided the deceased's net estate does not exceed £30,000.

STAMP DUTIES, CHEQUES, AND RECEIPTS

THE FINANCE ACT 1984, reduced the stamp duties payable on the conveyance of property. For the transfer of shares the stamp duty payable is 1 per cent. So far as property is concerned, if the purchase money does not exceed 30,000, no stamp duty is payable. Over 30,000 the rate is 1 per cent. Leases of furnished premises for any definite term less than one year are exempt from stamp duty if the rent does not exceed 400.

The Finance Act 1970 abolished the stamp duty on agreements, on accident and non-life insurance policies and on life policies for 50 or less. It also reduced the stamp duty on mortgage deeds to 10p per 100. Rates of stamp duty are varied from time to time. The Stamp Duty (Exempt) Instruments Regulations 1987 also exempt certain classes of conveyance and transfers of property.

Since the passing of the Cheques Act 1957, an unendorsed paid cheque is evidence of the receipt by the payee of the money.

REGISTRATION

BIRTHS must be notified to the registrar of the district within 42 days.

DEATHS must be registered by authorised persons within five days, or where written notice is given, within 14 days.

MARRIAGE

A MARRIAGE celebrated between persons either of whom is under the age of 16 years is void and therefore no marriage at all. Before a person over the age of 16 but under 18 can be married the consent of both parents is required or that of the Court. In certain circumstances the consent of one parent is sufficient.

Banns must be published on three Sundays preceding the date of the marriage. The parties must be resident in the parish 21 days and, if they reside in different parishes, the banns must be published in each. The marriage may take place in either parish.

For a **Common Licence** application should be made to the Registrat of the Diocese concerned. The current fee is £38. Residential requirements are the same as for Banns.

A **special licence** may be applied for at the Faculty Office, 1 The Sanctuary, Westminster, London SW1P

3JT. The fee is £75. This Licence is issued at the Archbishop of Canterbury's discretion in cases of emergency or exceptional circumstances for marriage elsewhere than in the Parish Church of either party.

For a common licence (fee £33) apply to the Bishop of the diocese.

At Register Office, by certificate (and including £2 for certificate of marriage), £29.50 or £42.50, by licence, fee £67.50. For a certificate the parties must have resided seven days in the district and must give 21 clear days' notice. If they live in different registration districts, notice must be given in each district. For a licence, one of the parties must have resided 15 days in the district, and one clear day, other than a Sunday, Christmas Day or Good Friday, must intervene between the day notice is given and the day the licence is issued. Hours for solemnisation: 8 a.m. to 6 p.m.

In a Registered Building, e.g. a non-conformist church or a Roman Catholic church registered for solemnisation of marriage. A Superintendent Registrar's certificate is required with or without a licence as for marriage in a Register Office and there are the same requirements as to residence and notice. Marriage usually takes place at a registered building within the district of residence of one of the parties, but it may take place in a building outside that district in certain circumstances. Similar provisions apply where the marriage is between members of the **Society of Friends (Quakers)**, or **Jews**, the marriage in each case being solemnised on the authority of a Superintendent Registrar's certificate with or without licence, and in accordance with the usages of the parties' religion.

A special provision was introduced on January 1, 1971 for the issue of a Registrar General's Licence to allow a marriage, otherwise than according to the rites of the Church of England or Church in Wales, to take place at any time on unregistered premises (e.g. in a hospital or at home), where one of the parties is seriously ill and is not expected to recover. Application must be made and notice given to the Superintendent Registrar of the district in which it is intended the marriage shall be solemnised.

The Marriage Act 1983 enables marriages of housebound and detained persons to be solemnised where they reside.

A marriage before witnesses at Gretna Green or elsewhere in Scotland is no longer valid, but marriage by cohabitation with habit and repute is still possible in that country.

AGE OF MAJORITY

MOST of the provisions of the Family Law Reform Act 1969 came into force on January 1, 1970, the most notable being that the age of majority is now 18 instead of 21. Apart from removing the necessity to obtain parental consent to marry after the age of 18, a very important effect of this Act is that contracts made by a person who is 18 but not 21 can no longer be avoided on the grounds that they are against the interests of the young person concerned. A young man or woman of this age can now make a will, grant a lease or tenancy or become a tenant. He or she can also enter into a hire purchase agreement, give a valid receipt or release a legal claim and any contract entered into is fully binding: such a person can sue or be sued in the Courts like anyone else.

S. 8 of this Act also provides that anyone over the age of 16 can now give a valid consent to surgical, medical or dental treatment and this is so even in the face of objection by the parent or guardian.

HUSBAND AND WIFE

THE LAW REFORM (Husband and Wife) Act, 1962, amended the old law relating to civil proceedings which formerly much restricted actions between spouses. Subject to certain safeguards, a husband or a wife may now sue each other as strangers. The Court has, however, a discretion to refuse to hear the action and to insist that the parties adopt the procedure laid down in the Married Women's Property Act, 1882 in order to resolve the dispute.

Housekeeping Money. For many years the law regarded savings from housekeeping money given to the wife by her husband as the property of the husband. The Married Women's Property Act 1964 altered this and now in disputes between husbands and wives regarding property any such savings have to be treated by the courts as belonging to both the husband and the wife in equal shares, unless there has been some agreement to the contrary.

MATRIMONIAL HOMES ACT 1983

THIS ACT concerns the rights of husbands and wives over the matrimonial home and is especially concerned with the not uncommon situation where either the freehold or the tenancy is in the name of one party to the marriage only. In such a case the other party now has a number of enforceable rights in respect of the matrimonial home which he or she did not have before. The Court may grant the other party the right to occupy the dwelling house. If the matrimonial home is a dwelling house held on a tenancy within the Rent Acts and the marriage is ended by divorce, the courts have power to make an order vesting the tenancy in either of the parties irrespective of whether the original tenancy was in the name of the husband or the wife or both jointly.

The Court now has power to order the sale of property belonging to either spouse in support of an order for financial relief.

ABORTION ACT, 1967

THIS ACT legalises abortion in certain circumstances, the principal requirements being (a) that in the opinion of two doctors the continuance of the pregnancy would involve risk to the life of the woman or injury to her mental or physical health, or (b) that in the opinion of two doctors there is a substantial risk that if the child were born it would suffer from such physical or mental abnormalities as to be seriously handicapped and (c) the abortion is carried out by a doctor in a hospital under the National Health Service Acts or in some other place approved by the Ministry of Health. In cases of emergency if a doctor considers that an abortion is immediately necessary to save life or to prevent serious injury to health, he may carry out an abortion without waiting for the second opinion required in (a) or (b) above. The Act also makes it clear that no doctor or anyone else is obliged to participate in an abortion if he or she does not wish to do so because of conscientious objection to it.

DIVORCE

SINCE January 1, 1971 great changes have been made in the law of divorce. The consolidating Matrimonial Causes Act 1973 provides that the sole ground for divorce is that the marriage has irretrievably broken down. S.2 provides that proof of such a breakdown can only be afforded if one or more of the following conditions are fulfilled:

(a) the respondent has committed adultery and the petitioner finds it intolerable to live with him or her;
(b) the respondent has behaved in such a way that the petitioner cannot reasonably be expected to live with him or her;
(c) the respondent has deserted the petitioner for a period of two years;
(d) the parties have lived apart for two years and the respondent consents to a decree;
(e) the parties have lived apart for five years.

Unless the Court considers the marriage has not broken down irretrievably a decree must be granted on proof of one of the above conditions except in the case of (e) above. This last ground permits one spouse to obtain a divorce against the wishes of the other even if the petitioner has broken up the marriage but in such a case a decree may be refused if it would result in grave financial hardship to the respondent.

S.6 of the Act contains provision for a possible reconciliation. The petitioner's solicitor has to certify whether reconciliation has been discussed and the Court also has power to adjourn divorce proceedings if there is a reasonable prospect of reconciliation.

In most undefended cases, it is now unnecessary for the parties to attend Court, except in relation to arrangements for the children and disputed matters as to maintenance and property.

As from October 12, 1984, with transitional exceptions, proceedings for divorce can be started after one year of marriage instead of three.

Apart from orders in the High Court, a spouse may apply for maintenance to a Magistrates Court under the Domestic Proceeding and Magistrates Court Act, 1978 and apply also for an order for custody of the children.

Decrees of Judicial Separation can still be made under the 1973 Act but the Law Reform (Miscellaneous Provisions) Act 1970 abolishes claims by husbands for damages for adultery after December 31, 1970. This last Act also abolishes actions for breach of promise to marry and actions for enticement or seduction. It also deals with the property of engaged couples and gifts between them.

DOMESTIC VIOLENCE

UNDER the Domestic Violence and Matrimonial Proceedings Act 1976, either partner to a marriage or a person living, unmarried, with another as husband and wife, may apply to the County Court for an order restraining the other from molesting the applicant and a child living with the applicant and excluding the other party from the matrimonial home, or requiring the other party to permit the applicant to enter and remain in the matrimonial home.

WAGES ACT 1986

FORMERLY wages had to be paid in cash to artificers and labourers. But now the Truck Acts have been fully repealed by the Wages Act 1986. The Act provides for restrictions in deductions from wages, and the new right of the employee to appeal to an independent tribunal.

UNFAIR DISMISSAL

AN EMPLOYEE who has been unfairly dismissed may be entitled to compensation or in some cases to reinstatement or re-engagement by the employer if the employee has been continuously employed in most cases for at least two years unless the employers have more than 30 employees. Application must be made to the Secretary, Central Office of Industrial Tribunals, 93 Ebury Bridge Road, London, S.W.1. Industrial tribunals also have jurisdiction to hear complaints of sex or racial discrimination in employment.

ABANDONMENT OF ANIMALS ACT 1960

UNDER this Act if any person who is the owner of a domestic or captive animal or who has charge and control of any such animal abandons it in circumstances likely to cause it unnecessary suffering, that person can be proceeded against for cruelty to the animal.

BADGERS AND OTTERS

BADGERS are protected from cruelty by the Badgers Act, 1973, and by the Wildlife and Countryside Act 1981. Also except in the case of authorised persons, it is an offence to take, keep, sell or kill badgers. It is also an offence to dig for badgers. The common otter is protected fully by the 1981 Act.

BATS

A BAT is a wild animal protected from cruelty and interference by the Wildlife and Countryside Act 1981. It is, for example, a criminal offence intentionally to kill, injure or take a bat. The taking, however, is not an offence if the bat has been disabled and was taken solely for the purpose of tending and releasing it, when recovered, or if it has been so seriously injured that there is no reasonable chance of its recovery. Furthermore, it is an offence to damage, destroy or obstruct access to any structure or place which the bat uses for shelter or protection, even in a dwelling house, unless it be in the living area, or the act was incidental to and unavoidable in the course of a lawful operation. In relation to any proposed action involving a bat outside the living area, e.g. a loft, the Nature Conservancy Council (Northminster House, Peterborough PE1 1UA. Phone no. 0733 40345) must be notified of the proposed action and given a reasonable time to advise whether such action should be carried out, and if so, the method to be used.

DEER

DEER are protected by the Deer Acts 1963 and 1980, including the prevention of poaching and the control of sale of venison. The Deer Act 1987 makes it lawful for deer kept on farms in England and Wales for food stock or breeding to be killed during the close season.

THE DANGEROUS WILD ANIMALS ACT 1976

NO PERSON can keep a dangerous wild animal without a licence granted by the local authority which has a limited discretion. There are exceptions to the requirements of a licence, e.g. dangerous wild animals kept in a circus, licensed pet shops and places registered for performing experiments. Zoos are now subject to licensing and control by the Zoo Licensing Act 1981.

DOG BREEDING

UNDER the Breeding of Dogs Act 1973, a licence is required by a dog breeder to keep premises, including a private dwelling house, where more than two bitches are kept for breeding. The breeder must comply with specific conditions for the welfare of all the animals as set out in the Act. There is a right of appeal to the Magistrates' Court if the local authority refuses a licence. There are special provisions for breeding for scientific research establishments in the Animals (Scientific Procedures) Act 1986.

DANGEROUS DOGS ACT 1989

WHERE a Court directs a dog to be destroyed under the Dogs Act 1871, it may also under the 1989 Act disqualify the owner from having custody of a dog for such period as it thinks fit.

JURY SERVICE

UNDER the Juries Act 1974, every person, with exceptions, between the ages of 18 and 65 inclusive is qualified to serve if registered as a parliamentary or local government elector and has resided in the United Kingdom, Channel Isles, or Isle of Man for at least five years since the age of 13.

Certain classes of persons are ineligible for jury service, among them:

(1) Clergymen, R.C. priests, and regular ministers of any religious denominations.
(2) Judges, Magistrates, Barristers and Solicitors, and Solicitors' legal executives.
(3) Officers of the Court, Sheriff's Officers, Prison Officers and Police Officers, including Special Constables.
(4) Persons receiving regular treatment for mental illness or subnormality.
(5) A person who has already served on a jury within less than two years or for such longer period as the Court may have excused him.

Other classes of persons may be excused from attendance, including:

(1) Peers, M.P.s.
(2) Full-time serving members of the armed services (if certified by his or her C.O.).
(3) Doctors, dentists, nurses, midwives, veterinary surgeons and chemists.

Under the Juries (Disqualification) Act 1984 (by amendment of the 1974 Act), the following are disqualified from serving on a jury and are liable to fines of 400 if they do so:

(a) Anyone who has at any time been sentenced to life imprisonment, to a term of five years or more or been detained lawfully during the Queen's or Secretary of State's pleasure.
(b) Anyone who at any time in the last ten years had served any part of sentence, custody or detention order, or had made in respect of him a Community Service order, or who during the last five years had been placed on probation.

A summons to serve on a jury has to be obeyed and fines of up to £100 can be imposed for non-attendance unless he can show reasonable cause for not attending. Attendance is excused on the grounds of illness and pregnancy, but medical certificates must be produced. There is also provision for excusing those who cannot act effectively by reason of physical disability or insufficient knowledge of English. Provided application is made in good time before the date of attendance, jury service can sometimes be postponed if very good grounds for this can be shown. Jurors are entitled to be paid travelling and subsistence allowance, and compensation for loss of earnings in accordance with scale and conditions prescribed.

There are special provisions relating to Coroner's juries.

VOTES

PARLIAMENTARY and Local Government. The Representation of the People Act 1969 permits everyone over the age of 18 to vote in a Parliamentary or Local Government election if he or she has a residence qualification. There is provision for voting by post and proxy voting.

Only persons whose names appear upon the voters' register may vote. In addition to everyone who is now over 18 people are also entitled to have their names upon the register if they will become 18 years of age during the 12 months following the day of publication of the register. In such cases the register will give the date on which 18 years is attained so that if an election is held on or after that day he or she may vote in it. The registers are open to public inspection and you should check that your name is on the list.

HIRE PURCHASE AND CREDIT SALES

HIRE PURCHASE, conditional sales, credit sales and other forms of instalment credit are established features of modern life. They are now controlled by the Consumer Credit Act 1974 which replaced the Hire Purchases Acts on May 19, 1985. The protection of the Act covers a large number of agreements including where the credit in a hire purchase agreement does not exceed £15,000.

Hire-Purchase is the hiring of goods with the option of purchase. The physical possession of the goods passes to the hirer upon his signing a Hire-Purchase Agreement: but the legal ownership remains vested in the owner until such time as all the instalments are paid and the option to purchase has been exercised by the payment of the option money specified in the Agreement.

Hire-Purchase Agreement: This is the document which legally binds the hirer and the owner, and is signed by the hirer. It sets out the terms under which the goods are hired. Any prospective hirer should always read such an agreement with great care before signing it.

Protection for the Hirer. The 1974 Act applies to most hire- purchase transactions where the credit does not exceed £15,000 and it provides protection for the hirer in the following ways:

(1) The person supplying goods must show on the agreement the cash price, the hire charge, the number of instalments, the amount of each and the date on which they become due, the sum paid as deposit and the cost of the option.
(2) The agreement must either be signed by the owner immediately after the hirer and a copy then handed to the hirer, or if the owner does not then sign, a copy of the agreement must immediately be given to the hirer when he signs.
(3) If the agreement is sent by post to the hirer for his signature then a copy of it must be enclosed with it for the hirer.
(4) A statutory notice must be inserted in the agreement setting out:

The Rights of Hirer to Cancel or Terminate, on terms set out in the Act.

The Rights of Owner to Repossess is restricted after one third of the hire-purchase price has been paid. Unless the hirer himself has put an end to the agreement the owner will have to apply to the Courts which have a wide discretion as to terms and conditions of repossession.

(5) Warranties and conditions are now imposed by the Sale of Goods Act 1979. The goods must be saleable when the time comes to transfer the ownership, normally at the end of the hiring. Where the owner hires out the goods in the course of business, the goods must be of merchantable quality, except as to defects known to the hirer. When the hirer makes known the purpose for which he requires the goods, they must be reasonably fit for such purpose, except where it is unreasonable for the hirer to rely upon the owner's skill or judgement. The conditions as to saleability cannot be excluded. The other conditions and warranties cannot be excluded if the goods are of a type ordinarily supplied for private use and consumption.

In other cases, excluding terms are unenforceable if not fair or reasonable.

(6) Door to Door Salesmen. This important feature of the 1974 Act applies where a hire-purchase agreement is not signed at the trade premises (e.g. a shop or office) of the owner or seller.

A second statutory copy of the agreement must be supplied to the hirer within seven days and where, for example, the agreement is signed at the home of the hirer, the agreement may be cancelled at any time within five days of the receipt of this second statutory copy of the agreement. Furthermore, this right to cancellation must be clearly stated in the agreement and the notice of cancellation may be sent by post. The purpose of this provision is to prevent housewives and others from being stampeded into entering into hire-purchase agreements and to give time for consideration. If the goods have been delivered and a notice of cancellation is given, then the prospective hirer is under an obligation to take reasonable care of them until collected and any money paid is recoverable.

Motor Vehicles. The Hire Purchase Act 1964 still gives some protection to persons who buy motor vehicles that are afterwards found to have been sold in breach of the terms of some earlier hire-purchase agreement. In such a case, provided the car was bought in good faith, the private purchaser usually obtains a good title to the vehicle.

The Owner Undertakes that the hirer will have quiet possession of the goods and that when the agreement has been fully paid up and the option to purchase exercised that he will have the right to sell the goods and no other person will have any claim on the goods; and the goods (second-hand ones excepted) are of merchantable quality, i.e. saleable.

The Hirer can Terminate the agreement by giving notice in writing to the person to whom he pays his instalments. His liability is then restricted to one-half of the total hire-purchase price.

Default by hirer. The owner or creditor must serve a default notice on the hirer, giving him an opportunity to remedy the breach, where possible.

What the Court may order. Where an owner brings an action against the hirer for the return of the goods after one-third has been paid the Court may order:

(a) Return of the goods to the owner;
(b) Return of the goods to the owner subject to the order being suspended, provided the unpaid balance is paid in accordance with the Court Order; or
(c) Delivery of part of the goods to the owner and the hirer allowed to keep part.

Credit Sales. In a Credit Sale the physical possession and legal ownership passes to the buyer at the outset, and in the case of default, action has to be taken in the County Court for the unpaid balance only. Many of the protection safeguards in respect of hire purchase transactions are also applicable to credit sale agreements, in particular (6) above, provided that the total credit does not exceed 15,000.

Where goods are advertised as being available on hire purchase or credit sale, particulars shown in the advertisement should include the deposit payable, if any, the amount, length and number of the instalments and the cash price and the hire-purchase price of the goods.

Control limits in Hire Purchase and Credit Sales agreements are liable to variation.

> **We are sorry but the editor is unable to answer any personal enquiries**

SOCIAL SECURITY

THE MINISTRY of Health and the Ministry of Social Security were merged in November 1968 to form the Department of Health and Social Security under a Secretary of State for Social Services. The Department carries out the functions of the two former Ministries, i.e. the central administration of the National Health Service and the administration of the various Social Security schemes, including National Insurance, Industrial Injuries, Supplementary Benefits (which have replaced National Assistance), Child Benefits (which have replaced Family Allowances), War Pensions, Family Income Supplements and Attendance Allowances. These schemes are administered through a network of about 600 local offices which are open to the public.

On April 6, 1975 the collection of Class 1 flat rate contributions by stamp card and graduated contributions through the PAYE income tax system was replaced by wholly earnings related contributions collected through the PAYE income tax system. There are 2 contributions corresponding to the old employee's and employer's contributions:

Primary Class 1 contributions, from employed earners i.e. those employed under a contract of service or office-holders with emoluments chargeable to tax under Schedule E and Secondary Class 1 contributions, from employers and other persons paying earnings.

No contributions are payable for employees whose earnings do not reach a specified minimum level (£46.00 a week from April 6, 1990). For all other employees contributions are payable on all their earnings up to a limit (£325 a week from April 6, 1990). There is no upper earnings limit for secondary contributions. Contribution rates and earnings limits are reviewed periodically and any consequent changes are given in leaflet NI 196 available from local offices of Department of Social Security and Crown Post Offices.

The Social Security Pensions Act 1975, abolished the right of married women and certain widows to choose reduced contribution liability. Reduced liability is now available only to those women who had an established right to it at the end of the 1977/78 tax year. Reduced liability continues until age 60 unless it is changed, marriage ends in divorce or annulment or, in the case of a widow title to national insurance, war or industrial injuries widow's benefit ceases (other than on remarriage). It will automatically end however, if, at any time after April 5, 1978, there are two consecutive tax years during which the woman had no earnings on which she was liable to pay Class 1 contributions and she has not been self-employed. For further information see leaflets N.I.1 (Married woman), N.I.151 (Widows).

It is compulsory for people who are self-employed to pay a weekly flat rate Class 2 contribution (unless exception on the grounds of low earnings has been applied for, and granted) either by stamping a contribution card with adhesive stamps purchased from the Post Office or by direct debit of their bank or National Girobank accounts. Authorisation forms for the latter method can be obtained from any local office of the Department of Social Security. Additionally, self-employed people may be liable to pay an earnings-related Class 4 contribution on profits and gains between specified limits, chargeable to income tax under Cases I and II of Schedule D. Class 4 contributions are assessed and collected by the Inland Revenue.

Class 3 contributions are paid voluntarily by persons who are not liable to pay Class 1 or Class 2 contributions to qualify for a limited range of benefits, particularly basic retirement pension, and by persons who do not have a full record of Class 1 or Class 2 contributions. Where Class 3 contributions are payable they may be paid either by the stamped card method, the direct debit of a bank or National Girobank account or a lump sum payment.

From April 6, 1983 men will not usually need to pay Class 3 contributions for their 60th birthday year or subsequent years. Contributions will be credited to them automatically for any periods in those years where there is no other liability. They cannot be given for any part of a tax year in which a man spends more than 182 days abroad.

New Pensions

From April 6, 1978, when the Social Security Pensions Act 1975 came into effect, certain changes were made to Class 1 contributions. Contracted-out pension scheme members paid a lower rate of NICs and the scheme guaranteed to pay a pension at 60 as good as SERPS. From April 6, 1979 flat-rate pensions for retirement, widowhood, and invalidity have been replaced by earnings-related pensions. The pensions consist of two parts a 'basic pension' and an additional amount, related to that part of a person's earnings between the qualifying earnings level for the basic pension (i.e. above the lower earnings limit) and below the employee's upper earnings limit. For those reaching pension age before 6.4.99 the rate is one-fiftieth of the surplus earnings between 9.75/79 and the tax year before the one in which pension age is reached. For those reaching pension age after 6.4.99 the additional pension is worked out in two parts. The surplus earnings for the years 1978/88 is multiplied by 2590 and divided by the number of years 1975/79 (tax year last birthday) and the one bfore that pension age is reached. The surplus earnings for years 1988/89 are calculated as above using a percentage between 25 and 20 depending on the date of pensionable age. The two amounts are added together to get the rate due (See leaflet N.D. 46).

The Social Security Act 1986 modified the calculation of additional pension for people retiring next century. Instead of being calculated on 25% of the best 20 years' relevant earnings it will be calculated on 20% of a person's lifetime average relevant earnings since 1978. The reduction from 25% to 20% will be phased in gradually over the first ten years of the next century.

Employees who are members of occupational pension schemes which meet specific requirements may be contracted out, by their employers, of the additional retirement pension. These occupational pension schemes then become responsible for providing a pension which must not be less than what is known as the guaranteed minimum pension (GMP). This is a substitute for, and broadly equivalent to the additional retirement pension. In return for providing the GMP a smaller national insurance contribution is payable. Contracted-out employees and their employers pay the normal rate of contribution on earnings up to the lower earnings limit plus a lower rate of contribution on that part of their earnings which is between the lower and upper earnings limits. From October 1985 all employers are liable to pay contributions at the normal rate on employees earnings above the upper earnings limit whether or not the employee is contracted-out.,

The Social Security Act 1986 makes it easier for employers to set up contracted-out schemes. Instead of having to promise a pension related to salary they will be able to pay a set amount of contributions into a scheme. Every employee will have a choice to take out a personal pension (PP) which can be used to contract-out of the State earnings related pension scheme (SERPS) or instead of membership of an occupational scheme. PP holders will pay full-rate national insurance contributions like employees not contracted-out who are full members of SERPS but the DSS will pay over a set amount into their PP scheme.

There were also some changes to the rules on liability from 6 April, 1978. The main change was that people over pension age (65 men, 60 women) do not have to pay any contributions at all, whether or not they have retired from work. The employer does however have to pay his share of a contribution at the not contracted-out rate in all cases.

The new scheme makes provision for protecting the rights to basic pension of people who are unable to pay sufficient contributions because they are at home raising a family or caring for a severely disabled person. This home responsibilities protection is not available to married women and widows while they have retained their right to pay reduced-rate contributions. (See leaflet NP 27.) Similar protection will be available for the additional pension rights of people retiring next century.

BENEFITS

BEFORE flat-rate benefit can be awarded certain conditions as to the number and class of contributions paid have to be complied with. These conditions vary for different benefits. Details can be found in the leaflets available free at local offices of the Department of Social Security.

Sickness Benefit - £35.20 a week: £22.10 for a dependent wife/husband or person looking after the claimant's children. People incapacitated as the result of an industrial accident or prescribed disease do not have to satisfy the contribution condition.

Invalidity Benefit. This usually replaces sickness benefit after 168 days of entitlement. If SSP was paid instead of sickness benefit, invalidity benefit is payable provided that the contribution conditions for sickness benefit were satisfied. It consists of a pension at the rate of £46.90 weekly; £28.20 for a dependent wife/husband or person looking after the claimant's children, £9.65 for each dependent child for whom child benefit is in payment. In addition, an invalidity allowance will be payable to those whose incapacity began more than five years before pension age. The rate of the allowance is £10.00 if incapacity began before age 40; £6.10 if it began before age 50; £3.10 if it began before age 55 for a woman and 60 for a man. There is also an additional earnings-related pension called Additional Pension which may be payable where entitlement to invalidity benefit began on or after April 6, 1979.

From September 16, 1985 Invalidity Allowance has been reduced or extinguished by any additional earnings-related pension and/or guaranteed minimum pension to which there is entitlement and only the balance of Invalidity Allowance if any, is payable.

Unemployment Benefit (Class 1 only). £37.35 a week; £23.05 for a dependent wife/husband or person looking after the claimant's children. Unemployment benefit is limited in duration to 312 days in any one period of interruption of employment. Once entitlement has been exhausted a claimant must work as an employee for at least 16 hours in each of 13 weeks in the 26 weeks before unemployment benefit is claimed again. These weeks need not be consecutive. The unemployment benefit payable to occupational pensioners age 55 or over is reduced by 10p for each 10p of their occupational pension in excess of £35 a week.

Waiting days. Sickness Benefit and Unemployment Benefit are not usually payable for the first three days of a period of interruption of employment.

Maternity Benefit. Statutory maternity pay (SMP) is administered by employers but there is still a state maternity allowance (MA) scheme for women who are self-employed or otherwise do not qualify for SMP.

In general, employers pay SMP to pregnant women who have been employed by them for at least six months and earned at least the lower earnings limit for the payment of NI contributions. For those who have been employed for at least two years, payment of SMP for the first six weeks is related to earnings, followed by up to twelve weeks at a standard rate of £39.25. Those who have been employed for at least six months but less than two years receive payment at standard rate only for the 18 weeks. Part-time working women also qualify for the earnings-related element if employed for at least five years. Women have some choice in deciding when to begin maternity leave but SMP is not payable for any week in which any work is done.

A woman may qualify for MA if she has been working and paying contributions at the full rate for at least 26 weeks in the 52-week period which ends 15 weeks before the baby is due. She also has an element of choice in deciding when to stop work and receive MA which is not payable for any period she works.

Widow's Benefit. Major changes in benefits were introduced for women widowed from 11 April 1988. From that date the three main widow's benefits will be: Widow's Payment, Widowed Mother's Allowance and Widow's Pension. Widow's benefit is used to mean all three of the benefits. Widows may be able to get a Widow's Payment and at the same time, a Widowed Mother's Allowance or a Widow's Pension. Widows cannot get a Widowed Mother's Allowance and a Widow's Pension at the same time.

Widow's benefit's are based on the National Insurance (NI) contributions of the man who had died. Widow's benefits are not based on the contributions of the widow. A widow cannot get any widow's benefit based on the man's NI if:

(a) she has been divorced from the man who has died
(b) she was living with the man as if she were married to him but without being legally married to him.
(c) she is living with another man as if she is married to him

A widow can only get widow's benefit if her husband has paid enough NI contributions. The rules about the number of NI contributions that are needed for these benefits can be complicated.

Widow's payment: A widow may be able to get a Widow's Payment if her husband has paid enough NI contributions and:

(a) she was under 60 when her husband died
(b) her husband was under 65 when he died

NATIONAL INSURANCE CONTRIBUTION RATES FROM 6 APRIL 1990

From October 1985 the upper earnings limit for employer's Class 1 contributions was abolished. There is still an upper earnings limit for contribution liability for employees.

The tables below and overleaf show the Class 1 rates and earnings limits for employees and employers from 6 April 1990. To find the total rate of national insurance due add together the rates from the employee's and the employer's columns.

	Lower Earnings Limit	**Upper Earnings Limit**
Weekly	£46.00	£350.00
Monthly	£200.00	£1517.00
Yearly	£2392.00	£18200.00

Not contracted-out employment

Not contracted-out earnings brackets			Employee				Employer
			On first £46.00 weekly or equivalent		Over £46.00 weekly or equivalent		
			Standard	Reduced	Standard	Reduced	
£46.00 or £200.00 or £2392.00	to £79.99 to £346.99 to £4159.99	weekly monthly yearly	2%	3.85%	9%	3.85%	5%
£80.00 or £347.00 or £4160.00	to £124.99 to £541.99 to £6499.99	weekly monthly yearly	2%	3.85%	9%	3.85%	7%
£125.00 or £542.00 or £6500.00	to £174.99 to £758.99 to £9099.99	weekly monthly yearly	2%	3.85%	9%	3.85%	9%
£175.00 or £759.00 or £8580.00	to £350.00 to £1517.00 to £16900.00	weekly monthly yearly	2%	3.85%	9%	3.85%	10.45%
Over or over or over	£350.00 weekly £1517.00 monthly £18200.00 yearly		2%	3.85%	9% up to £350.00 weekly or equivalent	3.85% up to £350.00 weekly or equivalent	10.45%

Class 2 contributions for the self-employed (see leaflet NI41)

Flat-rate for men under 65 and women under 60 £4.55 a week.

Small earnings exception from liability (apply if you expect to earn less than this from self-employment in the 1990/91 tax year £2,600 a year (from 6 April 1990 to 5 April 1991)

(c) if her husband was 65 or over when he died and was not getting a State Retirement Pension.

Widow payment is also payable if the widow is 60+ but only in certain circumstances i.e. husband must not have retired.

A widow who is entitled to a Widow's Payment will get a single payment of £1,000.00. This will be tax-free.

A widow may be able to get a **Widowed Mother's Allowance** if her husband has paid enough NI contributions and:

(a) she is receiving Child Benefit for one of her children
(b) her husband was receiving Child Benefit
(c) she is expecting her husband's baby.

A widow who is entitled to a Widowed Mother's Allowance will get an amount that is based on her husband's NI contributions. The maximum will be £46.90 a week. She will also get a £9.65 a week for each of her children and

she may also get an Additional Pension based on her husband's earnings since 1978. Widowed Mother's Allowance is usually paid as long as the widow is getting Child Benefit. Widowed Mother's Allowance will be taxable.

A widow may be able to get a **Widow's Pension** if her husband has paid enough NI contributions. She must be 45 or over when her husband died or when her Widowed Mother's Allowance ends. A widow cannot get a Widow's Pension at the same time as a Widowed Mother's Allowance.

A widow who is entitled to a Widow's Pension will get an amount that depends on two things:

(a) her age when her husband died or when her Widowed Mother's Allowance ends. If she was 55 or over she will get the full rate of Widow's Pension. Otherwise she will get less.
(b) the number of NI contributions her husband paid.

Contracted-out employment

Total earnings			Employee				Employer	
			On first £46.00 or equivalent		On earnings over £46.00 or equivalent		On first £46.00 or equivalent	On earnings £46.00 or equivalent
			Standard	Reduced	Standard	Reduced		
	£46.00 to £ 79.99 weekly		2%	3.85%	7%	3.85%	5%	1.2%
or	£200.00 to £346.99 monthly							
or	£2392.00 to £4159.99 yearly							
	£80.00 to £124.99 weekly		2%	3.85%	7%	3.85%	7%	3.2%
or	£347.00 to £541.99 monthly							
or	£4160.00 to £6499.99 yearly							
	£125.00 to £174.99 weekly		2%	3.85%	7%	3.85%	9%	5.2%
or	£542.00 to £758.99 monthly							
or	£6500.00 to £9099.99 yearly							
	£175.00 to £350.00 weekly		2%	3.85%	7%	3.85%	10.45%	6.65%
or	£759.00 to £1517.00 monthly							
or	£9100.00 to £18200.00 yearly							
over	**£350.00** weekly*		2%	3.85%	7% up to £350.00 or equivalent	3.85% up to £350.00 or equivalent	10.45% or equivalent	6.65% up to £350.00 and 10.45% thereafter
or over	£1517.00 monthly							
or over	£18200.00 yearly							

*Employees do not pay contributions on any earnings over £350.00 a week or the monthly or yearly equivalent.

Class 3 voluntary contributions to help qualify for basic retirement pension and a limited range of other benefits (see leaflet NI42).

Flat-rate for men and women £4.45 a week

Class 4 contributions for the self-employed (see leaflet NP18)

Rate payable 6.3% on Profits or gains between £5,050 and £16,900 a year

The maximum amount of Widow's Pension will be £46.90 per week. She may also get an Additional Pension based on her husband's earnings since 1978. Widow's Pension is usually paid until the widow is entitled to a State Retirement Pension, when she is 60 or older. Widow's Pension will be taxable.

Guardian's Allowance A weekly tax-free payment of £8.95 payable in addition to child benefit of £7.25 (to which the claimant must be entitled). It is payable to a person who takes into his or her family a child both of whose parents are dead, provided one of the parents satisfied a residence condition or was born in England, Wales, Scotland or Northern Ireland. In certain special circumstances the allowance may be paid where only one parent is dead. (See DSS leaflet NI 14.)

Child's Special Allowance (all classes) £9.65 a week for each child for whom child benefit is in payment. Payable to a woman whose marriage has been dissolved or annulled, on the death of her former husband, if she has not remarried and has a child towards whose support he was contributing at least 25p a week, or if she has taken reasonable steps to obtain maintenance. This benefit is abolished for all new claims where a former husband died on or after 6 April 1987.

Retirement Pension (all classes) The basic retirement pension is £46.90 a week payable on retirement for an insured man aged 65 or insured woman aged 60. The basic retirement pension for a married woman aged 60, based

on her husband's contribution is £28.20 provided her husband has also claimed his own pension. Increases of retirement pension may be payable in respect of a spouse, and in certain limited circumstances a husband or for a woman having care of the pensioner's children, at £28.20 a week and at £9.65 for each dependent child for whom child benefit is in payment. Where the date of retirement or claim is on or after April 6, 1979 an earnings-related pension called Additional Pension may also be payable.

The graduated scheme was wound up on April 5, 1975. Graduated Pension earned up to that date is however preserved and paid in the usual way on retirement. It was earned at the rate of 2 1/2p per week for every unit of 7.50 (9 for a woman) of graduated contributions paid by an employee and is paid in addition to the basic retirement pension. It can however be paid on its own where there is no entitlement to a basic pension. There is no increase of graduated pension for a wife or other dependent but a widow on her retirement at or after 60 will get half of the graduated pension which her late husband was receiving, or had earned, added to her retirement pension. A widower may get half of the graduated pension earned by his wife provided she died on or after April 6, 1979 and both of them were over pension age at the date of death. Since April 1978 graduated pensions in payment, and the rights earned by people who have not yet retired, have been increased in line with price rises. Currently they are payable at the rate of 6.14p for each unit of graduated contribution paid. Persons who postpone claiming and so do not receive their pensions at 65 (60 for women) can increase the rate of basic additional and graduated pension for which they may ultimately qualify when they claim or reach age 70 (65 for women). The earning Rule was abolished on 1st October 1989, therefore from that date pensioners' earnings will not affect their retirement pension.

From November 2, 1970 a non-contributory pension was provided for people who, because they were over pension age on July 5, 1948, were excluded from the National Insurance scheme, and for the wives, and in some cases, for the widows of men who were alive and over pension age on July 5, 1948. These pensions are subject to a residence test. The present rate is £28.20. From September 20, 1971 pensions at the same rate but without any provisions for dependants were introduced for all persons over age 80 (and who subsequently reach 80) who fail to qualify for a contributory pension or who qualify for one at a lower rate than these non-contributory pensions which are also subject to residence conditions. No new claims can be made for this allowance where a former husband dies on or after 6th April 1987.

Attendance Allowance This is a tax free allowance for severely disabled people, including children, who require a lot of help from another person. There are two rates of attendance allowance, the higher rate of £37.55 per week and the lower rate of £25.05 per week. To qualify for the higher rate a person must be so severely disabled physically or mentally that for six months or more he has required by day frequent attention or continual supervision to avoid substantial danger to himself or others and at night, prolonged or repeated attention or has required another person to be awake for a prolonged period or at frequent intervals for the purpose of watching over the disabled person to avoid substantial danger. The lower rate is payable where either one of the day conditions or one of the night conditions is satisfied. For children there is an additional condition that the attention or supervision required is substantially in excess of that normally required by a child of the same age and sex. Whether the medical conditions are satisfied is decided by the Attendance Allowance Board, an independent statutory authority. There are no contribution conditions for receipt of the allowance but simple tests of residence and presence in Great Britain. Further details and a claim form are contained in leaflet NI205, available from any DSS local office.

Invalid Care Allowance This is an allowance for people of working age who are unable to work because of the need to stay at home and care for a severely disabled person in receipt of attendance allowance or constant attendance allowance. It is payable at the rate of £28.20 a week with increases of £16.85 for an adult dependent; £9.65 for each dependent child for whom child benefit is in payment. There are no contribution conditions for receipt of the benefit. Beneficiaries of the allowance are awarded a Class I National Insurance Credit for each week of their entitlement. Further details and a claim form are contained in the leaflet NI212, available from any DSS local office.

Severe Disablement Allowance (SDA) This is a benefit which is not dependent on contributions and might be payable if the claimant does not qualify for contributory benefit. The weekly rates are the same as those for invalid care allowance and the benefit is payable to people of working age subject to the satisfaction of conditions as to residence and presence in the U.K. and proof of incapacity for work. A person who becomes incapable of work after their 20th birthday, in addition to satisfying the other conditions must be assessed as at least 80% disabled. People who are in receipt of a passport benefit such as Attendance Allowance or Mobility Allowance will automatically satisfy the 80% Disablement Test.

Mobility Allowance This is a non taxable allowance of 24.40 a week for those who are unable or virtually unable to walk because of physical disablement and are likely to remain so for at least a year. People aged 5 or over but under 66 can claim, but if they are already 65 they must have satisfied the conditions for receipt immediately before their 65th birthday. Once awarded, payment can continue up to age 75 as long as the conditions for receipt continue to be fulfilled. There are no contribution conditions but, in addition to the medical conditions there are simple tests of residence and presence in Great Britain.

INDUSTRIAL INJURIES
(Employed earners only)

BENEFIT may be payable to an employed earner suffering personal injury by accident arising out of and in the course of his employment or suffering from a prescribed disease due to his employment. There are no contribution conditions.

Industrial Injuries benefits are quite separate and distinct from any right to damages in respect of personal injuries and the receipt of such benefit in no way prevents a claim for damages being brought. But where a claim for Industrial Injuries benefits is made after 31.12.88 and compensation of £2,500 or more is awarded after 2.9.90 the provisions of reg. 2 of the Social Security (Recoupment) Regulations 1990 apply. This means the lesser of all the benefit paid up to the date of settlement or for the first 5 years will be deducted from the compensation before it is paid. The amount withheld will be repaid to the DSS by the compensator. If these Regulations do not apply then by virtue of the Law Reform (Personal Injuries) Act, 1948, the damages have to be reduced by one-half of the value of the Industrial Injuries benefits already received or calculated as due to be received, for from five years from the date of the injury.

Disablement Benefit. Usually paid 15 weeks after the date of accident or onset of the disease a weekly pension according to degree of disablement; £76.60 a week for 100 per cent assessment to £14.24 a week for 14 per cent. No benefit is payable for disablement below 14 per cent except for certain progressive respiratory diseases. There are various increases in special circumstances.

Reduced Earnings Allowance. Paid where disablement assessed at one per cent or more causes a reduction in earnings capacity weekly pension; maximum £30.64 a week.

Death Benefit. Widow if widowed before 11 April 1988 £14.07 or £46.90 a week depending on circumstances in each case. Allowances for dependent children, £9.65 for each child.

OTHER BENEFITS

Child Benefit. This replaced family allowances in April 1977 and is payable for all children including the first. The benefit is tax free at the rate of 7.25 a week for each child. There is a weekly addition of £5.60 per family for certain one-parent families.

Family Credit. Family Credit is a tax-free benefit for working families with at least one child under 16 (or under 19 if in full-time education up to and including A level or equivalent standard. If it is not a loan and does not have to be repaid). The claimant, or partner, if there is one, must be working 24 hours or more per week; they may be employed or self employed. Family credit may be claimed by a couple or a lone parent. No benefit is payable where the claimant and partner together have capital of over £8,000. Where the capital held is more than £3,000 but not more than £8,000 the rate of benefit is affected.

The Sue Ryder Foundation

For the sick and disabled

Founder – Lady Ryder of Warsaw, CMG, OBE.

The Sue Ryder Foundation was established by Sue Ryder during the post-war years after she had been doing social relief work on the Continent. Its purpose was, and is, the relief of suffering on a wide scale by means of personal service, helping sick and disabled in Britain and overseas, irrespective of race, religion or age, and thus serving as a **Living Memorial** to all those who suffered or died in the two World Wars and to those who undergo persecution or die in defence of human values today.

At present there are Homes in Britain in **Berkshire, Bedfordshire, Cambridgeshire, Cumbria, Gloucestershire, Hampshire, Hertfordshire, Lancashire, Norfolk, Suffolk, Yorkshire, Berwickshire** and **West Lothian**, but many more are needed. They care for the **physically handicapped, cancer** patients both terminal and convalescent, those with Huntington's chorea, the **mentally ill** and the **elderly**. Domiciliary care is also undertaken from some Homes. These and all our patients desperately need your help – with a legacy, deed of covenant or donation in finance or kind.

New Homes are planned in Birmingham, Manchester, London and North-East England.

Please write for any further information to:

The Sue Ryder Foundation
Cavendish
Sudbury
Suffolk, CO10 8AY

ROSEMARY FOR REMEMBRANCE

The method of assessment of family credit is as follows. A maximum credit is calculated comprising an adult credit (the same for one and two-parent families) plus an age-related child credit for each child. The maximum credit is payable where the family's income does not exceed the applicable amount, currently £57.60. Where net income does exceed the applicable amount, the maximum credit is reduced by 70% of any excess, and the result is the family credit payable.

Family credit is paid for 26 weeks at a time and is usually unaffected by changes in circumstances. Payment can be made either by orderbook, cashable weekly, or every 4 weeks direct into a bank or building society account. Family credit is claimed by post on claim form Family Credit FC1 (available from post offices or local social security offices). Claims are dealt with centrally at Family Credit Unit, Warbreck Hill, Blackpool

Free Milk and Vitamins. Free milk and vitamins are available to expectant and breast-feeding mothers and children under 5 in families receiving income support. Breastfeeding mothers can drink themselves any milk to which their breastfed baby is entitled. Beneficiaries receive tokens which can be exchanged for seven pints or eight half- litres of milk per week (or 900 grammes of dried baby milk if the child is under 1). Income support families may also obtain two bottles of vitamin drops every 13 weeks for each child under 5, two containers of vitamin tablets every 13 weeks for expectant mothers and 5 containers of vitamin tablets for breastfeeding mothers.

It is an offence to exchange milk tokens for anything other than milk.

Low Cost Baby Milk Families receiving family credit and who have a baby under 1 can buy 900 grammes per week of dried baby milk at a reduced cost from NHS maternity and child health clinics.

Full details are included in leaflet AB11 available at local offices of the Department Social Security and maternity and child health centres.

NATIONAL HEALTH SERVICE

The National Health Service comprises services provided by hospitals; general practitioners doctors, dentists, chemists and opticians; community health services, e.g. the district nursing and health visitor services, the ambulance service, maternity and child health care. A comprehensive health service is provided on behalf of the Secretary of State for Social Services by 14 Regional Health Authorities, 190 District Health Authorities, 90 Family Practitioner Committees and 16 Special Health Authorities. The present health authority boundaries were established in 1982 and as far as possible DHA boundaries correspond with local authority boundaries. But in some areas, such as London, this would be impracticable. RHAs include between eight and 22 DHAs and cover a number of local authorities. Health and local authorities work very closely together in the provision of total health care.

The service is available to everyone normally resident in the country. There is no insurance qualification. Charges are made for some items of treatment but these can be waived or reduced in cases of hardship.

Drugs and Appliances supplied under the National Health Service. There is a charge of £3.05 for each item supplied on prescription (other than tights at £6.10 per pair) unless the patient is exempt and the declaration on the back of the prescription form is completed. Children under 16, students under age 19 in full time education, men aged 65 or over and women aged 60 or over are automatically exempt.

Certain other people are eligible for exemption but must first obtain an exemption certificate. These are expectant mothers, and women who have borne a child in the previous 12 months; patients suffering from certain medical conditions; war or MOD disablement pensioners for prescriptions for their accepted disability; and people (and their dependants) in receipt of Income Support or Family Credit; other people whether in work or not, can claim exemption on low income grounds. Claim form AG1 is available from local Social Security Offices, doctors' surgeries, hospitals, dentists & opticians. (children 16 and over can claim on their own low income grounds).

People who are not exempt but who need frequent prescriptions can limit the amount they have to pay by purchasing a prepayment certificate (season ticket) which covers all charges for a fixed period. Certificates cost £15.80 for 4 months or £43.50 for 12 months. A prepayment certificate is worthwhile for anyone who needs more than five items on prescription in 4 months, or more than 14 items in 12 months. Prepayment certificate applications FP95 (EC95 in Scotland) are available from Post Offices, leaflet P11 containing information on prescription charges is available from local Social Security Offices, family doctors and chemists. There are separate arrangements for the payment of charges by hospital out-patients for wigs and fabric supports which are only supplied through the hospital service. The charges are £97 for each full bespoke human hair wig, £67 for each partial human hair wig, £26 for each stock wig, £17 for each abdominal or spinal support and £13 for each surgical brassiere. The following are exempt from charges for wigs and fabric supports: patients in hospital on the day of supply, war or MOD disablement pensioners in respect of their accepted disability, recipients (and their dependants) of Income Support, Family Credit, or holders (and their dependants) of a valid certificate of exemption from prescription charges on income grounds and young people under 16 or students under age 19 in full-time education. However, anyone who is not covered by these exemptions and whose income after paying their net housing costs is at or below the Income Support level can obtain full remission of the charges; and help with part of the charges may be given even where the income is a little higher. Claims for remission of charges on low income grounds are made on forms AG1, available at hospitals and local social security offices and doctors' surgeries.

Spectacles. From 1 April 1989 only patients in eligible categories can get a National Health service sight test which is free. These are children under 16, full-time students under age 19, people or their partners who are receiving Income Support or Family Credit, people with certificate AG2 from department of Social Security, the registered blind and partially sighted, those prescribed complex lenses as defined under the NHS voucher scheme, diagnosed diabetic and glaucoma sufferers and parents, brothers, sisters and children age 40 and over of glaucoma sufferers. Anyone not in one of the above categories has to seek a private eye test for which they will have to pay. Opticians will set the charge for private sight tests and this means prices will vary. Help with the cost of a private sight test is however available to some people with certificate AG1 from the Department of Social Security. Patients have a right to a copy of any prescription resulting from the test, whether the test is NHS or private. The new sight testing arrangements will be monitored to determine the pattern of private sight tests and fees charged for them.

The six basic voucher values are:

Optical Power	single vision	bifocal
low	£18.00	£34.75
intermediate	£28.75	£59.75
high	£47.00	£100.00

Values may be increased by additional amounts for prisms prescribed as clinically necessary (£4.00 per single vision lens and £4.75 per bifocal lens) and similarly for tints (£4.00 per single vision pair and £5.00 per bifocal pair). The voucher values for people qualifying only on complex lenses grounds are £3.50 and £18.00 respectively towards glasses with single vision lenses and bifocal glasses, with additions for prisms and tints where clinically necessary.

Leaflet G11 obtainable from local offices of the Department of Social Security explains how people can see whether they are eligible to NHS vouchers for glasses.

Repair and Replacement Under the Voucher Scheme
Help with the repair or replacement of damaged spectacles is available under the NHS voucher scheme. Help for children is available without regard to the circumstances the damage took place in. others will only get help with the loss or damage which has occurred as a direct result of illness. The Family Practitioner Committee must approve these cases before payment.

Charges for Dental Examination and Treatment. You will be asked to pay three-quarters of the cost of your NHS dental examination and treatment and about three-quarters of the cost of standard bridges and dentures. The maximum charge for a course of treatment is £150. There is no charge for arrest of bleeding, repairs to dentures, home visits by the dentist or reopening his surgery in an emergency (in these two cases you will have to pay for treatment given in the normal way). The following are exempt from dental charges:

> people under 18
> full time students under 19
> expectant mothers who were pregnant when accepted for treatment
> women who have had a child in the previous 12 months

The following are automatically entitled to full remission of charges:

> people getting Income Support or Family Credit and the partner of someone who gets Income Support or Family Credit.

Leaflet AB11 available from post offices and leaflet D11 available from local Social Security Offices and dentists' surgeries explain how other people on a low income can, depending on their financial circumstances, get free treatment or help with charges.

Medical Treatment Abroad. U.K. residents planning visits abroad should apply well beforehand to their local Post Office for leaflet T.I. 'The Travellers Guide to Health' or obtain a copy by ringing Freephone 0800 555 777. This explains how to get free or reduced cost emergency medical treatment in most European and some other countries. Visitors to Belgium, France, the Federal Republic of Germany (West Germany) Greece, Italy, Luxembourg, the Netherlands and Spain, have to apply for a Certificate of Entitlement to treatment (form E111) well before they go. The application form and the form E111 are available from the post office. British visitors to Denmark, Ireland and Portugal, do not need form E111 and treatment is generally available on the production of a UK passport. Further details are in leaflet 'T1 The Travellers Guide to Health'.

The arrangements for people planning to live or to work abroad are different. In this case they should write giving full details (including their National Insurance number) to the Department of Social Security Overseas Branch, Newcastle upon Tyne NE98 1YX who will give guidance on rights to Social Security. Overseas Branch should be contacted as soon as possible before leaving the U.K.

INCOME TAX

INCOME TAX is charged on the total income of an individual for a year of assessment commencing on April 6 and ending on the following April 5. The deductions which may be made from total income when calculating liability to income tax, and the rates of tax to be used, are frequently changed. The following comments apply to the calculation of income tax payable for the year of assessment 1990-91, ending on April 5, 1991. A new system of taxing husband and wife was introduced on April 6, 1990 and brief details of this system are given below.

INDEPENDENT TAXATION

Throughout a period of many years the income of a married woman 'living with', and not separated from her husband, was treated as that of the husband for income tax purposes. Thus it was the husband who was required to provide the Inland Revenue with details of his wife's income and to account for any outstanding income tax on that income. There were a number of notable exceptions to this general approach. It did not apply in the year of marriage and the wife was required to discharge her own commitments for that year. For subsequent years it was possible to exercise an option for separate assessment. This did not affect the aggregate amount of income tax payable but allocated the liability between husband and wife. Where the combined income of husband and wife was substantial an election for separate assessment of wife's earnings could also be made. As the result of such an election the wife was taxed as a single person on her earned income, receiving a lower personal allowance but not a wife's earned income allowance. The husband was taxed as a single man on his own earned income, together with the investment income of himself and his wife.

This system of taxing husband and wife 'living together' ceased to apply after April 5, 1990, with the introduction of independent taxation. For 1990-91 and future years a husband and wife will be independently assessed whether they are living together or living apart. All individuals, whether married or single, receive a personal allowance. In addition, a married man 'living with' his wife receives a married couple's allowance. Any unused personal allowance cannot usually be transferred from one spouse to the other, but where a husband cannot use, or fully use, the married couple's allowance he may transfer the unused portion to his wife.

There are three groups of special transitional allowances which have been introduced to ensure that the inception of independent taxation does not increase the tax liability incurred by a married couple.

ALLOWANCES

The availability and application of some allowances may be governed by whether a husband and wife are 'living together'. This relationship between a married couple is maintained unless -

i)   they are separated under an order of a court of competent jurisdiction;
ii) they are separated by deed of separation; or
iii) they are in fact separated in such circumstances that the separation is likely to be permanent.

(a) Personal Allowance.
For 1990-91 all individuals receive a basic personal allowance of £3,005. Individuals who were sixty-five years of age or more at any time in the year ended April 5, 1991, are entitled to an increased allowance of £3,670. The allowance is further increased to £3,820 for those

9

aged seventy-five years or over in the same year. In both cases the increased allowance is available for an individual who died before achieving the age of sixty-five or seventy-five if that age would otherwise have been reached before April 6, 1991.

The increased personal allowance otherwise available to older taxpayers will be reduced if the total income of the individual exceeds £12,300 for 1990-91. The personal allowance is then reduced by one-half of the income in excess of £12,300. This process continues until the allowance is reduced to the basic amount of £3,005, when no further reduction is necessary.

Apart from special transitional measures discussed below, any unused personal allowance of one spouse cannot be transferred to the other.

(b) Married Couple's Allowance.
Where a husband and wife are 'living together' at any time during the year ended April 6, 1991, the husband is entitled to a basic married couple's allowance of £1,720. This may be increased to £2,145 if either spouse is sixty-five years or over at any time in the year ending April 6, 1991. A further increase to £2,185 will be forthcoming if either spouse is seventy-five or over at any time in the year. In the case of a spouse who died during the year but would otherwise have reached the age of sixty-five or seventy-five before April 6, 1991, the appropriate increase will be forthcoming.

The increased married couple's allowance may require some restriction if the husband's income exceeds £12,300. Where this amount is exceeded the allowance will be reduced by -

a) one-half of the husband's total income (not including any income of his wife) in excess of £12,300, less
b) the amount of any reduction made to the husband's increased personal allowance by reason of income exceeding £12,300.

For the year of marriage the full allowance is available, at the appropriate level, if marriage takes place before May 6, 1990. The allowance must then be reduced by one-twelfth for each complete month preceding the date of marriage. Only one married couple's allowance can be obtained for 1990-91, notwithstanding that one marriage may terminate and a second marriage take place in the same year.

The married couple's allowance is given to the husband and not to the wife. If the allowance cannot be fully utilised by the husband the unused balance may be transferred to the wife.

After subtracting personal allowances and any other available deductions the first £20,700 of taxable income is chargeable to income tax at the basic rate of 25 per cent. Should income exceed £20,700, the excess will be taxable at the higher rate of 40 per cent. Income arising to trustees administering a discretionary or accumulation trust is chargeable at both the basic rate of 25 per cent and the additional rate of 10 per cent, thereby producing an aggregate liability of 35 per cent.

INCOME ASSESSABLE TO INCOME TAX

THE MAIN items of income which must be included in the calculation of total income and charged to income tax comprise the following:
(a) Benefits in kind enjoyed by most company directors and employees earning 8,500 per annum or more. Some benefits available to the lower paid are also taxable.
(b) Furnished letting income.

(c) Dividends and annuities.
(d) Interest.
(e) Pensions.
(f) Premiums from letting premises for periods which do not exceed fifty years.
(g) Profits from businesses and professions.
(h) Rents and other income from land and property.
(i) Salaries, wages, bonuses, commissions and all other emoluments from offices and employments. Up to one half of earnings arising from an approved profit-related pay scheme may be exempt from tax.
(j) Some Social Security benefits and pensions, including retirement pensions, widows' pensions, widows and widowed mothers' allowances, invalid care allowances, maternity pay and most unemployment benefits. Additions for children generally remain exempt and many other social security benefits are not liable to taxation (see paragraph (j) below). Unemployment benefits are taxable, but tax is only collected through the PAYE deduction scheme once the period of unemployment ends. Short-term statutory sick pay, payable by an employer, is taxable, but long-term sickness benefit which the employer is not required to pay incurs no liability to taxation.

INCOME NOT ASSESSABLE TO INCOME TAX

AMONG ITEMS not assessable to income tax are the following:

(a) Annuities paid to holders of the Victoria Cross, George Cross, Albert Medal, Edward Medal and certain other gallantry awards.
(b) Bounty payments to members of the armed forces.
(c) Building society interest, together with most interest received from banks and local authorities. (This may be chargeable at the higher rate of 40 per cent where income is substantial).
(d) Scholarship income.
(e) Compensation for loss of office and redundancy, unless the aggregate receipts exceed 30,000.
(f) Interest on contractual savings under the Save As You Earn Scheme.
(g) Interest on National Savings Certificates.
(h) Interest on TESSA deposit accounts after December 31, 1990.
(i) National Savings Bank interest. (Exemption is limited to the first 70 received and is restricted to interest on ordinary deposits.)
(j) Most Social Security pensions and benefits, including attendance allowances, child benefits, child's special allowances, family credit. family income supplement, guardian's allowances, invalidity benefits, maternity allowance, non-contributory invalidity benefits, long-term sickness benefits and mobility allowances. Those Social Security pensions and benefits which are chargeable to tax have been listed under paragraph (i) in the preceding section concerning assessable income.

(c) Additional Personal Allowance.
A widow, widower or other single person not entitled to the married personal allowance but who has a qualifying child resident with him or her for the whole or any part of the year ended on April 5, 1991, may receive an additional personal allowance of £1,720. The allowance is also available to a married man if throughout that year his wife was totally incapacitated by physical or mental infirmity and a qualifying child was similarly resident. A qualifying child means a child born during the year ended on April 5, 1991, a child under the age of sixteen years on April 6, 1990, or a child over the age of sixteen on April 6, 1990, and either receiving full-time instruction at a university, college, school or other educational establishment or undergoing training for a trade, profession or vocation

9

throughout a minimum two year period. It is also necessary to show that the qualifying child is a child of the claimant or, not being such a child, was either born during the year ended April 5, 1991, or under the age of eighteen years on April 6, 1990, and maintained for the whole or part of the succeeding twelve-month period by the claimant at his own expense. Only one allowance of £1,720 can be obtained, notwithstanding the number of qualifying children. Where an unmarried couple are living together as husband and wife only one individual can obtain the allowance of £1,720. The allowance is only available to the claimant and cannot be transferred.

(d) Blind Person's Allowance.
A blind person's allowance of £1,080 is available if the taxpayer is registered as blind on a register maintained by a local authority. Where husband and wife are 'living together' and either spouse cannot fully utilise the allowance the unused allowance may be transferred to the other spouse.

(e) Widow's Bereavement Allowance. A widow's bereavement allowance of £1,720 may be obtained by a widow for the year of assessment in which her husband dies. A similar allowance is also available for the year following that in which death occurred, unless the widow remarried in the year of her late husband's death. To obtain the allowance for either of these two years it must be shown that at the time of the husband's death the parties were 'living together'.

RELIEF FOR INTEREST PAID

INCOME TAX relief for payments of interest is restricted to loans or advances which satisfy a number of requirements. No relief can be obtained for interest payable on a bank overdraft. In addition, relief is limited to payments of annual interest or to other interest paid to a bank, stockbroker or discount house. No relief will be forthcoming to the extent that interest is paid at a rate exceeding a reasonable commercial level.

Relief is confined to interest on loans or advances used for one of the following purposes:

(i)   A loan applied for the purchase of an interest in land occupied by the borrower as his only or main residence. 'Land', which must be located in the United Kingdom or the Republic of Ireland, may comprise a house, flat, maisonette or similar building, together with large houseboats or caravans. If the loan was obtained before April 6, 1988 it could also be used to finance home improvements. New loans obtained after this date will not be recognised unless they are applied to finance the erection of a new building. Loans applied before April 6, 1988 to provide an only or main residence for a dependent relative, a separated spouse or a former spouse also enable relief to be obtained but loans applied for a similar purpose subsequently will longer qualify. If the loan exceeds £30,000 for 1990-91, relief is restricted to interest on that sum. Loans used to acquire some other residence or a property to be occupied on retirement may also qualify if the borrower is an employee, or carrying on business, and compelled to occupy premises in connection with his or her work. For loans obtained before August 1, 1988 each individual was subject to the £30,000 limitation, although this applied in aggregate to husband and wife living together. In the case of loans taken out after this date the limitation of £30,000 is applied to the aggregate of all loans on a single property.

(ii) A loan applied to purchase an annuity ending on death, if the borrower is at least sixty-five years of

age and the loan is secured on land used as an only or main residence. The £30,000 restriction also applies to loans of this nature.

(iii) A loan to acquire an interest in a partnership or, in the case of a loan to a partner, to acquire machinery or plant for use in the partnership business.

(iv) A loan to acquire an interest in a closely controlled company.

(v)   A loan to an employee for the purpose of acquiring machinery or plant used in his employment.

(vi) A loan made to acquire an interest in a co-operative or an employee controlled company.

(vii) A loan to personal representatives to discharge capital transfer tax or inheritance tax.

Interest paid on a loan to purchase or improve an interest in land which is let at a commercial rent, or available to be so let, may obtain relief. However, the interest can only be deducted from rental income and cannot be offset against other income of the borrower.

Any interest paid, whether on a loan or overdraft, wholly and exclusively for the purposes of a trade, profession or vocation is not affected by the above rules and may be deducted in arriving at business profits.

Relief for many payments of mortgage interest is given through a special scheme, namely MIRAS (mortgage interest relief at source). This scheme applies to most payments of interest made to building societies, banks, insurance companies, local authorities and some other persons. When making payments of mortgage interest under the MIRAS arrangements the payer deducts, and retains, income tax at the basic rate of 25 per cent. This effectively ensures that tax relief is obtained when making payment and not through the normal tax system.

Where loans exceed £30,000 or there is some other restriction, the operation of MIRAS will be limited to the interest qualifying for relief. MIRAS does not extend to payments of interest on all qualifying loans. For interest payments outside the MIRAS scheme, relief will then be available through the normal tax system. Borrowers within MIRAS who suffer income tax at the higher rate of 40 per cent, obtain relief at the excess rate in the normal manner.

BENEFITS IN KIND

CERTAIN benefits enjoyed by all employees, whatever their level of earnings, are chargeable to income tax. These include benefits from the occupation of an employer's property, the provision of season tickets, transport vouchers and credit cards, together with all other advantages capable of being turned into money.

Special provisions exist for charging income tax on the value of additional benefits enjoyed by company directors and also employees whose emoluments are at the rate of £8,500 or more annually. The taxable benefits include expenses reimbursed by the employer and expenditure incurred by an employer when providing the benefit. Where a motor car belonging to an employer is made available for use by an employee a scale charge will determine the amount of the taxable benefit. This is governed by the age of the vehicle, cost when new, and the amount of business mileage. A further scale charge also applies where an employer finances the cost of petrol or other fuel used for private motoring.

The ability to use other assets, and the provision of loan facilities on advantageous terms, may all create taxable benefits. No benefit arises from the provision of child care facilities where these are available on prenises provided by an employer.

ALLOWABLE EXPENSES OF EMPLOYEES

ANY EXPENSES which the holder of an office or employment is necessarily obliged to expend wholly, exclusively and necessarily in the performance of the duties of the office, including expenses of travelling, may be deducted from earnings assessable to income tax. The cost of travelling from home to the place of employment cannot be allowed, as travelling is not undertaken whilst performing the duties of the office but to place the individual in a position from which to carry out those duties. On the other hand, once the place of employment has been reached the cost of any further business journeys will usually qualify for relief.

Hotel expenses for travellers and others who have to go from place to place in the performance of their duties will usually be allowed. However expenses incurred in providing entertainment must usually be excluded.

Fees and subscriptions paid to professional societies carrying on activities relating to an employee's work may be deducted from the emoluments of an office.

PROPERTY INCOME

RENTAL and other income arising to the owner of land in the United Kingdom is chargeable to income tax. Liability is governed by entitlement and will not necessarily be limited to income actually received. Relief for lost rents and other deficiencies of income may be obtained if certain conditions are satisfied.

Expenses on maintenance, repairs, insurance and management may be deducted from gross income, leaving only the balance assessable.

Income tax is payable on January 1 for each year ending on the following April 5. As an accurate determination of property income cannot usually be made on the payment date, the assessment will be based on income arising in the previous year of assessment. Once the following April 5 has been reached, accurate figures of net income can be established and this will result in either an additional tax liability or some repayment of tax.

Special provisions apply to tax premiums payable on the granting of leases for periods not exceeding fifty years. Where such a premium is received the person granting the lease is treated as having derived an amount of income equal to the premium, less one-fiftieth for each year of the lease, disregarding the first year. Thus a premium of £20,000 paid for a lease of twenty-one years will involve a charge to tax on £12,000 (£20,000 less twenty-fiftieths).

DIVIDENDS

DIVIDENDS paid by United Kingdom companies are not subject to deduction of income tax. However, each dividend is treated as having attached to it a tax credit equal, for 1990-91, to one third of the dividend paid. For the purpose of calculating the total income of an individual who receives such a dividend the tax credit must be added

AMOUNT OF INCOME TAX FOR 1990-91

| On total income of | SINGLE PERSON | | | MARRIED MAN OR WOMAN | |
| | Persons under 65 years of age | | | | |
	One Person[2]	One parent family[3]	Persons over 65[2]	Persons under 65[2]	Persons over 65(2)
£	£	£	£	£	£
3,500	123.75	-	-	-	-
4,000	248.74	-	82.50	-	-
4,500	373.75	-	207.50	-	-
5,000	498.75	68.75	332.50	68.75	-
5,500	623.75	193.75	457.50	193.75	-
6,000	748.75	318.75	582.50	318.75	46.25
7,000	998.75	568.75	832.50	568.75	296.25
8,000	1,248.75	818.75	1,082.50	818.75	546.25
9,000	1,498.75	1,068.25	1,332.50	1,068.75	796.25
10,000	1,748.75	1,318.75	1,582.52	1,318.75	1,046.25
12,000	2,248.75	1,818.75	2,082.50	1,818.75	1,546.25
14,000	2,748.75	2,318.75	2,748.75	2,318.75	2,278.75
16,000	3,248.75	2,818.75	3,248.75	2,818.75	2,818.75
18,000	3,748.75	3,318.75	3,748.75	3,318.75	3,318.75
20,000	4,248.75	3,818.75	4,248.75	3,818.25	3,818.75
25,000	5,693.00	5,068.75	5,693.00	5,068.75	5,068.75
30,000	7,693.00	7,005.00	7,693.00	7,005.00	7,005.00
35,000	9,693.00	9,005.00	9,693.00	9,005.00	9,005.00
40,000	11,693.00	11,005.00	11,693.00	11,005.00	11,005.00
45,000	13,693.00	13,005.00	13,693.00	13,005.00	13,005.00
50,000	15,693.00	15,005.00	15,693.00	15,005.00	15,005.00
75,000	25,693.00	25,005.00	25,693.00	25,005.00	25,005.00
100,000	35,693.00	35,005.00	35,693.00	35,005.00	35,005.00
150,000	55,693.00	55,005.00	55,693.00	55,005.00	55,005.00

NOTES

1   The same amount of tax becomes payable whether income is earned or unearned.
2   The tax shown is that due where there are no allowances other than the lower personal allowance and the married couple's allowance, as appropriate. Rather less tax may be payable by elderly persons aged 75 or over.
3   A single person with a qualifying child receives both the lower personal allowance and an additional personal allowance of £1.720:

9 HOUSEHOLDERS' GUIDE

to the dividend received. The tax credit will be regarded as income tax suffered on the aggregate dividend at the rate of 25 per cent and an individual who is not liable, or not fully liable, to tax at this rate may obtain a complete or partial repayment of the tax credit. Those liable to tax at the higher rate of 40 per cent must suffer additional liability on the dividend received.

MAINTENANCE PAYMENTS

Payments of maintenance will often be made following the breakdown of marriage. The significance of these payments for taxation purposes is somewhat complex but in the case of binding maintenance agreements and Court Orders made not later than March 15, or perhaps June 30, 1988 the payer should obtain full income tax relief on the outlay. If the recipient is the spouse, or former spouse, of the payer the first £1,720 received in 1990-91 is exempt from income tax. This treatment will broadly continue in future years.

For new agreements and Court Orders, however the payer will only obtain tax relief if payments are made to a separated or former spouse. Relief cannot exceed 1,590. The recipient of such payments will not be required to suffer income tax. This situation also will continue in future years.

HOW INCOME TAX IS PAYABLE

THE PAYMENT of income tax is governed by the nature of income, profits or gains liable to that tax. As a general rule, tax will be payable on January 1 in the year of assessment, or thirty days after the date on which the assessment is made, whichever is the later.

Tax on income arising from a trade, profession or vocation is payable by two equal instalments, namely:

(i)   on January 1 in the year of assessment; and
(ii) on July 1 following.

Any higher rate tax attributable to the following income will be separately charged and become payable on December 1 following the end of the year of assessment to which the charge relates, or on the expiration of thirty days from the date of making the assessment, whichever is the later:

(i)   Dividends from United Kingdom companies.
(ii) Investment income taxed by deduction at the basic rate of 25 per cent.
(iii) Investment income deemed to have borne tax at the basic rate (e.g. building society interest received and most interest received from banks and local authorities, among others where that income arises before April 6, 1991).

Failure to satisfy income tax on the due date may incur a liability to account for interest. The rates of interest change from time to time in a manner which reflects movements in the money market.

PAY AS YOU EARN

PAY AS YOU EARN is not a separate tax but merely a scheme whereby income tax on wages and salaries is collected as and when emoluments are paid or, if earlier, when an employee becomes entitled to those emoluments. There are additional rules for establishing the date of payment for company directors. Employers are supplied with tax tables and code numbers for employees which enable income tax to be calculated and deducted from each payment of emoluments. The scheme takes account of personal allowances and deductions due to individual employees and where an employee has no other source of income Pay As You Earn deductions should exhaust his full tax liability. Many adjustments may be required where, for example, an employee retains two or more employments simultaneously or suffers some change in his personal circumstances during the year.

The P.A.Y.E. scheme is also applied to recover income tax on maternity pay and short-term sick benefits paid by an employer.

SUB-CONTRACTORS

MANY sub-contractors engaged in the construction industry have obtained certificates issued by the Board of Inland Revenue. Where these certificates are available any payments made to the sub-contractor by a contractor suffer no deduction of income tax. In the absence of a certificate, a contractor must deduct income tax at the rate of 25 per cent when making payments for the supply of labour by a sub-contractor. The sub-contractor will be assessable to income tax on his full profits, disregarding income tax deducted. However, the deductions may then be offset against income tax otherwise payable, thereby reducing the balance due or perhaps creating some repayment.

NON-RESIDENTS

THE PERSONAL allowances mentioned earlier are not usually granted to individuals who normally live outside the United Kingdom. These allowances may, however, be obtained where the taxpayer:

(i)   is a British subject or a citizen of the Republic of Ireland;
(ii)   is a person employed in the service of the Crown or of any missionary society;
(iii) is a resident of the Isle of Man or the Channel Islands;
(iv)   has previously resided within the United Kingdom and is resident overseas for health reasons;
(v)   is a widow whose late husband was in the service of the Crown; or
(vi)   is a resident of a country which has a reciprocal agreement with the United Kingdom.

Non-residents can claim exemption from United Kingdom income tax for interest paid on a restricted list of Government securities. Dividends and interest arising from United Kingdom resident companies and paid to a non-resident may be exempt from tax, or chargeable to tax at reduced rates, as required by the provisions of a double taxation agreement.

DOUBLE TAXATION

PERSONS resident in the United Kingdom who receive income from overseas may be chargeable to United Kingdom income tax on that income. It may well be found that the income has also borne tax in the country of origin, thereby creating double taxation. To avoid this situation, double taxation agreements have been concluded between the United Kingdom and many overseas territories. These agreements contain a variety of different features. Some exempt income from tax liability in one territory, others impose tax at reduced rates, and many allow a credit for foreign tax suffered to be set against United Kingdom tax payable. In no case can relief for overseas taxation exceed the tax otherwise payable in the United Kingdom and where unrelieved foreign tax arises no claim for repayment can be made to the United Kingdom tax authorities.

In those cases where no double taxation agreement exists between the United Kingdom and the overseas country of origin, a form of unilateral relief may often be used to mitigate the effect of double taxation.

REPAYMENT CLAIMS

MANY persons who receive income from investments are entitled to recover income tax deducted, or deemed to have been deducted, from dividends and interest. This situation will arise where the income tax suffered by deduction exceeds the recipient's personal liability. A claim for repayment should be forwarded to H.M. Inspector of Taxes in the locality where the taxpayer resides, enclosing dividend vouchers and other documents. It is necessary for repayment claims to be submitted within a period of six years following the end of the tax year to which they relate. Should the repayment be delayed, the taxpayer may be entitled to receive interest.

Interest received before April 6, 1991 from building societies, together with most interest received from banks, local authorities and some others, does not incur liability to income tax at the basic rate. Interest is paid under a composite rate scheme and depositors not liable to tax at the basic rate are unable to obtain any repayment of the notional tax suffered. The corporate rate scheme has no application for interest received after April 5, 1991. Most interest will then be paid after deducting income tax at the basic rate.

LIFE ASSURANCE PREMIUMS

FOR MANY years life assurance premium relief has been available for individuals paying premiums on qualifying policies. While this relief continues on many policies it is not available for premiums on policies made after March 13, 1984.

On paying premiums under an approved policy made before March 12, 1984 the individual will deduct and retain income tax at the rate of 12.5 per cent. It is immaterial whether the individual is liable to income tax or exempt on the grounds that his or her income is insufficient to create liability. In all cases the deduction can be made and retained. A restriction arises where the premiums paid in any year exceed £1,500 as relief must be limited to deductions on £1,500 or one-sixth of the individual's total income, whichever is the greater.

The availability of relief for premiums on pre-1984 policies may be lost if the terms of the policy are altered to provide increased benefits.

CORPORATION TAX

INCOME TAX is not charged on the income of a United Kingdom resident company. In place of this tax a company suffers liability to corporation tax on profits, gains and income. Corporation tax is charged on profits, gains and income of an account ing period, and this will usually be the period for which accounts are prepared annually.

Rates of corporation tax apply for a twelve month 'financial year' ending on March 31. Where the accounting period of a company overlaps this date, results must be apportioned to establish the amount falling in each financial year. Recent rates, and those which apply for future years, are as follows:

	Per cent
Year ending March 31, 1984	50
Year ending March 31, 1985	45
Year ending March 31, 1986	40
Years ending March 31, 1987 to 1991	35

Where the profits of a company do not exceed stated limits tax is payable at the small companies rate as follows:

	Per cent
Years ending March 31, 1984 to 1986	30
Year ending March 31, 1987	29
Year ending March 31, 1988	27
Year ending March 31, 1989 and 1991	25

These limits have altered on several occasions but for the year to March 31, 1991 the limit is £200,000. Marginal small companies rate relief is available for the same year where profits fall between £200,000 and £1 million.

Adjustment must be made to the small companies rate calculation if there are other companies under common control, or the accounting period overlaps March 31. The special rate cannot apply to certain investment companies.

Profits derived by a company, and chargeable to corporation tax, are broadly calculated on income tax principles. There are, however, several important exceptions to this rule, particularly where interest and annual payments are made.

Chargeable gains arising on the disposal of assets and accruing to individuals are assessable to capital gains tax. Similar gains derived by a company incur liability to corporation tax. For disposal taking place before March 17, 1987 only a fraction of the chargeable gains incurred liability at the full rate to ensure that tax was imposed at an effective rate of 30 per cent on the full gains. Chargeable gains on disposals occurring after this date are not reduced by a fraction but are added to the other profits of a company. The aggregate profits are then taxed at the full rate, small companies rate, or marginal rate as appropriate.

When making a qualifying distribution a United Kingdom resident company is required to account to the Inland Revenue for advance corporation tax. For the year ended April 5, 1991, the rate of advance corporation tax is one-third of the distribution. This tax may usually be deducted from the company's main corporation tax liability, if any, and really represents a payment in advance of that liability.

Each dividend paid by a United Kingdom resident company carries a tax credit and the significance of this to the recipient is shown on under the heading of 'DIVIDENDS'.

CAPITAL GAINS TAX

LIABILITY to capital gains tax was introduced on April 6, 1965 but there have been many changes in the concept and application of the tax in subsequent years. The following comments are confined to events taking place after April 5, 1988.

Capital gains tax liability arises where chargeable gains are derived on the disposal of assets. The expression 'disposal' usually involves a change in ownership but certain deemed disposals are treated as having taken place and these also may produce liability to capital gains tax. Assets include nearly all forms of property, an expression which incorporates stocks, shares, unit trust holdings, land, buildings, jewellery, antiques many others.

The potential scope of liability to capital gains tax is extremely wide, but numerous exemptions are available. Gains arising on the disposal of private motor vehicles, an individual's principal private residence, National Savings Certificates, Premium Bonds, together with sums received on the maturity or surrender of normal policies of life assurance, and sums received from the sale of most chattels which have a predictable life of less than fifty years, are usually exempt. The disposal of gilt edged securities issued by the Government, together with securities (not shares) issued by a company, will not produce liability. Gains arising on the disposal of goods and chattels not otherwise exempted, usually those with a life expectation of more than fifty years, will be excluded if the disposal proceeds do not exceed £6,000.

Transfers of assets between husband and wife living together produce no liability to capital gains tax, and a similar exemption applies to assets retained at the time of an individual's death.

Where gains arise from the disposal of assets used for the purposes of a business, these may often be rolled over and offset against the cost of acquiring replacement assets. Hold-over relief may be available on the transfer of a limited range of assets, including business assets, shares in trading companies and agricultural land.

An individual who has reached the age of sixty years before completing the disposal of business assets may obtain retirement relief, reaching a maximum in excess of £300,000 for disposals after April 5, 1988, which reduces or eliminates the gains otherwise chargeable to capital gains tax. Similar relief may be available to an individual compelled to retire on ill health grounds before reaching the age of sixty.

The calculation of gains arising on the disposal of assets made after April 5, 1988 will often proceed by comparing the cost of acquisition with the disposal proceeds. However, in those cases where the assets have been acquired before March 31, 1982 it must usually be assumed those assets were acquired for a consideration representing market value on that date.

The amount of any gain arising on the disposal may be reduced by subtracting an indexation allowance. This allowance is determined by applying the percentage increase in the retail prices index between March 1982 (or the month in which expenditure was subsequently incurred, if later) and the month of disposal, to cost. For those assets acquired before March 31, 1982 the 'cost' factor will reflect market value on that date.

The gain arising, after subtracting the indexation allowance, becomes the chargeable gain assessable to capital gains tax. Losses arising on disposal are calculated on a similar basis although the indexation allowance will clearly increase the amount of any loss.

The amount of capital gains tax payable by an individual for 1990-91 will be governed by the net gains (chargeable gains less losses) arising in the year. If the net gains do not exceed £5,000 no liability to tax will arise. Should this figure be exceed the excess will be charged to capital gains tax but liability must be calculated using income tax rates. In effect the excess is added to the amount on which an individual suffers income tax for the year of assessment to determine the rate of tax which must be applied. Although income tax rates are used, capital gains tax remains a completely separate tax which is not absorbed into the income tax system.

Losses brought forward from an earlier year must be set against chargeable gains for the current year but this is not to reduce the net gains below the exemption level of £5,000.

For 1989-90 only one combined exemption of £5,000 was available for husband and wife living together. Following the introduction of independent taxation on April 6, 1990 each spouse will be assessed to tax and may separately enjoy the annual £5,000 exemption.

INHERITANCE TAX

Introduced in 1974, capital transfer tax applied to many lifetime gifts and dispositions and also to the value of an individual's estate at the time of death. Substantial changes were introduced for events occurring after March 17, 1986, and the tax was renamed inheritance tax. The following comments outline the scope and application of inheritance tax but no attempt is made to review the former capital transfer tax.

Inheritance tax liability may affect assets located in the United Kingdom. Assets located overseas may also be affected if, but only if, the person concerned is domiciled in the United Kingdom. There are two main occasions of possible charge affecting individuals, one arising from lifetime gifts and dispositions and the other affecting the value of an estate at the time of death.

Lifetime transfers
Lifetime gifts or transfers which deplete the value of an individual's estate may fall into one of four broad categories, namely, transactions disregarded, exempt transfers, potentially exempt transfers and chargeable transfers.

Transactions disregarded
A range of transactions must be totally disregarded and will incur no liability to inheritance tax, notwithstanding that the value of an individual's estate has been reduced. These include transactions not intended to confer gratuitous benefit, the provision of family maintenance, the waiver of the right to receive remuneration or dividends and the grant of agricultural tenancies for full consideration.

Exempt transfers
Transfers of value which comprise exempt transfers will also avoid liability to inheritance tax. These include the following:

(i) A transfer by an individual to his or her spouse. This is subject to modification if the transferee is not domiciled in the United Kingdom.
(ii) The first £3,000 of transfers made in a year ending on April 5. If the total of the transfers made in any year falls below £3,000 the excess may be carried forward for one year only and utilised in that year.
(iii) Transfers of value made by a transferor to any one person in a year ending on April 5 if the values transferred do not exceed £250.
(iv) A transfer made as part of the normal expenditure of the transferor and satisfied out of income.
(v) Outright gifts in consideration of marriage, to the extent that the value transferred by any one transferor in respect of a single marriage does not exceed:

   (a) £5,000 if the transferor is the parent of either party to the marriage;
   (b) £2,500 if the transferor is a party to the marriage or a grandparent or remoter ancestor of either party to the marriage;
   (c) £1,000 if the transferor is any other person.

(vi) Transfers of value to charities, certain national bodies and political organisations.

Potentially exempt transfers
A potentially exempt transfer must be made by an individual to

(i) a second individual;
(ii) trustees administering an accumulation and maintenance trust; or
(iii) trustees administering a disabled person's trust.

Transfers affecting settled property where an individual retains, acquires or relinquishes an interest in possession may also comprise potentially exempt transfers if the transaction occurs after March 16, 1987.

As the title suggests, potentially exempt transfers are potentially exempt from liability and no inheritance tax will become payable at the time of the transfer. Freedom from liability will be confirmed should the transferor survive throughout a period of seven years from the date of the gift. However, if the transferor dies within the seven-year period inheritance tax becomes payable at the full rates in force on death. The amount of tax due may then be reduced to the following percentages by applying tapering relief:

Period of years before death	Percentage
Not more than 3	100
More than 3 but not more than 4	80
More than 4 but not more than 5	60
More than 5 but not more than 6	40
More than 6 but not more than 7	20

Chargeable transfers

Finally, a restricted range of lifetime transfers will incur liability to inheritance tax. These are limited to transfers involving trusts, other than the three types of trust falling within the potentially exempt transfer rules, transfers to non- individuals and transfers affecting close companies. Tax is payable at one-half of the full rate or rates. However, should the transferor die within a period of seven years from the date of the lifetime chargeable transfer, additional tax may become payable by substituting the full rates, less a deduction for tapering relief.

Gifts with reservation

Special rules apply where a lifetime gift is made but the transferor continues to enjoy some benefit in the subject matter of the gift. This may arise, for example, where a parent gifts a home to his or her children and continues to occupy the property rent- free. Where a gift with reservation is made it becomes necessary to establish the period during which the transferor continued to enjoy any benefit. There are three broad possibilities. Firstly, if the benefit ceased to be enjoyed more than seven years before the transferor's death there can be no liability. Secondly, if the benefit was enjoyed at the time of death the value of the asset must be added to the value of the deceased's estate on which inheritance tax is payable. Finally, if the transferor ceased to enjoy the benefit within a period of seven years before death, the transferor is treated as having made a potentially exempt transfer equal to the value of the asset at the time of cessation.

Transfers on death

Immediately before the time of death an individual is deemed to make a transfer of value equal to the value of his or her estate (assets less liabilities). However, exempt transfers involving transfers to the surviving spouse, if any, charities, national bodies and political organisations will not incur liability to inheritance tax, subject to limited exceptions. Inheritance tax is calculated by applying the full rate or rates. In addition, death may result in liability to tax on potentially exempt transfers and additional liability may arise on chargeable lifetime transfers made within a period of seven years before death.

Valuation

The value transferred by lifetime transfers will usually reflect the fall in the value of a person's estate. This is not necessarily the value of the actual gift made. For example, an individual may retain 51 per cent of the shares issued by a closely controlled company and gift 2 per cent, thereby reducing his holding to 49 per cent. The fall in value from a 51 per cent controlling interest to a 49 per cent minority interest will substantially exceed the actual value of a 2 per cent holding.

The value transferred on death will reflect the value of the deceased's estate.

In general, the value of property comprised in an individual's estate will represent the price which that property might reasonably have been expected to fetch on a sale in the open market. However, where the transfer relates to certain assets the value transferred, both by lifetime transfers and on death, may be reduced by a percentage. The percentage deductions for events occurring after March 16, 1987 are as follows:

Asset	Percentage Deduction
Business or interest in a business	50
Controlling shareholding interest in any company	50
Minority shareholding interest exceeding 25% in an unquoted company	50
Minority shareholding interest not exceeding 25% in an unquoted company	30
Land, buildings, machinery or plant used by a controlled company or by a partnership	30

The value of agricultural property transferred may also qualify for a percentage deduction. This is limited to the agricultural value and where, for example, property retains an excessive development value no deduction will be available for the excess. The percentage deductions are:

Asset	Percentage Deduction
Land subject to a tenancy not terminating within 12 months	30
Other land	50

In the case of lifetime chargeable transfers, unless inheritance tax is payable by the transferee the value transferred on which tax becomes due must usually be increased by the amount of that tax.

Calculation of tax payable

Inheritance tax is calculated by using a seven-year cumulative table. Each successive chargeable life -time transfer is added to earlier transfers made within the previous seven-year period to establish the rate band into which the current transfer falls. At the time of death there will also be added potentially exempt transfers becoming chargeable transfers and the value of the estate at death. These final additions will only be made to lifetime chargeable transfers taking place within the previous seven-year period.

Rates of tax

For events occurring after April 5, 1990 the first £128,000 is taxed at a nil rate. Any excess above this amount is taxed at 40 per cent. Therefore only one positive rate applies. When calculating tax on chargeable life transfers the half rate of 20 per cent must be used.

Settled property

Complex rules apply to settled property held by trustees. In general, where a beneficiary retains an interest in possession the settled property to which that interest extends will be treated as being in the effective ownership of the beneficiary. Property held on discretionary trusts is subject to a ten-year periodic charge, with interim charges where property leaves the trust before the first ten- year anniversary or between anniversaries. An accumulation and maintenance trust will not be subject to the ten-year periodic charge nor will liability to inheritance tax usually arise on the removal of property from such a trust.

9

POST OFFICE SERVICES

The following services and charges are for 1990 but are liable to modification. Up-to-date information can be obtained at any post office.

Inland Letter Post (including Cards) First class letters will normally be delivered next day and second class take up to two days longer.

Letter Post:

Not over	First Class	Second Class
g	p	p
60	22	17
100	33	27
150	41	32
200	49	38
250	59	46
300	68	55
350	78	63
400	88	71
450	99	79
500	1.10	87
600	1.35	1.05
700	1.60	1.25
750	1.70	1.30
800	1.80	not
900	1.95	admissible
1000	2.10	over
Each extra 250g		750g
(or part of)	55	

Parcel Post:

Not over	National Rate
kg	£
1	1.85
2	2.30
3	2.85
4	3.10
5	3.30
6	3.60
7	3.80
8	3.95
9	4.20
10	4.40
25*	5.50

*Parcels over10kg and up to 25kg are accepted at most post offices.

Newspapers: Copies of publications including any supplements which have been registered as newspapers at the Post Office may be sent by the inland newspaper post and are given the same service as first class letters. The publications must be specially posted by the publishers, printers or agents. All other newspapers are transmitted as first or second class letters according to the postage paid. Annual fee for registration as a newspaper £6.00

Cash on Delivery. Inland (Great Britain, Northern Ireland, the Channel Islands, and Isle of Man). The service applies to parcels and to registered packets, compensation fee parcels and Inland Datapost packages. COD items may not be sent by the Second Class Letter Service. The service is not in operation with the Irish Republic in either direction or to persons serving in H.M. ships.

Compensation Fee (C.F. Parcels). Inland fee, in addition to postage, 40p up to £70; 50p up to £130; 70p up to £230; 85p up to £360. Compensation up to £20 is available in the ordinary letter and parcel services in the event of loss or damage due to Post Office negligence. (It is advisable to obtain a free certificate of posting however.) Claims for lost or damaged parcels of higher value will be considered only if a Compensation Fee has been paid and the relevant conditions of the Service have been complied with.

Registered Letters, etc. Inland fee, in addition to postage, £1.75 for compensation up to £950; £1.70 up to £1,850; £1.80 up to £2,200. Registered letters may not be sent by the Second Class Service.

Recorded Delivery This service provides a record of posting and delivery for letters and packets (but not parcels and railway letters). Fee, 28p; in addition to ordinary postage. A Recorded Delivery packet must not contain an uncrossed postal order in which the name of the payee has not been inserted, a cheque or dividend warrant which is not crossed and payable to bearer, a bearer security, a bank or currency note, postage, revenue, etc., or savings stamps, coin or jewellery. The service does not extend to the Irish Republic or to H.M. ships outside Home Waters. Compensation for loss or damage in the post, £22 (max.).

Datapost. A guaranteed courier service, offering rapid delivery within or between major U.K. business centres (Datapost Sameday); overnight to any U.K. address (Datapost Overnight); and fast to 100 countries overseas, including most of Europe and North America (Datapost International). Items may be handed in at post offices or collected from sender's premises. Minimum fee for Datapost Sameday and Datapost Overnight £14 up to 10kg; £14 + 60p per extra kg or part kg over 10kg.

Royal Mail Special Delivery. Items can be posted at any post office where staff will check that they are in time i.e. in advance of the latest recommended posting time as set out in leaflets available at P.O. counters. Should the item arrive too late for ordinary deliveries it will be taken out by special messenger.

The fee for the service is £1.85 in addition to the ordinary first class postage rate. This fee would be refunded should items posted in time not be delivered on the next working day.

Royal Mail Facsimile. The service provides a range of options for sending urgent copies of documents by facsimile transmission between designated U.K. post offices as well as to participating post offices in more than 40 countries around the world.

On arrival documents may either be collected by the recipient or delivered the same day to addresses within defined delvery areas around each office by Post Office Messenger. Telephone advice of a document's availability for collection and the option of postal delivery are also available. Documents can also be sent from designated offices to compatible facsimile machines in the U.K. and overseas.

Redirection of Mail. Customers who change address may have their mail redirected to the new location. The fees are: £3.25 for one calendar month; £7.25 for three calendar months; £17.50 for twelve calendar months; and £60 for twelve calendar months in cases where mail has already been redirected for twelve months or more.

Postal Orders. Fees on issue of a postal order are as follows: 25p to £1, 23p; £2 to £10, 38p; £20, 58p.

OVERSEAS POST

Airmail Letters: Outside Europe *Zone A: not over 10g, 32p; each 10g after or part thereof, 14p; Zone B: not over 10g, 34p; each 10g after or part thereof, 16p; Zone C: not over 10g, 37p; each 10g after or part thereof, 18p.

Aerogrammes. All zones, one size only (A4), 30p.

Swiftair. This is an express service for letters to Europe and for air mail letters and printed papers to countries outside Europe. It provides accelerated treatment in the U.K. and express delivery abroad where available.

Items must either be handed over a post office counter or included in a firm's collection; if the latter, they must be kept separate. They should bear a Swiftair label and also air mail labels where appropriate. A certificate of posting (advisable in case of subsequent enquiries) is issued on request for items handed over at a post office counter. A fee of 1.75 is payable in addition to the normal postage.

The size and weight limits are the same as for ordinary letters and printed papers. Items can be registered or insured.

Postcards: To all zones, 29p.

Printed Papers (up to 2kg), Small Packets (up to 1kg) *Zone A: not over 10g, 25p; each additional 10g, 6p; Zone B: not over 10g, 26p; each additional 10g, 7p; Zone C: not over 10g, 27p; each additional 10g, 9p.

Newspapers/Periodicals (up to 2 kg) *Zone A: not over 10g, 25p; each additional 10g, 3p; Zone B: not over 10g, 26p; each additional 10g, 4p; Zone C: not over 10g, 27p; each additional 10g, 7p.

* Key to airmail zones
Zone A: North Africa; Middle East; Zone B: The Americas; most of Africa; India and neighbouring countries; South East Asia; Indonesia; Zone C: Australasia; China; Japan; Philippines.

Letters to Europe (Western & Eastern, including Cyprus, U.S.S.R. and Turkey) are prepaid at surface letter rates (see below) and given All-up treatment, i.e. are sent by airmail whenever this will result in earlier delivery. Letters to EC countries at first weight step, 20p.

OVERSEAS POSTAL RATES

Surface Mail Letters and postcards (All Countries)

Not over g	p	Not over g	p
20	24	450	2.05
60	41	500	2.25
100	60	750	3.15
150	80	1000	4.00
200	1.00	1250	4.65
250	1.20	1500	5.25
300	1.40	1750	5.85
350	1.65	2000	6.50
400	1.85		

Printed papers (unsealed printed matter without letters):

Not over g	Full rate p	Reduced rate p
20	20	20
60	34	30
100	47	36
150	60	46
200	74	57
250	85	67
300	1.00	78
350	1.15	93
400	1.25	1.01
450	1.40	1.12
500	1.55	1.23
750	2.10	1.56
1000	2.60	1.99
2000	3.65	3.62
3000	5.50	5.16
4000	7.35	6.92
5000	9.15	8.63

Small packets:

Not over g	p	Not over g	p
100	47	350	1.15
150	60	400	1.25
200	74	450	1.40
250	85	500	1.55
300	1.05	750	2.10
1000	2.60		

H.M. Forces Overseas: Surface Mail - Letters outside Europe:

Not over g	p	Not over g	p
60	15	300	47
100	24	350	56
150	28	400	63
200	34	450	70
250	41	500	78
750	1.15		

Postcards: 14p.

Printed papers and small packets:

Not over g	p	Not over g	p
60	15	350	55
100	23	400	67
150	26	450	68
200	33	500	73
250	41	750	1.05
300	48	1000	1.42

(Minimum charge for small packets 23p)

H.M. Forces Overseas: Europe:
There is only one class of mail available for letters to and from Europe. All items are sent by air wherever this will result in earlier postal delivery.

Not over g	p	Not over g	p
60	20	450	90
100	30	500	1.02
150	37	750	1.55
200	45	1kg.	1.95
250	54	1.25kg.	2.45
300	62	1.50kg.	2.95
350	71	1.75kg.	3.45
400	80	2kg.	3.95

Letters outside Europe Airmail: Not over 40g, 20p; each additional 10g or part, 10p. ──
Forces Aerogrammes: 15p each. Postcards; 20p each

9

BRITISH TELECOM

TELEPHONE INFORMATION

Exchange Lines
Exclusive service. Each exchange line:

	Quarterly Line Only
Business line	£27.75
Non-business	£17.13

Shared service Exchange connection (see below).

A connection charge up to £141.65 is payable for each business exchange line. (£129.26 for a residential line.)

Unless otherwise stated, all British Telecom (BT) charges are subject to VAT at the current rate.

Linkline
Linkline services enable businesses to offer customers or contacts free calls on an 0800 number or local rate call on an 0345 number. The caller dials the 0800 or 0345 code followed by a six-digit number from anywhere in the UK and will be connected to the business. The business pays a specified rate per minute for these services.

Companies in travel, distribution finance and transport services in particular are benefiting from Linkline. The service can help build business by improving response rates to advertising and promotions, build customer loyalty and enhance communications with staff and agents and is increasingly being used for customer service applications.

Advanced Linkline
Advanced Linkline is a sophisticated call management system made up of a range of features which will route calls depending on a variety of factors eg., time of day or day of the week in which the call is made, geographical origin of the call, or even the relative size of a customer's answering centres. These are some of the features which can combined to meet the customer's exact call handling requirements to ensure that incoming calls can always receive an answer.

British Telecom Chargecard
The British Telecom Chargecard service allows users to make calls from almost any phone and charge them automatically to a nominated home or office phone bill. Several Chargecards can be billed to one number, calls made with each card are separately identifiable on an unitemised statement which accompanies the usual telephone bill. Calls are dialled direct from Payphones and other Touchtone phones, or may be placed via the operator from other phones. Chargecard calls can also be made to the UK from over 120 countries via the local operator or via UK Direct.

Telephone Guidelines
Timeline, the speaking clock, is now the only service available under the Guideline name. Other services which were offered at ordinary call rates were withdrawn progressively up to September 1989, in accordance with the requirement that they should not be subsidised by other network services.

Callstream Services
Callstream 0898 is a British Telecom service which enables a customer to provide information services via the telephone and to receive an income from calls. The information is then available to the calling customer by dialling a special access code 0898 from the UK followed by the service number. Calls to these services are charged at 25p per minute in the cheap rate and at 38p at all other times.

N.B. British Telecom wish to point out that the charges for services above were correct at the time of going to press, but cannot be guaranteed to remain at these levels indefinitely.

Inland Call Charges
FOR the calculation of call charges exchanges are grouped. Calls to exchanges within the same or adjacent charge groups are local calls. National call charges are based on distance and a central point within each charge group is nominated for measurement of chargeable distance.

Local and dialled national calls are charged in units of 4.4p (10p, VAT inclusive, from payphone lines) for periods of time depending on the chargeable distance of calls and the time of day.

INTERNATIONAL TELEPHONE SERVICES

INTERNATIONAL DIRECT DIALLED (IDD) calls can be made from all parts of the U.K. to over 195 countries around the world and more countries are being added all the time.

IDD is also available from over 150 countries to the U.K. and collect (reverse charge) calls can be made from 140 countries.

Detailed information about IDD, including codes to dial, charges and general guidance about dialling direct overseas and reference handbooks, can be obtained by dialling 0800 272172.

There is an IDD Cheap or Economy rate to most of the countries. The Cheap rate applies to countries in International Charge Bands A, A2, B, C, D and F. For Charge Band D the cheap rate operates from 8.0pm to 8.0am every day. The Economy rate applies to countries in International Charge Band E and operates from 2.30p.m. to 7.30p.m. and from midnight to 7a.m. every day. (for further information or the latest editions of the booklets 'The Everyday Guide to Phoning Abroad' and 'Phoning Abroad - the Business Handbook' call 0800 272172.

There is no minimum charge. IDD calls are charged in whole units of 5.06p including V.A.T. The number of units recorded depends on the length of the call, the country dialled and the time of day the call is made. IDD calls can now also be made by using a BT Chargecard. Calls to countries not yet available by IDD can be made via the international operator.

The BT international operator service on 155 also provides facilities such as Collect (reverse charge), BT Chargecard and a wide selection of international Telephone Credit Card calls. Calls via the operator are subject to a 3 minute minimum charge. Further time is charged in minutes, with part of a minute possibly being rounded up to the next minute. Special facility calls attract an additional charge.

U.K. Direct
U.K. Direct enables collect or BT Chargecard calls to be made via a BT operator in the U.K., so there are no language or procedural difficulties. The service is currently available toll-free from 14 countries. For more information call 0800 272172.

Telephone Chargecards can be used to make calls to over 200 countries and to call the U.K. from 120 countries. For further information or to apply for a BT Chargecard, call 0800 272172.

CHARGES FROM ORDINARY LINES - NOT PAYPHONES OR MOBILE PHONES (V.A.T. Exclusive)

Dialled Calls To:		Peak Rate Mon. Fri. 9 a.m. 1 p.m.	Standard Rate Mon. Fri. 8 a.m. 9 a.m. and 1 p.m. 6 p.m.	Cheap Rate At all other times
Local area		60 seconds	85 seconds	5.5 minutes
National:	Up to 56.4 kilometres	25.7 seconds	34.3 seconds	96 seconds
	Over 56.4 kilometres and Channel Islands	18 seconds	24 seconds	45 seconds
*Low cost routes		22.5 seconds	30 seconds	1 minute
Irish Republic		8 seconds	8 seconds	12 seconds

Operator Connected Calls To:			These charges are for a 3 minute call unless otherwise stated)		
Local area:	normal		48p	45p	44p for 6 minutes
	lower rate		15p	12p	5p for 6 minutes
National:	Up to 56.4 kilometres:	normal	75p	69p	60p
		lower	30p	24p	9p
	Over 56.4 kilometres	normal	90p	78p	69p
	and Channel Islands:	lower	45p	33p	18p
*Low cost routes		normal	81p	72p	66p
		lower	36p	27p	15p
Irish Republic			£1.44	£1.44	£1.17

CHARGES FROM PAYPHONE LINES (V.A.T. Inclusive)

		Peak Rate Mon.-Fri. 9 a.m.-1 p.m.	Standard Rate Mon.-Fri. 8 a.m.-9 a.m. and 1 p.m.-6 p.m.	Cheap Rate At all other times
Local area ( )		60 seconds	85 seconds	2 minutes
National:	Up to 56 kilometres	25.7 seconds	34.3 seconds	96 seconds
	Over 56 kilometres and Channel Islands	18 seconds	24 seconds	45 seconds
*Low cost routes		22.5 seconds	30 seconds	1 minute
Irish Republic		8 seconds	8 seconds	12 seconds

			(Charge for each 3 minutes or part)		
Local area:		normal	80p	80p	80p
		lower	30p	30p	20p
National:	Up to 56 kilometres:	normal	1.30	1.20	1.00
		lower	.70p	.60p	.20p
	Over 56 kilometres	normal	1.60	1.40	1.20
	and Channel Islands:	lower	1.00	.80p	.40p
*Low cost routes		normal	1.40	1.20	1.10
		lower	.80p	.60p	.30p
Irish Republic			2.90	2.90	2.30

* Details of local low cost routes are available from local general manager's office.

The above rate periods may be changed on certain days at Christmas, Boxing Day and New Year's Day. Calls to the Irish Republic from Northern Ireland are charged at the Local or Inland National rates as appropriate.

Lower operator charges (roughly equivalent to a 3 minute dialled call) apply to calls that have to be passed to the operator because a dialled call has failed.

The lower operator charge does not apply to calls from Great Britain and Isle of Man to the Irish Republic, Channel Islands, most mobile telephones, Mercury numbers, numbers beginning 0898 and calls on which special services are required.

Normal operator charges apply to:

Calls which the caller chooses not to dial.
Special services (Transferred charge, Personal call, ADC, etc.).
Calls where both you and the operator get no reply or the engaged tone at the first attempt, but the operator subsequently connects the call.

Notes:

(i) For calls from telephones without a coinbox unless otherwise shown the charge is for the first 3 minutes (or part), each additional minute (or part) being of the charge shown.
(ii) For calls from telephones with a coinbox the charge is for each period of three minutes or part.
(iii) The charge for all calls connected by the operator is that in force when the call is originated.

INTERNATIONAL TELEGRAMS

International Telegrams can be filed by telephone or telex to most countries and are delivered the same day or the next. They are charged for on a per word basis according to the country of destination. To send an International Telegram, dial 100 (190 in London, Birmingham and Glasgow) and ask for International Telegrams. See Telex Directory for telex access codes. For more information, including charges, call free on 0800 282298.

INTERNATIONAL 0800

INTERNATIONAL 0800 is a direct-dialled, international call-free service. Companies in the U.K. rent call-free numbers abroad which, when dialled, connect the caller to the U.K. company free of charge or in some countries for no more than the cost of a local call. The company receiving the calls pays the charges.

The service is currently available from 25 countries including U.S.A., Canada, Hong Kong, Japan, Australia and most countries in western Europe.

International 0800 numbers cost £82.50 rental per quarter per country plus call charges.

For more information please call free on 0800 890800 or fax, also free, on 0800 898989.

TELEX

TELEX is the largest dedicated text messaging network in the world, giving access to over 200 countries and almost 2 million businesses worldwide. Telex is reliable, fast and provides evidence that a message has been delivered through its unique system of terminal identity codes known as telex 'answerbacks'.

Modernisation continues and currently over 60,000 U.K. telex lines are connected to the new digital exchanges. Within the next few years all customers will be served by digital exchanges.

TELEX PLUS is a store and forward facility which can deliver both single and multi-address messages to any direct dial destination in the U.K. and the world. Telex Plus is a particularly useful service for contacting difficult destinations, and for broadcasting the same message to a number of different companies. It is available to all BT telex customers; there is no subscription charge and no minimum usage. The service can be used by calling the Telex Plus computer on a set code and Telex Plus takes on the task of sending the message. It automatically makes repeat attempts to deliver, and gives the sender a delivery advice, freeing the customer's line to send and receive other calls.

For multi-address messages Telex Plus can handle up to 100 addresses with a single input. There is also a Pre Recorded Address (PRA) list facility available to those customers who regularly send a message to the same list of destinations. By using PRA it is possible to send the same message on to all the telex numbers on the list by inputting a simple code. Contact 0800 272172 for information on Telex plus.

British Telecom supplies a range of new technology, microprocessor-controlled terminals, the Leopard and the Cheetah Super Plus. All have advanced features and facilities including text editing, automatic calling, electronic message storing, message timing and the option to access the telex line from PCs, word processors or other office terminals.

INTERNATIONAL FACSIMILE

BT's international facsimile service is a rapid and reliable

means of transferring almost any type of documentary message, including type, handwriting, graphics and drawings, from one fax machine to another anywhere in the world.

Fax is available to virtually all IDD destinations from over 500,000 fax machines in the U.K. There are 8.5 million machines worldwide. These figures are almost doubling every year.

Fax costs and is billed in just the same way as an IDD phone call. And a typical A4 page is transmitted in considerably less than 60 seconds.

BT's official U.K. Fax Book , containing well over 150,000 numbers, is published annually in the autumn. BT also provides directories from over 60 countries.

Technical issues: In the U.K., customers can use any BABT approved fax machine for connection to the phone network. Group 3 fax machines operate at speeds up to 9.6k bit/s. Virtually all machines in use in the U.K. belong to this group.

Contacts:
For all enquiries including fault reporting, tariff and code information and directory orders call on 0800 272172.

TELEMESSAGES

Telemessage is BT's high impact written message service which can be accessed by telephone or telex and offers delivery to any address in the UK or USA. If filed by 10 p.m. (7 p.m. Sundays and Bank Holidays) Telemessages are delivered the next working day or BT offers a money back guarantee. From June 11, 1990 a Telemessage costs £7.95 for up to 50 words and £3.95 for each additional 50 words, up to a maximum of 35 single spaced lines of text (approximately 350 words), with the name and address free. Special occasion cards are available costing £1.45 each. To the USA Telemessages cost £11.95 for up to 50 words and £5.95 for each additional 50 words. All prices are inclusive of VAT.

To send a Telemessage, dial 100 (190 in London, Birmingham and Glasgow) and ask for the Telemessage service. See Telex Directory for telex access codes.

A range of special services is available for the business user. Telephone free on 0800 282298 for full details.

BUREAU SERVICES

BT Bureau Services offer a range of messaging facilities: Bureaufax, Telex Bureau, Multi-messaging and Translation and Interpreting Services. For further details call 071 492 7222/7444/7111.

INTERNATIONAL DATEL

DATEL enables data terminals and computers large and small to be directly connected via the telephone network to similar terminals in the U.K. and more than 100 overseas countries. Because DATEL works on the telephone network, data can be exchanged between terminals for the same price as a phone call.

It is ideal for transferring information such as text, spreadsheets, graphics and CAD/CAM files, as well as bulk data transfer where speeds of up to 9.6k bit/s (approximately 4 megabytes per hour) are suitable, and investment in leased circuits is not justified.

A free BT International Data Services handbook explains the terminology and provides guidance on setting up terminal equipment and making calls by both Datel and

Packet Switching (see below). It details data transmission standards and lists countries to which both services are available.

Contact: 0800 272172.

INTERNATIONAL PACKET SWITCHING SERVICE

THE International Packet Switching Service (IPSS) is British Telecom's international public data communications service. It links BT's U.K. Public Data Network (PDN) with over 135 similar networks in more than 85 countries worldwide.

IPSS conforms to internationally agreed standards and offers modem speed and protocol conversion, allowing an extensive range of otherwise incompatible computer equipment to communicate.

Based on packet switching techniques, IPSS is a reliable and cost-effective transmission medium for a wide variety of business applications. These include information retrieval, electronic mail, database access and the transfer of files, funds and software codes.

There are a large number of access speeds and methods to the PSS to suit individual requirements - from simple dial-up access using a terminal, modem and telephone line, to high-speed access using dedicated datalines.

Usage charges are based on the volume of data transferred. There is no charge for call duration. It would cost approximately 9.33p to send a screen containing 2000 characters to Europe and 23.3p to send it to North America. Details of usage are as follows:

Charge Band	Standard charge charge (per segment*)	Minimum call call charge (10 segments)
EUROPE	0.28p	2.8p
NORTH AMERICA	0.7p	7.0p
REST OF WORLD	0.82p	8.2p

* each segment can contain 1-64 characters.

Cost quoted exclude VAT.

For more information about IPSS call Network Specialist Sales on 0800 282444

INTERNATIONAL PRIVATE SERVICES

To accommodate the needs of virtually every business, BT has a range of analogue and digital services: Leaselines; International KiloStream; International MegaStream and SatStream. Primex is a comprehensive service which combines network design, lines, equipment, personnel and all the other components needed for operating a private, secure 24 hours a day communications network. International City Direct is a private switched, transatlantic business telecommunications service offering efficient voice and low-speed data access overseas. It blends the flexibility of the public telecommunications network with the security and cost effectiveness of private circuits. For further details call free on 0800 890909.

MARITIME COMMUNICATIONS

British Telecom provides world-wide communication services for shipping, aircraft, oil and gas platforms and some remote land stations. HF, MF and VHF radio frequency bands are used as well as satellite. Services include telephone, telex, morse telegraphy and data transmission.

MARITIME RADIO SERVICE

Global radio communications are handled by PORTISHEAD RADIO. A series of smaller stations around the U.K. coast provide medium and short range services.

MARITIME RADIOTELEPHONE

(For communications with ships equipped with Satellite Earth Stations, see British Telecom Inmarsat)

TO SHIP: Call free on 0800 378389, give your name, telephone number, the name of the person being called, the name of the ship and its callsign and position, if known.

FROM SHIP: Long Range HF communications are handled by PORTISHEAD RADIO. A series of coast stations around the U.K. provide medium and short range services on MF and VHF.

Charges, excluding VAT are :-

To ship from the U.K., per minute: VHF £1.05; MF £1.25; HF £2.16 (three minute minimum).
From ship to the U.K., per minute: VHF £1.05; MF £1.25; HF £2.16 (three minute minimum).

From 2400 hours GMT Friday to 2359 hours GMT Sunday, both to and from ship for the U.K. for HF radio telephone only, the price is £1.73 per minute (three minute minimum).

Prices for from-ship calls apply to sterling registered ships only. Other ships are billed at the appropriate Gold Franc rate.

Prices of calls from ship to other countries and from ship to ship via coast radio stations are available on request.

Further information and instruction booklets are available on request. Tel: 0278 781111 (Long Range).

MARITIME RADIOTELEX

(For communications with ships equipped with Satellite Earth Stations, see British Telecom Inmarsat).

TO SHIP: All Short and Long Range terrestrial Radiotelex services are controlled from PORTISHEAD RADIO.

Access to the fully automatic equipment is gained via telex 46116 (answerback 46116 BTGKA G).

To set up a two-way conversational mode, use 46300 (answerback BTGKA G). The automatic equipment will prompt you for information and advise you if direct connection is possible.

INFORMATION: To obtain ship and aircraft information, e.g. call-sign, SELCALL of satellite identity number, telex 46300 BTGKA G and, in response to the first prompt, key 'SNF+'.

ENQUIRIES: If you have difficulty or require assistance, call telex 46506 BTGKA G or telephone 0278 781111.

FOR SHIPS NOT EQUIPPED FOR RECEIVING RADIOTELEX: You may submit your message as a Radiotelegram by calling telex 46441 BTGKA G. Provide the name of the vessel, call-sign, and, if known, the name of the radio station through which you would like the message delivered.

9

PHONETEX: Messages may be telephoned direct to PORTISHEAD RADIO for onward transmission to the vessel by telex. Call PORTISHEAD RADIO free on 0800 378398.

FROM SHIP: The automatic system allows ships direct access to national and international telex routes.

VOICEBANK: By HF Radio, a vessel may telex PORTISHEAD from where the message is dictated into the customer's Voicebank.

TELEX LETTER: Telexes received from ship at PORTISHEAD may be forwarded to their destination by post.

MULTI ADDRESS FACILITY: A vessel may send an identical message to any number of destinations.

Charges, excluding VAT are :-

To and from ship for the U.K., per minute: MF £1.75; HF £2.05 (six second minimum).

Prices for from-ship calls apply to sterling registered ships only. Other ships are billed at the appropriate Gold Franc rate.

Prices of manually connected calls, connections to other countries, ship to ship and special facilities such as Phonetex, Voicebank and Telex Letter AND THE MULTI ADDRESS FACILITY are available on request.

For the full range of Radiotex services available, ships should key 'HELP+'. Further information and instruction booklets are available on request. Tel: 0278 781111.

MARITIME RADIOTELEGRAMS

TO SHIP: Telegrams can be accepted by telex or telephone.

TELEX: Call 46441 BTGKA G. Provide the name of the vessel, call-sign, and, if known, the name of the radio station through which you would like the message delivered.

TELEPHONE: Call FREE ON 0800 378389 AND ASK FOR SHIPS AND TELEGRAMS. If known, give the name and telephone number of the coast station through which the call should be made.

FROM SHIP: Long Range communications by HF are handled at PORTISHEAD RADIO. A series of coast stations around the U.K. provide a medium range service by MF. On VHF, telegrams may be dictated by radiotelegram.

VOICEBANK: By HF Radio, a vessel may call PORTISHEAD from where the message is dictated into the customer's VOICEBANK.

Charges, excluding VAT, are :-

To ship from the U.K.: 0.48 per word plus 2.00 per message.
From ship to the U.K.: 0.54 per word (7 word minimum). Prices for from-ship calls apply to sterling registered ships only. Other ships are billed at the appropriate Gold Franc rate.

Prices to other countries and for ship to ship charges are available on request. Further information and instruction booklets are available on request. Tel: 0278 781111.

BRITISH TELECOM INMARSAT

British Telecom Inmarsat provides for suitably equipped ships via its coast earth station at Goonhilly which covers the Atlantic Ocean Region, while reciprocal arrangements with Norway and Singapore provide access to the Indian and Pacific Ocean Regions respectively.

TO SHIP: TELEPHONE: Dial the International Operator on 155, ask for an INMARSAT call, quote the ship's name, its identification number and, if known, the ocean region it is in then wait to be connected.

If your exchange has to-ship direct access facilities, dial 010, followed by the Ocean Region Code and the ship's Identification Number. British Telecom Inmarsat enquiry point will be able to tell you whether or not your exchange is suitably equipped.

Ocean Region Codes are:
Atlantic Ocean   871
Pacific Ocean   872
Indian Ocean   873

Facilities include Facsimile, Data Transmission, International Packet Switching and Phonetex.

Phonetex: Call Portishead Radio, free on 0800 378389 and dictate the message which will then be telexed to the vessel.

TELEX: The procedure for sending messages to ships is the same as for sending direct international telex messages. Enter the code 00, followed by the Ocean Region Code and then the Ship Earth Station (SES) Identification Number.

Ocean Region Codes are :
Atlantic Ocean   571
Pacific Ocean   572
Indian Ocean   573

Telex Plus Store and Forward facilities are also available.

Phonetex: Call Portishead Radio, free on 0800 378389 and dictate the message which will then be telexed to the vessel.

FROM SHIP TELEPHONE: Select the Goonhilly Identification code 02. After receiving the dial tone, key 00, followed by the country code (44 for the U.K.) and the required number. For other services, key the appropriate two digit code after the 00.

Other facilities include Facsimile, Data Transmission, International Packet Switching, Prestel, Telecom Gold, Radiopaging and Voicebank.

TELEX: Select the Goonhilly Identification code 02. After the prompts, key 00, followed by the country code (51 for the U.K.) and the required number. For other services, key the appropriate two digit code after the 00.

Charges, excluding VAT, are :-

To ship: Telephone, including Data & Facsimile, 5.19 per minute, with 3 minute minimum for manually connected calls and 6 second minimum for automatic.
Telex (Automatic), 2.47 per minute, 6 seconds minimum.
From ship to U.K.: Telephone (Automatic), 5.19 per minute, 6 seconds minimum.
Telex (Automatic), 2.47 per minute, 6 seconds minimum.
Prices for from-ship calls apply to sterling registered ships only. Other ships are billed at the appropriate Gold Franc rate.

9

Prices to other countries, for automatic to-ship calls and operator controlled telex calls and for communications between ships are available on request.

Further information and instruction booklets are available on request. Tel: 071-936 4996.

AERONAUTICAL RADIO SERVICE

British Telecom provides a public air-to-ground radio telephone service through Portishead Radio.

SKYPHONE

Skyphone is the world's first satellite communications service for aircraft. It provides direct dial air-to-ground and ground-to-air telecommunications links to an from aircraft to anywhere in the world.

The service is provided on a worldwide basis. British Telecom operates Skyphone through Goonhilly earth station and the Inmarset satellite network.

The service is charged at $6.70 per minute. For further information call free on 0800 378983.

HOLIDAYS ABROAD - DUTY FREE AND TAX-FREE ALLOWANCES

You are entitles to the allowances in either Column 1 or Column 2, but not both. The countries of the EC (European Community) are Belgium, Denmark, France, West Germany, Greece, the Irish Republic, Italy, Luxembourg, The Netherlands, Portugal, Spain (but not the Canary Island) and the UK (but not the Channel Islands).

Column 1

Goods obtained duty & tax-free in the EC, or duty and tax-free on a ship or aircraft, or goods obtained outside the EC:

Tobacco products
200 cigarettes
or
100 cigarillos   double if you
or   live outside
50 cigars   Europe
or
250 grams of tobacco

Alcoholic drinks
2 litres of still table wine   plus
1 litre of alcoholic
    drink over 22% vol.   or
2 litres of alcoholic drink
    not over 22% vol.   or
fortified or sparkling wine
                           plus
a further 2 litres of still table wine

Perfume
50 grams (60 cc or 2 fl.oz.)

Toilet Water
250 cc (9 fl.oz.)

Other Goods
£32.00 worth

Column 2

Goods obtained duty and tax paid in the EC;

Tobacco products
300 cigarettes   or
150 cigarillos   or
75 cigars   or
400 grams of tobacco

Alcoholic drinks
5 litres of still table wine   plus
1.5 litres of alcoholic
    drinks over 22% vol.   or
3 litres of alcoholic
drinks not over 22% vol.   or
fortified or sparkling wine
                           plus
a further 3 litres of still table wine

The tobacco and alcoholic drinks allowance are not for persons under 17.

Perfume
75 grams (90cc or 3 fl.oz)

Toilet Water
375 cc (13 fl.oz.)

Other Goods
£50.00 worth but not more than 50 litres of beer and 25 mechanical lighters.

REDUNDANCY PAYMENTS

THE REDUNDANCY Payments Scheme covers nearly all employees who work under a contract of service. The main exceptions are employees who normally work less than eight hours a week; those whose employment ends on or after their 65th birthday. People who are self-employed are not covered by the scheme.

An employee is entitled to redundancy pay if dismissal is wholly or mainly due to disappearance of the job or because the employer needs fewer employees to do work of a particular kind.

To qualify for redundancy pay an employee must complete either:

(i) Two years continuous employment of not less than 16 hours a week or
(ii) Five years continuous employment of not less than eight hours a week.

Service before the age of 18 does not count. Payment is calculated on the basis of age, length of service and weekly earnings with a limit of £184 a week. The maximum service which can be taken into account is 20 years. If the total is more, then the last 20 years count.

The basis of payment is:

	Weeks' pay
(a) For each complete year of service after 41st birthday	1.5
(b) For each complete year of service (excluding those covered by (a)) after 22nd birthday	1
(c) For each complete year of service (excluding those covered by (a) and (b)) after 18th birthday	.5

Information about the Redundancy Payments Scheme can be obtained from any Redundancy Payments Office.

EUROPEAN COMMUNITY

Members: Belgium, Denmark, France, Federal Republic of Germany, Greece, Ireland, Italy, Luxembourg, The Netherlands, Portugal, Spain, United Kingdom.

COUNCIL OF MINISTERS

The Foreign Secretary or other Minister concerned, according to the subject discussed, from each of the ten member countries.

EUROPEAN COMMISSION

There are seventeen Commissioners and their term of office ran until the end of 1988. The Commission's headquarters are at 200 Rue de la Loi, B-1049 Brussels. There are 17 commissioners appointed for terms of four years, two years for the president and the vice-president. The responsibilities of the 17 commissioners are as follows:

President:

Jacques Delors (France)
Secretariat General; Legal Services; Monetary Affairs; Spokesman's Affairs; Joint Interpreting and Conference Service; Onward Studies Unit; Security Office.

Commissioners:

Frans Andriessen, Vice President (Netherlands)
External relations and Trade Policy; Co-ordination with other European countries

Henning Christopherson, Vice President (Denmark)
Economic and Financial Affairs; Co-ordination of Structural Instruments; Statistical Office

Manuel Marin, Vice President (Spain)
Co-operation and Development; Fisheries

Filippo Maria Pandolfi, Vice President (Italy)
Research and Science; Telecommunications; Information Technology and Innovation; Joint Research Centre

Martin Bangemann, Vice President (Federal Republic of Germany)
Internal Market and Industrial Affairs; Financial Institutions

Sir Leon Brittan, Vice President (United Kingdom)
Competition Policy; Financial Institutions

Carlo Ripa Di Meana (Italy)
Environment; Nuclear Safety; Civil Protection

Antonio Cardosa E Cunha (Portugal)
Personnel and Administration; Energy; Euratom Supply Agency; Policy on Small and Medium Sized Enterprises; Tourism; Social Economy

Abel Matutes (Spain)
Mediterranean Policy; Relations with Latin America and Asia; North-South Relations

Peter Schmidhuber (Federal Republic of Germany)
Budget; Financial Control

Christiane Scrivener (France)
Taxation; Customs Union; Questions relating to obligatory levies (fiscal or social levies)

Bruce Millan (United Kingdom)
Regional Policy

Jean Dondelinger (Luxembourg)
Audio-visual Policy; Cultural Affairs; Information and Communication Policy; Citizens' Europe; Office for Official Publications

Ray MacSharry (Ireland)
Agriculture; Rural Development

Karel Van Miert (Belgium)
Transport; Credit, Investments and Financial Instruments

Vasso Papandreou (Greece)
Social Affairs and Employment; Education and Training; Human Resources

EUROPEAN COURT OF JUSTICE

Kirchberg, Luxembourg

The new Court of First Instance was established by a Council Decision of 24 October 1988 under powers conferred by the Single European Act. The new Order of Precedence (below) takes effect 7 October 1990.

President: Judge O. Due
President of 4th & 6th Chambers: Sir Gordon Slynn
President of 1st & 5th Chambers: Judge C.N. Kakouris
President of 2nd Chamber: F.A. Schockweiler
President of 3rd Chamber: M. Zuleeg
First Advocate General: W. Van Gerven
Judge, G.F. Mancini
Advocate General: C.O. Lenz
Advocate General: M. Darmon
Judge: R. Joliet
Judge: T.F. O'Higgins
Advocate General: J Mischo
Advocate General: J.C. Moitinho De Almeida
Judge: G.C. Rodriguez Iglesias
Judge: F. Grevisse
Judge: M. Diez De Velasco
Advocate General: F.G. Jacobs
Advocate General: M.G. Tesauro
Judge: P.J.G. Kapteyn
Registrar: J-G Giraud

EUROPEAN PARLIAMENT

President:

Lord Plumb (United Kingdom)

The United Kingdom has 81 of the 518 seats in the European Parliament and voted in the third direct elections on June 15, 1989. Conservatives won 32 seats (13 less than in 1984), Labour 45 seats and the Scottish National Party one. Three members for Northern Ireland were elected by the single transferable voting system, the 17 Westminster constituencies forming one constituency. There were some boundary changes, but the number of constituencies remained at 78. Members elected are shown below in Constituency order and are also shown alphabetically at the end of this list. Political affiliations of Members and Opponents are as follows:

C	Conservative
G	Green Party
Lab	Labour
PC	Plaid Cymru
SDP	Social Democratic Party
SLD	Social and Liberal democrats
O	Others

Constituency	Member	Party	Votes
1 Bedfordshire South	Peter G. Beazley	C	72406
2 Birmingham East	Mrs. Christine M. Crawley	Lab	96588
3 Birmingham West	John E. Tomlinson	Lab	85545
4 Bristol	Ian White	Lab	87753
5 Cambridge and Bedfordshire North	Sir Frederick Catherwood	C	84044
6 Cheshire East	Brian Simpson	Lab	74721
7 Cheshire West	Lyndon Harrison	Lab	102962
8 Cleveland and Yorkshire North	David Bowe	Lab	94953
9 Cornwall and Plymouth	Christopher Beazley	C	88376
10 Cotswolds	The Lord Plumb	C	94852
11 Cumbria and Lancashire North	Lord Inglewood	C	84035
12 Derbyshire	Geoffrey W. Hoon	Lab	106018
13 Devon	The Lord O'Hagan	C	110518
14 Dorset East and Hampshire West	Bryan Cassidy	C	111469
15 Durham	Stephen S. Hughes	Lab	124448
16 Essex North-East	Anne McIntosh	C	92758
17 Essex South-West	Patricia Rawlings	C	77408
18 Glasgow	Mrs. Janey Buchan	Lab	107818
19 Hampshire Central	Edward Kellett-Bowman	C	78651
20 Hereford and Worcester	Sir James Scott-Hopkins	C	87898
21 Hertfordshire	Derek Prag	C	86898
22 Humberside	Peter Crampton	Lab	74163
23 Kent East	Christopher Jackson	C	85667
24 Kent West	G. B. Patterson	C	82519
25 Lancashire Central	M. J. Welsh	C	81125
26 Lancashire East	Michael J. Hindley	Lab	96946
27 Leeds	Michael McGowan	Lab	97385
28 Leicester	Mel Read	Lab	90798
29 Lincolnshire	W. F. Newton Dunn	C	92803
30 London Central	Stan Newens	Lab	78561
31 London East	Ms Carole Tongue	Lab	92803
32 London North	Pauline Green	Lab	85536
33 London North-East	Alfred Lomas	Lab	76085
34 London North-West	The Lord Bethell	C	74900
35 London South and Surrey East	James O. Moorhouse	C	78256
36 London South-East	Peter Price	C	80619
37 London South Inner	Richard A. Balfe	Lab	90378
38 London South-West	Anita Pollack	Lab	74298

10

Constituency	Member	Party	Votes
39 London West	M. N. Elliott	Lab	92959
40 Lothians	David W. Martin	Lab	90840
41 Manchester Central, Greater	Norman Eddy	Lab	86914
42 Manchester East, Greater	Glynn Ford	Lab	93294
43 Manchester West, Greater	Gary Titley	Lab	109228
44 Merseyside East	Terence Wynn	Lab	107288
45 Merseyside West	Kenneth Stewart	Lab	93717
46 Midlands Central	Christine Oddy	Lab	76736
47 Midlands West	John Bird	Lab	105529
48 Norfolk	Paul Howell	C	92385
49 Northamptonshire	Anthony M. H. Simpson	C	86695
50 Northern Ireland	Rev Ian Paisley	DUP*	160110
	John Hume	SDLP*	136335
	Jim Nicholson	OUP*	118785
51 Northumbria	Gordon J.Adam	Lab	110688
52 Nottingham	Ken Coates	Lab	92261
53 Oxford and Buckinghamshire	James Elles	C	92483
54 Scotland Mid and Fife	Alex Falconer	Lab	102246
55 Scotland North-East	Henry McGubban	Lab	65375
56 Scotland South	Alex Smith	Lab	81366
57 Sheffield	Roger Barton	Lab	109677
58 Shropshire and Stafford	Christopher J. Prout	C	85896
59 Somerset and Dorset West	Mrs. Margaret Daly	C	106716
60 Staffordshire East	G. W. Stevenson	Lab	94873
61 Strathclyde East	K. D. Collins	Lab	109170
62 Strathclyde West	Hugh McMahon	Lab	89627
63 Suffolk	A. E. Turner	C	82481
64 Surrey West	Tom Spencer	C	89674
65 Sussex East	Sir Jack Stewart-Clark	C	96388
66 Sussex West	R. Madron Seligman	C	95821
67 Thames Valley	John Stevens	C	73070
68 Tyne and Wear	Alan Donnelly	Lab	126682
69 Wales Mid and West	D. R. Morris	Lab	105670
70 Wales North	Anthony Wilson	Lab	83638
71 Wales South	David Wayne	Lab	108550
72 Wales South-East	Llewellyn Smith	Lab	138872
73 Wight and Hampshire East	R. J. Simmonds	C	90200
74 Wiltshire	Dr. Caroline Jackson	C	93200
75 York	Edward MacMillan Scott	C	81453
76 Yorkshire South	Norman West	C	121060
77 Yorkshire South-West	Thomas Megahy	Lab	108444
78 Yorkshire West	B. H. Seal	Lab	1086444

Three Members for Northern Ireland, a single constituency, were elected on a system of proportional representation. Figures are for numbers of votes cast.

The European Parliament meets in Strasbourg and has an office in London at: 2 Queen Anne's Gate, London, SW1H 9AA. 071-222 0411. Members are elected for a five-year term and their salaries are the same as those of members of their national parliaments.

The Commission of the European Communities has information offices in:

Belfast: Windsor House, 9/15 Bedford Street, Belfast BT2 7EG. Belfast 240708.
Cardiff: 4 Cathedral Road, Cardiff CF1 9SG. Cardiff 371631.
Edinburgh: 7 Alva Street, Edinburgh EH2 4PH. 031-225 2058.
London: 8 Storey's Gate, London SW1P 3AT. 071-222 8122.

MEMBERS OF THE EUROPEAN PARLIAMENT

(Listed alphabetically by Members' names.) Numbers refer to the constituency lists on pages 193 - 194.

A

Adam, G. J.; (Lab) *Northumbria*, 51

B

Balfe, R. A., (Lab) *London South Inner*, 37
Barton, Roger; (Lab) *Sheffield*, 57
Battersby, R.; (C) *Humberside*, 22
Beazley, Christopher; (C) *Cornwall and Plymouth*, 9
Beazley, P. G.; (C) *Bedfordshire South*, 1
Bethell, The Lord; (C) *London North-West*, 34
Bird, John; (Lab) *Midlands West*, 47
Bowe, David; (Lab) *Cleveland and Yorkshire North*, 8
Buchan, Mrs. J.; (Lab) *Glasgow*, 18

C

Cassidy, B.; (C) *Dorset East and Hampshire West*, 14
Catherwood, Sir Frederick; (C) *Cambridge and Bedfordshire North*, 5
Coates, Ken; (Lab) *Nottingham*, 52
Collins, K. D.; (Lab) *Strathclyde East*, 61
Crawley, Mrs. C. M.;(Lab) *Birmingham East*, 2

D

Daly, Mrs. M.; (C) *Somerset and Dorset West*, 59
Donnelly, Alan; (Lab) *Tyne and Wear*, 68
Dunn, W. F. Newton; (C) *Lincolnshire*, 29

E

Elles, James; (C) *Oxford and Buckinghamshire*, 53
Elliott, M. N.; (Lab) *London West*, 39

F

Falconer, Alex; (Lab) *Scotland Mid and Fife*, 54
Ford, J. G.; (Lab) *Greater Manchester East*, 42

G

Green, Pauline; (Lab) *London North*, 32

H

Harrison, Lyndon; (Lab) *Cheshire West*, 7
Hindley, M. J.; (Lab) *Lancashire East*, 26
Hoon, G. W.; (Lab) *Derbyshire*, 12
Howell, Paul; (C) *Norfolk*, 48
Hughes, S. S.; (Lab) *Durham*, 15
Hume, John ; (SDLP) *Northern Ireland*, 50

J

Jackson, Christopher; (C) *Kent East*, 23
Jackson, Dr. Caroline; (C) *Wiltshire*, 74

L

Lomas, Alfred; (Lab) *London North-East*, 33
Lord Ingelwood; (C) *Cumbria and Lancashire North*, 11

M

Macmillan-Scott, E.; (C) *York*, 75
Martin, D. W.; (Lab) *Lothians*, 40
McGowan, M.; (Lab) *Leeds*, 27
McGubban, Henry; (Lab) *Scotland North-East*, 55
McIntosh, Anne; (C) *Essex North-East*, 16
McMahon, Hugh; (Lab) *Strathclyde West*, 62
Megahy, T.; (Lab) *Yorkshire South-West*, 77
Moorhouse, C. J. O.; (C) *London South and Surrey East*, 35
Morris, D. R.; (Lab) *Wales Mid and West*, 69

N

Newens, A. S.; (Lab) *London Central*, 30
Newman, E.; (Lab) *Greater Manchester Central*, 41

O

Oddy, Christine; (Lab) *Midlands Central*, 46
O'Hagan, The Lord; (C) *Devon*, 13

P

Paisley, Ian ; (DUP) *Northern Ireland*, 50
Patterson, G. B.; (C) *Kent West*, 24
Plumb, The Lord ; (C) *The Cotswolds*, 10
Pollack, Anita; (Lab) *London South-West*, 38
Prag, Derek; (C) *Hertfordshire*, 21
Price, Peter; (C) *London South-East*, 36
Prout, C. J.; (C) *Shropshire and Stafford*, 58

R

Rawlings, Patricia; (C) *Essex South-West*, 17
Read, Mel; (Lab) *Leicester*, 28

S

Scott-Hopkins, Sir James; (C) *Hereford and Worcester*, 20
Seal, B. H.; (Lab) *Yorkshire West*, 78
Seligman, R. M.; (C) *Sussex West*, 66
Simmonds, R. J.; (C) *Wight and Hampshire East*, 73
Simpson, A. M. H.; (C) *Northamptonshire*, 49
Simpson, Brian; (Lab) *Cheshire East*, 6
Smith, Alex; (Lab) *Scotland South*, 56
Smith, L.; (Lab) *Wales South-East*, 72
Spencer, Tom; (C) *Surrey West*, 64
Stevens, John; (C) *Thames Valley*, 67
Stevenson, G. W.; (Lab) *Staffordshire East*, 60
Stewart, Kenneth; (Lab) *Merseyside West*, 45
Stewart-Clark, Sir Jack; (C) *Sussex East*, 65

T

Taylor, John; (OUP) *Northern Ireland*, 50
Titley, Gary; (Lab) *Greater Manchester West*, 43
Tomlinson, J. E.; (Lab) *Birmingham West*, 3
Tongue, Miss C.; (Lab) *London East*, 31
Turner, A. E.; (C) *Suffolk*, 63

W

Wayne, David; (Lab) *Wales South*, 71
Welsh, M. J.; (C) *Lancashire Central*, 25
West, N.; (Lab) *Yorkshire South*, 76
White, Ian; (C) *Bristol*, 4
Wilson, Anthony; (Lab) *Wales North*, 70
Wynn, Terence; (Lab) *Merseyside East*, 44

10

SECTION 11

INTERNATIONAL

UNITED NATIONS

THE United Nations Conference on International Organisation was held at San Francisco from April 25 to June 26, 1945, when 50 Allied nations signed the Charter of the United Nations. The preamble to the Charter reads:

"We, the peoples of the United Nations determined to save succeeding generations from the scourge of war, which twice in our lifetime has brought untold sorrow to mankind, and

"To reaffirm faith in fundamental human rights, in the dignity and worth of the human person, in the equal rights of men and women and of nations large and small, and

"To establish conditions under which justice and respect for the obligations arising from treaties and other sources of international law can be maintained, and

"To promote social progress and better standards of life in larger freedom, and for these ends

"To practise tolerance and live together in peace with one another as good neighbours, and

"To unite our strength to maintain international peace and security, and

"To ensure, by the acceptance of principles, and the institution of methods, that armed force shall not be used, save in the common interest, and

"To employ international machinery for the promotion of the economic and social advancement of all peoples, have resolved to combine our efforts to accomplish these aims.

"Accordingly our respective Governments, through representatives assembled in the city of San Francisco, who have exhibited their full powers found to be in good and due form, have agreed to the present Charter of the United Nations and do hereby establish an international organisation to be known as the United Nations."

The Charter became effective on October 24, 1945, when the United Nations formally came into existence. It was decided that the seat of the organisation should be in New York.

There are six main organs of the United Nations:

1. The General Assembly;
2. The Security Council;
3. The Economic and Social Council;
4. The Trusteeship Council;
5. The International Court of Justice;
6. The Secretariat.

THE GENERAL ASSEMBLY

This consists of the 159 members of the United Nations. Each member is entitled to only one vote. The General Assembly meets once a year in regular session, beginning on the third Tuesday in September. It may also meet in special session and in emergency special session. Any matter within the scope of the Charter may be brought before the General Assembly, which may make recommendations on all problems, disputes or situations currently under consideration by the Security Council.

There are seven main Committees on which each member has the right to be represented. They are:

(i) Political and Security;
(ii) Special Political;
(iii) Economic and Financial;
(iv) Social, Humanitarian and Cultural;
(v) Trusteeship and Decolonisation;
(vi) Administrative and Budgetary; and
(vii) Legal.

The Assembly elects its President for each session.

THE SECURITY COUNCIL

The Security Council has 15 members, of which five are designated as permanent members in the Charter. The ten non-permanent members are elected for two-year terms by the General Assembly. A State may not immediately succeed itself on the expiration of its term. The Security Council's function is to maintain international peace by settling disputes and stopping aggression. Decisions need nine affirmative votes, but on important questions decisions require concurring votes of the permanent members. If, therefore, any one of them votes against the motion, it cannot be enforced. An abstention is not in practice regarded as a vote against.

Permanent Members: China, France, Union of Soviet Socialist Republics, United Kingdom of Great Britain and Northern Ireland, United States of America.

Non-permanent members: Canada (1990), Colombia (!990), Cote d'Ivoire (1991), Cuba (1991), Democratic Yemen (1991), Ethiopia (1990), Finland (1990), Malaysia (1990), Romania (1991) and Zaire (1991).

THE ECONOMIC AND SOCIAL COUNCIL

This consists of 54 members elected by the General Assembly for periods of three years. The Council, under the authority of the General Assembly, is responsible for promoting higher standards of living, full employment and conditions of economic and social progress and development; international cultural and educational co-operation, and universal respect for, and observance of human rights and fundamental freedoms for all without distinction as to race, sex, language, or religion.

Members of the Economic and Social Council:

Algeria (1992), Bahamas (1991), Bahrain (1992), Brazil (1991), Bulgaria (1992), Burkino Faso (1992), Cameroon (1991), Canada (1992), China (1992), Colombia (1990), Cuba (1990), Czechoslovakia (1991), Ecuador (1992), Finland (1992), France (1990), German Democratic Republic (1992), Fed Rep of Germany (1990), Ghana (1990), Greece (1990), Guinea (1990), India (1990), Indonesia (1991), Iran (1992), Iraq (1991), Ireland (1990), Italy (1991), Jamaica (1992), Japan (1990), Jordan (1991), Kenya (1991), Lesotho (1990), Liberia (1990), Libya (1990), Mexico (1992), Netherlands (1991), New Zealand (1991), Nicaragua (1991), Niger (1991), Portugal (1990), Rwanda (1992), Saudi Arabia (1990), Soviet Union (1992), Sweden (1992), Thailand (1991), Trinidad & Tobago (1990), Tunisia (1991), Ukraine (1991), United Kingdom (1992), U.S.A. (1991), Venezuela (1990), Yugoslavia (1990), Zaire (1992) and Zambia (1991).

Officers:
The President of the Council, elected at the Council's organisational session in February, is Kjeld Mortensen (Denmark). The Vice Presidents are Chandrashekhar Dasgupta (India), Hassan Elghouayel (Tunisia), Guennadi Oudovenko (Ukraine) and Felipe Hector Paolillo (Uruguay).

TRUSTEESHIP COUNCIL

The Trusteeship Council has five members: China, France, USSR, United Kingdom and United States. The United States administers the Trust Territory of the Pacific Islands, the only remaining Trust.

THE INTERNATIONAL COURT OF JUSTICE

This is the principal judicial organ of the United Nations. All members of U.N. are ipso facto parties of the Statute of the Court. A State which is not a member of the United Nations may become a party to the Statute on conditions determined in each case by the General Assembly upon recommendation of the Security Council. Decisions of the Court are final, but are binding only between the parties concerned. The judges are elected for nine-year terms.

11

President: Jose Maria Ruda (Argentina) 1991.
Vice President: Keba Mbaye of Senegal (1991).
Judges of the court are: Roberto Ago, Italy (1997); Stephen Schwebel, U.S.A.(1997); Mohammed Bedjaoui, Algeria (1997); Sir Robert Y. Jennings, United Kingdom (1991); Kebu Mbaye, Senegal (1991); Manfred Lachs, Poland (1994); Jens Evensen, Norway (1994); Shigeru Oda, Japan (1994); Ni Zhengyu, China (1994); Taslim Olawale Elias, Nigeria (1994); Mohamed Shahabuddeen, Guyana (1997); Nikolai K. Tarasov, Soviet Union (1997); Gilbert Guillaume, France (1991). Raghunandan Swarup Pathak, India (1991).

(All terms expire on February 5 of the year designated.)

THE SECRETARIAT

This is composed of the Secretary-General, who is the chief administrative officer of the organisation, and such staff as the organisation requires. The Secretary-General makes an annual report to the General Assembly on the work of the organisation and is appointed for a five-year term.

Principal Secretary-General:
Javier Perez de Cuellar (Peru)

Officers of U.N. Secretariat:
Director General for Development and International Economic Co- operation: Antoine Blanca (France).
Chef de Cabinet: Virendra Dayal (India).
Under-Secretaries-General for Special Political Affairs: Marrack Goulding (United Kingdom).
Under-Secretary-General for Special Political Questions, Regional Cooperation, Decolonization and Trusteeship: Abdulrahim A. Farah (Somalia).
Under-Secretary-General for Political and General Assembly Affairs: Ronald I. Spiers (U.S.A.).
Under-Secretary-General for Technical Co-operation Development: Xie Qimei (China).
Under-Secretary-General Legal Counsel: Carl-August Fleischhauer (Federal Republic of Germany).
Under-Secretary-General for Political and Security Council Affairs: Vasiliy S. Safronchuk (U.S.S.R.).
Under-Secretary-General of the Department of International Economic and Social Affairs: Rafeeuddin Ahmed.
Under-Secretary-General, Office of Public Information: Mrs. Therese Paquet-Sevigny (Canada).
Under-Secretary-General, Conference Services: Eugeniusz Wyzner (Poland).
Under-Secretary-General, Director-General of the United Nations Office at Geneva: Jan Martenson.
Under-Secretary-General, Secretary-General of the United Nations Conference on Trade and Development (UNCTAD): Kenneth Dadzie (Ghana).
Acting Under-Secretary-General, Department of Administration and Management: Luis Maria Gomez - also Assistant Secretary-General for Programme Planning, Budget and Finance.
Direcor-General of the United Nations Industrial Development Organisation (UNIDO): Domingo L. Siazon.
Executive Secretary, Economic Commission for Europe (ECE): Gerald Hinteregger.
Executive Secretary, Economic and Social Commission for Asia and the Pacific (ESCAP): Shah A. M. S. Kibria (Bangladesh).
Executive Secretary, Economic Commission for Latin America and the Caribbean (ECLAC): Gert Rosenthal.
Executive Secretary, Economic and Social Commission for Africa (ECA): Adebayo Adedeji (Nigeria).
Executive Secretary, Economic and Social Commission for Western Asia (ESCWA): Tayseer Abdel Jaber.
Assistant-Secretary-General, Human Resources Management: Kofi Annan.
Assistant-Secretary-General, General Services: Richard J. Foran.
Administrator, United Nations Development Programme (UNDP): William H. Draper III (U.S.A.).
High Commissioner for Refugees (UNHCR): Thorvald Stoltenberg (Sweden).
Executive Director of the United Nations Children's Fund (UNICEF): James P. Grant (U.S.A.).
Commissioner-General of the United Nations Relief and Works Agency for Palestine Refugees in the Near East (UNRWA): Giorgio Giacomelli (Italy).
U.N. Environment Programme Executive Director (UNEP): Mostafa Kamal Tolba (Egypt).

Under-Secretary-General for Disarmament Affairs: Yasushi Akashi (Japan).
Assistant Secretary-General for Research and the Collection of Information: James Jonah.
Director-General of the United Nations Office at Vienna: Margaret Joan Anstee (UK).
United Nations Disaster Relief Co-ordinator: M'hamed Essaafi (Tunisia).

SPECIALISED AGENCIES OF THE UNITED NATIONS

FAO
Food and Agriculture Organisation of the United Nations
Viale delle Terme di Caracalla, Rome, Italy

FAO provides a world centre for information and cooperation in the fields of agriculture, forestry and fisheries development, mainly in the less-developed world. During 1989, FAO carried out 2,583 field projects in 140 countries and territories. These had a total combined project budgets of US dollars 2.28 billion. More than half of field expenditure was met by trust funds from donor countries and agencies. The United Nations Development Programme (UNDP) covered nearly 40 percent. FAO financed 76 field projects that were executed under the Technical Cooperation Programme (TCP) from the Organization's regular working budget.

Director-General: Edouard Saouma (Lebanon)

FUND
International Monetary Fund
Washington, D.C. 20431, U.S.A.

Established on December 27, 1945, to promote international monetary co-operation and expansion of international trade; to promote exchange stability; to assist in the establishment of a multi-lateral system of payments in respect of current trans - actions between Members.

Managing Director and Chairman of the Executive Board: Michel Camdessus (France)

GATT
General Agreement on Tariffs and Trade
Centre William Rappard, Rue de Lausanne 154, CH- 1211 Geneva 21, Switzerland

The General Agreement on Tariffs and Trade is a multi-lateral treaty through which most trading countries (96 contracting parties - full members - one acceded provisionally) co-operate to expand international trade and promote economic development. Member countries account for nearly 90 percent of world trade. GATT provides a forum for discussion of trade issues and multilateral negotiations (e.g. Tokyo Round negotiations 1973-79 and, currently, the Uruguay Round) to reduce tariffs and other obstacles to trade. Special attention is given to trade problems of developing countries.

Director-General: Arthur Dunkel (Switzerland)

IAEA
International Atomic Energy Agency
Vienna International Centre, Wagramerstrasse 5, A-1400 Vienna, Austria

IAEA came legally into being on July 29, 1957. During 1989-90 IAEA continued its work of applying safeguards to States in connection with the Treaty on the Non-Proliferation of Nuclear Weapons (NPT) which came into force on March 5, 1970, and to States outside the scope of NPT; advising on siting and safety of power reactors and assisting Member States in their nuclear power planning studies; promoting research and use of isotopes in medicine, agriculture, hydrology, and industry; increasing facilities for international computerisation of present knowledge on reactor physics for power and research purposes; scanning, classifying, and coding other scientific and technical information for the International Nuclear Information System; arranging for technical assistance and training by sending experts and equipment, granting fellowships, arranging courses, making research funds available and participating in the UN Development Programme; organising international conferences and symposia; investigating radioactivity and pollution in the seas; and providing a central point for the advancement of theoretical physics; preparing publications in various fields of nuclear science, and expanding its programme on environmental operations such as, radiological safety, waste management and nuclear safety and preparing a comprehensive set of safety codes and guides for nuclear power plants. The IAEA has established a system to facilitate emergency assistance to Member States in the event of radiation accidents. Two international conventions, namely the convention on Early Notification of a Nuclear Accident and the Convention on Emergency Assistance in the case of a Nuclear Accident or Radiological Emergency came into force respectively on 27 October 1986 and 25 February 1987 in which the IAEA plays a central role. In the light of the Chernobyl accident an expanded nuclear safety programme was endorsed. The programme covers the following specific areas: safety of nuclear installations, radiation protection, human health, review of operational safety of nuclear power plants, an incident reporting system and incentives for international cooperation on nuclear safety research.

Director-General: Hans Blix (Sweden)

ICAO
International Civil Aviation Organisation
1000 Sherbrooke Street West, Montreal, Canada, H3A 2R2

A specialised Agency of the United Nations since April 4, 1947, to ensure that international civil aviation should be developed in a safe and orderly manner and that international air transport services should be established on the basis of equality of opportunity and operated soundly and economically.

President of the Council: Dr. Assad Kotaite (Lebanon)
Secretary-General: Dr. Shivinder Singh Sidhu (India)

IDA
International Development Association
1818 H. Street, N.W. Washington D.C. 20433, U.S.A.
European Office: 66 Avenue d'I na, 75116 Paris, France

Established on September 24, 1960, as an affiliate of the World Bank, to provide finance for high-priority investment projects in less- developed member countries on terms which bear less heavily on their balance of payments than conventional loans. Membership: 138 countries. By June 30, 1989, IDA had lent $52,700 million. IDA development credits are for 35 or 40 years, free of interest.

President: Barber B. Conable (U.S.A.)

IFC
International Finance Corporation
1818 H. Street, N.W. Washington D.C. 20433, U.S.A.
European Office: New Zealand House, Haymarket, London, S.W.1.

Established on July 24, 1956, as an affiliate of the World Bank, to assist the economic growth of developing Member countries, by investing in private enterprises, in association with private capital. Membership: 134 countries. By June 30, 1989, IFC approvals totalled $10.1 billion.

President: Barber B. Conable (U.S.A.)

ILO
International Labour Organisation
International Labour Office, Geneva, Switzerland. Vincent House, Vincent Square, London SW1P 2NB. 071 828 6401.

Established on April 11, 1919, when it was constituted as an autonomous institution under Part XIII of the Treaty of Versailles. It entered into relationship with the United Nations as a specialised agency in 1946. Its objectives are to contribute to the establishment of lasting peace by promoting social justice; to improve, through

international action, labour conditions and living standards; to promote economic and social progress. The ILO was awarded the Nobel Peace Prize in 1969. It has launched a World Employment Programme to stimulate national and international efforts to create productive employment for the world's rapidly growing population; and an International Programme for improvement of working conditions and environment. Technical cooperation activities in the developing countries form an important part of the ILO's work. 150 countries were Members of the organisation in May, 1990. The structure of ILO is tripartite; delegates representing employers and workers take part in its deliberations alongside those representing governments.

Director-General: Michael Hausenne (Belgium)

IMO
International Maritime Organization
4 Albert Embankment, London SE1 7SR

Convention establishing IMO drawn up by the United Nations Maritime Conference held at Geneva from February 19 to March 6, 1948, and came into effect on March 17, 1958, after 21 nations, of which seven each had a total of at least one million gross tons of shipping, ratified the Convention.

IMO's purposes are to promote cooperation among governments in technical and legal problems of international shipping, to adopt safety measures and safety regulations for international shipping, and to prevent marine pollution caused by ships. Structure: Assembly (all Member States), Council (32 States), Maritime Safety Committee, Legal Committee, Facilitation Committee, Technical Cooperation Committee and Marine Environment Protection Committee (open to all Member States). Membership: 134 States in April 1990; budget 190 £12 million.

Secretary-General: W.A. O'Neil (Canada)

ITU
International Telecommunication Union
Place des Nations, Geneva, Switzerland

Established on May 17, 1865, when the International Telegraph convention was signed. In 1906 an International Radiotelegraph Convention was signed in Berlin. The International Telegraph Union changed its name in 1932 in Madrid to the International Telecommunication Union after the amalgamation of the Telegraph Convention and the Radiotelegraph Convention. It became the United Nations Specialised Agency for Telecommunications in 1947. Its object is to maintain and extend international cooperation for improvement and rational use of all kinds of telecommunications and promote the development of telecommunications facilities and services.

Secretary-General: Dr. Pekka Tarjanne (Finland)

UNESCO
United Nations Educational, Scientific and Cultural Organisation
Unesco House, 7 Place de Fontenoy, 75700 Paris, France

Established on November 4, 1946 for the purpose of advancing through the educational, scientific and cultural relations of the peoples of the world, the objectives of international peace and the common welfare of mankind. UNESCO's activities are funded through a regular budget provided by Member States, and also through other U.N. sources.

UNESCO assists the interchange of experience, knowledge and ideas, through a world network of specialists; coordinates international scientific efforts; organises various research projects on racial problems, and is concerned with prevention of discrimination in education, and improving access for women to education. It also assists Member States in their efforts to preserve their cultural and natural heritage and to develop their communication systems.

In May, 1989, the total number of Member States was 158.

Director-General: Federico Mayor(Spain)

UNHCR
Office of the United Nations High Commissioner for Refugees
Case Postale 2500, CH-1211 Geneva 2, Depot, Switzerland

The Office of the United Nations High Commissioner for Refugees (UNHCR), came into existence on January 1, 1951. UNHCR is entrusted with two main tasks: extending international protection and promoting permanent solutions to the problems of refugees through voluntary repatriation, resettlement in another country or local settlement. Since 1971 UNHCR has been asked to undertake a succession of special operations in the field of man-made disasters. In that year it coordinated humanitarian aid to East Bengali refugees in India; in 1972 it carried out an emergency relief programme for returning refugees and displaced persons in the Sudan. In more recent years it has been charged with similar tasks in newly-independent Angola, Guinea-Bissau, Mozambique, and lately in the Horn of Africa, the Sudan, Zaire, Zimbabwe, Pakistan, South East Asia and Central America and in the southern African region, notably Malawi. In April 1981 and July 1984 UNHCR co-sponsored International Conferences on Assistance to Refugees in Africa (ICARA) in order to focus attention on the plight of some 5 million refugees in Africa, to mobilise additional resources for refugees, and to assist countries of asylum to obtain international assistance for projects aimed at strengthening the ability of those countries to carry the extra burden placed on them. Following the signing of the Peace Accords in April 1987 between Afghanistan and Pakistan, and the Tripartite Agreement between Angola, Cuba and the Republic of South Africa in December 1988, UNHCR is participating in United Nations projects for those countries, and in the case of Namibia successfully carried out an operation under which some 43,000 Namibian refugees were successfully repatriated to their country of origin.

Both in areas where prospects for solutions to refugee problems have recently occurred, or where possibilities for such solutions were more qualified, it became clear that the efforts of UNHCR in responding to those challenges and opportunities have to be complemented more and more by increased international co-operation, consultations and solidarity. In this connection, three important international conferences have been held recently to address the problems of refugees in the relevant regions. The first of these was the International Conference on the Plight of Refugees, Returnees and Displaced Persons in Southern Africa (SARRED) which took place in Oslo, Norway in August 1988. This was followed by the International Conference on Central American Refugees (CIREFCA) which was held in Guatemala City in May 1989. A month later, in June 1989, the International Conference on Indo-Chinese Refugees (ICIR) took place in Geneva, Switzerland. UNHCR is closely involved in the implementation or follow-up of the respective Plans of Action adopted by those conferences.

A recently concluded meeting of the organization's Executive Committee approved a budget to finance UNHCR's assistance programmes in 1990 amounting to $378,885,900 which includes a carry-over in unliquidated obligations from 1989 amounting to some $38 million.

High Commissioner: Mr. Thorvald Stoltenberg of Norway

U.K. COMMITTEE FOR UNICEF
United Nations Children's Fund
55 Lincoln's Inn Fields, London WC2A 3NB. 071-405 5592. Greeting Card Operation: Unit 1 Rignalls Lane, Galleywood, Chelmsford. 0245 76315.

Established by the United Nations in 1946 to meet the emergency needs of children, particularly in war-devastated countries. In 1950 emphasis was shifted to long-range needs of children and young people in underdeveloped areas and in 1953 the United Nations indefinitely extended the Fund's mandate. The Fund is financed voluntarily, from governments and private individuals and from the sale of greeting cards and stationery (brochure available from addresses above), for activities in the fields of maternal and child welfare, disease control, the improvement of nutrition, education, vocational training and the development of social services for children, as well as assistance in the case of emergencies. A substantial portion of UNICEF's resources are devoted to the training of nationals of the countries in those activities which UNICEF is aiding.

UPU
Universal Postal Union
Weltpoststrasse 4, 3000 Berne 15, Switzerland
Telephone: 4131 432211. Telex: 912761 UPU CH. Telefax: 4131 432210

Established on October 9, 1874, by the Postal Convention of Berne, and came into effect on July 1, 1875. Its object is to assure organisation and to improve postal services and thus promote the development of international collaboration. Member-countries are therefore united in a single postal territory for the reciprocal exchange of mail.

The number of Member-countries is at present 170.

Director-General: A. C. Botto de Barros (Brazil)

WORLD BANK
International Bank for Reconstruction and Development
1818 H. Street, N.W., Washington D.C. 20433, U.S.A.
European Office: 66 Avenue d'I na, 75116 Paris, France

Created on December 27, 1945, the World Bank assists the economic development of its member countries by making loans, in cases where private capital is not available on reasonable terms, to finance productive investments. It also provides a wide variety of technical assistance to its members. Membership: 152 countries. Loans made by the World Bank since its inception to June 30, 1989, totalled $171,482 million.

President: Barber B. Conable (U.S.A.)

WHO
World Health Organization
Avenue Appia, Geneva, Switzerland

World Health Organization (WHO) is a specialised agency of the United Nations, but has its own governing body, the World Health Assembly, composed of representatives of its 166 Member States and its own budget (U.S. $653,740,000 for the biennium 1990-91) contributed directly by its Members.

WHO's objective is the improvement of health of all peoples. It assists governments to strengthen health services, to train health workers, to carry out disease control programmes, and to promote environmental and family health; it supports medical research; sets up international standards for drugs, vaccines, etc.; establishes regulations to prevent the spread of certain communicable diseases internationally, and runs a telex service providing warnings of outbreaks of diseases subject to International Sanitary Regulations.

Director-General: Dr. Hiroshi Nakajima (Japan)

WMO
World Meteorological Organisation
Case postale 2300, CH-1211 Geneva 2, Switzerland

Established on March 23, 1950, and succeeding the former IMO (International Meteorological Organisation). WMO is an inter-governmental specialised agency of the United Nations with present Membership of 156 States and five territories. Its objects are to facilitate world-wide cooperation and to promote standardisation in the making and exchange of meteorological and hydrological observations, to further the application of meteorology to various human activities, to promote activities in operational hydrology and to encourage research and training in meteorology and related fields.

WMO activities are directed through six programmes: World Weather Watch; World Climate Programme; Research and Development; Hydrology and Water Resources; Meteorological Applications and Education and Training. President: Zou Jingmeng (China)

Secretary-General: G. O. P. Obasi (Nigeria)

COMPARATIVE TIME

The following table gives the standard time in various cities of the world, compared with 12 noon G.M.T.

Fast on Greenwich

Algiers	1.00 p.m.	The Hague	1.00 p.m.	Sofia	2.00 p.m.	La Paz	8.00 a.m.
Amsterdam	1.00 p.m.	Hamburg	1.00 p.m.	Suva, Fiji	12 Midnight	Lima	4.00 a.m.
Ankara	2.00 p.m.	Helsinki	2.00 p.m.	Sydney	10.00 p.m.	Los Angeles	4.00 a.m.
Athens	2.00 p.m.	Hong Kong	8.00 p.m.	Tel Aviv	2.00 p.m.	Mexico City	6.00 a.m.
Baghdad	3.00 p.m.	Jerusalem	2.00 p.m.	Tokyo	9.00 p.m.	Montreal	7.00 a.m.
Bangkok	7.00 p.m.	Johannesburg	2.00 p.m.	Tunis	1.00 p.m.	New Orleans	6.00 a.m.
Beirut	2.00 p.m.	Kuala Lumpur	7.30 p.m.	Valletta	1.00 p.m.	New York	7.00 a.m.
Belgrade	1.00 p.m.	Luxembourg	1.00 p.m.	Vienna	1.00 p.m.	Ottawa	7.00 a.m.
Berlin	1.00 p.m.	Madras	5.30 p.m.	Warsaw	1.00 p.m.	Panama	7.00 a.m.
Berne	1.00 p.m.	Madrid	1.00 p.m.	Wellington	a.m.	Philadelphia	8.00 a.m.
Bombay	5.30 p.m.	Manila	8.00 p.m.	New Zealand	12 Midnight	Port of Spain	
Bonn	1.00 p.m.	Melbourne	10.00 p.m.			Trinidad	8.00 a.m.
Brussels	1.00 p.m.	Moscow	3.00 p.m.	**Slow on Greenwich**		Quebec	7.00 a.m.
Bucharest	2.00 p.m.	Nairobi	3.00 p.m.	Asuncion	8.00 a.m.	Quito	7.00 a.m.
Budapest	1.00 p.m.	New Delhi	5.30 p.m.	Baltimore	7.00 a.m.	Regina	5.00 a.m.
Cairo	2.00 p.m.	Nicosia	2.00 p.m.	Boston, Mass.	7.00 a.m.	Reykjavik	11.00 a.m.
Calcutta	5.30 p.m.	Oslo	1.00 p.m.	Calgary	5.00 a.m.	Rio de Janeiro	9.00 a.m.
Canberra	10.00 p.m.	Paris	1.00 p.m.	Chicago	6.00 a.m.	San Francisco	4.00 a.m.
Cape Town	2.00 p.m.	Peking	8.00 p.m.	Hamilton	00 a.m.	Santiago, Chile	8.00 a.m.
Colombo	5.30 p.m.	Perth, Western		Bermuda	8.00 a.m.	Sao Paulo	9.00 a.m.
Copenhagen	1.00 p.m.	Australia	8.00 p.m.	Havana	7.00 a.m.	Seattle	4.00 a.m.
Dar es Salaam	3.00 p.m.	Prague	1.00 p.m.	Honolulu	2.00 a.m.	Toronto	7.00 a.m.
Darwin	9.30 p.m.	Rome	1.00 p.m.	Kingston		Vancouver	4.00 a.m.
Gibraltar	1.00 p.m.	Stockholm	1.00 p.m.	Jamaica	7.00 a.m.	Winnipeg	6.00 a.m.

THE COMMONWEALTH

The Commonwealth is a voluntary association of 50 independent nations, each responsible for its own policies, consulting together and co-operating in the common interests of their peoples. The Association spans five continents and all levels of economic development. By race, language, faith and culture, the peoples of the Commonwealth - a quarter of the world's population - are of infinite variety. However, they share certain traditions, working techniques and attitudes, and all member countries subscribe to certain ideals, set out in the Declaration of Commonwealth Principles, and rely on unwritten conventions and accepted procedures.

ANGUILLA - British dependency in the Caribbean, formerly part of Associated State of St. Christopher-Nevis-Anguilla; area 35 sq. miles; pop. 7,000; the main town is known as The Valley. Governor: G.O.Whitaker.

* ANTIGUA AND BARBUDA - Three islands in the Caribbean (and including small island of Redonda), independent since 1981; area of Antigua 108 sq. miles and Barbuda 62 sq. miles; pop.84,000 (1988); cap. St.John's. Governor-General: Sir Wilfred Jacobs, Prime Minister Rt.Hon. Vere C.Bird.

* AUSTRALIA (Commonwealth of) - An independent member of the Commonwealth occupying the whole of the continent of Australia and certain outlying islands; area 7,682,300 sq. km.; pop.16.1 million; cap. Canberra; Governor-General Mr William Hayden; Prime Minister: The Hon. Robert James Lee Hawke; High Comm.in the U.K.: Hon. Douglas MClelland, Australia House, Strand, London WC 2. British High Comm. in Australia: Sir John Coles.

Australian States:-

Australian Capital Territory - Area 939 sq. miles.; pop. 253,085 (1985); cap. Canberra; Minister for the Arts and Territories: Hon. Gary F. Punch.

New South Wales - Area (excluding the Australian Capital Territory) 309,433 sq. miles; pop.5,474,288 (1985); cap. Sydney; Governor: Air Marshal Sir James Rowland; Premier: Nicholas F. Greiner.

Northern Territory - Area 1,346,200 sq. km.; pop.143,801 (1985); cap. Darwin; Chief Minister: Hon. S.P. Hatton, M.L.A.; Administrator: Cdre. E.E. Johnston.

Queensland - Area 667,000 sq. miles; pop.2,546,442 (1985); cap. Brisbane; Governor: Sir Walter Campbell, Q.C.; Premier: Hon. Michael J. Ahern.

South Australia - Area 380,070 sq. miles; pop. 1,362,876 (1985); cap. Adelaide; Governor: Lt. Gen. Sir Donald Dunstan.; Premier: Hon. John Bannon.

Tasmania - Area 26,383 sq. miles; pop.442,111 (1985); cap. Hobart; Governor: General Sir Phillip Bennett.

Victoria - Area 87,884 sq. miles; pop. 4,121,456 (1985); Governor: His Excellency Dr.Davis McCaughey; Premier: Hon J. Cain.

Western Australia - Area 975,920 sq. miles; pop. 1,407,451 (1985); cap. Perth; Governor: Prof. Gordon Reid; Premier: Hon. Peter Dowding.

AUSTRALIAN ANTARCTIC TERRITORY - Consists of all islands and territories (except Adelie Land) which are situated south of the 60th degree of South Latitude and lying between the 160th degree of East Longitude and the 45th degree of East Longitude.

* BAHAMAS (Commonwealth of) - An archipelago of about 700 islands, 30 of which are inhabited, in the West Atlantic; an independent member of the Commonwealth since 1973; area 5,380 sq. miles; pop. 247,000; cap. Nassau; Governor-General: Mr. Henry Milton Taylor (acting); Prime Minister: Rt.Hon. Sir Lynden Pindling; High Comm. for Bahamas in U.K.: Dr. Patricia E.J. Rodgers, 10 Chesterfield Street, London W1X 8AH. British High Comm.in the Bahamas: Colin G. Mays.

* BANGLADESH - Formerly East Pakistan, an independent republic since 1971 and member of the Commonwealth since 1972; area 55,598 sq. miles; pop. 108.851 million (1988); cap. Dacca (Dhaka). President and Chief Martial Law Administrator: Lt. Gen. H.M. Ershad; High Comm. in U.K.: Maj. Gen. K.M. Satiullah, 28 Queen Anne's Gate, London SW7 5JA; British High Comm. in Bangladesh: C.H. Imery.

* BARBADOS - An island in the Caribbean and independent member of the Commonwealth since 1966; area 166 sq. miles; pop. 255,000; cap. Bridgetown; Governor-General: Dame Nita Barrow; Prime Minister: Rt. Hon. L. Erskine Sandiford; High Comm. in the U.K.: Sir Roy Marshall, 1 Great Russell Street, London WC1B 3NH; British High Comm. in Barbados: K.F.X. Burns.

* BELIZE - A sovereign state on east coast of Central America, independent since 1981; area 8,866 sq. miles; pop. 182,000; cap. Belmopan. Governor-General: Dame Minita E. Gordon; Prime Minister: Rt.Hon. George Price; High Comm. for Belize in U.K.: Sir Edney Cain, O.B.E., 200 Sutherland Avenue, London W9 1RX. British High Comm. in Belize: P.A.B. Thompson.

BERMUDA (or Somer's Islands) - Dependent territory, a group of about 150 islands in the Western Atlantic; area 21 sq. miles; pop. 79,000; cap. Hamilton; Governor: The Viscount Dunrossil, C.M.G.

* BOTSWANA - Formerly Bechuanaland Protectorate. Republic in Southern Africa, independent since 1966; area 220,000 sq. miles; pop. 1.164 million (1988); cap. Gaborone; President: Dr. Quett Masire; High Comm. in the U.K.: Mrs. M. Nanyane Nasha, 6 Stratford Place, London W1; British High Comm. in Botswana: Mr B. Smith.

BRITISH VIRGIN ISLANDS - Chain of about 40 islands, islets and cays, 16 inhabited, lying at E end of Greater Antilles chain; area 153 sq. kms; pop. 13,000; Governor: H.E. Mr. J.M.A. Herdman; Chief Minister: Hon. Cyril Romney.

* BRUNEI (DARUSSALAM). - Sultanate on north-west coast of Borneo, independent since 1984; area 2,226 sq. miles; pop. 243,000 (!988); cap. Bandar Seri Bagawan; reigning Sultan: Paduka Seri Baginda and Yang di-Pertuan Sultan Hassanal Bolkiah Mu'izzaddin Waddaulah; High Comm. in U.K.: Pengiran Mustapha Pengiran Metasah, 49 Cromwell Road, London SW7 2ED; British High Comm. in Brunei: Roger Westbrook.

* CANADA - An independent member of the Commonwealth occupying most of the N. half of the N. American continent; area: 3,851,809 sq. miles; pop. 26,104,000 (1988); cap. Ottawa; Governor-General: Ramon Hnatsluyn; Prime Minister: Brian Mulroney; High Comm. in the U.K.: The Hon. Donald S. NacDonald, Macdonald House, Grosvenor Square, London W1; British High Comm. in Canada: Mr B J P Fall.

Canadian Provinces:-

Alberta - Area 255,285 sq. miles; pop.2,375,278 (1986); cap. Edmonton; Lt. Gov.: Hon. Helen Hunley; Premier: Hon. Donald Getty.

British Columbia - Area 366,255 sq. miles; pop. 2,889,207 (1986); cap. Victoria; Lt. Gov.: Hon. Robert Gordon Rogers; Premier: Hon. William Vander Zalm.

Manitoba - Area 251,000 sq. miles; pop. 1,071,232 (1986); cap. Winnipeg; Lt. Gov.: Hon. George Johnson; Premier: Hon. Gary Filmon

New Brunswick - Area 28,354 sq. miles; pop. 710,422 (1986); cap. Fredericton; Lt. Gov.: Hon. Gilbert Finn; Premier: Hon. Frank McKenna

Newfoundland - Area 156,185 sq. miles; pop. 568,349; cap. St.John's; Lt. Gov.: Hon. James McGrath; Premier: Hon. Brian Peckford.

Nova Scotia - Area 21,425 sq. miles; pop. 873,199 (1986); cap. Halifax; Lt. Gov.: Hon. Alan R. Abraham; Premier: Hon. John M. Buchanan.

Ontario - Area 412,582 sq. miles; pop. 9,113,515 (1986); cap. Toronto; Lt. Gov.: Hon. Lincoln Alexander; Prime Minister: David Peterson.

Prince Edward Island - Area 2,184 sq. miles; pop.126,646 (1986); cap. Charlottetown; Lt. Gov.: Hon. Lloyd MacPhail; Premier: Hon. Joseph Ghiz.

Quebec - Area 594,860 sq. miles; pop. 6,540,276 (1986); cap. Quebec City; Lt. Gov.: Hon. Gilles Lamontagne; Premier: Hon. Robert Bourassa.

Saskatchewan - Area 251,700 sq. miles; pop. 1,010,198 (1986); cap. Regina; Lt. Gov.: Hon. Frederick W. Johnson; Premier: Hon. Grant Devine.

Canadian Territories :-

Northwest Territories - Area 1,304,903 sq. miles; pop. 52,238 (1986); cap. Yellowknife; Govt. Leader Dennis Patterson.

Yukon Territory - Area 207,076 sq. miles; pop. 23,504 (1986); cap. Whitehorse; Govt. Leader Tony Penikett.

CAYMAN ISLANDS - Dependent territory; 3 islands in Caribbean Sea; area 100 sq. miles;pop. 20,300; cap. George Town; Governor: Alan J. Scott.

CHANNEL ISLANDS - A group of islands off the N.W. coast of France, the only remaining part of the Dukedom of Normandy under the British Crown; area 75 sq. miles; pop.132,724 (1981 census); consisting of the following:-

Jersey - Area 45 sq. miles; pop. 80,212; cap. St.Helier; Lt.Gov. & C.in C.: Admiral Sir William Pillar.

Guernsey and Dependencies - Area Guernsey 24.5 sq. miles, Alderney 3 sq. miles, Sark 2 sq. miles; pop. Guernsey, Alderney & Sark 55,902; cap. St.Peter Port; Lt.Gov. & C.in C.: Lt.Gen. Sir Alexander Boswell; dependencies Alderney, Brechou, Sark, Herm, Jethou, Lihou; President of Alderney: J. Kay- Mouat; Seigneur de Serk (Sark): Michael Beaumont.

CHRISTMAS ISLAND - Territory in the Indian Ocean, formerly part of Singapore; area 52 sq. miles; pop. 2,800. Authority over the island was transferred from the U.K. to Australia in October 1958. Administrator: Hon. A.D. Taylor.

COCOS (KEELING) ISLAND - A group of 27 small coral islands in the Indian Ocean; area 5.5 sq. miles; pop. 616. Administration of the islands was transferred from the United Kingdom to Australia in 1955. In 1984 the Cocos voted for integration with Australia. Administrator: Ms. Carolyn Stuart.

COOK ISLANDS - A group of 15 islands in the Pacific in free association with New Zealand, but internally self-governing since 1965; area 240 sq. km; pop. 23,000; cap. Avarua, Rarotonga; Prime Minister: Dr. Pipuke Robarti.

* CYPRUS - Independent republic in the Mediterranean; area 3,572 sq. miles; pop. 686,000 (1988); cap. Nicosia; President: George Vassiliou; Cyprus High Comm. in the U.K.: Tasos Panayides, 93 Park Street, London W1; British High Comm. in Cyprus: Humphrey Maud, C.M.G.

* DOMINICA (Commonwealth of) - An island in the eastern Caribbean, independent republic since 1978, formerly an associated state; area 290 sq. miles; pop. 81,000 (1988); cap. Roseau; President: Clarence A. Seignoret; Prime Minister: Mary Eugenia Charles; High Comm. F.A.M. Baron, non-resident. Honorary Consulate, 1 Collingham Gardens, London SW5 0HW; British High Comm. in Dominica (resident in Barbados): K.F.X. Burns.

ELLICE ISLANDS See TUVALU

ENGLAND - See UNITED KINGDOM

FALKLAND ISLANDS - Dependent territory of the South Atlantic; area (excluding dependencies) 4,700 sq. miles; pop. 2,000; cap. Stanley; dependencies South Georgia and South Sandwich Group; Governor: Gordon Jewkes.

* THE GAMBIA - Independent republic on the west coast of Africa; area 4,004 sq. miles; pop. 822,000 (1988); cap. Banjul; President: Hon. Sir Dawda Jawara; High Comm. in U.K.: Mr. Horace R. Monday Jnr., 57 Kensington Court, London W8; British High Comm. in the Gambia: Mr A Ibbott.

* GHANA - An independent republic of West Africa; area 92,000 sq. miles (approx); pop. 14,040,000 (1988); cap. Accra; Chairman of Provincial National Defence Council: Flt.Lieut. Jerry John Rawlings; High Comm. in U.K.: Dr.Joseph L. Sekoh Abbey, 13 Belgrave square, London SW1; High Comm. in Ghana: A M Goodenough.

GIBRALTAR - Dependent territory, a narrow peninsular on the S.W. coast of Spain; area 2.25 sq. miles; pop. 29,000; Governor and C.in C.: Air Chief Marshal Sir Peter Terry.

GILBERT ISLANDS See KIRIBATI

GREAT BRITAIN See UNITED KINGDOM

11

* GRENADA - An island in the Caribbean, part of the Windward group and independent since 1974; area, incl. island of Carriacou and Petit Martinique, 133 sq. miles; pop.102,000; cap. St.George's; Governor- General: Sir Paul Scoon; Prime Minister: The Rt. Hon. Nicholas Braithwaite; High Comm. in the U.K.: 1 Collingham Gardens, Earls Court, London SW5 OHW; British High Comm. in Grenada (resident in Barbados): K.F.X. Burns.

GUERNSEY - See CHANNEL ISLANDS

* GUYANA - Only English-speaking country on the mainland of South America, independent member of the Commonwealth since 1966 and a republic since 1970; area 83,00 sq miles; pop. 799,000 (1988); cap. Georgetown; President: H. Desmond Hoyte; High Comm. in the U.K.: Cecil S. Pilgrim, 3 Palace Court, Bayswater Road, London W2; British High Comm. in Guyana: D P Small.

HONG KONG - Dependent territory at mouth of Canton River, China, consisting of island of Hong Kong, a portion of the Chinese mainland and over 200 adjacent islands, some of them uninhabited; area approx. 403 sq. miles; pop. 5,500.000; cap. Victoria; Governor: Sir David Wilson.

* INDIA - A sovereign socialist secular democratic republic of Asia; area 3,287,263 sq. km; pop. 813,990,000; cap. New Delhi; President: Ramaswamy Venkataraman; Prime Minister: V. P. Singh; High Comm. in the U.K.: Ku;dip Nayar, India House, Aldwych, London WC2B 4NA; British High Comm. in India: Sir David Goodall.

Indian States (Populations Figures, 1981 census) :-

Andhra Pradesh - Area 275,068 sq. km; pop. 53,549,673; cap. Hyderabad.

Arunachal Pradesh - Area 83,743 sq. km; pop. 631,839; cap. Itanagar.

Assam - Area 78,438 sq. km; pop. 19,896,843; cap. Dispur.

Bihar - Area 67,196 sq. km; pop. 69,914,734; cap. Patna.

Gujarat - Area 96,024 sq. km; pop. 34,085,799; cap. Gandhinagar.

Haryana - Area 44,212 sq. km; pop. 12,922,618; cap. Chandigarh.

Himachal Pradesh - Area 55,673 sq. km; pop. 4,280,818; cap. Shimla.

Jammu & Kashmir - Area 222,236 sq. km, including 78,114 sq. km under Pakistani occupation, 5,180 sq. km handed over to China by Pakistan, and 37,555 sq. km under occupation of China; pop. 5,987,389; cap. Srinagar (summer), Jammu (winter).

Karnataka - Area 74,210 sq. km; pop. 37,135,714; cap. Bangalore.

Kerala - Area 38,863 sq. km; pop. 25,453,680; cap. Trivandrum.

Madhya Pradesh - Area 443,446 sq. km; pop. 52,178,844; cap. Bhopal.

Maharashtra - Area 307,690 sq. km; pop. 62,784,171; cap. Bombay.

Manipur - Area 8,628 sq. km; pop. 1,420,953; cap. Imphal.

Meghalaya - Area 22,429 sq. km; pop. 1,335,819; cap. Shillong.

Mizoram - Area 21,081 sq. km; pop. 493,757; cap. Aizawl.

Nagaland - Area 16,579 sq. km.; pop. 774,930; cap. Kohima.

Orissa - Area 60,162 sq.km; pop. 26,370,271; cap. Bhubaneswar.

Punjab - Area 50,362 sq. km; pop. 16,788,915; cap. Chandigarh.

Rajasthan - Area 132,150 sq. km; pop. 34,261,862; cap. Jaipur.

Sikkim - Area 7,096 sq. km; pop. 316,385; cap. Gangtok.

Tamil Nadu (formerly Madras) - Area 130,058 sq. km; pop. 48,408,077; cap. Madras.

Tripura - Area 10,486 sq. km; pop. 2,053,058; cap. Agartala.

Uttar Pradesh - Area 294,411 sq. km; pop. 110,862,013; cap. Lucknow.

West Bengal - Area 88,752 sq. km; pop. 54,580,647; cap. Calcutta.

Union Territories :-

Andaman & Nicobar Is. - Area 8,249 sq. km; pop. 188,741; cap. Port Blair.

Chandigarh - Area 114 sq. km; pop. 451,610; cap. Chandigarh.

Dadra & Nagar Haveli - Area 491 sq. km; pop. 103,676; cap. Silvassa.

Delhi - Area 1,483 sq. km; pop. 6,220,406; cap. Delhi.

Goa, Daman & Diu - Area 3,814 sq. km; pop. 1,086,730; cap. Panaji.

Lakshadweep - Area 32 sq. km; pop. 40,249; cap. Kavaratti.

Pondicherry - Area 185 sq. km; pop. 604,471; cap. Pondicherry.

THE ISLE OF MAN - An island in the Irish Sea, having its own legislature; area 227 sq. miles; pop. 64,282; cap. Douglas; Lt.Gov.: Major General Laurence New.

* JAMAICA - An independent state in the Caribbean within the Commonwealth since 1962; area 4,411 sq. miles; pop. 2,429,000; cap. Kingston; Governor-General: Sir Florizel Glasspole; Prime Minister: Michael Manley; High Comm. in the U.K.: Douglas Saunders, 1-2 Prince Consort Road, London SW1 2BJ; British High Comm. in Jamaica: D F Milton.

JERSEY - see CHANNEL ISLANDS

* KENYA - Independent republic in East Africa; area 224,960 sq. miles including 5,171 sq. miles of water; pop. 23,021,000 (1988); cap. Nairobi; President: Daniel T. arap Moi; High Comm. in U.K.: Dr. Sally Kosgei, 24/25 New Bond Street, London W1 9/HD; High Comm. in Kenya: J.R.Johnson.

* KIRIBATI - Republic of 33 islands in the central Pacific, independent since 1979, consisting of the Gilbert Islands, including Banaba (Ocean Island), Phoenix and Line Islands; area 264 sq. miles; pop. 67,000 (1988); cap. Tarawa. President: Ieremia Tabai; British High Comm. in Kiribati: Charles Thompson; High Commissioner in London: Peter Timeon.

LEEWARD ISLANDS see ANGUILLA, ANTIGUA AND BARBUDA, MONTSERRAT, ST.CHRISTOPHER-NEVIS.

* LESOTHO - Formerly Basutoland. Independent sovereign state in Southern Africa; area 11,716 sq. miles; pop. 1,673.000 (1988); cap. Maseru; Head of State: H.M. King Moshoeshoe II; Prime Minister: Major General J.M. Lekhanga; High Comm. in U.K.: H.E. Mr M K Tsekoa, 10 Collingham Road, London SW5 0NR; British High Comm. in Lesotho: J C Edwards.

* MALAWI - Formerly Nyasaland. An independent republic in central Africa; area 45,757 sq. miles; pop. 8,155,000 (1988); cap. Lilongwe; Head of State: Ngwazi Dr. Hastings Kamuzu Banda; High Comm. in U.K.: (Vacant), 33 Grosvenor Street, London W1; British High Comm. in Malawi: Dr D G Osborne.

* MALAYSIA - A federation established in September 1963 consisting of Peninsular Malaysia and the Borneo states of Sabah (former North Borneo) and Sarawak. Federal cap. Kuala Lumpur; Head of State: His Majesty Paduka Seri Sultan Azlan Muhibbuddin Shah of Perak; Prime Minister: The Rt. Hon. Datuk Seri Dr. Mahathir Mohamad; High Comm. in U.K.: Tan Sri Islan Sidek, 45 Belgrave Square, London SW1X 8QT; British High Comm. in Malaysia: J.N.T.Spreckley, C.M.G.Peninsular Malyasia - Eleven states comprising Johore, Kedah, Kelantan, Malacca, Negri Sembilan, Pahang, Penang, Perak, Perlis, Selangor and Trengganu; total area 50,600 sq. miles; pop. 15,611,000. Sabah and Sarawak - Total area 77,440 sq. miles; Total pop. 16,291,000 (1988).

* **THE MALDIVES** - Republic, a group of over 1,200 islands in the Indian Ocean about 200 of which are inhabited. Member of the Commonwealth since 1982. Area 115 sq. miles (approx); pop. 203,000 (1988); cap. Male; President: Maumoon Abdul Gayoom; British High Comm. (resident in Sri Lanka): D.A.S. Gladstone.

* **MALTA** - Islands in the Mediterranean, independent since 1964 and a republic since 1974; area: Malta 95 sq. miles, Gozo 26 sq. miles, Comino 1 sq. mile; pop. 345,000 (1988); cap. Valletta; President: Dr. Censu Tabone; Prime Minister: Dr. E. Fenech Adam.; High Comm. for Malta in U.K.: John A.Manduca, 16 Kensington Square, London W8 5HH; British High Comm. in Malta: Brian Hitch.

* **MAURITIUS** - An island in the Indian Ocean and independent member of the Commonwealth since 1968; area (including Rodrigues and lesser dependencies) 778 sq. miles; pop. 1,048,000 (1988); cap. Port Louis; Governor-General: Sir Veerasamy Ringadoo; Prime Minister: Rt. Hon. Aneerood Jugnauth; High Comm. in the U.K.: Dr. Boodhun Teelock, 32-33 Elvaston Place, London SW 7; British High Comm. in Mauritius: Mr M E Howell.

MONTSERRAT - Dependent territory in eastern Caribbean; area 39.5 sq. miles; pop. 12,034; principal town Plymouth; Governor: A.C. Watson.

* **NAURU** - An independent republic since 1968; an island in the Pacific almost on the Equator, formerly administered by the governments of Australia, New Zealand, and the United Kingdom; area 8.25 sq. miles; pop. 8,042; cap. Nauru; President: Hammer deRoburt.; British High Comm. in Nauru (resident in Fiji): A B P Smart.

NEW HEBRIDES see VANUATU

* **NEW ZEALAND** - An independent member of the Commonwealth in the S. Pacific consisting of the North and South Islands, Stewart Island, Chatham Islands and some other minor islands; area 268,000 sq. kilometres; pop. 3,339,000 (1988); cap. Wellington; Governor-General: HE Dame Catherine Anne Tizard; Prime Minister: The Rt. Hon Michael Moore; High Comm. in the U.K.: Bryce Harland, New Zealand House, Haymarket, London SW1Y 4TQ; British High Comm. in New Zealand: R.A.C. Byatt.

* **NIGERIA (Federal Republic of)** - An independent republic on west coast of Africa; area 356,669 sq. miles; pop. 110,131,000 (1989); cap. Lagos; Head of State: His Excellency General Ibrahim Babangida; High Comm. in the U.K.: George Dove-Edwin, 9 Northumberland Avenue, London WC2N 5BX; British High Comm. in Nigeria: B L Barder.

NIUE - An island in the Pacific in free association with New Zealand, but internally self-governing; area 258 sq. miles; pop. 3,002; Premier: Sir Robert R. Rex.

NORFOLK ISLAND - A territory of the Australian Commonwealth in the W.Pacific; area 36 sq. km; pop. 2,175; cap. Kingston; Administrator: Cdre. J.A. Matthew.

NORTHERN IRELAND see UNITED KINGDOM

* **PAPUA NEW GUINEA** - Independent since 1975, the country consists of eastern part of island of New Guinea, separated from Australia by Torres strait, and other islands including Bismarck archipelago, area 178,260 sq. miles; pop. 3,84,000 (1988); cap. Port Moresby; Governor- General: H.E. Sir Vincent Serei Eri; Prime Minister: The Hon. Rabbie Namaliu; High Comm. in the U.K.: Philip Bouraga, 14 Waterloo Place, London SW 1; British High Comm. in Papua New Guinea: E J Sharland.

PITCAIRN ISLANDS - Colony of the Pacific, originally settled by mutineers from H.M.S. Bounty; area 1.75 sq. miles; pop. approx 67. Three uninhabited islands, Oeno, Henderson and Ducie form part of the Pitcairn settlement; Governor (resident in New Zealand): T.D.O'Leary.

RHODESIA See ZIMBABWE

ROSS DEPENDENCY - An area of the Antarctic under the jurisdiction of New Zealand; area 154,440 sq. miles land and 127,410 sq. miles of permanent ice shelf; no settled population but there are bases for scientific personnel.

* **ST. KITTS & NEVIS** - Two islands in the Caribbean which became independent in 1983; area of St.Kitts 65 sq. miles; pop; 43,000; area of Nevis 36 sq. miles; pop.43,000 (1988); cap. Basseterre; Governor- General: Sir Clement Arrindell; Prime Minister: The Rt. Hon. Dr. Kennedy Simmonds; Acting High Comm. in U.K.: Mr Richard Gunn; British High Comm. in St.Christopher-Nevis (resident in Barbados): K.F.X. Burns.

ST.HELENA - Dependent territory, an island in the South Atlantic; area (excluding dependencies) 47 sq. miles; pop. 5,895; cap. Jamestown; Governor: Francis Baker, C.B.E. Dependencies Ascension and Tristan da Cunha (q.v.)

* **ST.LUCIA** - An island in the eastern Caribbean, independent since 1979, formerly an associated state; area 238 sq. miles; pop. 145,000 (1988); cap. Castries. Acting Governor-General: Stanilaus James; Prime Minister: Rt.Hon. John G.M. Compton; High Commissioner in the U.K.: H.E. Richard Gunn, 10 Kensington Court, London W8 5DL; British High Comm. in St.Lucia (resident in Barbados): K.F.X. Burns.

* **ST.VINCENT AND THE GRENADINES** - Island in the eastern Caribbean which with northern Grenadines became independent 1979. Total area 150 sq. miles (St.Vincent 133 sq. miles); pop. 122,000 (1988); cap. Kingstown. Acting Governor-General: Henry Williams; Prime Minister: Hon. James Mitchell; High Commissioner in U.K.: H.E. Mr Richard Gunn, 10 Kensington Court, London W8 5DL; High Comm. in St.Vincent (resident in Barbados): K.F.X. Burns.

SCOTLAND See UNITED KINGDOM

* **SEYCHELLES** - Archipelago of over 100 islands covering about 400,000 sq. miles of western Indian Ocean; an independent republic since 1976; total land area 170 sq. miles; pop. 68,000 (1988); cap. Victoria on island of Mahe. President: France Albert Rene; High Comm.: R.F. De lpech, 50 Conduit Street, London W1A 4PE; High Comm. in Seychelles: G W P Hart.

* **SIERRA LEONE** - independent republic on west coast of Africa; area 27,925 sq. miles; pop. 3,938,000 (1988); cap. Freetown. Executive President: Major-General Dr. Joseph Saidu Momoh; High Comm. in the U.K.: Caleb B.Aubee, 33 Portland Place, London W1; British High Comm. in Sierra Leone: D.W. Partridge.

* **SINGAPORE** - An island republic on the southern extremity of the Malay peninsula; area 620.5 sq. km; pop. 2,639,000 (1988); cap. Singapore; President: Mr Wee Kim Wee; Prime Minister: H.E. The Hon. Lee Kuan Yew; High Commissioner in the U.K.: Mr. Aziz Mahmood, 2 Wilton Crescent, London SW1X 8RW; British High Comm. in Singapore: Michael Pike.

* **SOLOMON ISLANDS** - A group of islands in the west Pacific, independent since 1978; land area 11,500 sq. miles; pop. 304,000 (1988); cap. Honiara (Guadalcanal); Governor-General: H.E. Sir George Lepping; Prime Minister: The Hon. Solomon Mamaloni; British High Comm. in Solomons: D J Young.

* **SRI LANKA** - Democratic Socialist Republic. Formerly Ceylon. An island to the south of India; area 25,332 sq. miles; pop. 16,561,000 (1989); cap. Colombo; President: Ranasinghe Premadasa; High Comm. in U.K.: General Don Sepala Attygalle, 13 Hyde Park Gardens, London W2; British High Comm. in Sri Lanka: D.A.S. Gladstone.

* **SWAZILAND** - Kingdom in Southern Africa, independent member of the Commonwealth since 1968; area 6,704 sq. miles; pop. 737,000 (1988); cap. Mbabane; Head of State: H.M. King Mswati III; Prime Minister: The Hon. Obed Dlamini (acting); High Comm. in U.K.: H.E. Mboni N. Dlamini, 58 Pont Street, London SW1 0A3; British High Comm. in Swaziland: John Flynn.

* **TANZANIA** - United republic. A union in East Africa between Tanganyika and Zanzibar. Formed April 1964 within the Commonwealth; area 945,087 sq. km; pop. 24,739,000 (1988); cap. Dar es Salaam; President: A.H. Mwinyi; High Comm. in U.K.: John S Malecela, 43 Hertford Street, London W1Y 8DB; British High Comm. in Tanzania: J T Masefield.

TOKELAU - A group of three atolls, Atafu, Fakaofo and Nukunonu, in the Pacific, belonging to New Zealand; area 12.2 sq. km; pop. 2,000; Administrator: Mr. H.H. Francis.

* TONGA (or Friendly Islands) - A group of islands in the southwest Pacific and independent member of the Commonwealth since 1970; area 270 sq. miles; pop. 101,000 (1988); cap. Nuku'alofa; reigning King: Taufa'ahau Tupou IV; Prime Minister: Prince Fatafehi Tu'ipelehake; High Comm. in U.K.: S.M. Tuita, New Zealand House, Haymarket, London SW1; British High Comm. in Tonga: A.P. Fabian.

* TRINIDAD AND TOBAGO - A twin island republic off the north coast of South America; area 1,864 and 116 sq. miles respectively; pop. 1,241,000 (1988); cap. Port-of-Spain; main town of Tobago, Scarborough; President: His Excellency Noor Hassanali; Prime Minister: Hon. A.N.R. Robinson; High Comm. in the U.K.: Justice Ulric Cross, 42 Belgrave Square, London SW1 8NT; British High Comm. in Trinidad and Tobago: Sir M.S. Berthoud, C.M.G.

TURKS AND CAICOS ISLANDS - Group of islands in Caribbean Sea; area 193 sq. miles; pop. 10,000; cap. Grand Turk. Governor: M.J. Bradley.

* TUVALU - Nine islands, formerly the Ellice Islands, in the south- western Pacific, independent since 1978; area 10 sq. miles spread over 500,000 sq. miles of ocean; pop. 9,000 (1988); cap. Funafuti; Governor-General: H.E. Tupua Leupena, M.B.E.; Prime Minister: Rt. Hon. Dr. Tomasi Puapua; U.K. High Comm. (resident in Fiji): A B P Smart.

* UGANDA - A republic in eastern Africa, independent member of the Commonwealth since 1962; area 94,000 sq. miles; pop. 16.195 million (1988); President: Yoweri Museveni; High Comm. in U.K.: William S.K. Matoru; British High Comm. in Uganda: Derek M. March.

* UNITED KINGDOM - Kingdom of N.W. Europe; area 94,214 sq. miles; pop. 57,019,000 (1988); cap. London; Reigning sovereign: H.M. Queen Elizabeth II; Prime Minister: Rt.Hon. Mrs Margaret Thatcher, M.P.The United Kingdom consists of England, Scotland, Wales and N. Ireland; the term Great Britain denotes England, Scotland, and Wales; the term British Isles denotes all of the above with the addition of the Irish Republic. This last term is solely a geographical one.

Countries of the U.K. :

England - Kingdom occupying the S. half of Great Britain; area 50,327 sq. miles; pop. 46,220,955; cap. London.

Northern Ireland - Area 5,459 sq. miles; pop. 1,543,300; cap. Belfast.

Scotland - Kingdom occupying the N. half of Great Britain; area 30,411 sq. miles; pop. 5,117,146; cap. Edinburgh.

Wales - Principality of the W. of Great Britain; area 8,017 sq. miles; pop. 2,790,462; cap. Cardiff.

* VANUATU - Independent republic consisting of a number of islands (including the Bank and Torres Islands) in the south-west Pacific, formerly Anglo-French condominium of the New Hebrides; area 5,700 sq. miles; pop. 151,000 (1988); cap. Vila; President: George Sokomanu; Prime Minister: Walter Hadye Lini; British High Comm. in Vanuatu: Malcolm Creek.

WALES See UNITED KINGDOM

* WESTERN SAMOA - Nine islands in the south west Pacific, a former Trust Territory of New Zealand, now an independent sovereign state; area 1,090 sq. miles; pop. 168,000 (1988); cap. Apia on island of Upolu; Head of State: His Higness Malietoa Tanumafili; Prime Minister: The Hon Tofilau Eti Alesana; High Comm. (resident in New Zealand): R.A.C. Byatt.

WINDWARD ISLANDS See DOMINICA, GRENADA, ST.LUCIA, ST.VINCENT.

* ZAMBIA - Formerly Northern Rhodesia. Independent republic of central Africa; area 290,587 sq. miles; pop. 7.486 million

(1988); cap. Lusaka; President: Dr.Kenneth Kaunda; High Comm. in U.K.: Edward M Lubinda, Zambia House, 2 Palace Gate, London W8 5NG; British High Comm. in Zambia: J. Wilson.

* ZIMBABWE - Formerly Southern Rhodesia. A republic of southern Africa, independent member of the Commonwealth since 1980; area 150,820 sq. miles; pop. 8,420,000; cap. Harare (formerly Salisbury); President: Robert Mugabe; High Comm. in U.K.: W K Prendagast, Zimbabwe House, 429 Strand, London WC 2; British High Comm. in Zimbabwe: Vacant.

* These countries are full members of the Commonwealth.

Population figures have been taken from the World Bank Atlas 1989.

FOREIGN COUNTRIES
A gazetteer of foreign countries of the world, with Colonies, Protectorates and self-governing States

AFGHANISTAN (Republic of). Republic, former monarchy, lying in central Asia; area 250,000 sq. miles; pop. 15,551,358. Capital Kabul. President of the Republic of Afghanistan & General Secretary of the People's Democratic Party of Afghanistan: Dr. Sayid Mohammed Najibullah. Prime Minister: Sultan Ali Kishtmand.

ALBANIA. Republic of the Balkans; area 10,600 sq. miles; pop. 3,800,00. Capital Tirana. Chairman of the Presidium of the People's Assembly: Ramiz Alia. Prime Minister: Foto Cami, Prokop Murra.

ALGERIA. Republic of North Africa; area 919,590 sq. miles; pop. 22,600,000 . Capital Algiers. President of Republic: Benjedid Chadli. Prime Minister: Abdlehamid Brahimi.

ANDORRA. A little country of the Pyrenees under suzerainty of the French Republic and the Spanish Bishop of Urgel; area 180 sq. miles; pop. 42,172 (1984 est.). Capital Andorra-la-Vielle. Head of Government: Josef Pintat Solans.

ANGOLA. A republic of west Africa, until 1975 a Portuguese overseas territory; area 481,351 sq. miles; pop. 8,960,000. Capital Luanda. President: Jose Eduardo dos Santos.

ARGENTINA. South American republic; area 1,079,418 sq. miles; pop. 31,060,000. Capital Buenos Aires. President: Senor Menem.

AUSTRIA. Republic of central Europe; area 32,374 sq. miles; pop, 7,555,338. Capital Vienna. President Dr. Kurt Waldheim. Chancellor Dr. Franz Vranitzky.

BAHRAIN, State of. A group of islands, of which Bahrain island is the largest, in the Arabian Gulf; area 265.5 sq. miles; pop. 416,275. Capital Manama. Crown Prince and Minister of Defence: Shaikh Hamad bin Isa Al-Khalifa. Prime Minister: Emir Shaikh Isa bin Sulman Al-Khalifa.

BELGIUM. Kingdom of western Europe; area 30,518 sq.km.; pop. 9,859,000. Capital Brussels. Reigning king: Baudouin I. Prime Minister: Wilfried Martens.

BENIN (People's Republic of Benin) (formerly Dahomey). A republic of west Africa; area 47,000 sq. miles; pop. 3,338,240. Capital Porto Novo. President: Ahmed Mathieu Kerekou.

BHUTAN. Independent state in eastern Himalayas; area 18,000 sq. miles approx.; pop. 1,300,000. Capital Thimphu. Reigning king: Jigme Singye Wangchuk. Bhutan, while retaining internal independence, agreed to be guided by the Government of India on external affairs.

BOLIVIA. South American republic; area 424,000 sq. miles; pop. 6,252,250. Legal capital Sucre. Seat of Government La Paz. President Victor Paz Estenssoro.

BRAZIL (Federative Republic of Brazil). South American republic; area 3,287,000 sq. miles; pop. 141,300,000. Largest independent nation in S. America. Capital Brasilia. President: Fernando Collor de Melo.

BULGARIA (People's Republic of). Area 42,797 sq. m.; pop. over 8,950,000. Capital Sofia. Chairman of State Council: Todor Zhivkov. Chairman of Council of Ministers: Georgy Atanasoff.

BURKINA FASO (formerly Upper Volta). Independent republic of west Africa; area 105,900 sq. miles; pop. 8,330,000. Capital Ouagadougou. President of CNR, Head od State and Government: Capt. Blaise Compaore.

BURMA (Socialist Republic of the Union of Burma). Republic of south- east Asia; area 261,228 sq. miles; pop. 37,850,000. Capital Rangoon. President and Chairman of Council of State: U San Yu. Prime Minister: U Maung Kha.

BURUNDI. Republic in central Africa formerly part of the Belgian Trust Territory of Ruanda-Urundi; area 10,747 sq. miles; pop. 4,923,000. Capital Bujumbura. President of the republic, Minister of Defence: Major Pierre Buyoya.

CABINDA. An autonomous enclave with Angola (q.v.).

CAMBODIA. People's Republic of Kampuchea; area 70,000 sq. miles; pop. 6,000,000. Capital Phnom Penh. President of the Coalition Government: Prince Norodom Sihanouk. Deputy President: Khieu Samphan. Prime Minister: Son Sann.

CAMEROON, Republic of. Independent republic of west Africa; area 179,558 sq. m.; pop. 9.880,000. Capital Yaounde. President: Paul Biya.

CAPE VERDE ISLANDS. A republic off the west coast of Africa, consisting of 15 islands in two groups; until 1975 a Portuguese overseas territory; area 1,557 sq. miles; pop. 350,000. Capital Praia. President: Aristides Maria Pereira.

CENTRAL AFRICAN REPUBLIC. Independent republic of Equatorial Africa within French community; area 238,200 sq. miles; pop. 2,780,000. Capital Bangui. Chairman of CMRN, Head of State and Governement, Minister of Defence and Veterans' Affairs: General Andre Kolingba.

CHAD. Independent republic of Equatorial Africa within French community; area 487,290 sq. miles; pop. 5,240,000. Capital N'djamena. President: Hissene Habr.

CHILE. South American republic; area 2,006,626 sq.km.; pop. 12,070,000. Capital Santiago. President: General Augusto Pinochet Ugarte.

CHINA (People's Republic of China). Republic of south-east Asia; area 3,700,000 sq. miles (est.); pop. 1,072,200,000. Capital Beijing (Peking). Premier: Li Peng. (Acting) General Secretary of Chinese Communist Party Central Committee: Jiang Zemin.

COLOMBIA. South American republic; area 440,505 sq. miles; pop. 29,500.000. Capital Bogota. President Dr. Virgilio Barco Vargas.

COMOROS (Comoro Republic). An archipelago in the Indian Ocean, formerly an overseas territory of France, independent since 1975, consisting of islands of Great Comoro, Anjouan and Moheli. The island of Mayotte in the archipelago rejected independence and voted in a referendum to remain a part of the French Republic. Area 849 sq. miles; pop. 422,500. Capital Moroni. President: Ahmed Abdallah Abderemane.

CONGO (People's Republic of the). Independent republic of Equatorial Africa within French community; area 130,000 sq. miles; pop. 2,180,000. Capital Brazzaville. President Colonel Denis Sassou- Nguessou. Prime Minister: Ange-Deouard Poungui.

COSTA RICA. Republic of southern part of central America; area 19,653 sq. miles; pop. 2,660,000. Capital San Jose. President: Oscar Arias Sanchez.

COTE D'IVOIRE. Independent republic of west Africa; area 124,324 sq. miles; pop. 10,600,000. Capital Abidjan. President Felix Houphouet Boigny.

CUBA. Republic, largest island of West Indies; area 44,000 sq. miles; pop. 10,190,000. Capital Havana. President: of the State's Council Dr. Fidel Castro Ruz.

CZECHOSLOVAKIA. Republic of central Europe; area 49,372 sq. miles; pop. 15,500,00. Capital Prague. President Vaclav Havel. Prime Minister: Marian Calsa.

DAHOMEY. See Benin.

DENMARK. Kingdom of northern Europe; area 17,028 sq. miles; pop. 5,116,273. Capital Copenhagen. Reigning queen: Margrethe II. Prime Minister: Poul Schluter.

DJIBOUTI. Formerly the French overseas territory of the Afars and Issas on the north-east coast of Africa, an independent republic since 1977; area 8,878 sq. m.; pop. 470,000. Capital Djibouti. President: Hassan Gouled Aptidon. Prime Minister: Barkat Gourad Hamadou.

DOMINICAN REPUBLIC. Republic of the West Indies, occupying eastern two-thirds of island of Hispaniola; the republic of Haiti occupying the west part; area 19,300 sq. miles; pop. 6,588,000. Capital Santo Domingo. President: Dr. Joaquin Balaguer.

ECUADOR. South American republic; area 226,000 sq. miles; pop. 9,647,107. Capital Quito. President: F. Christiani.

EGYPT (Arab Republic of Egypt). Republic of north-east Africa; area 386,900 sq. miles; pop. 49,200,000. Capital Cairo. President: Hosni Mubarak. Prime Minister: Dr. Atef Mohamed Naguib Sidki.

EL SALVADOR. Smallest of central American republics; area 8,236 sq. m.; pop. 5,480,000 (19830. Capital San Salvador. President: S. Christiani.

EQUATORIAL GUINEA. Republic of west Africa, independent since 1968, consisting of the former Spanish mainland province of Rio Muni and islands of Bioco (formerly Fernando Poo), Pagalu (formerly Annobon), Corisco, Elobey Grande and Elobey Chico; area 10,832 sq. miles; pop. 3758400. Capital Malabo (formerly Santa Isabel). President: Teodoro Obiang Nguema Mbasogo.

ETHIOPIA. (Eritrea united with Ethiopia in 1952). People's Democratic Republic of Ethiopia; area 1,223,600 sq. kms; pop. 46,000,000. Capital Addis Ababa. President of the People's Democratic Republic of Ethiopia: Mengistu Haile Mariam. Prime Minister: Fikre-Selaisse Wogderess.

FAROE ISLANDS. A territory of Denmark enjoying home rule, lying between north Scotland and Iceland; area 540 sq. miles; pop. 45,728. Capital Thorshavn. There are 18 islands altogether; 17 are inhabited.

FIJI. Fiji gained independent status on October 10, 1970, having been ceded to Britain on October 10, 1874; area 7,078 sq. miles; pop. 714,000. Capital Suva. President: Ratu Sir Penaia Ganilau. Prime Minister: Ratu Sir Kamisese Mara.

FINLAND. Republic of northern Europe; area 130,129 sq. miles; pop. 4,930,000. Capital Helsinki. President: Dr. Mauno Koivisto. Prime Minister: Harri Holkeri.

FORMOSA. See Taiwan.

FRANCE. Republic of western Europe; area 212,751 sq. miles; pop. 55,620,000. Capital Paris. President: Francois Mitterand. Prime Minister: Michel Rocard.

FRENCH ANTARCTICA. Territory comprising the Kerguelen and Crozet archipelagos, the islands of Saint Paul and New Amsterdam and Adelie Land; area Kerguelen 2,786 sq. miles; Crozet 195 sq. miles; Saint Paul 3 sq. miles; New Amsterdam 21 sq. miles Capital Port-aux-Francais, Kerguelen. Administrator: Admiral Claude Pieri.

FRENCH GUIANA. Overseas department of France on north-east coast of South America; area 34,750 sq. miles; pop. 85,800. Capital Cayenne. Commissioner: Jacques Dewatre.

FRENCH POLYNESIA. French overseas territory in the east Pacific, including the Society Is., Marquesas Is., Tuamotu Group, Iles sous le Vent, Austral Is., etc.; area 1,544 sq. miles; pop. 180,000. Capital Papeete on island of Tahiti. High Commissioner: Pierre Angeli.

11

GABON. Independent republic of Equatorial Africa within the French community; area 103,088 sq. miles; pop. 1,220,000. Capital Libreville. President: Omar Bongo.

GERMAN DEMOCRATIC REPUBLIC. Area 48,830 sq. miles; pop. 16,624,400. Capital Berlin. Prime Minister: Lothar de Maizière.

GERMANY, FEDERAL REPUBLIC OF. West Germany; area 248,694 sq. kms; pop. 61,140,000, (inc. Berlin - West). Greater Berlin is divided into West Berlin (British, French and U.S. sectors) and East Berlin (Soviet sector). Capital Bonn. President: Richard von Weizsacker. Chancellor: Helmut Kohl.

GREECE. Republic in south-east Europe; area 50,960 sq. miles; pop. 9,970,000. Capital Athens. President: Constantinos Karamalis. Prime Minister: Constantino Mitsotakis.

GREENLAND. World's largest island in the north Atlantic, a territory of Denmark enjoying home rule; area 840,000 sq. miles; pop. 53,406. Capital Nuuk.

GUADELOUPE. Overseas department of France, two islands in West Indies; area 688 sq. miles; pop. 330,600. Capital Point-a-Pitre. Commissioner: Yves Bonnet.

GUAM. A U.S. territory in the Pacific, largest of the Mariana Is.; area 209 sq. miles; pop. 106,000. Capital Agana. Governor: Ricardo Bordallo.

GUATEMALA. Central American republic; area 42,000 sq. miles; pop. 8,990,000. Capital Guatemala City. President: Marco Vinicio Cerezo Arevalo.

GUINEA. An independent republic of west Africa; area 94,926 sq. miles; pop. 6,407,000. Capital Conakry. President: Brig. Gen. Lansan Conte.

GUINEA-BISSAU. Republic of west Africa, formerly Portuguese Guinea; became independent 1974. Area 13,948 sq. miles; pop. 935,000. Capital Bissau. President: Gen. Joao Bernardo Vieira.

HAITI. Republic of the Caribbean, forming western third of island of Hispaniola; area 10,714 sq. miles; pop. 5,300,000. Capital Port-au- Prince. President: Gen. Henri Namphy.

HONDURAS. Central American republic; area 44,000 sq. miles; pop. 4,300,000. Capital Tegucigalpa. President: Ing. Jose Azcona-Hoyo.

HUNGARY. Republic of central Europe; area 35,902 sq. miles; pop. 10,622,000. Capital Budapest. President Arpai Gonez. Prime Minister: Jozsef Antall.

ICELAND. Republic in the north Atlantic Ocean. An island close to Arctic Circle; area 40,000 sq. miles; pop. 244.009. Capital Reykjavik. President: Mrs Vigdis Finnbogadottir. Prime Minister: Thorsteinn Palasson.

INDONESIA. A republic of south-east Asia, an archipelago consisting of 13,677 islands which are grouped into Sumatra Islands, Java and Madura, Kalimantan Islands (formerly called Borneo), Sulawesi (formerly Celebes), Maluku Islands, Nusa Tenggara Islands (Bali is located in the west of these islands) and Irian-Jaya; area 735,000 sq. miles; pop. 172,000,000. Capital Jakarta. President: General Suharto.

IRAN. Islamic republic in Asia; area 636,290 sq. miles; pop. 49,860,000. Capital Tehran. President: Ali Khamenei.

IRAQ. Republic in Asia; area 175,100 sq. miles; pop. 17,090,000. Capital Baghdad. President: Saddam Hussein al-Takriti.

IRELAND. Republic of northern Europe; area 27,136 sq. miles; pop. 3,540,000. Capital Dublin. President: Patrick J. Hillery. An Taoiseach (Prime Minister): Charles J. Haughey.

ISRAEL. A parliamentary democracy in the Middle East. Area 21,501 sq. kms.; pop, 4,331.300. Capital Jerusalem. President: Chaim Herzog. Prime Minister: Yitzhak Shamir.

ITALY. Republic of southern Europe; area 130,000 sq. miles; pop. 57,038,796. Capital Rome. President: Francesco Cossiga. Prime Minister: Giulio Andreotti.

IVORY COAST. See Cote D'Ivoire.

JAPAN. Country of Asia consisting of four main islands (Hokkaido, Honshu, Shikoku, Kyushu) and small adjunct islands; total area 145,834 sq. miles pop. 120,720,542. Capital Tokyo. Emperor: Akihito. Prime Minister: Yasuhiro Nakasone.

JORDAN. Hashemite Kingdom of. Kingdom of south-west Asia; area 36,500 sq. miles; pop. 2,497,000. Capital Amman. Reigning King Hussein, G. C. V. O. Prime Minister: Zaid Rifai.

KOREA. Republic of east Asia; area 38,452 sq. miles; pop. 42,082,000. Capital Seoul. President: Roh Tae Woo. Prime Minister Lee Hyon Jae. North Koreans established a Communist republic in the northern part of Korea; area 47,225 sq. miles; pop. 16,978,000. Capital Pyongyang. The country is now divided at the Truce Line of July, 1953, which corresponds roughly with the 38th Parallel.

KUWAIT. A country of the Arabian Peninsula, on the Arabian Gulf; area 7,820 sq. miles; pop. 1,770,000. Capital Kuwait. Prime Minister: HRH Crown Prince Shaikh Saad al-Abdullah as Salim as Sabah.

LAOS (Lao People's Democratic Republic). A republic, formerly a constitutional monarchy in south-east Asia; area 91,000 sq. miles; pop. 3,670,000. Capital Vientiane. Acting President: Phoumi Vongvichit. Prime Minister: Kaysone Phomvihane.

LEBANON. Republic of the east Mediterranean; area 4,000 sq. miles; pop. 3,500,000. Capital Beirut. President: Amin Gemayel. Prime Minister: Selim El-Hoss.

LIBERIA. Republic of west Africa; area 43,000 sq. miles; pop. 2,500,000. Capital Monrovia. President: Samuel K. Doe.

LIBYA (Socialist People's Libyan Arab Jamahariya). Jamahariyah (State of the masses) in north Africa of 25 municipalities; area 685,450 sq. miles; pop. 3,935,000. Capital Tripoli. Leader of the Revolution:Colonel Muammar Al Qadhafi.

LIECHTENSTEIN. Principality on Upper Rhine; area 62 sq. miles; pop. 27,076. Capital Vaduz. Head of Government: Hans Brunhart.

LUXEMBOURG. Grand Duchy of western Europe; area 999 sq. miles; pop. 369,500. Capital Luxembourg. Reigning Grand Duke: Jean. Prime Minister Jacques Santer.

MACAO. A territory under Portuguese administration in China on the Canton River; area 5 sq. miles; pop. 408,500. Capital Macao. Governor: Carlos Melancia.

MADAGASCAR (Democratic Republic of Madagascar) (Malagasy Republic). An island off the south-east coast of Africa; area 228,000 sq. miles; pop. 10,570,000. Capital Antananarivo. President: Didier Ratsiraka. Prime Minister: Lieut.-Col. Victor Ramahatra.

MALI. An independent republic in west Africa (formerly Sudan); area 464,890 sq. miles; pop. 8,730,000. Capital Bamako. Chairman of National Liberation Committee: Brig. Gen. Moussa Traore.

MARTINIQUE. Overseas department of France, an island in West Indies; area 417 sq. miles; pop. 327,716. Capital Fort-de-France. Prefect Edouard Lacroix.

MAURITANIA (Mauritanian Islamic Republic). Independent republic of west Africa; area 419,230 sq. miles; pop. 2,010,000. Capital Nouakchott. President: Lt.-Col. Moaouiaa Ould Sid Mohamed Taya.

MEXICO (United Mexican States). Federal republic of north America; area 762,000 sq. miles; pop. 76,000,000. Capital Mexico City. President: Carlos Salinas de Gortari.

MIDWAY ISLANDS. A group of islands in the north Pacific under the jurisdiction of the United States Navy Dept.; area 2 sq. miles; pop. 2,256.

MONACO. Principality on Mediterranean coast; area 453 acres; pop. 27,000. Capital Monaco-Ville. Ruling prince Rainier III.

MONGOLIA (Mongolian People's Republic). Republic of central Asia; area 1,565,000 sq. km; pop. 2,000,000. Capital Ulan Bator. President Jambyn Batmounkh. Prime Minister: Dumaagiin Sodnom.

MOROCCO. Kingdom in north Africa (includes former Spanish province of Ifni and Spanish Sahara); area 710. 850 sq. km.; pop. 22,061,000. Capital Rabat. Reigning King: Hassan II. Prime Minister: N. Azzeddine Laraki.

MOZAMBIQUE (People's Republic of Mozambique). A republic on east coast of Africa; formerly Portuguese East Africa, independent since 1975; area 297,731 sq. miles; pop. 14,540,000. Capital Maputo (formerly Lourenco Marques). President: Joaquim Alberto Chissano.

NAMIBIA (South-West Africa). Territory administered by the Transitional Government of National Unity instituted on June 17, 1985; area 318,261 sq. miles; pop. 1,184,000. Capital Windhoek. Administrator Louis Pienaar.

NEPAL. Independent Kingdom on southern slopes of Himalayas; area 54,362 sq. miles; pop. 16,630,000. Capital Kathmandu. Ruling King: Birendra Bir Bikram Shah Dev. Prime Minister: Marich Man Singh Shrestha.

NETHERLANDS. Kingdom of north-west Europe; area 15,900 sq. miles; pop. 14,614,000. Capital Amsterdam. Reigning queen: Beatrix. Prime Minister: R. F. M. Lubbers.

NETHERLANDS ANTILLES. Islands forming a statutory partner in the realm of the Netherlands in the West Indies consisting of Cura[accent]cao (172 sq. miles; capital Willemstad), Bonaire (111 sq. miles; capital Kralendijk), St. Martin (13 sq. miles; capital Philipsburg), St. Eustatius (11 sq. miles; capital Oranjestad), and Saba (4 sq. miles; capital The Bottom). Total area 383 sq. miles; pop. 183.000. Governor: Dr. R. A. Romer.

NEW CALEDONIA. French overseas territory in the Pacific, including the Loyalty Is.; area 7,335 sq. miles; pop. 143,000. Capital Noumea. Dependencies of New Caledonia: Is. of Pines (58 sq. miles; pop. 978), Loyalty Is. (800 sq. miles; pop. 12,248), Houn Is. , Belep Archipelago, Chesterfield Is. , Walpole Is. High Commissioner: Jean Montpezat.

NICARAGUA. Republic of central America; area 57,145 sq. miles; pop. 3,500,000. Capital Managua. The current government was elected on the 4 November 1984. President: Violetto Barios de Chamorro.

NIGER. Independent republic of west Africa; area 484,075 sq. miles; pop. 6,608,000. Capital Niamey. Head of State and President of Supreme Military Council: Colonel Ali Seybou.

NORWAY. Constitutional monarchy of northern Europe on Scandinavian peninsula; area 125,064 sq. miles; pop. 4,159,335. Capital Oslo. Reigning King Olav: V. Prime Minister: J. P. Syse.

OMAN. A sultanate on the south-eastern end of the Arabian peninsula; area 115,830 sq. miles; pop. 1,500,000. Capital Muscat. Ruler: Sultan Qaboos bin Said.

PAKISTAN. Independent Islamic Republic of Indo-Pakistan sub continent in South Asia situated to the north-west of the republic of Bharat (India). Consists of four provinces: Punjab (cap. Lahore), North-West Frontier (cap. Peshawar), Sind (cap. Karachi) and Baluchistan (cap. Quetta); area 310,403 sq. miles; pop. 102,002,000. Capital Islamabad. Prime Minister: Muhammed Khan Junejo.

PANAMA. Republic on the isthmus which connects north and south America; area 29,761 sq. miles; pop. 2,280,000. Capital Panama. President: Manuel Solis Palma.

PARAGUAY. South American republic; area 157,000 sq. miles; pop. 3,790,000. Capital Asuncion. President: Andres Rodrigues.

PERU. South American republic; area 496,221 sq. miles (including part of Lake Titicaca and islands off the coast); pop. 20,200,00. Capital Lima. President: Alan Garcia Perez.

PHILIPPINES. Republic, a group of islands, of south-east Asia; area 300,008 sq. km.; pop. 57,360,000. Capital Manila. President: Corazon C. Aquino.

POLAND. Polish People's Republic - Republic of central Europe; area 312. 683 sq. km.; pop. 37,345,000. Capital Warsaw. Chairman of Council of State: Wojciech Jaruzelski. Prime Minister: Tadeusz Mazowiecka.

PORTUGAL. Republic of western Europe; area 34,500 sq. miles; pop. 10,128,900. Capital Lisbon. Prime Minister: Prof. Anibal Cavaco Silva.

PUERTO RICO. A free commonwealth associated with the United States whose citizens hold U. S. citizenship. An island of the Greater Antilles group between the Atlantic and the Caribbean; area 3,435 sq. miles; pop. 3,196,520. Capital San Juan. Governor: Rafael Hernandez Colon.

QATAR. An independent sovereign Arab state, a peninsula on the western coast of the Arabian Gulf; area 4,402 sq. miles; pop. 371,863. Capital Doha. Ruler: Shaikh Khalifa Bin Hamad al-Thani.

REUNION. An overseas department of France, an island in the Indian Ocean; area 965 sq. miles; pop. 515,814. Capital St. Denis. Prefect Jean Ancuaux.

ROMANIA. Republic of south-east Europe; area 91,699 sq. m.; pop. 22,553,074. Capital Bucharest. President: Ion Iliescu.

RWANDA. Republic in central Africa, formerly part of the Belgian Trust Territory of Ruanda-Urundi; area 10,169 sq. miles; pop. 6,324,000. Capital Kigali. President: Maj. Gen. Juvenal Habyarimana.

ST. PIERRE AND MIQUELON. French overseas 'collectivite territoriale', eight small islands off south coast of Newfoundland; area 93 sq. miles; pop. 6,041. Capital St. Pierre. Prefect: Jean-Rene Garnier.

SAMOA, AMERICAN. U. S. island territory in the Pacific; seven islands area 76 sq. miles; pop. 31,171. Seat of government Fagatogo. Governor: A.P. Lutali.

SAN MARINO. Republic in Apennines near Rimini, Italy; area 23 sq. miles; pop. 22,700. Claims to be oldest republic in Europe. Capital San Marino. Captains Regent: two, appointed six-monthly.

SAO TOME AND PRINCIPE. A republic in the Gulf of Guinea, two islands formerly an overseas province of Portugal, independent since 1975; area 372 sq. miles; pop. 113,000). Capital Sao Tome. President: Dr. Manuel Pinta da Costa.

SAUDI ARABIA. Kingdom occupying major part of Arabian peninsula; area 927,000 sq. miles; pop. 11,520,000. Capital Riyadh. Ruling King: Fahd ibn Abdul Aziz. Custodian of the Two Holy Mosques: Fahd Ibn Abdul Aziz Al-Saud.

SENEGAL. Independent republic in west Africa; area 77,800 sq. miles; pop. 5,800,000. Capital Dakar. President of the Republic: Abdou Diouf.

SIKKIM. See under India in Commonwealth section.

SOMALIA (Somali Democratic Republic). Republic of east Africa, comprising the former British Somaliland Protectorate and the former Italian trust territory of Somalia; area 246,155 sq. miles; pop. 6,248,000. Capital Mogadishu. President: Maj.-Gen. Mohamed Siyad Barre.

SOUTH AFRICA (Republic of). Area 443,678 sq. miles; pop. 23,400,000. Capital (administration) Pretoria; (legislature) Cape Town. State Acting President: F.W. de Klerk. Provinces of the Republic. Cape. Area 247,637 sq. miles; pop. 5,373,781. Capital Cape Town. Administrator Eugene Louw. Natal. Area 35,272 sq. miles; pop. 6,098,000. Capital Pietermaritzburg. Administrator D. Hough. Orange Free State. Area 49,418 sq. miles; pop. 1,932,000. Capital Bloemfontein. Administrator L. J. Botha. Transvaal. Area 101,351 sq. miles; pop. 8,351,000. Capital

11

Pretoria. Administrator W. Cruywagen. National States given independence by South Africa, but not recognised as independent states by other countries. Bophuthatswana. Became independent of South Africa in December, 1977 and made up of six separate areas totalling 44,000 sq. km.; pop. 1,700,000. Capital Mmabatho. President Chief Lucas Mangope. Ciskei. Part of eastern Cape Province which became independent of South Africa in December, 1981; area 9,000 sq. km.; pop. 728,441. Capital Bisho. President Lennox Sebe. Transkei. A part of Cape Province which became independent of South Africa in October, 1976; area 44,630 sq. km.; pop. 3,00,000; cap. Umtata. President Paramount Chief Tudor Ndamase. Venda. Part of the Transvaal which became independent of South Africa in September, 1979; area 2,861 sq. miles; pop. 376,470. Cap. Thoyoyandou. President Paramount Chief Patrick Mphephu.

SOUTH WEST AFRICA. See Namibia.

SPAIN. Kingdom of western Europe; area 195,988 sq. miles including the Balearics and Canaries; pop. 38,400,000. Capital Madrid. On General Franco's death in 1975, Juan Carlos became King Juan Carlos I of Spain. Prime Minister: Felipe Gonzalez Marquez.

SUDAN. A republic of north-east Africa; area 967,500 sq. miles; pop. 25,500,000. Capital Khartoum. Prime Minister: Sadiq Al Mahdi.

SURINAME. A republic on north coast of south America, formerly Netherlands Guiana, independent since 1975; area 63,250 sq. miles; pop. 370,000. Capital Paramaribo. President: Ramsewak Shankar.

SVALBARD. An archipelago under Norwegian sovereignty in the Arctic Ocean; consists of Spitsbergen (15,200 sq. miles), North-East Land, Edge Island, Barents Island, Prince Charles Foreland, Wilhelm Island, White Island, King Charles Land, Bear Island and other smaller islands; area of group about 62,700 sq.km.

SWEDEN. Kingdom of northern Europe covering the largest and eastern part of Scandinavian peninsula; area 173,654 sq. miles; pop. 8,358,000. Capital Stockholm. Reigning king: Carl XVI Gustaf.

SWITZERLAND. Confederation of 26 cantons and half-cantons in central Europe; area 15,937 sq. miles; pop. 6,484,800. Capital Berne. President: Otto Stich; Vice President: Arnold Koller.

SYRIAN ARAB REPUBLIC. Republic in the Levant; area 71,498 sq. miles; pop. 10,960,000. Capital Damascus. President: Hafez al-Assad.

TAIWAN. Island off coast of China mainland, province of the Republic of China (Nationalist); area 13,885 sq. miles; pop. 19,500,000. Capital Taipei. President: Lee Teng-hui. Prime Minister: Yu Kuo-hwa.

THAILAND. Constitutional monarchy of south-east Asia; area 198,247 sq. m.; pop. 53,397,745. Capital Bangkok. Reigning king: Bhumibol Adulyadej. Prime Minister: Prem Tinsulanond.

TOGO. An independent republic of west Africa; area 21,000 sq. miles; pop. 3,160,000. Capital Lome. President: General Gnassingbe Eyadema.

TUNISIA. An independent republic of north Africa; area 63,378 sq. miles; pop. 7,320,000. Capital Tunis. President: Zein El Abidine Ben Ali.

TURKEY. Republic in Asia Minor and Europe; area 301,380 sq. miles; pop. 50,670,000. Capital Ankara. President: Kenan Evren. Prime Minister: Turgut Ozal.

UNITED ARAB EMIRATES. A federation, established in 1971, of seven of the former British-protected Trucial States in the Arabian Gulf comprising Ajman, Al Fujayrah, Abu Dhabi, Dubai, Ras al Khaimah, Sharjah and Umm al Qaiwain. Area 32,000 sq. miles; pop. 1,622,464. President: Shaikh Zayed bin Sultan al-Nahyan (Ruler of Abu Dhabi).

UPPER VOLTA. See Burkina Faso.

URUGUAY. Smallest South American republic; area 72,172 sq. miles; pop. 2,930,564. Capital Montevideo. President: Dr. Julio Maria Sanguinetti.

U.S.A. (United States of America). Federal republic of north America; area 3,615,211 sq. miles; pop. 238,700,000. Capital Washington, District of Columbia. President George Bush. The States of the Union (1980 census pop. figures) are:

Alabama (Ala.). Area 51,609 sq. miles; pop. 3,893,888. Capital Montgomery.

Alaska. Area 586,400 sq. miles; pop. 401,851. Capital Juneau.

Arizona (Ariz.). Area 113,956 sq. miles; pop. 2,718,215. Capital Phoenix.

Arkansas (Ark.). Area 53,104 sq. miles; pop. 2,286,435. Capital Little Rock.

California (Cal.). Area 158,693 sq. miles; pop. 23,667,902. Capital Sacramento.

Colorado (Colo.). Area 104,247 sq. miles; pop. 2,889,964. Capital Denver.

Connecticut (Conn.). Area 5,009 sq. miles; pop. 3,107,576. Capital Hartford.

Delaware (Del.). Area 2,057 sq. miles; pop. 594,338. Capital Dover.

* District of Columbia (D.C.). Area 69 sq. miles; pop. 638,333. Capital the whole is the Federal Capital of the U.S.

Florida (Fla.). Area 58,560 sq. miles; pop. 9,746,324. Capital Tallahassee.

Georgia (Ga.). Area 58,876 sq. miles; pop. 5,463,105. Capital Atlanta.

Hawaii. Area 6,424 sq. miles; pop. 964,691. Capital Honolulu.

Idaho. Area 83,557 sq. miles; pop. 943,935. Capital Boise.

Illinois (Ill.). Area 56,400 sq. miles; pop. 11,426,518. Capital Springfield.

Indiana (Ind.). Area 36,291 sq. miles; pop. 5,490,224. Capital Indianapolis.

Iowa. Area 56,290 sq. miles; pop. 2,913,808. Capital Des Moines.

Kansas (Kan.). Area 82,264 sq. miles; pop. 2,363,679. Capital Topeka.

Kentucky (Ky.). Area 40,395 sq. miles; pop. 3,660,777. Capital Frankfort.

Louisiana (La.). Area 48,523 sq. miles; pop. 4,205,900. Capital Baton Rouge.

Maine (Me.). Area 33,215 sq. miles; pop. 1,124,660. Capital Augusta.

Maryland (Md.). Area 10,577 sq. miles; pop. 4,216,975. Capital Annapolis.

Massachusetts (Mass.). Area 8,093 sq. miles; pop. 5,737,037. Capital Boston.

Michigan (Mich.). Area 58,216 sq. miles; pop. 9,262,078. Capital Lansing.

Minnesota (Minn.). Area 84,068 sq. miles; pop. 4,075,970. Capital St. Paul.

Mississippi (Miss.). Area 47,716 sq. miles; pop. 2,520,638. Capital Jackson.

Missouri (Mo.). Area 69,686 sq. miles; pop. 4,916,686. Capital Jefferson City.

Montana (Mont.). Area 147,138 sq. miles; pop. 786,690. Capital Helena.

Nebraska (Nebr.). Area 77,227 sq. miles; pop. 1,569,825. Capital Lincoln.

Nevada (Nev.). Area 110,540 sq. miles; pop. 800,493. Capital Carson City.

New Hampshire (N.H.). Area 9,304 sq. miles; pop. 920,610. Capital Concord.

New Jersey (N.J.). Area 8,219 sq. miles; pop. 7,364,823. Capital Trenton.

New Mexico (N.M.). Area 121,666 sq. miles; pop. 1,302,894. Capital Santa Fe.

New York (N.Y.). Area 49,576 sq. miles; pop. 17,558,072. Capital Albany.

North Carolina (N.C.). Area 52,712 sq. miles; pop. 5,881,766. Capital Raleigh.

North Dakota (N.D.). Area 70,665 sq. miles; pop. 652,717. Capital Bismarck.

Ohio. Area 41,222 sq. miles; pop. 10,797,630. Capital Columbus.

Oklahoma (Okla.). Area 69,919 sq. miles; pop. 3,025,290. Capital Oklahoma City.

Oregon (Ore.). Area 96,891 sq. miles; pop. 2,633,105. Capital Salem.

Pennsylvania (Pa.). Area 45,333 sq. miles; pop. 11,863,895. Capital Harrisburg.

Rhode Island (R.I.). Area 1,214 sq. miles; pop. 947,154. Capital Providence.

South Carolina (S.C.). Area 31,055 sq. miles; pop. 3,121,820. Capital Columbia.

South Dakota (S. Dak.). Area 77,047 sq. miles; pop. 690,768. Capital Pierre.

Tennessee (Tenn.). Area 42,244 sq. miles; pop. 4,591,120. Capital Nashville.

Texas (Tex.). Area 267,339 sq. miles; pop. 14,229,191. Capital Austin.

Utah. Area 84,916 sq. miles; pop. 1,461,037. Capital Salt Lake City.

Vermont (Vt.). Area 9,609 sq. miles; pop. 511,456. Capital Montpelier.

Virginia (Va.). Area 40,815 sq. miles; pop. 5,346,818. Capital Richmond.

Washington (Wash.). Area 68,192 sq. miles; pop. 4,132,156. Capital Olympia.

West Virginia (W. Va.). Area 24,181 sq. miles; pop. 1,949,644. Capital Charleston.

Wisconsin (Wisc.). Area 56,154 sq. miles; pop. 4,705,767. Capital Madison.

Wyoming (Wyo.). Area 97,914 sq. miles; pop. 469,557. Capital Cheyenne.
* Not a State but a Federal District.

U.S.S.R.. Union of Soviet Socialist Republics, consisting of the following 15 republics (in Europe and Asia):

Armenian S.S.R. Area 29,800 sq.km.; pop. 3,410,000. Capital Yerevan.

Azerbaijan S.S.R. Area 86,600 sq.km.; pop. 6,808,000. Capital Baku.

Byelorussian S.S.R. Area 207,600 sq.km.; pop. 10,082,000. Capital Minsk.

Estonian S.S.R. Area 45,100 sq.km.; pop. 1,557,000. Capital Tallin.

Georgian S.S.R. Area 69,700 sq.km.; pop. 5,272,000. Capital Tbilisi.

Kazakh S.S.R. Area 2,717,300 sq.km.; pop. 16,227,000. Capital Alma-Ata.

Kirghiz S.S.R. Area 198,500 sq.km.; pop. 4,141,000. Capital Frunze.

Latvian S.S.R. Area 63,700 sq.km.; pop. 2,600,000. Capital Riga.

Lithuanian S.S.R. Area 65,200 sq.km.; pop. 3,641,000. Capital Vilnius.

Moldavian S.S.R. Area 33,700 sq.km.; pop. 4,190,000. Capital Kishinev.

Russian Federation (R.S.F.S.R.). Area 17,075,400 sq.km.; pop. 145,320,000. Capital Moscow.

Tadjik S.S.R. Area 143,100 sq.km.; pop. 4,805,000. Capital Dushambe.

Turkmen S.S.R. Area 488,100 sq.km.; pop. 3,352,000. Capital Ashkhabad.

Ukrainian S.S.R. Area 603,700 sq. miles; pop. 51,211,000. Capital Kiev.

Uzbek S.S.R. Area 447,400 sq.km.; pop. 19,013,000. Capital Tashkent.

Total area 22,402,200 sq.km.; total pop. 284,500,000. Capital of U.S.S.R. Moscow, President: Mikhail Gorbachev.

VATICAN CITY. A sovereign state in Rome under the sovereignty of the Holy See; area 108.7 acres; pop. about 1,000. Supreme Pontiff Pope John Paul II (Karol Wojtyla) as Head of the Roman Catholic Church exercises temporal power in the Vatican City State.

VENEZUELA. South American republic; area 352,143 sq. miles; pop. 17,320,000. Capital Caracas. President: Carlos Andres Perez.

VIETNAM. (Socialist Republic of Vietnam). A republic in south-east Asia; area 127,259 sq. miles; pop. 61,950,000; Capital Hanoi. President of Council of State: Vo Chi Cong. Acting Chairman of Council of Ministers (Premier): Vo Van Kiet.

VIRGIN ISLANDS (U.S.). A U.S. territory in the West Indies; formerly the Danish West Indies; area 133 sq. miles; pop. 95,000. Capital Charlotte Amalie. Governor: Juan Luis. See also British Virgin Islands in Commonwealth section.

WAKE ISLAND. A U.S. territory in the Pacific administered by the U.S. Air Force. Area, with Wilkes and Peale islands, 3 sq. miles

WALLIS AND FUTUNA. Islands forming a French overseas territory in the Pacific; area 50 sq. miles; pop. 11,943 (1982). Capital Mata Utu. Administrator M. Le Henaff.

YEMEN, PEOPLE'S DEMOCRATIC REPUBLIC OF (South Yemen). A republic on the southern end of the Arabian peninsula consisting of the former British colony of Aden, islands and protectorates, independent since 1967; area 110,000 sq. miles; pop. 2,500,000 (est.). Capital Aden. President and Chairman of Supreme People's Council: Heider Abubakr Al-Attas.

YEMEN ARAB REPUBLIC (North Yemen). Republic in the south-west of Arabian peninsula. Area 75,000 sq. miles; pop. 6,273,272. Capital Sana'a. President: Ali Abdullah Saleh.

YUGOSLAVIA (Socialist Federal Republic of Yugoslavia). A republic of south-eastern Europe; area 98,725 sq. miles; pop. 23.270,000. Capital Beograd (Belgrade). President of Federal Assembly: Marjan Rozic.

ZAIRE (Formerly Congo Democratic Republic). A republic in central Africa. Until 1960, a Belgian colony; area 914,550 sq. miles; pop. 31,7800,000. Capital Kinshasa. President: Marshal Mobutu Sese Seko Kuku Ngbendu wa Zabanga.

11

POPULATION OF THE WORLD

Current U.N. estimates put the total world polulation in mid-1990 at 5,292,177,000 and 8,466,516,000 by the year 2,025.

NORTH ATLANTIC TREATY ORGANISATION

THE North Atlantic Treaty was signed in Washington on April 4, 1949, by the Foreign Ministers of Belgium, Canada, Denmark, France, Iceland, Italy, Luxembourg, Netherlands, Norway, Portugal, the United Kingdom, and the United States. Greece and Turkey acceded to the Treaty in 1952, the Federal Republic of Germany in 1955 and Spain in 1982. The Treaty is an agreement for collective self-defence as provided for in Article 51 of the Charter of the United Nations.

The North Atlantic Council meets regularly throughout the year at the level of Permanent Representatives of member governments, twice-yearly at Ministerial level, and on occasion at the level of Heads of State of Government.The Secretary General is the Chairman of the Council.

The NATO defence area is divided into three military commands - **the Atlantic Ocean, Europe, Channel** - plus a Regional Planning Group for the North American area.

Address: NATO 1110 Brussels, Belgium.
Secretary-General: Mr. Manfred Worner (Fed.Rep. of Germany)

SACEUR (Allied Command Europe): Supreme Commander: General John R. Galvin (U.S.).

SACLANT (Allied Command Atlantic): Supreme Commander: Admiral Leon A. Edmey. (U.S.).

CINCHAN (Allied Command Channel): C.-in-C. Admiral Sir Benjamin Bathurst K.C.B. (U.K.).

EMBASSIES AND AMBASSADORS

Country	Embassy in London	Ambassador or Minister	British Ambassador or Minister
Afghanistan	31 Princes Gate, SW7 1QQ	Ahmad Sarwar Charge d'Affaires	I. W.Mackley
Algeria	54 Holland Park, W.11	Ahmed Laidi	P. E. C. Eyers, C.M.G., L.V.O.
Apostolic Nunciature	54 Parkside, Wimbledon, SW19 5NF	Archbishop Luigi Barbarito Apolistic Pro-Nuncio	J. K. E. Broadley
Austria	18 Belgrave Mews West, SW1X 8HU	Dr. Walter F. Mayrutsek	Robert O'Neill
Bahrain	98 Gloucester Road, SW7 4AU	Salman Abdul Wahab Al Sabbagh	J. Shepherd
Belgium	103 Eaton Sq., S.W.1	Jean Paul van Bellinghen	P.C.Petrie, C.M.G.
Bolivia	106 Eaton Sq., S.W.1	Eduardo Arauco Paz	C. J. Sharkey, C.M.G., M.B.E.
Brazil	32 Green St., W1.	Celso de Souza e Silva Charge d'Affaires	M.J. Newington, C.M.G.
Bulgaria	186-188 Queen's Gate, S.W.7.	Dimitar Zhulev	John Fawcett
Burma	19A Charles St., W.1	U.Tin Hlaing	Martin Morland
Cameroon, Republic of	84 Holland Park, W11 3SB	Dr. Gibering Bol-Alima	Martin Reith
Chile	12 Devonshire St., W1N 2DS	Juan Carlos Delano	Alan White.
China	49-51 Portland Pl., W1	Ji Chaozhu	Sir Alan Donald
Colombia	Flat 3A, 3 Hans Cres., SW1X 0LR	Dr. Fernando Cepeda	R.A. Neilson, L.V.O.
Costa Rica	93 Star Street, W2 1QF	Miguel T. Yamuni	Michael F.Daly
Cote D'Ivoire	2 Upper Belgrave St., S.W.1	Theodore de Mel	Mrs. V.E. Sutherland
Cuba	167 High Holborn, W.C.1	(Vacant)	David Brighty
Czechoslovakia	25 Kensington Palace Gdns.W.8	H.E. Jan Fidler	Lawrence O'Keefe.
Denmark	55 Sloane St., SW1X 9SR	(Vacant)	Peter Unwin, C.M.G.
Ecuador	Flat 3B, 3 Hans Cres., SW1X 0LN	Rafael Perez y Reyna	M.W. Atkinson, C.M.G.
Egypt, Arab Republic of	26 South Street, W1Y 8EL	Mohamed I. Shaker	W.J. Adams, C.M.G.
Ethiopia	17 Princes Gate, S.W.7	Ato Teferra Haile-Selassie	H.B. Walker
Finland	38 Chesham Place, S.W.1	Ilkka Pastinen	Justin Staples
France	58 Knightsbridge, SW1X 7JT	Viconte Luc de la Barre de Nanteuil	Sir Ewen Fergusson, K.C.M.G.
Gabon	48 Kensington Court, W8 5DB	Charles Mamadou Diop	M.A. Goodfellow
German Democratic Republic	34 Belgrave Square, S.W.1	Dr. Joachim Mitdank	Nigel Broomfield.
Germany Federal Republic of	21-23 Belgrave Sq., SW1X 8PZ	Baron Hermann von Richtofen	Sir Christopher Mallaby, K.C.M.G.
Greece	1A Holland Park, W.11	Stephanos Stathatos	Sir J.C. Thomas, K.C.M.G.
Haiti	Embassy office closed in London		A.J. Payne.
Honduras	47 Manchester Street, W.1	Max Velasquez-Diaz	David Joy
Hungary	35 Eaton Pl., S.W.1	Dr. Matyas Domokos	Leonard Appleyard

Country	Embassy in London	Ambassador or Minister	British Ambassador or Minister
Iceland	1 Eaton Ter., SW1W 8EY	Olafur Egilsson	M.F. Chapman, C.V.O.
Indonesia	38 Grosvenor Sq., W.1	S. Suhartoyo	W.K.K. White
Iran	Diplomatic relations broken on 7th March 1989		
Iraq	21 Queen's Gate, S.W.7	Dr. Mohamed Sadiq Al-Mashat	T.J. Clark, C.M.G., C.V.O.
Ireland	17 Grosvenor Place, SW1X 7HR	Andrew O'Rourke	Nicholas M. Fenn, C.M.G.
Israel	2 Palace Green, W.8	Yoav Biran	C.W. Squire, C.M.G., M.V.O.
Italy	14 Three Kings Yard, Davies St., W.1	Boris Biancheri	Sir Derek Thomas, K.C.M.G.,
Japan	46 Grosvenor St., W.1	Kazuo Chiba	Sir John S. Whitehead, K.C.M.G., C.V.O.
Jordan	6 Upper Phillimore Gardens, W8 7HB	Dr. Albert Butros	Anthony Reeve
Korea	4 Palace Gate, W8 5NF	Jay Hee Oh	Lawrence Middleton
Kuwait	46 Queen's Gate, S.W.7	Ghazi Al-Rayes	P. R. M. Hincliffe
Laos	Embassy closed (Resident in Paris)	Thongsay Bodishane Derek Tonkin	
Lebanon	21 Kensington Palace Gdns,W.8	General Ahmad Ahmad El-Hajj	John Gray, C.M.G., K.B.E, C.M.G.
Liberia	2 Pembridge Gate, W2	Willie A. Givens	M.E.J. Gore
Luxembourg	27 Wilton Cres., SW1X 8SD	Jean Wagner d'Auvergne Campbell	Mme. Juliet Jeanne
Mexico	8 Halkin St., S.W.1	Bernardo Sepulveda	John Morgan, C.M.G.
Monaco	4 Audley Square, W1Y 5DR	I.S. Ivanovic, Consul-General	T.E.J. Mound
Mongolia	7 Kensington Court, W.8	Ishetsogyin Ochirbal	G.W.P. Hart
Morocco	49 Queen's Gate Gdns., S.W.7	Abdesselam Zenined	J.W.R. Shakespeare.
Nepal	12A Kensington Palace Gdns., W.8	Maj. Gen. Bharat K. Simha	R.E.G. Burges Watson, C.M.G. K.C.V.O.
Netherlands	38 Hyde Park Gate, SW7 5DP	P.J.H. Jonkman	Michael Jenkins, C.M.G.
Nicaragua	8 Gloucester Road, SW7 4PP	Francisco d'Escoto	Michael F. Daly (resident in Costa Rica)
Norway	25 Belgrave Sq., S.W.1	Kjell Eliassen	J.A. Robson, C.M.G.
Oman, Sultanate of	44A/B Montpelier Sq, S.W.7	Hussain Bin Mohamed Bin Ali	R.J. Alston, C.M.G.
Pakistan	35 Lowndes Square, SW1X9JN	Shaharyar M. Khan	N. J. Barrington C.M.G.,C.V.O.
Panama	119 Crawford St, W1	Guillermo Vega	Mrs Margaret Bryan
Paraguay	Braemar Lodge, Cornwall Gdns., S.W.7	Antonio Zuccolillo	John MacDonald
Peru	52 Sloane St., S.W.1	Dr. Carlos Raffo	Adrian Beamish.
Philippines	9A Palace Green, W.8	Tomas T. Syquia	
Keith Gordon MacInnes C.M.G.			
Poland	47 Portland Pl., W.1	Dr. Zbigniew Gertych	Brian Barder
Portugal C.M.G.	11 Belgrave Sq., S.W.1	(Vacant)	M.K.O. Simpson-Orlebar,
Qatar, State of	27 Chesham Place, S.W.1	Sherida Sa'ad Jubran Al Ka'abi	M. Nixon, O.B.E.
Romania	4 Palace Green, Kensington, W.8	Stan Soare	Hugh J. Arbuthnott, C.M.G.
El Salvador	Flat 9, 62 Welbeck St., W.1	Dr. Maurico Rosales-Rivera	David Joy
San Marino	166 High Holborn, WC1V 6TT.	I.J. Rawlinson Consul-General	Miss Mary Croll
Saudi Arabia	30 Belgrave Sq., S.W.1	Sheikh Nasser Almanqour	Stephen Egerton
Senegal	11 Phillimore Gardens., W.8	General Idrissa Fall	John Macrae
Somalia	60 Portland Place, W.1	Ahmed Jama Abdulle	Jeremy Varcoe.
South Africa	South African Embassy, Trafalgar Sq., WC2N 5DP	P.R. Killen	Robin Renwick, C.M.G.,L.V.O.
Spain	24 Belgrave Sq., S.W.1	Jose J. Puig de la Bellacasa	Lord Nicholas Gordon Lennox, C.M.G., M.V.O.
Sudan	3 Cleveland Row, W.1	Ibrahim Mohamed Ali	J. L. Beavan, C.M.G., C.V.O.
Sweden	11 Montagu Place, W1H 2AL	Leif Leifland, G.C.V.O.	Sir John Ure, K.C.M.G., L.V.O.
Switzerland	16-18 Montagu Place, W1H 2BQ	Franz E. Muheim	Christopher Long
Thailand	29-30 Queen's Gate, SW7 5JB	Sudhee Prasasvinitchai	Derek Tonkin
Tunisia	29 Princes Gate, S.W.7	Abdelwaheb Abdallah	S.P. Day
Turkey	43 Belgrave Sq., SW1X 8PA	Nurver Nures	T.L.A. Daunt, C.M.G.
United Arab Emirates	30 Princes Gate, S.W.7	Dr. Khalifa Mohamed Sulaiman	M.L. Tait, L.V.O.
United States	24-32 Grosvenor Square, W1A 2LH	Henry E. Catto	Sir Antony Acland, G.C.M.G., K.C.V.O.
Uruguay	48 Lennox Gdns., S.W.1	Luis Alberto Sole-Romeo	Eric Vines
U.S.S.R.	13 Kensington Palace Gdns. W.8	Leonid M. Zamyatin	Sir Bryan Cartledge, K.C.M.G.
Venezuela	1 Cromwell Road, SW7 5JB	Dr. Francisco Kerdel-Vegas	Giles Fitzherbert
Vietnam, Socialist Republic of	12-14 Victoria Road, W.8	Tran Van Hung	E.T. Davies, O.B.E.
Yemen, People's Democratic Republic of	57 Cromwell Rd., SW7 2ED	Ahmed Abdo Rageh	Arthur Marshall
Yemen Arab Republic	41 South Street, W1Y 5PD	Ahmed Daifellah AlAzeib	M.A. Marshal
Yugoslavia	5-7 Lexham Gdns., W.8	Mitko Calovski	Andrew Wood
Zaire	26 Chesham Pl., SW1X 8HG	W.J. Phiri	R.L.B. Cormack

11

UNITED KINGDOM REPRESENTATIVES

Ambassador and Permanent Representative to the EC: Sir David Hannay, K.C.M.G.

Permanent Representative to NATO: Sir Michael Alexander, C.M.G.

Permanent Representative to the UN: Sir Crispin Tickell, K.C.V.O.

COMMONWEALTH SECRETARIAT

Marlborough House, Pall Mall, London SW1Y 5HX. 01-839 3411.

Established in 1965 as an international body at the service of all member countries of the Commonwealth, the Commonwealth Secretariat provides the central organisation for joint consultation and co- operation in many fields. It is responsible to Commonwealth governments collectively and is the main agency for multilateral communciation between them. Staffed by officers from member countries and financed by contributions from member governments, the Secretariat is headed by the Commonwealth Secretary-General who has access to Heads of Governments. It promotes consultation and disseminates information on matters of common concern, organises and services meetings of Heads of Government and other conferences, and provides expert technical assistance for economic and social development through the multilateral Commonwealth Fund for Technical Co-operation.

Commonwealth Secretary-General: Chief Emeka Anyoaku (Nigeria).

Deputy Secretaries-General: Sir Anthony Siaguru (Papua New Guinea); Sir Peter Unwin (United Kingdom).

WESTERN EUROPEAN UNION

9 Grosvenor Place, London, SW1X 7H

WESTERN European Union was formally inaugurated on May 6, 1955, and comprises the following members: the United Kingdom, Belgium, France, the Federal Republic of Germany, Italy, Luxembourg, and the Netherlands. It originated in a Treaty signed at Brussels on March 17, 1948, by the United Kingdom, France, and the three Benelux countries for economic, social and cultural collaboration and collective self- defence. This Treaty was modified and completed by the Agreements signed in Paris on October 23, 1954. Following the decision taken in 1984 to revitalise the Organisation, a part of previous armaments control activity was terminated on January 1, 1986. As part of the reforms the Council of W.E.U. (Ministers of Foreign Affairs and Defence) now meet twice a year, and regularly as required at Ambassador level. On 13th November 1989, WEU organisers decided to set up a <169>WEU - Institute for Security Studies<170> in Paris which is to carry out research and promotes a greater awareness of European security issues. A Parliamentary Assembly sitting twice a year is also located in Paris together with the Institute at 43 Avenue du President Wilson, 75775 Paris Cedex 16.

Secretary-General: Wim van Eekelen (NL)

OVERSEAS CURRENCIES (AT AUGUST 7 1990)

Country	Currency			Average equivalent to £1 sterling
Afghanistan	100 puls	=	1 Afghani	Af. 99.25
Algeria	100 centimes	=	1 Dinar	Din. 16.35
Argentina	100 centavos	=	1 Austral	Austral. 10235.10
Australia (1)	100 cents	=	1 Australian Dollar	Aus. $2.37
Austria	100 groschen	=	1 Schilling	Sch. 20.73
Bahrain	1,000 fils	=	1 Dinar	BD 0.7
Bangladesh	100 paisa	=	1 Taka	T. 64.0
Barbados	100 cents	=	1 Barbados	$ B.$ 3.77
Belgium	100 centimes	=	1 Franc	Fr. 60.55*
Bolivia	1m pesos	=	1 Boliviano	Boliviano 5.95
Botswana	100 thebe	=	1 Pula	Pula 3.36
Brazil	100 cruzeiros	=	1 Cruzado	Crs. 129.11
Bulgaria	100 stotinki	=	1 Lev	Levas 5.30
Burma	100 pyas	=	1 Kyat	Ky. 10.77
Canada	100 cents	=	1 Dollar	$2.15
Chile	100 centavos	=	1 Chilean Peso	Pesos 586.78
China	100 fens	=	1 Renminbi	RMB 8.80
Colombia	100 centavos	=	1 Peso	Pesos 961.38
Costa Rica	100 centimos	=	1 Colon	Cols. 172.25
Cuba	100 centavos	=	1 Cuban Peso	Pesos 1.49
Cyprus	1,000 mils	=	1 Cyprus (pound)	C. 0.83
Czechoslovakia	100 halers	=	1 Koruna	Kcs. 29.39*
Denmark	100 re	=	1 Danish Krone	Krs. 11.24
Dominican Republic	100 centavos	=	1 Peso	Pesos 19.53
Ecuador	100 centavos	=	1 Sucre	Suc. 1639.2+
Egypt, Arab Republic of	100 piastres	=	1 Egyptian (pound)	E. 5.03
El Salvador	100 centavos	=	1 Colon	Cols. 11.93
Ethiopia	100 cents	=	1 Birr	Birr 3.85
Fiji	100 cents	=	1 Fiji $	$2.76
Finland	100 pennia	=	1 Markka	Mks. 6.9
France (3)	100 centimes	=	1 Franc	Frs. 9.90
Gambia	100 bututs	=	1 Dalasi	Dalasi 15.63
German Democratic Republic	100 pfennig	=	1 Ostmark	M. 2.95
Germany (Federal Republic)	100 pfennig	=	1 Deutsche Mark	DM. 2.95
Ghana	100 pesew	=	1 Cedi	Cedi 608.50
Greece	100 lepta	=	1 Drachma	Dr. 290.60
Guatemala	100 centavos	=	1 Quetzal	Qu. 8.48
Guyana	100 cents	=	1 Guyanese $	G.$ 83.35
Haiti	100 centimes	=	1 Gourde	G. 9.38
Honduras	100 centavos	=	1 Lempira	L. 0.19
Hong Kong	100 cents	=	1 Dollar	HK $14.59
Hungary	100 filler	=	1 Forint	Ft. 116.96

Country	Currency			Average equivalent to £1 sterling
Iceland	100 aurar	=	1 Krona	Kr. 107.55
India	100 paise	=	1 Rupee	Rs. 32.00
Indonesia	100 sen	=	1 Rupiah	Rp. 3,448.15
Iran	100 dinars	=	1 Rial	Rls. 127.75
Iraq	1,000 fils	=	1 Dinar	Din. 0.57
Ireland	100 pence	=	1 Irish Punt	1.1
Israel	100 agorot	=	1 Shekel	Sh. 3.82
Italy (4)	100 centesimi	=	1 Lira	Lire 2,160.75
Jamaica	100 cents	=	1 Jamaica $	J$ 12.80
Japan	100 sen	=	1 Yen	Yen 149.53
Jordan	1,000 fils	=	1 Dinar	Din. 0.65
Kenya	100 cents	=	1 Kenya Shilling	Sh. 42.90
Korea (South Korea)	100 chon	=	1 Won	W. 1,325.75
Kuwait	1,000 fils	=	1 Dinar K.	n/a @ 7.8.90
Lebanon	100 piastres	=	1 Lebanese Pound	1329.10
Liberia	100 cents	=	1 Dollar	$1.87
Libya	1,000 dirhams	=	1 Dinar	D. 0.52
Luxembourg	100 centimes	=	1 L Franc	L.F. 60.55
Malawi	100 tambala	=	1 Kwacha	Kwacha 4.86
Malaysia	100 cents	=	1 Malaysian Dollar (Ringgit)	$5.06
Mexico	100 centavos	=	1 Peso	Pesos 5399.75//
Morocco	100 centimes	=	1 Dirham (Morocco)	DH. 15.78
Netherlands	100 cents	=	1 Guilder (Florin)	Fls. 3.32
New Zealand	100 cents	=	1 N.Z. Dollar	$3.13
Nigeria	100 Kobo	=	1 Naira	Naira 14.82
Norway	100 re	=	1 Krone	Krs. 11.53
Oman	1,000 baiza	=	1 Rial Omani	R.O. 0.38
Pakistan	100 paisa	=	1 Rupee	Rs. 40.00
Panama	100 centesimos	=	1 Balboa	Bals. 1.87
Papua New Guinea	100 toea	=	1 Kina	K. 1.79
Paraguay	100 centimos	=	1 Guarani	Gus. 2,248.30
Peru	100 centavos	=	1 Inti72952.10	
Philippines	100 centavos	=	1 Peso	Pesos 43.00
Poland	100 groszy	=	1 Zloty	Zl. 17600.00
Portugal (5)	100 centavos	=	1 Escudo	Esc. 260.60
Qatar	100 dirham	=	1 Qatar Riyal	R.Q. 6.81
Romania	100 bani	=	1 Leu	Lei 35.32i
Saudi Arabia	100 halalas	=	1 Riyal	R. 6.07
Sierra Leone	100 cents	=	1 Leone	Leone 297.80
Singapore	100 cents	=	1 $ Singapore	$3.38
Somalia	100 cents	=	1 Somali shilling	Sh. So. 769.36
South Africa (6)	100 cents	=	1 Rand	Rand 4.84*
Spain (7)	100 centimos	=	1 Peseta	Ptas. 181.50
Sri Lanka	100 cents	=	1 Rupee	Rs. 74.00
Sudan	100 piastres	=	1 Sudan Pound	Sudan 21.48
Swaziland	100 cents	=	1 Lilangeni	L. 4.84
Sweden	100 re	=	1 Krona	Krs. 10.83
Switzerland	100 centimes	=	1 Franc	Frs. 2.49
Syria	100 piastres	=	1 Syrian Pound	39.40
Taiwan	100 cents	=	1 New Taiwan Dollar	$50.65
Tanzania	100 cents	=	1 Shilling	Sh. 362.17
Thailand	100 satang	=	1 Baht, or Tical	Baht 47.00
Trinidad and Tobago	100 cents	=	1 Trinidad and Tobago Dollar	$7.99
Tunisia	1,000 millimes	=	1 Dinar	D. 1.60
Turkey	100 kurus	=	1 Turkish Lira	T.L. 4,920.34
United Arab Emirates	100 fils	=	1 Dirham	DH 6.87
Uruguay	100 centesimo	s=	1 Peso	Pesos 2294.30
U.S.A.	100 cents	=	1 Dollar	$1.87
U.S.S.R.	100 kopeks	=	1 Rouble	Rs. 1.07
Venezuela	100 centimos	=	1 Bolivar	Bols. 92.84
Yugoslavia	100 paras	=	1 Dinar	Din. 20.69
Zaire	100 makuta	=	1 Zaire	Z. 1112.00
Zambia	1 dollar	=	1 Kwacha	K. 72.30
Zimbabwe	100 cents	=	1 Zimbabwe Dollar	Z. $4.59

In view of the absence of fixed parities for many of these currencies, rates are liable to considerable fluctuation. They must be taken only as an approximate guide applicable as at August 7 1990.

*   Commercial rate.
+   Official rate
//   Free rate
i   Non commercial rate

(1) Also applies to Cocos (Keeling) Islands, Christmas Island and Nauru.
(2) New currency introduced 1 January 1987.
(3) Also applies to Monaco.
(4) Also applies to San Marino, Vatican City.
(5) Also applies to Azores, Madeira.
(6) Also applies to Namibia.
(7) Also applies to Andorra, Balearic Islands, Canary Islands and Spanish ports in North Africa.

11

11 INTERNATIONAL

MEMBERS OF UNITED NATIONS

	Date of Admission
Afghanistan	Nov.19.1946
Albania	Dec.14.1955
Algeria	Oct. 8.1962
Angola	Dec. 1.1976
Antigua and Barbuda	Nov.11.1981
*Argentina	Oct.24.1945
*Australia	Nov. 1.1945
Austria	Dec.14.1955
Bahamas, The	Sept.18.1973
Bahrain	Sept.21.1971
Bangladesh	Sept.17.1974
Barbados	Dec. 9.1966
*Belgium	Dec.27.1945
Belize	Sept.25.1981
Benin	Sept.20.1960
Bhutan	Sept.21.1971
*Bolivia	Nov.14.1945
Botswana	Oct.17.1966
*Brazil	Oct.24.1945
Brunei	Sept.21.1984
Bulgaria	Dec.14.1955
Burkina Faso	Sept.20.1960
Burma	Apr.19.1948
Burundi	Sept.18.1962
*Byelorussian Soviet Socialist Republic	Oct.24.1945
Cameroon	Sept.20.1960
*Canada	Nov. 9.1945
Cape Verde	Sept.16.1975
Central African Rep	Sept.20.1960
Chad	Sept.20.1960
*Chile	Oct.24.1945
*China	Oct.24.1945
*Colombia	Nov. 5.1945
Colmoros	Nov.12.1975
Congo	Sept.20.1960
*Costa Rica	Nov. 2.1945
*Cuba	Oct.24.1945
Cyprus	Sept.20.1960
*Czechoslovakia	Oct.24.1945
*Denmark	Oct.24.1945
Djibouti	Sept.20.1977
Dominica	Dec.18.1978
*Dominican Rep	Oct.24.1945
*Ecuador	Dec.21.1945
*Egypt, Arab Rep of	Oct.24.1945
*El Salvador	Oct.24.1945
Equatorial Guinea	Nov.12.1968
*Ethiopia	Nov.13.1945
Fiji	Oct.13.1970
Finland	Dec.14.1955
*France	Oct.24.1945
Gabon	Sept.20.1960
Gambia	Sept.21.1965
German Democratic Rep	Sept.18.1973
Germany Federal Rep of	Sept.18.1973
Ghana	Mar. 8.1957

	Date of Admission
*Greece	Oct.25.1945
Grenada	Sept.17.1974
*Guatemala	Nov.21.1945
Guinea	Dec.12.1958
Guinea-Bissau	Sept.17.1974
Guyana	Sept.20.1966
*Haiti	Oct.24.1945
*Honduras	Dec.17.1945
Hungary	Dec.14.1955
Iceland	Dec.19.1946
*India	Oct.30.1945
Indonesia	Sept.28.1950
*Iran	Oct.24.1945
*Iraq	Dec.21.1945
Ireland	Dec.14.1955
Israel	May.11.1949
Italy	Dec.14.1955
Ivory Coast	Sept.20.1960
Jamaica	Sept.18.1962
Japan	Dec.18.1956
Jordan	Dec.14.1955
Kampuchea, Dem	Dec.14.1955
Kenya	Dec.16.1963
Kuwait	May 14.1963
Laos	Dec.14.1955
*Lebanon	Oct.24.1945
Lesotho	Oct.17.1966
*Liberia	Nov. 2.1945
Libya	Dec.14.1955
*Luxembourg	Oct.24.1945
Madagascar	Sept.20.1960
Malawi	Dec. 1.1964
Malaysia	Sept.17.1957
Maldive Islands	Sept.21.1965
Mali	Sept.28.1960
Malta	Dec. 1.1964
Mauritania	Oct.27.1961
Mauritius	Apr.24.1968
*Mexico	Nov. 7.1945
Mongolia	Oct.27.1961
Morocco	Nov.12.1956
Mozambique	Sept.16.1975
Namibia	Apr.23 1990
Nepal	Dec.14.1955
*Netherlands	Dec.10.1945
*New Zealand	Oct.24.1945
*Nicaragua	Oct.24.1945
Niger	Sept.20.1960
Nigeria	Oct. 7.1960
*Norway	Nov.27.1945
Oman	Oct. 7.1971
Pakistan	Sept.30.1947
*Panama	Nov.13.1945
Papua New Guinea	Oct.10.1975
*Paraguay	Oct.24.1945
People's Democratic Rep of Yemen	Dec.14.1967
*Peru	Oct.31.1945

	Date of Admission
*Philippines	Oct.24.1945
*Poland	Oct.24.1945
Portugal	Dec.14.1955
Qatar	Sept.21.1971
Romania	Dec.14.1955
Rwanda	Sept.18.1962
St Christopher and Nevis	Sept.23.1983
St Lucia	Sept.18.1979
St Vincent and the Grenadines	Sept.16.1980
Samoa	Dec.15.1976
Sao Tome and Principe	Sept.16.1975
*Saudi Arabia	Oct.24.1945
Senegal	Sept.28.1960
Seychelles	Sept.21.1976
Sierra Leone	Sept.27.1961
Singapore	Sept.21.1965
Solomon Islands	Dec.18.1978
Somalia	Sept.20.1960
*South Africa	Nov. 7.1945
Spain	Dec.14.1955
Sri Lanka	Dec.14.1955
Sudan	Nov.12.1956
Surinam	Dec. 4.1975
Swaziland	Sept.24.1968
Sweden	Nov.19.1946
*Syria	Oct.24.1945
Tanzania	Dec.14.1961
Thailand	Dec.16.1946
Togo	Sept.20.1960
Trinidad and Tobago	Sept.18.1962
Tunisia	Nov.12.1956
*Turkey	Oct.24.1945
Uganda	Oct.25.1962
*Ukrainian Soviet Socialist Republic	Oct.24.1945
*Union of Soviet Socialist Republics	Oct.24.1945
United Arab Emirates	Dec. 9.1971
*United Kingdom	Oct.24.1945
*United States	Oct.24.1945
*Uruguay	Dec.18.1945
Vanuatu	Sept.15.1981
*Venezuela	Nov.15.1945
Vietnam	Sept.20.1977
#Yemen Arab Rep	Sept.30.1947
*Yugoslavia	Oct.24.1945
Zaire	Sept.20.1960
Zambia	Dec. 1.1964
Zimbabwe	Aug.25.1980

*Original mambers of United Nations
#On 23 May 1990, the two Yemens were welcomed as the Republic of Yemen

CURRENT AFFAIRS

EVENTS OF THE PAST YEAR FROM OCTOBER 1, 1989

OCTOBER 1989

1. The Archbishop of Canterbury warned of the dangers of Britain becoming a "pharisee" society based on self-interest and intolerance in which the pursuit of quick wealth becomes an obsession.

2. More than 7,000 East German refugees travelled second-class to a new life in West, under an agreement which raised hopes that the hardline regime in East Berlin would reluctantly accept the need for reform.

3. The Labour Party voted to scrap the unilateralist defence policy on which it had fought the previous two general elections, a move which was regarded as a vital step in Mr. Neil Kinnock's programme of reforms to improve the party's chances of winning next time.

4. Figures were released that showed revised estimates of revenue expected from the Channel tunnel when it opens in 1993 had failed to keep pace with the increase in the cost of the project which had spiralled £2 billion.

5. The Government announced plans for a far-reaching crackdown on "acid house" parties, including tough laws covering noise nuisance and stiffer licensing requirements. The legislation would outline legislative proposals to make noise pollution a criminal offence for the first time and to vastly increase penalties.

12

6. The Government was to forced raise interest rates to 15 per cent following a one-point raise in West German interest rates to 8 per cent.

7. President Gorbachev began a two-day visit to East Germany with a plea to East Germans not to flee their country but ruled out Soviet intervention in their affairs.

8. The leader of the House of Commons, Sir Geoffrey Howe, decided that MPs should be the only group to be exempted from the paying poll tax on their second homes.

9. Twenty-eight soldiers from the Ulster Defence Regiment were arrested during raids in Belfast and Co. Down in connection with the wave of security leaks to "loyalist" paramilitary groups of secret files on suspected IRA terrorists.

10. Journalists at The Daily Telegraph and The Sunday Telegraph started a 36-hour strike after the newspapers' management proposed 33 redundancies and wide-ranging changes in working conditions, including new contracts.

11. The Government was expected to move swiftly to introduce legislation to curb the growing increase of computer hacking after a Law Commission report urged the creation of three types of offence to combat the activity.

12. Mr. David Hunt, Minister of State for Local Government, announced at the Conservative Party conference that the Government would provide an extra £1.3 billion to soften the impact of the poll tax.

13. Mr. John Gummer, Minister of Agriculture, Fisheries and Food, unveiled plans for a Food Safety Directorate following criticism of the Government's handling of food poisoning scares.

14. Inflation in the year to September 1989 rose from 7.3 per cent to 7.6 per cent in the previous month.

15. The British Medical Association threatened a work-to-rule in protest at the imposition of new contracts for GPs.

16. Family doctors threatened to resign en masse from the health service and charge patients fees, in a rebellion against the new contracts the Government imposed on them formally.

17. Stock markets pulled back from the brink of collapse when a rally on Wall Street prompted a surge in share prices. More than £2O billion had been wiped off the value of shares in London.

18. It was announced that policemen involved in the investigation of the IRA Guildford pub bombings were to be prosecuted and the 14-year convictions of three men and a women, jailed for the terrorist attack, would be quashed.

19. The death toll in northern California rose towards 300 as a big rescue operation got under way after the second worst earthquake ever to hit the United State.

20. Britain and Argentina formally declared an end to all hostilities and announced a comprehensive package of agreements to normalise relations.

21. A fraud enquiry was launched into the merger between Ferranti, the British defence contractor and the International Signal and Control group of the United States, after an estimated shortfall of £215 millions in Ferranti's assets was announced the previous month.

22. It was reported that the Government was to adopt an official abortion policy for the first time, and would be likely to support a reduction in the period during which abortion is allowed from 28 weeks to 24 weeks of pregnancy.

23. It was reported that the Prince of Wales would write and present an important BBC television documentary aimed at confronting threats to the world's environment.

24. Ambulance services to 10 million Londoners were at a virtual standstill as the Government faced calls from doctors and Conservative MPs to intervene in a worsening dispute and bring in the armed forces.

25. Mr. Nigel Lawson and senior backbench Conservative MPs called on the Prime Minister, Mrs. Margaret Thatcher, to silence Sir Alan Walters, her personal economic adviser following Sir Alan's criticism of the European Monetary System.

26. Mr. John Major, the Foreign Secretary announced to the Commons that 40,000 Vietnamese boat people would be forced to return home from Hong Kong.

26. Mr. Nigel Lawson resigned as Chancellor of the Exchequer prompting an immediate reconstruction of the most senior Cabinet posts. Mr. John Major was appointed Chancellor, Mr. Douglas Hurd became Foreign Minister and Mr. David Waddington became Home Secretary.

28. The East German Government announced a sweeping amnesty covering demonstrators, refugees and several thousand people imprisoned for trying to flee to the West.

29. It was reported that police investigating the Lockerbie air disaster, had uncovered evidence which suggested that the bomb which destroyed the American jumbo jet was originally loaded on to the plane at Malta.

30. At least eight people died as high winds, gusting to hurricane force in places, battered much of Britain, producing havoc on land and at sea.

31. A leaked Cabinet memorandum revealed that about a third of Britain's miners could lose their jobs in the first three years after the privatisation of the electricity industry.

NOVEMBER 1989

1. It was announced that the cost of a television licence would go up by £5.00 to £71.00 for a colour set and by £2.00 to £24.00 for a black and white set from April 1990.

2. Ford, the world's second largest car maker, bid £1.6 million for Jaguar, the luxury car maker and the Jaguar board, led by Sir John Egan, its chairman, recommended the offer to shareholders.

3. Mr. Christopher Patten, Secretary of State for the Environment, launched the Government's £5 billion water privatization, claiming that it was the first privatization designed to improve the environment.

6. An internal Home Office report stated that Britain was not becoming a more violent society, but that it was becoming less tolerant of violence and readier to report it to the police who were readier to record it.

7. Troops stood on standby to cover gaps in Britain's accident and emergency services as Mr. Kenneth Clarke, the Health Secretary, ordered the Army to prepare to step into the two-month old dispute involving 22,500 ambulance crews and officers.

8. The Government of East Germany resigned suddenly throwing the country's political future into turmoil as the flood of dissidents leaving for the West accelerated.

9. Mrs Thatcher called for "a vast, international co-operative effort" to save the global environment and announced plans for a multi-million pound British centre to monitor climatic change.

10. In an historic announcement which rendered the Berlin Wall irrelevant, East Germany declared that its citizens could leave the country directly at all crossing points through the Wall and over the 1,000-mile border with West Germany.

11. Conservative MPs called on the Government to rethink its electricity privatization proposals in the wake of its decision to abandon the nuclear industry sale.

12. It was reported that the first grammar schools in Britain since the comprehensive revolution began in the 1960s would be created in a move by Conservative councillors in Buckinghamshire to set up a national network of schools selecting pupils by an 11-plus examination funded from Whitehall.

13. A British crewman in the Whitbread Round the World yacht race, Mr. Anthony Phillips, died after being swept overboard in the south Atlantic.

14. The Government announced that everyone in Britain is to be asked to which ethnic group they belong in the next national census in April 1991, to provide for the first time a complete breakdown of the country's racial composition.

15. Scotland Yard issued an urgent warning to politicians, VIPs and senior servicemen to be extra vigilant after the discovery of a powerful IRA booby-trap bomb intended for Lieutenant-General Sir David Ramsbotham, commander UK Field Army.

16. Plans for a substantial increase in road and rail investment to relieve congestion were approved by the Chancellor. Spending would go up by £1.8 billion over the next three years, bringing total investment in the road, rail and Underground networks to more than £13 billion.

17. Britain's carbon dioxide emissions, which contribute to the greenhouse effect, would increase by 37 per cent by the year 2005, according to a forecast from the Department of Energy - despite the fact that the Government was committed to reducing them by 20 per cent.

18. A British correspondent for The Sunday Correspondent, Mr. David Blundy, was killed while reporting intense fighting between government forces and left-wing guerrillas in El Salvador that had left more than 800 dead and 1,600 injured in the previous six days.

19. It was reported that extensive British and American defence reviews were being planned in response to the political upheavals in eastern Europe, and evidence that the Soviet Union had recently trimmed its military budget.

20. It was announced that the Government would be introducing anonymous testing of men, women and babies for traces of the Aids virus.

12

21. MPs began a new session of Parliament under the glare of television lights with the outside world getting its first on- screen glimpse of the Commons at work.

22. Six former Chiefs of the Defence Staff joined together to complain about the Government's "neglect" of the 53,500 war widows who did not receive a Ministry of Defence pension because their husbands died before March 13, 1973.

23. A devastating explosion ripped through the motorcade of President Rene Muawad of Lebanon in west Beirut, killing him and 16 other people, including five members of his bodyguard.

24. The Government announced that it was giving an extra £19 million to help haemophiliacs who had contracted the HIV Aids virus after receiving NHS treatment with infected blood.

25. Czechoslovakia's ruling Communist politburo elected Mr. Karol Urbanek as their new leader, after Mr. Milos Jakes, the former leader, and the entire party Secretariat had resigned.

26. It was reported that Sir Anthony Meyer, Conservative MP for Clwyd Northwest, intended to oppose Mrs Thatcher for the party leadership vote on December 5th.

27. Mr. Rajiv Gandhi's governing Congress (I) party had its huge parliamentary majority wiped out in the Indian general election, and for the first time the world's largest democracy was to have a coalition government.

28. Britain's national newspaper editors agreed on a common Code of Practice and declared that they would introduce readers' representatives, or ombudsmen, to deal with complaints.

29. Mr. Ladislav Adamec, the Czechoslovak Prime Minister, began a new era in his country's history by formally renouncing the Communist Party's monopoly of power.

30. A television viewer who proved he watched only Sky satellite broadcasts did not need a television licence, a court ruled in the first case of its kind.

DECEMBER 1989

1. Record libel damages of £1.5 million were awarded to Lord Aldington, a former Conservative Party deputy chairman, in a trial where he defeated accusations of being a war criminal.

2. President Gorbachev became the first leader of the Soviet Union to meet the Pope in an historic meeting in Italy.

3. Mikhail Gorbachev and George Bush met for summit talks on the Soviet cruiseliner Maxim Gorky, which was docked off Malta.

4. The East German Politburo and the Central Committee of the Communist Party resigned as the country slipped into political chaos.

5. A top civil servant admitted that the Government did not reveal details of the £38 million in "sweeteners" to British Aerospace for buying the Rover Group because of fears that they would damage relations with the European Commission.

6. Mrs Thatcher won 314 votes in the first Conservative leadership election since 1975 while sixty MPs either voted against her or abstained from the contest.

7. Mr. Bob Reid, the chairman and chief executive of Steel UK, was formally appointed chairman of British Rail for a five-year term at a salary of £200,000.

8. The bronze dancing faun by the Dutch-born sculptor Adrien de Vries was sold by an elderly couple at Sotheby's for a record £6.8 million. Bought for £100 in the 1950s, it had stood in their garden for nearly 40 years.

9. Medical experts announced that Britain was in the throes of "substantial influenza epidemic", following a threefold increase in the number of reported flu cases.

10. EC leaders declared their support for German unity through "free self-determination" of the German people.

11. In Prague Castle, President Husak swore in Czechoslovakia's first non-communist majority Government in 41 years and then resigned.

12. Britain's 55,000 pre-1973 war widows won their battle for a better pension when the Government announced a £40 a week increase from April 1990.

13. The Government faced an onslaught from the White House, the Opposition and refugee organizations over the forced repatriation of Vietnamese boat people from Hong Kong.

14. It was announced that a key parliamentary committee would reopen its investigation into the controversial British Aerospace takeover of Rover and that Lord Young of Graffham, former Secretary for Trade and Industry, would be asked to appear before it.

15. An unknown buyer paid £160,000, plus £16,000 in commission, for 1A, one of a collection of registration number plates held back by the Driver and Vehicle Licensing Centre and sold in an auction.

16. The Government suffered a setback to its prime aim of beating inflation with the release of figures showing an annual inflation rate the previous month of 7.7 per cent - its highest for four months.

17. According to government sources up to 300,000 Hong Kong professional people and their families were to be offered "copper-bottomed guarantees" of a safe haven in Britain but without full British passports.

18. The Labour leadership announced that its support for the new European Community social charter meant that Labour would accept its provision that workers would have the right to join or not to join unions, thereby burying its traditional support for the "closed shop".

19. Dr. Andrei Sakharov was buried at a small Moscow cemetery after a day in which Soviet leaders and people from all over the Soviet Union and abroad had paid their separate tributes to his memory.

20. Mr. Nicholas Ridley, Secretary of State for trade and Industry, announced that the Government would pay £150 million compensation to 18,500 small investors who lost their savings in the Barlow Clowes collapse.

21. Panama was under American military control after an invasion which installed a democratic government but failed to capture the Panamanian dictator, General Noriega.

22. The Government decided to end the "no-discrimination" rule operated by the credit card companies and create a dual-price system under which retailers can charge customers using plastic more than those paying cash.

23. Hundreds of people were reported killed in Bucharest when pro-Ceausescu forces launched an abortive counter-attack after the overthrow of Romania's hard-line leader, President Ceauscescu, who was reported having fled the country.

24. Shops were besieged from dawn to dusk as last-minute Christmas shoppers defied gloomy retail predictions and set new spending records.

25. Former Romanian President Ceauscescu and his wife Elena were executed at 4pm by a firing squad.

26. Samuel Beckett, a giant of twentieth century literature and drama, died aged 83 in Paris and was buried at a private ceremony.

26. Desert Orchid equalled the record of Wayward Lad by winning the King George VI Rank Chase for the third time at Kempton Park. The Cheltenham Gold Cup winner gained victory by eight lengths.

28. Police reported a drop in the number of people failing breath tests for drunken driving over Christmas.

29. In the first fatal earthquake to hit Australia, 11 people died and 21 were missing beneath the rubble in the city of Newcastle on the New South wales coast.

30. After 13 years as Czechoslovakia's leading dissident, five of them spent in prison, Mr. Vaclav Havel, the playwright and human rights activist, was elected the country's first non-communist President in 41 years.

31. Figures published by the Meteorological Office showed that in 1989 Britain had enjoyed its warmest year since records began 330 years previously.

JANUARY 1990

1. The Panamanian Government sought to bring murder charges against General Manuel Noriega fuelling speculation that the filing of charges could be a prelude to the general's trial in the United States for drug offences.

3. It was disclosed that nearly half a million businesses would face rate increases of more than 50% when the uniform commercial rate was introduced in April 1990.

4. Mr. Norman Fowler resigned from the Cabinet insisting that his resignation as Secretary of State for Employment had not been provoked by policy differences with the Prime Minister and had been planned for five months. He stated that he wished to spend more time with his young daughters.

5. In an unprecedented gesture, the Queen honoured the son of Field Marshal Erwin Rommel (the Desert Fox), Herr Manfred Rommel, Mayor of Stuttgart, by making him a C.B.E. for his considerable contribution to reconciliation between the former adversaries following the war.

6. The Football Association charged Swindon Town, Mr. Lou Macari, its former manager, and Mr. Brian Hillier, its chairman, with a breach of rules relating to unauthorized betting.

12

7. It was reported that American drug investigators had warned that Britain could face a cocaine epidemic as Colombian drug barons find it increasingly difficult to smuggle drugs into the saturated United States market.

8. Crises increased for President Gorbachev as the Kremlin sent troop reinforcements to keep the peace between rival communities in Georgia.

9. Strong signs emerged that South Africa would release Nelson Mandela within weeks, a move seen as the beginning of the end of its diplomatic isolation.

10. Ron Brown, the Labour MP for Edinburgh, Leith, left Lewes Crown Court after being fined £1,000 for causing criminal damage at the home of his former mistress but was acquitted of theft. Judge Gower said he should be "thoroughly ashamed" but the MP described the outcome as "a moral victory".

11. Patrick Ryan, the Irish priest wanted in Britain on charges of conspiracy to murder and possession of explosives, was expelled from his Order, the Pallottine Fathers, for defying his superiors.

12. It was announced that RAF Molesworth, the former cruise missile site in Cambridgeshire, was to be converted into American wartime emergency headquarters and a special centre for US intelligence analysis.

13. The Romanian Communist Party was outlawed by the interim administration after a day of anti-government protests in the streets of Bucharest.

14. It was reported that Britain's family doctors would receive a 13% pay rise under the terms of an independent pay review.

15. The Government denied that security forces in Ulster were conducting a "shoot-to-kill" policy as military forces said the soldiers who gunned down three men in a Belfast street thought the suspects would open fire.

16. A supermarket check-out girl was released from prison where she had spent two weeks with her baby after a widely criticized sentence by Judge James Pickles for theft. Lord Chief Justice Lane said that Miss Tracey Scott, aged 19, should have been put on probation.

17. Civil war raged unabated along the frontier between Armenia and Azerbaijan with troops sent in by the Kremlin to quell the violence came under fire from both sides.

18. Following the resignation of Lord Devaird in the wake of allegations of homosexual behaviour put to him by Lord Hope, the President of the Court of Session, equivalent to the Lord Chief Justice in England, it was reported that five of Scotland's 24 High Court judges had been under investigation after allegations of homosexuality.

19. A leading kidney surgeon astonished a disciplinary hearing of the General Medical Council by admitting that for 14 years he had behaved unethically by operating on donors without first meeting them and ascertaining their background and medical history.

20. The Director of Public Prosecutions urged Greater Manchester Police to investigate the trial of Mr. Kevin Taylor, the Manchester businessman linked to Mr. John Stalker and cleared of fraud that week.

21. A MORI poll found that only half the population believed that the British monarchy would survive another century. Although the royal family kept a strong hold on the nation's affections, many believed our last monarch had already been born.

22. The Government's chief veterinary officer acknowledged that the cattle disease, bovine spongiform encephalopathy, could have been prevented if a ban imposed two years previously on feeding to cattle products derived from sheep had been introduced a decade earlier.

23. The Metropolitan Police officially became Britain's first force to scrap all height requirements and dispense with the rule that policemen must be 5ft 8in tall and policewomen 5ft 4in in an attempt to attract more recruits from ethnic communities.

24. It was announced that Ferranti International was to sell its defence systems division to GEC for £310 million, just after winning a share of the £2 billion European Fighter Aircraft radar contract, and following the earlier disclosure that the company had been the victim of a £215 million fraud by one of its subsidiaries.

25. Nearly 32,000 Ford workers snubbed their union demands for a national strike and accepted a two-year deal worth 10.2 per cent this during 1990.

26. Severe gales and storms left 47 people dead and hundreds injured as well as causing millions of pounds of damage.

27. It was disclosed that the BBC would be scrapping plans for a £200 million radio centre and would make savings of £75 million a year by 1993 as part of a radical reorganisation of the corporation.

28. Mr. David Waddington, the Home Secretary, announced that all 92 football clubs in England and Wales would be ordered by the government to convert their grounds to all-seat stadiums by the year 2000. Clubs that did not comply would be closed.

29. Princess Margaret, setting off for a holiday on the Caribbean island of Mustique, was forced to spend the night in a Manchester hotel after her British Airways jumbo jet was disabled by lightning.

30. East Germany's disgraced former leader Herr Erich Honecker, aged 77 and suffering from cancer of the kidney, was released from hospital and taken straight to an East German jail to face charges of treason, corruption and abuse of office.

31. The Welsh weightlifter, Ricky Chaplin, who won a gold medal in the middleweight match, was disqualified from the Commonwealth Games and stripped of his title after being tested positive for drugs.

FEBRUARY 1990

1. It was reported that government ministers were considering plans to bring greater competition into Post Office operations, including an end to its monopoly on delivering letters.

2. East Germany's Prime Minister Herr Hans Modrow called for a united German fatherland governed from Berlin stating that "Germany should once again become the unified fatherland of all citizens of the German nation."

3. President de Klerk of South Africa lifted the 30-year ban on the African National Congress and announced the imminent release of Nelson Mandela in a speech that stunned the world with the extent of its reforms.

4. Doctors at Guy's hospital, London, appealed for women considering abortion because they have been told their baby will have cleft lips to volunteer for the world's first "out of womb" surgery to correct the condition, a new technique involving removing the head and neck from the womb to allow surgery.

5. Tests completed by a team of French doctors confirmed disturbing statistics, covered up by the late Nicolae Ceausceu, which showed that Romania was suffering from an Aids epidemic among young children and was in need of urgent assistance to monitor and control it.

6. The Chief Inspector of Schools disclosed that one in three schoolchildren was "getting a raw deal" from the state education system, and that whilst standards of teaching were satisfactory or better for the majority there were serious problems of low achievement and poor teaching to be tackled.

7. The Home Secretary announced a shake-up of sentencing policy to make sure hardened criminals spent longer in jail, while keeping petty offenders out of prison.

8. The Soviet Communist Party leadership decided to back proposals for a new style executive presidency with a cabinet to see policy through and to abolish the ruling Politburo.

9. In a move to ensure survival in the face of a spiralling deficit, the Royal Shakespeare Company announced that would close its two London theatres during the following winter.

10. Salman Rushdie, author of The Satanic Verses, was condemned to remain in hiding for his life as Ayatollah Khameneni, spiritual leader of Iran, reaffirmed the death sentence imposed the previous year.

11. Michele Vermilio, the first baby in the world to undergo heart surgery inside the womb, died in his parents' arms after doctors at Guy's Hospital switched off the ventilator keeping him alive.

12. Nelson Mandela emerged from more than a quarter of a century in jail to tell tens of thousands of supporters that the armed struggle against apartheid must continue. At the same time Britain signalled the end to sanctions on South Africa.

13. The Guinness trial got underway at Southwark Crown Court with the swearing-in of the jury for a hearing expected to last up to six months.

14. Midland Bank admitted that it was having merger talks with the Hong Kong and Shanghai Bank, the closest an overseas bank had come to taking over one of the big four high street banks.

15. All bottles of Perrier, the French mineral water, were withdrawn from sale worldwide after traces of benzene, a solvent linked to cancer, were discovered in supplies of the drink in Britain and several other European countries.

16. An urgent investigation of safety at nuclear power stations was ordered by the Government after experts found that men working in the plants might father children with leukaemia.

17. Nationwide Anglia, the country's second-biggest building society, followed the Abbey National's lead and raised its mortgage rate to 15.4 per cent.

18. It was reported that British Telecom was receiving a record 1 million complaints a year despite charging more for its local calls than any other industrialised country.

19. Mrs Thatcher made an announcement insisting that American troops must continue to be stationed in a unified Germany which remained part of NATO.

20. Mr. John Browne, Conservative MP for Winchester, who faced disciplinary action and possible expulsion by the Commons for breaking rules, denied that he had set out to deceive Parliament.

21. Amid fears of a new IRA onslaught, Scotland Yard's anti- terrorist branch issued an urgent warning for increased public and military vigilance after an IRA attempt

22. The director of health and safety at the Cumbrian Sellafield nuclear plant, Dr. Roger Berry, advised workers at the plant who feared that their children might develop cancer that it might be best not to have a family.

23. President de Klerk of South Africa removed the final obstacle to talks with the African National Congress when he welcomed a proposed ANC visit to discuss negotiations on ending apartheid.

24. Militant ambulancemen were reported as going ahead with an all-out strike in spite of the settlement agreed after 20 hours of talks between health service and union negotiators.

25. A MORI poll reported that Labour had gained a record 17-point lead over the Conservatives, the biggest since Margaret Thatcher had come to power nearly 11 years earlier.

26. First results of the elections in Baltic republic of Lithuania showed that the breakaway Communist Party was suffering a crushing defeat at the hands of nationalists.

27. President Ortega of Nicaragua relinquished power to Senora Violeta Chamorro after her American-backed coalition won a stunning electoral victory over the Sandinistas who had run the country for a decade.

28. It was reported that household insurance premiums might have to rise by 10 per cent in the wake of the storms that killed 18 people in the British Isles in the previous two days.

MARCH 1990

1. The Prime Minister announced an extra £500 million of funding for the Government's inner-city programme, taking spending on regeneration schemes during the year to a record £4 billion.

2. The Government came under heavy fire from critics after announcing that prescription charges would rise by 8.9 per cent, taking the cost of a prescription up to £3.05.

3. The Medical Research Council announced that the most promising anti-Aids drug since the development of AST was to be tested on hundreds of British patients. The investigation would be into the potential benefits of a drug called dideoxyinosine, or DDI, which appeared to be capable of slowing down the replication of the Aids virus.

4. The environment secretary, Chris Patten, announced an end to the dumping of sewage in the seas around Britain, in a move designed to shed Britain's reputation as "the dirty man of Europe".

5. Mr. Peter Walker disclosed that he would leave the Cabinet shortly and would not be a candidate at the next election. His resignation was the third Cabinet resignation in less than six months.

6. Mr. Arthur Scargill, the president of the National Union of Mineworkers, vigorously denied that Libyan money was used to pay off mortgages on his home and that of the union's general secretary.

7. Town halls across the country were besieged by thousands of protesters as anti-poll tax demonstrations - many organized by Militant - erupted into violence.

8. Mr. Nicholas Ridley announced that the Fayed brothers were to be allowed to keep Harrods in spite of a damning official report which said that they had lied persistently to win approval for their £615 million takeover of the House of Fraser stores.

9. The Government introduced legislation which meant that suspected Nazi war criminals living in Britain could be prosecuted in British courts within two years.

11. Farzad Bazoft, the Observer correspondent accused by Iraq of spying, was sentenced to death by a revolutionary court in Baghdad. Daphne Parish, a British nurse accused of helping him, was jailed for 15 years.

12. Lithuania declared independence from the Soviet Union and renamed itself the Supreme Council of the Sovereign Republic of Lithuania, thereby becoming the first republic to take the step of legal separation from the Soviet Union.

13. A report by the National Society for the Prevention of Cruelty to Children said that children as young as five were being forced to take part in bizarre sex and satanic rituals involving drugs, animal sacrifices and the drinking of urine and blood.

14. Five judges of the Irish Supreme Court decided to free and not to extradite two convicted terrorists to Northern Ireland on the grounds that the men faced a "probable risk" of assault by Northern Ireland prison officers.

15. The head of sculpture at Christie's, Dr. Charles Avery, resigned after admitting that he personally tried to buy a work that he had valued at around £3,000, and which was on the market for an estimated £5 million.

16. Britain reacted with anger and shock at the execution of Farzad Bazoft by Iraq, but refrained from breaking off diplomatic relations or imposing trade sanctions.

17. The widow of a money broker killed in the Clapham rail disaster was awarded £106,881 agreed damages against British Rail. The husband of Mrs Carol Perry-Lewis of Bournemouth was among the 35 who died in the crash in December 1988.

18. Thousands of Britons took to the roads and headed for the coast as one of the warmest March days on record brought the first sunbathing and swimming weather of the year.

19. East Germany's first free elections since the Nazi takeover of 1933 ended with an overwhelming victory for Herr Lothar de Maiziere and his conservative Alliance for Germany party.

20. The Tass news agency reported that President Gorbachev had ordered his Government to take priority measures in response to Lithuania's decision to ignore the demands of the Soviet Parliament.

21. Mr. John Major's first budget was met with approval by the Conservative Party with the Chancellor feeling that economic problems could be solved if the City believed the Government would win the next election.

22. The Home Secretary, Mr. David Waddington, announced that Devon and Cornwall detectives were to begin a fresh but limited inquiry into new evidence put forward on behalf of the "Birmingham Six".

23. Mrs Sylvia Heal overturned a 14,654 Conservative majority to win the Mid Staffordshire by-election by 9,449 votes.

24. The Duchess of York gave birth to a second daughter after a Caesarean section operation performed the previous night at the Portland Hospital, London.

25. Soviet tanks rolled through the streets of Vilnius, the Lithuanian capital, as the Kremlin and the rebel republic appeared to be heading ever closer to confrontation.

25. The Archbishop of Canterbury, Dr. Robert Runcie, announced his retirement and launched the Church of England into a period of intense in-fighting and uncertainty, with its whole future at stake.

27. Negotiations between the South African Government and the African National Congress were jeopardized by clashes between police and huge crowds of demonstrators, in which at least three people died and about 300 were injured.

28. Glenda Jackson, the award winning actress, was selected as Labour candidate for the marginal north London constituency of Hampstead and Highgate at the next general election.

29. British and American Customs officers foiled an attempt to smuggle trigger devices for nuclear bombs on to an Iraqi airliner.

30. It was announced that petrol prices would move to their highest level for five years at more than £2 a gallon.

31. Lord Rothschild, chairman of the National Gallery trustees, presented to the nation a major Dutch 17th century painting, "View of the Westerkerk, Amsterdam" by Jan van der Heyden, in lieu of inheritance tax of 2.8 million pounds on the estate of his late cousin.

APRIL 1990

1. Violence erupted at Britain's biggest poll tax rally in central London as 2,000 police fought to control crowds. More than 30 people were arrested and six policemen hurt.

2. It was reported that at least three prisoners died and dozens of inmates and prisons officers were injured as riot police and staff fought to regain control of Strangeways Prison in Manchester after a day of rioting.

3. Large areas of Britain were shaken by the second biggest earthquake to hit the U.K. in 100 years. The 20-second tremor, which was centred on Wrexham, Clwyd, North wales, was recorded at 2.46 pm by the seismic research group of the British Geological Survey in Edinburgh, and measured 5.2 on the Richter scale.

4. The Bishop of Durham, The Right Rev. David Jenkins, said that the legal link between the state and the Church of England was a vestigial rigmarole left over from the Middle Ages - a kind of Gilbert and Sullivan performance - and must go.

5. Dr. Raymond Crockett, a Harley Street specialist involved in the sale of kidneys, was ordered to be struck off the medical register. The General Medical Council said he had bought disgrace upon himself and dishonour upon his profession in his conduct towards four Turks paid for their kidneys.

6. Mr. Bryan Gould, the Opposition's chief environment spokesman, in an important shift in policy, said that the Labour Party would introduce a "modernised and updated" version of the domestic rates in place of the community charge.

7. The captain of a British Airways Boeing 747 Jumbo jet resigned and his two fellow flight-deck crew members were demoted after an internal inquiry into how they almost flew into a hotel on an approach to Heathrow airport.

8. It was reported that secret contingency plans had been approved by Britain's police chiefs to allow SAS-trained police marksmen to fire on gunmen who shoot at officers during street riots. It was the first time that police on the mainland had considered using firearms during outbreaks of public disorder.

9. Unrest in Britain's jails spread to a total of 11 institutions as the disturbances claimed the life of another prisoner. The latest victim was found dead in a fire-damaged cell at Dartmoor when 100 rioting inmates gave themselves up after 24 hours.

10. Ford cancelled a £225 million investment in South Wales that would have made Britain its key European engine production centre. The move was seen as a reprisal for disputes which cost the car company more than £800 million in lost production earlier in the year.

11. It was reported that in the first quarter of the year, receivers were appointed to 543 companies, most of them in London and the South. This more than doubled the figure for the previous year.

12. Customs officers discovered what they believed to be a 140- ton gun capable of firing nuclear or chemical shells hundreds of miles, packed in boxes on board a merchant ship bound for Iraq.

13. It was reported that average earnings were starting to climb again after holding steady for four months, confirming fears that persistent and rising inflation was fuelling wage demands when the Government was hoping for slower pay growth.

14. International tension mounted after President Gorbachev told Lithuania that essential supplies would be halted in two days if the republic failed in that time to rescind laws passed since its declaration of independence.

15. Britain's river pollution watchdog told the government that a financial crisis was threatening its work. The National Rivers Authority said it was so short of staff, equipment and money that many rivers would remain polluted unless the government made more resources available.

16. It was confirmed that Mr. Nelson Mandela, the African National Congress leader, would meet Mrs Thatcher and Mr. Douglas Hurd, the Foreign Secretary, for official talks later in the year.

17. The manufacturer of what was alleged to be a "super-gun barrel" for Iraq, Sheffield Forgemasters, confirmed that it had been working on the contract with the Space Research Corporation, which was run by Gerald Bull, the ballistics expert who was murdered outside his Brussels flat on March 22.

18. The financial services group British and Commonwealth Holdings had to write off £550 million on a computer company, Atlantic Computers, it bought for £416 million less than two years previously.

19. The seven remaining rioters at Strangeways prison continued their mocking contempt of the authorities for the 18th day.

20. A backbench rebellion on plans to give 50,000 Hong Kong residents British passports was beaten off after a passionate Commons debate. The revolt led by Mr. Norman Tebbit was defeated in spite of a dramatic appeal by the former party chairman to MPs to stand by election promises on immigration, and a warning that it could increase racial tension.

21. The draft report into the Boeing 737 crash on the M1 near Kegworth in 1989 was critical of British Midland's operating and training procedures and contained 27 separate safety recommendations.

22. A survey revealed that one in three secondary school children thought the sun revolved around the earth and that sound travelled faster than light. Nearly as many thought radioactive milk was safe when boiled and did not know that oxygen came from plants.

23. An American hostage, Professor Robert Pothill, was handed over to the American Ambassador in Syria, after he was released by his Iranian kidnappers at a Beirut hotel. He had been in captivity in Lebanon for nearly 39 months.

24. Britain's biggest takeover bid ended after Sir James Goldsmith dropped plans to renew his £13.4 billion bid for the tobacco-based conglomerate BAT Industries.

25. Charles Wilson, one of the Great Train Robbers, who gained notoriety by escaping from prison and avoiding detection for more than three years, was murdered at his Spanish home.

26. The siege at Strangeways Prison ended after 25 days when the final five inmates to hold out dictated their terms for surrender.

27. It was reported that the master of the dredger Bowbelle, which collided with the Marchioness on the Thames last August, was to be prosecuted and that Captain Douglas Henderson would face charges of a breach of duty in that he failed to ensure a proper lookout was posted.

28. Two Irishmen and a woman convicted of being part of an IRA reconnaissance unit plotting the murder of Mr. Tom King, the Secretary of State for Defence, were back in Dublin after the Court of Appeal quashed their convictions after deciding that Mr. Kings comments on the right to silence made during their trial should have led to a retrial.

29. A water company, Anglian Water, admitted that 1.25m people in parts of Leicestershire, Northamptonshire, Cambridgeshire, Buckinghamshire and Hertfordshire, may have drunk supplies contaminated by toxic algae, mycrocystin.

30. The first hosepipe ban of the new season coincided with southern England basking in temperatures higher than those in Spanish holiday resorts with temperatures in London reaching 23C (73F) against 17C (63F) on the rainy Costa del Sol.

MAY 1990

1. The Ministry of Defence set up a board of inquiry after an RAF early-warning Shackleton aircraft plunged into a hillside in the Western Isles killing all 10 crew members.

2. Some 40,000 demonstrators waved banners and placards condemning the Communist leadership and Mr. Gorbachev personally, calling for an end to the economic blockade on Lithuania and supporting Mr. Boris Yeltsin for president, at the Red Square May Day parade.

3. Families and friends of Mr. John McCarthy and Mr. Brian Keenan heard from Mr. Frank Reed -

the American hostage released the previous Monday - that the two men kidnapped in Beirut in April 1986 were well and that he had had a long conversation with them.

4. It was reported that a ban on the ownership of certain breeds of dangerous dog including Rottweilers, Dobermans and American pit bull terriers, was to be considered by the Government in response to the increase in attacks on humans.

5. Latvia declared itself "an independent democratic republic" in the first stage of a process intended to take it out of the Soviet Union.

6. A mob of 2,000 Leeds United soccer fans hurled beer cans, bottles and stones at police in riot gear before the Second Division match at Bournemouth.

7. Four and a half million telephone subscribers were faced with the advent of new dialling codes for the capital - 071 for central London and 081 for outer areas.

8. It was reported that more than a million people a year were being vetted by prospective employers with access to police records from the police national computer.

9. The Estonian supreme soviet brought its republic in line with Latvia, strengthening the legal basis of Estonian independence and changing its name to the Estonian Republic removing the words "Soviet Socialist".

10. It was announced that an investigation of British car prices, claimed to be as much as a third higher than the rest of Europe, was to be mounted by the Monopolies and Mergers Commission.

11. Relatives of the 11 people killed on the ground in the 1988 Lockerbie disaster, and those who suffered injury or damage to property, reached an out-of-court settlement with Pan Am believed to be worth more than £7 million.

12. The poll tax, higher electricity and water charges and excise increases pushed Britain's inflation rate to 9.4% in April, the worst for eight years.

13. A leading food scientist, Professor Richard Lacey, was reported as saying that the risks of humans catching "mad cow" disease were now so great that 6 million cattle needed to be slaughtered.

14. More cases of bogus social workers trying to examine children came to light on the eve of a conference to co-ordinate investigations.

15. Seven people were injured when an IRA time bomb buried in a flower bed exploded outside the front door of the headquarters of the Directorate of Army Education in Eltham, south London, catching the largely civilian workforce at their desks.

16. It was reported that amid continuing fears over "mad cow" disease, more than 1,000 schools, and some hospitals and old people's homes were preparing to take British beef off their menus in spite of repeated government assurances that it posed no risk to health.

17. An army sergeant was killed and another injured after a bomb blew up a military van in Wembly. It was the fourth mainland attack of the year.

18. A "landmark ruling" from the European Court of Justice found that company pension schemes which discriminated between men and women on redundancy payments were in breach of the Treaty of Rome.

19. A report from The Samaritans reported that the number of men who commit suicide before they reach middle age had increased by 50% over the past 10 years, with farmers and doctors most likely to take their own lives.

20. It was reported that a drug, tamoxifen, that could prevent breast cancer had been pioneered by British doctors and was to be offered to thousands of women.

21. An air-sea rescue was effected in the Atlantic to pick up a seriously ill crewman in the Whitbread Round the World Race, after Mr. Andrew Dibsdall was diagnosed by doctors over a radio link to the yacht Liverpool Enterprise as he showed signs of rejecting a kidney transplanted four years earlier.

22. The judicial inquiry by Sir John May, the former appeal court judge, into the Guildford and Maguire cases, found that new forensic tests by a professor of analytical chemistry had made the convictions of the Maguire seven unsafe and unsatisfactory 14 years after their trial.

23. It was reported that cattle sales dropped by 38% in Britain as farmers withheld their animals from market in anticipation of a fall in demand and prices because of fears that "mad cow" disease, bovine encephalopathy, could pass to humans through infected meat.

24. Family doctors were given the go-ahead by the General Medical Council to advertise on television, radio and in newspapers to attract patients.

25. Mr. Nicholas Ridley blamed a "breakdown in communication" for the Department of Trade and Industry's blunder in prematurely releasing a monopolies report on Kingfisher's proposed £568 million takeover of Dixons and in a short press release the Secretary of Trade said: "I apologise to all concerned on behalf of the Government."

26. Mrs Margaret Thatcher called for a "giant international effort" to save the Earth from the consequences of global warming, and committed Britain to curbing its emissions of carbon dioxide.

27. It was reported that the USA and the Soviet Union were deeply alarmed about the possibility of a nuclear war breaking out between India and Pakistan over the disputed state of Kashmir.

28. Soviet officials insisted that President Gorbachev would go to the United States for his summit with President Bush despite growing chaos in Moscow and an upsurge of ethnic violence in Armenia, where troops shot dead six Armenian militants.

29. Dutch police hunted armed IRA terrorists who gunned down two young London-based Australian lawyers, on holiday in the border town of Roermond, after mistaking them for off-duty British servicemen.

30. Mr. Boris Yeltsin swept to power as President of the Russian Federation, three years after being sacked by President Gorbachev.

31. Britain accused France of undermining European Community law by announcing a ban on imports of British beef and cattle because of concern that "mad cow" disease could harm French consumers.

JUNE 1990

1. A warning was issued by the Department of Health that people should not eat shellfish caught off the north-east coast between the Humber and Montrose, after traces of a potentially fatal toxin were found in samples of crab meat.

2. The first mass prosecutions in England for the non-payment of the poll tax collapsed because a Tory-controlled council, Medina in the Isle of Wight, sent final demands by 2nd-class post.

3. The Social Democratic Party was wound up after Dr. David Owen and his two fellow MPs said it was not large enough to continue as a national force.

5. Sunday trading convictions against two D.I.Y. stores were quashed at the High Court in an important judgement which was felt would lead to a campaign to clarify the law on the point.

6. President Gorbachev faced mounting troubles with serious clashes between Uzbeks and Kirghiz in Soviet Central Asia left 11 dead.

8. France, West Germany and Italy lifted their bans on British beef, thereby removing the threat of a trade war that had been hanging over the Community for the previous week.

9. A government scientist, who had received repeated death threats for her work on laboratory animals at the Ministry of Defence's Chemical Defence Establishment at Porton Down in Wiltshire,

narrowly escaped death when a bomb destroyed her car as she drove to work.

10. The British government gave approval for four politicians to visit Iran to try to break the diplomatic impasse over the fatwa, or death sentence, issued against Salman Rushdie.

11. An aircraft carrying 81 holidaymakers from Birmingham to Malaga made an emergency landing at Southampton with its captain seriously injured and members of the crew struggling to stop him being sucked through the windscreen.

12. John Poindexter, the former United States National Security adviser, became the first and only member of the Reagan administration to receive a prison sentence for his role in the Iran-Contra affair.

13. A parliamentary enquiry disclosed that the defence ministry's £1.6 billion project for a new anti-aircraft missile system was three years behind schedule and nearly £300 million over budget.

14. Figures from the Office of Population Censuses and Surveys showed that divorce was rising after a two year fall.

15. The home secretary, David Waddington, announced that the convictions of the Maguire Seven for running an IRA bomb factory could not be allowed to stand after a statement by the director of public prosecutions that the 1976 convictions were unsafe and unsatisfactory.

16. The biggest legal challenge mounted against the poll tax failed when the High Court ruled that the government acted lawfully in charge-capping 21 councils.

17. Italian police fired tear gas and baton-charged English soccer fans who rioted in the streets of Cagliari, the Sardinian capital, on their way to the World Cup match between England and Holland.

18. A manhunt was under way in The Netherlands and Belgium for a suspected IRA terrorist as West Germany announced that it would seek the extradition of Donna Maguire over the possible involvement in the murder of a British soldier.

19. Orders for 33 Tornado aircraft were cancelled, giving the first firm indication of the direction the government was taking in its review of Britain's defence needs after the upheaval in eastern Europe.

20. Mr. John Patten announced that courts were to be empowered to make attachment of earnings orders to ensure that absent fathers support their children.

22. More than 25,000 people were killed and tens of thousands injured when an earthquake struck north-western Iran near the Caspian Sea.

23. Two women priests, Kathleen Young and Irene Templeton, became the first in Europe to be ordained priest in the Anglican communion.

26. Four people were seriously injured after an explosion caused by a terrorist bomb, damaged the ground floor of the Carlton Club in London.

27. A report by HM Inspectorate concluded that schools were ill-equipped to meet the demands of the National Curriculum and the 1992 single European Act. A survey of 25 schools indicated that teachers had inadequate knowledge of modern languages, which are compulsory for pupils from the aged 11.

28. It was reported that the government was unlikely to appeal against a ruling by the European Commission that British Aerospace would have to repay £44.4 million of illegal 'sweeteners' received as part of the sale of the Rover car company.

29. The Prince of Wales was detained in hospital after breaking his right arm in a fall from his polo pony during a match at Cirencester Park, Gloucestershire.

30. David Trippier, the environment minister, announced that India and China would sign the Montreal Protocol on protecting the ozone layer.

JULY 1990

1. The Queen, after calling on Canadians to remain united, braved protesters and entered Quebec to help celebrate Canada's national holiday.

2. A police officer was forced to strangle a Rottweiler to release himself from its jaws after being attacked when called to an incident in Aylesford, Kent.

3. It was announced that Swindon Town football club was to stay in the second division after a Football Association appeal board decided against relegating it to the third following an inquiry into serious breaches of league regulations.

4. Saudi Arabia's interior minister, Prince Nayef Ibn Abdulaziz, announced that a total of 1,426 pilgrims died during a stampede in a tunnel near the Muslim holy city of Mecca.

5. It was reported that Arthur Scargill, president of the National Union of Mineworkers, was to face a fresh enquiry into what became of £1 million donated by Soviet miners to help their British counterparts during the year-long strike.

6. A re-examination of patient records and tissue specimens by virologists at Manchester University

12

medical school showed that a former Royal Navy seaman, died of full-blown Aids in 1959.

7. NATO leaders presented the new face of a transformed Western alliance, signalling the end of the Cold War.

8. West Germany were the World Cup winners after beating Argentina 1-0 in Rome in one of the worst-tempered finals in the history of the tournament.

9. Plans for a network of children's courts in England and Wales, where for the first time children's cases would be handled by specially trained judges, were announced by the Lord Chancellor.

10. UEFA, the European football governing body, unconditionally readmitted English clubs to competition from which they had been exiled since the Heysel stadium disaster.

11. It was reported that, in the first big encroachment of the private sector into the criminal justice system, the government would be privatising prisoner escort duties in England and Wales and the running of a remand centre on Humberside.

12. President Gorbachev faced open revolt from radical Communist reformers as first Boris Yeltsin, the rebel president of the Russian Federation, and then leaders of the reformist Democratic Platform group announced that they were leaving the Communist party.

13. The West German press reacted with universal outrage to Nicholas Ridley's comments about Germany's alleged designs for an economic takeover of Europe.

14. Nicholas Ridley resigned as trade and industry secretary after senior ministers said his continued presence in the cabinet threatened Britain's influence in Europe and couple cripple the government. His replacement was named as Peter Lilley, financial secretary to the Treasury.

15. Nigel Mansell, Britain's most successful racing driver since James Hunt, declared he would retire from grand prix racing at the end of the season.

16. Iraq unexpectedly freed Daphne Parish, the British nurse jailed for 15 years for assisting Farzad Bazoft, the Observer journalist executed for spying.

17. It was reported that British Airways was now 40% owned by foreign investors, raising fears over its future standing as a British airline.

18. British Telecom announced increases in charges averaging 9 per cent for domestic consumers from September.

19. Two British girls arrested in Thailand on drug-smuggling charges appeared in court in Bangkok, after being detained for carrying 67lb of top-grade heroin with an estimated street value of £4 million.

20. John MacGregor, the education secretary, announced that councils were to be able to opt out of national pay bargaining and strike their own deals with local leaders of teachers' unions under sweeping reforms designed to let market forces solve the growing problem of staff shortages.

21. Labour announced that the poll tax would be abolished within weeks if the Labour party won the next general election and that it would be replaced by a system called 'fair rates', which it claimed would cut the poll tax bills of 72% of households.

22. Leaders of Britain's Muslims accused the authorities of double-standards for banning a controversial film which depicted Salman Rushdie's death when they failed to act over Muslims' claims that the Satanic Verses was blasphemous to the Islamic religion.

23. Thirty-one ministers were involved in a complicated reshuffle of the middle ranks of the government, which strengthened the education and transport departments and increased the pro-European tendency at the Foreign Office.

24. A Roman Catholic nun in her 30s and three policemen were killed in an IRA landmine explosion near Armagh.

25. It was announced that the Right Reverend George Carey, Bishop of Bath and Wells, was to succeed Dr. Robert Runcie as Archbishop of Canterbury.

26. Scotland Yard began an investigation into the financial affairs of the National Union of Mineworkers after serious allegations of untraced money were made by a Soviet miners' leader.

28. It was reported that some of the Royal Navy's oldest frigates and submarines were expected to be paid off immediately to save £600 million in the financial year.

29. The government faced Labour demands for an independent commission of enquiry into recent privatizations, after John Wakeham, the energy secretary, confirmed that the Hanson group might be paid a fee for its expenses in bidding for PowerGen.

31. Mr. Ian Gow, a close friend of the prime minister, and with outspoken views on Northern Ireland, was killed when a 5lb IRA car bomb exploded at his home in East Sussex.

12

SECTION 13

SPORT

RESULTS IN 1989-90

COMMONWEALTH GAMES
Auckland, New Zealand, 24th January - 3 February 1990

ATHLETICS

Men

100 metres	L Christie, England 9.93s
200 metres	M Adam, England 20.10s
400 metres	D Clark, Australia 44.60s
800 metres	S Tirop, Kenya 1m 45.98s
1500 metres	P Eliott, England 3m 33.39s
5000 metres	A Lloyd, Australia 13m 24.86s
10000 metres	E Martin 28m 08.57s
Marathon	D Wakiihuri, Kenya 2m 10.27s
3000 metres steeplechase	J Kariuka, Kenya 8m 20.64s
110 metres hurdles	C Jackson, Wales 13.08s
400 metres hurdles	K Akabusi, England 48.89s
4 x 100 metres relay	England 38.67s
4 x 400 metres relay	Kenya 3m 02.48s
High jump	N Saunders, Bermuda 2.36m
Pole vault	S Arkell, Australia 5.35m
Long jump	Y Alli, Nigeria 8.39m
Triple jump	M Hadjiandreou, Cyprus 16.95m
Shot	S Williams, England 18.54m
Discus	A Olokoju, Nigeria 62.62m
Hammer	S Carlin, Australia 75.66m
Javelin	S Backley, England 86.02m
Decathlon	M Smith, Canada 8525 pts
20 miles road walk	G LeBlanc, Canada 2h 08m 08s

Women

100 metres	M Ottey, Jamaica 11.02s
200 metres	M Ottey, Jamaica 22.76s
400 metres	F Yusuf, Nigeria 51.08s
800 metres	D Edwards, England 2m 00.25s
1500 metres	A Chalmers, Canada 4m 08.41s
3000 metres	A Chalmers, Canada 8m 38.38s
10000 metres	L McColgan, Scotland 32m 23.56s
Marathon	L Martin, Australia 2m 25.28s
80 metres hurdles	K Morley, Wales 12.91s
400 metres hurdles	S Gunnell, England 55.38s
4 x 100 metres relay	Australia 43.87s
4 x 400 metres relay	England 3m 28.88s
High jump	T Murray, New Zealand 1.88m
Long jump	J Flemming, Australia 6.78m
Shot	M Augee, England 18.48m
Discus	L-M Vizaniari, Australia 56.38m
Javelin	T Sanderson, England 65.72m
Pentathlon	J Flemming, Australia 6695 pts
10 kilometres walk	K Saxby, Australia 45m 03s

BADMINTON

Men's singles	R Sidek, Malaysia
Men's doubles	J Sidek & R Sidek, Malaysia
Women's singles	F Smith, England
Women's doubles	F Smith & S Samkey, England
Mixed doubles	C C Chan & A Chan, Hong Kong

BOWLS

Men

Singles	R Parella, Australia
Pairs	T Morris & Ischuback, Australia
Fours	Scotland

Women

Singles	G Tau, Papua New Guinea
Pairs	M Watson & J Howat, New Zealand
Fours	Australia

BOXING

48kg (Light-flyweight)	J Juko, Uganda
51kg (Flyweight)	W McCollough, Northern Ireland
54kg (Bantamweight)	S Mohammed, Nigeria
57kg (Featherweight)	J Irwin, England
60kg (Lightweight)	G Nyakana, Uganda
63.5kg (Light-welterweight)	C Kane, Scotland
67kg (Welterweight)	D Defiagbon, Nigeria
71kg (Light-middleweight)	R Woodhall, England
75kg (Middleweight)	C Johnson, Canada
81kg (Light-middleweight)	J Akhasamba, Nigeria
91kg (Heavyweight)	G Onyango, Kenya
Over 91kg (Super-heavyweight)	M Kenny, New Zealand

CYCLING

1000 metres time trial	M Vinnicome, Australia 1m 05.572s
4000 metres individual pursuit	G Anderson, New Zealand 4m 44.610s
4000 metres team pursuit	New Zealand 4m 22.76s
Sprint	G Neiwand, Australia
10 mile track	G Anderson, New Zealand 19m 44.20s
Points	R Burns, Australia 81 pts
Road race	G Miller, New Zealand 4h 34m 00.19s
100 kilometre road team time trial	New Zealand 2h 06m 46.5s

Women

Women's sprint	L Jones, Wales
Women's 3000m individual pursuit	M Harris, New Zealand 3m 54.67s
Women's road race (72km)	K Watt, Australia 1h 55m 11.60s

GYMNASTICS

Men

Team	Canada
Individual all round	C Hibbert, Canada
Rings	C Hibbert, Canada
Parallel bars	C Hibbert, Canada
Horizontal bars	C Hibbert, Canada & A Nolet, Canada

Floor exercises .... N Thomas, England
Vault .... J May, England
Pommel horse .... D Dowrick, Australia

Women
Team .... Canada
Individual all round .... L strong, Canada
Beam .... L Strong, Canada
Floor Exercises .... L Strong, Canada
Vault .... N Perkins, New Zealand
Asymmetrical Bars .... M Allen, Australia

Rythmic
Overall .... M Fuzesi, Canada
Ribbons .... M Fuzesi, Canada
Hoop .... M Fuzesi, Canada
Rope .... A Walker, New Zealand

JUDO
Men
60kg .... C Finney, England
65kg .... B Cooper, New Zealand
71kg .... R stone, England
78kg .... D Southby, England
86kg .... D White, England
95kg .... R Stevens, England
Over 95kg .... E Gordon, England
Open .... E Gordon, England

Women
48kg .... K Briggs, England
52kg .... S Rendle, England
56kg .... L Cusak, Scotland
61kg .... D Bell, England
66kg .... S Mills, England
72kg .... J Morris, England
Over 72kg .... S Lee, England
Open .... S lee, England

SHOOTING
Individual
Free pistol .... P Adams, Australia 554
Centre fire pistol .... A Pandit, India 583
Rapid fire pistol .... A Breton, Guernsey 583
Air pistol .... B Sandstrom, Australia 580
Small bore rifle (prone) ...... R harvey, New Zealand 591
Small bore rifle (3-positions) M Klepp, Canada 1157
Full bore rifle .... C Mallet, Jersey 394
Air rifle .... G Lorian, Canada 583
Clay pigeon .... J Maxwell, Australia 184
Skeet .... K Harman, England 187
Running boar .... C Robertson, Australia 539

Pairs
Free pistol .... P Adams & B Sandstone,
 Australia 1106
Centre fire pistol .... P Adams & B Quick,
 Australia 115
Rapid fire pistol .... B Farrell & P Murray,
 Australia 1153
Air pistol .... A Rahman & A Sattar,
 Bangladesh 1183
Small bore rifle (prone) ...... S Petterson & R Harvey,
 New Zealand 1185
Small bore rifle (3-positions) J-F Senecal & M Klepp,
 Canada 2272
Full bore rifle .... S Belither & A Tucker,
 England 580
Air rifle .... G Lorian & M Klepp,
 Canada 1163
Clay pigeon .... K Gill & I peel, England 181
Skeet .... I Marsden & J Dunlup,
 Scotland

SWIMMING
Men
50 metres freestyle .... A Baildon, Australia 22.76s

100 metres freestyle .... A Baildon, Australia 49.80s
200 metres freestyle .... M Roberts, Australia 1m
 49.58s
400 metres freestyle .... I Brown, Australia 3m
 49.91s
1500 metres freestyle .... G Houseman, Australia 14m
 55.25s
4 x 100 metres freestyle relay Australia 3m
 20.05s
4 x 200 metres freestyle relay Australia 7m
 21.17s
100 metres backstroke .... M Tewksbury, Canada
 56.07s
200 metres backstroke .... G Anderson, 2m 01.69s
100 metres breaststroke ...... A Moorhouse, England 1m
 01.49s
200 metres breaststroke ...... J Cleveland, Canada 2m
 14.96s
100 metres butterfly .... A Baildon, Australia 52.98s
200 metres butterfly .... A Mosse, New Zealand 1m
 57.33s
200 metres individual medley G Anderson,
 Canada 2m 02.94s
400 metres individual medley R Bruce, Australia
 4m 20.26s
4 x 100 metres medley relay Canada 3m 42.45s
Springboard diving .... 3m C Rogerson, Australia
 .... 1m R Butler, Australia
Highboard diving .... R Morgan, Wales

Women
50 metres freestyle .... L Curry-Kenny, Australia
 25.80s
100 metres freestyle .... K Van Wirdum, Australia
 56.48s
200 metres freestyle .... M Roberts, Australia 2m
 00.79s
400 metres freestyle .... H Lewis, Australia 4m 38.8s
800 metres freestyle .... J McDonald, Australia 8m
 30.27s
4 x 100 metres freestyle relay Australia 3m
 46.85s
4 x 200 metres freestyle relay Australia 8m
 08.95s
100 metres backstroke .... N Livingstone, Australia 1m
 02.46s
200 metres backstroke .... A Simic, New Zealand 2m
 12.32s
100 metres breaststroke ...... K Duggan, Canada 1m
 10.74s
200 metres breaststroke ...... N Giguere, Canada 2m
 32.16s
100 metres butterfly .... L Curry-Kenny, Australia
 1m 00.66s
200 metres butterfly .... H Lewis, Australia 2m
 11.15s
200 metres individual medley N Sweetman,
 Canada 2m 15.61s
400 metres individual medley H Lewis, Australia
 4m 42.65s
4 x 100 metres medley relay Australia 4m 10.87s
Springboard diving .... 3m J Donnet, Australia
 .... 1m M De Piero, Canada
Highboard diving .... A Dacyshyn, Canada
Synchronised swimming-solo S Frechette,
 Canada
Synchronised swimming-duet K Glen & C
 Larsen, Canada

WEIGHTLIFTING
Flyweight - up to 52kg ...... C Raghavan, India 232.5
Bantamweight - up to 56kg R Punnuswamy, India 274.5
Featherweight up to 60kg .. C Sharma, India 257.5
Lightweight - up to 67.5kg P Sharma, India 295
Middleweight - up to 75kg R Laycock, Australia 310
Light-heavyweight -
 up to 82.5kg .... D Morgan, Wales 347.5

Middle heavyweight -
up to 90kg .... D Dawkins, England 357.5
Sub-heavyweight -
up to 100kg .... A Saxton, England 362.5
Heavyweight - up to 110kg M Thomas, England 357.5
Super Heavyweight -
over 110kg .... A Davies, Wales 402.50

MEDAL TABLE

Total		G	S	B
162	Australia	52	54	56
129	England	47	40	42
112	Canada	35	41	36
58	New Zealand	17	14	27
32	India	13	8	11
25	Wales	10	3	12
25	Nigeria	5	13	7
22	Scotland	5	7	10
18	Kenya	6	9	3
9	N Ireland	1	3	5
5	Hong Kong	1	1	3
4	Malaysia	2	2	0
4	Jamaica	2	0	2
4	Uganda	2	0	2
3	Nauru	1	2	0
3	Zimbabwe	0	2	1
3	Tanzania	0	1	2
3	Zambia	0	0	3
2	Cyprus	1	1	0
2	Bangladesh	1	0	1
2	Jersey	1	0	1
2	Ghana	0	2	0
2	Bahamas	0	0	2
2	W. Samoa	0	0	2
1	Bermuda	1	0	0
1	Guernsey	1	0	0
1	Papua NG	1	0	0
1	Guyana	0	0	1
1	Malta	0	0	1

AMERICAN FOOTBALL

US Superbowl .... San Francisco 49ers

ATHLETICS

European Indoor Championships, Glasgow
Men
60 metres .... L Christie, Great Britain,
6.56s
200 metres .... S Floris, Italy, 21.01s
400 metres .... N Dobeleit, West Germany,
46.08s
800 metres .... T McKean, Great Britain,
1m 46.22s
1500 metres .... J-P Herold, East Germany,
3m 44.2s
3000 metres .... E Dubus, France, 7m 53.9s
5000 metres walk .... M Schennikov, USSR, 19m
00.62s
60 metres hurdles .... I Kazanov, USSR, 7.52s
High jump .... A Partyka, Poland, 2.33m
Long jump .... D Haaf, West Germany,
8.11m
Triple jump .... I Lapshin, USSR, 17.14m
Pole vault .... R Gautaulin, USSR, 5.80m
Shot .... K Bodenmueller, Austria,
21.03m

Women
60 metres .... U Sarvari, West Germany,
7.10s
200 metres .... U Sarvari, West Germany,
22.96s
400 metres .... M Shonina, USSR, 51.22s

800 metres .... L Gurina, 2m 01.63s
1500 metres .... D Melinte, Romania, 4m
09.73s
3000 metres .... E Van Hulst, Holland, 8m
57.28s
3000 metres walk .... B Anders, East Germany,
11m 59.36s
60 metres hurdles .... L Narozhilenko, USSR,
7.74s
High jump .... G Christiakova, USSR,
14.4m
Long jump .... G Christiakova, USSR,
6.85m
Shot .... C Losch, West Germany,
20.64m

National Indoor Championships

Men
60 metres .... L Christie, 6.61s
200 metres .... M Adam, 21.25s
400 metres .... D Harris 46.73s
800 metres .... T McKean, 1m 46.49s
1500 metres .... K Cheruiyot, 3m 44.12s
3000 metres .... R Denmark, 7m 54.41s
60 metres hurdles .... C Jackson, 7.43s
High jump .... N Saunders, 2.25m
Long jump .... S Faulkener, 8.00m
Triple jump .... F Payepong, 16.05m
Pole Vault .... A Ashurst, 5.20m
Shot ....

Women
60 metres .... B Kinch, 7.26s
200 metres .... M Ottey 23.07s
400 metres .... S Guise 55.24s
800 metres .... D Gandy 2m 07.65s
1500 metres .... D Gunning 4m 27.55s
3000 metres ....
60 metres hurdles .... J Agyepong, 8.16s
High jump .... J Bennett 1.92m
Long jump .... K Hagger 6.28m
Shot .... J Oakes 18.55m

BADMINTON

All-England championships:
Singles, men .... Z Jianhua, China
Singles, women .... S Susanti, Indonesi
Doubles, men .... Lee Moon-Soo and Park
Joo-Bong, South Korea
Doubles, women .... Chung Myung-Hee and H
Hye-Yung, South Korea
Doubles, mixed .... Park Joo-Bong and Chung
Myung-Hee, South Korea

World Team Championships
Thomas Cup .... China
Uber Cup .... China

European Championships, Moscow:
Singles .... S Baddeley, England
Singles, women .... P Nedegaard, Denmark
Doubles, men .... H Suarrer & J Paulson,
Denmark
Doubles, women .... D Kjaar & N Neilsen,
Denmark
Doubles, mixed .... J-H Christiansen & G
Mogensen, Denmark

BASEBALL

1989 World Series .... Oakland Athletics

13

BASKETBALL

Men:

NBA Champions	Detroit Pistons
European Champions Cup	Jugoplastika, Split, Yugoslavia
European Cup-Winners Cup	Virtus Bologna, Italy
European Korac Cup	Joventut Badalona, Spain
National Championship	Kingston Kings
National Cup	Kingston Kings
Carlsberg League	Kingston Kings
National League - Division 1	Oldham Celtics
Division 2	Doncaster Eagles

Women:

Women's World Champions	United States
European Ronchetti Cup	Parma Primizie, Italy
National Championship	T Roos, Northampton
National League - Division 1	T Roos, Northampton
Division 2	T Roos, Northampton
National Cup	Sheffield Hatters

BILLIARDS AND SNOOKER

Ranking Tournaments

Honk Kong Open	S Hendry, Scotland
555 Asian Open	S Hendry, Scotland
Rothmans Grand Prix	S Davis, England
BCE International	S Davis, England
Dubai Classic	S Hendry, Scotland
Stormseal UK Open	S Hendry, Scotland
Mercantile Credit Classic	S James, England
Pearl Assurance British Open	B Chaperon, Canada
European Open	J Parrott, England
EMbassy World Professional	S Hendry, Scotland

Non Ranking Tournaments

Everest World Matchplay	J White, England
Regal Masters	S Hendry, Scotland
Norwich Union Grand Prix	J Johnson, England
Benson & Hedges Masters	S Hendry, Scotland
Welsh Professional	D Morgan
British Car Rentals World Cup	Canada
Benson & Hedges Irish Masters	S Davis, England
Matchroom League	S Davis, England
World Amateur (1989)	K Doherty, Republic of Ireland

Billiards 1988/89

United Kingdom	M Russell, England
British Open	P Gilchrist, England

BOWLS

Men:
Nat West British Isles Championships

Fours	England
Triples	Ireland
Pairs	Wales
Singles	J Ottaway, England
Home Internationals	England

Indoor

Embassy World Championship

Singles	J Price, Wales
Pairs	D Bryant and T Allcock, England
Bristol & West Building Society Denny Cup	Cambridge Park

Anglia Secure Homes International	Ely

British Championships:

Fours	England
Triple	Wales
Pairs	M Craig & J Baker, Ireland
Singles	G Robertson, Scotland
Home Internationals	England

English Championships

Fours	Cyphers
Triples	Sunderland
Pairs	T Scott & D Webb, Gateshead
Singles	A Thomson, Cyphers

County Champions

(Liberty Trophy)	Middlesex

CIS Insurance British Isles International Series

(Hilton Trophy)	England

Women

Outdoor

British Isles Championships

Fours	Wales
Triples	Wales
Pairs	England
Singles	L Wren, Scotland
Home Internationals	England

Indoor

CIS Home International

Champions	England

British Championship

Fours	England
Triples	England
Pairs	A McFarlane & M Spink, Scotland
Singles	M. Johnston, N. Ireland

Cornwallis English Championships

Fours	Teeside
Triples	Boston
Pairs	D Wilson & J Cammack, Boston
Singles	G Smith, Bentham
Champion of Champions	G Thomas, West Cornwall
Yetton Trophy	Essex County

British Isles Championships

Fours	England
Triples	England
Pairs	Scotland
Singles	M Johnston, N. Ireland
Home Internationals	England

BOXING (Amateur)

A.B.A Championships

Light-flyweight	N Tooley, Dawlish
Flyweight	J Armour, St Marys
Bantamweight	P Lloyd, Vauxhall
Featherweight	B Carr, Auchengeich
Lightweight	P Gallagher, Angel
Light-welterweight	J Pender, St Francis
Welterweight	A Carew, Lynn
Light-middleweight	T Taylor, Newco-Repton
Middleweight	S Wilson, Haddington
Light-heavyweight	J McCluskey, Croy Miners
Heavyweight	K Inglis, Tunbridge Wells
Super-heavyweight	K McCormack, Coed-Eva

13

CANOEING

National Sprint Championships

Men

K-1 500m	G Bourne, Elmbride
K-1 1,000m	G Bourne, Elmbridge
K-2 500m	I Lawler & G Bourne, Elmbridge
K-2 1,000m	I Lawler & G Bourne, Elmbridge
K-4 500m	GB National Squad
K-4 1,000m	GB National Squad

Women

K-1 500m	A Dallaway, Elmbridge
K-1 1,000m	A Thoroughgood, Newham
K-1 4,500m	H Dresser, Royal
K-2 500m	H Dresser, Royal & A Dallaway, Elmbride
K-2 1,000m	A Thoroughgood & S Troup, GB National Squad
K-4 500m	GB National Squad

CRICKET

ENGLAND TEST RESULTS

ENGLAND v WEST INDIES 1989-90

First Test (Kingston) England won by 9 wickets
WEST INDIES 164 and 240
ENGLAND 364 and 41-1

Second Test (Georgetown) Abandoned without a ball being bowled

Third Test (Port of Spain) Match drawn
WEST INDIES 199 and 120-5
ENGLAND 288 and 120-5

Fourth Test (Barbados) West Indies won by 164 runs
WEST INDIES 446 and 267
ENGLAND 358 and 191

Fifth Test (Antigua) West Indies won by an innings and 32 runs
ENGLAND 260 and 154
WEST INDIES 446

ENGLAND V NEW ZEALAND 1990

First Test (Trent Bridge) Match drawn
NEW ZEALAND 208 and 36-2
ENGLAND 345-9 declared

Second Test (Lord's) Match drawn
ENGLAND 334 and 272-4
NEW ZEALAND 462

Third Test (Edgbaston) England won by 114 runs
ENGLAND 435 and 158
NEW ZEALAND 249 and 230

TEXACO TROPHY

Headingly, New Zealand won by 4 wickets
ENGLAND 295-6 (55 overs)
NEW ZEALAND 298-6 (54.5 overs)

The Oval, England won by 6 wickets
NEW ZEALAND 212-6 (55 overs)
ENGLAND 213-4 (49.3 overs)

England won the two-match series on faster run rate

ICC TROPHY FINAL

The Hague, Zimbabwe won by 6 wickets

HOLLAND 197-9 (60 overs)
ZIMBABWE 198-4 (54.2 overs)

BENSON AND HEDGES CUP FINAL

Nottinghamshire beat Essex by 3 wickets in the final at Lord's on July 16. ESSEX made 243-7 off their 55 overs. NOTTINGHAMSHIRE made 244-7, winning off the last ball of the match.

Lord's July 14.
Lancashire beat Worcestershire by 69 runs.
Lancashire (55 overs) 241-8 (M. Watkinson 50), (M. Atherton 40)
Worcestershire (54 overs) 172 all out.
Man of the Match Gold Award: M. Watkinson (Lancashire)

CROQUET

British Championships

Men	R Fulford
Women	F Ransome
Mixed Doubles	M Saurin & F McCoig

Inter-Counties Champions .. Eastern Counties

CROSS COUNTRY RUNNING

World Championships:

Individual, men	K Shah, Morocco
Team, men	Kenya
Individual, women	L Jennings, United States
Team, women	USSR

Provincial Insurance National Championships:

Individual, men	R Nerurker, Bingley
Team, men	Valli, Tyneside
Individual, women	A Whitcombe, Parkside
Team, women	Parkside

Inter-Counties individual men   B. Rushworth, North East
Inter-Counties team, men .... North East

CURLING

World Championships Vasters, Sweden

Men	Canada
Women	Norway

CYCLING

Major Overseas Races:

Tour de France, men	G LeMond, United States
Tour of Italy	G Bugno, Italy
Tour of Spain	M Giovanetti, Italy
Paris-Nice	M Indurain, Spain
Milan-San Remo	G Bugno, Italy
Paris-Roubaix	E Planckaert, Belgium
Fleche-Wallonne	M Argentin, Italy
Liege-Bastogne-Liege	E Van Lancker, Belgium
Amstel Gold Race	A Van Der Poel, Holland
Dunkirk Four Day Race	S Roche, Ireland
Dauphin Libre	R Millar, Great Britain

MAJOR BRITISH RACES

Tour of Britain Milk Race
Individual .... S Sutton, Australia
Team .... Banana-Falcon

Scottish Provident League
Race 1 .... C Lillywhite, Banana-Falcon
Race 2 .... J McLoughlin, Ever Ready-
                                           Halfords
Race 3 .... C Lillywhite, Banana-Falcon
Race 4 .... C Walker, Banana-falcon
Race 5 .... C Walker, Banana-Falcon
Race 6 .... D Mann, PCA
Race 7 .... C Walker, Banana-Falcon
Race 8 .... S Sutton, Banana-Falcon
Race 9 .... M Elliott, Teka
Overall .... D Rayner, Banana-falcon

British Professional Road
Race Champs .... C Stugess, Tulip Computers

Wincanton Classic .... G Bugno, Italy

National Road Champions

25 miles .... C Boardman, Manchester
                                              Wheelers
25 miles, team .... Manchester Wheelers
50 miles .... D Smith, Horwich CC
50 miles, team .... Manchester Wheelers
24 hours .... P Oxborough, St Ives CC
24 hours, team .... St Ives CC
Amateur Road Race .... S Hempsall, Chesterfield
                                              Couriers

Cyclo-cross

World professional .... H Baars, Holland
World amateur
Individual .... A Busser, Switzerland
Team .... Switzerland
British Open .... D Baker, Cycles, Pegeot

National Champion

Men
100 Mile Indivvidual .... P Longbottom, Manchester
                                              Wheelers
100 Mile Team .... Manchester Wheelers

Women
100 Mile Individual .... C Roberts, Team Kronos

DARTS

Embassy World Professional Championship
                                P Taylor, England
British Open .... A Warriner, England
News of the World Championship
Men .... P Cook
Women .... L Ormond
BSB World Champions Challenge
Men .... E Bristow, England
Women .... S Colclough, England
1989 World Cup - Overall   England
Team .... Canada
Individual (Men) .... E Bristow, England
Individual (Women) ...... E Grisby, United States
Pairs (Men) .... J Lowe & E Bristow,
                                              England
Pairs (Women) .... S Colclough & S Edwards,
                                              England

EQUESTRIANISM

Show Jumping:

Volvo World Cup
individual .... J Whitaker, Great Britain on
                                              Henderson Milton
British Nations Cup .... Great Britain

Royal International Horse Show, Birmingham

King George V Cup .... J Whitaker, Great Britain on
                                              Henderson Milton
Queen Elizabeth II Cup ...... E-J Mac, Great Britain on
                                              Everest Oyster

Three-Day Eventing

Badminton Horse Trials .... N McIrvine, Great Britain on
                                              Middle Road

FOOTBALL

14th World Cup
Italy, 8th June - 8th July 1990

Group A
Rome
Italy   1 (0)   Austria   0 (0)
Schillaci

Florence
Czechoslovakia 5 (2)   United States   0 (1)
Skuhravy 2, Hasek, Caliguri
Bilek (pen), Luhovey

Rome
Italy   1 (1)   United States   0 (0)
Giannini

Florence
Czechoslovakia 1 (1)   Austria   0 (0)
Bilek (pen)

Rome
Italy   2 (1)   Czechoslovaki   0 (0)
Schillaci, Baggio

Florence
Austria   2 (0)   United States   0 (0)
Ogris, Rodax   Murray

Final Table

	P	W	D	L	F	A	PTS
Italy	3	3	0	0	4	0	6
Czecholsovakia	3	2	0	1	6	3	4
Austria	3	1	0	2	2	3	2
United States	3	0	0	3	2	8	0

Group B
Milan
Cameroon   1 (0)   Argentina 0 (0)
Oman Biyik

Bari
Romania   2 (1)   Soviet Union   0 (0)
Lacatus 2 (1 pen)

Naples
Argentina   2 (1)   Soviet Union   0 (0)
Troglio, Burruchage

Bari
Cameroon   2 (0)   Romania   1 (0)
Milla 2

Bari
Soviet Union　　4 (2)　　Cameroon　　　0 (0)
Protasov, Zygmantovich,
Zavarov, Dobrovlsky

Naples
Argentina1 (0)　　Romania 1 (0)
Monzon　Balint

Final Table

	P	W	D	L	F	A	PTS
Cameroon	3	2	0	1	3	5	4
Romania	3	1	1	1	4	3	3
Argentina	3	1	1	1	3	2	3
Soviet Union	3	1	0	2	4	4	2

Group C

Turin
Brazil　　2 (1)　　Sweden　1 (0)
Careca 2　Brolin

Genoa
Costa Rica　　1 (0)　　Scotland　0 (0)
Cayaso

Turin
Brazil　　1 (1)　　Costa Rica　0 (0)
Muller

Genoa
Scotland　2 (1)　　Sweden　　1 (0)
McCall, Johnston (pen)　　Stromberg

Genoa
Costa Rica　2 (1)　　Sweden　　1 (0)
Flores, Medford　　Ekstrom

Turin
Brazil　　1 (0)　　Scotland　0 (0)
Muller

Final Table

	P	W	D	L	F	A	PTS
Brazil	3	3	0	0	4	1	6
Costa Rica	3	2	0	1	3	2	4
Scotland	3	1	0	2	2	3	2
Sweden	3	0	0	3	3	6	0

Group D

Bologna
Colombia2 (0)　　United Arab Emirates　　1 (0)
Redin, Valderrama

Milan
West Germany　4 (2)　　Yugoslavia　　1 (0)
Mattaus 2, Voller, Klinsman　Jozic

Bologna
Yugoslavia　　1 (0)　　Colombia　　0 (0)
Jozic

Milan
West Germany　5 (2) United Arab Emirates　1 (0)
Voller 2, Klinsman,　　Khalid Ismail Mubarak
Matthaus, Bein

Milan
Colombia1 (0)　　West Germany　　1 (0)
Rincon　　Litbarski

Bologna
Yugoslavia　4 (2)　　United Arab Emirates 1 (1)
Pancev 2, Susic, Prosinecki　Ali Thani Jumaa

Final Table

	P	W	D	L	F	A	PTS
West Germany	3	2	1	0	10	3	5
Yugoslavia	3	2	0	1	6	5	4
Colombia	3	1	1	1	3	2	3
United Arab Emirates	3	0	0	3	2	11	0

Group E

Verona
Belgium　2 (0)　　South Korea　　0 (0)
Degryse De Wolf

Udine
Spain　　0 (0)　　Uruguay　0 (0)

Udine
Spain　　3 (1)　　South Korea　　1 (0)
Michael 3　　Hwang Bo-Kwan

Verona
Belgium　3 (2)　　Uruguay　1 (0)
Clijsters, Scifo, Ceulmana　　Bengoechea

Verona
Spain　　2 (2)　　Belgium　1 (1)
Michel (pen), Gorriz　　Vervoort

Udine
Uruguay 1 (0)　　South Korea　　0 (0)
Fonseca

Final Table

	P	W	D	L	F	A	PTS
Spain	3	2	1	0	5	2	5
Belgium	3	2	0	1	6	3	4
Uruguay	3	1	1	1	2	3	3
South Korea	3	0	0	3	1	6	0

Group F

Caligari
England　1 (1)　　Rep. of Ireland　　1 (0)
Lineker　Sheedy

Palermo
Egypt　　1 (0)　　Holland　1 (0)
Abedelghani (pen)　　Kieft

Caligari
England　0 (0)　　Holland　0 (0)

Palermo
Egypt　　0 (0)　　Rep. of Ireland　0 (0)

Caligari
England　1 (0)　　Eqypt　0 (0)
Wright

Palermo
Holland　1 (1)　　Rep. of Ireland　1 (0)
Gullit　　Quinn

Final Table

	P	W	D	L	F	A	PTS
England	3	1	2	0	2	1	4
Rep. of Ireland	3	0	3	0	2	2	3
Holland	3	0	3	0	2	2	3
Egypt	3	0	2	1	1	2	2

Round Two

Naples
Cameroon　2 (0)(0)　　Colombia1 (0)(0)
Milla 2　　Redin

Bari
Czechoslovakia 4 (1)   Costa Rica   1 (0)
Skuhravy 3, Kubic   Gonzalez

Turin
Argentina 1 (0)   Brazil   0 (0)
Caniggia

Milan
West Germany   2 (0)   Holland   1 (0)
Klinsman, Brehme   R Koeman (pen)

Genoa
Rep. of Ireland   0 (0)(0)   Romania   0 (0)(0)

Rome
Italy   2 (0)   Uruguay   0 (0)
Schilaci, Serena

Verona
Yugoslavia   2 (0)(1)   Spain   1 (0)(1)
Stojkovic 2   Salina

Bologna
England 1 (0)(0)   Belgium   0 (0)(0)
Platt

Quarter Finals

Florence
Argentina 0 (0)(0) Yugoslavia 0 (0)(0)
Argentina won 3-2 on pens

Rome
Italy   1 (1) Rep. of Ireland   0 (0)
Schillaci

Milan
West Germany   1 (1) Czechoslovakia   0 (0)
Matthaus (pen)

Naples
England   3 (1)(2) Cameroon   2 (0)(2)
Lineker (2 pens), Platt   Kunde (pen), Ekeke

Semi Finals

Naples
Argentina 1 (0)(1) Italy   1 (1)(1)
Caniggia Schillaci
Argentina won 3-2 on pens

Turin
West Germany   1 (0)(1) England   1 (0)(1)
Brehme   Linekar
West Germany won 3-2 on pens

Third Place Play-off

Bari
Italy   2 (0)   England 1 (0)
Baggio, Schillaci (pen)   Platt

Final

Rome
West Germany   1 (0)   Argentina 0 (0)
Brehme (pen)

Leading Scorers:

6 Schillaci (Italy); 5 Shukravy (Czechoslovakia); 4 Lineker (England); Matthaus (West Germany); Milla (Cameroon); Michel (Spain)

NOTES ON THE 1989/90 FOOTBALL SEASON

	Winners	Runners-up
World Club Championship	AC Milan	Atletico Nacional
European Super Cup	AC Milan	Barcelona
European Cup	AC Milan	Benfica
European Cup Winnters' Cup	Sampdoria	Anderlecht
UEFA Cup	Juventus	Fiorentina
FA Cup	Manchester U	Crystal P
Football League (Littlewoods) Cup	Nottingham F	Oldham A
Scottish FA Cup	Aberdeen	Celtic
Scottish League (Skol) Cup	Aberdeen	Rangers
Zenith Data Systems Cup	Chelsea	Middlesborough
Welsh FA Cup	Hereford U	Wrexham
Lyeland DAF Cup	Tranmere R	Bristol R
FA Challenge Trophy	Barrow	Leek T
FA Challenge Vase	Reading	Bridlington T
FA Youth Cup	Tottenham H	Middlesborough
Womens' FA Cup	Doncaster B	Friends of Fulham

FOOTBALL LEAGUE

Division 1

		HOME					AWAY					
	P	W	D	L	F	A	W	D	L	F	A	Pts
1 LIVERPOOL	38	13	5	1	38	15	10	5	4	40	22	79
2 Aston Villa	38	13	3	3	36	20	8	4	7	21	18	70
3 Tottenham H	38	12	1	6	35	24	7	5	7	24	23	63
4 Arsenal	38	14	3	2	38	11	4	5	10	16	27	62
5 Chelsea	38	8	7	4	31	24	8	5	6	27	26	60
6 Everton	38	14	3	2	40	16	3	5	11	17	30	59
7 Southampton	38	10	5	4	40	27	5	5	9	31	36	55
8 Wimbledon	38	5	8	6	22	23	8	8	3	25	17	55
9 Nottingham F	38	9	4	6	31	21	6	5	8	24	26	54
10 Norwich C	38	7	10	2	24	14	6	4	9	20	28	53
11 QPR	38	9	4	6	27	22	4	7	8	18	22	50
12 Coventry C	38	11	2	6	24	25	3	5	11	15	34	49
13 Man. Untd	38	8	6	5	26	14	5	3	11	20	33	48
14 Man. City	38	9	4	6	26	21	3	8	8	17	31	48
15 Crystal P	38	8	7	4	27	23	5	2	12	15	43	48
16 Derby C	38	9	1	9	29	21	2	6	9	14	19	46
17 Luton T	38	8	8	3	24	18	2	5	12	19	39	43
18 Sheffield W	38	8	6	5	21	17	3	4	12	14	34	43
19 Charlton A	38	4	6	9	18	25	3	3	13	13	32	30
20 Millwall	38	4	6	9	23	25	1	5	13	16	40	26

Division 2

		HOME					AWAY					
	P	W	D	L	F	A	W	D	L	F	A	Pts
1 LEEDS U	46	16	6	1	46	18	8	7	8	33	34	85
2 Sheffield U	46	14	5	4	43	27	10	8	5	35	31	85
3 Newcastle U	46	17	4	2	51	26	5	10	8	29	29	80
4 Swindon T	46	12	6	5	49	29	8	8	7	30	30	74
5 Blackburn R	46	10	9	4	43	30	9	8	6	31	29	74
6 Sunderland	46	10	8	5	41	32	10	6	7	29	32	74
7 West Ham U	46	14	5	4	50	22	6	7	10	30	35	72
8 Oldham A	46	15	7	1	50	23	4	7	12	20	34	71
9 Ipswich T	46	13	7	3	38	22	6	5	12	29	44	69
10 Wolves	46	12	5	6	37	20	6	8	9	30	40	67
11 Port Vale	46	11	9	3	37	20	4	7	12	25	37	61
12 Portsmouth	46	9	8	6	40	34	6	8	9	22	31	61
13 Leicester C	46	9	5	9	34	29	5	6	12	33	50	59
14 Hull C	46	7	8	8	27	31	7	8	8	31	34	58
15 Watford	46	11	6	6	41	28	3	9	11	17	32	57
16 Plymouth A	46	8	6	9	30	23	5	5	13	28	40	54
17 Oxford U	46	8	7	8	35	31	7	2	14	22	35	54
18 Brighton HA	46	10	6	7	28	27	5	3	15	28	45	54
19 Barnsley	46	7	9	7	22	23	6	6	11	27	44	54
20 West Brom	46	6	8	9	35	37	6	7	10	32	34	51
21 Middlesboro'	46	10	3	10	33	29	3	8	12	19	34	50
22 Bournemouth	46	8	6	9	30	31	4	6	13	27	45	48
23 Bradford C	46	9	6	8	26	24	0	8	15	18	44	41
24 Stoke C	46	4	11	8	20	24	2	8	13	15	39	37

Division 3

	P	HOME W	D	L	F	A	AWAY W	D	L	F	A	Pts
1 BRISTOL R	46	15	8	0	43	14	11	7	5	28	21	93
2 Bristol C	46	15	5	3	40	16	12	5	6	36	24	91
3 Notts C	46	17	4	2	40	18	8	8	7	33	35	87
4 Tranmere R	46	15	5	3	54	22	8	6	9	32	27	80
5 Bury	46	11	7	5	35	19	10	4	9	35	30	74
6 Bolton W	46	12	7	4	32	19	6	8	9	27	29	69
7 Birmingham	46	10	7	6	33	19	8	5	10	27	40	66
8 Huddersfield	46	11	5	7	30	23	6	9	8	31	39	65
9 Rotherham U	46	12	6	5	48	28	5	7	11	23	34	64
10 Reading	46	10	9	4	33	21	5	10	8	24	32	64
11 Shrewsbury	46	10	9	4	38	24	6	6	11	21	30	63
12 Crewe A	46	10	8	5	32	24	5	9	9	24	29	62
13 Brentford	46	11	4	8	41	31	7	3	13	25	35	61
14 Leyton O	46	9	6	8	28	24	7	4	12	24	32	58
15 Mansfield T	46	13	2	8	34	25	3	5	15	16	40	55
16 Chester C	46	11	7	5	30	23	2	8	13	13	32	54
17 Swansea C	46	10	6	7	25	27	4	6	13	20	36	54
18 Wigan A	46	10	6	7	29	22	3	8	12	19	42	53
19 Preston NE	46	10	7	6	42	30	4	3	16	23	49	52
20 Fulham	46	8	8	7	33	27	4	7	12	22	39	51
21 Cardiff C	46	6	9	8	30	35	6	5	12	21	35	50
22 Northampton	46	7	7	9	27	31	4	7	12	24	37	47
23 Blackpool	46	8	6	9	29	33	2	10	11	20	40	46
24 Walsall	46	6	8	9	23	30	3	6	14	17	42	41

Division 4

	P	HOME W	D	L	F	A	AWAY W	D	L	F	A	Pts
1 Exeter C	46	20	3	0	50	14	8	2	13	33	34	89
2 Grimsby T	46	14	4	5	41	20	8	9	6	29	27	79
3 Southend U	46	15	3	5	35	14	7	6	10	26	34	75
4 Stockport C	46	13	6	4	45	27	8	5	10	23	35	74
5 Maidstone U	46	14	4	5	49	21	8	3	12	28	40	73
6 Cambridge U	46	14	3	6	45	30	7	7	9	31	36	73
7 Chesterfield	46	12	9	2	41	19	7	5	11	22	35	71
8 Carlisle U	46	15	4	4	38	20	6	4	13	23	40	71
9 Peterborough	46	10	8	5	35	23	7	9	7	24	23	68
10 Lincoln C	46	11	6	6	30	27	7	8	8	18	21	68
11 Scunthorpe U	46	9	9	5	42	25	8	6	9	27	29	66
12 Rochdale	46	11	4	8	28	23	9	2	12	24	32	66
13 York C	46	10	5	8	29	24	6	11	6	26	29	64
14 Gillingham	46	9	8	6	28	21	8	3	12	18	27	62
15 Torquay U	46	12	2	9	33	29	3	10	10	20	37	57
16 Burnley	46	6	10	7	19	18	8	4	11	26	37	56
17 Hereford U	46	7	4	12	31	32	8	6	9	25	30	55
18 Scarborough	46	10	5	8	35	28	5	5	13	25	45	53
19 Hartlepool	46	12	4	7	45	33	3	6	14	21	55	55
20 Doncaster R	46	7	7	9	29	29	7	2	14	24	31	51
21 Wrexham	46	8	8	7	28	28	5	4	14	23	39	51
22 Aldershot	46	8	7	8	28	26	4	7	12	21	43	50
23 Halifax T	46	5	9	9	31	29	7	4	12	26	36	49
24 Colcheater U	46	9	3	11	26	25	2	7	14	22	50	43

FA CUP FINAL

Crystal Palace (2) 3   Manchester United (2) 3
after extra time: end of 90 mins, 2-2

Crystal Palace: Martyn, Pemberton, Shaw, Gray (Madden), O'Reilly, Thorn, Barber (Wright), Thomas, Bright, Salako, Pardew
Scorers: Wright 2, O'Reilly

Manchester United: Leighton, Ince, Martin (Blackmore), Bruce, Phelan, Pallister (Robins), Robson, Webb, McClair, Hughes, Wallace
Scorers: Hughes 2, Robson

Ref: A Gunn (Sussex)   Att: 80,000

Replay
Manchester United (0) 1   Crystal Palce (0) 0

Manchester United: Sealey, Ince, Martin, Bruce, Phelan, Pallister, Robson, Webb, McClair, Hughes, Wallace
Scorer: Martin

Crystal Palace: Martyn, Pemberton, Shaw, Gray, O'Reilly, Thorn, Barber (Wright), Thomas, Hughes, Wallace

Ref: A Gunn (Sussex)   Att: 80,000

LITTLEWOODS CUP FINAL

Nottingham Forest (0) 1   Oldham Athletic (0) 0

Nottingham Forest: Sutton, Laws, Pearce, Walker, Chettle, Hodge, Crosby, Parker, Clough, Jemson, Carr
Scorer: Jemson

Oldham Athletic: Rhodes, Irwin Barlow, Henry, Barrett, Warhurst, Adams, Ritchie, Bunn (Palmer), Milligan, Holden

Ref: J E. Martin (Alton)   Att: 74,343

SCOTTISH FA CUP FINAL

Aberdeen (0) 0   Celtic (0) 0
(After extra time, Aberdeen won 9-8 on penalties)

Aberdeen: Snelders, McKimmie, Robertson, B. Grant, McLeish, Irvine, Nicholas, Bett, Mason (Watson), Connor, Gilhaus

Celtic: Bonner, Wdowczyk, Rogan, P. Grant, Elliott, Whyte, Stark (Galloway), McStay, Dziekanowski, Walker (Coyne), Miller

Ref: G Smith (Edinburgh)   Att: 60,493

AWARDS

European Footballer of the Year :	M Van Basten (AC Milan)
PFA Player of the Year:	D Platt (Aston Villa)
PFA Young Player of the Year:	M. le Tissier (Southampton)
PFA Merit Award:	P Shilton (Derby C)
FWA Footballer of the Year:	J Barnes (liverpool)
Scottish FWA Player of the Year:	A McLeish (Aberdeen)
Barclays Bank Manager of the Year:	K Dalglish (Liverpool)

GOLF

Professional - Men

Major Tournaments

British Open	
US Open	H Irwin, United States
US Masters	N Faldo, Great Britain

European PGA Tour

Tenerife Open	V Fernandez, Argentina
AGF Open	B Ogle, Australia
British Open	N Faldo, Great Britain
Volvo Open	E Romero, Argentina
Credit Lyonnaise Cannes Open	K McNulty, Zimbabwe
Cepsa Madrid Open	B langer, West Germany
Peugot Spanish Open	R David Australia
Lancia Italian Open	R Boxall, England
Volvo PGA Championship	M Harwood, Australia
Dunhill British Masters	M James, England
Wang Four Stars National	C Davis, Australia
Carrolls Irish Open	J-M Olazabal, Spain
Peugeot French Open	P walton, Ireland
Torras Monte Carlo Open	I Woosnam, Ireland
Bell's Scottish Open	Ian Woosnan, Great Britain

13

KLM Dutch Open .... S McAllister, Great Britain
Scandinavian Enterprise
   Open .... C Stadler, United States
Benson & Hedges
   International .... J-M Olazabal, Spain
Vinho Verde Atlantic Open. S McAllister, Scotland
Emirates Airline Desert
   Classic .... E Darcy, Ireland
American Express
   Mediterranean Open ...... I Woosnam, Wales
Renault Mallorcan Open .... S Ballesteros, Spain
EL Bosque Open, Valencia V Singh, Fiji
Peugeot-Trends
   Belgian Open .... O Sellberg, Sweden

Others

Zimbabwe Open .... G Turner, England
Zambia Open .... G J Brabnd, England
555 Kenya Open .... C O'Connor, Ireland
Australian Open .... P Senior, Australia
Australian PGA .... P Senior, Australia
Australian Masters .. G Norman, Australia
Million Dollar Challenge .. D Frost, South Africa
Japanese Masters .... J-M Olazabal, Spain
PGA Seniors .... G Player, South Africa
Trushouse Forte PGA
   Seniors .... B Waites, Notts
Volvo Seniors British
   Open .... G Player, South Africa

Amateur - Men

British Amateur .... R Munz, Holland
President's Putter .... G Woullett, United States
Halford Hewitt Cup .... Tonbridge
English Amateur .... O Edmond, France & G
                              Evans, England (shared)

Women

British Women's Open ...... J Hall, Felexstowe Ferry
European Masters .... K Lunn, Australia
English Womens'
   Match-play .... A Uzielli, The Berkshire
Scottish Amateur .... E Farquarharson, Dundee
Welsh Amateur .... S Roberts, Maesdy
Women's County
   Championship .... Cheshire

Teams

Curtis Cup .... United States
Ryder Cup .... Europe & US (match drawn)
Dunhill Cup (1989) .... United States
Suntory Worlf Match Play
   Championship (1989) .... N Falso
World Cup (1988 - team ... Australia
   - individual .... P Fowler, Australia

GREYHOUND RACING

Daily Mirror Derby .... Slippy Blue
Daily Mirror Grand
   National .... Gizmo Pasha
David Richardson Scurry
   Cup ....
BBC TV Trophy .... Shropshire Lass

GYMNASTICS

European Championships:

Men

Overall .... V Mogilny, USSR
Floor .... V Sherbo, USSR

Pommel Horse .... V Mogilny, USSR
Rings .... Y Chechi, Italy
Parallel Bars .... V Mogilny, USSR & D
                              Giubellini, Italy
Vault .... V Sherbo, USSR
High Bars .... V Sherbo, USSR

Women

Overall .... S Boginskaya, USSR
Vault .... S Boginskaya, USSR
Beam .... S Boginskaya, USSR
Asymmetrical Bars .... S Boginskaya, USSR
Floor .... S Boginskaya, USSR

Daily Mirror Champions All:

Men .... T Bartlett, Great Britain
Women .... L Homma, Canada

British Championships:

Men .... N Thomas, Lilleshall
Women .... S Mercer, Leatherhead
Women's team rythmic ...... Coventry

HANDBALL

National Cup - Men .... Ruislip Eagles
   - Women .... Wakefield Metros

HOCKEY

Men

World Cup .... Holland
European Club Champions Uhlenhorst Mulheim, West
                              Germany
European Cup-winners' cup Hounslow, England
European Indoor Cup .... Rotweiss Cologne, West
                              Germany
County Champions .... Middlesex
H.A. Cup .... Havant

Poundstretcher League

Division 1 .... Hounslow
Division 2 .... St. Albans

Poundstretcher Cup

Division 1 .... Havant
Division 2 .... Neston
Champions Trophy .... Australia
Divisional Champions .... East
National Inter-League
   Champions .... Trojan, Hampshire
Royal Bank Indoor Club
   Champions .... St. Albans
Indoor Home International
   Championship .... Austria (they took the place
                              of Ireland)

Women

World Cup .... Holland
European Club Champions Amsterdam
European Indoor Club
   Champions .... Brandenburg Berlin, West
                              Germany
National Club Champions .. Sutton Coldfield
National Indoor Club
   Champions .... Ipswich
Indoor Home International
   Champions .... Ireland
National County Indoor
   Champions .... Lancashire

HORSE RACING

Classic winners and starting prices for the last five years

Year	Owner	Horse/Price	Jockey
One Thousand Guineas			
1986	H. Ranier	Midway Lady, 10-1	R. Cochrane
1987	Stavros Niachros	Miesque, 15-8	F. Head
1988	Ecurie Aland	Ravinella, 4-5 fav	G. Moore
1989	Sheikh Mohammed	Musical Bliss, 7-2	W. Swinburn
1990	Hamid A-Makhtoum	Salsabil, 6-4 fav	W. Carson
Two Thousand Guineas			
1986	K. Abdulla	Dancing Brave, 15-8	G. Starkey
1987	Jim Hogan	Don't Forget Me, 9-1	W. Carson
1988	HH Aga Khan	Doyoun, 4-5 fav	W. Swinburn
1989	Hamdan Al-Maktoum	Nashwan, 3-1 fav	W. Carson
1990	J. Horgan	Tirol, 9-1	m. Kinane
The Derby			
1986	H.H. Aga Khan	Shahrastani, 11-2	W. Swinburn
1987	Louis Freedman	Reference Point, 6-4	S. Cauthen
1988	Luca Cumani	Kahyas, 11-1	R. Cochrane
1989	Hamdan Al-Maktoum	Nashwan, 5-4 fav	W. Carson
1990	Prince Khalid Abdulla	Quest for Fame, 7-1	P. Eddery
The Oaks			
1986	H. Ranier	Midway Lady, 15-8	R. Cochrane
1987	Sheikh Mohammed	Unite, 11-1	W. Swinburn
1988	Sheikh Mohammed	Diminuendo, 7-4 fav	S. Cauthen
1989	Aga Khan	Aliysa, 11-10 fav	W. Swinburn
1990	Hamdam Al-Makhtoum	Salsabil, 2-1 fav	W. Carson
St. Leger			
1985	Sheikh Mohammed	Oh So Sharp, 8-11	S. Cauthen
1986	Lavinia Duchess of Norfolk	Moon Madness, 9-2	P. Eddery
1987	Louis Freedman	Reference Point, 4-11	S. Cauthen
1988	Lady Beaverbrook	Minster Son, 15-2	W. Carson
1989	C St. George	Michelozzo, 6-4 fav	S. Cauthen

BIG RACE WINNERS

Flat - Group One Races

Race	Horse	SP
Coronation Cup	In the Wings	15-8f
St. James's Palace Stakes	Shavian	11-1
Coronation Stakes	Chimes of Freedom	11-2
Ascot Gold Cup	Ashal	14-1
King's Stand Stakes	Dayjur	11-2
Coral Eclipse Stakes	Elaamud	13-2
Carroll Foundation July Cup	Royal Academy	7-1
King George VI and Queen Diamond Stakes	Belmez	15-2

Flat - Principal Handicaps

Race	Horse	SP
William Hill Lincoln Handicap	Evichstar	33-1
Ladbroke European Free Handicap	Ashnan	9-2
Jubilee Handicap	Langtry Lady	14-1
Ladbroke Chester Cup	Travelling Light	5-2f
Royal Hunt Cup	Pontenuovo	50-1
Wokingham Stakes	Knight of Mercy	16-1
Northumberland Plate	Al Maheb	9-2
John Smith's Magnet Cup	Eradicate	15-2
William Hill Steward's Cup	Kinight of Mercy	14-1

National Hunt

Race	Horse	SP
Mackeson Gold Cup (1989)	Joint Sovereignty	10-1
Hennessy Cognac Gold Cup (1989)	Ghofar	5-1
Coral Welsh Grand National (1989)	Bonanza Boy	15-8f
Waterford Crystal Champion Hurdle	Kribesis	95-40
Queen Mother Champion Chase	Barnbrrok Again	11-10f
Daily Express Triumph Hurdle	Rare Holiday	25-1
Tote Cheltenham Gold Cup	Norton's Coin	100-1
Seagram Grand National	Mr Frisk	16-1
William Hill Scottish Grand National	Four Trix	25-1
Jameson Irish Grand National	Desert Orchid	evens f
Whitbread Gold Cup	Mr Frisk	9-2f

Abroad

Race	Horse
Irish 1000 Guineas	Heart of Joy
Irish 2000 Guineas	Tirol
Irish Derby	Salsabil
Irish Oaks	Knight's Baroness
Irish St Leger	Petite Ile
French 1000 Guineas	Houseproud
French 2000 Guineas	Linamix
French Derby	Sanglamore
French Oaks	Rahfa

13

French St Leger (1989) ...... Top Sunrise
Prix de l'Arc de
   Triomphe (1989) .... Carroll House

US Triple Crown:
Kentucky Derby .... Unbridled
Preakness Stakes .... Summer Squall
Belmont Stakes .... Go and Go

ICE HOCKEY

World Championships .... USSR
Heineken British
   Championship .... Cardiff Devils
Stanley Cup .... Edmonton Oilers
Heineken League Champions Cardiff Devils

JUDO

European Championships, Helsinki:
Men
Under 60kg .... P Pradaurol, France
Under 65kg .... B Carabetta, France
Under 71kg .... G Schumacher, FRG
Under 78kg .... B Varayev, USSR
Under 86kg .... W Legien, Poland
Under 95kg .... S Traineau, France
Over 95kg .... S Kosorotov, USSR
Open .... L Tolnai, Hungary

Women
Under 48kg .... C Nowak, France
Under 52kg .... S Rendle, Great Britain
Under 56kg .... C Arnaud, France
Under 61kg .... B Gomez, Spain
Under 66kg .... A Schreiber, FRG
Under 72kg .... K Krueger, FRG
Over 72kg .... C Cicot, France
Open .... S lee, Great Britain

British Open Championships

Men
Under 60kg .... T Dibert, France
Under 65kg .... M Preston, Great Britain
Under 71kg .... C M'Bani, France
Under 78kg .... R Birch, Great Britain
Under 86kg .... M Leibnitz, France
Under 95kg .... R Stevens, Great Britain
Over 95kg .... D Douillet, France

Women
Under 48kg .... K Briggs, Great Britain
Under 52kg .... S rendle, Great Britain
Under 56kg .... N Fairbrother, Great Britain
Under 61kg .... D Bell, Great Britain
Under 66kg .... K Howey, Great Britain
Under 72kg .... E Esscombe, France
Over 72kg .... S lee Great Britain

LACROSSE

Men
Men's World Championship United States
English Clubs (Iroquois Cup) .... Cheadle
Northern Flags .... Cheadle
Southern Senior Flags .... Hampstead
Brine Northern League .... Heaton Mersey
English Club Championship Cheadle

Women
Home International .... England
Hattersley Salvar .... East

SAC Clubs and
   Colleges Trophy .... West London
National School's
Championship .... Queen Anne's

LAWN TENNIS

Wimbledon:
Singles, men .... S Edberg, Sweden
Singles, women .... M Navratilova, United States
Doubles, men .... R Leach & J Pugh, United
   States
Doubles, women .... J Novotna and H Sukova,
   Czechoslovakia
Doubles, mixed .... R leach & Z Garrison,
   United States

British Rankings:

Men .... J Bates
Women .... M Javier
Prudential County Cup,
   men .... Surrey
Prudential County Cup,
   women .... Surrey

International Championships:

Wightman Cup .... United States
Federation Cup (1989) .... United States
World Team Cup (1989) .. West Germany
Davis Cup (1989) .... West Germany
1989 Men's Grand Prix Masters
  - Singles .... S Edberg, Sweden
  - Doubles .... P McEnroe & J Grabb,
   United States
1989 Virginia Slims Series
  - Singles .... S Graf, West Germany
  - Doubles .... M Natratilova, & P Shriver,
   United States
1989 WCT Singles .... J McEnroe, United States
1989 ITF World Champions
  - Men .... B Becker, West Germany
  - Women .... S Graf, West Germany

Australian Open:
Singles, men .... I Lendl, Czechoslovakia
Singles, women .... S Graf, W Germany
Doubles, men .... P Aldrich & D Visser, South
   Africa
Doubles, women .... J Novotna & H Sukova,
   Czechoslovakia
Doubles, mixed .... J Pugh, United States & N
   Zvereva, USSR

French Open:
Singles, men .... A Gomez, Ecuador
Singles, women .... M Seles, Yugoslavia
Doubles, men .... S Casal & E Sanchez, Spain
Doubles, women .... J Novotna & H Sukova,
   Czechoslovakia
Doubles, mixed .... J Lozano, Mexico & A
   Sanchez Vicario, Spain

Italian Open:
Singles, men .... T Muster, Austria
Doubles, men .... M Seles, Yugoslavia

MODERN PENTATHLON

Men

World Championship
   team .... Soviet Union
   individual .... G Tiberti, Italy

MOTORCYCLING

Isle of Man TT:

Senior	C Fogarty, Honda
Junior 250cc	I Lougher, Yamaha
125cc	R Dunlop, Honda
Formula I	C Fogarty, Honda
Supersport 600	B Reid, Yamaha
Supersport 400	D Leach, Yamaha
Sidecar (Race A)	D Saville & N Roche, Yamaha
Sidecar (Race B)	D Saville & N Roche, Yamaha

Speedway:

World Championships:

British League Riders Championship (1989)	S Moran, Belle Vue
British League (1989)	Oxford
National League (1989)	Poole

MOTOR RACING

1989 World Championship:

Drivers:
1 A Prost, France 76 pts
2 A Senna, Brazil 60 pts
3 R Patrese, Italy 40 pts

Constructors:
1 McLaren 141 pts
2 Williams 77 pts
3 Ferrari 59 pts

1990 World Championship:

Brazilian GP	A Prost, France, Ferrari
San Marino GP	R Patrese, Italy, Williams
Monaco GP	A Senna, Brazil, NcLaren
Mexican GP	A Prost, France, Ferrari
United States GP	A Senna, Brazil, McLaren
Canadian GP	A Senna, Brazil, McLaren
French GP	A Prost, France, Ferrari
British GP	A Prost, France
German GP	A Senna, Brazil

International

Le Mans 24 hours	J Nielsen, Denmark; P. Cobb, United States; M Brundle, Great Britain, Jaguar
Indianapolis 500	A Luyendik, Holland, Lola
Daytona 500	D Cope, United States, Chevrolet

Major International Rallies

Lombard RAC (1988)	P Arikkala, Finland, Mitsibushi
Swedish Rally	I Carlsson,Sweden
Monte Carlo Rally	D Auriol, France, Lancia
Portuguese Rally	M Biasion, Italy, Lancia
Safari Rally	B Waldegaard, Sweden, Toyota
Tour of Corsica	D Auriol, France, Lancia
Acropolis Rally	C Sainz, Spain, Toyota
New Zealand Rally	C Sainz, Spain, Toyota
Argentine Rally	M Biasion, Italy
Paris-Dakar Rally	A Vatinen, Finland, Peugeot

British Open Rally Championship

Cartel International	C McRae/D Ringer, Ford Sierra
BIF Circuit of Ireland	D Llwewllin/P Short, Toyota
Fram Welsh Rally	
RSAC Scottish Rally	D Llewellin/P Short, Toyota
British Midland Ulster Rally	D Llewellin

NETBALL

English Counties League

Division 1	Bedfordshire
Division 2	South Yorkshire
National Clubs Knockout Cup	New Campbell Grasshoppers (Essex Met)

ORIENTEERING

British Championships

Men	S Hale, Perth
Women	Y Hague, Edinburgh University

RACKETS

Lacoste Open Singles	N. Smith
Lacost Open Doubles	J Male and J Prenn, Great Britain
Lacoste Amateur Doubles	J Prenn and J Male,Great Britain
Rank Xerox Professional Singles	S Hazell
British Amateur Singles	W Boone
British Amateur Doubles	J Prenn & J Male
British Open Singles	N Smith
British Open Doubles	N Smith and W Boone

REAL TENNIS

Conrad Construction World Tournament

Men	L Deuchar
Men's Doubles	L Deuchar & W Davies
Women	A Warren-Piper & S Jones
Women's Doubles	A Warren-Piper & S Jones
George Wimpey Amateur Singles	J Male
British Professional Singles	L Deuchar
George Wimpey Under-24 Singles	C Bray
George Wimpey Under-24 Doubles	C Bray & A Phillips
George Wimpey Women's Masters	F Syson
Henry Leaf Cup	Radley
Bathurst Cup	England
Taylor Cup	M Devine
Seacourt Silver Racket	I Snell
Holyport Inter Club Doubles	Hatfield (R Lake & J Gibbs)

ROWING

British Championships:

Men

Eights	Nottingham County 5m 38.05s
Coxed fours	Lea 'A' 6m 17.62s
Coxless fours	Nottingham County 6m 03.86s

Coxed pairs .... Thames Tradesmens 7m
26.88s

Coxless pairs .... Lea/Tyrian 6m 48.57s
Quad sculls .... Upper Thames 'A' 6m
07.47s
Double sculls .... Molesey 6m 32.03s
Single sculls .... S Larkin, Nottingham
County 7m 02.38s
Lightweight Single sculls .. P Ashmore, St. Ives 7m
10.45s
Lightweight Double sculls Nottingham County 6m
37.38s
Lightweight Quad sculls .... Kensington Auriol 6m
19.11s
Lightweight Coxless Fours Nottingham County 6m
06.55s
Lightweight Eights .... Nottingham County 5m
47.37s

Women
Eights .... Cambridge University 'A'
6m 30.99s
Coxed fours .... University of London 7m
11.82s
Coxless pairs .... GB National Squad 'B' 7m
31.38s
Quadruple sculls .... Tideway Scullers 'A' 6m
49.37s
Double sculls .... GB National Squad 7m
03.75s
Single sculls .... P Reid, GB National Squad
7m 58.86s
Lightweight Single sculls .. C Parker, Nottingham
County 7m 84.63s
Lightweight Double sculls. Marlow/Thames 7m 15.36s
Lightweight Coxless Pairs. Birmingham 7m 45.08s
Lightweight Coxless Fours. Thames Tradesmens 7m
05.41s

Henley Royal Regatta:
Grand Challenge Cup .... RC Hansa Dortmund, West
Germany
Ladies' Challenge Plate .... Harvard University
Prince Philip Challenge
Cup .... Hansa Dortmund, West
Germany
Stewards' Challenge Cup .. Star Lub and Leander 'A'
Wyfold Challenge Cup ...... London Rowing Club 'A'
Silver Goblets and
Nickalls' Challenge Cup K Sinzinger & H Bauer,
Austria
Double Sculls Challenge
Cup .... A Rudkin & P Kittermaster,
Tideway Scullers'
Diamond Challenge
sculls .... E Verdonk, New Zealand
Visitors' Challenge Cup .... University of London
Brittania Challenge Cup .... Uni versity College, Galway,
Ireland
Princess Elizabeth
Challenge Cup .... Eton College
Queen Mother
Challenge Cup .... Danmark Rocenter Roklub,
Denmark
Thames Cup .... Nottingham County
Henley Prize (new 1990) .... Imperial College, London

Thames races
Head-of-River, eights .... GB National Squad
Head-of-River, scullers ...... R henderson, Leander
Oxford v. Cambridge .... Oxford
Oxford v. Cambridge,
women .... Cambridge
Wingfield Sculls .... R Henderson, Imperial
College

RUGBY FOOTBALL

Rugby Union

International Championship - Final Table

	P	W	D	L	F	A	Pts
Scotland	4	4	0	0	60	26	8
England	4	3	0	1	90	26	6
France	4	2	0	2	67	78	4
Ireland	4	1	0	3	36	72	2
Wales	4	0	0	4	42	90	0

Courage Championship
Division 1 .... Wasps
Division 2 .... Northampton
Division 3 .... London Scottish
Toshiba County champions Lancashire
Inter-Services .... Army
Pilkington Cup .... Bath
Schweppes Welsh Cup ...... Neath
Hospitals Cup .... St Mary's
U.A.U. Champions .... Loughborough University
Middlesex Sevens .... Harlequins
Cathay Pacific Hong Kong
Sevens .... Fiji
1989 Varsity Match .... Cambridge
Women's Cup Final .... Wasps

Rugby League
Silk Cut Challenge Cup ...... Wigan
Stones Bitter Premiership. Widnes
Regal Trophy .... Wigan
Stones Bitter 2nd
Division Premiership .... Oldham
Division One Champions .. Wigan
Division Two Champions .. Hull KR
Lancashire Cup .... Warrington
Yorkshire Cup .... Bradford Northern
War of the Roses .... Yorkshire

SHOOTING

Bisley
National Rifle Association Meeting:
Queen's Prize .... J Bloomfield, North London
RC
St George's Vase .... A Ringer, Uppingham
Veterans
Prince of Wales Prize .... Miss T Fitsimmons,
Manchester
Mackinnon Tophy .... Canada
Land Rover Grand
Aggregate .... A Marion, Canada
Daily Telegraph
Challenge Cup .... P Kent, Old Epsomians
Daily Mail Cup .... G Feast, Radlett

SKATING

World Figure Skating Championship, Paris:
Men .... K Browning, Canada
Women .... J Trenary, Unites States
Pairs .... E Gordeyeva and S Grinkov,
USSR
Dancing .... M Klimova and S
Ponomarenko, USSR

European Figure Skating Championship, Birmingham:
Men .... V Petrenko, USSR
Women .... E Grossman, East Germany
Pairs .... E Gordeeva & S Grinkov,
USSR
Dancing .... M Klimova and S
Ponomarenko, USSR

SKIING

Alpine World Cup

Men:

Overall	P Zurbriggen, Switzerland
Downhill	H Hohflehner, Austria
Super-Giant Slalom	M Zurbriggen, Switzerland
Giant Slalom	O C Furuseth, Norway
Slalom	A Bittner, West Germany

Women:

Overall	P Kronberger, Austria
Downhill	K Gutensholn-Knopl, Austria
Super-Giant Slalom	C Merle, France
Giant Slalom	A Wachter, Austria
Slalom	C Schneider, Switzerland
Nations Cup	Austria

British Championships

Freestyle

Moguls - men	N Munro
women	J Curry
Ballet - men	I Wilcox
- women	J Snell
Aerials - men	R Cobbing
- women	J Curry
Combined - men	R Harrison
- women	J Curry

SWIMMING

TSB National Championships:

Men:

50m freestyle	N. Sanders, New Zealand 23.51s
100m freestyle	J Steel, New Zealand 51.45s
200m freestyle	P Howe, Birmingham 1m 51.07s
400m freestyle	P Howe, Birmingham 3m 55.10s
1500m freestyle	I Wilson, Sunderland 15m 25.92s
100m backstroke	M Harris, Barnet Copthall 57.87s
200m backstroke	T Deutsch, Hun 2m 04.92s
100m breaststroke	A Moorhouse, Leeds 1m 01.49s
200m breaststroke	N Gillingham, Birmingham 2m 16.48s
100m butterfly	N Sanders, New Zealand 54.97s
200m butterfly	P Howe, Birmingham 2m 04.23s
200m medley	G Robins, Portsmouth Northsea 2m 05.99s
400m medley	J Munro, New Zealand 4m 26.84s

Women:

50m freestyle	C Woodcock, Barnet Copthall 26.54s
100m freestyle	K Pickering, Ipswich 57.60s
200m freestyle	K Pickering, Ipswich 2m 03.02s
400m freestyle	K Mellor, Sheffield 4m 17.96s
800m freestyle	K Mellor, Sheffield 8m 44.98s
100m backstroke	S Page, Wigan Wasps 1m 04.34s
200m backstroke	A Simcic, New Zealand 2m 15.53s
100m breaststroke	L Hooiveld, Leeds 1m 11.03s
200m breaststroke	S Brownsdon, Wigan Wasps 1m 2m 36.15s
100m butterfly	M Scarborough, Portsmouth Northsea 1m 02.00s
200m butterfly	m Scarborough, Portsmouth Northsea 2m 15.71s
200m medley	Z Long, Beckenham 2m 19.74s
400m medley	Z Long, Beckenham 4m 54.34s
4x100 metres freestyle medley	Portsmouth Northsea 4m 00.93s
4x100 Medley relay	Southampton 4m 21.40s

TABLE TENNIS

World Team Cup

Men	Sweden
Women	China

European Championships

Singles, men	M Applegren, Sweden
Singles, women	D Guerguelcheva, Bulgaria
Doubles, men	I Lupelesku & Z Primorac, Yugoslavia
Doubles, women	G Wirth * C Batorfi, Hungary

Leeds National Championships

Singles, men	D Douglas, Warwicks
Singles, women	F Elliott, Staffs
Doubles, men	A Cooke, Derbys & D Douglas, Warwicks
Doubles, women	L Lomas, Beds & F Elliott, Staffs
National League (Alan Rensen Cup)	Ashford 1

TRAMPOLINING

British Championships

Men	R Cobbing, Gateshead
Women	S Challis, Portsmouth
Pairs, men	A Harrison, Hull & K Young, London
Pairs, women	V Webb, Isle of Wight & L Lyon, Liverpool

VOLLEYBALL

National League, men	Mizuno Malory
National Cup, men	Mizuno Malory
National League, women	Brixton Knights
National Cup, women	Brixton Knights
British Championship	Scotland
European Cup	Phillips Modena, Italy
British Championship	
- men	Scotland
- women	England

WATER SKIING

British Championships

Men

Overall	S Bronson, West Wickham
Slalom	J Battleday, Chiswick
Jump	A Rooke, West Bridgeford
Tricks	J Battleday, Chiswick

13

Women

Overall	P Roberts, Windsor
Slalom	P Roberts, Windsor
Jump	P Roberts, Windsor
Tricks	P Roberts, Windsor

Carlsberg European Masters

Men

Slalom	P Carmin, France
Jump	F Oberleitner, Austria
Tricks	N le Forestier, France

Women

Slalom	G Semiglia, Italy
Jump	P Roberts, Great Britain
Tricks	N Ivanova, USSR

WRESTLING

British Freestyle Champions

up to 48kg	A Airlie, East Kilbride
up to 52kg	D Connelly, Cumbernauld
up to 57kg	P Morris, Bolton
up to 62kg	J Melling, Leigh
up to 68kg	P Keech, Bolton
up to 74kg	F Walker, Manchester YMCA
up to 82kg	S Morley, Wirksworth
up to 90kg	G English, East Kilbride
up to 100kg	A Singh, BAI
over 100kg	M Clempner, Manchester YMCA

YACHTING

Whitbread Round the World Race

P Blake, New Zealand, skipper of Steinlager II in 128d 9h 40m

BOAT RACE RESULTS

Year	Winner	Time	Won by
1988	Oxford	17m 35s	5 lengths
1989	Oxford	18m 27s	2.5 lengths
1990	Oxford	17m 15s	24 lengths

Score to date: Oxford 67 wins; Cambridge 69 wins; dead-heat 1 (in 1877)

MARATHONS

London Marathon

Men	A Hutton, Great Britain
Women	W Panfil Poland

Boston Marathon

Men	G Bordin, Italy
Women	R Mota, Portugal

Chicago Marathon (1989)

Men	P Davies-Hale, Great Britain
Women	L Weidenbach, United States

New York Marathon (1989)

Men	J Ikangaa, Tanzania
Women	I Kristiansen, Norway

Rotterdam Marathon (1989)

Men	B Dinsamo, Ethiopia
Women	E Murgoci, Romania

SPORTING BODIES

Given below are the addresses of the secretaries

Angling: National Anglers Council, 11 Cowgate, Peterborough PE1 1LZ. Peterborough 54084.
National Federation of Sea Anglers, 26 Downsview Crescent, Uckfield, East Sussex TN22 1UB. Uckfield 3589.
National Federation of Anglers, Halliday House, 2 Wilson Street, Derby DE1 1PG. Derby 362000.
Salmon and Trout Association, Fishmongers' Hall, London Bridge, London EC4R 9EL. 071-626-3531.
Shark Angling Club of Great Britain. The Quay, Looe, Cornwall. 050 36 3375/2642.

Archery: Grand National Archery Society, National Agricultural Centre, Stoneleigh, Kenilworth, Warwickshire CV8 2LG. Coventry 696631.
English Field Archery Association, 64 Macauley Road, Dunstable Road, Luton, Bedfordshire. 0582 68716.

Association Football: Football Association (England), 16 Lancaster Gate, London W2 3LW. 071-262-4542.
Football Association (Scotland) 6 Park Gardens, Glasgow G3 7YF. 041-332- 6372.
Football Association (Irish) 20 Windsor Avenue, Belfast BT9 6EG. N.I. Belfast 669458.
Football Association (Eire), 80 Merion Square, Dublin 2. Dublin 76684.
Football Association (Wales), 3 Westgate Street, Cardiff, South Glamorgan CF1 1JF. Cardiff 372325.
Football League, Lytham St Annes, Lancs. FY8 1JG. Lytham 729421.
Women's Football Association, 448/450 Hanging Ditch, The Corn Exchange, Manchester M4 3ES. 061-832-5911.

Athletics: British Amateur Athletic Board, Edgbaston House, 3 Duchess Place, Hagley Road, Birmingham B16 8NM. 021-456-4050.
Athletic Association, Francis House, Francis Street, London SW1P 1DE. 071-828 9326.
Women's Amateur Athletic Association, Francis House, Francis Street, London SW1P 1DL. 071-828-4731.

Badminton: Badminton Association of England, National Badminton Centre, Bradwell Road, Loughton Lodge, Milton Keynes MK8 9LA. Milton Keynes 568822.

Baseball: British Amateur Baseball and Softball Federation. 197 Newbridge Road, Hull, Humberside HU9 2LR. Hull 76169.

Basketball: English Basketball Association, Calomax House, Lupton Avenue, Leeds LS9 7EE. Leeds 496044.

Billiards and Snooker: Billards and Snooker Control Council, Coronet House, Queen street, Leeds LS1 2TN. Leeds 440586.

Board Sailing: U.K. Board Sailing Association, Masons Road, Stratford upon Avon. Warwickshire. Stratford 299574.

Bobsleigh: British Bobsleigh Association, 111 Cheyne Walk, London SW10 0DJ. 071-351-5120.

Bowling: English Indoor Bowling Association, 290a Barking Road, London E6 3BA. 071-470-1237.

Bowls: British Crown Green Bowling Association, 14 Leighton Avenue, Maghull, Liverpool L31 0AH. 051-526-8367.
English Women's Bowling Association, 'Daracombe', The Clays, Market Lavington, Devizes, Wiltshire SN10 4AY. 0380-813774.

Boxing: Amateur Boxing Association, Francis House, Francis Street, London SW1P 1DE. 071-828-8568.
British Boxing Board of Control (1929), 7d Vauxhall Bridge Road, London SW1V 2RP. 071-828-2133.

Canoeing: British Canoe Union, Mapperley Hall, Lucknow Avenue, Nottingham, NG3 5FA. 0602-691994.

Caving: National Caving Association, c/o The White Lion, Ynys Uchaf, Ystradgyniais, Swansea, SA9 1RWQ. 0639-849519.

Cricket: The Cricket Council, Lord's Ground, London NW8 8QN. 071-286-4405.
National Cricket Association, Lord's Ground, London NW8 8QN. 071-289 6098.
Women's Cricket Association, 16 Upper Woburn Place, London WC1H 0QF. 071-387 3423

Croquet: The Croquet Association, Hurlingham Club, Ranelagh Gardens, London SW6 3PR. 071-736 3148.

Curling: Royal Caledonian Curling Club, 2 Coates Crescent, Edinburgh EH3 7AN. 031-225 7083.
English Curling Association, 66 Preston Old Road, Freckleton, Preston, Lancashire. Preston 634154.

Cycling: British Cycling Federation, 36 Rockingham Road, Kettering, Northants. NN16 8HG. 0536 412211
Cyclists' Touring Club, Cotterell House, 69 Meadow, Godalming, Surrey GU7 7HS. Godalming 7217.
Road Time Trials Council, Dallacre, Mill Road, Yarwell, Peterborough PE8 6PS. Stamford 782464.

Darts: British Darts Organisation, 2 Pages Lane, Muswell Hill, London N10 1PS. 01-883 5544.

Equestrianism: British Horse Society, British Equestrian Centre, Stoneleigh, Kenilworth, Warwickshire CV8 2LR. Coventry 696697.

Fencing: Amateur Fencing Association. The de Beaumont Centre, 83 Perham Road, West Kensington, London W14 9SP. 071-385 7442.

Fives: Rugby Fives Association, 1 Kennington Road, London SE1 7QR. 071-620-0383.
Eton Fives Association, Saintbury Close, Saintbury, Nr. Broadway, Worcestershire. 038685-3564.

Gliding: British Gliding Association, Kimberley House, 47 Vaughan Way, Leicester LE1 4SG. Leicester 531051.
British Hang Gliding Association, Cranfield Airfield, Cranfield, Bedford MK43 0YR. Bedford 751688.

Golf: Royal and Ancient Golf Club, St. Andrews, Fife KY16 9JD. St.Andrews 72112.
Ladies' Golf Union, 'The Scores', St.Andrews, Fife, KY16 9AT. 0334- 75811.
English Golf Union, 1-3 Upper King Street, Leicester LE1 6XF. Leicester 553042.

Greyhound Racing: National Greyhound Racing Club Ltd., 24/28 Oval Road, London NW1 7DA. 071-267 9256.

Gymnastics: British Amateur Gymnastics Association, Ford Hall, Lilishall National Sports Centre, Nr Newport, Shropshire. TF10 9NB. 0952-820330.

Handball: British Handball Association, Bridgefield Forum Leisure Centre, Cantbridge Lane, Halewood, Liverpool L26 6LH.

Hang Gliding: British Hang Gliding Association, Cranfield Airfield, Cranfield, Beds MK43 0YR. 0234-751688.

Hockey, Field: Hockey Association, 16 Northdown Street, London N1 9BG. 071-837 8878.
All-England Women's Hockey Association, Argyle House, 29-31 Euston Road, London NW1. 071-278 6340.

Hockey, Ice: British Ice Hockey Association, 40 Hambledon Road, Boscombe East, Bournemouth, Dorset BH7 6PQ. 0202-303946.

Horse Racing: The Jockey Club, 42 Portman Square, London W1H 0EN. 071-486 4921.

Jogging: National Jogging Association, Newstead Abbey Park, Newstead, Nottinghamshire. Mansfield 793496.

Judo: British Judo Association, 9 Islington High Street, London N1 9LQ. 071-833 4424.

Lacrosse: English Lacross Union, Ryecroft Mills, Smith Street, Ashton-under-Lyne, Greater Manchester OL7 0DB. 061-339 7508.
All-England Women's Lacrosse Association, Francis House, Francis Street, London SW1P 1DE. 071-931 8899.

Lawn Tennis: All-England Lawn Tennis and Croquet Club, Church Road, Wimbledon, London SW19 5AE. 01-946 2244.
Lawn Tennis Association, Baron's Court, West Kensington, London W14 9EG. 071-385 2366.

Motor Cycling: Auto-Cycle Union, Millbuck House, Corporation Street, Rugby CV21 2DN. Rugby 70332.

Motor Racing: RAC Motor Sports Association Ltd., Riverside Park, Colnbrook, Slough, SL3 0HG 0753-681736.

Mountaineering: British Mountaineering Council, Crawford House, Precinct Centre, Booth Street East, Manchester M13 9RZ. 061-273 5835.

Netball: All-England Netball Association, Francis House, Francis Street, London SW1P 1DE. 071-828 2176.

Olympic Games: British Olympic Association, 1 Church Row, Wandsworth Plain, london SW18 1EH. 071-871 2677.

Orienteering: British Orienteering Federation, Riversdale, Dale Road North, Darley Dale, Matlock, Derbyshire DE4 1JB. Matlock 734042.

Parachuting: British Parachute Association, Kimberley House, 47 Vaughan Way, Leicester LE1 4SG. Leicester 519635 or 519778.

Petanque: British Petanque Association, PO Box 87, Leatherhead, Surrey. KT22 8LA. 0372-386860.

Physical Recreation, Central Council of: Francis House, Francis Street, London SW1P 1DE. 071-828 3163.

Polo: Hurlingham Polo Association, Ambersham Farm, Ambersham, Midhurst, West Sussex GU29 0BX. 077985 277.

Racketball: British Racketball Association, 50 Tredegar Road, Wilmington, Dartford, Kent DA2 7AZ. Dartford 72200.

Roller Hockey: National Roller Hockey Association of Great Britain, 528 Loose Road, Maidstone, Kent. ME15 9YF. Maidstone 43155.

Rounders: National Rounders Association, 3 Denehurst Avenue, Nottingham NG8 5DA. Nottingham 785514.

Rowing: Amateur Rowing Association, 6 Lower Mall, Hammersmith, London W6 9DL. 01-748 3632/3.

Rugby Football: Rugby Football Union, Whitton Road, Twickenham, Middlesex. TW2 7RQ. 081-892 8161.
British Amateur Rugby League Association, Britannic Building, 3 Upperhead Row, Huddersfield, West Yorkshire HD1 2JL. Huddersfield 44131.
Rugby Football League, 180 Chapeltown Road, Leeds. LS7 4HT. Leeds 624637.

Shooting: National Rifle Association, Bisley Camp, Brookwood, Woking, Surrey GU24 0NY. 04867-2213.

13

13 SPORT

National Smallbore Rifle Association, Lord Robert's House, Bisley Camp, Brookwood, Woking, Surrey GU24 0NP. Brookwood 6969.

Clay Pigeon Shooting Association, 107 Epping New Road, Buckhurst Hill, Essex. IG9 5TQ. 01-505 6221.

Show Jumping: British Show Jumping Association, British Equestrian Centre, Stoneleigh, Kenilworth, Warwickshire CV8 2LR. 0203 969516.

Skateboarding: English Skateboard Association, 2 Northcliffe Heights, Marlpool Lane, Kidderminster, Worcs. DY11 5DA. 0562-74493.

Skating: National Skating Association of Great Britain. 15-27 Gee Street, London EC1V 2RU. 071-253 3824.

Ski-ing: British Ski Federation, Brocades House, Pyrford Road, West Byfleet, Weybridge, Surrey. KT14 6RA. 0932-336488.

Speedway: Speedway Control Board, 'Larchmont', Skinners Lane, Ashtead, Surrey. KT21 2NN. Ashtead 76905.

Sports Council: 16 Upper Woburn Place, London WC1H 0QP. 071-388 1277.

Squash Rackets: Squash Rackets Association, Francis House, Francis Street, London SW1P 1DE. 071-828 3064.

Women's Squash Rackets Association, 345 Upper Richmond Road West, London SW14 8QN. 01-876 6219.

Surfing: British Surfing Association, Room G5, Burrows Chambers, East Burrows Road, Swansea. SA1 1RF. Swansea 461476.

Swimming: Amateur Swimming Association, Harold Fern House, Derby Square, Loughborough. LE11 0AL. Loughborough 230431.

Table Tennis: English Table Tennis Association, 21 Claremont, Hastings, East Susex. TN34 1HA. Hastings 0424-722525.

Tenpin Bowling: British Tenpin Bowling Association, 19 Canterbury Avenue, Ilford, Essex. IG1 3NA. 071-478 9173.

Trampolining: British Trampoline Federation, 152a College Road, Harrow, Middlesex. 01-863 7278.

Tug of War: Tug of War Association, 57 Lynton Road, Chesham, Bucks. AP5 2BT. 0494 783057.

Volleyball: English Volleyball Association, 13 Rectory Road, West Bridgford, Nottingham NG2 6BE. Nottingham 816324.

Water Ski: British Water Ski Federation, 390 City Road, London EC1V 2QA. 071-833 2855.

Weightlifting: British Amateur Weighlifters Association, 3 Iffley Turn, Oxford. Oxford 778319.

Wrestling: English Olympic Wrestling Association, 2 Huxley Drive, Bramhall, Stockport, Cheshire. 061-439 5749. 061-832 9209 (Office).

British Amateur Wrestling Association. 061-226 2641.

Yachting: Royal Yachting Association, Victoria Way, Woking, Surrey. GU21 1EQ. Woking 5022.

Royal Ocean Racing Club, 20 St James's Palace, London SW1A 1NN. 071-493 5252/071-499 4264.

Yoga: British Wheel of Yoga, Grafton Grange, Grafton. York. YO5 9QQ. Boroughbridge 3386.

WORLD RECORDS

ASSOCIATION FOOTBALL
Peter Shilton. England. In 1989 he became England's most capped footballer when he surpassed Bobby Moore's record of 108 caps. Has played over 800 Football League games for Leicester City, Stoke City, Nottingham Forest, Southampton and Derby County. He retired from International football after the 1990 World Cup having won a world record 125 caps.

ATHLETICS
Men:
Alfred A. Oerter, U.S.A. Only athlete to win same title at four successive Olympic Games - Discus, 1956, 1960, 1964 and 1968.
Women:
Fanny Blankers Koen, Netherlands. Only woman to win four track and field gold medals at one Olympics (London 1948).

BADMINTON
Men:
Eddie Choong, Malaya. Only man to win more than 60 senior international championships (1950-58).
Women:
Judy Hashman, U.S.A. Only woman to win All-England and U.S.A. championships 10 or more times (1953-67).

BOBSLEIGH
Men:
Eugenio Monti, Italy. Only man to win two Olympic gold medals and 11 world titles (1957-68).

BOWLS (LAWN)
Men:
David Bryant, England. Only man to win world championship titles at singles (1966, 1980, 1988), triples (1980), fours (1972) and team titles (1980 and 1988). Has won Commonwealth Games singles title four times (1962, 1970, 1974, 1978) and British singles title seven times (1964-1979).
Women:
Mavis Steele, England. Only woman to win national singles championship three times (1961, 1962, 1969) and share titles at pairs, triples and fours.

BOXING
Amateur:
Oliver Kirk, U.S.A. Only man to win two titles at one Olympics - bantam and featherweight, (St. Louis 1904).
Professional:
Joe Louis, U.S.A. remained unbeaten in record 12 years as heavyweight champion of world in which he made a record 25 defences (1937-1949).

CANOEING
Men:
Gert Fredriksson, Sweden. Only man to win six gold medals at four Olympic Games (1948-60).
Women:
Ludmila Pinayeva (nee Khvedosyuk), U.S.S.R. Only woman to win three Olympic gold medals (1964, 1968, 1972).

CRICKET
Men:
Sir Garfield Sobers, Barbados. Only man to have captained West Indies in 39 successive Tests in a world record 80 consecutive appearances; to have hit six successive sixes, to have exceeded 25,000 runs in first-class cricket; and to have taken more than 1,000 wickets.

CYCLING
Eddie Merckx, Belgium. Only rider to win world amateur and three professional world championships accompanied by five successes in Tour de France and 350 major races.

GOLF
Amateur:
Robert Jones, U.S.A. Only golfer to win British Open and Amateur and U.S. Open and Amateur in the same year (1930). He was unbeaten in five Walker Cup matches (1922-30).

Professional:

Jack Nicklaus, U.S.A. Winner of more major golf titles than anyone else in the world - U.S. Masters six times; U.S. Open four times; U.S. P.G.A. five times; British Open three times and U.S. Amateur twice. (1959-80).

Women:

Catherine Lacoste, France. Only woman to win U.S. Open, U.S. Amateur, British Open and French Open championships (1965-69).

LAWN TENNIS

Men:

Rod Laver, Australia. Only champion to win Wimbledon, United States, French and Australian titles in same years twice (1962, 1969).

Women:

Margaret Court, Australia. Won a record 66 Grand Slam events 1960-75 (Wimbledon, United States, Australian and French titles), including a record 24 at singles. The only woman to have won Grand Slam at singles (1970) and mixed doubles (1963).

MOTOR RACING

Men:

Juan Fangio, Argentina. Only man to win world racing drivers' championship five times (1951-57).

ROWING

Men:

Jack Beresford, Great Britain. Only man to win Olympic gold medals for sculls, double sculls and fours and silvers for eights and sculls (1920- 36).

RUGBY FOOTBALL

Amateur:

Mike Gibson, Ireland. Only man to have represented his country in 69 international matches (1964-79). He has also equalled his fellow countryman Willie John McBride's record of five Lions tours.

Professional:

James Sullivan, Wales. Made a record 60 international appearances 1921-39 and kicked a record 160 goals. Made record 921 appearances in his career 1921-46, kicked record 2859 goals and scored 6006 points.

SKATING (FIGURE)

Men:

Richard Button, U.S.A. Only man to win two individual gold medals and five world championships (1948-1952).

Women:

Sonja Henie, Norway. Only woman to win solo gold medals at three successive Olympics (1928-32-36) and ten world and eight European titles.

SKATING (SPEED)

Men:

Eric Heiden, U.S.A. Only skater to win all five gold medals at one Olympic Games (Lake Placid 1980).

Women:

Lidija Skoblikova, U.S.S.R. Only woman to win four gold medals at one Olympics (1964).

SKI-ING (ALPINE)

Men:

Toni Sailer, Austria. Only man to win seven world championships including three Olympic gold medals (1958-66).

Women:

Marielle Goitschel, France. Only woman to win two Olympic and three world gold medals (1964-68).

SKI-ING (NORDIC)

Men:

Sixtern Jenberg, Sweden. Only man to win four Olympic and four world gold medals (1956-64).

Women:

Galina Koulakova, U.S.S.R. Only woman to collect gold (3), silver and bronze Olympic medals (1968, 1972).

SWIMMING

Men:

Mark Spitz, U.S.A. Only swimmer to win seven gold medals at one Olympic Games (1972). Spitz won all his medals in world record times.

Women:

Greta Andersen, Denmark and U.S.A. Only woman to win Olympic sprint gold medal, win English cross-Channel race against men; and set England-France record (1948-1957).

SWIMMING (ENGLISH CHANNEL)

Men:

Desmond Renford, Australia. Only man to have swum the Channel 14 times, including both directions, and twice within five days (1970-79).

Women:

Cynthia Nicholas, Canada. Only woman to have swum the Channel eight times, including twice two-way non-stop in record times (1975-79).

TABLE TENNIS

Men:

Victor Barna, Hungary and England. Only player to win 21 world titles, including singles five times (1928-39).

Women:

Angelica Rozeanu, Romania. Only woman to win 16 world titles, including singles six times (1948-56).

WEIGHT LIFTING

Tommy Kono, U.S.A. Only man to win six world titles and Olympic medals at three different weights (1952-60).

SPORTSMAN AND WOMAN OF THE YEAR

The Sports Writers Association elect by ballot each year the Sportsmen and the Sportswomen of the Year. The winners since 1975 have been :

1976	**James Hunt** (Motor racing)
	Gillian Gilks (Badminton)
1977	**Barry Sheene** (Motor cycling)
	Virginia Wade (Tennis)
1978	**Daley Thompson** (Athletics)
	Sharron Davies (Swimming)
1979	**Sebastian Coe** (Athletics)
	Caroline Bradley (Show jumping)
1980	**Sebastian Coe** (Athletics)
	Sharron Davies (Swimming)
1981	**Sebastian Coe** (Athletics)
	Jayne Torvill (Ice dancing)
1982	**Daley Thompson** (Athletics)
	Wendy Norman (Modern pentathlon)
1983	**Steve Cram** (Athletics)
	Joe Durie (Tennis)
1984	**Sebastian Coe** (Athletics)
	Tessa Sanderson (Athletics)
1985	**Steve Cram** (Athletics)
	Virginia Holgate (Equestrian)
1986	**Lloyd Honeyghan** (Boxing)
	Fatima Whitbread (Athletics
1987	**Nick Faldo** (Golf)
	Fatima Whitbread (Athletics)
1988	**Sandy Lyle** (golf)
	Liz McColgan (Athletics)
1989	**Nick Faldo** (Golf)
	Y Murray (Athletics)

HISTORY OF THE COMMONWEALTH GAMES

THE 'COMMONWEALTH Olympics' were inaugurated at Hamilton, Ontario, in 1930 following a get-together of British Empire competitors at the Olympic Games of 1928, in Amsterdam. They wanted a less formal and more friendly festival of sport. After 1930 it was agreed to stage a four-yearly series alternating with the Olympics. In 1934 London was host; in 1938 Sydney, Austrlia; in 1950 Auckland, New Zealand; 1954 Vancouver, B.C; 1958 Cardiff, Wales; 1962 Perth, Western Australia; 1966 Kingston, Jamaica; 1970 Edinburgh, Scotland; 1974 Christchurch, New Zealand; 1978 Edmonton, Canada; 1982 Brisbane, Australia; 1986 Edinburgh Scotland; 1990 Auckland, New Zealand. The sports contested at Auckland were: Athletics, Badminton, Bowls, Boxing, Cycling, Gymnastics, Judo, Shooting, Swimming, Weightlifting. The 1994 Games are scheduled for Victoria, Canada.

13

GENERAL INFORMATION

ABBREVIATIONS

A.A.	Autombile Association
A.A.A.	Amateur Athletic Association
A.C.A.	Associate of the Institute of Chartered Accountants
A.C.A.S.	Advisory Conciliation and Arbitration Service
A.C.C.A.	Associate of the Association of Certified Accountants
A.C.I.I.	Associate of the Chartered Insurance Institute
A.C.T.	Australian Capital Territory
A.D.	Anno Domini, in the year of our Lord
A.D.C.	Aide-de-Camp
A.E.R.E.	Atomic Energy Research Establishment
A.F.C.	Air Force Cross
A.F.M.	Air Force Medal
A.G.	Adjutant General
A.G.S.M.	Associate of the Guildhall School of Music
A.I.B.	Associate of the Institute of Bankers
A.I.D.S.	Acquired Immune Deficiency Syndrome
A.K.C.	Associate of King's College
A.L.A.	Associate of the Library Association
A.L.C.D.	Associate of London College of Divinity
A.M.	Ante Meridiem, before noon
A.M.I.C.E.	Associate Member of Institution of Civil Engineers
A.N.C.	African National Congress
A.O.C.	Air Officer Commanding
A.R.A.	Associate of the Royal Academy
A.R.A.M.	Associate of the Royal Academy of Music
A.R.C.M.	Associate of the Royal College of Music
A.R.I.B.A.	Associate of the Royal Institute of British Architects
A.R.I.C.S.	Associate of the Royal Institution of Chartered Surveyors
A.R.P.S.	Associate of Royal Photographic Society
A.S.A.	Amateur Swimming Association
A.S.E.A.N.	Association of South East Asian Nations
A.S.L.E.F.	Associated Society of Locomotive Engineers and Firemen
B.A.	Bachelor of Arts
B.A.A.S.	British Association for the Advancement of Science
B.A.O.R.	British Army of the Rhine
B.B.C.	British Broadcasting Corporation
B.C.	Before Christ
B.Ch.	Bachelor of Surgery
B.C.L.	Bachelor of Civil Law
B.D.A.	British Dental Association
B.Ed.	Bachelor of Education
B.E.M.	British Empire Medal
B.F.P.O.	British Forces Post Office
B.M.A.	British Medical Association
B.Mus.	Bachelor of Music

B.N.O.C.	British National Oil Corporation
B.O.T.B.	British Overseas Trade Board
B.R.C.S.	British Red Cross Society
B.Sc.	Bachelor of Science
B.S.T.	British Summer Time
Bt.	Baronet
C.	Conservative
C.A.	Chartered Accountant
C.B.	Companion of the Bath
C.B.E.	Commander of Order of the British Empire
C.B.I.	Confederation of British Industry
C.E.G.B.	Central Electricity Generating Board
C.Eng.	Chartered Engineer
C.E.N.T.O.	Central Treaty Organisation
C.F.	Chaplain to the Forces
C.G.M.	Conspicuous Gallantry Medal
C.G.S.	Chief of General Staff
C.H.	Companion of Honour
Ch.B.	Bachelor of Surveyor
Ch.M.	Master of Surgery
C.I.	Channel Islands
C.I.A.	Central Intelligence Agency
C.I.D.	Criminal Investigation Department
C.-in-C.	Commander-in-Chief
C.Lit.	Companion of Literature
C.M.G.	Companion of the Order of St Michael and St George
C.N.A.A.	Council for National Academic Awards
C.N.D.	Campaign for Nuclear Disarmament
C.O.	Commanding Officer
C.O.D.	Cash on Delivery
C.O.I.	Central Office of Information
C.R.E.	Commission for Racial Equality
C.V.O.	Commander of the Royal Victorian Order
D.B.E.	Dame Commander of the Order of the British Empire
D.C.B.	Dame Commander of the Bath
D.C.L.	Doctor of Civil Law
D.C.M.	Distinguished Conduct Medal
D.C.M.G.	Dame Commander of St Michael and St George
D.C.V.O.	Dame Commander of the Royal Victorian Order
D.D.	Doctor of Divinity
D.F.C.	Distinguished Flying Cross
D.F.M.	Distinguished Flying Medal
D.H.S.S.	Department of Health and Social Security
D.Lit.or Litt.	Doctor of Letters or Literature
D.Phil.	Doctor of Philosophy
D.S.C.	Distinguished Service Cross
D.S.O.	Distinguished Service Order
E.C.S.C.	European Coal and Steel Community
E.E.C.	European Economic Community
E.F.T.A.	European Free Trade Association
E.N.G.	Enrolled Nurse General
E.R.D.	Emergency Reserve Decoration
E.R.N.I.E.	Electronic Random Number Indicator Equipment
F.A.	Football Association
F.A.O.	Food and Agriculture Organisation
F.B.A.	Fellow of the British Academy

F.B.I.	Federal Bureau of Investigation
F.C.A.	Fellow of the Institute of Chartered Accountants
F.C.C.A.	Fellow of the Association of Certified Accountants
F.C.I.I.	Fellow of the Chartered Insurance Institute
F.C.I.S.	Fellow of the Chartered Institute of Secretaries
F.I.A.	Fellow of the Institute of Actuaries
F.I.B.	Fellow of the Institute of Bankers
F.I.C.E.	Fellow of Institution of Civil Engineers
F.L.S.	Fellow of the Linnaean Society
F.M.	Field Marshal
F.R.Ae.S.	Fellow of the Royal Aeronautical Society
F.R.A.S.	Fellow of the Royal Astronomical Society
F.R.C.M.	Fellow of the Royal College of Music
F.R.C.O.	Fellow of the Royal College of Organists
F.R.C.O.G.	Fellow of the Royal College of Obstetricians and Gynaecologists
F.R.C.P.	Fellow of the Royal College of Physicians
F.R.C.P.E.	Fellow of the Royal College of Physicians of Edinburgh
F.R.C.S.	Fellow of the Royal College of Surgeons
F.R.C.S.E.	Fellow of the Royal College of Surgeons of Edinburgh
F.R.C.V.S.	Fellow of the Royal College of Veterinary Surgeons
F.R.G.S.	Fellow of the Royal Geographical Society
F.R.H.S.	Fellow of the Royal Horticultural Society
F.R.I.B.A.	Fellow of the Royal Institute of British Architects
F.R.I.C.	Fellow of the Royal Institute of Chemistry
F.R.I.C.S.	Fellow of the Royal Institution of Chartered Surveyors
F.R.S.	Fellow of the Royal Society
F.R.S.A.	Fellow of the Royal Society of Art
F.R.S.C.	Fellow of the Royal Society of Chemistry
F.R.S.E.	Fellow of the Royal Society of Edinburgh
F.R.S.L.	Fellow of the Royal Society of Literature
F.S.A.	Fellow of the Sceoity of Antiquaries
F.Z.S.	Fellow of the Zoological Society
G.A.T.T.	General Agreement on Tariffs and Trade
G.B.E.	Knight or Dame Grand Cross of the Order of the British Empire
G.C.	George Cross
G.C.B.	Knight or Dame Grand Cross of the Bath
G.C.E.	General Certificate of Education
G.C.I.E.	Knight Grand Commander of the Indian Empire
G.C.M.G.	Knight or Dame Grand Cross of St Michael and St George
G.C.S.E.	General Certificate of Secondary Education
G.C.S.I.	Knight Grand Commander of the Star of India
G.C.V.O.	Knight or Dame Grand Cross of Royal Victorian Order
G.D.R.	German Democratic Republic
G.H.Q.	General Headquarters
G.M.	George Medal
G.M.T.	Greenwich Mean Time
G.O.C.	General Officer Commanding
H.E.	His Excellency: His Eminence
H.M.L.	Her Majesty's Lieutenant
H.M.S.	Her Majesty's Ship or Service
H.M.S.O.	Her Majesty's Stationery Office
I.A.T.A.	International Air Transport Association
I.B.A.	Independent Broadcasting Authority
I.C.A.O.	International Civil Aviation Organisation
i.d.c.	Graduate of Imperial Defence College
I.D.D.	International Direct Dialling
I.F.C.	International Finance Corporation
I.L.E.A.	Inner London Education Authority
I.L.O.	International Labour Organisation
I.M.F.	International Monetary Fund
I.M.O.	International Maritime Organisation
I.N.L.A.	Irish National Liberation Army
I.R.A.	Irish Republican Army
I.T.U.	International Telecommunication Union
J.P.	Justice of the Peace
K.B.E.	Knight Commander Order of the British Empire
K.C.	King's Counsel
K.C.B.	Knight Commander of the Bath
K.C.M.G.	Knight Commander of St Michael and St George
K.C.V.O.	Knight Commander of the Royal Victorian Order
K.G.	Knight of the Garter
K.St.J.	Knight of Order of St John of Jerusalem
K.T.	Knight of the Thistle
L.	Liberal
Lab.	Labour
L.C.J.	Lord Chief Justice
L.D.S.	Licentiate in Dental Surgery
L.G.S.M.	Licentiate of the Guildhall School of Music
Lit.or Litt.D.	Doctor of Letters or Literature
LL.B.	Bachelow of Laws
LL.D.	Doctor of Laws
LL.M.	Master of Laws
L.R.A.M.	Licentiate of the Royal Academy of Music
L.R.C.M.	Licentiate of the Royal College of Music
L.R.C.P.	Licentiate of the Royal College of Physicians
L.R.I.B.A.	Licentiate of the Royal Institute of British Architects
L.S.E.	London School of Economics
L.T.A.	Lawn Tennis Association
L.V.O.	Lieutenant of Royal Victorian Order
M.A.	Master of Arts
M.A.F.F.	Ministry of Agriculture, Fisheries and Food
M.A.O.T.	Member of the Association of Occupational Therapists
M.B.	Bachelor of Medicine
M.B.E.	Member of the Order of the British Empire
M.C.	Military Cross
M.Ch.	Master of Surgery
M.C.C.	Marylebone Cricket Club

M.D.	Doctor of Medicine
M.Ed.	Master of Education
M.E.P.	Member of the European Parliament
M.G.S.M.	Member of the Guildhall School of Music
M.I.C.E.	Member of Institution of Civil Engineers
M.I.C.W.	Member of Institute of Clerks of Works
M.I.Mech.E.	Member of Institution of Mechanical Engineers
M.I.R.A.S.	Mortgage Interest Relief at Source
M.L.R.	Minimum Lending Rate
M.M.	Military Medal
M.O.D.	Ministry of Defence
M.O.H.	Medical Officer of Health
M.P.	Member of Parliament
M.P.S.	Member of Pharmaceutical Society
M.R.A.M.	Member of the Royal Academy of Music
M.R.C.	Medical Research Council
M.R.C.M.	Member of the Royal College of Music
M.R.C.O.G.	Member of Royal College of Obstetricians and Gynaecologists
M.R.C.P.	Member of the Royal College of Physicians
M.R.C.P.E.	Member of Royal College of Physicians Edinburgh
M.R.C.S.	Member of Royal College of Surgeons
M.R.C.S.E.	Member of Royal College of Surgeons Edinburgh
M.R.C.V.S.	Member of Royal College of Veterinary Surgeons
M.R.S.C.	Member of Royal Society of Chemistry
M.S.	Master of Surgery
M.S.C.	Manpower Services Commission
M.Sc.	Master of Science
M.V.O.	Member of Royal Victorian Order
N.A.A.F.I.	Navy, Army and Air Force Institutes
N.A.T.O.	North Atlantic Treaty Organisation
N.C.O.	Non-commissioned Officer
N.E.B.	Natonal Enterprise Board
N.E.D.C.	National Economic Development Council
N.E.R.C.	Natural Environment Research Council
N.P.	Notary Public
N.R.D.C.	National Research Development Corporation
N.S.P.C.C.	National Society for the Prevention of Cruelty to Children
O.B.E.	Officer of Order of the British Empire
O.D.M.	Ministry of Overseas Development
O.E.C.D.	Organisation for Economic Co-operation and Development
O.H.M.S.	On Her Majesty's Service
O.M.	Order of Merit
O.P.E.C.	Organisation of Petroleum Exporting Countries
O.S.B.	Order of St Benedict
O.St.J.	Officer of Order of St John of Jerusalem
P.C.	Privy Counsellor
P.D.S.A.	People's Dispensary for Sick Animals
p.f.c.	Graduate of R.A.F.Flying College
Ph.D.	Doctor of Philosophy
P.L.A.	Port of London Authority
P.L.C.	Public Limited Company
P.M.	Post Meridiem, after noon
P.M.R.A.F.N.S.	Princess Mary's Royal Air Force Nursing Service
P.P.S.	Parliamentary Private Secretary
P.R.A.	President of the Royal Academy
P.R.S.	President of the Royal Society
P.R.S.A.	President of the Royal Scottish Academy
P.R.S.E.	President of the Royal Society of Edinburgh
P.S.B.R.	Public Sector Borrowing Requirement
Q.A.R.A.N.C.	Queen Alexandra's Royal Army Nursing Corps
Q.A.R.N.N.S.	Queen Alexandra's Royal Naval Nursing Service
Q.C.	Queen's Counsel
Q.H.C.	Queen's Honorary Chaplain
Q.H.N.S.	Queen's Honorary Nursing Sister
Q.M.G.	Quartermaster-General
Q.P.M.	Queen's Police Medal
R.A.	Royal Academician: Royal Artillery
R.A.E.	Royal Aircraft Establishment
R.Ae.S.	Royal Aeronautical Society
R.B.A.	Member Royal Society of British Artists
R.B.S.	Royal Society of British Sculptors
R.C.M.	Royal College of Music
R.G.N.	Registered General Nurse
R.H.S.	Royal Horticultural Society
R.I.	Member Royal Institute of Painters in Water Colours
R.M.A.	Royal Military Academy
R.S.A.	Royal Society of Arts
R.S.C.N.	Registered Sick Children's Nurse
R.S.E.	Royal Society of Edinburgh
R.S.P.C.A.	Royal Society for the Prevention of Cruelty to Animals
R.W.S.	Member Royal Society of Painters in Water Colours
S.D.L.P.	Social Democratic and Labour Party
S.E.A.T.O.	South East Asia Treaty Organisation
S.E.N.	State Enrolled Nurse
S.N.P.	Scottish National Plan
S.R.N.	State Registered Nurse
T.A.	Territorial Army
Toc.H.	Talbot House
T.U.C.	Trades Union Congress
U.E.F.A.	Union of European Football Associations
U.G.C.	University Grants Committee
U.K.	United Kingdom
U.K.A.E.A.	United Kingdom Atomic Energy Authority
U.N.	United Nations
U.N.C.T.A.D.	United Nations Commission for Trade and Development
U.N.E.S.C.O.	United Nations Educational Scientific and Cultural Organisation
U.N.I.C.E.F.	United Nations International Children's Emergency Fund
U.S.A.	United States of America
U.S.S.R.	Union of Soviet Socialist Republic
V.A.T.	Value-added Tax
V.C.	Victoria Cross
V.R.D.	Volunteer Reserve Decoration
W.E.A.	Workers' Educational Association
W.H.O.	World Health Organisation
Wh.Sch.	Whitworth Scholar
W.M.O.	World Meteorological Organisation
W.R.A.C.	Women's Royal Army Corps
W.R.A.F.	Women's Royal Air Force
W.R.N.S.	Women's Royal Naval Service
W.R.V.S.	Women's Royal Voluntary Service
W.S.	Writer to the Signet
Y.H.A.	Youth Hostels Association
Y.M.C.A.	Young Men's Christian Association
Y.W.C.A.	Young Women's Christian Association

14

ROMAN NUMERALS

I	1	XXX	30
II	2	XL	40
III	3	L	50
IV	4	LX	60
V	5	LXX	70
VI	6	LXXX	80
VII	7	XC	90
VIII	8	C	100
IX	9	CC	200
X	10	CCC	300
XI	11	CD	400
XII	12	D	500
XIII	13	DC	600
XIV	14	DCC	700
XV	15	DCCC	800
XVI	16	CM	900
XVII	17	M	1000
XVIII	18	MCM	1900
XIX	19	MM	2000
XX	20	MMM	3000

Note - A dash line over a numeral multiplies the value by 1,000: thus $\overline{X} = 10,000$; $\overline{L} = 50,000$; $\overline{C} = 100,000$; $\overline{D} = 500,000$; $\overline{M} = 1,000,000$; $\overline{CLIX} = 159,000$; $\overline{DLIX} = 559,000$. Other general rules in Roman numerals are:
1. A letter repeated once or twice repeats its value that many times. (XXX = 30, CC = 200, etc.).
2. One or more letters placed after another letter of greater value increases the greater value by the amount of the smaller. (VI = 6, LXX = 70, MCC = 1,200, etc.)
3. A letter placed before another letter of greater value decreases the greater value by the amount of the smaller. (IV = 4, XC = 90, CM = 900, etc.)

THE ARMED FORCES AND DEFENCE

Chief of the Defence Staff
Marshall of the Air Force Sir David Craig, C.C.B., O.B.E.
Vice-Chief of the Defence Staff
General Sir Richard Vincent, K.C.B., D.S.O.

THE ROYAL NAVY

Chief of Naval Staff and First Sea Lord
Admiral Sir Julian Oswald, G.C.B., A.D.C.
Chief of Naval Personnel and Second Sea Lord
Vice Admiral Sir Brian Brown, K.C.B., C.B.E.
Controller of the Navy
Vice-Admiral Sir Kenneth Baton, K.C.B.
Chief of Fleet Support
Vice-Admiral Sir Jock Slater, K.C.B., L.V.O.
Director of Women's Royal Naval Service
Commandant Larken, A.D.C., W.R.N.S.
Matron-in-Chief Queen Alexandra's Royal Naval Nursing Service
Miss J. Titley, R.R.C., Q.H.N.O.
Chaplain of the Fleet
MHQ Henley, Q.H.C., L.T.H.
Commandant-General, Royal Marines
Lt. Gen. Henry Beverley, O.B.E., D.S.O.

ADMIRALS OF THE FLEET
(in order of appointment)

His Royal Highness the Prince Philip, Duke of Edinburgh, K.G., K.T., O.M., G.B.E.
Sir Varyl Begg, G.C.B., D.S.O., D.S.C.
Lord Hill-Norton, G.C.B.
Sir Michael Pollock, G.C.B., M.V.O., D.S.C.
Sir Edward Ashmore, G.C.B., D.S.C.
Lord Lewin, K.G., G.C.B., M.V.O., D.S.C.
Sir Henry Leach, G.C.B.
Sir John Fieldhouse, G.C.B., G.B.E. (Chief of Defence Staff)
Sir William Staveley, G.C.B.

NAVAL COMMANDS AND COMMANDERS

Commander-in-Chief Fleet
Admiral Sir Benjamin Bathurst, K.C.B.
Commander-in-Chief Naval Home Command
Admiral Sir Jeremy Black, K.C.B., D.S.O., M.B.E., A.D.C.
Flag Officer Scotland and Northern Ireland
Vice-Admiral Sir Michael Livesay, K.C.B.
Flag Officer Plymouth
Vice-Admiral Sir Alan Grose, K.C.B.
Flag Officer Naval Aviation
Rear-Admiral M.H.G. Layard, C.B.E.
Flag Officer (Submarines), also Comsub Eastlant (NATO)
Vice admiral Sir John Coward, K.C.B., D.S.O.

STRENGTH OF THE FLEET, 1990

Operational, preparing for service or engaged in trials or training

27	Submarines	38	Mine countermeasures vessels
2	ASW carriers		
2	Assault ship	23	Patrol craft
12	Guided missile destroyers	2	Support ships
		1	Royal yacht/hospital ship
33	Frigates	4	Training ships
8	Offshore patrol vessels	6	Survey ships
		1	Ice Patrol Ship

Undergoing long refit or conversion, or on standby

6	Submarines	1	Offshore patrol vessel
1	ASW carrier	3	Mine countermeasures vessels
1	Guided missile destroyers	2	Patrol craft
3	Frigates	2	Survey ship

(Strengths at 1 April 1990. Includes ships for completion or disposal during 1990/91)

THE ARMY

Chief of the General Staff
General Sir John Chapple, G.C.B., C.B.E., M.A.
Adjutant-General
General Sir Robert Pascoe, K.C.B., M.B.E.
Quarter-Master-General
Lt.-Gen. Charles Jones, C.B.E.
Master-General of the Ordnance
Lt.-Gen. Sir John Stibbon, K.C.B., O.B.E.
Director, Women's Royal Army Corps
Brigadier Gail Ramsey, M.B.E.
Chaplain-General to the Forces
The Reverend J. Harkness, O.B.E., Q.H.C.
Matron-in-Chief (Army) and Director of Army Nursing Services
Brigadier Jill Field, R.R.C.

FIELD MARSHALS
(in order of appointment)

His Royal Highness the Prince Philip, Duke of Edinburgh, K.G., K.T., O.M., G.B.E.
Lord Harding of Petherton, G.C.B., C.B.E., D.S.O., M.C
Sir Richard A. Hull, K.G., G.C.B., D.S.O., M.A., LL.D.
Sir James Cassels, G.C.B., K.B.E., D.S.O.
Lord Carver, G.C.B., C.B.E., D.S.O., M.C.
Sir Roland Gibbs, G.C.B., C.B.E., D.S.O., M.C.
H.M. King Birendra Bir Bikram Shah Deva of Nepal
Lord Bramall, G.C.B., O.B.E., M.C.
Sir John Stanier, G.C.B., M.B.E.

GENERALS

Sir John Chapple, G.C.B., C.B.E.
Chief of the General Staff
Sir Richard Vincent, K.C.B., D.S.O.
Vice Chief of the Defence Staff

14

Sir Antony Walker
Commandant Royal College of Defence Studies
Sir Peter Inge
Commander in Chief British Army of the Rhine
Sir Robert Pascoe, K.C.B., M.B.E.
Adjutant General
Sir John Stibbon, K.C.B., C.B.E.
Master General of the Ordnance
Sir Charles Huxtable, K.C.B., C.B.E.
Commander in Chief United Kingdom Land Forces
Sir John Akehurst, K.C.B., C.B.E.
Deputy Supreme Allied Commander Europe
Sir Patrick Palmer, K.B.E.
Commander in Chief Allied Forces Northern Europe

LIEUTENANT GENERALS

Sir Edward Jones, K.C.B., C.B.E.
Quartermaster General
Sir Garry Johnson
Commander Training and Arms Director
Sir David Ramsbotham, K.C.B., C.B.E.
Commander United Kingdom Field Army
Sir Charles Guthrie
Commander 1st British Corps
Sir Peter de la Billiere, K.C.B., C.B.E., D.S.O.
General Officer Commanding South East District
Sir John Macmillan, K.C.B., C.B.E.
General Officer Commanding Scotland
Sir John waters, K.C.B., C.B.E.
General Officer Commanding and Director of Military Operations Northern Ireland
Sir John Learmont, K.C.B., C.B.E.
Military Secretary
Sir Anthony Mullens, K.C.B., O.B.E.
Deputy Chief of the Defence Staff (Systems)

THE ROYAL AIR FORCE

Chief of the Air Staff
Air Chief Marshal Sir Peter Harding, G.C.B., F.R.Ae.S., C.B.I.M.

Air Member for Personnel
Air Chief Marshal Sir David Parry-Evans, K.C.B., C.B.E.
Air Member for Supply and Organisation
Air Chief Marshal Sir Brendan Jackson, K.C.B., B.A.
Director, Women's Royal Air Force
Air Commodore R.M.B. Montague, A.D.C.

Matron-in-Chief
Group Capt. E.A.I. Sanderson, Q.H.N.S, R.R.C.
Chaplain-in-Chief
The Venerable B.N. Halfpenny, Q.H.C., M.A.
Director-General of Security and Commandant-General, Royal Air Force Regiment
Air Vice-Marshal G.C. Williams, A.F.C.

MARSHALS OF THE ROYAL AIR FORCE

(in order of appointment)

His Royal Highness the Prince Philip, Duke of Edinburgh, K.G., K.T., O.M., G.B.E.
Sir Dermot Boyle, G.C.B., K.C.V.O., K.B.E., A.F.C.
Lord Elworthy, K.G., G.C.B., C.B.E., D.S.O., M.V.O., D.F.C., A.F.C., M.A.
Sir John Grandy, G.C.B., K.B.E., D.S.O.
Sir Denis Spotswood, G.C.B., C.B.E., D.S.O., D.F.C.
Sir Michael Beetham, G.C.B., C.B.E., D.F.C., A.F.C.
Sir Keith Williamson, G.C.B., A.F.C.
Sir David Craig, G.C.B., O.B.E.

R.A.F. COMMANDS AND COMMANDERS

Air Officers Commanding-in-Chief
Strike
Air Chief Marshal Sir Patrick Hine, K.C.B., A.D.C., C.B.I.M., F.R.Ae.S.
No. 18 (Maritime) Group
Air Marshal Sir Michael Stear, K.C.B., C.B.E.
Support
Air Marshal Sir Michael Graydon, K.C.B., C.B.E.
Air Officers Commander in Chief
Royal Air Force Germany
Air Marshal Sir Roger Palin, K.C.B., O.B.E., M.A.

STRENGTH OF THE ARMED FORCES

As at 1st January 1990

Royal Navy	57,000
Royal Marines	7,900
Army	158,400
Royal Air Force	89,609
Total	**312,909**

COMPARATIVE RANKS IN THE FORCES

ROYAL NAVY AND W.R.N.S.	ARMY AND W.R.A.C.*	ROYAL AIR FORCE AND W.R.A.F.*
Admiral of the Fleet	Field-Marshal	Marshal of the Royal Air Force
Admiral	General	Air Chief Marshal
Vice-Admiral	Lieutenant-General	Air Marshal
Rear-Admiral	Major-General	Air Vice-Marshal
Commodore/Commandant W.R.N.S.	Brigadier	Air Commodore
Captain/Superintendent W.R.N.S.	Colonel	Group Captain
Commander/Chief Officer W.R.N.S.	Lieutenant-Colonel	Wing Commander
Lieutenant-Commander/First Officer W.R.N.S	Major	Squadron Leader
Lieutenant/Second Officer, W.R.N.S	Captain	Flight-Lieutenant
Sub-Lieutenant/Third Officer, W.R.N.S	Lieutenant	Flying Officer
Acting Sub-Lieutenant	Second Lieutenant	Pilot Officer

* Officers in the Royal Marines and in the Women's Royal Army Corps are titled similarly to the Army ranks. Royal Marine officers' ranks ashore are of equal seniority with Army officers' ranks. When afloat, ranks of Major and below in the Royal Marines are considered one grade higher, i.e. a Major is equivalent to a Commander, R.N.
Officers in the Women's Royal Air Force are titled similarly to the R.A.F. ranks.

BRITAIN'S TALLEST BUILDINGS

The tallest building in Britain is the 183 m (600 ft) National Westminster Tower in Old Broad Street, London. The Tower was topped out in March 1077, completed in 1981 and opened by the Queen on June 11, 1981.

The London Telecom Tower, in Maple Street W1 was opened in 1965 and is 177 m (580 ft) high. The mast which surmounts it adds another 12 m (40 ft). The Tower provides microwave radio channels to carry telehone calls and TV programmes between London and all parts of the country. The IBA mast at Belmont 385 m (1m265 ft) is the UK's tallest structure. The Emley Moor mast 329.18 m (1080 ft) is the tallest concrete structure, the concrete section being 274 m (900 ft) high and made of 20,000 tons of concrete

14

GOVERNMENT, PUBLIC OFFICES, SOCIETIES, INSTITUTES AND CHARITIES

Advertising Association: Abford House, 15 Wilton Road, London SW1V NJ. 071-828 2771. Director-General: R.H. Underhill.

Advisory Conciliation and Arbitration Service: 27 Wilton Street, London SW1X 7AX. 071-210 3000. Chairman: D.B. Smith, C.B.

Agricultural and Food Research Council: Central Office, Wiltshire Court, Farnsby Street, Swindon SN1 5AT. 0793 514242. Chairman: The Earl of Selborne, D.L.

Amnesty International (British section), 99-110 Roseberry Avenue, London EC1R 4RD. 071 278 6000. Director: Marie Staunton.

Architectural Association (Inc.): 34-36 Bedford Square, **London WC1B 3ES. 071-636 0974. President:** Gerald Levin, B. Arch. (CT), A.R.I.B.A., M.R.T.P.I.

Arts Council of Great Britain: 105 Piccadilly, London W1V 0AU. 071- 629 9495. Chairman: Christopher Palumbo. Secretary General: Luke Rittner. The Arts Council Shop, 8 Long Acre, London WC2E 9LG. 071-836 1359. Hayward Gallery, South Bank, London SE1. 071-928 3144. Serpentine Gallery, Kensington Gardens, London W2. 071-402 6075.

Association for Protection of Rural Scotland: 14A Napier Road, Edinburgh EH10 5AY. 031-229 1898. Director: Robert L. Smith, O.B.E., F.R.I.C.S.

Atomic Energy Authority, United Kingdom: 11 Charles II Street, London SW1Y 4QP. 071-930 5454.

Attorney General's Chambers: Law Officers' Department, Royal Courts of Justice, London WC2A 2LL. 071-936 6602. Attorney General: The Rt. Hon. Sir Patrick Mayhew, Q.C., M.P.

Baltic Exchange Ltd.: St. Mary Axe, London EC3A 8BU. 071-623 5501. Chairman: R.B. Hunt. Vice Chairman: D.W. Frame. Secretary: D.J. Walker.

Bank of England: Threadneedle Street, London EC2R 8AH. 071-601 4444. Governor: Rt. Hon. Robin Leigh-Pemberton.

Bankruptcy Court: Thomas More Building, Royal Courts of Justice, Strand, London WC2A 2LL. Chief Registrar: John Bradburn.

Biological Engineering Society: Royal College of Surgeons, Lincoln's Inn Fields, London WC2A 3PN. 071-242 7750. President: Dr. S.A. Meldrum, B.Sc., Ph.D.

Blood Transfusion (Scottish National Service): Headquarters Unit, 21 Ellen's Glen Road, Edinburgh EH17 7QT. 031-664 2317.

Blood Transfusion Service: England and Wales: Health Services Division, Dept. of Health and Social Security, Hannibal House, Elephant and Castle, London SE1 6TE. 071-703 6380. Northern Ireland: 89 Durham Street, Belfast BT12 4GE. 0232 46464.

Board of Customs and Excise: King's Beam House, 22 Upper Ground, London SE1 9pJ. 071-62 1313. Chairman: J.B. Unwin.

Board of Inland Revenue: Somerset House, London WC2R 1LB. 071-438 6622. Chairman: Sir Anthony Battishill. Edinburgh: Chief Valuer Scotland, Meldrum House, 15 Drumsheugh Gardens, Edinburgh EH3 7UN. 031-225 8511. Chief Valuer: J.A. Sutherland.

Book Trust: Book House, 45 East Hill, London SW18 2QZ. (An independent charitable organisation that exists to promote books and reading.) 081-870 9055/8. Director: Martyn Goff, O.B.E.

British Aerospace plc: 11 The Strand, London WC2. Chairman: Sir Austin Pearce. Secretary: B. Cookson.

British Airports Authority: Corporate Office, Gatwick Airport, Gatwick, West Sussex RH6 0HZ. Gatwick 517755. Chairman: Sir Norman Payne, C.B.E. Managing Director: John Mulkern. Responsible for: Heathrow, Gatwick, Stansted, Glasgow, Edinburgh, Prestwick and Aberdeen Airports.

British Airways plc: Head Office: Speedbird House, P.O. Box 10, London Airport Heathrow, Hounslow, Middlesex. 081-759 5511. Chairman: Lord King of Wartnaby. Chief Executive: Sir Colin Marshall.

British Archaeological Association: 61 Old Park Ridings, Winchmore Hill, London N21 2ET. Hon. Assistant Treasurer and Secretary: Miss I.B. McClure.

British Association for the Advancement of Science : Fortress House, 23 Savile Row, London W1X 1AB. 071-734 6010. President 1986-87: Sir Kenneth Durham. Executive Secretary: Dr. D.W. Morley.

British Association of Social Workers: 16 Kent Street, Birmingham B5 6RD. 021-622 3911. General Secretary: David N. Jones, B.A.(Hons.), M.A., C.Q.S.W.

British Board of Film Classification: 3 Soho Square, London W1V 5DE. 071-439 7961. President: The Earl of Harewood. Director: James Ferman, M.A.

British Broadcasting Corporation: Broadcasting House, Portland Place, London W1A 1AA. 071-580 4468. Director-General: Michael Checkland.

British Coal: Hobart House, Grosvenor Place, London SW1X 7AE. 071-235 2020. Chairman: Sir Robert Haslam.

British Computer Society (Incorporated by Royal Charter 1984): 13 Mansfield Street, London W1M 0BP. 071-637 0471.

British Council: 10 Spring Gardens, London SW1A 2BN. 071-930 8466. Chairman: Sir David Orr, M.C., LL.D. Director-General: Sir John Burgh, K.C.M.G., C.B.

British Council of Productivity Associations (British Productivity Council): The Management College, Green lands, Henley-on-Thames, Oxon. RG9 3AU. Henley-on-Thames 571676. Company Secretary: Ron Edwards.

British Dental Association: 64 Wimpole Street, London W1M 8AL. 071- 935 0875. Secretary: N.H. Whitehouse, B.Ch.D.

British Film Institute: 27 Stephen Street, London W1P 1PL. 071 255 1444. Chairman: Sir Richard Attenborough C.B.E.

British Gas Corporation: Rivermill House, 152 Grosvenor Road, London SW1V 3JL. 071-821 1444. Chairman: Sir Denis Rooke, C.B.E., F.R.S., F.Eng.

British Heart Foundation: 102 Gloucester Place, London W1H 4DH. 071- 935 0185. Director General: Brigadier Peter Tower. Secretary: Marion Grainge, F.C.A.

British Library: National library for the U.K. and centre for reference, lending, bibliographic and other information services based on its vast collections of books, manuscripts, music, newspapers, stamps, patents and recorded sound. Temporary and permanent exhibitions are mounted in the Library's galleries in Great Russell Street, London WC1B 3DG. The Library's reference collections are open to those who need material not readily available elsewhere. Admission for most areas is by a Reader's Pass. There is open access to the Science Reference and Information Service and the National Sound Archive, where a free listening service for its oldings operates. Details of all Library services, addresses and opening times are available from Press and Public Relations, 2 Sheraton Street, London W1V 4BH. 071-323 7111. Chairman: The Lord Quinton.

British Medical Association: B.M.A. House, Tavistock Square, London WC1H 9JP. 071-387 4499. President: Sir Christopher Booth. Secretary: Dr. J.D.J. Havard, M.A., M.D., LL.B.

British Museum: Great Russell Street, London WC1B 3DG. 071-636 1555. Director: Sir David Wilson.

British Overseas Trade Board: 1 Victoria Street, London SW1H 0ET. 071-215 5000.

British Post Office Philatelic Bureau: 20 Brandon Street, Edinburgh EH3 5TT. 031-556 8661.

British Rail: Eastern Region: York YO1 1HT. York 53022. General Manager: D.E. Rayner.

British Rail: London Midland Region: Stanier House, 10 Holliday Street, Birmingham B1 1TG. 021-643 4444. General Manager: C. Bleasdale.

British Rail: Scottish Region: ScotRail House, 58 Port Dundas Road, Glasgow G4 0HG. 041-332 9811. General Manager: J.S. Corvell.

British Rail: Southern Region: Waterloo Station, London SE1 8SE. 071-928 5151. General Manager: Gordon Pettitt.

British Rail: Western Region: 125 House, 1 Gloucester Street, Swindon SN1 1DL. Swindon 26100. General Manager: S.B. Newey.

British Railways Board: Euston Square, P.O. Box 100, London NW1 2DZ. 071-262 3232. Chairman: Sir Robert Reid, C.B.E.

British Red Cross Society: 9 Grosvenor Crescent, London SW1X 7EJ. 071-235 5454. Director-General: J.C. Burke-Gaffney.

14

14 GENERAL INFORMATION

Societies and Institutes

British Shipbuilders: 197 Knightsbridge, London SW7 1RB. 071-581 1393. Chairman and Chief Executive: P.D.G. Hares, C.B.E. Corporation Secretary: M. Day. Benton House, 136 Sandyford Road, Newcastle upon Tyne NE2 1QE. Newcastle upon Tyne 091-232 6772.

British Steel Corporation: 9 Albert Embankment, London SE1 7SN. 071- 735 7654. Chairman: Sir Robert Scholey.

British Technology Group (Formerly the National Research Development Corporation): 101 Newington Causeway, London SE1 6BU. 071-403 6666. Chairman: Colin Barker. Secretary: John Morton.

British Technology Group: Northern Office: 9 Hunters Mews, Wilmslow, Cheshire SK9 2AR. 0625 532343.

British Technology Group: Scottish Office: 87 St. Vincent Street, Glasgow G2 5TF. 041-221 1820.

British Telecom: British Telecom Centre, 81 Newgate Street, London EC1A 7AJ. 071-356 5000. Chairman: Sir George Jefferson, C.B.E.

British Theatre Association: Darwin Infill Building, Regent's College, Regent's Park, London NW1 4NS. 071-387 2666. Director: Jane Hackworth-Young.

British Tourist Authority: Thames Tower, Black's Road, London W6 9EL. 081-846 9000. Chairman: Duncan Bluck, O.B.E.

British and Foreign Bible Society: Stonehill Green, Westlea, Swindon, Wiltshire SN5 7DG. Swindon 617381. General Director: Rev. Neville B. Cryer. Executive Director: Richard Worthing-Davies.

Britoil plc: 150 St. Vincent Street, Glasgow G2 5LJ. 041-204 2525; Stornoway House, 13 Cleveland Row, St. James's, London SW1A 1DH. 071- 409 2525; Britoil House, Hill of Rubislaw, Anderson Drive, Aberdeen AB9 8XB. Aberdeen 574555. Chairman: Sir Philip Shelbourne.

Building Societies Association: 3 Savile Row, London W1X 1AF. 071-437 0655. Secretary-General: Richard S. Weir, M.A.

Building Societies Commission (a function of the Registry of Friendly Societies): 15 Great Marlborough Street, LondonW1V 2AX. 071-437 9992, Chairman and First Commissioner: J.M. Bridgeman. Deputy Chairman: G.W. Watson. Commissioner: R.L. Devlin.

Cabinet Office: Whitehall, London SW1A 2AS. 071-270 3000. Secretary of the Cabinet, Permanent Secretary to the Management and Personnel Office and Head of the Home Civil Service: Sir Robin Butler, K.C.B., C.V.O.

Cabinet War Rooms (Imperial War Museum): Clive Steps, King Charles Street, London SW1A 2AQ. 071-930 6961.

Cable and Wireless plc: Mercury House, Theobalds Road, London WC1X 8RX. 071-242 4433. Chairman and Chief Executive: Sir Eric Sharp.

Campaign for Nuclear Disarmament: 22 Underwood Street, London N1 7GA. 071 250 4010. General Secretary: Meg Beresford.

Central Electricity Generating Board: Sudbury House, 15 Newgate Street, London EC1A 7AU. 071-634 5111. Chairman: The Lord Marshall of Goring, Kt., C.B.E., F.R.S.

Central Office of Information: Hercules Road, London SE1 7DU. 071-928 2345. Director-General: G.M. Devereau.

Charity Commission: St. Alban's House, 57-60 Haymarket, London SW1Y 4QX. 071-210 3000. Chief Commissioner: R.I.L. Guthrie.

Chartered Association of Certified Accountants: 29 Lincoln's Inn Fields, London. WC2A 3EE. 071-242 6855. Telex: 24381. President: N. Cannon, F.C.C.A.

Chartered Insurance Institute: 20 Aldermanbury, Lon don EC2V 7HY. 071-606 3835. Secretary-General: P.V. Saxton, F.C.I.I., F.I.T.D., F.B.I.M., F.I.C.O.

Child Poverty Action Group: Bath Street, London EC1V 9PY. 071 253 3406. Director: Fran Bennett

Church Commissioners: 1 Millbank, Westminster, London SW1P 3JZ. 071- 222 7010. Secretary: J.E. Shelley.

City of London Police: 26 Old Jewry, London EC2R 8DJ. 071-601 2222. Commissioner: Owen Kelly, Q.P.M.

Civic Trust (encourages the protection and improvement of the environment): 17 Carlton House Terrace, London SW1Y 5AW. 071-930 0914. Director: M. H. Middleton.

Civic Trust for Wales: Room 4, Llandaff Court, Fairwater Road, Llandaff, Cardiff CF5 2LN. 0222 552388.

Civil Aviation Authority: CAA House, 45-59 Kingsway, London WC2B 6TE. 071-379 7311. Chairman: Christopher Tugendhat. Secretary: Miss G.M.E.White.

Civil Service Commission: Alencon Link, Basingstoke,

Hants RG21 1JB. Basingstoke 0256 29222. First Commissioner: J.H. Holroyd.

College of Arms: Queen Victoria Street, London EC4V 4BT. 071-248 2762. Earl Marshal: The Duke of Norfolk, K.G. C.B., C.B.E.; Garter Principal King of Arms: Sir Colin Cole K.C.V.O., T.D.

College of Occupational Therapists Ltd: 20 Rede Place, Bayswater, London W2 4TU. 071-229 9738. Secretary: Air Commodore G.J.B. Claridge, C.B.E.

College of Radiographers: 14 Upper Wimpole Street, London W1M 8BN. 071-935 5726. Secretary: R. M. Jordan.

Commission for Racial Equality: Elliot House, 10-12 Allington Street, London SW1E 5EH. 071-828 7022. Chairman: Sir Peter Newsam.

Commissioners of Northern Lighthouses: 84 George Street, Edinburgh EH2 3DA. 031-226 7051. Telex: 72551 (NLBG). General Manager: Cdr.J.M. Mackay, M.B.E., R.N. (Ret'd).

Commonwealth Development Corporation: 33 Hill Street, London W1A 3AR. 071-629 8484. Chairman: The Lord Kindersley.

Commonwealth Institute: Kensington High Street, London W8 6NQ. 071-603 4535. Exhibition galleries, Arts Centre (including theatre, cinema, art gallery) licensed restaurant, library and Resources Centre. Recorded information about special events: 071-602 3257. Director: J.F.Porter, M.A., B.Sc., F.C.P. Scottish enquiries to: 8 Rutland Square, Edinburgh 1.

Commonwealth Secretariat: Marlborough House, Pall Mall, London SW1Y 5HX. 071-839 3411. Secretary-General: Shridath Ramphal.

Commonwealth War Graves Commission: 2 Marlow Road, Maidenhead, Berkshire SL6 7DX. 0628 34221. Director-General (Secretary to the Commission): J. Saynor.

Confederation of British Industry: Centre Point, 103 New Oxford Street, London WC1A 1DU. 071-379 7400. Telex: 21332. President: Sir James Cleminson, M.C.

Corporation of London: Guildhall, London EC2P 2EJ. 071-606 3030. Lord Mayor: Elected September each year. Sheriffs: Alderman Hugh Charles Philip Bidwell and Alderman Alexander Michael Graham. Recorder: Sir James William Miskin, Q.C. Chamberlain: Bernard P. Harty. Town Clerk: Geoffrey W. Rowley. Common Cryer and Sergeant-at-Arms: Col. John Cecil Marcus Ansell.

Council for the Protection of Rural England: 4 Hobart Place, London SW1W 0HY. 071-235 9481. Director: Robin Grove-White.

Council for the Protection of Rural Wales(CPRW): Cymdeithas Diogelu Cymru Wledig, Ty Gwyn, 31 High Street, Welshpool, Powys SY21 7JP. Welshpool 2525. Director: Simon Meade.

Countryside Commission: John Dower House, Crescent Place, Cheltenham, Glos. 0242 521381. Chairman: Sir Derek Barber. Director: Adrian Phillips.

Court of the Lord Lyon: H.M. New Register House, Edinburgh EH1 3YT. 031-556 7255. Lord Lyon King of Arms: Malcolm Rognvald Innes of Edingight, C.V.O., W.S.

Criminal Injuries Compensation Board: Whittington House, 19 Alfred Place, London WC1E 7LG. 071-636 9501. Chairman: Lord carlisle of Bucklow, Q.C.

Crown Agents for Oversea Governments and Administrations: St.Nicholas House, St.Nicholas Road, Sutton, Surrey SM1 TEL. 081-643 3311., Chairman: Peter A. Graham, O.B.E.

Crown Estate Commissioners: Crown Estate Office, 13-15 Carlton House Terrace, London SW1Y 5AH. 071-210 3000. First Commissioner and Chairman: The Rt. Hon The Earl of Mansfield. Second Commissioner and Deputy Chairman: C.K. Howes.

Crown Office, Scotland: 5-7 Regent Road, Edinburgh EH7 5BL. 031-557 3800. Crown Agent: I. Dean.

Cystic Fibrosis Research Trust: Alexandra House, 5 Blyth Road, Bromley, Kent BR1 3RS. 081-464 7211. Executive Director: Barbara Bentley.

Department for National Savings: Charles House, 375 Kensington High Street, London W14 8SD. 071-603 2000. Director: Stuart Gilbert, C.B.

Department of Education and Science: Elizabeth House, York Road, London SE1 7PH. 071-934 9000. Permanent Under-Secretary of State: Sir David Hancock, K.C.B.

Department of Employment: Caxton House, Tothill Street, London SW1H 9NF. 071-213 3000. Permanent Secretary: Sir Michael Quinlan, K.C.B.

Department of Energy: Thames House South, Millbank, London SW1P 4QJ. 081-211 3000. Permanent Under-Secretary: Peter Gregson, C.B.

Department of Social Security: Alexander Fleming House, Elephant and Castle, London SE1 6BY. 071-407 5522. Permanent Secretaries: Sir Kenneth Stowe, K.C.B., C.V.O. Sir Geoffrey Otton, K.C.B. Chief Medical Officer: Dr. E.D. Acheson, D.M.

Department of Trade and Industry: 1-19 Victoria Street, London SW1H 0ET. 071-215 7877. Telex: 8811074 DTHQG. Permanent Secretary: Sir Brian Hayes, K.C.B.

Department of Trade and Industry, Services Organisation: 29, Bressenden Place, London SW1E 5DT. 071-215 7877. Telex: 8813148 DIHQG. Regional Organisation: North Eastern: Stangate House, 2 Groat Market, Newcastle upon Tyne NE1 1YN. 091-2324722; North-Western: Sunley Tower, Piccadilly Plaza, Manchester M1 4BA. 061-236 2171. Yorkshire and Humberside: Priestley House, Park Row, Leeds LS1 5LF. Leeds 443171. West Midlands: Ladywood House, Stephenson Street, Birmingham B2 4DT. 021-632 4111. East Midlands: Severns House, 20 Middle Pavement, Nottingham NG1 7DW. Nottingham 506181, South-Western: The Pithay, Bristol BS1 2PB. Bristol 272666. South West Industrial Development Office: Phoenix House, Notte Street, Plymouth PL1 2HF. Ply mouth 221891, South Eastern Region: Ebury Bridge House, Ebury Bridge Road, London SW1W 8QD. 071-730 9678.

Department of Transport: 2 Marsham Street, London SW1P 3EB. 071-212 3434. Permanent Secretary of State: Alan M. Bailey, C.B.

Department of the Environment: 2 Marsham Street, London SW1P 3EB. 071-212 3434. Permanent Secretary: T.M. Heiser, C.B. Second Permanent Secretary: Sir Peter Harrop, K.C.B. Property Services Agency: Chief Executive: A.G.Manzie, C.B.

Design Centre, Scotland: 72 St. Vincent Street, Glasgow G2 5TN. 041- 221 6121.

Design Council: The Design Centre, 28 Haymarket, London SW1Y 4SU. 071-839 8000. Director: Keith Grant.

Design Council, Wales: Pearl Assurance House, Greyfriars Road, Cardiff CF1 3JN. Cardiff 395811/2.

Director of Public Prosecutions: 4/12 Queen Anne's Gate, London SW1H 9AZ. 071-213 3000. Director: Sir Thomas C. Hetherington, K.C.B., C.B.E., T.D., Q.C.

Duchy of Cornwall: 10 Buckingham Gate, London SW1E 6LA. 071-834 7346.

Duchy of Lancaster: Lancaster Place, Strand, London WC2E 7ED. 071-836 8277. Chancellor: Rt. Hon. Kenneth Baker, M.P.

Duxford Airfield (Imperial War Museum): Duxford, Cambs. CB2 4QR. Cambridge 833963.

Ecology Party see Green Party.

Economic and Social Research Council: 160 Great Portland Street, London W1N 6BA. 071-637 1499. Chairman: Professor Sir Douglas Hague, C.B.E. Secretary: Mrs. Suzanne Reeve.

Edinburgh Royal Observatory: Blackford Hill, Edinburgh EH9 3HJ. 031- 667 3321. Director: Professor M. S. Longair, B.Sc., M.A., Ph.D., LL.D., F.R.S.E., Astronomer Royal for Scotland.

Electricity Council: 30 Millbank, London SW1P 4RD. 071-834 2333. Chairman: Philip Jones, C.B.

English Folk Dance and Song Society: Cecil Sharp House, 2 Regent's Park Road, London NW1 7AY. 071-485 2206. Director: James Lloyd.

English Heritage: See Historic Buildings and Monuments Commission for England.

English National Board for Nursing, Midwifery and Health Visiting: Victory House, 170 Tottenham Court Road, London W1P 0HA. 071-388 3131. Chief Executive Officer: Dr. E. Bendall.

English-Speaking Union: (International Council, Commonwealth Board and National Committee for England and Wales), Dartmouth House, 37 Charles Street, London W1X 8AB. Club and Offices: 071-629 8995/4931. Director General: Alan Lee Williams, O.B.E.

Equal Opportunities Commission: Overseas House, Quay Street, Manchester M3 3HN. 061-833 9244. Press Office: 1 Bedford Street, Strand, London WC2E 9HD. 071-379 6323. Regional Offices : Scotland: 249 West George Street, Glasgow G2 4QE. 041-226 4591. Wales: Caerwys House, Windsor Lane, Cardiff CF1 1LB. Cardiff 43552. Commission's work is directed towards the elimination of sex discrimination and the promotion of equality of opportunity between men and women. Chairman: The Baroness Platt of Writtle.

Export Credits Guarantee Department: Aldermanbury House, Aldermanbury, London EC2P 2EL. 071-382 7000. Chief Executive: Jack Gill, C.B.

Family Planning Association: 27-35 Mortimer Street, London W1N 7RJ. 071-636 7866. General Secretary: Alastair Service.

Family Welfare Association: 501-505 Kingsland Road, Dalston, London E8 4AU. 071-254 6251. Director: R.E. Morley, B.A.

Federation of British Artists: 17 Carlton House Terrace, London SW1Y 5BD. 071-930 6844. Administrators of The Mall Galleries, The Mall, SW1Y 5BD. Secretariat for the major London Art Societies. Chief Executive: Oliver Warman, R.B.A.

Fellowship Houses Trust: Clock House, Byfleet, Weybridge, Surrey KT14 7RN. Byfleet 43172. Secretary: L.P. Leech.

Fire Protection Association: 140 Aldersgate Street, London EC1A 4HX. 071-606 3757. Director: C.D. Woodward, F.I. Fire. E.

Folklore Society: c/o University College London, Gower Street, London WC1E 6BT. 071-387 5894. Hon. Secretary: A. Roy Vickery.

Foreign and Commonwealth Office: London SW1A 2AH. 071-233 3000. Permanent Under-Secretary: Sir Patrick Wright, K.C.M.G.

Forestry Commission: 231 Corstorphine Road, Edin burgh EH12 7AT. 031-334 0303. Chairman: Sir David Montgomery, Bt.

Friends of the Earth Ltd: 26-28 Underwood Street, London N1 7JQ 071 490 1555.

Gaming Board for Great Britain: Berkshire House, 168-173 High Holborn, London WC1V 7AA. 071-240 0821. Chairman: Sir Anthony Rawlinson, K.C.B.

General Council of British Shipping: 30-32 St. Mary Axe, London EC3A 8ET. 071-283 2922. President: W. G. Runciman. Vice-President: K. St. Johnston. Director-General: P. Le Cheminant, C.B. Deputy Director- General: F. J. Whitworth.

General Dental Council: 37 Wimpole Street, London W1M 8DQ. 071-486 2171. Registrar: Norman Davies, M.B.E., B.A.

General Medical Council: 44 Hallam Street, London W1N 6AE. 071-580 7642. President: Sir John Walton, T.D., F.R.C.P.

General Register Office: England and Wales: See Population Censuses and Surveys, Office of. Scotland: New Register House, Edinburgh EH1 3YT. 031-556 3952. Registrar General: Dr. C.M. Glennie.

Geological Museum (Part of the British Museum (Natural History)): Exhibition Road, South Kensington, London SW7 2DE. 071-589 3444. Director: Dr. R.H. Hedley. Curator: F.W. Dunning, O.B.E.

Geological Society: Burlington House, Piccadilly, London W1V 0JU. 071-734 2356. President: Professor B.E. Leake. Executive Secretary: R.M. Bateman.

Government Actuary: 22 Kingsway, London WC2B 6LE. 071-242 6828. E.A. Johnston, C.B., B.A., F.I.A.

Government Chemist: Department of Trade and Industry, Laboratory of the Government Chemist, Cornwall House, Waterloo Road, London SE1 8XY. 081-211 7900. Ronald Coleman, D.Sc., C.Chem., F.R.S.C.

Green Party: 36-38 Clapham Road, London SW9 0JQ. 071-735 2485. Office Manager: John Bishop.

Guild of British Newspaper Editors: Whitefriars House, 6 Carmelite Street, London EC4Y 0BL. 071-583 3311. President: G. Lloyd. Secretary-Treasurer: C. Gordon Page, A.C.I.S.

Guildhall School of Music and Drama: Barbican, London EC2Y 8DT. 071- 628 2571. Principal: John Hosier, C.B.E., M.A., Hon.D.Mus., F.G.S.M., F.R.C.M., F.R.N.C.M., Hon.R.A.M., Hon.F.T.C.L. Director of Music: Damian Cranmer, B.Mus., M.A. Artistic Director (Drama): Tony Church, M.A., F.G.S.M. Director of Technical Theatre Studies: Geoff Pope, F.G.S.M. Director of Administration: George Derbyshire, LL.B., Hon.G.S.M.

H.M. Coastguard: Department of Transport, Sunley House, 90 High Holborn, London WC1V 6LP. 071-405 6911. Chief Coastguard: Lt.-Cdr. J.T. Fetherston-Dilke, R.N. (retd.)

H.M. Land Registry: Lincoln's Inn Fields, London WC2A 3PH. 071-405 3488. Chief Land Registrar: E.J. Pryer.

H.M. Stationery Office Bookshops: 13a Castle Street, Edinburgh EH2 3AR.

H.M. Stationery Office Bookshops: 49 High Holborn, London WC1V 6HB. (Post orders to P.O. Box 276, London SW8

5DT); 258 Broad Street, Birmingham B1 2HE.

H.M. Stationery Office Bookshops: 80 Chichester Street, Belfast BT1 4JY.

H.M. Stationery Office Bookshops: Princess Street, Manchester M60 8AS.

H.M. Stationery Office Bookshops: Southey House, Wine Street, Bristol BS1 2BQ.

H.M. Stationery Office: St. Crispins, Duke Street, Norwich NR3 1PD. Norwich 622211. Controller and Chief Executive: J. A. Dole.

H.M. Treasury: Parliament Street, London SW1P 3AG. 071-270 3000. Permanent Secretary: Sir Peter Middleton, K.C.B.

H.M.S. Belfast (Imperial War Museum): Symons Wharf, Vine Lane, London SE12JH. 071-407 6434.

Hansard Society for Parliamentary Government: 16 Gower Street, London WC1E 6DP. 071-323 1131. General-Secretary: Mary Goudie.

Historic Buildings and Monuments Commission for England (English Heritage): Fortress House, 23 Savile Row, London W1X 2HE. 071-734 6010. Chairman: The Lord Montagu of Beaulieu. Chief Executive: Peter Rumble, C.B.

Home Office: 50 Queen Anne's Gate, London SW1H 9AT. 071-213 3000. Permanent Under-Secretary of State: Sir Brian Cubbon, G.C.B. Prison Department: Cleland House, Page Street, London SW1P 4LN. 081-211 3000. Director General of the Prison Service (Chairman of Prison Board): C.J. Train. Deputy Director General: G.H. Lakes, M.C. Director of Regimes and Services: T.C. Platt. Director of Operational Policy: A.J. Langdon. Director of Personnel and Finance: E. Caines. Director of Prison Medical Services: Dr.J. Kilgour.

Horserace Totalisator Board: Tote House, 74 Upper Richmond Road, London SW15 2SU. 081-874 6411. Chairman: Sir Woodrow Wyatt. Chief Executive: Brian M.McDonnell.

Hospital Saving Association: Hambleden House, Andover, Hants SP10 1LQ. Andover 53211. General Secretary: I. Forbes, M.B.E., D.F.C.

Housing Corporation: 149 Tottenham Court Road, London W1P 0BN. 071-387 9466. Responsible for registering, supervising and funding non-profit making housing associations throughout England, Scotland and Wales. In addition to housing for rent, now promoting shared ownership, improvement for sale, leasehold for the elderly and other methods of making full use of the resources available. Chairman: Sir Hugh Cubitt, C.B.E., F.R.I.C.S., D.L. Chief Executive: D.A. Edmonds.

Imperial War Museum: Lambeth Road, London SE1 6HZ. 071-735 8922. Director: Dr. A.C.N. Borg.

Incorporated Society of Valuers and Auctioneers: 3 Cadogan Gate, London SW1X 0AS. 071-235 2282-4. President (1987-88): James Shaw. President Elect (1988-89): Donald Magennis. Secretary: M. H. R. Astbury, M.A.

Independent Broadcasting Authority: 70 Brompton Road, London SW3 1EY. 071-584 7011. Chairman: The Lord Thomson of Monifieth, K.T., P.C.

Industrial Society: Peter Runge House, 3 Carlton House Terrace, London SW1Y 5DG. 071-839 4300. Director: Alistair Graham. Secretary: Michael Hyde.

Institute of Actuaries: Staple Inn Hall, High Holborn, London WC1V 7QJ. 071-242 0106. Secretary-General: C.D. Mackie, F.C.A., F.S.S., F.B.I.M.

Institute of Agricultural Secretaries: National Agricultural Centre, Stoneleigh, Kenilworth, Warwickshire CV8 2LZ. Coventry 20623. Secretary: Mrs. A. Dymond.

Institute of Chartered Accountants in England and Wales: P.O.Box 433, Chartered Accountants' Hall, Moorgate Place, London EC2P 2BJ. 071-628 7060. President: D.A. Boothman, F.C.A.

Institute of Chartered Secretaries and Administrators: 16 Park Crescent, London W1N 4AH. 071-580 4741. Secretary and Chief Executive: B. Barker, M.B.E., M.A., F.C.I.S.

Institute of Clerks of Work of Great Britain Incorporated: 41 The Mall, Ealing, London W5 3TJ. 081-579 2917. General Secretary: A.P. Macnamara, Hon. F.I.C.W., F.S.A.E., M.A.C.E.

Institute of Cost and Management Accountants: 63 Portland Place, London W1N 4AB. 071-637 2311. President: Peter Lawrence. Secretary: T.B. Degenhardt.

Institute of Export: Export House, 64 Clifton Street, London EC2A 4HB. 071-247 9812. President: The Earl of Limerick, K.B.E. Chairman: Derek Langham. Director-General: J.R. Wilson.

Institute of Marine Engineers: 76 Mark Lane, London EC3R 7JN. 071-481 8493. Secretary: J.E. Sloggett, B.Sc., C.Eng., F.I.Mar.E., F.R.I.N.A., F.I.C.S., C.Dip.A.F.

Institute of Marketing: Moor Hall, Cookham, Berkshire SL6 9QH. Bourne End 24922. Director General: Tony McBurnie, M.A., F.Inst.M. Secretary: W.E. Hinder, F.C.I.S., F.B.I.M.

Institution of Civil Engineers: Great George Street, London SW1P 3AA. 071-222 7722. President: D.G.M. Roberts, M.A., C.Eng., F.I.C.E., F.I.Mech.E., F.I.W.E.S., F.I.P.H.E., M.I.W.P.C.

Institution of Electrical Engineers: Savoy Place, London WC2R 0BL. 071-240 1871. Secretary: H.H.W. Losty, B.Sc., F.Eng., F.I.E.E.

Institution of Mechanical Engineers: 1 Birdcage Walk, London SW1H 9JJ. 071-222 7899. President: Mr. O. Roith, C.B., M.A., F.Eng., F.R.S.

Kew Gardens: See Royal Botanic Gardens, Kew

Land Charges and Agricultural Credits Department: Burrington Way, Plymouth, Devon PL5 3LP. Plymouth 779831.

Law Society: The Law Society's Hall, 113 Chancery Lane, London WC2A 1PL. 071-242 1222.

Law Society of Scotland: 26 Drumsheugh Gardens, Edinburgh EH3 7YR. 031-226 7411. Telex: 72436 LawscoG. Secretary: K.W. Pritchard, B.L., S.S.C.

Library Association: 7 Ridgmount Street, London WC1E 7AE. 071-636 7543. Chief Executive: George Cunningham, B.A., B.Sc.

Lloyd's Register of Shipping (Ship classification society and independent inspection agency): 71 Fenchurch Street, London EC3M 4BS. 071-709 9166. Chairman: H.R. Mac Leod.

Lloyd's of London (Insurance Market): Lime Street, London EC3M 7HA. 071-623 7100. Chairman: Peter Miller.

Local Government Boundary Commission for England: Room 122, 20 Albert Embankment, London SE1 7TJ. 081-211 6389. Chairman: G.J. Ellerton, C.M.G., M.B.E. Deputy Chairman: J.G. Powell, F.R.I.C.S.

London Chamber of Commerce and Industry: 69 Cannon Street, London EC4N 5AB. 071-248 4444. Telex No. 888941. President: Sir Anthony Jolliffe, G.B.E., D.Sc. Director: A.M.W. Platt.

London Regional Transport: 55 Broadway, London SW1H 0BD. 071-222 5600. Chairman: Sir Keith Bright.

Lord Advocate's Department: Fielden House, 10 Great College Street, London SW1P 3SL. 071-212 7676. Legal Secretary: N.J. Adamson, C.B., Q.C.

Lord Chamberlain's Office: St. James's Palace, London S.W.1. 071-930 3007. Lord Chamberlain: The Earl of Airlie, P.C., Kt., G.C.V.O.

Lord Chancellor's Office: House of Lords, London S.W.1. 071-219 3000. Permanent Secretary to the Lord Chancellor: Sir Derek Oulton, K.C.B., Q.C.

Lord Great Chamberlain's Office: House of Lords, London SW1A 0PW. Lord Great Chamberlain: The Marquess of Cholmondeley, G.C.V.O., M.C. Black Rod's and Sergeant-at-Arms' Office: House of Lords, London SW1A 0PW. 071-219 3100. Black Rod and Sergeant-at-Arms: Air Chief Marshal Sir John Gingell, G.B.E., K.C.B.

Lord's Day Observance Society: 5 Victory Avenue, Morden, Surrey SM4 6DL. 081-648 0529. Secretary: J.G. Roberts.

Loss Prevention Council: 140 Aldersgate Street, London EC1A 3HY. 071-606 1050. Chief Executive: J.L. Hill, M.A., C.Eng., M.I.Mech.E., M.I.M.C.

Low Pay Unit: 9 Upper Berkeley St., London W1H 8BY. 071 071-242 7278.

Manpower Services Commission: Moorfoot, Sheffield S1 4PQ. Sheffield 753275. Chairman: Bryan Nicholson. Director: Geoffrey Holland.

Medical Research Council: 20 Park Crescent, London W1N 4AL. 071-636 5422. Chairman: The Earl Jellicoe, K.B.E., D.S.O., M.C., P.C. Secretary: Dr. D. A. Rees, D.Sc., F.R.S.

Medicines Commission: Market Towers, 1 Nine Elms Lane, London SW8 5NQ. 071-720 2188. Chairman: Professor R. Hurley, M.D., F.R.C.Path.

Mersey Docks and Harbour Company: Port of Liverpool Building, Liverpool L3 1BZ. 051-200 2020. Telex No. 627013. Managing Director and Chief Executive: P.T. Furlong.

Meteorological Office: London Road, Bracknell, Berks. RG12 2SZ. Bracknell 420242. Director-General: Professor John Houghton, C.B.E., D.Phil., F.R.S.

Metropolitan Police Office: New Scotland Yard, Broadway, London SW1H 0BG. 071-230 1212. Commissioner: Mr. Peter Imbert, Q.P.M.

Ministry of Agriculture, Fisheries and Food: Whitehall Place, London SW1A 2HH. 071-233 3000. Permanent Secretary: Sir Michael Franklin, K.C.B. Fisheries Laboratory: Pakefield Road, Lowestoft, Suffolk NR33 0HT. Lowestoft 62244. Central Veterinary Laboratory, New Haw, Weybridge, Surrey KT15 3NB. Byfleet 41111.

Ministry of Defence: Main Building, Whitehall, London SW1A 2HB. 071- 218 9000. Permanent Under-Secretary of State: Sir Clive Whitmore, K.C.B., C.V.O. Second Permanent Under-Secretary of State: J. N.H. Blelloch, C.B.

Monopolies and Mergers Commission: New Court, 48 Carey Street, London WC2A 2JT. 071-831 6111. Chairman: Sir Godfray Le Quesne, Q.C.

Muscular Dystrophy Group of Great Britain and Northern Ireland: Nattrass House, 35 Macaulay Road, London SW4 0QP. 071-720 8055. President: Sir Richard Attenborough, C.B.E., D.Litt., D.C.L., Executive Director: Paul F.Walker.

Museum of London: London Wall, EC2Y 5HN. 071-600 3699. Director: Max Hebditch, M.A., F.S.A., F.M.A.

National Association of Citizens' Advice Bureaux: Myddelton House, 115-123 Pentonville Road, London, N1 9LZ. 071-833 2181. Director: Elizabeth Filkin.

National Association of Local Councils: 108 Great Russell Street, London WC1B 3LD. 071-637 1865/8. Secretary: J.E. Clark.

National Audit Office: Buckingham Palace Road, London SW1W 9SP. 071- 798 7000. Comptroller and Auditor General: Sir Gordon Downey, K.C.B.

National Board for Nursing, Midwifery and Health Visiting for Northern Ireland: RAC House, 79 Chichester Street, Belfast BT1 4JE., Belfast 652713. Chief Executive Officer: J. Walsh.

National Board for Nursing, Midwifery and Health Visiting for Scotland: 22 Queen Street, Edinburgh EH2 1JX. 031-226 7371. Chief Executive Officer: Miss L. W. Coutts.

National Book League: see Book Trust.

National Bus Company: 172 Buckingham Palace Road, London SW1W 9TN. 071-730 3453.

National Council for Civil Liberties: 21 Tabard St., London, SE1 4LA. 071 405 3888. General Secretary: Sarah Spencer.

National Consumer Council: 18 Queen Anne's Gate, London SW1H 9AA. 071-222 9501. Chairman: Michael Montague, C.B.E.

National Council of Women: 34 Lower Sloane Street, London SW1W 8BP. 071-730 0619. President: (1986-88): Mrs. E. Martin. Secretary: Mrs. June Norman.

National Debt Office: Royex House, Aldermanbury Square, London EC2V 7LR. 071-606 7321. Secretary and Comptroller-General: P. A. Goodwin, C.B.E.

National Dock Labour Board: 22-26 Albert Embank ment, London SE1 7TE. 071-735 7271. Chairman: R. H. Thompson.

National Economic Development Office: Millbank Tower, Millbank, London SW1P 4QX. 081-211 3000. Director-General: John Cassels, C.B.

National Farmers Union: Agriculture House, Knightsbridge, London SW1X 7NJ. Tel: 071-235 5077. President: Sir Simon Gourlay.

National Federation of Women's Institutes: 39 Eccleston Street, London SW1W 9NT. 071-730 7212.

National Freight Consortium plc.: The Merton Centre, 45 St. Peters Street, Bedford. MK40 2UB. Bedford 272222. Chairman: Sir Peter Thompson.

National Gallery: Trafalgar Square, London WC2N 5DN. 071-839 3321. Director: Robert Neil MacGregor.

National Girobank: 10 Milk Street, London EC2V 8JH. 071-600 6020.

National Girobank: Bootle, Merseyside GIR 0AA. 051-928 8181.

National Heritage Memorial Fund: Church House, Great Smith Street, London, SW1. 071-212 5414. Chairman of Trustees: The Lord Charteris of Amisfield, P.C., G.C.B., G.C.V.O., Q.S.O., O.B.E., Secretary: Brian Lang, Ph.D.

National Institute for Medical Research: The Ridgeway, Mill Hill, London NW7 1AA. 081-959 3666. Director: D.A.Rees, D.Sc., F.R.S.C., F.I.Biol., F.R.S.

National Maritime Museum: Greenwich, London SE10 9NF. 081-858 4422. Director: Richard Ormond.

National Marriage Guidance Council: Headquarters and Training Centre, Herbert Gray College, Little Church Street,

Rugby, Warwickshire CV21 3AP. Rugby 73241. Chief Officer: Nicholas Tyndall, B.A.

National Monuments Record (incorporating the National Monuments Record) (Royal Commission on the Historical Monuments of England): Fortress House, 23 Savile Row, London W1X 1AB. 071-734 6010. Director: T.G. Hassall, M.A., F.S.A., M.I.F.A.

National Museum of Wales: Cathays Park, Cardiff CF1 3NP. Cardiff 397951. Director: D. W. Dykes, M.A., Ph.D., F.S.A., F.R.Hist.S.

National Museums of Scotland: Royal Scottish Museum, Chambers Street, Edinburgh EH1 1JF. 031-225 7534. Royal Museum of Scotland, Queen Street, Edinburgh EH2 1JD. 031-225 7534. Plus the Scottish United Services Museum, the Scottish Agricultural Museum, East Fortune Museum of Flight, Shambellie House Museum of Costume, Leith Custom House Gallery and Biggar Gasworks Museum. Director: R.G.W. Anderson, M.A., D.Phil.

National Physical Laboratory: Teddington, Middlesex TW11 0LW. 081-977 3222. Director: Dr. P. Dean, C.B., Secretary: Dr. Walter Vickers.

National Portrait Gallery: St. Martin's Place, Charing Cross Road, London WC2H 0HE. 071-930 1552. Director: John Hayes, M.A., Ph.D., F.S.A.

National Society for the Prevention of Cruelty to Children: National Headquarters, 67 Saffron Hill, London EC1N 8RS. 071-242 1626. Director: Dr. Alan Gilmour, C.B.E., M.B., B.S., F.R.C.G.P.

National Trust for Places of Historic Interest or Natural Beauty: 36 Queen Anne's Gate, London SW1H 9AS. 071-222 9251. Chairman: Dame Jennifer Jenkins. Director General: Angus Stirling.

National Trust for Scotland: 5 Charlotte Square, Edin burgh EH2 4DU. 031-226 5922. Director: Lester Borley.

Natural Environment Research Council: Polaris House, North Star Avenue, Swindon SN2 1EU. Swindon 40101. Chairman: Hugh Fish, C.B.E., Secretary: J.C. Bowman, C.B.E., B.Sc., Ph.D., F.I.Biol.

Nature Conservancy Council: Northminster House, Peterborough PE1 1UA. Peterborough 40345. Director-General: R.C.Steele.

Navy, Army and Air Force Institutes: Imperial Court, Kennington Lane, London SE11 5QX. 071-735 1200. Chairman Board of Management: Malcolm D.Field. Managing Director: James Rucker.

New English Art Club: 17 Carlton House Terrace, London SW1Y 5BD. Hon. Secretary: William Bowyer.

Newspaper Publishers Association Ltd.: 6 Bouverie Street, London EC4Y 8AY. 071-583 8132. Director: J. LePage.

Newspaper Society: Whitefriars House, 6 Carmelite Street, London EC4Y 0BL. 071-583 3311. President: Christopher Dicks. Director: Dugal Nisbet-Smith.

North East Civic Trust: 3 Old Elvet, Durham DH1 3HL. 0385 61182.

North West Civic Trust: The Environmental Institute, Greaves School, Bolton Road, Swinton, Manchester M27 2UX. 061-794 9314.

Northern Ireland Office: Whitehall, London SW1A 2AZ. 071-210 3000. Stormont Castle, Belfast BT4 3ST. Belfast 63011. Stormont House, Belfast BT4 3ST. Belfast 63255. Dundonald House, Belfast BT4 3SU. Belfast 63255. Permanent Under-Secretary of State: Sir Robert John Andrew, K.C.B

Office of Fair Trading: Field House, Bream's Buildings, London EC4A 1PR. 071-242 2858. Director General: Sir Gordon Borrie.

Office of Manpower Economics: 22 Kingsway, London WC2B 6JY. 071-405 5944. Director: N. Covington. Assistant Secretaries: D.R. Bower; K.R. Perry; D.A. Roberts.

Office of Population Censuses and Surveys: St. Catherines House, 10 Kingsway, London WC2B 6JP. 071-242 0262.

Offshore Energy Technology Board: Department of Energy, Thames House South, Millbank, London SW1P 4QJ. 081-211 7312. Chairman: Rt. Hon. Alick Buchanan-Smith, M.P. Minister of State for Energy. Secretary: J. Roddie.

Ordnance Survey: Romsey Road, Maybush, Southampton SO9 4DH. Southampton 792000. Director-General: Peter McMaster, B.Sc., A.R.I.C.S.

Overseas Development Administration: Eland House, Stag Place, London SW1E 5DH. 071-213 4451. Permanent Secretary: Sir Crispin Tickell, K.C.V.O.

Pastel Society: 17 Carlton House Terrace, London SW1Y 5BD. President: Leigh Parry.

Patent Office: State House, 61-71 High Holborn, London WC1R 4TP. 071-831 2525. Comptroller-General: P. J. Cooper. Sales Branch (for Information Retrieval Services), Block C Station Square Hse, St Mary Cray Orpington, Kent BR5 3RD.

Paymaster General's Office: Sutherland House, Russell Way, Crawley, West Sussex RH10 1UH. Crawley 27833. Assistant Paymaster General: L. A. Andrews.

Pensions Appeal Tribunals: St. Dunstans House, Fetter Lane, London EC4A 1BT. 071-936 7033. President: Sir Geoffrey Briggs. Secretary: K. R. Abbott.

Performing Right Society Ltd.: 29-33 Berners Street, London W1P 4AA. 071-580 5544. Chief Executive: M. J. Freegard, F.C.I.S. Public Relations Manager: Miss L. A. Bray.

Pharmaceutical Society of Great Britain: 1 Lambeth High Street, London SE1 7JN. 071-735 9141. President: Dr. T. G. Booth. Secretary and Registrar: John Ferguson.

Pilgrim Trust: Fielden House, Little College Street, London SW1P 3SH. 071-222 4723. Chairman: The Lord Richardson of Duntisbourne, K.G. Secretary: Hon. A. Hoyer Millar.

Playing Fields Association, National: 25 Ovington Square, London SW3 1LQ. 071-584 6445. Chairman: A. C. Gilmour. Director General: Colin W. McFadyean.

Port of London Authority: International House, 1 St. Katharine's Way, London E1 9UN. 071-481 4887. Chairman: Sir Brian Kellett.

Post Office: 33 Grosvenor Place, London SW1X 1PX. 071-235 8000. Chairman: Sir Ronald Dearing, C.B.

Post Office Users' Council for Wales: Caradog House, (First Floor), St. Andrews Place, Cardiff CF1 3BE. Cardiff 374028. Chairman: Professor J. Roger Webster. Secretary: B. Lewis.

Post Office Users' National Council: Waterloo Bridge House, Waterloo Road, London SE1 8UA. 071-928 9458. Chairman: Thomas S. Corrigan. Secretary: Brian R. Jones.

Press Association: 85 Fleet Street, London EC4P 4BE. 071-353 7440. Chairman: P. W. Gibbings.

Press Council: 1 Salisbury Square, London EC4Y 8AE. 071-353 1248. Independent Chairman: Rt. Hon. Sir Zelman Cowen, A.K., G.C.M.G., G.C.V.O., Q.C., Director: Kenneth Morgan, O.B.E.

Privy Council Office: Whitehall, London SW1A 2AT. 071-233 5031. Clerk of the Council: G. I. de Deney, C.V.O.

Public Trustee: Stewart House, Kingsway (entrance in Sardinia Street), London WC2B 6JX. 071-405 4300. Public Trustee: J. A. Boland.

Public Works Loan Board: Royex House, Aldermanbury Square, London EC2V 7LR. 071-606 7321. Chairman: J. E. A. R. Guinness. R.H.S. Wisley Garden: Wisley, nr. Ripley, Surrey. 0483 224234.

Rainer Foundation (formerly London Police Court Mission): 227-239 Tooley Street, London SE1 2JX. 071-403 4434. President: The Lord Henniker, K.C.M.G., M.C., C.V.O. Director: Richard Kay.

Record Offices: Public Record Office: Ruskin Avenue, Kew, Richmond, Surrey TW9 4DU. 081-876 3444; Chancery Lane, London WC2A 1LR. 071-405 0741. Keeper: G. H. Martin. Corporation of London Records Office: Guildhall, London EC2P 2EJ. 071-606 3030. Deputy Keeper: James Reid Sewell, M.A., F.S.A., Scottish Record Office: General Register House, Edinburgh EH1 3YY. 031-556 6585. Keeper: Dr. Athol L. Murray.

Registry of Friendly Societies: 15 Great Marlborough Street, London W1V 2AX. 071-437 9992. Chief Registrar: J.M. Bridgeman. Scotland: 58 Frederick Street, Edinburgh EH2 1NB. 031-226 3224.

Royal Academy of Dramatic Art: 62-64 Gower Street, London WC1E 6ED. 071-636 7076. Founded 1904 by Sir Herbert Beerbohm Tree. Incorporating Vanbrugh Theatre Club. Principal: Oliver Neville. Administrator-Registrar: Richard O'Donoghue.

Royal Academy of Music: Marylebone Road, London NW1 5HT. 071-935 5461. Principal: Sir David Lumsden, M.A., D.Phil. (Oxon. et Cantab.), Mus.B., Hon.R.A.M., F.R.C.M., F.R.N.C.M., F.R.S.A.M.D., Hon.G.S.M., Hon.F.L.C.M., Hon.F.R.C.O., F.R.S.A.

Royal Aeronautical Society: 4 Hamilton Place, London W1V 0BQ. 071-499 3515. President (1986-89): Dr. J.W. Fozard, O.B.E., F.Eng., F.I.Mech.E., F.R.Ae.S., F.A.I.A.A.

Royal Agricultural Society of England: National Agricultural Centre, Stoneleigh, Kenilworth, Warwickshire CV8 2LZ. Royal Show (0203) 555100. Chief Executive: J.D.M. Hearth. Agricultural Director: G.H. Jackson. Marketing Director: C.H. Richardson. Showground Director: J. Perrott.

Royal Anthropological Institute: 56 Queen Anne Street, London W1M 9LA. 071-486 6832. President: Professor Michael Banton.

Royal Archaeological Institute: President: F.H. Thompson, M.C., M.A., F.S.A. Asst. Secretary: Miss W.E. Phillips, 304 Addison House, Grove End Road, St. John's Wood, London NW8 9EL.

Royal Astronimical Society: Burlington House, London W1V 0NL. 071-734 4582. President: Professor D. Lynden-Bell.

Royal Ballet School: 155 Talgarth Road, London W14 9DE. 081-748 3123, and at White Lodge, Richmond. Director: Merle Park, C.B.E.,Associate Director and Ballet Principal: Barbara Fewster.

Royal Botanic Gardens, Kew: Kew, Richmond, Surrey TW9 3AB. 081-940 1171; Wakehurst Place, Ardingly, Haywards Heath, Sussex RH17 6TN. Ardingly 892701. Director: Professor E. Arthur Bell.

Royal British Legion: 48 Pall Mall, London SW1Y 5JY. 071-930 8131. President: General Sir Patrick Howard-Dobson, G.C.B.

Royal British Legion, Scotland: New Haig House, Logie Green Road, Edinburgh EH7 4HR. 031-557 2782. President: General Sir Michael Gow, G.C.B. Chairman: Maj. Gen. Sir John Swinton, K.C.V.O., O.B.E., D.L. General Secretary: Brig. R.W. Riddle, O.B.E.

Royal College of General Practitioners: 14 Princes Gate, London SW7 1PU. 071-581 3232. President: Professor V.W.M. Drury O.B.E. General Administrator: Mrs. S. Fountain, M.A.

Royal College of Music: Prince Consort Road, London SW7 2BS. 071-589 3643. Director: Michael Gough Matthews, F.R.C.M., Hon.R.A.M., Hon.F.L.C.M., A.R.C.O., F.R.S.A.

Royal College of Obstetricians and Gynaecologists: 27 Sussex Place, Regent's Park, London NW1 4RG. 071-262 5425. President: Professor Sir Malcolm Macnaughton, M.D., F.R.C.P., F.R.C.O.G., F.R.S.E. College Adminis trator: A. G. S. Taylour, F.A.A.I., F.B.I.M

Royal College of Organists: Kensington Gore, London SW7 2QS. 071-589 1765. Clerk: K. B. Lyndon.

Royal College of Pathologists: 2 Carlton House Terrace, London SW1Y 5AF. 071-930 5861. President: Professor Barbara E. Clayton, C.B.E., D.Sc., Ph.D., M.D., F.R.C.P., F.R.C.P.E., P.R.C.Path.

Royal College of Physicians: 11 St. Andrews Place, London NW1 4LE. 071-935 1174. President: Sir Raymond Hoffenberg, K.B.E., M.D., P.R.C.P.

Royal College of Physicians of Edinburgh: 9 Queen Street, Edinburgh EH2 1JQ. 031-225 7324. Library: 031-225 5968. President: M. F. Oliver, C.B.E., M.D., P.R.C.P.(Ed.)., F.R.C.P., F.F.C.M. Secretary: T. M. Chalmers, M.B., Ch.B., F.R.C.P.(Ed.)

Royal College of Psychiatrists: 17 Belgrave Square, London SW1X 8PG. 071-235 2351. Registrar: Prof. R. G. Priest, F.R.C.Psych.

Royal College of Surgeons of Edinburgh: Nicolson Street, Edinburgh EH8 9DW. 031-556 6206. President: T.J. McNair, Q.H.S., M.D., F.R.C.S.Ed. Secretary: Peter Edmond, C.B.E., Q.H.S., T.D., F.R.C.S.Ed.

Royal College of Surgeons of England: Lincoln's Inn Fields, London WC2A 3PN. 071-405 3474. President: Ian P. Todd, P.R.C.S.

Royal College of Veterinary Surgeons: 32 Belgrave Square, London SW1X 8QP. 071-235 4971. President: Professor Leslie Clifford Vaughan, D.Sc., D.V.R., F.R.C.V.S.

Royal Commission on Ancient and Historical Monuments in Wales: (including the National Monuments Record for Wales) Edleston House, Queen's Road, Aberystwyth SY23 2HP. Aberystwyth 4381/2. Chairman: Professor Glanmor Williams, C.B.E., M.A., F.S.A.

Royal Commission on Environmental Pollution: Church Hse, Great Smith Street, London SW1P 3BL. 071-212 8620. Chairman: Sir Jack Lewis, F.R.S. Secretary: G. I. Fuller.

Royal Commission on the Ancient and Historical Monuments of Scotland: 54 Melville Street, Edinburgh EH3 7HF. 031-225 5994. Chairman: The Earl of Crawford and Balcarres, P.C. Secretary: J.G. Dunbar, M.A., F.S.A., Hon. F.R.I.A.S.

Royal Commission on the Historical Monuments of England: Fortress House, 23 Saville Row, London W1X 1AB. 071-734 6010. Chairman: The Earl Ferrers, P.C. Secretary: T.G. Hassall, M.A., F.S.A., M.I.F.A.

Royal Commonwealth Society: 18 Northumberland Avenue, London WC2N 5BJ. 071-930 6733. Secretary-General: Sir Michael Scott, K.C.V.O., C.M.G.

Royal Fine Art Commission: 7 St. James's Square, London SW1Y 4JU. 071-839 6537. Chairman: Rt. Hon. Norman St. John-Stevas, M.P. Secretary: Sherban Canta cuzino, M.A., F.R.I.B.A.

Royal Fine Art Commission for Scotland: 9 Atholl Crescent, Edinburgh EH3 8HA. 031-229 1109. Chairman: Professor Alexander J. Youngson, M.A., D.Litt., Hon.F.R.I.A.S. Secretary: Charles Prosser, D.F.A., D.A.Ed.

Royal Forestry Society of England, Wales and Northern Ireland: 102 High Street, Tring, Herts HP23 4AH. Tring 2028. President: R. M. Harley, B.Sc. Director: E.H.M. Harris, B.Sc.

Royal Geographical Society: 1 Kensington Gore, London SW7 2AR. 071- 589 5466. Director and Secretary: Dr. John Hemming.

Royal Greenwich Observatory: Herstmonceux Castle, Hailsham, East Sussex BN27 1RP. Herstmonceux 833171. Director: Prof. A. Boksenberg, F.R.S.

Royal Historical Society: University College London, Gower Street, London WC1E 6BT. 071-387 7532. President: G.E.Aylmer, M.A., D.Phil., F.B.A.

Royal Horticultural Society: Vincent Square, London SW1P 2PE. 071-834 4333. Director General: C. D. Brickell, N.D.H.

Royal Humane Society (encourages and rewards the saving of human life): Brettenham House, Lancaster Place, London WC2E 7EP. 071-836 8155. Secretary: Major A. J. Dickinson.

Royal Institute of British Architects: 66 Portland Place, London W1N 4AD. 071-580 5533. President: Larry Rolland.

Royal Institute of International Affairs: Chatham House, 10 St. James's Square, London SW1Y 4LE. 071-930 2233. Director: Admiral Sir James Eberle, G.C.B.

Royal Institute of Oil Painters: 17 Carlton House Terrace, London SW1Y 5BD. President: Krome Barratt, R.B.A.

Royal Institute of Painters in Water Colours: 17 Carlton House Terrace, London SW1Y 5BD. President: Charles Bone.

Royal Institution of Chartered Surveyors: 12 Great George Street, Parliament Square, London SW1P 3AD. 071-222 7000. President: D. A. G. Troup, F.R.I.C.S., C.A.A.V. Secretary-General: M. A. Pattison, B.A.

Royal Institution of Great Britain: 21 Albemarle Street, London W1X 4BS. 071-409 2992. President: H.R.H. The Duke of Kent, K.G., G.C.M.G., G.C.V.O. Director: Professor J. M. Thomas, F.R.S. Hon. Secretary: Professor E. A. Ash, C.B.E., F.R.S.

Royal Life Saving Society: Mountbatten House, Studley, Warwickshire B80 7NN. Studley 3943/4. President: Sir David McNee, Q.P.M. Director and Chief Commonwealth Secretary: Keith H. Sach.

Royal Meteorological Society: James Glaisher House, Grenville Place, Bracknell, Berkshire RG12 1BX. Bracknell 422957. President: R.S. Scorer, Ph.D.

Royal Mint: Llantrisant, Pontyclun, Mid Glamorgan CF7 8YT. Llantrisant 222111. Deputy Master: Dr. D.J. Gerhard, C.B. London Office: 7 Grosvenor Gardens, London SW1W 0BH. 071-828 8724.

Royal National Lifeboat Institution: West Quay Road, Poole, Dorset. BH15 1HZ. Poole 671133. Chairman: The Duke of Atholl. Director: Lieutenant-Commander B. Miles, R.D., M.N.I., R.N.R.

Royal Observer Corps: Bentley Priory, Stanmore, Middlesex. 081-950 4000 ext. 450. Commandant: Air Commodore I. Horrocks, R.A.F.

Royal Photographic Society of Great Britain: R.P.S. National Centre of Photography, The Octagon, Milsom Street, Bath BA1 1DN. Bath 62841. President: Arthur Downes. Secretary: Kenneth R. Warr.

Royal Scottish Country Dance Society: 12 Coates Crescent, Edinburgh EH3 7AF. 031-225 3854. Secretary: M. M. Gibson.

Royal Scottish Forestry Society: 11 Atholl Crescent, Edinburgh EH3 8HE. 031-229 8180 or 8851. Secretary and Treasurer: W.B.C. Walker, LL.B., N.P.

Royal Scottish Geograhcial Society: 10 Randolph Crescent, Edinburgh EH3 7TU. 031-225 3330. Secretary: Alistair B. Cruickshank, M.A.

Royal Scottish Society for Prevention of Cruelty to Children: 41 Polwarth Terrace, Edinburgh EH11 1NU. 031-337 8539/0. General Secretary: Arthur M. M. Wood, O.B.E., M.A., LL.B.

Royal Society: 6 Carlton House Terrace, London SW1Y 5AG. 071-839 5561. President: Sir George Porter, F.R.S. Executive Secretary: Dr. P.T. Warren.

Royal Society for the Prevention of Cruelty to Animals: The Causeway, Horsham, Sussex RH12 1HG. Horsham 64181. Executive Director: Frank Dixon Ward.

Royal Society of Arts: 6-8 John Adam Street, Adelphi, London WC2N 6EZ. 071-930 5115. Chairman: Sir Peter Baldwin, K.C.B. Secretary: Christopher Lucas.

Royal Society of British Artists: 17 Carlton House Terrace, London SW1Y 5BD. President: Peter Garrard, R.P.

Royal Society of British Sculptors: 108 Old Brompton Road, London SW7 3RA. 071-373 5554. President: Michael Rizzello, O.B.E. Secretary: Maureen O'Connor.

Royal Society of Chemistry: Burlington House, London W1V 0BN. 071-437 8656. President: Professor Sir Jack Lewis, Ms.C., Ph.D., C.Chem., F.R.S.C., F.R.S., Secretary General: J.S., Gow, B.Sc., Ph.D., C.Chem., F.R.S.C., F.R.S.E.

Royal Society of Edinburgh: 22 George Street, Edinburgh EH2 2PQ. 031-225 6057. President: Sir Alwyn Williams.

Royal Society of Marine Artists: 17 Carlton House Terrace, London SW1Y 5BD. President: John Worsley.

Royal Society of Medicine: 1 Wimpole Street, London W1M 8AE. 071-408 2119. President: Sir Gordon Robson, C.B.E., F.F.A.R.C.S., Executive Director: Robert N. Thomson, M.A.

Royal Society of Miniature Painters, Sculptors and Gravers: 17 Carlton House Terrace, London SW1Y 5BD. President: Suzanne Lucas.

Royal Society of Portrait Painters: 17 Carlton House Terrace, London SW1Y 5BD. President: David Poole, A.R.C.A.

Royal Statistical Society: 25 Enford Street, London W1H 2BH. 071-723 5882. President: Professor J. Durbin.

Royal Zoological Society of Scotland (Scottish National Zoological Collection): Murrayfield, Edinburgh. EH12 6TS. 031-334 9171/2. Director: R.J. Wheater, F.R.S.E.

Science Museum: South Kensington, London SW7 2DD. 071-589 3456. Director: Dr. Neil Cossons, O.B.E., M.A., F.S.A., F.M.A.

Science and Engineering Research Council: Polaris House, North Star Avenue, Swindon SN2 1ET. Swindon 26222. Chairman: Professor E.W.J. Mitchell, C.B.E., F.R.S. Secretary: Dr. J.A. Catterall.

Scottish Arts Council: 19 Charlotte Square, Edinburgh EH2 4DF. 031- 226 6051. Director: Timothy Mason.

Scottish Civic Trust: 24 George Square, Glasgow G2 1EF. 041-221 1466.

Scottish Office: New St. Andrew's House, Edinburgh EH1 3DG. 031-556 8400. Dover House, Whitehall, London SW1A 2AU. 071-270 3000. Permanent Under-Secretary of State: R.R. Hillhouse. Industry Department for Scotland: New St. Andrew's House, Edinburgh EH1 3TA. 031-556 8400. Secretary: J.A. Scott, C.B., L.V.O. Scottish Development Department: St. Andrew's House, Edinburgh EH1 3DE. 031-556 8400. Secretary and Chief Economic Advisor: R.G.L. McCrone, C.B., F.R.S.E., Ph.D. Scottish Education Department: New St. Andrew's House, Edinburgh EH1 3SY. 031- 556 8400. Secretary: G.R. Wilson. Scottish Home and Health Department: St. Andrew's House, Edinburgh EH1 3DE. 031-556 8501. Secretary: W.K. Reid, C.B.

Scottish Information Office: New St. Andrews House ,Edinburgh EH1 3TD. 031-556 8400., Director: C.F. Corbett.

Sea Fish Industry Authority: 10 Young Street, Edinburgh EH2 4JQ. 031-225 2515. Telex: 727225. Chairman: J.P. Rettie, T.D. Chief Executive: J.C.H. Richman.

SHELTER: National Campaign for the Homeless, 157 Waterloo Road, London, SE1. 071 633 9377.

Social Security Advisory Committee: New Court, Carey Street, London WC2A 2LS. 071-831 6111 ext. 2636.

Social Security Advisory Committee: See Social Security, Department of.

Society for the Assistance of Ladies in Reduced Circumstances: Lancaster House, 25 Hornyold Road, Malvern, Worcs. WR14 1QQ. Malvern 4645.

Society of Antiquaries: Burlington House, London W1V 0HS. 071-734 0193. President: Professor J.D. Evans, M.A., Ph.D., F.B.A.

14

Society of Antiquaries of Scotland: Royal Museum of Scotland, Queen Street, Edinburgh EH2 1JD. 031-557 3550 ext. 268. Secretary: Trevor F. Watkins, B.A., Ph.D.

Society of Apothecaries: Black Friars Lane, London EC4V 6EJ. 071-236 1180. Clerk: Major J.C. O'Leary.

Society of Graphic Artists: 9 Newburgh Street, London W1V 1LH. President: Lorna B. Kell.

Society of Wildlife Artists: 17 Carlton House Terrace, London SW1Y 5BD. President: Robert Gilmore.

Society of Women Artists: 17 Carlton House Terrace, London SW1Y 5BD. President: Barbara Tate.

Spastics Society: 12 Park Crescent, London W1N 4EQ. 071-636 5020. Chairman: Mrs. Joyce Smith, O.B.E. Director: Sir John Cox, K.C.B. Secretary: P. G. Lockley, F.C.I.S.

St. John Ambulance: 1 Grosvenor Crescent, London SW1X 7EF. 071-235 5231. Director of Public Relations: John Mills, M.B.E., M.I.P.R.

St. Peter's Research Trust for the Cure of Kidney Disease: 172-176 Shaftesbury Avenue, London WC2H 8JE. 071-240 9115. Hon. Secretary: Mrs. A. M. Joekes.

Statute Law Society: 186 City Road, London EC1V 2NU. 071-251 1644. President: The Lord Renton, P.C., Q.C. Chairman: Rt. Hon. Sir Edward Eveleigh. Acting Secretary: Clifford Shanbury, LL.B., F.C.A.

Stock Exchange: London EC2N 1HP. 071-588 2355. Chairman: Sir Nicholas Goodison.

Tate Gallery: Millbank, London SW1P 4RG. 071-821 1313. Recorded information 071-821 7128. Director: Alan Bowness, C.B.E. Comprises the national collection of British painting and twentieth century sculpture.

Thames Water Authority: Nugent House, Vaston Road, Reading, Berks., RG1 8DB. 0734 593333. Chairman: Roy Watts, C.B.E. Managing Director: William Harper.

The British Academy: 20-21 Cornwall Terrace, London NW1 4QP. 071-487 5966. President: Sir Randolph Quirk.

Toc H: 1 Forest Close, Wendover, Buckinghamshire. HP22 6BT. Wendover 623911. General Secretary: Dr. J.M.A. Kilburn.

Translators' Guild (1986) Ltd.: c/o 13 Fidler Place, Bushey, Herts. WD2 3UF. 071-831 6550. Chairman: Dr. John Sykes. Secretary: Mrs Dimity Castellano.

Transport Tribunal: Golden Cross House (4th floor), Duncannon Street, London WC2N 4JF. 071-210 4601. President: Judge Inskip, Q.C. Secretary: D.T.R. Evans.

Treasury Solicitor: Queen Anne's Chambers, 28 Broadway, London SW1H 9JS. 071-210 3000. H.M. Procurator-General and Treasury Solicitor: Sir John Bailey, K.C.B.

Trinity House: Tower Hill, London EC3N 4DH. 071-480 6601. General Lighthouse Authority for England, Wales and Channel Islands and Gibraltar; Principal Pilotage Authority for the U.K.; a charitable maritime organisation. Deputy Master: Captain Sir Miles Buckley Wingate, K.C.V.O., F.N.I. Secretary: J.R. Backhouse

TRUST: 59 Caledonian Road, London, N1 9BU. 071 273 9315. Director: Dr. Stephen Shaw.

United Kingdom Central Council for Nursing, Midwifery and Health Visiting: 23 Portland Place, London W1N 3AF. 071-637 7181. Chief Executive Officer: Miss M. Storey.

United Nations Association of Great Britain and Northern Ireland: 3 Whitehall Court, London SW1A 2EL. 071-930 2931. Director: Malcolm Harper.

United Society of Artists: 17 Carlton House Terrace, London SW1Y 5BD. President: Robert Hill.

University Grants Committee: 14 Park Crescent, London W1N 4DH. 071- 636 7799. Chairman: Sir Peter Swinnerton-Dyer, Bt., K.B.E., F.R.S.

Victoria Cross and George Cross Association: Room 04, Archway Block South, Old Admiralty Building, Whitehall, London SW1A 2BE. 071-930 3506. Chairman: Rear Admiral B.C.G. Place, V.C., C.B., D.S.C.

Victoria and Albert Museum, Bethnal Green Museum of Childhood: Cambridge Heath Road, London E2, 081-980 2415.

Victoria and Albert Museum, Ham House, Nr. Richmond, Surrey. 081-940 1950.

Victoria and Albert Museum, National Museum of Art & Design: South Kensington, London SW7 2RL. 071-589 6371. Director: Elizabeth Esteve-Coll.

Victoria and Albert Museum, Osterley Park House, Osterley, Middlesex. 081-560 3918.

Victoria and Albert Museum, Theatre Museum, The Flower Market, Covent Garden, London (Opening April 1987.)

Victoria and Albert Museum, Wellington Museum at Apsley House: Hyde Park Corner, London W1. 071-499 5676.

Wallace Collection: Hertford House, Manchester Square, London W1M 6BN. 071-935 0687.

Water Authorities Association: 1 Queen Anne's Gate, London SW1H 9BT. 071-222 8111. Chairman: Len Hill, C.B.E. Secretary: Andrew Semple.

Welsh Arts Council: Holst House, 9 Museum Place, Cardiff CF1 3NX. Cardiff 394711. Director: Thomas Arfon Owen. Oriel Bookshop and Gallery: 52 Charles Street, Cardiff CF1 4ED. Cardiff 395548.

Welsh National Board for Nursing, Midwifery and Health Visiting: Floor 13, Pearl Assurance House, Greyfriars Road, Cardiff CF1 3AG. Cardiff 395535. Chief Executive Officer: Wyndham Preece.

Welsh Office: Gwydyr House, Whitehall, London SW1A 2ER. 071-233 3000. Cathays Park, Cardiff. Cardiff 825111. Permanent Secretary: R. A. Lloyd-Jones, C.B. Deputy Secretary: I.H. Lightman, C.B.; J. W. Preston.

Women's Royal Voluntary Service: WRVS Headquarters, 17 Old Park Lane, London W1Y 4AJ. 071-499 6040. Chairman: Dame Barbara Shenfield, D.B.E.

Zoological Society of London: Regent's Park, London NW1 4RY. 071-722 3333. President: Sir William Henderson, D.Sc., F.R.C.V.S., F.I.Biol., F.R.S.E., F.R.S. Secretary: Dr. R.M. Laws, C.B.E., Ph.D., F.I.Biol., F.R.S.

THE ROYAL SOCIETY FOR THE PREVENTION OF ACCIDENTS (ROSPA)

THE SOCIETY, founded in 1916 as the London Safety First Council, has as its object the prevention of accidents on the roads, in the home, in leisure pursuits, in commerce, industry and agriculture, by educational means.

The Society produces posters, leaflets, and other forms of publicity. It has an information service and film library, and an industrial safety training centre at 22 Summer Road, Acocks Green, Birmingham B27 7UT. A list of publications is available. It is non-profit making, and relies on the subscriptions of its members, contributions from other interested bodies and, for certain activities grants from Government Departments. The whole of its funds are used in promoting the prevention of accidents.

Patron: H.M. The Queen.

President: Lord Keith of Castleacre

Hon. Treasurer: J. Adcock.

Director-General: J.F.B. Wethered

Secretary: J. Newton

Head Office: Cannon House, The Priory Queensway, Birmingham, B4 6BS. 021-200 2461.

ACCIDENTS IN GREAT BRITAIN

Every day in Great Britain, about 38 people die from accidental injuries. Another six people die from injuries resulting in 'open-verdicts' at inquest (i.e. injuries undetermined whether accidentally or not).

During 1988, there were 13,898 accidental deaths (24 deaths per 100,000 peoplw) and 2,284 deaths resulting in 'open-verdicts'. In comparison, there were 13,945 accidental deaths during 1987 and 2,167 'open-verdicts'.

The number of people non-fatally injured in acciodents is not precisely known. However, it is estimated that some seven million people are treated for injuries at hospital accident/ emergency departments every year of whom some 600,000 people are detained in hospital.

The breakdown of the deaths and injuries by place of occurrence, based on recent annual figures, is shown in the accompanying tables. Further details for selected areas of accident occurrence are provided below:

Place	Deaths	Hospital cases
Road	5,600	400,000
Home	5,100	2,400,000
Work	650	1,200,000
Sport/leisure	400	1,000,000
Other - transport	250	
Other - falls	1,000	2,000,000
Others	1,000	
Total	**14,000**	**7 million**

ROAD ACCIDENTS

Provisional figures published by the Department of Transport based on police reports show that there were 5,230 deaths in road traffic accidents in Great Britain during 1989 (just over nine deaths per 100,000 population). There were 61,800 serious injuries and 261,100 slight injuries. A breakdown of deaths by class of road user for 1989 is:

Class of Road User	Killed	Injured
Pedestrians	1,671	57,100
Pedal cyclists	295	27,200
Motorcyclists	659	40,500
Car users	2,304	178,400
Bus/coach users	28	9,800
Goods vehicle users	253	13,700
Others, e.g. horse riders	20	1,300
All Casualties,	**5,230**	**327,900**
of whom		
Children under 15	378	41,700
Adults 15 to 59	3,377	247,700
Adults 60 & over	1,466	34,500
Age not reported	9	4,100

The overall trends in road casualties since 1985 are shown in the accompanying table:

Year	Killed	Seriously Injured	Slightly Injured	Total Casualties
1985	5,165	71,000	241,400	317,500
1986	5,382	68,800	247,300	321,500
1987	5,125	64,300	242,100	311,500
1988	5,041	63,000	250,000	318,000
1989*	5,230	61,800	266,100	333,200

* *Provisional figures*

The number of vehicles in use and the volume of traffic on the roads have been increasing steadily. The latest census figure (based on a full count at DLVC in Swansea of all currently licensed vehicles) is 24.2 million vehicles on 31 December 1989 (including 19.7 million cars and 875,000 motorcycles). This total compares with 23.3 million vehicles one year before and 20.8 million vehicles, five years ago, in 1984.

HOME ACCIDENTS

Accidental deaths in the home totalled just over 5,000 per year. During 1988, some 5,248 people in the UK died in accidents in the home (including residential institutions). The total represents some nine deaths per 100,000 population. The trend in home accident deaths over recent years (and the death rate per 100,000 people) is:

Year	Deaths	Rate
1985	5,901	(10)
1986	5,685	(10)
1987	5,149	(9)
1988	5,248	

The breakdown by cause of death in the UK during 1988 is:

Cause of death	Under 15	15-64	65 & over	All ages
Accidental falls	25	373	2,775	3,173
Fire/flames/burns *	128	284	423	835
Accidental poisoning	9	412	88	524
Suffocation/choking	52	199	155	406
Other causes	39	121	165	310
Total	**253**	**1,389**	**3,606**	**5,248**

* *Includes suffocation by smoke*

Non-fatal injuries in the home/garden involving hospital treatment are estimated to number over two million cases each year. The distribution by age is markedly different from accidental deaths. For example, children comprise five per cent of the accidental deaths in the home but 40 per cent of the hospital cases.

The breakdown of the home/garden injuries involving hospital treatment by type of accident with national estimates for Rngland and Wales during 1987 is shown in the accompanying table. The whole spectrum of injury is covered from 'no diagnosed injury' to the severe fractures, burns etc.

Type of Accident	All Ages
Falls	825,000
Cutting/piercing	362,000
Struck by obj/person	397,000
Burning	92,000
Foreign body	97,000
Poisoning	40,000
Over exertion	25,000
Other	86,000
Unknown	176,000
Total	**2,102,000**

WORK ACCIDENTS

There were 620 accidental deaths reported at work in Great Britain over a 12 month period commencing 1 April 1987. This total includes employees, the self-employed and others (e.g. child trespassers killed on construction sites, farmers' wives and children, etc.). The trend in the figures since 1981 (when The Notification of Accidents and Dangerous Occurrences Regulations, 1980, came into force) is:

1981	654
1982	673
1983	646
1984	627
1985	659

14

New reporting regulations were introduced on 1 April 1986 (The Reporting of Injuries, Diseases and Dangerous Occurrences Regulations, 1985). The trend since 1986 (figures subsequently collected on a financial year basis) is:

1986/7	535
1987/8	620

The breakdown of the 1987/8 accidental deaths by sector is:

Agriculture	63
Energy & water	35
Manufacturing	103
Construction	158
Distributive trades	41
Transport & communication	54
Banking/insurance, etc	6
Other services	84
Merchant shipping	60
Civil aviation	2
Unclassified	15
TOTAL	**620**

Regarding non-fatal injuries, it has been estimated that around one million people are injured at work each year and subsequently seek hospital treatment. However, only injuries involving more than three days' absence from normal employment are counted as reportable cases under the regulations.

The 1985 regulations re-introduced the requirement on employers to directly report injuries at work and this change has resulted in an estimated 50% under-reporting when compared with figures collected under the 1980 regulations via DHSS injury benefit claims data. For example, during 1982 (the last full year based on DHSS claims data), there were less than one-half this number recorded in 1986/7 and 1987/8. The current injury rates for manufacturing and construction are, respectively, around 1,200 and 2,000 injuries of over three days' absence per 100,000 employees per year.

Major injuries were first defined in the 1980 regulations and include most fractures, spells in hospital, etc. These injuries averaged over 7,000 cases per year in manufacturing industries over the first two years under the 1985 reporting regulations and 2,600 injuries per year in construction. The trend in the major injury rate per 100,000 employees since 1981 is:

	Manufacturing	*Construction*
1981	71	164
1982	75	204
1983	79	221
1984	88	234
1985	91	232

A greater proportion of the reported injuries came under the scope of "major" when the definition was changed in the 1985 regulations. This change artificially inflated the most recent incidence rates:

1986/7	141	264
1987/8	138	261

NATIONAL NEWSPAPERS

DAILY NEWSPAPERS

Daily Express. Express Newspapers plc, Ludgate House, 245 Blackfriars Road, London SE1 9UX. 071-928 8000. (1,561,754).
Daily Mail. Mail Newspapers plc, Northcliffe House, 2 Derry Street, London W8 5TS 071-938 6000. (1,670,036).
The Daily Mirror. Mirror Group Newspapers, Holborn Group Newspapers, London EC1P 1DQ 071-353 0246. (3,129,890).
The Daily Star. Express Newspapers plc, Ludgate House, 245

Blackfriars Road, London SE1 9UX. 071-928 8000. (919,133).
The Daily Telegraph. Peterborough Court at South Quay, 181 Marsh Wall London E14 9SR. 071-538 5000. (1,113,033).
Financial Times. Number One, Southwark Bridge Road, London SE1 9HL. 071-873 3000. (291,531).
The Guardian. Guardian Newspapers Ltd., 119 Faringdon Road, London EC1R 3ER. 071-278 2332. (430,458).
The Independent. Newspaper Publishing plc, 40 City Road, London EC1Y 2DB. 071-253 1222. (414,357).
The Sun. News International Distribution Ltd., 1 Virginia Street, London E19XP. 071-782 4000 (3,936,692).
The Times. News International Distribution Ltd., 1 Pennington Street, London E1 9XN. 071-782 5000. (432,453).
Today. News (UK) Ltd., 70 Vauxhall Bridge Road, Pimlico, London SW1V 2RP. 071-630 1333. (581,240)

SUNDAY NEWSPAPERS

The Mail on Sunday. Northcliffe House, 2 Derry Street, Kensington, London W8 5TS. 071-938 6000 (1,889,431).
News of the World. News International Distribution Ltd., 1 Virginia Street, London E1 9XR. 071-782 4000. (5,036,019).
The Observer. Chelsea Bridge House, Queenstown Road, London SW8 4NN. 071-627 0700. (566,854).
The People. Mirror Group Newspapers, Holborn Circus, London EC1P 1DQ. 071-353 0246. (2,588,468).
The Sunday Express. Express Newspapers plc, Ludgate House, 245 Blackfriars Road, London SE1 9UX. 071-928 8000. (1,727,376).
Sunday Mirror. Mirror Group Newspapers, Holborn Circus, London EC1P 1DQ. 071-353 0246. (2,910,867).
Sunday Telegraph. Peterborough Court at South Quay, 181 Marsh Wall, London E14 9SR. 071-538 5000. (656,120).
The Sunday Times. News International Distribution Ltd., 1, Pennington Street, London E1 9XW. 071-782 5000 (1,186,667).
Sunday Sport. Apollo Ltd., Administration Centre, 848b Melton Road, Thurmaston, Leicester LE4 8El. 0533 693861 (451,951)

The average daily circulation of each paper during the period January to June '90 is given in brackets with the permission of the newspaper concerned and/or from ABC published statistics.

ESPERANTO IN BRITAIN

140 Holland Park Avenue, London W11 4UF (071-727 7821) THE British Esperanto Association (Inc.) Ltd. was founded in 1904. A twin association, the Esperanto Association of Britain, is an educational charity at the same address. They both assist local groups and classes, hold examinations up to licentiateship, publish and retail books from a stock of several thousands, issue a bi- monthly magazine, organise lectures, conferences and seminars.

The Butler Library at the same address has books and other items indexed up to 30,000 entries. Members of the British and European Parliaments give support; in the world of education their efforts have given the GCSE in Esperanto; tuition is available in two British universities.

A youth section and a teacher's association have special fields of activity. Current activity involves encouraging the use of Esperanto as an easier common language among the nations of the European Community.

Secretary (BEA): M.H. McClelland, F.E.A.B.

Secretary (EAB): Will Green, L.B.E.A., F.B.E.A.

President: A Diaz, F.E.A.B.

The Universal Esperanto Association has its headquarters in Rotterdam and holds international congresses each year in a different country.

MORSE CODE

A	._	N	_.
B	_...	O	___
C	_._.	P	.__.
D	_..	Q	__._
E	.	R	._.
F	.._.	S	...
G	__.	T	_
H	....	U	.._
I	..	V	..._
J	.___	W	.__
K	_._	X	_.._
L	._..	Y	_.__
M	__	Z	__..
1	.____	6	_....
2	..___	7	__...
3	...__	8	___..
4	...._	9	____.
5	.....	0	_____

Å (German)	
A or Ä (Spanish and Scandinavian)	._._
ÇH (German and Spanish)	____
É (French)	.._..
Ñ (Spanish)	__.__
Ö (German)	___.
Ü (German)	.._

Note:
A dash is equal to three dots.
The space between parts of the same letter is equal to one dot.
The space between two letters is equal to three dots.
The space between two words is equal to seven dots.

Full stop	._._._
Comma	__..__
Colon or division sign	___...
Apostrophe	._____.
Hyphen	_...._
Fraction bar or division sign	_.._.
Left hand bracket	_.__.
Right hand bracket	_.__._
Break sign	_..._
Distress signal	...___...
Commencing signal	_._._
General call	_._._._
From (de)	_..
Invitation to transmit	_._
Question mark (note of interrogation or request for repetition)	..__..
Wait	._...
Double hyphen	_..._
Understood	..._.
Error	....
Received	._.
Position report	_._.
Cross or added sign	._._.
Transmission finished	..._._

SEVEN WONDERS OF THE WORLD

THE PYRAMIDS OF EGYPT. On the west bank of the Nile, the pyramids were built about 3000 B.C. by the Egyptian Pharaohs as royal tombs. The Great Pyramid at Cheops was originally 481 ft. high and 756 ft. square at the base. The pyramids are the only wonder now in existence.

THE HANGING GARDENS OF BABYLON. Reputed to have been built by Nebuchadnezzar about 600 B.C. 60 miles from Baghdad. The gardens were terraced, varying in height from 75 ft. to 300 ft. and were watered from the highest terrace.

THE TEMPLE OF DIANA AT EPHESUS. A marble temple erected by the cities of Ionia in honour of Diana (Artemis) about 480 B.C.

THE STATUE OF JUPITER OLYMPUS (ZEUS). Built by Phidias at Olympia in the fifth century B.C. The statue was made of marble, inlaid with gold and ivory.

THE TOMB OF MAUSOLUS. Built about 350 B.C. by Queen Artemisia in memory of her husband Mausolus, at Halicarnassuss, Asia Minor. The term mausoleum originated from this.

THE COLOSSUS OF RHODES. A bronze statue of Apollo, erected about 280 B.C. and said to have stood astride the harbour of Rhodes.

THE PHAROS OF ALEXANDRIA. A lighthouse built about 200 B.C. on the island of Pharos outside the port of Alexandria.

WEIGHTS AND MEASURES

IMPERIAL SYSTEM

MEASURE OF LENGTH

12 lines	= 1 inch (in.)
12 inches	= 1 foot (ft.)
3 feet	= 1 yard (yd.)
22 yards	= 1 chain
10 chains	= 1 furlong
8 furlongs	= 1,760 yards = 1 mile (ml.)
3 barleycorns	= 1 inch
2 1/4 inches	= 1 nail
4 inches	= 1 hand
9 inches	= 1 span
7.92 inches	= 1 link

CLOTH MEASURE

2 1/4 inches	= 1 nail
4 nails	= 1 quarter (of a yard)
3 quarters	= 1 Flemish ell
4 quarters	= 1 yard
5 quarters	= 1 English ell
6 quarters	= 1 French ell

MEASURES OF AREA

144 square inches (sq.in.)	= 1 square foot (sq.ft.)
9 square feet	= 1 square yard (sq.yd.)
484 square yards	= 1 square chain
1,210 square yards	= 1 rood (rd.)
4 roods	= 1 acre (ac.)
640 acres	= 1 square mile (sq.ml.)
4,840 square yards	= 1 acre

DRY OR LIQUID MEASURE

4 gills	= 1 pint
2 pints	= 1 quart
4 quarts	= 1 gallon = 8 pints
	= 277,274 cu.inches
2 gallons	= 1 peck
2 pecks	= 1 bushel
4 bushels	= 1 coomb
5 bushels (or porter's load)	= 1 sack of flour
8 bushels	= 1 quarter
4 1/2 quarters	= 1 chaldron
36 bushels	= 1 chaldron
5 quarters (40 bushels)	= 1 wey or horseload
2 weys (10 quarters) = 1 last	
1 gallon (U.S.)	= 0.833 Imperial gallons

FLUID MEASURE

60 minims (drops)	= 1 drachm
8 drachms	= 1 ounce
20 ounces	= 1 pint
1 teaspoonful	= 1 drachm
1 desertspoonful	= 2 drachms
1 tablespoonful	= 4 drachms

ALE AND BEER MEASURE

4 gills	= 1 pint
2 pints	= 1 quart
4 quarts	= 1 gallon
4 1/2 gallons	= 1 pin
9 gallons	= 1 firkin
2 firkins (18 gallons) = 1 kilderkin	
2 kilderkins	= 1 barrel
1 1/2 barrels	= 1 hogshead
2 hogsheads	= 1 butt
2 butts	= 1 tun

WINE MEASURE

4 gills	= 1 pint
2 pints	= 1 quart
4 quarts	= 1 gallon
10 gallons	= 1 anker
18 gallons	= 1 runlet
31 1/2 gallons	= 1 barrel
42 gallons	= 1 tierce
63 gallons	= 1 hogshead
84 gallons	= 1 puncheon
2 hogsheads	= 1 pipe or butt
2 pipes	= 1 tun

14

OTHER MEASURES

12 articles	= 1 dozen
12 dozen	= 1 gross
12 gross	= 1 great gross
20 articles	= 1 score
5 score	= 1 hundred
6 score	= 1 great hundred
1 tablespoon	= 1/2 fluid oz.
1 desertspoon	= 1/4 fluid oz.
1 teaspoon	1/8 fluid oz.

KITCHEN MEASURES

1 lb. of wheat flour	= 1 quart
1 lb.2 oz. of corn flour	= 1 quart
1 lb. butter	= 1 pint
1 lb.2 oz. brown sugar	= 1 pint
1 lb.1 oz. granulated sugar	= 1 pint
4 tablespoonfuls	= 1/2 gill
1 glass tumbler	= 1/2 pint
1 tea-cup	= 1 gill
1 tablespoonful	= 1/2 oz.

AVOIRDUPOIS WEIGHT

7,000 grains (gr.)	= 1 pound (lb.)
27,34375 grains	= 1 dram (dr.)
16 drams	= 1 ounce (oz.)
16 ounces	= 1 pound (lb.)_
14 pounds	= 1 stone (st.)
28 pounds	= 1 quarter (qr.)
4 quarters (112 pounds)	= 1 hundredweight (cwt.)
20 hundredweight	= 1 ton = 2,240 lb.
100 pounds	= 1 cental
20 centals	= 1 short ton = 2,000 lb.

TROY WEIGHT

Jewellery made of gold is described as of so many carats. This is not the weight of the article, but the proportion of gold used in its manufacture. Articles are not made of pure gold, the metal being too soft. Each article is supposed to be divided into 24 equal parts or carats, and is composed of so many parts gold and so many parts alloy. Thus 18 carat gold is made of 18 parts gold and 6 alloy. The gold in general use is either 9, 15, 18, or 22 carat.
The British sovereign is 22 carat gold. It weighs 123,274 grains, 113 of which is gold.

3,086 grains	= 1 carat
24 grains	= 1 pennyweight (dwt.)
20 pennyweights	= 1 ounce (oz.)

THE METRIC (SI) SYSTEM

The original metric system adopted first in France at the end of the 18th century was based on two units, the metre for length and the kilogram for weight. With developments of science and technology these two units have been found to be insufficient and other base units have been added to give the modernised metric system, known as the International System of Units, initials **SI** for short. The seven base units of **SI** are :

> The metre (m) for length
> The kilogram (kg) for mass or weight *
> The second(s) for time
> The ampere (A) for electrical current
> The kelvin (K) for thermo-dynamic temperature
> The candela (cd) for luminous intensity
> The mole (mol) for amount of substance

The mole is not likely to be met with except in theoretical physics and chemistry. For practical purposes the Celsius (°C) scale is used instead of the kelvin. They have identical scale intervals but the kelvin scale starts at absolute zero and the Celsius scale starts at the freezing point of water i.e. 0°C or 273 K.

There are two supplementary units, the radian for the plane angle and the steradian for the solid angle but the normal plane angle (degree, minute and second) is retained as well as the minute and hour of time. There are also units derived from the base units which define force (newton), pressure (pascal and bar), and the existing metric units, for work and energy (joule), power (watts), electrical quantities (volt and ohm etc.) and so on.

The whole system is "coherent"i.e. all the units are derived from the seven base units.

Prefixes are used to obtain multiples and sub-multiples of the units. The more commonly used of these SI prefixes are :

Prefix			*Symbol*
mega	one	million times (10^6)	M
kilo	one	thousand times (10^3)	k
hecto	one	hundred times (10^2)	h
deca	ten	times (10)	da
deci	one	tenth of (10^{-1})	d
centi	one	hundredth of (10^{-2})	c
milli	one	thousandth of (10^{-3})	m
micro	one	millionth of (10^{-6})	μ

For everyday life only a small selection of the units included in the International System will be needed. These are set out below.

LENGTH

metre (m)	
Centimetre (cm)	= one hundredth of a metre
millimetre (mm)	= one thousandth of a metre
kilometre (km)	= one thousand metres

WEIGHT*

kilogram (kg)	
gram (g)	= one thousandth of a kilogram
tonne (t)	= one thousand kilgrams

*Strictly speaking, the gram, kilogram and tonne are units of mass. For most people and ordinary trading purposes the distinction between weight and mass is unimportant.

VOLUME AND CAPACITY

litre	
mililitre (ml)	= one thousandth of a litre
cubic centimetre (cm^3)	
decilitre (dl)	= one tenth of a litre
centiletre (cl)	= one hundredth of a litre
cubic metre (m^3)	= 1000 litres

METRIC EQUIVALENTS OF BRITISH WEIGHTS AND MEASURES

Length

1 inch	2.54 centimetres
1 foot	30.48 centimetres
1 yard	0.9144 metre
1 mile	1.609 kilometres

Area

1 sq.inch	6.4516 sq.centimetres
1 sq.foot	929.03 sq.centimetres (cm^2)
1 sq.yard	0.836127 sq.metres (m^2)
1 acre (4.840 sq.yards)	0.40468 hectare
1 sq.mile (640 acres)	258.999 hectares

Volume

1 cu.inch	16.387 cu.centimetres (cm^3)
1 cu.foot (1.728 cu.inch)	0.028317 cu. metre (m^3)
1 cu.yard (27 cu.feet)	0.764555 cu. metre (m^3)

Capacity

1 gill	0.142 litre
1 pint	0.568 litre
1 quart	1.137 litres
1 gallon	4.546 litres
1 peck (2 gallons)	9.092 litres
1 quarter (8 bushels)	2,909 hectolitres

Note: one mililitre = 1 cm^3

Weight

1 grain	0.0648 gram
1 ounce (16 drams)	28.350 grams
1 pound (16 ounces or 7,000 grains)	0.45359237 kilogram
1 stone (14 lb.)	6.350 kilograms
1 quarter (28 lb.)	12.70 kilograms
1 cwt (112 lb.)	50.80 kilograms
1 ton (20 cwt.)	1.0160 tonnes or 1016 kilograms

14

METRIC CONVERSION TABLES

The figures in the central columns apply to either of the columns on each side. For example:
1 centimetre = 0.394 inches and 1 inch = 2.54 centimetres
1 litre = 1.76 pints and 1 pint = 0.568 litres.

LENGTH

Centimetres		Inches
2.54	1	0.394
5.08	2	0.787
7.62	3	1.181
10.16	4	1.575
12.70	5	1.969
15.24	6	2.362
17.78	7	2.756
20.32	8	3.150
22.85	9	3.543
27.94	11	4.330
30.48	12	4.724
38.1	15	5.91
50.8	20	7.87
76.2	30	11.81
101.6	40	15.75
127.0	50	19.69
152.4	60	23.62
177.8	70	27.45
203.2	80	31.49
228.6	90	35.43

Metres		Feet
0.305	1	3.281
0.610	2	6.562
0.914	3	9.843
1.219	4	13.123
1.524	5	16.404
1.829	6	19.685
2.134	7	22.966
2.438	8	26.247
2.743	9	29.528
3.048	10	32.808
6.096	20	65.617
9.144	30	98.425
12.192	40	131.233
15.240	50	164.042
18.288	60	196.850
21.336	70	229.658
24.384	80	262.467
27.432	90	295.275
31.751	70	154.324

Kilometres		Miles
1.609	1	0.621
3.219	2	1.243
4.828	3	1.864
6.437	4	2.486
8.047	5	3.107
9.656	6	3.728
11.265	7	4.350
12.875	8	4.971
14.484	9	5.592
16.093	10	6.214
32.187	20	12.427
48.280	30	18.641
64.374	40	24.855
80.467	50	31.069
96.561	60	37.282
112.654	70	43.496
128.748	80	49.710
144.841	90	55.923

CAPACITY

Litres		Pints
0.568	1	1.76
1.136	2	3.52
1.705	3	5.28
2.273	4	7.04
2.841	5	8.80
3.410	6	10.56
3.978	7	12.32
4.546	8	14.08
25.400	10	3.937

Litres		Pints
4.546	1	0.220
9.092	2	0.440
13.638	3	0.660
18.184	4	0.880
22.730	5	1.100
27.276	6	1.320
31.822	7	1.540
36.368	8	1.760
40.914	9	1.980
45.460	10	2.200

WEIGHT

Kilograms		Pounds
0.454	1	2.205
0.907	2	4.409
1.361	3	6.614
1.814	4	8.818
2.268	5	11.023
2.722	6	13.228
3.175	7	15.432
3.629	8	17.637
4.082	9	19.842
4.536	10	22.046
9.072	20	44.092
13.608	30	66.139
18.144	40	88.185
22.680	50	110.231
27.216	60	132.277
36.287	80	176.370
40.823	90	198.416

PRESSURE

Kilograms per sq.cm		Pounds per sq.in.
0.070	1	14.224
0.141	2	28.447
0.211	3	42.671
0.281	4	56.894
0.352	5	71.118
0.422	6	85.341
0.492	7	99.565
0.562	8	113.788
0.633	9	128.012
0.703	10	142.235

1 metre	39.37 inches
1 metre	3.2808 feet
1 metre	1.0936 yards
1 kilometreq	0.6214 mile

Area

1 sq. centimetre	0.155 sq.inch
1 sq. metre	10.764 sq.feet
1 sq. metre	1.196 sq.yards
1 are (100 sq.metres)	119.60 sq.yards
1 hectare (100 ares or 10000 sq. metres)	2.471 acres

Volume and Capacity

1 cu. centimetre	0.061 cu.inch
1 cu. decimetre (1000 cu. centimetres)	61.024 cu. inches
1 cu. metre	35.315 cu. feet
1 cu. metre	1.308 cu. yards
1 centilitre	0.070 gill
1 decilitre	0.176 pint
1 litre	1.76 pints
1 litre	0.22 gallon

ANGULAR OR CIRCULAR MEASURE

60 seconds (")	= 1 minute (')
60 minutes	= 1 degree (°)
90 degrees	= 1 right angle or quadrant

Diameter of circle x 3.1416 = circumference
Diameter squared x 0.7854 = area of circle
Diameter squared x 3.1416 = surface of sphere
Diameter cubed x 0.5236 - solidity of sphere

PAPER AND BOOK MEASURE

24 sheets	= 1 quire
20 quires (480 sheets)	= 1 ream
516 sheets	= 1 printer's ream
2 reams	= 1 bundle
10 reams	= 1 bale

PAPER SIZES

	Inches	Millimetres
2A	46.81 x 66.22	1189 x 1682
A0	33.11 x 46.81	841 x 1189
A1	23.39 x 33.11	594 x 841
A2	16.54 x 23.39	420 x 594
A3	11.69 x 16.54	297 x 420
A4	8.27 x 11.69	210 x 297
A5	5.83 x 8.27	148 x 210
A6	4.13 x 5.83	105 x 148
A7	2.91 x 4.13	74 x 105
A8	2.05 x 2.91	52 x 74
A9	1.46 x 2.05	37 x 52
A10	1.02 x 1.46	26 x 37

THERMOMETER COMPARISONS

Centigrade or Celcius	Fahrenheit	Centigrade	Fahrenheit or Celcius
100°	212°	50°	122°
95	203	45	113
90	194	40	104
85	185	35	95
80	176	30	86
75	167	25	77
70	158	20	68
65	149	15	59
60	140	10	50
55	131	5	41
		0	32

The Centigrade scale was devised by Anders Celsius (1701-44), a Swedish physicist and astronomer. The Fahrenheit scale was devised by Gabriel Daniel Fahrenheit (1686-1736), a German physicist. *Boiling point:* 100°C/212°F. *Freezing point:* 0°C/32°F.
To convert Centigrade into Fahrenheit: multiply by 9, divide by 5 and add 32.
To convert Fahrenheit into Centigrade: subtract 32, multiply by 5 and divide by 9.
Normal temperature of a human body is 98.4°F = 36.9°C.

METRIC WEIGHTS AND MEASURES WITH THE BRITISH EQUIVALENTS

Weight

1 miligram	0.015 grains
1 gram	15.432 grains
1 kilogram (1000 g)	2.2046 lb
1 tonne (1000 kg)	0.9842 ton

Length

1 millimetre	0.03937 inch
1 centimetre	0.3937 inch
1 decimetre	3.937 inches

14

PRESIDENTS OF THE UNITED STATES OF AMERICA

	Party	Born	Inaugurated	Died
George Washington	Fed.	1732	1789	1799
John Adams	Fed.	1735	1797	1826
Thomas Jefferson	Dem./Rep.	1743	1801	1826
James Madison	Dem./Rep.	1751	1809	1836
James Monroe	Dem./Rep.	1758	1817	1831
John Quincy Adams	Dem./Rep.	1767	1825	1848
Andrew Jackson	Dem.	1767	1829	1845
Martin Van Buren	Dem.	1782	1837	1862
William Henry Harrison*	Whig	1773	1841	1841
John Tyler	Whig	1790	1841	1862
James Knox Polk*	Dem.	1795	1845	1849
Zachary Taylor	Whig	1784	1849	1850
Millard Fillmore	Whig	1800	1850	1874
Franklin Pierce	Dem.	1804	1853	1869
James Buchanan	Dem.	1791	1857	1868
Abraham Lincoln [1]	Rep.	1809	1861	1865
Andrew Johnson [2]	Rep.	1808	1865	1875
Ulysses Simpson Grant	Rep.	1822	1869	1885
Rutherford Birchard Hayes	Rep.	1822	1877	1893
James Abraham Garfield [1]	Rep.	1831	1881	1881
Chester Alan Arthur	Rep.	1830	1881	1886
Grover Cleveland	Dem.	1837	1885	1908
Benjamin Harrison	Rep.	1833	1889	1901
Grover Cleveland	Dem.	1837	1893	1908
William McKinley[1]	Rep.	1843	1897	1901
Theodore Roosevelt	Rep.	1858	1901	1919
William Howard Taft	Rep.	1857	1909	1930
Woodrow Wilson	Dem.	1856	1913	1924
Warren Gamaliel Harding*	Rep.	1865	1921	1923
Calvin Coolidge	Rep.	1872	1923	1933
Herbert C. Hoover	Rep.	1874	1929	1964
Franklin Delano Roosevelt [3]	Dem.	1882	1933	1945
Harry S. Truman	Dem.	1884	1945	1972
Dwight D. Eisenhower	Rep.	1890	1953	1969
John F. Kennedy [1]	Dem.	1917	1961	1963
Lyndon B. Johnson	Dem.	1908	1963	1973
Richard M. Nixon [4]	Rep.	1913	1969	—
Gerald R. Ford	Rep.	1913	1974	—
James Earl Carter	Dem.	1924	1977	—
Ronald Reagan	Rep.	1911	1981	—
George H W Bush	Rep	1924	1989	—

[1] Assassinated.   [2] A Democrat but nominated Vice-President by Republicans and elected with Lincoln   [3] Re-elected Nov. 5, 1940; re-elected for fourth-term Nov. 7, 1944.   [4] Resigned August 1974   .* Died in office.
Fed. Federalist.   Dem. Democrat   Rep. Republican.

WEDDING ANNIVERSARIES

Anniversary	Wedding	Anniversary	Wedding
First	Cotton	Fifteenth	Crystal
Second	Paper	Twentieth	China
Third	Leather	Twenty-fifth	Silver
Fifth	Wooden	Thirtieth	Pearl
Seventh	Woollen	Fortieth	Ruby
Tenth	Tin	Forty-fifth	Sapphire
Twelfth	Silk and Fine Linen	Fiftieth	Golden
		Sixtieth	Diamond

14

INDEX

Not all individual items are separately indexed and reference should be made to entries in BOLD TYPE.